TABLE OF CONTENTS.

ISBN 978-0-265-67818-3
PIBN 11013010

1 MONTH OF
FREE
READING

at
www.ForgottenBooks.com

By purchasing this book you are eligible for one month membership to ForgottenBooks.com, giving you unlimited access to our entire collection of over 1,000,000 titles via our web site and mobile apps.

To claim your free month visit:

www.forgottenbooks.com/free1013010

English
Français
Deutsche
Italiano
Español
Português

www.forgottenbooks.com

Mythology Photography **Fiction**
Fishing Christianity **Art** Cooking
Essays Buddhism Freemasonry
Medicine **Biology** Music **Ancient
Egypt** Evolution Carpentry Physics
Dance Geology **Mathematics** Fitness
Shakespeare **Folklore** Yoga Marketing
Confidence Immortality Biographies
Poetry **Psychology** Witchcraft
Electronics Chemistry History **Law**
Accounting **Philosophy** Anthropology
Alchemy Drama Quantum Mechanics
Atheism Sexual Health **Ancient History**
Entrepreneurship Languages Sport
Paleontology Needlework Islam
Metaphysics Investment Archaeology
Parenting Statistics Criminology
Motivational

ELEVENTH ANNUAL REPORT
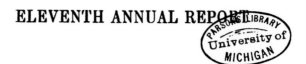

OF THE

POOR LAW COMMISSIONERS,

WITH

.

APPENDICES.

LONDON:

PRINTED BY W. CLOWES AND SONS, STAMFORD STREET,

For Her Majesty's Stationery Office.

1845.

PROCEEDINGS IN IRELAND.

LIST OF PAPERS IN THE APPENDIX.

APPENDIX B.—TABLES AND RETURNS.

ENGLAND AND WALES.

IRELAND.

APPENDIX C.

———

ENGLAND AND WALES.

ELEVENTH

ANNUAL REPORT.

TO THE RIGHT HON. SIR JAMES GRAHAM, Bart.,

*Her Majesty's Principal Secretary of State for the
Home Department.*

Poor Law Commission Office,
Somerset House, May 1, 1845.

Proceedings in England.

Sir,

1. In our last Annual Report we stated, upon the authority of the Returns which we received from the Unions and parishes of England and Wales, the amount of the expenditure for the relief of the poor, in the year ending at Lady-day, 1843; and we accompanied that statement with some details relative to the number and classes of paupers relieved during the same period. We proceed now to submit to you a similar statement with respect to the parochial year, ending at Lady-day, 1844.

2. The following statement exhibits the total amount of money levied in England and Wales under the denomination of poor's rate, in the parochial year 1844, together with the monies received from other sources in aid of the poor's rate.* These two sums amounted in that year to somewhat more than seven millions sterling. It likewise exhibits the manner in which this money was expended. Of the seven millions disposable as poor's rate, nearly five millions were applied to the relief of the poor. The payments made for the county and borough rate amounted to above 1,350,000*l.* The law charges incurred by Unions and parishes a little exceeded 100,000*l.*; and the payments made, under the Parochial Assessments Act, for surveys and valuations of parishes, were about 30,000*l.* The expenses under the Vaccination Act were about 16,000*l.*, and those under the Act for registering births, deaths, and marriages, were about 56,000*l.* The money returned to us as expended for " other purposes," not comprised in the preceding

---

* The following are the principal sources of this subsidiary revenue; viz., 1. Rents of parish estates; 2. Income of funds of parishes; 3. Payments by relations of paupers; 4. Payments by fathers and mothers of bastards; 5. Re-payments of loans to out-pensioners; 6. Payments under orders of removal; 7. Fines, &c., paid over by magistrates; 8. Parliamentary registration shillings and lists of voters sold.

B

heads, amounts to 359,106*l*. We believe that the payments included in this unspecified item were principally made for the following purposes: viz., 1. Removals of paupers and travelling expenses of overseers; 2. Constables' expenses; 3. Expenses of proceedings before magistrates; 4. Expenses on account of parish property; 5. Printing lists of voters, and making out lists of juries.

An Account of the Receipt and Expenditure of the Poor's Rate for the Year ended Lady-day, 1844.

Receipt.

Amount of money levied by assessment	£ 6,847,205
Received from other sources in aid of Poor Rate . .	219,592
Total Receipt . . .	£ 7,066,797

Expenditure.

For relief to the poor	£4,976,093
Law charges, parochial and Union	105,304
Payments under the Parochial Assessments Act (for surveys, valuations, &c.) and loans repaid under the same	30,083
Expenses under the Vaccination Act . . . ,	16,980
Expenses under the Act for Registering Births, Deaths, and Marriages	56,094
Payments for county and borough rate, and for county and local police forces . , . . .	1,356,457
Money expended for all other purposes . . .	359,106
Total Expenditure . . .	£ 6,900,117

3. We likewise annex at the end of this Report a comparative statement, showing the receipt and expenditure for all the above items since the year 1834 (below p. 44).

4. Both the amount received as poor's rate, and the expenditure for the relief of the poor, were less in the parochial year 1844, than in the preceding year. The amounts are as follows:—

Years ending Lady-day	Total Amount of Monies received as Poor's Rate.
1843	£7,304,601
1844	7,066,797
Diminution .	£237,804

Years ending Lady-day	Total Expenditure for the Relief of the Poor.
1843 . . .	£5,208,027
1844	4,976,093
Diminution .	£231,934

5. The expenditure for the relief of the poor, which diminished during the years 1835, 1836, 1837, began to increase in 1838, and continued to increase in each successive year until Lady-day, 1843. The parochial year 1844 is the first year

since 1837, which did not exhibit an increase of expenditure
over the preceding year. As compared with the expenditure
of the year 1834, the last parochial year previous to the passing
of the Poor Law Amendment Act, the following is the amount
for 1844 :—

Years ending Lady-day	Total Expenditure for the Relief of the Poor.
1834	£6,317,255
1844	4,976,093
Diminution .	£1,341,162

6. The diminution in the expenditure for the parochial year
1844, as compared with 1843, is distributed with tolerable
equality over all the counties. The highest rates of reduction
are in Lancashire, Cheshire, and the West Riding of Yorkshire;
owing to the improvement in manufactures, which took place
in the latter year. In some counties the expenditure of 1844
was slightly greater than that of the preceding year. The
principal of these are Lincolnshire, Shropshire, Durham and
Northumberland. The increase of expenditure in the two
latter counties was owing to the state of employment among
the colliers : with regard to Lincolnshire, the cause is probably
to be sought in a circumstance to which we shall advert in the
course of our Report (par. 51).

7. The chief items of which the expenditure for the relief of
the poor is composed, are shown in the following Table, which
relates to the two last parochial years, and comprises the Unions
and parishes under the Poor Law Amendment Act. From the
remaining parishes we receive no such returns as furnish the
information contained in this Table.

Years ended Lady-day	Expenditure of 585 Unions and Parishes under Boards of Guardians.						Rate per Head of Total on Population.
	In-Maintenance.	Out-Relief.	Establishment Charges and Salaries.	Workhouse Loans Repaid.	Other Charges connected with Relief to the Poor.	Total Expenditure for Relief, &c., to the Poor.	
	£.	£.	£.	£.	£.	£.	s. d.
1843	810,372	2,818,843	786,148	167,103	7,092	4,589,558	6 9½
1844	705,253	2,726,431	748,985	183,898	5,584	4,370,171	6 5½
Increase .	..	..	..	16,795	..	..	..
Decrease .	105,119	92,392	37,163	..	1,508	219,387	0 4

Decrease on Total Union Expenditure in 1844, compared with 1843   4·8 per cent.

8. The diminution in the expenditure for the relief of the
poor, with stationary prices of food, is naturally accompanied
by a diminution in the number of the persons relieved. The
following table exhibits the number of persons relieved during
each of the Lady-day quarters in 1843 and 1844.

COMPARATIVE STATEMENT of the Number of In-door and Out-door Paupers relieved in England and Wales, during each of the Quarters ended Lady-day, 1843 and 1844.

Quarters ended Lady-day	Number of Paupers Relieved.			Rate per Cent. of Total Number of Paupers on the Population in 1841.
	In-door.	Out-door.	Total.	
1843	238,748	1,307,642	1,546,390	9·7
1844	230,818	1,246,743	1,477,561	9·3
Decrease in 1844	7,930	60,899	68,829	·4

Population in 1841 15,906,741

From this statement it appears that the total number of persons relieved in the three months ending Lady-day, 1844, amounted to nearly a million and a-half, and were about 9¼ per cent. of the entire population, according to the census of 1841. Of the million and half persons thus relieved, a large proportion were permanent paupers; but the number of new cases in the other three-quarters may be safely estimated at half a million; so that the number of persons relieved in England and Wales, in the course of the parochial year 1844, may be taken at about two millions, or nearly one-eighth part of the actual population. In other words, about one person in eight, through the entire population, received relief from the poor's rate at some time during that year.

9. The same table shows that out of 1,477,561 paupers relieved in the quarter ending Lady-day, 1844, the number who were relieved in the workhouse was 230,818, and the number who received out-door relief was 1,246,743; that is to say, those who were relieved in the workhouse were 16 per cent, and those who received out-door relief were 84 per cent; or, in other words, those who were relieved in the workhouse were to those who received out-door relief about as 1 to 5.

10. The following table shows the number of adult able-bodied paupers relieved during each of the quarters ending Lady-day 1843 and 1844; from which it appears, that although t number of those who received relief, both in and out of the rkhouse, on account of sickness or accident, was greater in second of these two periods; the number of those who were rel   ed on other   ounds was considerably less. The decrease   number of   class of able-bodied paupers was not less   per cent;   result highly gratifying, when it is re-   t t the   ing was not obtained by any change in   ·   m   of the law, but arose solely from the   '   country.

Quarters ended at Lady-day	In-door.			Out-door.			Total In-door and Out-door.
	On Account of temporary Sickness or Accident.	All other Causes, including Vagrants.	Total In-door.	On Account of temporary Sickness or Accident.	All other Causes, including Vagrants.	Total Out-door.	
1843	10,888	88,308	99,196	146,704	220,685	367,389	466,585
1844	11,458	86,327	97,785	158,280	175,419	333,699	431,484
Increase per Cent.. .}	5·2	..	..	7·9	..	..	..
Decrease per Cent.. .}	..	2·2	1·4	..	20·5	9·2	7·5

NOTE.—An estimate is made for places not in Union under the Poor Law Amendment Act. The above results are obtained from the Union Quarterly Abstracts.

11. On the other hand, the number of persons of both sexes, partially or wholly disabled by age or infirmity, who received out-door relief in the quarter ending Lady-day, 1844, is greater than the number who received similar relief in the corresponding quarter of 1843.

	Quarters ended Lady day.	Wholly unable to Work.		Partially able to Work.		Total.		Grand Total.
		Males.	Females.	Males.	Females.	Males.	Females	
Aged and infirm paupers receiving out-door relief in 585 Unions . . .}	1843	64,246	117,806	34,716	74,306	98,962	192,112	291,074
	1844	67,262	119,655	34,407	73,258	101,669	192,913	294,582

12. It may be observed, that the variation of the expenditure for the five years ending at Lady-day, 1844, leads, on the whole, to a satisfactory view of the manner in which the administration of the fund for the relief of the poor has been conducted by the local authorities. During the early part of this period, particularly during the year 1841, severe distress prevailed in most of the manufacturing districts, including that important part of the country where the manufactures of cotton are carried on.* The depression of the manufacturing districts was, as a natural consequence, soon followed by distress in the agricultural parts of the country.† In the year ending Lady-day, 1844, however, the demand for labour both in the manufacturing and agricultural districts had revived, and the number of able-bodied persons incapable of obtaining employment was not considerable.‡ Owing to this state of things, the expenditure for the relief of the poor increased steadily in the parochial years 1839-1843, but diminished in the year 1844. This fact proves that the amount of the poor rate is not (as

* See Sixth Annual Report, p. 1. Eighth Annual Report, pp. 7 and 8, edit. 8vo.
† Ninth Annual Report, pp. 1-3.   ‡ Tenth Annual Report, p. 1.

some persons have feared) governed by a law of constant and irresistible progression; but that, when subjected to proper control, the amount of the expenditure may be adapted to the varying exigencies of the people; that after having increased with the augmentation of distress, it can be diminished upon the return of comparative prosperity.

13. Before we close our remarks upon the expenditure for the relief of the poor, we are desirous of again calling your attention to the magnitude of the sums annually levied in England and Wales for the purposes of local taxation. The total amount received for the poor's rate (which includes the county rate and part of the borough rate, and other miscellaneous items), was, as we have already seen, 6,847,205*l*. in the parochial year 1844. The amount of borough rate imposed by the municipal boroughs (independently of the payments made out of the poor's-rate, and the produce of the borough property and borough tolls and dues), exceeds 200,000*l*. per annum.* The entire expenditure of the municipal boroughs is about 1,000,000*l*. sterling a year. The annual expenditure of the turnpike trusts is about 1,500,000*l*.; and that defrayed out of the highway rate is about 1,200,000*l*. The sums annually levied in towns for sewers rate, and for watching, lighting, and paving rates, have never been ascertained and returned to Parliament; the annual amount of the former is about 75,000*l*.; as to the latter, there is not, we believe, any information on which even an approximate estimate can be founded. The annual expenditure of the church rate appears to be nearly 500,000*l*. sterling. Adding some other branches of local taxation (which it is unnecessary to specify),† the total amount of the local taxes annually levied and expended in England and Wales cannot, upon the most moderate computation, be placed at a less amount than 10,000,000*l*. sterling.

14. Now the amount of the revenue of the general government of the United Kingdom which is expended under the annual control of Parliament, may be measured by the sums included in the Appropriation Act. In the Appropriation Act for the year 1844, these sums amounted to 17,719,485*l*. Of this amount five-sixths may, in round numbers, be considered as having been contributed by England; the remaining sixth being paid by Ireland and Scotland. While therefore the share of the expenses of the general government, under the annual control of Parliament, which is borne by England, does not exceed 15,000,000*l*., the sum which is annually expended in England out of the local taxes amounts to at least 10,000,000*l*. This comparison, we think, places in a clear light the magni-

---

* See Tables of Revenue, Population, and Commerce for 1843. Sess. Paper, vol. 55, p. 366.
† See the Report of the Poor Law Commissioners on Local Taxation, pp. 27, 28, t. 8vo.

tude and importance of the expenditure out of the local rates, and proves the expediency of bringing their amounts under the periodical observation of Parliament.

15. We are aware that the system of our local taxation is generally organised on the assumption that the imposition of the tax and its disbursement, as well as the audit of its expenditure, are committed to the discretion and control of the local authorities; and that *their* inspection is a sufficient security against abuse or mismanagement, without the interference of Parliament. Experience, however, has shown the advantage of ascertaining the aggregate amount of the public income and expenditure of the various local bodies, and of submitting these accounts, properly arranged and classified, to the frequent review of Parliament. As an illustration of this advantage, we may cite the returns of the Poor Law expenditure which have been annually made to Parliament since 1813; the annual accounts of the expenditure of the turnpike trusts returned under the 3 and 4 Wm. IV., c. 80, since 1834; and the accounts of the expenditure of the county rate, prepared from the returns of the county treasurers, which have for the last few years been annually printed for the use of the House of Commons. The reason of this advantage is, we think, apparent. So long as the local expenditure is stated exclusively for each parish, township, or other small division, the produce of the rate is viewed for one of these separate portions singly; and thus the aggregate importance of the tax is likely to be overlooked. The expense actually considered is small; while the amount of the expenses incurred by all the other divisions which, taken together, would form an important sum, is unknown and perhaps unthought of. The apparent amount of some of the most productive of the taxes imposed by the general government, might be reduced by a similar process of insulation. If, for example, an estimate were made of the amount of the tax on sugar, or tea, or spirits, which is contributed by a single rural parish, and if this sum was looked at by itself, without reference to the amount levied in the rest of the country, its importance would seem inconsiderable.

16. Amongst the local taxes, the fund levied under the denomination of poor's rate stands first in magnitude. The monies expended from this fund have, since the passing of the Poor Law Amendment Act, been subjected to a regular audit by paid auditors; which will, we trust, be rendered still more effective by the provisions in the Poor Law Act of last session. The expenses for the survey and valuation of parishes, for vaccination, and for the registration of births, deaths, and marriages, which have been created by Acts of Parliament passed subsequently to 1834, have been imposed upon the poor's rate, and form a new charge upon that fund. Their aggregate

annual amount is about 100,000*l.*; and although this expenditure may be justly considered as of great public utility, the
fact of its recent creation ought not to be overlooked in comparing the present amount of the poor's rate with its amount
in former years. With respect to the law charges incurred by
parishes and Unions (which are not included in the expenditure
for the relief of the poor), it is to be observed that they have
undergone a great diminution since the passing of the Poor
Law Amendment Act. Their amount in 1834 was not less
than 258,604*l.*; in 1842 it had fallen to 68,051*l.*; in 1844 it
had risen to 105,304*l.*, which, however, is less than half the
amount in 1834. A further important saving due to the
operation of the same Act is that which has taken place in the
miscellaneous item returned to us under the unspecified head
of "*other purposes,*" as is shown in the following account:

Years ended Lady-day.	Money expended out of the Poor's Rate for all other Purposes.	Years ended Lady-day.	Money expended out of the Poor's Rate for all other Purposes.
1834	£1,021,941	1840	466,698
1835	935,362	1841	527,717
1836	823,213	1842	318,092
1837	637,043	1843	346,007
1838	507,929	1844	359,106*
1839	493,703		

The large reduction in this item must be attributed mainly
to the exclusion of irregular and illegal expenses of a miscellaneous nature which has been effected by the auditors appointed
under the Poor Law Amendment Act. Upon this subject we refer
to a passage contained in a Report which was made to us in the
year 1840 by our Assistant-Commissioner, Mr. Power, when
he was in charge of Lancashire and the West Riding of Yorkshire, and which was printed in the Appendix to our Sixth
Annual Report.†

* The metropolitan police rate (which amounts to nearly 200,000*l.* per annum)
is included in this item for the years 1834–41; but not in the three subsequent years.

† "The item entitled 'other purposes,' in the Annual Parliamentary Returns,
demands a few observations in reference to its enormous amount in the earlier years
of the comparison, and the considerable reductions of this item effected in later years
show the value of that part of the new system of management, whereby the expenditure of 20 or 30 townships, instead of being left separately in the hands of as many
paid assistant overseers, is brought into one focus, a clear and distinct system of
accounting introduced, and the whole submitted to the searching and effectual examination of an auditor every quarter. In the year 1835, no less a sum than
64,888*l.* was included in the Parliamentary Returns for Lancashire, under the head
of 'other purposes;' and the sum of 39,675*l.*, under the same head, for the West
Riding of York.

"This item appears to have undergone a gradual decrease immediately from the
passing of the Poor Law Amendment Act, the improper and illegal disbursements of
which it partly consisted, having begun to be discontinued by the Overseers through
fear of the impending change in the mode of examining and auditing the accounts.
Much, however, was left to be effected by the auditors of the Unions, which, from time
to time, have been brought into operation; and the labours of these officers have been
attended with most important effect in the exclusion of improper items of expenditure."—(Mr. Power on the Poor Rate Expenditure of Lancashire and the West
Riding; Sixth Annual Report, Appendix B. No. 2.)

17. The decrease in the expenditure for law charges, and in the miscellaneous item just mentioned, ought to be added to the decrease in the expenditure for the relief of the poor, in order to obtain a complete view of the saving produced by the operation of the Poor Law Amendment Act.

Years ended Lady-day.	Total Expenditure for the Relief of the Poor.	Law Charges, &c.	Money expended for all other Purposes.	Total.
1834	£6,317,255	£258,604	£1,021,941	£7,597,800
1844	4,976,093	105,304	359,106	5,440,503
Decrease . .	1,341,162	153,300	662,835	2,157,297

The actual reduction in the expenditure out of the poor's rate, under these three heads, for the year 1844, as compared with the year 1834, therefore exceeds two millions sterling.

18. The only expenditure charged upon the poor's rate, which has undergone a large increase since 1834, is that for the county and borough rates. The payments out of the poor's rate for county and borough rates, which amounted only to 604,203*l.* in the year 1837, had, in the year 1844, reached the sum of 1,356,457*l.*, that is to say, they have more than doubled in seven years. It is not within our province to inquire into the causes of this increase, or to consider whether the additional advantages afforded to the public service do not more than compensate the increased expenditure. We will, however, remark that in consequence of the manner in which the payments for the county and borough rates are mixed up in the returns made to us, and the imperfect accounts of the borough rate expenditure which have been laid before Parliament, it is impossible to make the payments for these two rates balance the expenditure. We have compared the sums returned from the Unions and parishes as paid for county and borough rates in the three years ending Lady-day 1840, 1841, 1842, with the sums acknowledged by the county treasurers to have been received as county rate in the three years ending Michaelmas 1840, 1841, 1842, as stated in the returns made to the House of Commons.* From these authorities it appears that the payments made for the county and borough rate during the above three years ending at Lady-day, amounted to 3,177,005*l.*, or to an average sum of 1,059,002*l.* per annum ; whereas the sums received as county rate by the county treasurers, during the three years ending at Michaelmas, amounted only to 2,376,473*l.*, or to an average sum of 792,158*l.* per annum. We presume, therefore, that the difference between these two sums, that is, about 260,000*l.* per annum, was paid by the overseers, out of the poor's rate, to the town councils in the municipal

---

* For the receipt and expenditure of the county rate, see Parliamentary Papers, No. 434, Sess. 1842, and No. 76, Sess. 1844.

boroughs. The exact amount of this payment cannot be ascertained from the returns of the expenditure of boroughs which have been presented to Parliament.* It is to be observed that the payments made from the poor's rate for the county rate are less than the county rate expenditure ; inasmuch as an annual contribution to certain of the expenses charged upon the county rate is made by the general government. The sum thus allowed amounted in 1842 to 114,734*l.*

19. But, notwithstanding the recent increase in the amount of the county and borough rates, and the creation of new expenses charged upon the poor's rate, the sum levied as poor's rate in the year 1844 is less than the sum levied as poor's rate in 1834. Moreover, the sum levied as poor's rate in 1844 is less than the sum levied as poor's rate in any year from 1813 to 1834, except the year 1824, when the amount was slightly inferior. This fact becomes the more important when the great increase of population, since 1813, is taken into the account. The following Table shows the population, the amount levied as poor's rate, and the ratio which this amount bore to the population, in each of the four years, 1813, 1824, 1834, and 1844.

Year ended Lady-day	Population of England and Wales.	Total Money levied for Poor Rates, and County and Borough Rates.	Rate per Head on the Population.
		£.	£. s. d.
1813	10,505,886	8,646,841	0 16 5
1824	12,517,921	6,836,505	0 10 11
1834	14,105,645	8,338,079	0 11 9
1844	16,543,010	6,847,205	0 8 3

If therefore the pressure of the sum levied as poor's rate is measured by the ratio of its amount to the population, its burden in 1844 would be half its burden in 1813, and only two-thirds of its burden in 1834.

If it should be objected that the pressure of this tax ought to be estimated by its ratio to property and not to population, this comparison leads to an equally satisfactory result. There is no doubt that the yearly produce of the rateable property of England has undergone a very great increase since 1813; and that its annual progress is now rapid. The total annual value of real property assessed to the property tax in 1815, in England and Wales, was 51,898,423*l.*,† whereas the amount in 1843

---

* Return of Parochial and Borough Rates, &c. (England and Wales), No. 635, Sess. 1844.

† Parl. Paper, No. 444, Sess. 1835.

was 85,802,735*l.** It is further to be observed, that the increase in the annual value of rateable property arises, not only from the improved cultivation of the land, and its consequently increased productiveness, but also, to a great extent, from the large number of new houses, and other buildings (such as manufactories and warehouses), as well as railways, canals, wharfs, &c., which are constructed from year to year. Accordingly, land, as such, pays a smaller proportion of the local rates in each successive year; and a larger proportion falls on the other sorts of rateable property. This fact appears from the table inserted in our Ninth Annual Report, par. 27, which shows, that whereas the proportion of the poor's rate falling upon land was 69 per cent., and that falling on other property was 31 per cent. in 1826; the proportion falling on land was only 52 per cent., and on other property 48 per cent. in 1841. The following is the statement to which we refer.

Years.	On Landed Property.	Proportion per Cent.	Dwelling Houses.	Proportion per Cent.	All other Property.	Proportion per Cent.	Total Amount of Poor Rate levied.
	£.		£.		£.		£.
1826	4,795,482	69	1,814,228	26	356,447	5	6,966,157
1841	3,316,593	52	2,375,221	37	660,014	11	6,351,828

20. The expenditure of the poor's rate and the county rate may, as it appears to us, be taken generally as affording some approximation to an index of the amounts of destitution and crime in the country; the former being applied solely to the relief of want, and the latter principally expended in the detection, prosecution, and punishment of crime. Tried by this test, the state of the country must be considered as presenting a favourable aspect; inasmuch as the ratio of this expenditure to population and property is at least as low as in any recent year, and is only half the amount at which it stood about the year 1813.

21. But although the pressure of the most important of the local taxes in England may be less at present than in previous years; it is nevertheless highly expedient that all practicable securities against the abuse or mismanagement of those taxes should be established, and that the mode and amount of their levy and expenditure should be brought periodically under the observation of Parliament. We have already stated that complete accounts of the expenditure of the poor's rate are annually presented by us to Parliament; and that similar accounts are presented of the county rate expenditure from the returns of

* Parl. Paper, No. 102, Sess. 1845. In the Parl. Paper, No. 316, Sess. 1844, this amount for the same period is returned at 82,233,844*l.* We presume that the latest return is most correct.

the county treasurers. Some returns of the borough rate expenditure have likewise been made; but the information which they afford is not complete. Ample returns of the expenses of the Turnpike Trusts are transmitted annually under the 3 and 4 Wm. IV., c. 80, to Sir James M'Adam, by whom they are digested for presentation to Parliament. We believe that the accounts thus obtained have been productive of much public benefit. On the other hand, there is no periodical return of the highway rate; a rate which is liable to great abuse, and is, we fear, in not a few parishes converted into a subsidiary poor's rate for the relief of able-bodied labourers. No return has ever been made to Parliament of the amounts levied and expended for the sewers rate, or for lighting, watching, and paving rates. Nor is any regular return made of the sums expended as church rate.

22. We have, perhaps, dwelt longer on this portion of our Report than was consistent with our strict duty; but we trust that the importance of the subject, and our official connexion with the poor's rate, the largest of the local taxes, as well as the intimate connexion which subsists between most of these taxes, will serve as a sufficient excuse for our venturing to submit to you the above remarks. We will merely state, in addition, that the general survey which we have taken of the present state of our system of local taxation seems to us to authorize the two following conclusions: viz., 1. That an account of the receipt and expenditure of all the more considerable local taxes ought to be annually prepared and laid before Parliament. 2. That the expenditure of all such taxes ought to undergo a strict and regular audit by competent auditors.

23. We are unable, on account of the delay which occurs in the transmission of the annual returns to our office, to state the amount of the expenditure for the parochial year ending at Lady-day, 1845. Indeed, the audit of the Poor Law accounts for the Lady-day quarter is, in many Unions, not yet completed. We can, however, say generally that the year since the first of May, 1844, has, on the whole, been favourable to the poorer classes of this country. In the manufacturing districts, the demand for labour has been extensive and constant; and even the iron and coal districts, which were the last to recover from the general depression, were prosperous during the last twelve months. The drought of last summer, and the length and severity of the cold during last winter, were unfavourable to the employment of agricultural labourers; but we rejoice to say that the number of rural Unions in which difficulty arose from the application of unemployed able-bodied men was not considerable. Amongst those in which the workhouses were filled, and it became necessary to give out-door relief to the able-

bodied, subject to a condition of labour, we may specify the Caxton and Arrington Union in Cambridgeshire, the Rye Union in Sussex, and the Highworth and Swindon Union in Wiltshire. The Guardians of the latter Union have, in order as far as possible to prevent a recurrence of the same state of things, agreed to build a new and enlarged workhouse. Moreover, in several Unions it has been necessary to give out-door relief to all applicants for a time, on account of the existence of small-pox in the workhouse. We have, however, the satisfaction of being able to state that, during the last year, the administration of the Poor Law, under the amended statutes and the regulations of the Commissioners, was conducted with general regularity on the part of the local authorities, and acquiescence on the part of the public.

24. An important part of our proceedings, since the date of our last annual Report, has consisted in the execution of the additional duties imposed upon us by the Poor Law Act of last session, the statue of the 7 and 8 Vict., c. 101, and in the measures which we took for giving effect to its provisions.

25. Our first step, after the conclusion of the session of Parliament, was to place in the hands of the Guardians and Officers throughout the country a circular letter, calling attention to the enactments contained in that statute. We did not attempt to affix an authentic interpretation to that which the superior courts are alone competent to interpret; our purpose was to state, as plainly and as briefly as we could, any new duties and liabilities imposed on Guardians, Overseers, and paid Officers, as well as to explain the principal changes effected by the recent statute. This circular letter will be found in the Appendix to this Report.*

26. Our next duty appeared to be to modify any of our own regulations which might either really or apparently conflict with the new statute. The only order which seemed to require alteration on this account was that which regulates the administration of out-door relief. Sections 25 and 26 of the Act placed married women whose husbands were absent under certain conditions, and a peculiar class of widows, in a position somewhat different from that in which they had previously stood. We have, therefore, so modified our regulations as to make them consistent with these clauses, and have re-issued the General Order with no other change in its provisions than was requisite for this purpose. The Order, as amended, will be found in the Appendix.†

27. In connexion with this subject we may state that, in December last, we issued an Order, of considerable importance,

---

* Appendix A. No. 8.   † Appendix A. No. 1.

with reference to the administration of relief to paupers not residing within the Union from which the relief is received. This order imposes no fresh restrictions as to the class of paupers to whom such relief may lawfully be given; nor does it diminish, in any degree, the discretion previously exercised by Boards of Guardians with reference to the persons who are to receive relief. Its sole object is to regulate the mode in which the money is to be transmitted from one Union to another, and that in which the accounts relating to it are to be kept, in cases in which a Board of Guardians voluntarily undertakes to administer relief for another Board.

28. It often happened that a relieving officer, acting for a large district in a manufacturing town, had constantly passing through his hands large sums payable to paupers belonging to other Unions, which were intrusted to him by the Officers or Guardians of these distant Unions to pay the paupers residing in his district. Now, for the due administration of all money placed in his hands by his own Board of Guardians, this officer had given security, and he and his sureties were accountable, under his bond, for any fraud or misapplication; but in respect to the money thus forwarded to him by Officers or Guardians with whom he was not officially connected, there existed no effectual responsibility of any kind. He was, to all intents and purposes, their private agent; and although, like any other private agent, he was liable to the ordinary proceedings for fraud, whether civil or criminal, there could not exist the same security against peculation, as in the case of monies delivered into his hands, as a public officer, by his official superiors.

29. These evils of agency are inseparably connected with any system of non-resident relief: they were not created by the Poor Law Amendment Act; on the contrary, we believe that they have been in every respect much diminished under the operation of that statute. We have found, however, by experience, that the opportunity thus thrown in the way of relieving officers not unfrequently led to misapplication of money over which no effectual control could be exercised. An officer was intrusted with a considerable sum to be paid away in half-crowns or shillings to a number of paupers living at a distance from the only persons who had any direct interest in ascertaining that he fulfilled his trust; he was not the officer of those paupers, and it was optional with him whether he undertook to distribute relief on their behalf. A temptation of this kind would often lead a man, hitherto honest, to keep back, at first perhaps for a short time with the intention of replacing it, some portion of the money in his hands; months might elapse before a complaint reached the distant Board of Guardians, and even then it was not easy for them to ascertain all the facts of the case.

30. These difficulties are in a great degree inseparable from a system in which the recipient lives at a distance from the persons making the allowance. We have, so far as we could, from time to time lent our aid in detecting and punishing by dismissal any cases of fraud brought to our notice; but we became satisfied of the necessity of applying some more general remedy to the evils arising from this state of things. To do so was not easy, inasmuch as a relieving officer of one Union cannot be treated as the officer of another Union; he cannot be the servant of two different Boards at the same time; and a complete official responsibility extending to his sureties can only be enforced in the cases in which he misconducts himself in his capacity of a public servant. It followed that such a responsibility could only be created by causing him to distribute, under the authority and direction of his own Board, the relief originally allowed by distant Boards of Guardians; but for this purpose it became necessary that the former body should constitute themselves the agents of the authorities transmitting the money on account of the parish in which the pauper was settled. We did not conceive that we were empowered to compel a Board of Guardians to act as the agents of another Board which requested them to do so. All we could do was to prohibit the officers from accepting such agency without the sanction of their own Board, and to regulate the mode of transmitting the money and keeping the accounts where they were directed to administer relief on behalf of other Unions or parishes.

31. The result is, that no officer can now lawfully administer relief to non-settled poor as from the parish of their settlement without being responsible for the proper application of monies, in the same manner as if he were relieving paupers settled and residing in his own district. Our Order (as is stated in the Instructional Letter sent with it) does not prohibit Boards of Guardians from employing any other agency, if they think proper to run the risk; all we have done is to regulate the proceedings of the Board of Guardians when the agency is accepted, and thus to secure the paid officers against the continual temptation to fraud thrown in their way by the extreme laxity of the system previously pursued. This Order, and the Instructional Letter accompanying it, will be found in the Appendix.*

32. In the Poor Law Amendment Act certain powers of making rules and regulations respecting parish apprentices were intrusted to the Commissioners; but some doubt existed as to the possibility of so exercising these powers as effectually

---

* Appendix A, No. 2.

to bind the masters who undertook the care of children thus situated. By the 12th section of the Act of last Session these doubts were removed; and specific authority was given to the Commissioners to prescribe the duties of the masters, as well as the terms and conditions to be inserted in the indentures of parish apprentices. In pursuance of this section we have issued a General Order, which will be found in the Appendix.*

33. In this Order we have, among other provisions, directed that no child shall be apprenticed until he can read and write; and we have endeavoured, so far as such an object can be attained by regulations, to protect the apprentice and to prevent that risk of his maltreatment which is, to a certain extent, inseparable from every system of parish apprenticeship.

34. Certain provisions of this Order have been objected to by some parishes and Unions. These are more especially the limitations as to premiums for apprentices above the age of 14 (Art. 2): the proposed payment to be made by the master to his apprentice after he is 17 years of age (Art. 18, No. 8), and the prohibition of causing the boy to be taken more than ten miles from the place of apprenticeship without the licence of the Guardians (Art. 18, No. 10). The principal ground on which these provisions are objected to is, that they are calculated seriously to impede apprenticeship, by imposing responsibilities on masters such as will deter a great number of persons from taking parish apprentices at all.

35. We certainly entertain opinions unfavourable to that state of servitude which is created by the apprenticeship of parish children; and we should not regret to find that the regulations imposed by us tended gradually to diminish the number of children thus dealt with. We feel satisfied that greater attention to the education and industrial training of poor children would more than compensate for any supposed inconvenience arising from an indisposition to take apprentices, and that the results of such an improvement would be beneficial both to the master and the child. We think we are fully justified in arriving at this conclusion by the evidence embodied in Mr. Kay Shuttleworth's Report† on "The improvements in Training of Pauper Children, and on Apprenticeship in the Metropolitan Unions." This Report will be found in the Appendix to that which in the year 1841 we had the honour to make to the Marquis of Normanby on the general subject of the training of pauper children, and we confidently refer to it as establishing the unsatisfactory results of pauper apprenticeship with a premium.

36. At the same time it is not our wish to inflict any great

---

* Appendix A. No. 3.
† "Report on Training of Pauper Children," 1841, 8vo., Appendix, pp. 127 to 194.

or sudden inconvenience on large and populous parishes by
regulations which may appear vexatious to the future masters,
and thereby impede the placing out of children now fit for
service. We have, therefore, collected such information on the
probable operation of the Order as we could readily procure;
we have, also, received a deputation from the parish of St.
Marylebone, as well as one from the clerks to the Guardians
of the Unions in the neighbourhood of London, on the subject.
We shall proceed to consider the representations of these parties,
whose practical experience necessarily gives great weight to any
expression of their opinion; and we are prepared to make such
changes in the regulations now issued as may appear advisable.

37. Perhaps the most important change effected by the Act
of 7 and 8 Vict., c. 101, was that relating to bastardy. It is
unnecessary for us to recite the various alterations in the law
respecting the affiliation of bastard children, which had been
made previously to the last session of Parliament. We expressed our views with reference to further legislation on the
subject, in a special Report which we had the honour of presenting to you on the 31st day of January, 1844.—(See Tenth
Ann. Rep., App. A. No. 7.)

38. The Legislature, in the Act of last session, departed
entirely from the principle on which the affiliation of bastard
children had previously been based. In all former provisions
on this subject, from the Act of Elizabeth downwards, the sole
object avowed by the statutes was indemnity to the parish for
the charge of supporting the bastard. This indemnity was to
be supplied both by the putative father and by the mother;
practically, it depended on the former of the two. In no Act
had the principle been recognised that redress to the woman
for a wrong inflicted on her was the object of the Legislature.
The fact, therefore, that the protection afforded was, in the
eye of the law, given solely for the purpose of meeting the
charge upon the rate-payers, necessarily connected the affiliation of bastard children with the question of relief.

39. We have always believed, and we still think, that the
indirect use of what professed to be a remedy for the parish
only, as a means of redressing any wrong supposed to be inflicted on the woman, was in every way most mischievous and
embarrassing in its operation. The question, how far direct
redress in such cases could properly be given, is not one which
we were called upon to raise. If redress were to be given at
all, it ought, in our opinion, as we had the honour of reporting
to you, to be direct only; and such it was made by the statute
of last session. The result of this enactment, therefore, has
been that the affiliation of bastards stands altogether uncon-
nected with the laws for the relief of the poor. Parish and

c

Union officers are forbidden to take part in the proceedings relating to it, and an entirely new principle has been established by the law; that is to say, it is now admitted that the mother of a bastard, not the parish, is the party by whom redress is to be sought from the putative father, and to whom indemnity is to be awarded for the charge of maintaining the child. The means placed at her disposal for obtaining such redress are the cheapest and most accessible known to the laws of this country; that is to say, a proceeding in petty sessions.

40. Our only duty, in this Report, is to state in what manner this new principle has been found to work in relation to the laws for the relief of the poor, with the administration of which we are intrusted.

41. We have been consulted on various points of bastardy law, arising under the recent statute, by Union and parish officers as well as by justices; and we have, in consideration of the former connexion of the subject with the Poor Laws, endeavoured to afford advice and assistance, even where it did not appear strictly within our province to do so. To Boards of Guardians we have uniformly stated that a bastard and the mother of a bastard were, like any other persons, entitled to relief when destitute; that the fact of the latter having affiliated the child did not of itself deprive her of such a right, although any payment made by the putative father to her necessarily formed part of those means the amount of which it was the duty of the Guardians to consider when they proceeded to decide on the fact of her destitution. We have no reason to think that any embarrassment or difficulty of importance will occur in administering the laws for the relief of the poor in the cases of illegitimate children or their mothers in consequence of the Act of last session.

42. We were, by the Act of last session, empowered to combine Unions and parishes, within certain limits, for the erection of district schools to be used for the education of pauper children. We accordingly proceeded, soon after the passing of the Act, to consider the arrangements which it would be expedient to make for the purpose of giving effect to this provision; and we have to express much regret that we have hitherto been unable to declare any such district. This has arisen mainly from the fact that when we had caused the probable cost of the buildings to be appropriated to such schools to be accurately calculated, we saw reason to fear that the limit imposed on the money to be raised or borrowed by the 44th section of the statute, viz., one-fifth of the average annual expenditure, would in most instances, though not perhaps in all, preclude our obtaining such a sum as would be adequate for the proper construction of the building in question.

43. We feel bound also to state that we find existing among the members of the various Boards of Guardians in and about the metropolis considerable reluctance to avail themselves of the powers conferred on them by the Legislature. This indisposition, we make no doubt, would, on further consideration of the subject, be greatly diminished, provided the preliminary obstacle of the narrow limit fixed for the cost of the building and site were previously enlarged by the authority of Parliament. It is clear that this might easily be done without authorizing the expenditure of any such sum as would cast a serious burthen on the rate-payers; and it will be remembered that the Commissioners have no power conferred on them to order the erection of any school without the consent of the majority of the Board to be constituted for each district.

44. With regard to the other class of districts authorized by 7 and 8 Vic., c. 101, those, namely, for the relief of casual poor within the limits of the metropolitan police, we have framed a scheme for the division of the whole of the metropolitan district in such a manner as will, we think, enable us to carry out the intention of the Legislature. In this case the cost to be actually incurred will probably fall very far short of that authorized by the Act; and we shall proceed to declare the districts in question at as early a period as possible. We have caused them to be arranged, as much as practicable, with reference to the great lines of road along which mendicants and vagrants find their way into the metropolis; and our hope is that they will be found such as will enable the metropolitan police to discharge, without inconvenience, the duties imposed upon them in connexion with these asylums.

45. Among the provisions of the Act of last session, to which we are required to give effect, some of the most important are those relating to the appointment of District Auditors throughout England and Wales.

46. In the Report to the Marquis of Normanby on the further amendment of the Poor Laws, which the Commissioners had the honour to present in 1839, attention was called to the following recommendations of the Select Committee of the House of Commons on the Poor Law Amendment Act, in 1838:—1. That Auditors should not be confined to one Union, but should act for large districts. 2. That the Poor Law Commissioners should have the power of appointing District Auditors.

The Commissioners, in that Report, proceeded to dwell on the importance of the duties of an Auditor, and on the qualifications which appeared necessary for the discharge of those duties. In our Report of last year, we recurred to the

c 2

defect in the existing system of audit, and to the cumbrous
nature of the proceedings to which, in certain cases, we had
been compelled to resort ;in order to protect the rate-payers
from illegal expenditure of their funds. It was therefore with
sincere satisfaction that we saw the Legislature, in the last
session of Parliament, proceed to make such changes in the
system of audit as will, in our opinion, secure far more efficient
protection against fraud and illegality in the administration of
the poor-rate than has ever yet existed in the case of any
local fund in this country. The authority to form districts
was conferred on the Commissioners, the powers of District
Auditors were fixed and settled, and the method of their
appointment to a certain degree defined by the Act. The
appointment, however, was not, as recommended by the Select
Committee of the House of Commons, vested in the Commissioners, but was placed in the hands of the Chairman and
Vice-Chairman of each Board of Guardians included in a
district. We think it right to state that we entertain no doubt
of the superior advantages of the mode of appointment selected
by the Legislature ; and the experience of the elections which
have taken place, though limited, has satisfied us that no
preferable mode of appointment could have been devised.
The Chairmen and Vice-Chairmen of Unions are usually
gentlemen of such weight and experience in the despatch of
business as to inspire a reliance on their judgment and their
integrity. The Guardians, the rate-payers, and the officers
must all alike feel that an Auditor, selected by such persons,
is in the first instance entitled to public confidence. Should
it be afterwards proved, by his misconduct or inefficiency, that
such confidence has been misplaced, the Commissioners are
empowered to remove the officer thus failing in the discharge
of his duty.

47. At the same time, although the nomination of the
Auditors generally is not vested in the Commissioners, they
were authorized to deal with certain peculiar cases in which
Auditors were already acting for more than one Union. In
these instances, the Commissioners have the power to continue
the existing Auditor in office, and to add to or alter his district
as they see fit. We have considered this provision as intended
to effect two objects :—1. It enabled us, in the case of persons
who had already devoted a large part of their time to the
performance of the duties of Auditor, and whose salary was not
inconsiderable in amount, to secure to them a continuance of
their present situation, provided that they had proved themselves competent to perform its duties, and that the existence
of their district was not incompatible with the main object of
the Legislature ; that is to say, the general establishment of
proper audit districts throughout the whole country. 2. It

enabled us at once to extend the services of a tried and meritorious officer, acting for a small district, to one of larger extent, instead of exposing that officer to the risk of a fresh election, and of causing a new and perhaps inexperienced auditor to be elected for Unions which might properly be annexed to an existing district.

48. It will be observed that this power of continuance and of annexation does not prejudice the right of the Chairmen and Vice-Chairmen to elect in the event of any future vacancy; and we only regret that the considerations necessarily pressing on us in dividing the whole country into districts have often made it impossible to continue District Auditors against whom no complaint has been made, but whose retention of office would have disturbed the general arrangements which we were called upon to make. In such cases we have reluctantly been compelled to allow the Act to take its course, and the services of persons so situated, as well as of the Auditors for single Unions, have terminated, or will necessarily terminate, as fresh districts are declared. With regard to the Auditors for single Unions, we have in some instances, in which the Board of Guardians have expressed confidence in them, felt especial regret at our inability to continue them. Upon the whole, however, the sacrifice of individual interest in each case is so trifling as to make the operation of the Act in respect of the Auditors for single Unions of less importance, inasmuch as their salary is always inconsiderable, and their duties as Auditor have occupied but a small portion of their time.

49. Since the passing of the Act we have declared 24 districts for the purpose of audit: of these, 16 are districts in which we have thought it right to continue the services of an Auditor already acting for more than one Union, and the remainder are districts in which an auditor either has been or will be elected by the Chairmen and Vice-Chairmen of the several Boards of Guardians. With regard to these latter districts, we insert in the Appendix* a copy of the order directing the mode of election; which we have endeavoured to frame so as to give the least possible trouble to the electors, and to leave in the hands of our Assistant Commissioner, acting as returning officer, as little discretion as is compatible with the proper conduct of the election.

50. Some important amendments of the law in matters relating to the election of Guardians (particularly in the scale of voting for owners and rate-payers) were made by the Act of last session; and we accordingly, in January last, issued a general order, regulating the manner of conducting the elec-

---

* Appendix A. No. 4.

tions of Guardians,* in which all the provisions arc adapted to the altered state of the law.

51. By the 66th section of the Act we were empowered to separate parishes from, or annex them to, existing Unions, without the consent of the Board of Guardians, required by the Poor Law Amendment Act. In pursuance of this provision, we have detached the parishes of Kensington and Paddington from the former Kensington Union, and have placed them under separate Boards of Guardians; the other two parishes of the Union, Fulham and Hammersmith, remain together, as the Fulham Union. Our attention has likewise been directed to other Unions in different parts of the country, which appeared to be inconveniently large, or otherwise to require modification, with a view to the exercise of the power just adverted to. We have reason to believe that some of the Unions in Lincolnshire, in particular, contain too large an area, and that the local circumstances will in several cases admit of their reduction. The recent continued increase of pauperism in that county has, as it appears to us, been partly caused by the difficulty of inspection, which arises from the extent of the district placed under the superintendence of a single Board of Guardians.

52. We have likewise exercised in many cases the power conferred upon us by the same Act (sect. 18), of altering the number of Guardians elected by a parish. In general this alteration has been effected by authorizing the election of an additional Guardian or Guardians, the object being to remove slight inequalities in the representation, which had either existed from the formation of the Union, or had been produced by the disproportionate increase of population in different parishes.

53. The 34th section of the Act gave the Commissioners the power of consenting to the discharge by the auditor of any outstanding balance struck against an officer before the passing of the Act, provided no proceedings had been taken for its recovery. We have been applied to for our consent to the discharge of such balances in many cases, and in the majority of them this consent has been given. In some we have felt a difficulty in interpreting the words which occur in the middle of the clause, and have hesitated to assume a power respecting which some doubt may exist. In one or two cases only we have reluctantly refused on different grounds; that is to say, because it appeared that the balance due arose from illegal

---

* Appendix A. No. 5.

payments knowingly persevered in after notice of their illegality. We have thought that it was the intention of the Legislature to relieve from embarrassment those officers only who had been exposed to loss through inadvertence or ignorance of the law, not such as had intentionally violated its provisions.

54. The powers in the Act (sections 61 and 62) for the appointment of collectors and assistant overseers, and the provisions with respect to their duties and the security to be given by them, have been found very useful. Applications are constantly made to us from Boards of Guardians and from parishes to be allowed to avail themselves of the power of appointment in section 62. Although this portion of the administration of the Poor Laws is still encumbered with some difficulties, we entertain a confident hope that there will gradually be established a degree of regularity and of responsibility on the part of those officers such as has not hitherto existed.

55. We have only, in conclusion, to state that, with the exception of the points expressly mentioned above, the statute of the 7th and 8th Vict., c. 101, is now in operation, without having deranged, in any important respect, the previous administration of the Poor Laws, and without any prospect, so far as we can see, of its provisions acting otherwise than beneficially, both as regards the poor and the rate-payers.

56. In our last Annual Report we stated that the difficulties which we had experienced in enforcing the provisions of our general medical order, of March, 1842, had principally arisen in connexion with one of the three following subjects, viz.—1. The qualifications of the medical officers. 2. The maximum amount of the area and population of medical districts. 3. The rates of payments for medical officers in certain surgical and midwifery cases.

57. During the last year, the size of the medical districts has not undergone much modification; a few districts, in which the previous arrangements were susceptible of improvement, have been divided, or otherwise altered. The rates of the surgical and midwifery fees have continued in several unions to create objection; but these payments are now generally acquiesced in, since the Boards of Guardians have learnt by experience that the increase of expenditure, and the various evils, which they anticipated from the introduction of the fees in question, have not, in fact, been produced. The following is the amount of the expenditure for medical relief in each year since 1838:—

Years ending Lady-day.	Amount of Medical Relief.
	£.
1838	136,775
1839	148,652
1840	151,781
1841	154,054
1842	152,006
1843	160,726
1844	166,257

58. In regulating the remuneration for medical relief, our object has been to secure to the medical officer such a payment as would enable him to discharge his duty to his pauper patients, and to furnish them with proper medicines. In fixing this amount, however, it is necessary that we should keep in view the value at which the services of a medical man are attainable for this purpose, under the existing circumstances of the profession. If the Commissioners were to attempt, by their regulations, to fix the salaries of medical officers at a rate higher than that at which competent medical men are willing to accept the office and perform its duties, the result would be that the medical offices of Unions would become the subjects of sale, more or less concealed, and the pauper patients would derive no benefit from the excessive payment. A case, which affords an illustration of this principle, has recently occurred in the South Dublin Union. It appears that upon the resignation of one of the medical officers for the workhouse, an arrangement was made by the retiring officer with another medical gentleman that the latter, if elected his successor, would pay him a sum of 300*l.*; the annual salary of the office being 100*l.* We insert in the Appendix* the correspondence relating to the case. We think that the transaction to which we now refer affords a sufficient proof that the mere act of fixing a higher salary by the Commissioners or the Guardians cannot, as a matter of course, bring about the result that the increase of salary to a medical officer will secure more attention to the duties of the office which he holds. The increase, instead of acting as a constant stimulus to the exertions of the medical man from day to day, with reference to the persons to be placed under his care, may have passed out of his pocket by anticipation, and have gone simply to enrich his predecessor; nay, he may by this very payment be left encumbered with debts and difficulties which would rather impede than facilitate the discharge of his duties, especially if he had to provide medicines at his own cost.

59. The subject of medical relief is surrounded with great practical difficulties, and it has accordingly occupied a large share of our attention. We do not, however, anticipate at present any serious obstacle to the administration of this

* Appendix A No. 14.

branch of relief under the provisions of our general medical order. The questions which at present create the chief embarrassment in connexion with medical relief, and which admit of the least satisfactory solution, are those which arise from the inconvenient, intricate, and obscure state of the law respecting medical qualifications.

60. In our last Annual Report (par. 40) we noticed the increase which had then taken place in the mortality from smallpox. It was with regret that we perceived from the Registrar-General's Quarterly Tables of Mortality, that the deaths from this cause continued on the increase, notwithstanding the extent to which vaccination was carried on throughout England and Wales.

61. Towards the end of the year we caused a form of return to be prepared and transmitted to the clerks of the several Unions and parishes, calling for a statement of the numbers vaccinated in each during the year ending 29th September, 1844. We have since received returns from 542 Unions and parishes, an abstract from which will be found in the Appendix to this Report.* The returns distinguish the number of children which have been successfully vaccinated; they also distinguish the places where the parties were vaccinated. In order that we might the more readily judge whether vaccination had kept pace in each Union with the increase and probable wants of the population in that respect, we required the clerks to state the number of births in their respective Unions during the year. We also invited the remarks of the Guardians and public vaccinators on the working of the Vaccination Extension Act.

62. The births in the 542 Unions from which returns were received (after estimating the births for those Unions the returns for which were imperfect), amounted to 452,235. Of the children born in the year 1842, $8\frac{7}{10}$ per cent. died under the age of three months. Assuming therefore that the ratio of deaths of children under that age in the 542 Unions during the year ended 29th September, 1844, was the same, 39,344 children died in that year before attaining the age at which vaccination is most usually performed. This leaves 412,891 children requiring to be vaccinated in the course of the year. By the abstract of the returns referred to, it appears that there were 290,453 persons vaccinated by the public vaccinators, leaving only 122,438 children to be vaccinated by private medical practitioners and at public institutions. We are aware that the children vaccinated were not all born within the year ended 29th September, 1844, indeed that many adults are included in

---

* Appendix B. No. 9.

the number, and also that there may have been a considerable number of cases of re-vaccination ; but we think we may assume that the relation which the number of births bears to the number vaccinated is a tolerably correct measure of the efficiency of the arrangements for promoting the object of the Act.

63. Whenever we found that the births in any Union greatly exceeded the numbers vaccinated, we requested the Guardians to call the attention of the vaccinators to the subject, with a view to the further extension of vaccination in their respective districts; and where we found that few or none had been vaccinated at the appointed stations, we suggested that the vaccinators should be directed, as opportunities offered, to visit the houses of the poorer classes for the purpose of vaccinating any unvaccinated children. We have also, where it was stated that great prejudice prevailed against vaccination, recommended the Guardians to address circular letters to the clergymen within the Union, requesting them to co-operate with the public vaccinators in the extension of vaccination; and we believe that the clergy have in many instances rendered important service in removing the objections of their poorer parishioners. We have also the satisfaction of knowing, from the information supplied to us by the vaccinators, that although many of the more ignorant are still averse to their children being vaccinated, from the erroneous apprehension that other eruptive and cutaneous diseases may thereby be communicated to them, the prejudice does not now prevail to so great an extent as it did in previous years.

64. The public vaccinators return 3954 cases of small-pox attended by them during the year, out of which they state that 1283 were previously vaccinated. The information which the returns supply, in respect to the deaths from small-pox, on comparison with the mortality as published by the Registrar-General, proved to be so inaccurate that we have altogether omitted it from the Abstract.

65. In the 542 Unions referred to there are 2614 public vaccinators, and the number of stations appointed is 7075, which number includes the vaccinators' residences; but, in many instances, the out-stations have been given up in consequence of the neglect of the people to take their children to them. In such cases the vaccinators perform the operation either at their own residences, or visit the parties' houses for that purpose. Of the 290,453 persons vaccinated, the vaccinators returned 278,192 as successful; so that, of the total number vaccinated, only 12,261, or 4 per cent., on inspection, proved unsuccessful.

66. The following table is a continuation of the one contained in our last Annual Report of the Mortality from Small-pox in the Metropolis, since 1840 :—

Years.	March.	June.	September.	December.	Total.
1840	104	170	253	708	1,235
1841	605	252	128	68	1,053
1842	71	59	126	104	360
1843	144	105	75	114	438
1844	252	425	556	571	1,804
1845	481	..	..	..	..

It is satisfactory to observe a decrease in the mortality of the March quarter of 1845, as compared with the two preceding quarters; and we trust that the steps which we have taken, with the view of increasing the diligence of the public vaccinators, and calling public attention to the subject of vaccination, will have the effect of lessening the mortality from this disease.

The mortality from small-pox in England and Wales, during the years 1840, 1841, and 1842, was as follows:—

1840	10,434
1841	6,368
1842	2,715

67. The fees paid to the public vaccinators in England and Wales, during the year ended 25th March, 1844, amounted to 16,694*l.*, being an increase of 675*l.* upon the amount paid in the previous year.

68. We regret to be compelled to state that, in some few Unions in Wales, and in the Todmorden and Hayfield Unions, the Guardians have omitted to make provision for the gratuitous vaccination of the residents generally. We believe, however, that in these Unions the medical officers vaccinate all poor persons who apply to them, without charge; and are required, in terms of their appointment, to vaccinate the children of all the paupers. In very few of the parishes which are not in union, or governed under the provisions of local Acts, have the parish officers contracted expressly for vaccination.

69. Since the date of our last Annual Report, we have issued our Workhouse Regulations to Chester, Southampton, Chichester, Exeter, and St. Mary's Newington, all which places are governed by Boards of Guardians appointed under the provisions of local Acts. We have likewise issued a general order to several of the metropolitan parishes, requiring the clerks to make a weekly return of the number of paupers relieved, and certain other particulars, to the Assistant Commissioner of the district. We subjoin a copy of this order in the Appendix.* Our general order on pauper apprenticeship

* Appendix A. No. 6.

(see above, par. 32,) was likewise issued to the Unions and parishes under local Acts; and we have included several places similarly situated, in districts for the audit of accounts.

70. In all the above orders which we have issued to Unions and parishes under local Acts, we have, acting upon the spirit of the decision of the Court of Queen's Bench in the case of the parish of St. Pancras, carefully abstained from interfering with the constitution of the Board of Guardians, and the mode of its appointment. Our regulations have been confined to a control of the powers exercised by the local Board. We have found that the strict observance of this distinction, coupled with the explanations which we have given in our recent Annual Reports, has removed much of the misunderstanding which previously existed in many of the local Act Boards, with respect to the extent of the powers of the Commissioners. The decision of the Court of Queen's Bench, in the case of the Queen v. the Guardians of the poor of the city of Oxford, in Easter Term, 1844, has likewise placed out of all doubt the power of the Commissioners to regulate the proceedings of Boards of Guardians appointed under a local Act. In this case (of which the material facts are stated in our last Annual Report, par. 50), the Court of Queen's Bench decided, upon argument, that an order issued by the Poor Law Commissioners to the Oxford Guardians (who are elected under a local Act), directing them to appoint a master of the workhouse, was valid and must be obeyed.* We have likewise the satisfaction of stating that the difficulties to which we adverted in our last Annual Report, as having arisen in the parish of Birmingham, with respect to the regulations which we had issued to the Guardians, have since that time been removed.

71. The 64th section of the 7 and 8 Vic., c. 101, provides that whenever, under any local Act, there is no person particularly designated or authorized to act as chairman or vice-chairman, the Guardians shall appoint annually a chairman or vice-chairman. In consequence of this provision, we issued a circular to the Boards of Guardians under local Acts, inquiring whether a chairman and vice-chairman had been appointed accordingly, and we believe that this direction of the statute has generally been complied with.

72. A considerable number of parishes in Derbyshire and Staffordshire had been left under the provisions of the 43 Eliz., in consequence of their vicinity to the Alstonefield Union, formed under Gilbert's Act. Having ascertained that many of the parishes which assumed to belong to this Union had not

* A full report of the case is given in the "Justice of the Peace," for October 26, 1844.

been included in it according to the forms prescribed by the statute, we submitted a case to the Solicitor-General and Mr. Tomlinson ; and, upon the authority of their opinion, we issued an order, dated the 4th of January last, by which we formed the Ashbourne Union, out of the two classes of parishes just described. We have likewise annexed to the Uttoxeter and Bakewell Unions some other of the parishes which claimed to be a part of the Alstonefield Union. Since the date of our order, two elections of Guardians for the Ashbourne Union have taken place ; and the Board have appointed their officers and divided the Union into districts for general and medical relief. We have, however, received notice on behalf of some of the parishes which consider themselves members of the Alstonefield Union, that it is their intention to apply for a writ of *certiorari* to bring up our order before the Court of Queen's Bench.

73. In the township of Leeds, containing a population of 88,741 persons, the relief of the poor had been administered by a body of Overseers, appointed under a provision in a local Act for lighting and cleansing the town. By an Order, dated the 21st of November, 1844, we placed the administration of relief in that township under a Board of Guardians; and by the same Order we divided the township into wards for the election of Guardians, in pursuance of the powers contained in s. 19 of the 7 and 8 Vic., c. 101. Some questions have arisen in consequence of the transfer of power from the overseers to the Board of Guardians; but we have the satisfaction of stating that the operations of the newly appointed Board of Guardians have been conducted in such a manner as to lead us to anticipate much benefit to this important town from the change.

74. We have stated in former Reports that there are in Lancashire three Unions (viz., the Rochdale, Ashton, and Oldham Unions), which were formed in the year 1837, for the purposes of the Act for registering Births, Deaths, and Marriages, but which had never been put in operation for the administration of relief to the poor. Having come to the conclusion that it was desirable to put an end to the anomalous state in which these Unions remained, we issued, in October last, an Order to the Rochdale Guardians, directing them to take upon themselves the administration of relief to the poor. As this order was not complied with, we caused an application to be made to the Court of Queen's Bench for a writ of mandamus to compel the Guardians to obey its directions. The mandamus was granted by the Court, and a return to it was made by the Guardians; which return was traversed on the part of the Crown, and the issues thus framed were tried at the last assizes at Liverpool. A verdict was, under the direction of the judge, given for

the Crown upon all the issues, with a power to the defendants
to move to set it aside. This motion has since been made in
Easter Term, and a rule *nisi* has been obtained. As soon as
the judgment of the Court upon the points reserved (which
relate to merely formal questions) shall have been given, we
shall be able to take such further steps as may be requisite for
bringing the general law into operation in this Union.

75. The Guardians of the Royston Union have never appointed a chaplain for their workhouse; and complaints having
been made to us with respect to the attendance of Protestant
dissenting ministers upon members of the Established Church,
being inmates of the workhouse (which complaints were afterwards investigated), we issued in February, and afterwards in
April, 1842, an Order directing that "no child under the age
of 16 years, being a pauper and an inmate of the workhouse
of the Royston Union, who shall be a member of the Established
Church, should be compelled, required, or permitted to attend
the religious service or instruction of any minister dissenting
from the principles of such Established Church, either in or
out of such workhouse."

76. In the letter which accompanied our General Workhouse
Order (dated February, 1842), we made the following remarks
in reference to the restrictions which we thought it advisable
to place upon the presence of members of the Established
Church at the religious services of dissenting ministers in the
workhouse:—

"It appears to the Commissioners that the section of the Poor Law
Amendment Act, just quoted (s. 19), does not contemplate the attendance of members of the Established Church at the Divine service
performed by a dissenting minister in a workhouse. If any adult members of the Established Church should desire to attend the service of a
dissenting minister, the Commissioners would not interfere to prevent
their attendance, provided that no improper influence was used to induce
them to attend, although they consider it objectionable ; but the Commissioners think that children, being members of the Established Church,
should never be permitted to attend on such occasions, and they would,
in case of necessity, prohibit any such practice by an Order."

We still think that a considerable difference exists between
the cases of children and adults ; and we are reluctant, without
strong reasons, to interfere for the purpose of controlling the
religious discretion of adults in a workhouse. But the peculiar
circumstances of the Royston workhouse, and the complaints
which we continued to receive after the issue of the Order to
which we have above referred, induced us to issue a further
Order to this Union in January last, extending the provisions
of the former Order to *all* pauper inmates of the workhouse,
without reference to their age.*

* Appendix A. No. 7.

77.. We have subsequently received a memorial from the Board of Guardians, containing a strong remonstrance against the last-mentioned Order. The chief ground upon which the Guardians rely in this memorial, is that the prohibition of adult inmates of a workhouse, belonging to the Established Church, from attendance upon the religious service of a dissenting minister, is an infraction of their religious liberty. It appears to us, however, that no serious invasion of the religious liberty of the adult inmates of workhouses can be said to have taken place, so long as every such inmate can change his religious profession whenever he thinks fit, and can cause the register of his religious creed to be altered upon a simple notice to the Guardians. It is, moreover, necessary that, in framing regulations on this subject, we should look to the state of things in the Irish as well as the English workhouses; and we fear that serious inconveniences might arise in Ireland, if the adult inmates of a workhouse were to be permitted, without restriction, sometimes to attend the religious services of the Protestant and sometimes of the Roman Catholic chaplain.

78. Representations were some time ago made to us that the quantity of needlework executed in the metropolitan workhouses by the pauper inmates was sufficient to affect the market price of the article, and to lower the wages of the women who were employed by the trade. We accordingly instructed our Assistant Commissioner, Mr. Hall, to make inquiry into the subject; and we insert in the Appendix his Report, containing the results of his investigation. It appears from his Report that the value of the needlework performed in the metropolitan workhouses is not sufficient to affect the general market price, inasmuch as the total average value of such work done in the 28 metropolitan workhouses under our regulations does not amount to 14*l.* per week. For further details we refer to Mr. Hall's Report, which we insert in the Appendix.*

79. We likewise insert in the Appendix† a communication which we received from the Guardians of the Honiton Union, in Devonshire, containing a Report, prepared by several of the Guardians, of the state of the cottages inhabited by paupers in a portion of their Union. Much advantage would, we think, be produced by a similar inspection of this class of cottages in other Unions.

80. With reference to the subject of the emigration of paupers during the past year, we have to state that the number of emigrants to Canada who went out under our regulations exceeded that of the previous year.‡

* Appendix A, No. 11. † Appendix A, No. 12. ‡ Appendix B, No. 12.

81. Mr. Buchanan, in his Report on Emigration for the year 1843, set forth 659 emigrants as having been sent out under the superintendence of the Poor Law Commissioners; while in a list appended to his Report for the last year, a copy of which has been forwarded to us by the Colonial Land and Emigration Commissioners, 813 persons are stated to have been sent out under our orders. We do not readily trace 50 of these, according to the names of the ships which are given by Mr. Buchanan; but we have occasionally some difficulty in doing so where the contracts for the passage are not entered into with the merchants usually engaged in the carriage of emigrants to the colonies.

82. In the course of last autumn one vessel was sent out to Australia under the directions of the Colonial Land and Emigration Commissioners as a bounty ship, and it contained many pauper emigrants, who were assisted by their parishes under our authority. Another vessel is about to sail this spring, and several pauper emigrants will proceed in it.

83. We have no knowledge of any intention on the part of the Colonial Land and Emigration Commissioners to recommend the resumption of the bounty emigration to the Australian Colonies; we observe, however, that though in their Fifth General Report which has been lately presented to Parliament, they state in reference to New South Wales, that there was still much demand for shepherds and agricultural labourers, the following passage occurs :—" At Port Philip the prospect for *single men* is described as good, although the immigration of married people with young children was considered very unadvisable." As for the most part pauper emigrants consist of families, it is of much importance that this recommendation should be attended to by persons who may be disposed to forward the emigration of persons of that class.

84. There is one subject connected with the emigration of paupers to which we referred in our Eighth Annual Report, p. 37 (8vo. edition), and which we consider it highly desirable to notice again. We there described a practice of men quitting England and procuring a passage to the United States, leaving their families to be forwarded to that country by the parish officers or private individuals; and we stated that we objected to sanction the emigration to the United States, and added our strong opinion of the great inexpediency of rendering the assistance to the families of persons so circumstanced, which it is the object of the parties to obtain by the desertion of their families.

85. The remarks there made have been frequently supposed to refer simply to the emigration of parties to the United States, and we have been often requested to sanction the emigration of the wives and children of men who have deserted them and have emigrated to Canada. It has appeared to us, however,

that the strongest objections exist to defraying from the funds
of the parish the charges of emigration for families left destitute in this country by the husband or father.   If anything
were wanting to show. the importance of adhering to a general
rule with regard to such cases, we would refer to the following
passage in the extract from the Annual Report of the Chief
Agent for Emigration in Canada, dated Quebec, 20th December, 1844, which is printed in the Appendix to the Report of
the Colonial Land and Emigration Commissioners above
referred to, No. 8, p. 36 :—

" There is another class of our emigrants in almost every instance
requiring assistance from this department on arrival.   I find, on referring
to the books of the office at this place, that 173 widows, accompanied
by 488 children and grandchildren, came out this season to join their
sons or daughters ; *and* 245 *women, having* 713 *children, came out to
join their husbands,* all of whom received more or less assistance from
their relatives here to enable them to reach this port."

This extract gives information only as to those who have been
sent for by their husbands and fathers, and we are left in
ignorance as to the numbers who have been totally deserted, or
who, in the expectation of being summoned to the colony, are
left either in charge upon the parochial funds or their poor
relations.

86. In the allowances which we have sanctioned from the
parish funds for the emigration of paupers, we have deemed
it advisable to make an addition, to enable the Guardians to
provide an outfit of bedding and utensils for the voyage.   It
was generally found that the emigrants arrived at the vessel
unprovided with these requisites ; and as the shipper's contract
did not stipulate. for the providing of them, they were to be
purchased on the spot.   This purchase not being according to
the terms of our order, often led to many irregularities.   We
might have required the shipper's contract to include these
articles ; but as it appeared that the emigrants might frequently
have what was wanted, it was considered inexpedient to make
a provision which would operate universally, though not always
required.

87. We deem it right to advert to the provision in the
statute of the last Session of Parliament, contained in sec. 29,
which enables the Guardians of the parish or Union to apply
the money raised for the purpose of defraying the expenses of
emigration in such parish or in any parish in the Union.   We
have been informed that some misapprehension has arisen upon
the effect of this clause, and that some Boards of Guardians
have entertained an idea that they could apply any money for
emigration purposes when it seemed fit to them to do so.   It
is however, we believe, quite clear that they have no power to
act in this matter, except to carry into effect the resolution of

D

the rate-payers and owners of property who agree to the expenditure.

Proceedings in Ireland.

88. The administration of the law in Ireland has proceeded satisfactorily, upon the whole, since the date of our last Report.

89. The cases in which resistance to the collection of the rate has occurred within the last 12 months are comparatively few; and but few cases have occurred in which violence has even been anticipated. On all those occasions the prompt attention afforded by Her Majesty's Government in Ireland to every local application for assistance, has permitted no difficulty of this kind to continue to embarrass the administration of the law.

90. In the Westport Union, in the county of Mayo, the collection of the rate was for a time delayed, through a combination of adverse circumstances upon which it is not necessary to dwell. By the persevering efforts of a stipendiary magistrate, Mr. Kelly, who received His Excellency the Lord-Lieutenant's directions to repair to that Union, and assist the local magistracy in asserting the law and enforcing the payment of the rate, every difficulty was finally overcome, and the whole of a large rate made before the passing of the 6 and 7 Vic. c. 92 has been collected, with the exception of such arrears as might scarcely be considered recoverable after so great a lapse of time.

91. In the Ballinasloe Union also, in the counties of Roscommon and Galway, special assistance was applied for by the Guardians to enable the arrears of a rate made before August, 1843, to be collected. In compliance with this requisition, the presence of a military force, and the special services of stipendiary magistrates were provided by His Excellency's command; and these arrangements were at once followed by a peaceable and satisfactory collection of the rates, and the complete vindication of the law. In Ballinrobe Union, situate in the counties of Galway and Mayo; in Castlebar Union, county of Mayo; and in Loughrea Union, in the county of Galway, special assistance was also afforded on the application of the Guardians, with the same successful and beneficial result.

92. The financial embarrassment which we remarked upon in our last Report, as one of the circumstances prejudicial to the working of the law in some Unions, has now ceased to exist in nearly all the Unions, the Guardians of which have not systematically opposed themselves to the introduction and progress of the law; and there is reason to believe that the alteration of the law, fixing the payment of rates made upon tenements at or under 4*l.* value upon the landlord, has been productive of much general advantage in this respect. The collection of the rates

which have been made under the statute 6 and 7 Vic., c. 92, has so far proceeded well; and the improved financial state of the Unions generally must be ascribed, in some measure, to the amended state of the law.   By the last monthly account of the collection, comprising returns from 121 Unions, the amount collected within the month ended 31st March last was 27,871*l.*; the net amount of the balances in the hands of the treasurers of all the 121 Unions was 32,714*l.*, and rates to the further amount of 145,703*l.* were in progress of collection.

93. Several Unions, namely, those of Carlow, Mountmelick, Dungarvan, Kanturk, Killarney, Listowel, Letterkenny, and Bantry, have been brought into operation during the last year; and effectual steps are being taken by the Guardians of Kenmare, Swineford, Enniskillen, Dunfanaghy, and Lowtherstown, to open their respective workhouses for the admission and relief of the destitute poor.   There are on the whole, at the present time, 118 workhouses out of the entire number, 130, open for the purposes of relief.   Of the remaining number of workhouses 3 are not yet declared to be ready for the reception of inmates; and in a few instances, which we shall proceed to specify, the Guardians still refuse or neglect to proceed duly in the administration of relief, although the workhouses have long since been declared fit for the reception of inmates.

94. The case of the Tuam Union was adverted to in our last Report.   Since that date the Guardians, although continually pressed by us to proceed in the performance of their duties, have made so little progress that the rate signed by them on the 24th October, 1842, amounting to 1796*l.*, has not yet been put in course of collection.   Collectors having been appointed to some of the electoral divisions, we urged the Guardians to cause the rates to be collected in those divisions; but they declined giving warrants to the collectors for this purpose, until the appointment of all the collectors should be made and their securities completed, which has not yet been done.   We deemed it our duty, under these circumstances, to apply to the Court of Queen's Bench for a mandamus to require the Guardians to proceed in this particular portion of their duty.   No cause having been shown against the conditional order, it was made absolute, and a writ of mandamus was served on the Guardians, returnable on the first day of Easter term.   The Guardians have made a return to the writ, and the suit is still in progress.
95. We can anticipate no other result than the final submission of the Guardians of Tuam Union to the authority of the law.   In the mean time many suits have been commenced against them for debts which they have not hesitated to incur, although neglecting to furnish themselves with any means of

payment. The first application therefore of this large rate, when collected, will be to defray the costs of proceedings taken by the creditors of the Union against the Guardians, and to repair the great waste of property incurred by permitting the goods of the Union to be seized and sold in payment of these debts. Many of the destitute poor, whom these rates were intended to relieve, have been permitted in the mean while to become a burden on the surrounding Unions.

96. We shall not fail to use every legal means available to us, of urging forward the administration of relief to the poor in Tuam workhouse.

97. The Guardians of Castlerea and Westport Unions have not yet proceeded, as they ought to have long since done, to open their respective workhouses and to commence the administration of relief; and the Guardians of Clifden and Cahirciveen Unions have not yet made any rate. We cannot, however, believe that a course of inaction so adverse to all interests, can be long persevered in by the Guardians of these Unions.

98. In our last Annual Report we adverted to the amended regulations issued by us for the guidance and government of the Guardians and officers of Unions in Ireland, and a copy of the General Regulations' Order was given in the Appendix to that Report.*

99. In the month of August last, shortly after the issue of this order, we were requested by the Guardians of Limerick Union to alter the 41st article of those regulations, in such a manner as to vest in the Guardians the power of suspending the clerk of the Union from the performance of his duties.

100. We explained, in reply to the representations of the Guardians, the grounds on which we doubted the propriety of our placing in the Union Boards, constituted under the Irish Poor Relief Amendment Act, the exercise of this function, referring particularly to those provisions of the Act which vest in the Poor Law Commissioners the responsiblity of determining the continuance in office of certain of the Union officers, and to other provisions, which confer upon the clerk of a Union functions which it appeared to be intended he should exercise on his own responsibility in fulfilment of the direct provisions of the Act.

101. The class of provisions last mentioned are those which make the counter-signature of the clerk necessary to perfect a legal record of the proceedings of the Guardians, as provided in the 28th section of the original Act; the provision in section 43, which makes the counter-signature of the clerk essential

---

* Annual Report, 1844, Appendix A. No. 19.

to the registration of paupers, a process by which their chargeability to particular electoral divisions is determined; and to
those may be added the section of the Irish Poor Relief Act,
which requires the clerk to certify on the rate, before it is
signed by the Guardians, that it is made in conformity with
the valuation then in force.

102. As the Guardians of the Limerick Union persisted in
the view which they had taken of the 41st article, we deemed
it right for our own satisfaction, as well as for that of the
Guardians, to obtain legal advice as to the extent of our powers
in reference to the point in question; and the Limerick and
Rathkeale Boards having determined to abandon the performance of their duties as Guardians, we took the further advice
of Counsel as to the applicability of the writ of mandamus to
these cases; notwithstanding the provisions of the 26th section of
the Relief Act, which enabled us under such circumstances to
dissolve the Board of Guardians, and cause another Board to
be elected.

103. On the first of the two points above stated we were advised by the Solicitor-General for Ireland, that the provisions
of the Irish Poor Relief Act contained nothing which could
prevent our legally imparting to the Board of Guardians the
power of suspending the Clerk of the Union from the exercise
of his duties as clerk.

104. Two English Counsel, viz., Mr. Erle (now Mr. Justice
Erle), and Mr. Tomlinson, advised us, on the contrary, that we
could not legally impart to the Guardians the function which
they claimed to exercise of suspending the clerk. We communicated this opinion to the Guardians of Limerick and
Rathkeale as soon as we received it. We were at the same
time, advised by Mr. Erle and Mr. Tomlinson that the writ of
mandamus was available to compel the Guardians to act in
execution of their office, notwithstanding the provisions of the
26th section.

105. We accordingly applied to the Court of Queen's Bench
in Ireland for writs of mandamus against the Guardians of
Limerick and Rathkeale Unions, requiring them to proceed in
the execution of their duties as Guardians, and to meet weekly
for the purpose, which for several weeks past the Guardians of
both Unions had ceased to do; and we obtained conditional
orders in both cases. Against these orders the Guardians
showed cause, and the Court refused, after argument, to issue
the writs, on the ground that the 26th section of the Act
afforded another remedy for the neglect of the Guardians, by
enabling the Poor Law Commissioners to dissolve the Union,
and to cause another Board of Guardians to be elected. The
Judges, at the same time, expressed their strong disapprobation
of the course taken by the Guardians in venturing to abandon

the performance of their duties, and expressed their opinion that the Guardians could not resign their offices without the consent of the Poor Law Commissioners, nor cease to act in discharge of their duties, without exposing themselves to indictment for a breach of the law.

106. After duly weighing the effect of these proceedings, and the observations made by the Court, the Guardians of Limerick and Rathkeale Unions resumed the discharge of their duties as Guardians of the poor.

107. During the progress of these proceedings, the Guardians of Limerick Union communicated their views regarding the 41st Article to the other Boards of Guardians in Ireland, and thereby caused an expression of similar views on the part of a large majority of the Unions. In reply to all the communications which reached us on this subject, we informed the Guardians fully of the view which we ourselves had taken of the intentions of the Legislature, and of the advice which we had received from Counsel; and we have always assured the Guardians of our readiness to inquire into any complaint against the conduct of their officers, and to afford immediate assistance and redress on every occasion of such complaint being shown to be well founded.

108. We shall only add further, in reference to this controversy, that neither at Limerick nor elsewhere has the question appeared to connect itself with the existence or supposed existence of any practical grievance on the part of the Guardians. Where the guardians have been willing to remove their clerk, we have almost invariably found occasion to coincide in that view. The cases, in which we have differed in opinion with a Board of Guardians regarding the conduct of their clerk, have nearly always been of an opposite nature; that is to say, when we have proposed to remove the clerk of a Union in Ireland on the ground of his unfitness for the office, we have very frequently found the majority of the Guardians desirous of retaining him.

109. Since the date of our last Report, the Guardians of many additional Unions have taken steps for providing relief to persons suffering from dangerous contagious disorders, under sections 15 and 16 of the Irish Poor Law Amendment Act. At the present point of time, the Guardians of 26 Unions have either already built a fever ward or have determined to do so. At Longford, Larne, Dundalk, Balrothery, and Lurgan, these buildings are now completed, and in nearly all the others the works are in progress. The Longford fever ward is open, and made use of for the reception and treatment of patients.

110. In 11 other Unions, the subject of building a fever ward is still under consideration. The course which we have

recommended and described in paragraph 154 of our last Report, has invariably been adopted hitherto; that is to say, the building of an out-ward on a part of the workhouse site sufficiently distant from the main building to avoid the risk of infection.

111. In a considerable number of Unions, arrangements have been made with the directors of fever hospitals for the reception and treatment of fever patients from the workhouse, under the provisions of section 15 of the Amendment Act; and in eight Unions, houses have been hired for fever hospitals, under section 16. A Return to an Order of the House of Commons is now in course of preparation, which will show these several arrangements in detail, and exhibit the number of cases already relieved under sections 15 and 16. A Copy of this Return will be included in the Appendix to this Report.*

112. The immediate operation of these provisions, there can be no doubt, has been very beneficial in many places. In Galway, for example, during a most severe epidemic, the Guardians erected a temporary hospital near the workhouse, and received into it, during a period of about six months, 1096 cases, of which 995 were discharged cured on or before the 14th February last.

113. Since the date of our last Report, we have taken no new steps, sufficiently important to be mentioned, under those sections of the 6 and 7 Vict., c. 92, which relate to the valuation of Unions. After the report of the Parliamentary Committee appointed last Session to inquire into the subject of valuations generally in Ireland, we have deemed it advisable to do no more than provide for the immediate exigencies of those Unions which required valuation or revision by making arrangements for these purposes of a temporary nature only.

114. We place in the Appendix† to this Report, returns which have been obtained in reference to the progress of the Vaccination Act in Ireland, which will show that this measure, although not duly carried into effect by the Guardians of many Unions, has nevertheless obtained a wide and beneficial operation, which we trust is in course of gradual extension.

115. The amount shown to have been expended for vaccination, in the half-year ended 29th September last, according to the audited abstracts of 104 Unions, is 1754*l.* The amount for the preceding half-year for 100 Unions was 2329*l.*; and the total amount therefore for the entire year, in all the Unions in Ireland, may be taken to exceed considerably the sum of 4000*l.*; the usual rate of payment being 1*s.* on each successful case for the first 100 cases in the year, and 6*d.* on each successful case for the remainder.

---

* Appendix B. No. 20.   † Appendix B. No. 19.

116. In our last Annual Report we exhibited a summary of the receipts and expenditure in 73 Unions, for the half-year ended on the 29th September, 1843; and we gave in the Appendix a series of Tables, showing the details of that expenditure in each of those Unions, and showing the nature and amount of the particular items of which the establishment charges were composed.* That statement was necessarily restricted to the Unions from which audited accounts had been obtained at the time the Report was framed; and we had much reason to regret that the state of the audits in Ireland did not at that time admit of a larger proportion of the whole expenditure being thus exhibited.

117. We are now enabled to give a similar but far more extended statement for the two half-years severally ended on the 25th March, 1844, and the 29th September following. For the former half-year we have received the accounts of 100 Unions duly audited, and for the latter half-year the accounts of 104 Unions; and we give, in the Appendix,† Tables which exhibit a minute analysis of that expenditure in all the Unions for which we have received accounts duly audited. It is obvious that information of this kind cannot be safely given for Unions, the accounts of which remain unclosed or unaudited; of which class we regret to say that several still remain. The satisfactory progress, however, which has been made in bringing up the arrears of the audits during the past year, gives us reason to hope that in our next Report we may be enabled to exhibit a similar analysis of the expenditure for the whole of the 130 Unions in Ireland.

118. We now subjoin for each of the two half-years above adverted to, a summary of the receipts and expenditure duly balanced, derived from the audited abstracts of the several Union accounts.

Summary of the Accounts of 100 *Unions, from which Audited Accounts have been received, for the Half-year ended 25th March,* 1844.

CHARGE.

	£.	s.	d.	£.	s.	d.
Balances in favour of electoral divisions at the close of last half-year. . . .		.	.	42,060	8	5½
Amount of poor-rates collected	128,312	11	8			
Repayment of relief by way of loan . .	47	2	5			
Other receipts	2,032	14	5			
Total receipts in the half-year		.	.	130,392	8	6
Balances against the electoral divisions at the close of this half-year . .				67,866	7	3¾
				£240,319	4	3½

---

* Annual Report, 1844, App. B. Nos. 15 and 16.
† Appendix B. Nos. 13, 14, and 15.

DISCHARGE.

	£.	s.	d.	£.	s.	d.
Balances against electoral divisions at the close of last half-year				65,650	1	8
Maintenance and clothing of electoral division paupers	59,354	15	7¾			
Ditto of Union paupers	8,551	16	8			
Establishment charges	35,923	13	1½			
Repayment of workhouse loans . . .	4,770	0	0			
Vaccination expenses	2,329	0	2½			
Expense of valuing or revising valuations	3,101	2	7			
Collectors' poundage	3,373	6	1½			
Funerals, election, law, and other expenses	8,130	2	9			
Total expenditure in the half-year . .				125,533	17	1
Balances in favour of electoral divisions at the close of this half-year . . .				49,135	5	6¼
				£240,319	4	3¼

Summary of the Accounts of 104 *Unions, from which Audited Accounts have been received for the Half-year ended 29th September,* 1844.

CHARGE.

	£.	s.	d.	£.	s.	d.
Balances in favour of electoral divisions at the close of last half-year . . .				51,075	16	7¾
Amount of poor-rates collected . . .	128,346	19	5			
Repayment of relief by way of loan . .	29	10	3¾			
Other receipts	1,493	4	3			
Total receipts in the half-year				129,869	13	11¾
Balances against the electoral divisions at the close of this half-year				60,627	19	1
				£241,573	9	8½

DISCHARGE.

	£.	s.	d.	£.	s.	d.
Balances against electoral divisions at the close of last half-year				64,561	17	7¾
Maintenance and clothing of electoral division paupers	68,202	14	4¾			
Ditto of Union paupers	10,278	13	8			
Establishment charges	34,983	1	3¾			
Repayment of workhouse loans . . .	4,584	3	4			
Vaccination expenses	1,754	17	7½			
Expense of valuing or revising valuations	1,720	6	5			
Collector's poundage	2,867	18	8½			
Amount expended on emigration . . .	101	13	11			
Funeral, election, law, and other expenses	3,910	15	0¼			
Total expenditure in the half-year . .				128,404	4	4¼
Balances in favour of electoral divisions at the close of this half-year. .				48,607	7	8½
				£241,573	9	8

119. In the first of these half-years the receipts exceed the expenditure by the sum of 4858*l.* 11*s.* 4½*d.*; in the second half-year, the receipts exceed the expenditure by the sum of 1465*l.* 9*s.* 7½*d.*

120. The accounts for the half-year ended 25th March, 1845, have not yet been audited: but we have every reason to believe, from the monthly returns of the collection, and of the balances reported to be in the hands of the treasurers, that the financial improvement above indicated is proceeding favourably.

121. The establishment charges for the first half-year amount to 35,923*l.*; in the second half-year to 34,983*l.* In the Appendix* will be found a minute statement of the nature and amount of the particular items included in this part of the expenditure for each half-year. They will be found, on examination, to consist of charges necessarily incidental to the system of relief established by the Irish Poor Relief Act, viz., relief afforded in a workhouse only.

122. In another part of the Appendix† will be found tables showing the amount of the cost of maintenance and clothing of paupers, the number of paupers relieved in each half-year, and the average weekly cost per head.

123. From a table now before us it appears that in the half-year ended on the 29th September, 1844, the number of paupers relieved in 103 Unions during the half-year was 67,487. The average number of days during which each pauper was relieved exceeded 92 days, or about one quarter of a year. The average weekly cost per head of maintenance appears to have been 1*s.* 5¾*d.*, and the average weekly cost of clothing, 3¼*d.*: total average weekly cost per head for maintenance and clothing 1*s.* 9*d.*

124. From a comparison of the expenditure with the net annual value of the property rateable in each Union we may safely infer that the current annual expenditure is at an average rate of less than 6*d.* in the £. at the present time.

125. Thus, in the first half-year, the proportion of expenditure to net annual value (11,188,204*l.*), gives an amount of 2½*d.* in the £. and a small fraction; in the second half-year also 2½*d.* in the £. and a small fraction, the net annual value being 11,324,511*l.*

126. It should be stated, however, that there is a great arrear of instalments due on account of the building loans in many of the Unions; and that very few workhouses at present contain the full complement of inmates which they are calculated to receive. On both these points some increase of the

---

* Appendix B. No. 14.   † Appendix B. No. 15.

average rate of poundage may be expected, as well as from the further extension of relief to persons suffering from dangerous contagious disorders.

127. The rates of poundage above specified include the sums paid in repayment of the instalments of loans borrowed for building and fitting up the workhouses, so far as those instalments have been paid. By a table given in the Appendix* it will be seen that the total amount of the sums borrowed for that purpose affords an average poundage on the net annual value of Ireland of 1*s.* 8¼*d.* in the £.; that is, a poundage of about 1*d.* in the £. per annum for repayment of the capital sums borrowed. It will be seen, from the details given in the same table, that the pressure of these loans on the property rated varies in the different Unions in which workhouses have been built so much as from 1*s.* to 9*s.* 4½*d.* in the £.; a variation arising from the great difference in the proportions which the building expenditure in the several Unions bears to their net annual value respectively.

128. Up to the present point of time rates have been made upon 126 Unions out of the entire number of 130; the Unions in which no rate has yet been made are Cahirciveen, Clifden, Glenties, and Milford.

129. In addition to the four Unions last mentioned, there are eight Unions in which the workhouses are not yet opened for the relief of the destitute poor, viz., Castlerea, Dunfanaghy Kenmare, Lowtherstown, Swineford, Enniskillen, Westport, and Tuam, making a total of 12 workhouses still remaining unopened.

130. We trust we may be enabled to report next year that the whole of the 130 workhouses in Ireland are open for the reception and relief of the destitute poor, in accordance with the intention of the Legislature, and the provisions of the Irish Poor Relief Act.

We have the honour to be,

Sir,

Your very faithful and obedient Servants,

(Signed)   GEORGE NICHOLLS,
GEORGE CORNEWALL LEWIS,
EDMUND WALKER HEAD.

---

* Appendix B. No. 18.

AMOUNT OF MONEY Levied, and Received from other Sources in Aid of POOR'S RATE, and expended for the RELIEF and MAINTENANCE of the Poor, and for other Purposes, in ENGLAND and WALES, during the Years ending 25th March, 1834, to 1844, with the Average Price of Wheat per Quarter in each Year.

Years ended at Lady-day.	Receipt.			Expenditure.										Medical Relief.	Average Price of Wheat per Quarter, in each Year ending at Lady-day.
	Amount of Money levied by Assessment. £.	Received from all other Sources in Aid of Poor's Rate. £.	Total Amount of Money received as Poor's Rate. £.	Amount of Money expended in Relief, &c., of the Poor.* £.	Amount of Money expended in Law Charges (Parochial and Union). £.	Amount of Fees paid to the Vaccinators under the Vaccination Extension Act. £.	Payments on Account of the Registration Act: viz. Fees to Clergymen and Registrars, Outlay for Register Offices, Books and Forms. £.	Payments under the Parochial Assessments Act, (for Surveys, Valuations, &c.,) and Loans repaid under the same. £.	Payments made under the Act for taking an Account of the Census of 1841. £.	Payments for or towards the County or Borough Rate. £.	Payments for or towards the County and Local Police Forces, (if any, and if not Paid out of the County or Borough Rate.) £.	Money expended for all other Purposes. £.	Total Parochial Rates expended. £.	£.	s. d.
1834†	8,388,079			6,317,255	258,604					691,548		1,021,941	8,289,348		51
1835	7,373,807			5,526,418	220,527					705,711		935,362	7,370,018		44 2
1836	6,334,538			4,717,630	172,432					699,845		823,213	6,413,120		39 5
1837	5,294,566			4,044,741	126,951					604,203		657,043	5,412,938		52 6
1838	5,186,389			4,123,604	93,982		35,662	25,680		681,842		507,929	5,468,699	136,775	53 3
1839	5,613,939	273,139	5,887,078	4,406,907	63,412		52,306	56,846		741,407		498,703	5,814,581	148,652	69 4
1840	6,014,605	227,966	6,242,571	4,576,965	67,020		51,228	49,963		855,532		466,698	6,067,426	151,781	68 6
1841	6,351,828	226,984	6,578,812	4,760,929	69,942	11,664	58,728	43,157	57,111	1,026,035		597,717	6,493,172	154,054	63 0
1842	6,552,890	201,514	6,754,404	4,911,498	68,051	33,744	52,379	40,178		1,003,651	227,067	318,092	6,711,771	153,491	64 4
1843	7,085,595	219,006	7,304,601	5,208,027	84,730	16,425	53,896	30,420		1,051,878	243,738	346,007	7,085,121	160,726	54 4
1844	6,847,205	219,592	7,066,797	4,975,093	103,304	16,990	56,094	20,083		1,111,236	245,221	359,106	6,900,117	166,257	51 5

* Including in-door and out-door relief and establishment charges; and since the passing of the Poor Law Amendment Act, in addition thereto building and emigration loans repaid, furnishing of Union workhouses, &c.

† The last parochial year previous to the passing of the Poor Law Amendment Act.

NOTE.—The above results are obtained from the annual Poor Rate Returns received from the clerks of Unions and Overseers of the Poor.

APPENDIX.

APPENDIX (A.)

ORDERS AND INSTRUCTIONAL LETTERS ISSUED BY THE POOR LAW COMMISSIONERS, REPORTS, &c.

ENGLAND.

No. 1.

AMENDED GENERAL ORDERS—REGULATING THE RELIEF OF ABLE-BODIED POOR PERSONS.

To THE GUARDIANS OF THE POOR of the several Unions named in the Schedule hereunto annexed;

To the Churchwardens and Overseers of the Poor of the several Parishes and Places comprised within the said respective Unions;

To the Clerk or Clerks to the Justices of the Petty Sessions held for the Division or Divisions in which the Parishes and Places comprised within the said respective Unions are situate;

And to all others whom it may concern.

We, the Poor Law Commissioners, in pursuance of the authorities vested in Us by an Act passed in the fifth year of the reign of his late Majesty King William the Fourth, intituled "An Act for the Amendment and better Administration of the Laws relating to the Poor in England and Wales," do hereby rescind an Order, being a general rule of the Poor Law Commissioners, bearing date the second day of August, in the year of our Lord one thousand eight hundred and forty-one, except so far as the same rescinds any Order or Orders theretofore issued by the Poor Law Commissioners.

And we do hereby also rescind the Orders relative to the relief of able-bodied Poor Persons, issued by the Poor Law Commissioners to the several Unions hereunder mentioned, except so far as the same rescind any Order or Orders theretofore issued by the said Commissioners, or relate to the out-door labour test for able-bodied male paupers, that is to say:—

The Order bearing date the ninth day of December, one thousand eight hundred and forty-one, and issued to the Guardians of the Poor of the Burgh of Bury St Edmunds;

The Order bearing date the tenth day of January, one thousand eight hundred and forty-two, and issued to the Guardians of the Poor of the Aberystwith Union;

The Order bearing date the fifteenth day of April, one thousand eight hundred and forty-two, and issued to the Guardians of the Poor of the Ruthin Union;

The Order bearing date the thirtieth day of April, one thousand eight hundred and forty-two, and issued to the Guardians of the Poor of the Llanfyllin Union;

The General Order bearing date the thirtieth day of July, one thousand eight hundred and forty-two, and issued to the Guardians of the Poor of the Longtown Union, the Guardians of the Poor of the Whitehaven Union, and the Guardians of the Poor of the Wigton Union;

The Order bearing date the fifth day of August, one thousand eight hundred and forty-two, and issued to the Guardians of the Poor of the Cockermouth Union;

The Order bearing date the ninth day of September, one thousand eight hundred and forty-two, and issued to the Guardians of the Poor of the Richmond Union, in the County of York;

The Order bearing date the thirtieth day of November, one thousand eight hundred and forty-two, and issued to the Guardians of the Poor of the Ormskirk Union;

The Order bearing date the seventeenth day of December, one thousand eight hundred and forty-two, and issued to the Guardians of the Poor of the Hailsham Union;

The Order bearing date the twenty-first day of January, one thousand eight hundred and forty-three, and issued to the Guardians of the Poor of the Chard Union.

And the General Order bearing date the twenty-seventh day of June, one thousand eight hundred and forty-three, and issued to the Guardians of the Poor of the Saint Asaph Union; the Guardians of the Poor of the Bala Union; the Guardians of the Poor of the Bridgend and Cowbridge Union; the Guardians of the Poor of the Corwen Union; the Guardians of the Poor of the Festiniog Union; and the Guardians of the Poor of the Pwllheli Union:

Provided that nothing herein contained shall apply to any relief given under or prohibited by any of the said Orders hereby rescinded.

And we do hereby order, direct, and declare, with respect to each and every of the Unions named in the Schedule hereunto annexed, as follows :—

Art. 1.—Every able-bodied person, male or female, requiring relief from any Parish within any of the said Unions, shall be relieved wholly in the Workhouse of the Union, together with such of the family of every such able-bodied person as may be resident with him or her, and may not be in employment, and together with the wife of every such able-bodied male person, if he be a married man, and if she be resident with him; save and except in the following cases :—

   1st.—Where such person shall require relief on account of sudden and urgent necessity.

   2nd.—Where such person shall require relief on account of any sickness, accident, or bodily or mental infirmity affecting such person, or any of his or her family.

   3rd.—Where such person shall require relief for the purpose of defraying the expenses, either wholly or in part, of the burial of any of his or her family.

4th.—Where such person, being a widow, shall be in the first six months of her widowhood.

5th.—Where such person shall be a widow, and have a legitimate child, or legitimate children dependent upon her, and incapable of earning his, her, or their livelihood, and have no illegitimate child born after the commencement of her widowhood.

6th.—Where such person shall be confined in any gaol or place of safe custody, subject always to the regulation contained in Article 4.

7th.—Where such person shall be the wife, or child, of any ablebodied man who shall be in the service of Her Majesty as a soldier, sailor, or marine.

8th.—Where any able-bodied person, not being a soldier, sailor, or marine, shall not reside within the Union, but the wife, child, or children of such person shall reside within the same, the Board of Guardians of the Union, according to their discretion, may, subject to the regulation contained in Article 4, afford relief in the Workhouse to such wife, child, or children, or may allow out-door relief for any such child or children being within the age of nurture, and resident with the mother within the Union.

Art. 2.—In every case in which out-door relief shall be given on account of sickness, accident, or infirmity, to any able-bodied male person resident within any of the said Unions, or to any member of the family of any able-bodied male person, an extract from the Medical Officer's Weekly Report (if any such officer shall have attended the case), stating the nature of such sickness, accident, or infirmity, shall be specially entered in the Minutes of the Proceedings of the Board of Guardians of the day on which the relief is ordered or subsequently allowed.

But if the Board of Guardians shall think fit, a certificate under the hand of a Medical Officer of the Union, or of the Medical Practitioner in attendance on the party, shall be laid before the Board, stating the nature of such sickness, accident, or infirmity, and a copy of the same shall be in like manner entered in the Minutes.

Art. 3.—No relief shall be given from the poor-rates of any parish comprised in any of the said Unions to any person who does not reside in some place within the Union, save and except in the following cases:—

1st.—Where such person, being casually within such parish, shall become destitute.

2nd.—Where such person shall require relief on account of any sickness, accident, or bodily or mental infirmity, affecting such person, or any of his or her family.

3rd.—Where such person shall be entitled to receive relief from any parish in which he or she may not be resident, under any order which justices may by law be authorized to make.

4th.—Where such person being a widow, shall be in the first six months of her widowhood.

5th.—Where such person is a widow, who has a legitimate child dependent on her for support, and no illegitimate child born after the commencement of her widowhood, and who at the time of her husband's death was resident with him in some place other than the parish of her legal settlement, and not situated in the Union in which such parish may be comprised.

6th.—Where such person shall be a child under the age of 16, maintained in a workhouse or establishment for the education of pauper children not situate within the Union.

7th.—Where such person shall be the wife or child residing within the Union, of some person not able-bodied, and not residing within the Union.

8th.—Where such person shall have been in the receipt of relief from some parish in the Union from which such person seeks relief, at some time within the twelve calendar months next preceding the date of that one of the several Orders hereinbefore recited which was applicable to that Union, being settled in such parish, and not being resident within the Union at the time of the allowance of the relief.

Art. 4.—Where the husband of any woman is beyond the seas, or in custody of the law, or in confinement in a licensed house or asylum as a lunatic or idiot, all relief which the Guardians shall give to his wife, or her child, or children, shall be given to such woman, in the same manner, and subject to the same conditions, as if she were a widow.

Art. 5.—It shall not be lawful for the Guardians, or any of their officers, or for the Overseer or Overseers of any parish in the Union, to pay, wholly or in part, the rent of the house or lodging of any pauper, or to apply any portion of the relief ordered to be given to any pauper in payment of any such rent, or to retain any portion of such relief for the purpose of directly or indirectly discharging such rent, in full or in part, for any such pauper.

Provided always, that nothing in this article contained shall apply to any shelter or temporary lodging, procured in any case of sudden and urgent necessity, or mental imbecility, or shall be taken to prevent the said Guardians, in regulating the amount of relief to be afforded to any particular person, from considering the expense to be incurred by such person in providing lodging.

Art. 6.—Provided always, that in case the Guardians of any of the said Unions depart in any particular instance from any of the regulations hereinbefore contained, and within fifteen days after such departure report the same, and the grounds thereof to the Poor Law Commissioners, and the Poor Law Commissioners approve of such departure, then the relief granted in such particular instance shall, if otherwise lawful, not be deemed to be unlawful, or be subject to be disallowed.

Art. 7.—No relief which may be contrary to any regulation in this Order shall be given by way of loan; and any relief which may be given to, or on account of, any person above the age of 21, or to his wife, or any part of his or her family under the age of 16, under Article 1, or any of the exceptions thereto, or under any of the exceptions to Article 3, or under Article 4, or under the proviso in Article 6, may, if the Guardians think fit, be given by way of loan.

Art. 8.—Whenever the word "parish" is used in this Order, it shall be taken to include any place separately maintaining its own poor, whether parochial or extra-parochial.

Art. 9.—Whenever the word "Union" is used in this Order, it shall be taken to include not only an union of parishes formed under the provisions of the hereinbefore-recited Act, but also any union of parishes incorporated or united for the relief or maintenance of the poor under any local Act of Parliament.

Art. 10.—Whenever the word "Guardians" is used in this Order, it shall be taken to include not only Guardians appointed, or entitled to act, under the provisions of the said hereinbefore-recited Act, but also any Governors, Directors, Managers, or Acting Guardians entitled to act in the ordering of relief to the poor from the poor-rates under any local Act of Parliament.

Art. 11.—Whenever in this Order any article is referred to by its number, the article of this Order bearing that number, shall be taken to be signified thereby.

SCHEDULE,

Containing the Names of the Unions to which the present Order applies.

Aberaeron	Bedale	Buntingford
Abergavenny	Bedford	Burton-upon-Trent
Aberystwith	Bedminster	Bury Saint Edmund's
Abingdon	Belford	Caistor
Alban's, St.	Belper	Calne
Alcester	Bellingham	Cambridge
Alderbury	Berkhampstead	Cardiff
Alnwick	Berwick-upon-Tweed	Cardigan
Alresford	Beverley	Carmarthen
Alton	Bicester	Castle Ward
Altrincham	Bideford	Catherington
Amersham	Biggleswade	Caxton and Arrington
Amesbury	Billericay	Cern
Ampthill	Billesdon	Chailey
Andover	Bingham	Chapel-en-le-Frith
Asaph, St.	Bishop's Stortford	Chard
Ashby-de-la-Zouch	Blaby	Cheadle
Ashford, East	Blandford	Chelmsford
Ashford, West	Blean	Cheltenham
Aston	Blofield	Chepstow
Atcham	Blything	Chesterfield
Atherstone	Bosmere and Claydon	Chesterton
Auckland	Boston	Chester-le-Street
Austell, St.	Bourn	Chippenham
Axbridge	Brackley	Chipping Norton
Axminster	Bradfield	Chipping Sodbury
Aylesbury	Bradford (Wilts)	Christchurch
Aylesford, North	Braintree	Church Stretton
Aylsham	Brampton	Cirencester
Bakewell	Brecknock	Cleobury Mortimer
Bala	Bridge	Clifton
Banbury	Bridgend and Cowbridge	Clun
Barnet	Bridgenorth	Clutton
Barnstaple	Bridgwater	Cockermouth
Barrow-upon-Soar	Bridport	Colchester
Basford	Brixworth	Columb Major, St.
Basingstoke	Bromley	Cookham
Bath	Bromsgrove	Corwen
Battle	Bromyard	Cosford
Beaminster	Buckingham	Cranbrook

E

Crediton
Crickhowel
Cricklade and Wootton Bassett
Croydon
Cuckfield
Darlington
Dartford
Daventry
Depwade
Derby
Devizes
Docking
Doncaster
Dorchester
Dore
Dorking
Dover
Downham
Drayton
Driffield
Droitwich
Droxford
Dudley
Dunmow
Durham
Dursley
Easingwold
Eastbourne
East Grinstead
Easthampstead
East Retford
East Ward
Eastry
Elham
Ellesmere
Ely
Epping
Epsom
Erpingham
Eton
Evesham
Faith, St.
Fareham
Faringdon
Faversham
Festiniog
Flegg, East and West
Foleshill
Fordingbridge
Forehoe
Freebridge Lynn
Frome
Gainsborough
Germans, St.
Glanford Brigg
Glendale
Glossop
Gloucester
Godstone
Goole
Grantham
Gravesend and Milton
Guildford

Guiltcross
Guisborough
Hailsham
Halstead
Haltwhistle
Hambledon
Hardingstone
Hartismere
Hartley Wintney
Hastings
Havant
Haverfordwest
Hay
Hayfield
Headington
Hemel Hempstead
Henley
Henstead
Hereford
Hertford
Hexham
Highworth and Swindon
Hinckley
Hitchin
Holbeach
Hollingbourn
Holywell
Honiton
Hoo
Horncastle
Horsham
Houghton-le-Spring
Howden
Hoxne
Hungerford
Huntingdon
Hursley
Ipswich
Ives, St.
Kettering
Keynsham
Kidderminster
Kingsbridge
Kingsclere
King's Norton
Kington
Knighton
Lanchester
Langport
Launceston
Ledbury
Leek
Leighton Buzzard
Leominster
Lewes
Lexden and Winstree
Leyburn
Lichfield
Lincoln
Linton
Liskeard
Llandilo Fawr
Llandovery
Llanelly

Llanfyllin
Loddon and Clavering
Longtown
Loughborough
Louth
Ludlow
Luton
Lutterworth
Lymington
Madeley
Maidstone
Maldon
Malling
Malmsbury
Malton
Mansfield
Market Bosworth
Market Harborough
Marlborough
Martley
Medway
Melksham
Melton Mowbray
Mere
Meriden
Midhurst
Mildenhall
Milton
Mitford and Launditch
Monmouth
Morpeth
Nantwich
Narberth
Neath
Neot's St.
Newark
Newbury
Newcastle-in-Emlyn
Newcastle-under-Lyne
Newent
New Forest
Newhaven
Newmarket
Newport (Monmouth)
Newport (Salop)
Newport Pagnell
Newton Abbott
Northampton
Northleach
Northwich
North Witchford
Nuneaton
Oakham
Okehampton
Ongar
Ormskirk
Orsett
Oundle
Patrington
Pembroke
Penkridge
Penrith
Penzance
Pershore

Peterborough
Petersfield
Petworth
Pewsey
Pickering
Plomesgate
Plympton, St. Mary
Pont-y-pool
Poole
Portsea Island
Potterspury
Pwllheli
Reading
Redruth
Reeth
Reigate
Richmond (Yorkshire)
Ringwood
Risbridge
Rochford
Romford
Romney Marsh
Romsey
Ross
Rothbury
Royston
Rugby
Ruthin
Rye
Saffron Walden
Samford
Scarborough
Sculcoates
Sedgefield
Seisdon
Selby
Sevenoaks
Shaftesbury
Shardlow
Sheppy
Shepton Mallet
Sherborne
Shiffnal
Shipston-upon-Stour
Skirlaugh
Sleaford
Solihull
Southam
South Molton
South Shields
South Stoneham
Southwell
Spalding

Spilsby
Stafford
Staines
Stamford
Steyning
Stockbridge
Stone
Stourbridge
Stow
Stow-on-the-Wold
Stratford-upon-Avon
Stroud
Sturminster
Sudbury
Swaffham
Swansea
Tamworth
Taunton
Tavistock
Teesdale
Tenbury
Tendring
Tenterden
Tetbury
Tewkesbury
Thakeham
Thame
Thanet, Isle of
Thetford
Thingoe
Thirsk
Thomas, St.
Thornbury
Thorne
Thrapston
Ticehurst
Tisbury
Tiverton
Tonbridge
Torrington
Totnes
Towcester
Tunstead and Happing
Tynemouth
Uckfield
Uppingham
Upton-upon-Severn
Uttoxeter
Uxbridge
Wallingford
Walsal
Walsingham
Wangford

Wantage
Ware
Wareham and Purbeck
Warminster
Warwick
Watford
Wayland
Weardale
Wellingborough
Wellington (Somerset)
Wellington (Salop)
Wells
Welwyn
Wem
Weobly
Westbourne
West Bromwich
Westbury-upon-Severn
Westbury and Whorwels-down
West Firle
West Ham
West Hampnett
West Ward
Weymouth
Wheatenhurst
Whitby
Whitchurch
Whitehaven
Wigton
Williton
Wilton
Wimborne and Cranborne
Wincanton
Winchcombe
Winchester, New
Windsor
Winslow
Wirrall
Wisbeach
Witham
Witney
Woburn
Wokingham
Wolverhampton
Woodbridge
Woodstock
Wolstanton and Burslem
Worcester
Worksop
Wrexham
Wycombe
Yeovil

Given under our hands and seal of office, this Twenty-first day of December, in the year of our Lord One thousand eight hundred and forty-four.

(Signed) GEO. NICHOLLS.
(L.S.) G. C. LEWIS.
EDMUND W. HEAD.

[This Order came into operation on the 31st day of January, 1845.]

To THE GUARDIANS OF THE POOR of the several Parishes named in
the Schedule hereunto annexed :—

To the Churchwardens and Overseers of the poor of the said several
Parishes ;—

To the Clerk or Clerks to the Justices of the Petty Sessions held
for the Division or Divisions in which the said several Parishes
are situate ;—

And to all others whom it may concern.

We, the Poor Law Commissioners, in pursuance of the authorities
vested in us by an Act passed in the fifth year of the reign of his late
Majesty King William the Fourth, intituled " An Act for the Amendment and better Administration of the Laws relating to the Poor in
England and Wales," do hereby rescind an Order, being a General
Rule of the Poor Law Commissioners, bearing date the twenty-second
day of September, in the year of our Lord One thousand eight hundred
and forty-one, addressed to the Guardians of the Poor of the several
Parishes mentioned in the Schedule annexed to the said Order, namely,
the Parishes of Alston with Garrigill, East Stonehouse, Stoke-upon-
Trent, Saint Mary and Saint Andrew Whittlesea, and Great Yarmouth,
except so far as the same rescinds any Order or Orders theretofore
issued by the Poor Law Commissioners.

Provided that nothing herein contained shall apply to any relief given
under or prohibited by the said Order hereby rescinded.

And we do hereby order, direct, and declare, with respect to each
and every of the parishes named in the Schedule hereunto annexed, as
follows :—

Art. 1.—Every able-bodied person, male or female, requiring relief
from any of the said parishes, shall be relieved wholly in the workhouse of the parish, together with such of the family of every such
able-bodied person as may be resident with him or her, and may not
be in employment, and together with the wife of every such able-bodied
male person, if he be a married man, and if she be resident with him ;
save and except in the following cases :—

1st.—Where such person shall require relief on account of sudden
and urgent necessity.

2nd.—Where such person shall require relief on account of any
sickness, accident, or bodily or mental infirmity affecting such
person, or any of his or her family.

3rd.—Where such person shall require relief for the purpose of
defraying the expenses, either wholly or in part, of the burial
of any of his or her family.

4th.—Where such person, being a widow, shall be in the first six
months of her widowhood.

5th.—Where such person shall be a widow, and have a legitimate
child or legitimate children dependent upon her, and incapable
of earning his, her, or their livelihood, and have no illegitimate child born after the commencement of her widowhood.

6th.—Where such person shall be confined in any gaol or place of
safe custody, subject always to the regulation contained in
Article 4.

7th.—Where such person shall be the wife, or child, of any able-bodied man who shall be in the service of Her Majesty as a soldier, sailor, or marine.

8th.—Where any able-bodied person, not being a soldier, sailor, or marine, shall not reside within the parish, but the wife, child, or children of such person shall reside within the same, the Board of Guardians of the parish, according to their discretion, may, subject to the regulation contained in Article 4, afford relief in the workhouse to such wife, child, or children, or may allow out-door relief for any such child or children being within the age of nurture, and resident with the mother within the parish.

Art. 2.—In every case in which out-door relief shall be given on account of sickness, accident, or infirmity, to any able-bodied male person resident within any of the said parishes, or to any member of the family of any able-bodied male person, an extract from the Medical Officer's Weekly Report (if any such Officer shall have attended the case), stating the nature of such sickness, accident, or infirmity, shall be specially entered in the Minutes of the Proceedings of the Board of Guardians of the day on which the relief is ordered or subsequently allowed.

But if the Board of Guardians shall think fit, a certificate under the hand of a Medical Officer of the parish, or of the Medical Practitioner in attendance on the party, shall be laid before the Board, stating the nature of such sickness, accident, or infirmity, and a copy of the same shall be in like manner entered in the Minutes.

Art. 3.—No relief shall be given from the poor-rates of any of the said parishes to any person who does not reside within the parish, save and except in the following cases:—

1st.—Where such person, being casually within such parish, shall become destitute.

2nd.—Where such person shall require relief on account of any sickness, accident, or bodily or mental infirmity, affecting such person, or any of his or her family.

3rd.—Where such person shall be entitled to receive relief from any parish in which he or she may not be resident, under any order which Justices may by law be authorized to make.

4th.—Where such person, being a widow, shall be in the first six months of her widowhood.

5th.—Where such person is a widow, who has a legitimate child dependent on her for support, and no illegitimate child born after the commencement of her widowhood, and who at the time of her husband's death was resident with him in some place other than the parish of her legal settlement.

6th.—Where such person shall be a child under the age of sixteen, maintained in a workhouse or establishment for the education of pauper children not situate within the parish.

7th.—Where such person shall be the wife or child residing within the parish, of some person not able-bodied, and not residing within the parish.

8th.—Where such person shall have been in the receipt of relief from the parish, at some time within the twelve calendar months next preceding the date of the said Order of the twenty-second day of September One thousand eight hundred and forty-one, being settled in such parish, and not being resident within the parish at the time of the allowance of the relief.

Art. 4.—Where the husband of any woman is beyond the seas, or in custody of the law, or in confinement in a licensed house or asylum as a lunatic or idiot, all relief which the Guardians shall give to his wife, or her child or children, shall be given to such woman, in the same manner, and subject to the same conditions, as if she were a widow.

Art. 5.—It shall not be lawful for the Guardians, or any of their Officers, or for the Overseer or Overseers of any of the said parishes, to pay, wholly or in part, the rent of the house or lodging of any pauper, or to apply any portion of the relief ordered to be given to any pauper in payment of any such rent, or to retain any portion of such relief for the purpose of directly or indirectly discharging such rent, in full or in part, for any such pauper.

Provided always, that nothing in this Article contained shall apply to any shelter or temporary lodging, procured in any case of sudden and urgent necessity, or mental imbecility, or shall be taken to prevent the said Guardians, in regulating the amount of relief to be afforded to any particular person, from considering the expense to be incurred by such person in providing lodging.

Art. 6.—Provided always, that in case the Guardians of any of the said parishes depart in any particular instance from any of the regulations hereinbefore contained, and within fifteen days after such departure report the same, and the grounds thereof, to the Poor Law Commissioners, and the Poor Law Commissioners approve of such departure, then the relief granted in such particular instance shall, if otherwise lawful, not be deemed to be unlawful, or be subject to be disallowed.

Art. 7.—No relief which may be contrary to any regulation in this Order shall be given by way of loan; and any relief which may be given to, or on account of, any person above the age of twenty-one, or to his wife, or any part of his or her family under the age of sixteen, under Article 1, or any of the exceptions thereto, or under any of the exceptions to Article 3, or under Article 4, or under the proviso in Article 6, may, if the Guardians think fit, be given by way of Loan.

Art. 8.—Whenever in this Order any Article is referred to by its number the Article of this Order bearing that number shall be taken to be signified thereby.

SCHEDULE,

Containing the names of the PARISHES to which the present Order applies.

Alston-with-Garrigill.	Stoke-upon-Trent.
East Stonehouse.	Whittlesea, St. Mary, and St.
Great Yarmouth.	Andrew.

Given under our hands and seal of office, this Thirty-first day of December, in the year of our Lord One thousand eight hundred and forty-four.

(Signed)   GEO. NICHOLLS.
(*L.S.*)   G. C. LEWIS.
                EDMUND W. HEAD.

[This Order came into operation on the 11th day of February, 1845.]

To THE GUARDIANS OF THE POOR of the Newtown and Llanidloes Union, in the County of Montgomery;—

To the Churchwardens and Overseers of the poor of the several Parishes and Places comprised within the said Union ;—

To the Clerk or Clerks to the Justices of the Petty Sessions held for the Division or Divisions in which the said Union is situate ;—

And to all others whom it may concern.

We, the Poor Law Commissioners, in pursuance of the authorities vested in Us by an Act passed in the fifth year of the reign of his late Majesty King William the Fourth, intituled "An Act for the Amendment and better Administration of the Laws relating to the Poor in England and Wales," do hereby order, direct, and declare, with respect to the Newtown and Llanidloes Union, in the County of Montgomery, as follows :—

Art. 1.—Every able-bodied person, male or female, requiring relief from any parish within the said Union, shall be relieved wholly in the workhouse of the Union, together with such of the family of every such able-bodied person as may be resident with him or her, and may not be in employment, and together with the wife of every such able-bodied male person, if he be a married man, and if she be resident with him ; save and except in the following cases :—

1st.—Where such person shall require relief on account of sudden and urgent necessity.

2nd.—Where such person shall require relief on account of any sickness, accident, or bodily or mental infirmity affecting such person, or any of his or her family.

3rd.—Where such person shall require relief for the purpose of defraying the expenses, either wholly or in part, of the burial of any of his or her family.

4th.—Where such person, being a widow, shall be in the first six months of her widowhood.

5th.—Where such person shall be a widow, and have a legitimate child, or legitimate children, dependent upon her, and incapable of earning his, her, or their livelihood, and have no illegitimate child born after the commencement of her widowhood.

6th.—Where such person shall be confined in any gaol or place of safe custody, subject always to the regulation contained in Article 4.

7th.—Where such person shall be the wife, or child, of any able-bodied man who shall be in the service of Her Majesty as a soldier, sailor, or marine.

8th.—Where any able-bodied person, not being a soldier, sailor, or marine shall not reside within the Union, but the wife, child, or children of such person shall reside within the same, the Board of Guardians of the Union, according to their discretion, may, subject to the regulation contained in Article 4, afford relief in the workhouse to such wife, child, or children, or may allow out-door relief for any such child or children being within the age of nurture, and resident with the mother within the Union.

Art. 2.—In every case in which out-door relief shall be given, on account of sickness, accident or infirmity, to any able-bodied male person

one, or with any fixed number of children, but will make a careful inquiry into every case thus to be relieved.

8.—*Exception* 6.]—It sometimes becomes necessary that the Guardians should be empowered to give relief to the wife and children in cases where the husband cannot be required to enter the workhouse on account of his being in a place of legal confinement.

9.—*Exception* 7.]—The state of the law, in reference to married women, explained in par. 10, and the peculiar rights and obligations of soldiers, sailors and marines, render it desirable to give great latitude to the proceedings of the Board of Guardians in respect of the families of persons in these departments of the Queen's service. The seventh exception therefore allows of relief of any kind being given to the wife or children of a soldier, sailor, or marine, whether in or out of the workhouse, without requiring the husband to come into the workhouse.

10.—*Exception* 8.]—The eighth exception provides for the case of a wife whose husband is absent from her, either by desertion or otherwise, and is necessary, in consequence of the state of the law applicable to women thus situated. It had been held that in such cases relief to the children was not relief to the wife; consequently the wife could not be compelled to come with her children into the workhouse, although a new provision has been made by the Statute, 7 Vict., c. 101, § 25, to be noticed at full hereinafter, in respect of certain women separate from their husbands. If, however, under any circumstances she require relief for herself, the Guardians may require her to receive it in the workhouse, and if she require relief for her children, the Guardians may require such of them as are above the age of nurture to receive it in the workhouse, whether she do or do not come into the workhouse. As regards, however, children under the age of nurture who may be living with the mother, the Guardians cannot remove them from her; so that if she require relief for them and them only, the Guardians must, except in the case hereafter provided for, give out-relief if relief be necessary.

11.—ARTICLE 2.—The regulation which requires the entry on the Minutes of the Medical Officer's Report, or a Medical Certificate in case of relief being given to an able-bodied pauper on account of sickness, accident, &c., has been introduced in consequence of a tendency which has displayed itself in various parts of the country, to make exceptions to the Prohibitory Order on too slight grounds, and the Commissioners think that this provision will have the useful effect of calling the special attention of the Guardians to every such case.

If the pauper should not have been attended by a Medical Officer of the Union, a certificate may be given either by the Medical Practitioner who may have attended him, or by a Medical Officer of the Union who may visit him for the purpose.

Relief of Non-residents.

12.—ARTICLE 3.—As respects the portion of the Order which relates to the relief of persons not resident within their Union, the Commissioners desire to point out that it prohibits new cases of relief of this sort, with the exceptions therein mentioned.

13.—Under the provisions of this article, the Guardians may relieve a pauper residing within the Union, though not residing in the parish to which he belongs; the Commissioners, however, are far from wishing to encourage even this species of non-resident relief. It is true that the frauds and evils which are incidental to non-resident relief, in consequence of the want of inspection and the difficulty of transmitting the relief, do not occur with reference to paupers resident within the Union, who are within the reach of the Relieving Officers; but, nevertheless, the rate-payers of the parish charged with the relief, who by means of the quarterly lists of paupers, can, by personal observation of those who reside in their parish, ascertain whether they are fit objects for relief, are deprived of this protection where the pauper for whom they pay is resident at a distant part of the Union. The relief of paupers out of their parish, and out of the relieving district in which the parish is comprised, is not unattended with difficulties both of a legal and practical nature, which are sufficient to make it desirable that the Guardians should not, without sufficient ground, permit new cases of this nature even within the Union.

14.—The Commissioners have stated fully their views on the subject of non-resident relief, as respects both its legality and expediency, in a Minute dated 26th of January, 1841, which is reprinted in the Appendix to their Seventh Annual Report, (App. A. No. 1.)

15.—*Article* 3. *Exception* 1.]—The Commissioners have introduced this exception in order to meet the cases of vagrants who may become casually destitute within the Union. It is the duty of the Guardians to relieve persons so situated, without reference to the place of their settlement or residence. The Commissioners have had occasion to address several communications to the Metropolitan Boards of Guardians, on the duty of the locality to relieve all cases of urgent destitution. [See the Commissioners' Fourth Annual Report, pages 154, 155, 156, and 157, Appendix A. No. 2.—and Fifth Annual Report, page 87, Appendix A. No. 10.]

The Commissioners have not introduced into this article an exception on account of sudden and urgent necessity. [See *paragraph* 2.] Cases of sudden and urgent necessity manifestly require the prompt attention and vigilant inspection which can only be exercised by the Guardians and their Officers in the district where the necessity arises.

16.—*Exception* 2.]—This exception corresponds to exception 2 to Article 1. [See *paragraph* 3.] The Commissioners introduced this exception on account of the difficulty which a want of the power of giving temporary relief to non-residents in cases of sickness has been found to create in some parts of the country. The Commissioners, however, desire to caution the Guardians against giving temporary relief in cases of sickness to persons not resident within the Union, unless they are able to obtain accurate information concerning the case, and can ensure adequate and prompt relief, both medical and otherwise. It may be observed that this exception permits poor persons to be sent to establishments out of the Union, intended for the treatment of their respective infirmities, as hospitals for the sick, asylums for the insane, and schools for the blind or deaf and dumb.

17.—*Exception* 3.]—The third exception is intended expressly to except from the operation of the Order the cases of relief given to non-resident lunatics in asylums under orders of justices, and to persons under orders of removal.

18.—*Exception* 4.]—This exception is similar to the fourth exception to Article 1, the reasons for which are stated above in paragraph 5.

19.—*Exception* 5.]—This exception is that which the Legislature has introduced in the 7 & 8 Vict. c. 101, § 26, and upon which the Commissioners have already made their remarks in their Circular Letter to Boards of Guardians, dated the 17th October last.

20.—*Exception* 6.]—This exception removes the restriction upon Guardians from sending children to a workhouse or establishment for the training of pauper children, which may be situated out of their Union, where, but for the prohibition of relief to non-residents contained in the Order, they might lawfully do so.

21.—*Exception* 7.]—This exception enables the Guardians to relieve the resident family of a non-resident man, provided he be not able-bodied, without requiring them to come into the workhouse.

22.—*Exception* 8.]—This exception permits the continuance of non-resident relief to all paupers (not being able-bodied persons within Article 1) who were in the receipt of relief from some parish in the Union, within the twelve calendar months next preceding the date of the several Orders issued to the different Unions set forth in the Schedule. Consequently, it permits the continuance of non-resident relief to the infirm through age or any other cause, and to able-bodied widows with a child or children, who were in the receipt of parochial relief from the Union within that period.

23.—Article 4.—This article is introduced in conformity with the new provision contained in the 7 & 8 Vict. c. 101, § 25, in regard to the relief of women separated from their husbands, in certain cases particularly specified who are by that provision to be treated as widows in respect to relief to be afforded to them by Guardians. The Commissioners refer again to their observations in the Circular Letter of the 17th of October last upon this subject.

24.—ARTICLE 5.—This article is intended to prevent a practice which has prevailed in some parts of the country, whereby the poor-rates have been made a fund for the payment of rents directly to the landlords. In all cases where the pauper is so far destitute as to require a lodging, or the means of paying for one, if the Guardians do not deem it expedient in the particular case to require the party to come into the workhouse, they should supply to the pauper the means of paying for such lodging.

Cases of peculiar Urgency.

25.—ARTICLE 6.—It is possible, although not probable, that cases may occasionally arise which present very peculiar circumstances, and which do not fall within any of the exceptions contained in the present Order. The Commissioners think it desirable in cases of that kind, in which the immediate withdrawal or denial of out-door relief might appear likely to produce serious evil to the applicant, that the Guardians should give out-door relief, or take a portion of the applicant's family into the workhouse, and report the case within fifteen days to the Poor Law Commissioners, as a case of peculiar urgency, in order that the Commissioners may give their opinion thereupon. The Commissioners have accordingly introduced this proviso, enabling the Guardians to pursue this course with respect to exceptional cases of this description.

Relief by way of Loan.

26.—ARTICLE 7.—The first part of Article 7 is introduced in order to put an end to a misapprehension of the law which existed in some

Boards of Guardians, viz.:—that although the Prohibitory Order prevented them from *giving* out-door relief, they might nevertheless *lend* it. The second part of the Article enables the Guardians to make all the relief which may be given to persons above twenty-one years of age, or their families, a loan under the 58th section of the Poor Law Amendment Act of 1834.

27.—ARTICLES 9 and 10.—These Articles are introduced because the Order is addressed to four Unions of Parishes formed, not under the Poor Law Amendment Act, but under local Acts of Parliament, viz.—East and West Flegg, Forehoe, Samford, and Tunstead and Happing.

Signed by order of the Board,

EDWIN CHADWICK,

To the Clerk of the Board of Guardians.　　　　　*Secretary.*

No. 2.

GENERAL ORDER RELATING TO THE ADMINISTRATION OF RELIEF TO NON-RESIDENT AND NON-SETTLED POOR.

To THE GUARDIANS OF THE POOR of the several Unions and Parishes named in the Schedules hereunto annexed ;—

To the Churchwardens and Overseers of the Poor of the several Parishes and places comprised in the said Unions ;—

To the Churchwardens and Overseers of the Poor of the said other Parishes ;—

To the Clerk or Clerks to the Justices of the Petty Sessions, held for the Division or Divisions in which all such Parishes and Places are situate :—

And to all others whom it may concern.

Whereas it is expedient that certain regulations should be made with respect to the mode in which relief is to be transmitted to poor persons who reside in Parishes or Unions, but are not settled therein, and respecting the accounts to be kept and rendered with regard to such relief.

Now therefore we, the Poor Law Commissioners, in pursuance of the authorities vested in us by an Act passed in the fifth year of the reign of His late Majesty King William the Fourth, intituled "An Act for the amendment and better administration of the Laws relating to the Poor in England and Wales," do hereby order, direct, and declare, with respect to each and every of the Unions named in the Schedule A. hereunto annexed, and of the Parishes named in the Schedule B. hereunto annexed, that from and after the *twenty-fifth* day of *March* next,

Art. 1.—If any Board of Guardians undertake or agree to administer relief allowed to a non-settled poor person living within the Parish or Union for which they act, on behalf of the officers, or of the Board of Guardians, of the Parish or Union in which such pauper is deemed to be settled, every such undertaking or agreement shall be made in conformity with the rules and regulations of the Poor Law Commissioners in force at the time.

Art. 2.—No relieving officer or other officer of any Board of Guardians, nor any assistant overseer or collector, shall receive money for the relief of any non-settled pauper on behalf of any officer, or of the Board of Guardians of any other Parish or Union, nor shall he constitute himself in any way the agent of the officers or Board of Guardians of such other Parish or Union, except as provided in this Order.

Art. 3.—Every relieving officer shall be bound to visit, relieve, and otherwise attend to non-settled poor, being within his district, according to the directions of the Board of Guardians whose officer he is, and in no other way, subject always to the obligation imposed on him in cases of sudden and urgent necessity, and to the rules, orders, and regulations of the Poor Law Commissioners; and every such relieving officer shall set apart one or more pages in his out-door relief list, in which he shall duly and punctually enter up the payments made by authority of his own Board of Guardians to non-settled poor, and shall take credit for such payments under the head of non-settled poor in his receipt and expenditure book.

Art. 4.—No money shall be transmitted by any Board of Guardians or parish officers to the relieving officer or other officer of any Union or any Parish in which the relief is administered by a Board of Guardians, in order to be applied to the relief of any non-settled pauper, except in conformity with the provisions of this Order; but if any money be so transmitted contrary to the provisions of this Order, such officer shall forthwith pay such money into the hands of the treasurer to the Guardians of the Parish or Union whose officer he is, and shall report to the Board of Guardians at their next meeting the fact that such money has been so received and paid, and shall make a true entry accordingly on both sides of his receipt and expenditure book.

Art. 5.—If the Board of Guardians of any Parish or Union undertake or agree to administer relief through their officer to any non-settled pauper on behalf of the officer or Guardians of any other Parish or Union, the clerk to such first-mentioned Board of Guardians shall open an account in their ledger, to be headed " Non-settled Poor Account," and he shall debit such account with the cost of all relief paid to such non-settled poor, and shall credit such account by all payments from time to time actually made to the treasurer on account of the Parish or Union to which such non-settled poor are supposed to belong.

Art. 6.—If any Board of Guardians authorize the administration of relief by any other Board of Guardians on their behalf to a non-resident pauper, the clerk to such first-mentioned Board of Guardians shall open an account in their ledger, to be headed " Non-resident Poor Account," and he shall debit such account with the amount of all money actually transmitted to any other Parish or Union in payment of non-resident relief, such amount to be credited to the treasurer or other officer by whom the same is paid, and the clerk shall credit the said non-resident poor relief account with the sums reported to have been paid as aforesaid, such sums to be carried to the debit of out-relief against the respective parishes for which the same were paid.

Art. 7.—The clerk to every Board of Guardians shall at the first meeting of the Guardians in each quarter lay before the Board of Guardians, or some Committee appointed by such Board, the non-settled poor account, and the non-resident poor account, posted in his ledger to the end of the preceding quarter, and shall take the directions of the Board of Guardians respecting the remittance of checks or post-office orders to the Guardians of any other Union or Parish, or the transmission of accounts due from other Unions or Parishes and requests for payment.

Art. 8.—The clerk shall, within fourteen days from the close of each quarter, transmit by post all accounts of relief administered in the course of the preceding quarter to non-settled poor to the Guardians of the Unions and Parishes on account of which such relief was given; and every account so transmitted shall state the names and class of the several paupers to whom the relief in question has been administered; and all accounts for the relief duly administered to non-resident poor shall be discharged before the end of one calendar month from the receipt of such accounts, by the transmission of the amount due in one of the modes prescribed in this Order.

Art. 9.—No money shall be paid to the officer of any Union or Parish in which the relief is administered by a Board of Guardians on account of non-resident poor, except in one of the three following ways :—

> No. 1.—By post-office order, payable to the treasurer or the banker of such treasurer of the Union or Parish to the account of which the money is to be paid.
>
> No. 2.—By check or order payable to the treasurer of such Parish or Union, or to his order.
>
> No. 3.—By check payable to bearer (where the same may lawfully be drawn), and crossed as payable through the treasurer of such Parish or Union, or his banker, or through the agent of such treasurer or banker; and every such check shall be so crossed by the clerk to the Guardians before it is signed by the presiding chairman.

Art. 10.—The Clerk to the Board of Guardians shall, in making up his account before each audit, include the cost of all relief to non-resident poor, the payment on account of which has been actually made in the cost of relief given by the Board of Guardians of the Parish or Union for which he is clerk.

He shall in like manner enter the non-resident poor, on account of whom the cost of relief has been transmitted, in their proper classes as paupers relieved by the Board of Guardians for which he is clerk, and shall deduct from the number of paupers so relieved all poor persons on account of whom any remittance may have been actually received from any other Parish or Union in the course of the period to which the account refers, notwithstanding that such poor persons may have received relief over and above the value of the remittance so made.

Art. 11.—The clerk to every Board of Guardians shall immediately after each audit lay before the Board of Guardians a statement of the following particulars, which shall be signed by the auditor in testimony that it appears consistent with the accounts audited by him, so far as is apparent on the face of such accounts :—

> No. 1.—The number of non-resident poor, and of the persons composing their families, on account of whom money has been actually transmitted during the period to which the accounts last audited relate, and the sum so transmitted, distinguishing the amount to each Parish or Union.

No. 2.—The number of accounts for relief given during the same period supposed to be outstanding on account of non-resident poor, but not yet received, distinguishing the Parishes or Unions from which they should have been sent.

No. 3.—The number of non-settled poor, divided into their proper classes, actually relieved in the course of the same period on account of other Parishes or Unions, and the sum expended in such relief, distinguishing the amount on account of each Parish or Union.

No. 4.—The sum actually received during the same period in repayment of relief to non-settled poor, distinguishing the sum for each Parish or Union.

No. 5.—The number of accounts for non-settled poor relieved during the same period, not yet discharged by other Parishes or Unions although sent in, distinguishing the amount due from each Parish or Union, and also distinguishing those cases in which the account has been sent in more than fourteen days before the audit.

Art. 12.—Nothing in this Order shall be taken to discharge any Board of Guardians, or any officer of a Parish or Union, from any legal obligation now incumbent on such Board of Guardians, or on such officer, to relieve poor persons destitute in such Parish or Union, but not settled therein, and nothing in this Order shall be taken either to authorize the allowance of relief to any poor person in any case in which such relief may otherwise be unlawful, or to prohibit the allowance of relief to any poor person in any case in which the same may otherwise be lawfully made, or to affect any repayment of relief administered under a suspended order of removal.

Art. 13.—The term *non-resident poor* in this Order shall be taken to mean all paupers in receipt of relief allowed on account of any Parish or Union in relation to which the term is used, but not residing therein.

The term "*non-settled poor*" in this Order shall be taken to mean all paupers residing in the Parish or Union in relation to which the term is used, but to whom relief has been or is to be allowed on account of some Parish or Union other than that in which they reside.

The terms "*allowance of relief*" and "*to allow relief*" in this Order shall be taken to refer to the order or authority of the Board of Guardians, or other persons, making themselves liable for the ultimate payment of such relief, or undertaking to repay the same.

The terms "*administration of relief*" and "*to administer relief*" in this Order shall be taken to refer to the payment or actual giving of relief to the pauper who is to receive the same.

The word "*Union*" in this Order shall be taken to include not only an Union of Parishes formed under the provisions of the hereinbefore-recited Act, but also an Union of Parishes incorporated or united for the relief or maintenance of the Poor under any local Act of Parliament.

The word "*Guardians*" in this Order shall be taken to include

F

not only Guardians appointed or entitled to act under the provisions of the said hereinbefore-recited Act, but also any Governors, Deputy Governors, Assistants, Directors, Managers, Acting Guardians, Trustees of the Poor, or Select Vestrymen, entitled to act in the ordering of relief to the poor from the poor rate under any local Act of Parliament, and the churchwardens and overseers of the poor of the several parishes in the city of Salisbury.

The word "*Parish*" in this Order shall be taken to include any place maintaining its own poor, whether parochial or extra parochial.

Whenever in describing any person or party, matter or thing, the word importing the singular number or the masculine gender only is used in this Order, the same shall be taken to include and shall be applied to several persons or parties, as well as one person or party, and females as well as males, and several matters or things, as well as one matter or thing respectively, unless there be something in the subject or context repugnant to such construction.

SCHEDULE A.

Containing the names of the UNIONS to which the present Order applies.

Aberaeron	Barrow-upon-Soar	Bradfield
Abergavenny	Basford	Bradford (Wilts)
Aberystwith	Basingstoke	Bradford (York)
Abingdon	Bath	Braintree
Alban's, St.	Battle	Brampton
Alcester	Beaminster	Brecknock
Alderbury	Bedale	Brentford
Alnwick	Bedford	Bridge
Alresford	Bedminster	Bridgend and Cowbridge
Alton	Belford	Bridgwater
Altrincham	Bellingham	Bridgnorth
Amersham	Belper	Bridlington
Amesbury	Berkhampstead	Bridport
Ampthill	Berwick-upon-Tweed	Bristol
Andover	Beverley	Brixworth
Anglesey	Bicester	Bromley
Asaph, St.	Bideford	Bromsgrove
Ashby-de-la-Zouch	Biggleswade	Bromyard
Ashford, East	Billericay	Buckingham
Ashford, West	Billesdan	Builth
Aston	Bingham	Buntingford
Atcham	Bishop's Stortford	Burnley
Atherstone	Blaby	Burton-upon-Trent
Auckland	Blackburn	Bury
Austel, St.	Blanford	Bury Saint Edmund's
Axbridge	Blean	Caistor
Axminster	Blofield	Calne
Aylesbury	Blything	Cambridge
Aylesford, North	Bodmin	Camelford
Aylsham	Bolton	Canterbury
Bakewell	Bootle	Cardiff
Bala	Bosmere and Claydon	Cardigan
Banbury	Boston	Carlisle
Bangor and Beaumaris	Boughton, Great	Carmarthen
Barnet	Bourn	Carnarvon
Barnstaple	Brackley	Castle Ward

Catherington
Caxton and Arrington
Cerne
Chailey
Chapel-en-le Frith
Chard
Cheadle
Chelmsford
Cheltenham
Chepstow
Chertsey
Chester
Chesterfield
Chester-le-Street
Chesterton
Chichester
Chippenham
Chipping-Norton
Chipping Sodbury
Chorley
Chorlton
Christchurch
Church Stretton
Cirencester
Cleobury Mortimer
Clifton
Clitheroe
Clun
Clutton
Cockermouth
Colchester
Columb, St. Major
Congleton
Conway
Cookham
Corwen
Cosford
Coventry
Cranbrook
Crediton
Crickhowel
Cricklade and Wootton
  Bassett
Croydon
Cuckfield
Darlington
Dartford
Daventry
Depwade
Derby
Devizes
Dewsbury
Docking
Dongelly
Doncaster
Dorchester
Dore
Dorking
Dover
Downham
Drayton
Driffield
Droitwich
Droxford

Dudley
Dulverton
Dunmow
Durham
Dursley
Easington
Easingwold
Eastbourne
East Grinstead
Easthampstead
East Retford
Eastry
East Ward
Ecclesall Bierlow
Edmonton
Elham
Ellesmere
Ely
Epping
Epsom
Erpingham
Eton
Evesham
Exeter
Faith, Saint
Falmouth
Fareham
Faringdon
Faversham
Festiniog
Flegg, East and West
Foleshill
Fordingbridge
Forehoe
Freebridge Lynn
Frome
Fylde
Gainsborough
Garstang
Gateshead
Germans, Saint
Glanford Brigg
Glendale
Glossop
Gloucester
Godstone
Goole
Grantham
Gravesend and Milton
Greenwich
Guildford
Guiltcross
Guisborough
Hackney
Hailsham
Halifax
Halsted
Haltwhistle
Hambledon
Hardingstone
Hartismere
Hartley Wintney
Haslingden
Hastings

Hatfield
Havant
Haverfordwest
Hay
Hayfield
Headington
Helmsley Blackmoor
Helston
Hemel Hempstead
Hendon
Henley
Henstead
Hereford
Hertford
Hexham
Highworth and Swindon
Hinckley
Hitchin
Holbeach
Holborn
Hollingbourn
Holsworthy
Holywell
Honiton
Hoo
Horncastle
Horsham
Houghton-le-Spring
Howden
Hoxne
Huddersfield
Hungerford
Huntingdon
Hursley
Ipswich
Ives, Saint
Keighley
Kendal
Kensington
Kettering
Keynsham
Kidderminster
Kingsbridge
Kingsclere
King's Lynn
King's Norton
Kingston-upon-Thames
Kington
Knighton
Lampeter
Lancaster
Lanchester
Langport
Launceston
Ledbury
Leek
Leicester
Leigh
Leighton Buzzard
Leominster
Lewes
Lewisham
Lexden and Winstree
Leyburn

Lichfield
Lincoln
Linton
Liskeard
Llandilo Fawr
Llandovery
Llanelly
Llanfyllin
Llanrwst
Loddon and Clavering
London, City of
London, East
London, West
Longtown
Loughborough
Louth
Ludlow
Luton
Lutterworth
Lymington
Macclesfield
Machynlleth
Madeley
Maidstone
Maldon
Malling
Malmesbury
Malton
Manchester
Mansfield
Market Bosworth
Market Harborough
Marlborough
Martley
Medway
Melksham
Melton Mowbray
Mere
Meriden
Merthyr Tidvil
Midhurst
Mildenhall
Milton
Mitford and Launditch
Monmouth
Morpeth
Mutford and Lothing-
   land
Nantwich
Narberth
Neath
Neot's, Saint
Newark
Newbury
Newcastle-in-Emlyn
Newcastle-under-Lyne
Newcastle-upon-Tyne
Newent
New Forest
Newhaven
Newmarket
Newport (Monmouth)
Newport (Salop)
Newport Pagnell

New Sarum (otherwise
   Salisbury)
Newton Abbot
Newtown Llanidloes
Northallerton
Northampton
Northleach
Northwich
North Witchford
Nottingham
Nuneaton
Oakham
Okehampton
Olave's, Saint
Ongar
Ormskirk
Orsett
Oswestry
Oundle
Oxford
Pately Bridge
Patrington
Pembroke
Penkridge
Penrith
Penzance
Pershore
Peterborough
Petersfield
Petworth
Pewsey
Pickering
Plomesgate
Plympton, Saint Mary
Pocklington
Pont-y-Pool
Poole
Poplar
Portsea Island
Potterspury
Prescot
Presteigne
Preston
Pwllheli
Radford
Reading
Redruth
Reeth
Reigate
Rhayadar
Richmond (Surrey)
Richmond (York)
Ringwood
Risbridge
Rochdale
Rochford
Romford
Romney Marsh
Romsey
Ross
Rothbury
Rotherham
Royston
Rugby

Runcorn
Ruthin
Rye
Saffron Walden
St. Margaret, and St
   John the Evangelist
   Westminster
Salisbury (otherwise New
   Sarum)
Salford
Samford
Saviour's, Saint
Scarborough
Sculcoates
Sedbergh
Sedgefield
Seisdon
Selby
Settle
Sevenoaks
Shaftsbury
Shardlow
Sheffield
Sheppey
Shepton Mallett
Sherborne
Shiffnall
Shipston-upon-Stour
Skipton
Skirlaugh
Sleaford
Solihull
Southam
Southampton
South Molton
South Shields
South Stoneham
Southwell
Spalding
Spilsby
Stafford
Staines
Stamford
Stepney
Steyning
Stockbridge
Stockport
Stockton
Stokesley
Stone
Stourbridge
Stow
Stow-on-the-Wold
Strand
Stratford-upon-Avon
Stratton
Stroud
Sturminster
Sudbury
Sunderland
Swaffham
Swansea
Tamworth
Taunton

Tavistock
Teesdale
Tenbury
Tendring
Tenterden
Tetbury
Tewkesbury
Thakeham
Thame
Thanet, Isle of
Thetford
Thingoe
Thirsk
Thomas, Saint
Thornbury
Thorn
Thrapston
Ticehurst
Tisbury
Tiverton
Todmorden
Tonbridge
Torrington
Totnes
Towcester
Tregaron
Truro
Tunstead and Happing
Tynemouth
Uckfield
Ulverstone
Uppingham
Upton-upon-Severn
Uttoxeter
Uxbridge

Wakefield
Wallingford
Walsal
Walsingham
Wandsworth and Clapham
Wangford
Wantage
Ware
Wareham and Purbeck
Warminster
Warrington
Warwick
Watford
Wayland
Weardale
Wellingborough
Wellington (Salop)
Wellington (Somerset)
Wells
Welwyn
Wem
Weobly
Westbourne
West Bromwich
Westbury-upon-Severn
Westbury and Whorwelsdown
West Derby
West Firle
West Ham
West Hampnett
West Ward
Weymouth

Wheatenhurst
Whitby
Whitchurch (Southampton)
Whitechapel
Whitehaven
Wigan
Wigton
Williton
Wilton
Wimborne and Cranborne
Wincanton
Winchcombe
Winchester, New
Windsor
Winslow
Wirrall
Wisbeach
Witham
Witney
Woburn
Wokingham
Wolstanton and Burslem
Wolverhampton
Woodbridge
Woodstock
Worcester
Worksop
Wortley
Wrexham
Wycombe
Yeovil
York

SCHEDULE B.

Containing the Names of the Parishes to which the present Order applies.

Alston with Garrigil
Birmingham
East Stonehouse
Great Yarmouth
Leeds
Liverpool
St. George-the-Martyr, Southwark
St. George-in-the-East

St. Giles, Camberwell
St. Leonard, Shoreditch
St. Luke, Chelsea
St. Luke, Middlesex
St. James, Clerkenwell
St. Martin-in-the-Fields
St. Mary Lambeth
St. Mary Magdalen, Bermondsey

St. Mary, Rotherhithe
St. Matthew, Bethnal Green
Stoke-upon-Trent
Whitchurch (Salop)
Whittlesea, St. Mary and St. Andrew

Given under our hands and seal of office, this Twenty-first day of December, in the year One thousand eight hundred and forty-four.

(Signed)   Geo. Nicholls.

(*L.S.*)   G. C. Lewis.

Edmund W. Head.

[This Order took effect on the 25th day of March, 1845.]

Poor Law Commission Office, Somerset House;
December 21, 1844.

SIR,

I am directed by the Poor Law Commissioners to enclose a copy of an order which they have issued on the subject of non-resident relief, which will come into operation on the 25th day of March next.

The Guardians will observe that the Order in question is entirely confined to regulating the agency by which the relief of non-resident poor in certain cases, and the mode in which the accounts respecting them, shall be managed, and that it does not permit, or forbid the allowance of non-resident relief in any case in which such relief is not now permitted, or is not now forbidden.

The Order, moreover, does not prevent the Guardians of any Union from transmitting relief to a poor person who is non-resident in cases where the same may lawfully be given, through any private channel or any means other than the officers of another Union or Parish, however objectionable such a course may generally be. When a course of this description is voluntarily resorted to by the Guardians, they cannot hereafter complain if cases of imposition and peculation on the part of the paupers and of the persons conveying the money should occur.

All that is done by the present Order is, to require that when the agency of another Board of Guardians is employed, certain rules shall be adhered to. Whether the Board of Guardians allowing the non-resident relief choose to employ that agency is a matter for their own consideration, and whether the Board of Guardians of the Union where the pauper resides choose to act in the capacity of agents, and direct their officers to administer the relief, is again a matter of choice.

If two Boards do so agree to act together, these regulations must be observed, since no contract in opposition to them could be enforced by one party against the other, and the officers of the respective Unions are of course bound to act in conformity with law.

The Guardians will see that the relieving officer is expressly prohibited from acting as the agent of any Board other than that whose officer he is. The Commissioners are persuaded that the Guardians will have seen and felt the inconveniences which have arisen in many places from a different practice too well to be surprised at a restriction of this kind.

These inconveniences, indeed, form the principal reasons on account of which the Commissioners have thought it expedient to issue this Order.

They have found that relieving Officers were apparently placed in an anomalous position, receiving orders as it were from more than one Board of Guardians, and often being liable in two ways for the relief of the same pauper; that is to say, in their capacity of agent to some distant Board, and in their position as relieving officers of their own district in which that pauper resides.

For reasons, in some measure similar to those which apply to the relieving officers, and for others of a more general character, the prohibition is extended to assistant overseers and collectors.

It is always to be remembered, that no undertaking to give relief to a pauper residing at a distance has any legal effect in lessening the obligation cast by the law on the Guardians and officers of the spot where the pauper dwells or becomes destitute. The Board of Guardians at a distance may incur a moral responsibility, by promising to provide for the case, and may transmit from time to time the means of subsistence but if by neglect or error, or peculation, those means fail, or owing to any change of circumstances become insufficient, it is on the authorities at the place where the pauper is, that the weight of legal responsibility will fall. A voluntary act on the part of one person, or one body, does not remove the positive legal duty already cast on another. Much of the ambiguity on this head will cease when this Order is acted upon, since the relieving officer can only act as the officer and agent of his own Board, though some misapprehension is inseparable from any system of non-resident relief.

A further advantage contemplated, is the removal of those opportunities for fraud and for wilful detention of money thus intrusted to a distant officer, which have so often acted as a temptation and a snare to persons who would otherwise have preserved an honest and trustworthy character. And as the money thus misapplied does not come into the officer's hands in the capacity of officer of the Parish or Union in which he acts, but as a private agent for distant Boards and for Overseers of other Parishes in general, in case of peculation, such money could not be recovered from his sureties, since they were answerable for him only in the capacity of relieving officer.

Another benefit will be the avoiding of errors and misstatements of a statistical nature which now occur, in consequence of the same persons and the same relief being charged in the accounts of two Unions.

The Commissioners feel satisfied that the regulations will ensure a better understanding of the duties and responsibilities connected with the relief of non-resident poor—that they will act as a powerful obstacle to peculation and fraud, and that they will prevent error in the returns of expenditure and the enumeration of paupers, which are now unavoidable. The relief of non-resident and non-settled poor administered under this Order, will of course become the subject of correspondence between the Board of Guardians of the Unions where they are relieved and where they reside; and this correspondence will be conducted by the clerks of the Unions concerned. The Commissioners regret that they should impose some trouble on the clerk to the Guardians, but they believe that the amount of *additional* trouble is greater in appearance than in reality. Wherever non-resident relief is now given, either the ordinary correspondence with reference to these cases is conducted by the clerk, or difficulties arise from time to time, which produce long and tedious disputes, by letter, leading probably to appeal to the Poor Law Commissioners, and terminating in no satisfactory result, the matter devolving upon the clerk in the more advanced stages, and when complicated by previous misunderstandings.

The return after the audit of the number and amount of accounts outstanding, and other particulars, will enable the Guardians to call the attention to any acts of gross neglect on the part of a distant Union or Parish, and will probably in the end be the means of saving much trouble to the clerk.

I am, Sir, your obedient Servant,

EDWIN CHADWICK, *Secretary.*

The Clerk to the Guardians.

No. 3.

General Orders relating to the Apprenticeship of Poor Children.

To the Guardians of the Poor of the several Unions and of the several Parishes under a Board of Guardians, named in the Schedule hereunto annexed, and the Officers of such Unions and Parishes;—

To the Churchwardens and Overseers of the several Parishes and Places comprised within the said Unions, and of the several other Parishes named in the said Schedule;—

To the Clerk or Clerks to the Justices of the Petty Sessions held for the Division or Divisions in which the Parishes and Places comprised within the said Unions, and the said other Parishes named in the said Schedule, are situate;—

And to all others whom it may concern.

In pursuance of the powers vested in us by an Act passed in the fifth year of the reign of His late Majesty King William the Fourth, intituled "An Act for the Amendment and better Administration of the Poor relating to the Poor in England and Wales," and an Act passed in the seventh and eighth year of the reign of Her present Majesty Queen Victoria, intituled "An Act for the further Amendment of the Laws relating to the poor in England," we, the Poor Law Commissioners, do make the following rules and regulations in regard to the apprenticing of poor children by the Guardians of the poor of the several Unions named in the Schedule A. hereunto annexed, and of the parishes named in the Schedule B. hereunto annexed.

The Parties.

Art. 1.—No child under the age of *nine* years shall be bound apprentice:
and no child that cannot read and write his own name.

No child shall be so bound to a person who is not a housekeeper, or assessed to the poor-rate in his own name;
　　or who is a journeyman, or a person not carrying on trade or business on his own account;
　　or who is under the age of twenty-one;
　　or a married woman.

The Premium.

Art. 2.—No premium other than clothing for the apprentice shall be given upon the binding of any person above the age of *fourteen,* unless such person be maimed, deformed, or suffering from some permanent bodily infirmity, so that the nature of the work or trade which such person is fit to perform or exercise is restricted.

Art. 3. Where any premium is given it shall consist in part of clothes supplied to the apprentice at the commencement of the binding, and in part of money, one moiety whereof shall be paid to the master at the binding, and the residue at the termination of the first year of the binding.

Term.

Art. 4.—No apprentice shall be bound for more than *eight* years.

Consent.

Art. 5.—No person above *fourteen* years of age shall be so bound without his *consent;*

and no child under the age of *sixteen* years shall be so bound without the consent of the father of such child, or if the father be dead, or be disqualified to give such consent, as hereinafter provided, or if such child be a bastard, without the consent of the mother, if living, of such child.

Provided, that where the parent of such child, whose consent would be otherwise requisite, is transported beyond the seas, or is in the custody of the law, having been convicted of some *felony,* or for the space of six calendar months before the time of executing the indenture has deserted such child, or for such space of time has been in the service of Her Majesty, or of the East India Company, in foreign parts, such parent, if the father, shall be deemed to be disqualified as hereinbefore stated, and if it be the mother, no such consent shall be required.

Place of Service.

Art. 6.—No child shall be bound to a master whose place of business whereat the child is to work and to live, shall be distant more than *thirty* miles, from the place in which the child is residing at the time of the binding;

Unless in any particular case the Poor Law Commissioners shall, on application to them, otherwise permit.

Preliminaries to the Binding.

Art. 7.—If the child, whom it is proposed to bind apprentice, be in the workhouse, and under the age of *fourteen,* the Guardians shall require a certificate in writing from the medical officer of the workhouse as to the fitness in regard to bodily health and strength of such child to be bound apprentice to the proposed trade, and shall also ascertain from the master of the workhouse the capacity of the child for such binding in other respects.

Art. 8.—If the child be not in the workhouse, but in the Union or Parish by the Guardians of which it is proposed that it shall be bound, the relieving officer of the district in which the child shall be residing shall examine into the circumstances of the case, the condition of the child, and of his parents, if any, and the residence of the proposed master, the nature of his trade, the number of other apprentices, if any, then bound to him, and generally as to the fitness of the particular binding, and shall report the result of his inquiry to the Board of Guardians.

Art. 9.—If the Board of Guardians think proper to proceed with the binding, they shall, when the child is under the age of *fourteen,* direct the relieving officer to take the child to the medical officer of the district, to be examined as to his fitness in respect of bodily health and strength for the proposed trade or business ; and such medical officer shall certify in writing according to his judgment in the matter, which certificate shall be produced by the said relieving officer to the next meeting of the Guardians.

Art. 10.—If the child be residing in some other Parish or Union, the Guardians who proposed to bind him shall not proceed to do so unless they receive such a report as is required in Article 8, from the relieving officer of the district in which such child is residing, and a certificate from some medical practitioner of the neighbourhood of the child's residence to the effect required in Article 9.

Art. 11. When a premium is proposed to be given, in a case within the provision of Article 2, the Guardians shall require a certificate in writing of some medical practitioner, certifying that the person is maimed, deformed, or disabled, to the extent 'specified in such Article, and shall cause a copy of such certificate to be entered on their minutes before they proceed to execute the indenture.

Art. 12.—When such certificate, as is required by Articles 7, 9, and 10, is received, or in case from the age of the child no such certificate is required, the Guardians shall direct that the child and the proposed master, or some person on his behalf, and in case the child be under the age of *sixteen*, the parent or person in whose custody such child shall be then living, shall attend some meeting of the Board to be then appointed.

Art. 13.— At such meeting, if such parties appear, the Guardians shall examine into the circumstances of the case ; and if, after making all due inquiries, and hearing the objections (if any be made) on the part of the relatives or friends of such child, they shall deem it proper that the binding shall be effected, they may forthwith cause the indentures to be prepared, and, if the master be present, to be executed, but if he be not present they shall cause the same to be transmitted to him for execution ; and when executed by him, and returned to the Guardians, the same shall be executed by the latter, and shall be signed by the child, as hereinafter provided.

Art. 14.—If the proposed master reside out of the Union, but in some other Union or parish under a Board of Guardians, whether formed under the provisions of the first recited Act or of the Act of the twenty-second year of the reign of King George the Third, intituled "An. Act for the better Relief and Employment of the Poor," or of any local Act, the Guardians shall, before proceeding to effect the binding, communicate in writing the proposal to the Guardians of such other Union or Parish, and request to be informed whether such binding is open to any objection ; and if no objection be reported by such Guardians within the space of one calendar month, or if the objection does not appear to the Guardians proposing to bind the child to be sufficient to prevent the binding, the same may be proceeded with ; and when the indentures shall have been executed, the clerk to the Guardians who executed the same shall send notice thereof in writing to the Guardians of the Union or Parish wherein the said apprentice is to reside.

Indentures.

Art. 15. The indentures shall be executed in duplicate by the master and the Guardians, and shall not be valid unless signed by the proposed apprentice, without aid or assistance, in the presence of the said Guardians ; and the consent of the parent, where requisite, shall be testified by such parent signing with his name or mark, to be properly attested, at the foot of the said indenture ; and where such consent is dispensed with under the provision contained in Article 5, the cause of such dispensation shall be stated at the foot of the indenture by the clerk to the said Guardians.

Art. 16.—The indenture shall contain mention of the place or places at which the apprentice is to work and live.

Art. 17.—One part of such indenture, when executed, shall be kept by the Guardians, the other shall be delivered to the master.

Duties of the Master.

Art. 18.—And we do hereby prescribe the duties of the master to whom such poor child may be apprenticed, and the terms and conditions to be inserted in the said indentures, as follows :—

No. 1.—The master shall teach the child the trade, business, or employment set forth in the indenture, unless the Board of Guardians authorize the substitution of another trade or business.

No. 2.—He shall maintain the said child with proper food and nourishment.

No. 3.—He shall provide a proper lodging for the said child.

No. 4.—He shall supply to the said child one suit of proper clothing every year during the term of the binding.

No. 5.—He shall, in case the said child be affected with any disease or sickness, or meet with any accident, procure, at his own cost, adequate medical or surgical assistance, to be supplied by some duly qualified medical man, for such child.

No. 6.—He shall, once at least on every Sunday, cause the child to attend some place of divine worship, if there be any such within a reasonable distance, according to the religious persuasion in which the child has been brought up, so, however, that no child shall be required by the master to attend any place of worship to which his parents or surviving parent may object, nor, when he shall be above the age of *sixteen*, any place to which he may himself object.

No. 7.—Where such parents, or parent, or next of kin shall desire it, he shall allow the said child, while under the age of *sixteen*, to attend any Sunday or other school which shall be situated within the same parish, or within *two* miles distance from his residence, on every Sunday ; and if there be no such school which such child can attend, shall, at some reasonable hour on every Sunday, allow any minister of the religious persuasion of the child to have access to such child for the purpose of imparting religious instruction.

No. 8.—Where the apprentice continues bound after the age of *seventeen* years the master shall pay to such apprentice, for and in respect of every week that he duly and properly serves the said master, as a remuneration, a sum to be inserted in the indenture, or to be agreed upon by the Guardians and the said master when that time arrives, or, if they cannot agree, to be settled by some person to be then chosen by the said master and the said Guardians ; and until such sum be agreed upon or settled, not less than *one-fourth* of the amount then commonly paid as wages to journeymen in the said trade, or business, or employment.

No. 9.—The master shall, by himself or by his agent, produce the apprentice to the Board of Guardians by whom such apprentice was bound at their ordinary meeting next preceding the end of the first year of the binding, and before the receipt of the remainder of the premium, if any, be due; and shall, in like manner, produce the said apprentice at some one of their ordinary meetings, to be held at or about the middle of the term, and whenever afterwards required to do so by the said Guardians.

Provided that, if the apprentice reside out of the Union, by the Guardians whereof he was bound, the apprentice shall be produced, as hereinbefore directed, to the Board of Guardians of the Union or Parish, as described in Article 14, in which the apprentice may be residing.

No. 10.—The master shall not cause the said apprentice to work or live more than *ten miles* from the place or places mentioned in the indenture, according to Article 16, without the leave of the Guardians so binding him, to be given under their common seal.

Art. 19.—These duties of the master shall be enforced by covenants and conditions to be inserted in the said indenture so to be executed by him.

Art. 20.—The master shall also covenant not to assign nor to cancel the indenture without the consent of the Guardians, under their common seal, previously obtained, under a penalty to be specified in the said covenant, and to pay to the said Guardians all costs and expenses that they may incur in consequence of the said apprentice not being supplied with medical or surgical assistance by the master, in case the same shall be at any time requisite.

Art. 21.—The indenture shall be made subject to the following provisoes:—

1.—That if the master take the benefit of any Act for the relief of insolvent debtors, or be discharged under any such Act, such indenture shall forthwith become of no further force or effect.

2.—That if, on a conviction for a breach of any one of the aforesaid covenants before a justice of the peace, in pursuance of the provisions of the statute in such case made and provided, the Guardians who may be parties to the said indenture shall declare by a resolution that the indenture shall be determined, and shall transmit a copy of such resolution, under the hand of their clerk or the person for the time being acting as such, by the post or otherwise to the said master, such indenture shall, except in respect of all rights and liabilities then accrued, forthwith become of no further force or effect.

Explanation of Terms.

Art. 22.—Whenever the word *Parish* is used in this order, it shall be taken to include any place maintaining its own poor, whether parochial or extra-parochial; and the word *Guardians* shall include the select vestry of the parish of *Liverpool*.

Art. 23.—Whenever, in describing any person or party, matter or thing, the word importing the singular number or the masculine gender only is used in this Order, the same shall be taken to include and shall be applied to several persons or parties as well as one person or party, and females as well as males, and several matters or things as well as one matter or thing, respectively, unless there be something in the subject or context repugnant to such construction.

Art. 24.—Whenever in this Order any article is referred to by its number, the article of this Order bearing that number shall be taken to be signified thereby.

Art. 25.—Provided that nothing herein contained shall apply to the apprenticing of poor children to the sea-service.

SCHEDULE A.

Containing the Names of the UNIONS to which the present Order applies.

Aberaeron	Bellingham	Burnley
Abergavenny	Belper	Burton-upon-Trent
Aberystwith	Berkhamstead	Bury
Abingdon	Berwick-upon-Tweed	Caistor
Albans, St.	Beverley	Calne
Alcester	Bicester	Cambridge
Alderbury	Bideford	Camelford
Alnwick	Biggleswade	Cardiff
Alresford	Billericay	Cardigan
Alton	Billesdon	Carlisle
Altrincham	Bingham	Carmarthen
Amersham	Bishop's Stortford	Carnarvon
Amesbury	Blaby	Castle Ward
Ampthill	Blackburn	Catherington
Andover	Blandford	Caxton and Arrington
Anglesey	Blean	Cerne
Asaph, St.	Blofield	Chaily
Ashby-de-la-Zouch	Blything	Chapel-en-le-Frith
Ashford, East	Bodmin	Chard
Ashford, West	Bolton	Cheadle
Aston	Bootle	Chelmsford
Atcham	Bosmere and Claydon	Cheltenham
Atherstone	Boston	Chepstow
Auckland	Boughton, Great	Chertsey
Austel, St.	Bourn	Chesterfield
Axbridge	Brackley	Chester-le-Street
Axminster	Bradfield	Chesterton
Aylesbury	Bradford (Wilts)	Chippenham
Aylesford, North	Bradford (York)	Chipping Norton
Aylsham	Braintree	Chipping Sodbury
Bakewell	Brampton	Chorley
Bala	Brecknock	Chorlton
Banbury	Brentford	Christchurch
Bangor and Beaumaris	Bridge	Church Stretton
Barnet	Bridgend & Cowbridge	Cirencester
Barnstaple	Bridgnorth	Cleobury Mortimer
Barrow upon-Soar	Bridgwater	Clifton
Basford	Bridlington	Clitheroe
Basingstoke	Bridport	Clun
Bath	Brixworth	Clutton
Battle	Bromley	Cockermouth
Beaminster	Bromsgrove	Colchester
Bedale	Bromyard	Columb, St. Major
Bedford	Buckingham	Congleton
Bedminster	Builth	Conway
Belford	Buntingford	Cookham

Corwen
Cosford
Cranbrook
Crediton
Crickhowel
Cricklade and Wootton
  Basset
Croydon
Cuckfield
Darlington
Dartford
Daventry
Depwade
Derby
Devizes
Dewsbury
Docking
Dolgelly
Doncaster
Dorchester
Dore
Dorking
Dover
Downham
Drayton
Driffield
Droitwich
Droxford
Dudley
Dulverton
Dunmow
Durham
Dursley
Easington
Easingwold
Eastbourne
East Grinstead
Easthampstead
East Retford
Eastry
East Ward
Ecclesall Bierlow
Edmonton
Elham
Ellesmere
Ely
Epping
Epsom
Erpingham
Eton
Evesham
Faith, St.
Falmouth
Fareham
Faringdon
Faversham
Festiniog
Foleshill
Fordingbridge
Freebridge Lynn
Frome
Fylde
Gainsborough
Garstang

Gateshead
German's, St.
Glanford Brigg
Glendale
Glossop
Gloucester
Godstone
Goole
Grantham
Gravesend and Milton
Greenwich
Guildford
Guiltcross
Guisborough
Hackney
Hailsham
Halifax
Halstead
Haltwhistle
Hambledon
Hardingstone
Hartismere
Hartley Wintney
Haslingden
Hastings
Hatfield
Havant
Haverfordwest
Hay
Hayfield
Headington
Helmsley Blackmoor
Helston
Hemel Hempstead
Hendon
Henley
Henstead
Hereford
Hertford
Hexham
Highworth and Swindon
Hinckley
Hitchin
Holbeach
Holborn
Hollingbourn
Holsworthy
Holywell
Honiton
Hoo
Horncastle
Horsham
Houghton-le-Spring
Howden
Hoxne
Huddersfield
Hungerford
Huntingdon
Hursley
Ipswich
Ives, St.
Keighley
Kendal
Kensington

Kettering
Keynsham
Kidderminster
Kingsbridge
Kingsclere
King's Lynn
King's Norton
Kingston-upon-Thames
Kington
Knighton
Lampeter
Lancaster
Lanchester
Langport
Launceston
Ledbury
Leek
Leicester
Leigh
Leighton Buzzard
Leominster
Lewes
Lewisham
Lexden and Winstree
Leyburn
Lichfield
Lincoln
Linton
Liskeard
Llandilo Fawr
Llandovery
Llanelly
Llanfyllin
Llanrwst
Loddon and Clavering
London, City of
London, East
London, West
Longtown
Loughborough
Louth
Ludlow
Luton
Lutterworth
Lymington
Macclesfield
Machynlleth
Madeley
Maidstone
Maldon
Malling
Malmsbury
Malton
Manchester
Mansfield
Market Bosworth
Market Harborough
Marlborough
Martley
Medway
Melksham
Melton Mowbray
Mere
Meriden

Merthyr Tidvil
Midhurst
Mildenhall
Milton
Mitford and Launditch
Monmouth
Morpeth
Nantwich
Narberth
Neath
Neots, St.
Newark
Newbury
Newcastle-in-Emlyn
Newcastle-under-Lyne
Newcastle-upon-Tyne
Newent
New Forest
Newhaven
Newmarket
Newport (Monmouth)
Newport (Salop)
Newport Pagnell
Newton Abbot
Newtown and Llanidloes
Northallerton
Northampton
Northleach
Northwich
North Witchford
Nottingham
Nuneaton
Oakham
Okehampton
Olave's, St.
Ongar
Ormskirk
Orsett
Oundle
Pateley Bridge
Patrington
Pembroke
Penkridge
Penrith
Penzance
Pershore
Peterborough
Petersfield
Petworth
Pewsey
Pickering
Plomesgate
Plympton, St. Mary
Pocklington
Pont-y-Pool
Poole
Poplar
Portsea Island
Potterspury
Prescot
Presteigne
Preston
Pwllheli
Radford

Reading
Redruth
Reeth
Reigate
Rhayader
Richmond (Surrey)
Richmond (York)
Ringwood
Risbridge
Rochdale
Rochford
Romford
Romney Marsh
Romsey
Ross
Rothbury
Rotherham
Royston
Rugby
Runcorn
Ruthin
Rye
Saffron Walden
Salford
Saviour's, St.
Scarborough
Sculcoates
Sedbergh
Sedgefield
Seisdon
Selby
Settle
Sevenoaks
Shaftesbury
Shardlow
Sheffield
Sheppey
Shepton Mallet
Sherborne
Shiffnal
Shipston-upon-Stour
Skipton
Skirlaugh
Sleaford
Solihull
Southam
South Molton
South Shields
South Stoneham
Southwell
Spalding
Spilsby
Stafford
Staines
Stamford
Stepney
Steyning
Stockbridge
Stockport
Stockton
Stokesley
Stone
Stourbridge
Stow

Stow-on-the-Wold
Strand
Stratford-upon-Avon
Stratton
Stroud
Sturminster
Sudbury
Sunderland
Swaffham
Swansea
Tamworth
Taunton
Tavistock
Teesdale
Tenbury
Tendring
Tenterden
Tetbury
Tewkesbury
Thakeham
Thame
Thanet, Isle of
Thetford
Thingoe
Thirsk
Thomas, St.
Thornbury
Thorne
Thrapston
Ticehurst
Tisbury
Tiverton
Todmorden
Tonbridge
Torrington
Totnes
Towcester
Tregaron
Truro
Tunstead and Happing
Tynemouth
Uckfield
Ulverstone
Uppingham
Upton-upon-Severn
Uttoxeter
Uxbridge
Wakefield
Wallingford
Walsal
Walsingham
Wandsworth and Clapham
Wangford
Wantage
Ware
Wareham and Purbeck
Warminster
Warrington
Warwick
Watford
Wayland
Weardale
Wellingborough

Wellington (Salop)	Wheatenhurst	Witham
Wellington (Somerset)	Whitby	Witney
Wells	Whitchurch	Woburn
Welwyn	Whitechapel	Wokingham
Wem	Whitehaven	Wolstanton and Burslem
Weobly	Wigan	Wolverhampton
Westbourne	Wigton	Woodbridge
West Bromwich	Williton	Woodstock
Westbury-upon-Severn	Wilton	Worcester
Westbury and Whorwels-down	Wimborne and Cranborne	Worksop
	Wincanton	Wortley
West Derby	Winchcombe	Wrexham
West Firle	Winchester, New	Wycombe
West Ham	Windsor	Yeovil
West Hampnett	Winslow	York
West Ward	Wirrall	
Weymouth	Wisbeach	

SCHEDULE B.

Containing the Names of the PARISHES to which the present Order applies.

Alston with Garrigill	Liverpool	St. Mary, Rotherhithe
East Stonehouse	St. Luke, Chelsea	St. Matthew, Bethnal
St. George-the-Martyr, Southwark	Saint Martin-in-the-Fields	Green
St. George-in-the-East	St. Mary, Lambeth	Stoke-upon-Trent
St. Giles, Camberwell	St. Mary Magdalen,	Whittlesea, St. Mary and
Leeds	Bermondsey	St. Andrew
		Great Yarmouth

Given under our hands and seal of office, this Thirty-first day of
December, in the year One thousand eight hundred and forty-four.

(Signed)   GEO. NICHÓLLS.

(*L.S.*)   G. C. LEWIS.

EDMUND W. HEAD.

[This Order came into operation on the 14th day of February, 1845.]

To THE GUARDIANS OF THE POOR of the several Unions and of
the several Parishes named in the Schedule hereunto annexed,
and the Officers of such Unions and Parishes ;—

To the Churchwardens and Overseers of the several Parishes and
Places comprised within the said Unions, and of the several
other Parishes named in the said Schedule ;—

To the Clerk or Clerks to the Justices of the Petty Sessions held
for the Division or Divisions in which the Parishes and Places
comprised within the said Unions, and the said other Parishes
named in the said Schedule, are situate ;—

And to all others whom it may concern.

IN pursuance of the powers vested in us by an Act passed in the fifth
year of the reign of His late Majesty King William the Fourth, intituled
" An Act for the Amendment and better Administration of the Laws
relating to the Poor in England and Wales," and an Act passed in the
seventh and eighth year of the reign of Her present Majesty Queen
Victoria, intituled " An Act for the further Amendment of the Laws

relating to the Poor in England," we, the Poor Law Commissioners, do make the following rules and regulations in regard to the apprenticing of poor children of the several Unions named in the Schedule A. hereunto annexed, and of the Parishes named in the Schedule B. hereunto annexed.

The Parties.

Art. 1.—No child under the age of *nine* years shall be bound apprentice ;
and no child that cannot read and write his own name.

No child shall be so bound to a person who is not a housekeeper, or assessed to the poor-rate in his own name ;
or who is a journeyman, or a person not carrying on trade or business on his own account ;
or who is under the age of twenty-one;
or a married woman.

The Premium.

Art. 2.—No premium other than clothing for the apprentice shall be given upon the binding of any person above the age of *fourteen,* unless such person be maimed, deformed, or suffering from some permanent bodily infirmity, so that the nature of the work or trade which such person is fit to perform or exercise is restricted.

Art. 3.—Where any premium is given it shall consist in part of clothes supplied to the apprentice at the commencement of the binding, and in part of money, one moiety whereof shall be paid to the master at the binding, and the residue at the termination of the first year of the binding.

Term.

Art. 4.—No apprentice shall be bound for more than *eight* years.

Consent.

Art. 5.—No person above *fourteen* years of age shall be so bound without his *consent.*

And no child under the age of *sixteen* years shall be so bound without the consent of the father of such child, or if the father be dead, or be disqualified to give such consent, as hereinafter provided, or if such child be a bastard, without the consent of the mother, if living, of such child.

Provided, that where the parent of such child, whose consent would be otherwise requisite, is transported beyond the seas, or is in the custody of the law, having been convicted of some *felony,* or for the space of six calendar months before the time of executing the indenture has deserted such child, or for such space of time has been in the service of Her Majesty, or of the East India Company, in foreign parts, such parent, if the father, shall be deemed to be disqualified as hereinbefore stated, and if it be the mother, no such consent shall be required.

Place of Service.

Art. 6.—No child shall be bound to a master whose place of business, whereat the child is to work and live, shall be distant more than *thirty* miles from the place in which the child is residing at the time of the binding.

G

Unless in any particular case the Poor Law Commissioners shall, on application to them, otherwise permit.

Preliminaries to the Binding.

Art. 7.—If the child, whom it is proposed to bind apprentice, be in the workhouse, and under the age of *fourteen*, the Guardians shall require a certificate in writing from the medical officer of the workhouse, or from some medical man duly licensed to practise, as to the fitness in regard to bodily health and strength of such child to be bound apprentice to the proposed trade, and shall also ascertain from the master of the workhouse the capacity of the child for such binding in other respects.

Art. 8.—If the child be not in the workhouse, but in the Union or Parish by the Guardians of which it is proposed that it shall be bound, a relieving officer or some other person authorized by the persons proposing to bind such child, shall examine into the circumstances of the case, the condition of the child, and of his parents, if any, and the residence of the proposed master, the nature of his trade, the number of other apprentices, if any, then bound to him, and generally as to the fitness of the particular binding, and shall report the result of his inquiry to the Board of Guardians.

Art. 9.—If the Board of Guardians think proper to proceed with the binding, they shall, when the child is under the age of *fourteen*, direct such child to be taken to a medical man duly licensed to practise, to be examined as to his fitness in respect of bodily health and strength for the proposed trade or business; in order that such medical man may certify in writing according to his judgment in the matter, which certificate shall be produced, previously to the binding, to the Guardians.

Art. 10.—If the child be residing in some other Parish or Union, the Guardians who propose to bind him shall not proceed to do so unless they receive such a report as is required in Article 8, from the relieving officer or some other officer administering the relief of the poor of the district in which such child is residing, and a certificate from some medical practitioner in the neighbourhood of the child's residence to the effect required in Article 9.

Art. 11.—When a premium is proposed to be given, in a case within the provision of Article 2, the Guardians shall require a certificate in writing of some medical practitioner, certifying that the person is maimed, deformed, or disabled, to the extent specified in such Article, and shall cause a copy of such certificate to be entered on their minutes before they proceed to execute the indenture.

Art. 12.—When such certificate, as is required by Articles 7, 9, 10, is received, or in case from the age of the child no such certificate is required, the Guardians shall direct that the child, and the proposed master, or some person on his behalf, and in case the child be under the age of *sixteen*, the parent or person in whose custody such child shall be then living, shall attend some meeting of the Board to be then appointed.

Art. 13.—At such meeting, if such parties appear, the said Guardians shall examine into the circumstances of the case ; and if, after making all due inquiries, and hearing the objections (if any be made) on the part of the relatives or friends of such child, they shall deem it proper that the binding shall be effected, they may forthwith cause the indentures to be prepared, and in such manner and with such sanction as the law shall require to be executed; provided that when the same shall have been executed by the master and the other parties lawfully authorized, the same shall be signed by the child, as hereinafter provided.

Art. 14.—If the proposed master reside out of the Union or Parish on account of which the binding is to be effected, but in some other Union or Parish under a Board of Guardians, whether formed under the provisions of the first-recited Act or of the Act of the twenty-second year of the reign of King George the Third, intituled "An Act for the better Relief and Employment of the Poor," or of any local Act, the Guardians shall, before proceeding to effect the binding, communicate in writing the proposal to the Guardians of such other Union or Parish, and request to be informed whether such binding is open to any objection, and if no objection be reported by such Guardians within the space of one calendar month, or, if the objection does not appear to the Guardians proposing to bind the child to be sufficient to prevent the binding, the same may be proceeded with; and when the indentures shall have been executed, the Guardians who executed the same shall cause notice thereof in writing to be sent to the Guardians of the Union or Parish wherein the said apprentice is to reside.

Indenture.

Art. 15.—The indenture shall be executed in duplicate, by the master and the Guardians, or the persons lawfully authorized to do so, and shall not be valid unless signed by the proposed apprentice, without aid or assistance, in the presence of the said Guardians; and the consent of the parent, where requisite, shall be testified by such parent signing with his name or mark, to be properly attested, at the foot of the said indenture, and where such consent is dispensed with under the provision contained in Article 5, the cause of such dispensation shall be stated at the foot of the indenture, by any clerk or other officer acting as clerk to the said Guardians.

Art. 16.—The indenture shall contain mention of the place or places at which the apprentice is to work and live.

Art. 17.—One part of such indenture, when executed, shall be kept by the Guardians; the other shall be delivered to the master.

Duties of the Master.

Art. 18.—And we do hereby prescribe the duties of the master to whom such poor child may be apprenticed, and the terms and conditions to be inserted in the said indentures, as follows:—

No. 1.—The master shall teach the child the trade, business, or employment set forth in the indenture, unless the Board of Guardians authorize the substitution of another trade or business.

No. 2.—He shall maintain the said child with proper food and nourishment.

No. 3.—He shall provide a proper lodging for the said child.

No. 4.—He shall supply to the said child one suit of proper clothing every year during the term of the binding.

No. 5.—He shall, in case the said child be affected with any disease or sickness, or meet with any accident, procure, at his own cost, adequate medical or surgical assistance, to be supplied by some duly qualified medical man, for such child.

No. 6.—He shall, once at least on every Sunday, cause the child to attend some place of divine worship, if there be any such within a reasonable distance, according to the religious persuasion in which the child has been bought up, so, however, that no child shall be required by the master to attend any place of worship to which his parents or surviving parent may object, nor, when he shall be above the age of *sixteen*, any place to which he may himself object.

No. 7.—Where such parents or parent or next of kin shall desire it, he shall allow the said child, while under the age of *sixteen*, to attend any Sunday or other school which shall be situated within the same parish or within *two* miles' distance from his residence, on every Sunday; and, if there be no such school which such child can attend, shall, at some reasonable hour on every Sunday allow any minister of the religious persuasion of the child to have access to such child for the purpose of imparting religious instruction.

No. 8.—Where the apprentice continues bound after the age of *seventeen* years, the master shall pay to such apprentice, for and in respect of every week that he duly and properly serves the said master, as a remuneration, a sum to be inserted in the indenture, or to be agreed upon by the Guardians and the said master when that time arrives, or, if they cannot agree, to be settled by some person to be then chosen by the said master and such Guardians, and, until such sum be agreed upon or settled, not less than *one-fourth* of the amount then commonly paid as wages to journeymen in the said trade, business, or employment.

No. 9.—The master shall, by himself or by his agent, produce the apprentice to the Board of Guardians by whom such apprentice was bound, or to their successors in office, at their ordinary meeting next preceding the end of the first year of the binding, and before the receipt of the remainder of the premium, if any be due, and shall in like manner produce the said apprentice at some one of their ordinary meetings, to be held at or about the middle of the term, and whenever afterwards required to do so by the said Guardians or their successors.

Provided that if the apprentice reside out of the Union or Parish by the Guardians whereof he was bound, the apprentice shall be produced, as hereinbefore directed, to any Board of Guardians of the Union or Parish, as described in Article 14, or if there be no such Board of Guardians, then to the overseers of the parish in which the apprentice may be residing.

No. 10.—The master shall not cause the said apprentice to work or live more than 10 *miles* from the place or places mentioned in the indenture, according to Article 16, without the leave of the Guardians so binding him, or their successors.

Art. 19.—These duties of the master shall be enforced by covenants and conditions, to be inserted in the said indenture so to be executed by him.

Art. 20.—The master shall also covenant not to assign nor to cancel the indenture, without the consent of the Guardians or their successors, previously obtained, under a penalty to be specified in the said covenant, and to pay to the said Guardians or their successors all costs and expenses that they may incur in consequence of the said apprentice not being supplied with medical or surgical assistance by the master, in case the same shall be at any time requisite.

Art. 21.—The indenture shall be. made subject to the following provisoes :—

    1.—That if the master take the benefit of any Act for the relief of insolvent debtors, or be discharged under any such Act, such indenture shall forthwith become of no further force or effect.

    2.—That if, on a conviction for a breach of any one of the aforesaid covenants before a Justice of the Peace in pursuance of the provisions of the statute in such case made and provided, the Guardians who may be parties to the said indenture, or their successors, shall declare by a resolution that the indenture shall be determined, and shall transmit a copy of such resolution, under the hand of their clerk, or the person for the time being acting as such, by the post or otherwise, to the said master, such indenture shall, except in respect of all rights and liabilities then accrued, forthwith become of no further force or effect.

Explanation of Terms.

Art. 22.—The word *Union* in this Order shall be taken to include any union of parishes incorporated. or united for the relief or maintenance of the poor under any local Act of Parliament.

Art. 23.—The word *Guardians* in this Order shall be taken to include any Governors, Deputy Governors, Assistants, Directors, Managers, Acting Guardians, Trustees of the poor, or Select Vestrymen, entitled to act in the ordering of relief to the poor from the poor rate under any local Act of Parliament.

Art. 24.—Whenever the word *Parish* is used in this Order it shall be taken to include any place maintaining its own poor, whether parochial or extra-parochial.

Art. 25.—The word *Child* in this Order shall signify any person under the age of 21 years.

Art. 26.—Whenever, in describing any person or party, matter, or thing, the word importing the singular number or the masculine gender only is used in this Order, the same shall be taken to include, and shall be applied to, several persons or parties as well as one person or party, and females as well as males, and several matters or things as well as one matter or thing, respectively, unless there be something in the subject or context repugnant to such construction.

Art. 27.—Whenever in this Order any article is referred to by its number, the article of this Order bearing that number shall be taken to be signified thereby.

Art. 28.—Provided that nothing herein contained shall apply to the apprenticing of poor children to the sea service.

Art. 29.—And, in pursuance of the provisions contained in the said first recited Act, we do direct, that wherever any justice or justices shall, under any authority of law, assent or consent, order or allow, of the binding of any poor child as apprentice, such justice or justices shall certify at the foot of the indenture and the counterpart thereof, in the form and manner following; that is to say :—

" I *or* we, [*as the case may be,*] Justice *or* Justices of the
Peace of and in the County [*or other jurisdiction, as the
case may be*] of   , who have assented
to, ordered, *or* allowed the above binding, do hereby
certify that we have examined and ascertained that the
Rules, Orders, and Regulations of the Poor Law Commissioners, for the binding of poor children apprentices,
and applicable to the above-named parish, [*or other
place, as the case may be,*] contained in their General
Order bearing date the Twenty-ninth day of January,
One thousand eight hundred and forty-five, have been
complied with.

" Signed this   day of
          Signature."

SCHEDULE A.

Containing the Names of the UNIONS to which the present Order applies.

Bury St. Edmund's	Forehoe Hundred	St. Giles-in-the-Fields and
Canterbury	Mutford and Lothingland	St. George, Bloomsbury
Chester	Hundred	Samford Hundred
Chichester	Norwich	Southampton
Coventry	Oswestry	Tunstead and Happing
Exeter	Oxford	Hundred
Flegg, East and West,	Plymouth	Wight, Isle of.
Hundred		

SCHEDULE B.

Containing the Names of the PARISHES to which the present Order
applies.

Birmingham	St. Mary, Islington	St. Pancras
Kingston-upon-Hull	St. Mary-le-bone	Stoke Damerel
St. George, Hanover-square	St. Mary, Newington	Whitchurch (Salop.)

Given under our hands and seal of office, this Twenty-
ninth day of January, in the year One thousand eight hundred and forty-five.

(Signed)   GEO. NICHOLLS.

(*L.S.*)   G. C. LEWIS.

[This Order came into operation on the 13th day of March, 1845.]

To THE CHURCHWARDENS AND OVERSEERS of the several
parishes and places named in the Schedule hereunto
annexed ;—

To the Clerk or Clerks to the Justices of the Petty Sessions
held for the division or divisions in which the parishes
and places named in the said Schedule are situate ;—

And to all others whom it may concern.

In pursuance of the powers vested in us by an Act passed in the fifth
year of the reign of His late Majesty King William the Fourth, intituled
" An Act for the Amendment and better Administration of the Laws relating to the Poor in England and Wales," and an Act passed in the
seventh and eighth year of the reign of Her present Majesty Queen

Victoria, intituled "An Act for the further Amendment of the Laws relating to the Poor in England," we, the Poor Law Commissioners, do make the following rules and regulations in regard to the apprenticing of the poor children of the several parishes named in the Schedule hereunto annexed.

The Parties.

Art. 1.—No child under the age of *nine* years shall be bound apprentice;

And no child that cannot read and write his own name;

No child shall be so bound to a person who is not a housekeeper, or assessed to the poor-rate in his own name;

Or who is a journeyman, or a person not carrying on trade or business on his own account;

Or who is under the age of twenty-one;

Or a married woman.

The Premium.

Art 2.—No premium other than clothing for the apprentice shall be given upon the binding of any person above the age of *fourteen*, unless such person be maimed, deformed, or suffering from some permanent bodily infirmity, so that the nature of the work or trade which such person is fit to perform or exercise is restricted.

Art. 3.—Where any premium is given it shall consist in part of clothes supplied to the apprentice at the commencement of the binding, and in part of money.

Term.

Art. 4.—No apprentice shall be bound for more than *eight* years.

Art. 5.—No person above *fourteen* years of age shall be so bound without his *consent*.

And no child under the age of *sixteen* years shall be so bound without the consent of the father of such child, or if the father be dead, or be disqualified to give such consent, as hereinafter provided, or if such child be a bastard, without the consent of the mother, if living, of such child.

Provided, that where the parent of such child, whose consent would be otherwise requisite, is transported beyond the seas, or is in the custody of the Law, having been convicted of some *felony*, or for the space of six calendar months before the time of executing the indenture has deserted such child, or for such space of time has been in the service of Her Majesty or of the East India Company, in foreign parts, such parent, if the father, shall be deemed to be disqualified as hereinbefore stated, and if it be the mother, no such consent shall be required.

Place of Service.

Art. 6.—No child shall be bound to a master whose place of business, whereat the child is to work and live, shall be distant more than *thirty* miles from the place in which the child is residing at the time of the binding;

Unless in any particular case the Poor Law Commissioners shall, on application to them, otherwise permit.

Preliminaries to the Binding.

Art. 7.—If the child, whom it is proposed to bind apprentice, be in the workhouse, and under the age of *fourteen*, the Overseers shall require a certificate in writing from some medical man duly licensed to practise, as to the fitness in regard to bodily health and strength of such child to be bound apprentice to the proposed trade, and shall also ascertain from the master of the workhouse the capacity of the child for such binding in other respects.

Art. 8.—If the child be not in the workhouse, but in the parish by which it is proposed that it shall be bound, the Overseers shall examine into the circumstances of the case, the condition of the child, and of his parents, if any, and the residence of the proposed master, the nature of his trade, the number of other apprentices, if any, then bound to him, and generally as to the fitness of the particular binding.

Art. 9.—The Overseers shall, when the child is under the age of *fourteen*, direct such child to be taken to a medical man duly licensed to practise, to be examined as to his fitness in respect of bodily health and strength for the proposed trade or business, in order that such medical man may certify in writing according to his judgment in the matter, which certificate shall be obtained by the said Overseers previously to the binding.

Art. 10.—If the child be residing in some other Parish or Union, the Overseers who propose to bind him shall not proceed to do so unless they receive such a report as is required in Article 8, from the relieving officer, or some other officer administering the relief of the poor of the district in which such child is residing, and a certificate from some medical practitioner of the neighbourhood of the child's residence to the effect required in Article 9.

Art. 11.—When a premium is proposed to be given, in a case within the provisions of Article 2, the Overseers shall require a certificate in writing of some medical practitioner, certifying that the person is maimed, deformed, or disabled, to the extent specified in such article, before they proceed to execute the indenture; and shall cause such certificate to be deposited with the books and documents of the parish.

Art. 12.—When such certificate as is required by Articles 7, 9, and 10 is received, or in case, from the age of the child, no such certificate is required, the Overseers shall direct that the child, and the proposed master, or some person on his behalf, and, in case the child be under the age of *sixteen*, the parent or person in whose custody such child shall be then living, shall attend some meeting of the Overseers to be appointed for such purpose.

Art. 13.—At such meeting, if such parties appear, and the said Overseers, after making all due inquiries, and hearing the objections (if any be made) on the part of the relatives or friends of such child, shall deem it proper that the binding shall be effected, they may forthwith cause the indentures to be prepared, and to be executed in such manner and with such sanction as the law shall require; provided that when the same shall have been executed by the master and the other parties lawfully authorized, the same shall be signed by the child, as hereinafter provided.

Art. 14.—If the proposed master reside out of the parish on account of which the binding is to be effected, but in some Union or Parish under a Board of Guardians, whether formed under the provisions of the first-recited Act or of the Act of the twenty-second year of the reign of King George the Third, intituled " An Act for the better Relief and Employment of the Poor," or of any local Act, the Overseers shall, before pro.

ceeding to effect the binding, communicate in writing the proposal to the Guardians of such Union or Parish, and request to be informed whether such binding is open to any objection; and if no objection be reported by such Guardians within the space of one calendar month, or if the objection does not appear to the overseers proposing to bind the child to be sufficient to prevent the binding, the same may be proceeded with; and when the indentures shall have been executed, the overseers who executed the same shall cause notice thereof, in writing, to be sent to the Guardians of the Union or Parish wherein the said apprentice is to reside.

Indenture.

Art. 15.—The indenture shall be executed in duplicate by the master and the overseers, and shall not be valid unless signed by the proposed apprentice, without aid or assistance, in the presence of the said overseers; and the consent of the parent, where requisite, shall be testified by such parent signing with his name or mark, to be properly attested, at the foot of the said indenture; and where such consent is dispensed with under the provision contained in Article 5, the cause of such dispensation shall be stated at the foot of the indenture by the said overseers.

Art. 16.—The indenture shall contain mention of the place or places at which the apprentice is to work and live.

Art. 17.—One part of such indenture, when executed, shall be kept by the overseers, the other shall be delivered to the master.

Duties of the Master.

Art. 18.—And we do hereby prescribe the duties of the master to whom such poor child may be apprenticed, and the terms and conditions to be inserted in the said indentures, as follows:—

No. 1.—The master shall teach the child the trade, business or employment set forth in the indenture, unless the overseers or their successors, or the Guardians of any Union in which the parish may hereafter be comprised, or of the parish itself, in case it shall be placed under a Board of Guardians, shall authorize the substitution of another trade or business.

No. 2.—He shall maintain the said child with proper food and nourishment.

No. 3.—He shall provide a proper lodging for the said child.

No. 4.—He shall supply to the said child one suit of proper clothing every year during the term of the binding.

No. 5.—He shall, in case the said child be affected with any disease or sickness, or meet with any accident, procure, at his own cost, adequate medical or surgical assistance, to be supplied by some duly qualified medical man for such child.

No. 6.—He shall, once at least on every Sunday, cause the child to attend some place of divine worship, if there be any such within a reasonable distance, according to the religious persuasion in which the child has been brought up; so, however, that no child shall be required by the master to attend any place of worship to which his parents or surviving parent may object, nor, when he shall be above the age of *sixteen*, any place to which he may himself object.

No. 7.—Where his parents or parent, or next of kin shall desire it, he shall allow the said child while under the age of *sixteen* to attend any Sunday or other school which shall be situated within the same parish, or within *two* miles' distance from his residence, on every Sunday; and if there be no such school which such child can attend, shall, at some reasonable hour on every Sunday, allow any minister of the religious persuasion of the child to have access to such child for the purpose of imparting religious instruction.

No. 8.—Where the apprentice continues bound after the age of *seventeen* years the master shall pay to such apprentice, for and in respect of every week that he duly and properly serves the said master, as a remuneration, a sum to be inserted in the indenture, or to be agreed upon by the overseers for the time being, or the Guardians of the Union in which such parish may then be included, or of the parish if it shall be under a Board of Guardians, and the said master when that time arrives, or, if they cannot agree, to be settled by some person to be then chosen by the said master and such overseers or guardians; and until such sum be agreed upon or settled, not less than *one-fourth* of the amount then commonly paid as wages to journeymen in the said trade, business, or employment.

No. 9.—The master shall, by himself or by his agent, produce the apprentice to the overseers by whom such apprentice was bound, or to their successors in office, at the end of the first year of the binding, and at the middle of the term, and whenever afterwards required to do so by the said overseers or their successors.

> Provided that, if the said parish shall at any time after the execution of the said indenture he comprised in any Union, or be placed under a Board of Guardians, the child shall be produced at such times to such Guardians instead of the overseers of the parish.

> Provided also, that if the apprentice reside out of the parish by the overseers whereof he was bound, the apprentice shall be produced, as hereinbefore directed, to any Board of Guardians of the Union or Parish, as described in Article 14; or if there be no such Board of Guardians, then to the overseers of the parish in which the apprentice may be residing.

No. 10.—The master shall not cause the said apprentice to work or live more than *ten* miles from the place or places mentioned in the indenture, according to Article 16, without the leave of the overseers so binding him, or their successors.

Art. 19.—These duties of the master shall be enforced by covenants and conditions to be inserted in the said indenture so to be executed by him.

Art. 20.—The master shall also covenant not to assign nor to cancel the indenture without the consent of the overseers or Guardians, as mentioned in the next Article, or their respective successors, previously obtained, under a penalty to be specified in the said covenant; and to pay to the said overseers or Guardians, or their respective successors, all costs and expenses that may be incurred on account of the said parish in consequence of the said apprentice not being supplied with medical or surgical assistance by the master, in case the same shall be at any time requisite.

Art. 21.—The master shall also further covenant that, if the parish shall at any time after the execution of the said indenture be comprised in any Union, or be placed under a Board of Guardians, he will discharge all the obligations incurred by him under the said indenture, in reference to the overseers, according to the directions of the Guardians of such Union or Parish, as though such Guardians had been the parties to the said indenture instead of the overseers.

Art. 22.—The indenture shall be made subject to the following provisoes:—

1.—That if the master take the benefit of any Act for the relief of insolvent debtors, or be discharged under any such Act, such indenture shall forthwith become of no further force or effect.

2.—That, if on a conviction for a breach of any one of the aforesaid covenants before a justice of the peace, in pursuance of the provisions of the statute in such case made and provided, the overseers who may be parties to the said indenture, or their successors, shall declare by a notice that the indenture shall be determined, and shall transmit a copy of such notice, under the hands of the majority of them, by the post or otherwise, to the said Master, such indenture shall, except in respect of all rights and liabilities then accrued, forthwith become of no further force or effect.

Explanation of Terms.

Art. 23.—Whenever the word *Parish* is used in this order it shall be taken to include any place maintaining its own poor, whether parochial or extra-parochial.

Art. 24.—The word *Overseers* shall include churchwardens, where there are any such for the parish.

Art. 25.—The word *Child* in this Order shall signify any person under the age of twenty-one years.

Art. 26.—Whenever in describing any person or party, matter or thing, the word importing the singular number or the masculine gender only is used in this Order, the same shall be taken to include and shall be applied to several persons or parties as well as one person or party and females as well as males, and several matters or things as well as one matter or thing, respectively, unless there be something in the subject or context repugnant to such construction.

Art. 27.—Whenever in this Order any Article is referred to by its number, the Article of this Order bearing that number shall be taken to be signified thereby.

Art. 28.—Provided that nothing herein contained shall apply to the apprenticing of poor children to the sea service.

Art. 29.—And, in pursuance of the provisions contained in the said first recited Act, we do direct, that wherever any justice or justices shall, under any authority of law, assent or consent, order or allow of the binding of any poor child as apprentice, such justice or justices shall certify, at the foot of the indenture and the counterpart thereof, in the form and manner following; that is to say:—

> " I, *or* We, [*as the case may be,*] Justice *or* Justices of the Peace of and in the county [*or other jurisdiction, as the case may be*] of , who have assented to, ordered, *or* allowed the above binding, do hereby certify that we have examined and ascertained that the Rules, Orders, and Regulations of the Poor Law Commissioners, for the binding of poor children apprentices, and applicable to the above-named parish, [*or other place, as the case may be,*] contained in their General Order bearing date the Twenty-ninth day of January, One thousand eight hundred and forty-five, have been complied with.
>
> " Signed this day of
>
> Signature."

THE SCHEDULE,

Containing the Names of the PARISHES and Places to which the present Order applies.

DERBY.

High Peake Hundred.

Blackwell
Rowland
Wormhill
Youlgrave.

Wirksworth Hundred.

Elton.

GLOUCESTER.

Bristol City.

All Saints
Augustine, St.
Castle Precincts
Christ Church
Ewin, St.
James, St.
John, St.
Leonard, St.
Mary-le-Port, St.
Mary 'Redcliffe, St.
Michael, St.
Nicholas, St.
Paul, St.
Peter, St.
Philip and Jacob, St.
Stephen, St.
Temple
Thomas, St.
Werburg, St.

LANCASTER.

Lonsdale Hundred.

Arkholm-with-Cawood
Bare
Bolton-le-Sands
Borwick
Burrow-with-Burrow
Cansfield
Caton
Claughton
Dalton-with-Hutton
Farleton
Gressingham
Halton-with-Aughton
Heysham
Hornby
Ireby
Kellett, Nether
Kellett, Over
Leck
Melling-with-Wrayton
Poulton
Quernmoor
Roburndale
Slyne-with-Hest
Tatham, Lower End
Tatham, Upper End
Torrisholme
Tunstal
Wennington
Whittington
Wray-with-Bolton

Salford Hundred.

Clifton
Worsley

LEICESTER.

Sparkenhoe Hundred.

Higham-on-the-Hill
Ratcliffe Culey
Sibson
Stapleton
Stoke Golding
Sutton Cheney
Witherley

MIDDLESEX.

Saint James, and Saint John, Clerkenwell
Saint James, Westminster
Saint Leonard, Shoreditch
Saint Luke
Saint Margaret, and Saint John the Evangelist

NORFOLK.

Holt Hundred

Brinton
Melton Constable, and Burgh Parva

SALOP.

: *Chirbury Hundred.*

Brompton and Riston
Chirbury
Worthen

Shrewsbury Town.

Alkmond, St.
Chad, St.
Holy Cross, and St. Giles
Julian, St.
Mary, St.
Meole, Brace

SOUTHAMPTON.

Bramshott
Dockenfield
Kingsley
Headley
Aldershott
Cove
Farnborough
Hawley
Long Sutton
Yateley
Avington
Laverstoke
Alverstoke

STAFFORD.

Offlow, North Hundred.

Haselour
Ronton Abbey
Alstonefield
Grindon
Butterton
Wetton

SURREY.

Farnham
Frensham
Seal and Tongham
Puttenham
Frimley
Ash and Normanby

SUSSEX.

Rape of Arundel, Arundel Hundred.

Arundel

'Avesford Hundred.'

Climping
Ford
South Stoke and Offham
Tortington

Bury Hundred.

Bignor
Bury and West Burton
Coates
Fittleworth
Houghton

Poling Hundred.

Angmering
Burgham
Ferring
Goring
Kingston
Leominster
Littlehampton
North Stoke
Poling
Preston, East
Rustington
Warningcamp

Rotherbridge Hundred.

Barlavington
Burton
Duncton
Egdean
Sutton

Westeasworth Hundred.

Amberley
Greatham
Rackham
Wiggenholt

Rape of Bramber, Brightford Hundred.

Broadwater
Clapham
Durrington
Heene
Lancing

Patching Hundred.

Patching

Tarring Hundred.

West Tarring

Rape of Chichester, Aldwick Hundred.

Slindon
South Berstead

Eastbourne Hundred.

Heyshott

Rape of Leeds, Whales.

Brighthelmston

WARWICK.

Hemlingford Hundred. Atherstone Division.

Hartshill

Knightlow Hundred, Kirby Division.

Bedworth
Brinklow
Pailton
Wolvey

YORK, EAST RIDING.

Ouse and Derwent Wapentake.

Menthorpe-with-Bow-thorpe

Liberty of St. Peter, York.

Helperby

Ainsty of the City of York.

Acaster Selby
Acomb
Angram
Appleton Roebuck
Askam Bryan
Bickerton
Bilbrough
Bilton
Bolton Percy
Catterton
Colton
Helaugh
Hessay
Hutton
Knapton
Long Marston
Moor Monckton
Oxton
Poppleton, Nether
Poppleton, Upper
Rufforth
Steeton
Tadcaster, East
Thorp Arch
Tockwith
Walton
Wighill
Wilstrop

YORK, NORTH RIDING

Allertonshire Wapentake.

Norton Conyers

Bulmer Wapentake.

Shipton
Skelton
Tollerton
Warthill
Youlton

Halfield Wapentake.

Asenby
Baldersby
Cundall and Leckby
Dishforth
Humberton
Kirby-on-the Moor, or
   Kirby Hill
Langthorpe
Marton-le-Moor
Melmerby
Middleton Quernhow
Norton-le-Clay
Rainton-with-Newby

Tanfield, East
Tanfield, West
Thornton Bridge
Wath

Hang, West, Wapentake.

Abbotside, Higher
Abbotside, Lower
Askrigg
Aysgarth
Bainbridge
Bishop Dale
Burton and Walden
Carperby
Hawes
Newbiggen
Thoralby
Thornton Rust

*Lanbaurgh Liberty, West
Division.*

Picton

YORK, WEST RIDING.

Agbrigg Wapentake.

Acton
Altofts
Crofton
Lofthouse and Carlton
Methley
Middleton
Normanton
Rothwell
Saddleworth-with-Quick
Snydale
Whitwood

*Barkston Ash Wapentake,
Lower Division.*

Birken
Burton Salmon
Byrome-with-Poole
Haddlesey, West
Hambleton
Hillam
Monk Fryston
Ryther-with-Ozendike
Sutton

*Barkston Ash Wapentake,
Upper Division.*

Barkston
Bramham
Brotherton
Clifford-with-Boston
Fairburn
Fenton-with-Biggin
Grimston
Huddleston and Lumby
Kirkby Wharf-with-Mil-
   ford
Kirk Fenton
Lead
Ledsham
Ledstone
Lotherton-with-Aberford
Micklefield
Micklethwaite
Milford, South
Newthorpe
Newton Kyme-with-Toul-
   ston
Saxton-with-Scarthing-
   well
Sherburn
Sutton-with-Hazlewood
Tadcaster, West
Towton
Ulleskelf

*Claro Wapentake, Lower
Division.*

Aldborough
Aldfield
Arkendale
Azerley
Bilton-with-Harrowgate
Birstwith
Blubberhouses
Boroughbridge
Brearton
Burton Leonard
Clifton-with-Norwood
Clint
Copgrove
Farnham
Felliscliffe
Ferensby
Fewston

Grewelthorpe
Hampsthwaite
Killinghall
Kirby Hall
Kirkby Malzeard
Knaresborough
Laverton
Milby
Minskip
Ouseburn, Great
Pannall
Rocliffe
Scotton
Scriven-with-Tentergate
Skelding
Stainley, South, with
   Clayton
Staveley
Studley Rog
Thornville
Timble, Great
Winksley

*Claro Wapentake, Upper
Division.*

Allerton Mauleverer with
   Hopperton
Askwith
Beamsley-in-Skipton
Castley
Cattall
Clareton
Coneythorpe
Cowthorpe,
Deighton, North
Denton
Dunkeswith
Dunsforth, Lower
Dunsforth, Upper, with
   Branton Green
Farnley
Flaxby
Follifoot
Goldsborough
Greenhammerton
Hunsingore
Kirkby-with-Netherby
Kirk Deighton
Kirby Overblows
Kirk Hammerton
Leathley
Lindley
Linton
Marton-with-Grafton
Middleton
Nesfield-with-Langbar
Newhall-with-Clifton
Nun Monkton
Ouseburn, Little
Plumpton
Ribston, Great, with
   Walshford
Ribston, Little

Rigton
Ripley
Sicklinghall
Spofforth
Stainburn
Thorpe Green, or Under-
wood
Timble, Little
Weeton
Weston
Wetherby
Whixley
Widdington

Morley Wapentake.

Churwell
Eccleshill
Gildersome

*Osgoldcross Wapentake,
Lower Division.*

Baln
Beaghall
Cridling Stubbs
Eggborough
Heck
Hensall
Kellington
Smeaton, Little
Walden Stubbs
Whitley
Womersley

*Osgoldcross Wapentake,
Upper Division.*

Ackworth
Badsworth
Carleton
Castleford
Darrington
Elmsall, North
Elmsall, South
Featherstone
Ferry Frystone
Hardwick, East
Hardwick, West
Hessle
Hilltop
Houghton Glass
Kirby, South
Kirksmeaton
Knottingley
Moukhill
Nostell, Huntwick, and
Foulby
Pontefract
Purston Jaglin
Skelbrooke
Stapleton
Tanshelf
Thorp Audlin
Upton

*Skyrack Wapentake,
Lower Division.*

Abberford
Allerton Bywater
Austhorpe
Bardsey-with-Rigton
Barwick-in-Elmet
Collingham
Garforth, West
Guiseley
Keswick, East
Kippax
Parlington
Preston, Great and Little
Roundhay
Scarcroft
Seacroft
Shadwell
Sturton Grange
Swillington
Temple Newsham
Thorner
Wothersome

*Skyrack Wapentake, Upper
Division.*

Addle-with-Eccup
Allwoodley
Arthington
Baildon
Bramhope
Burley
Carlton
Esholt
Harewood
Hawksworth
Horsforth
Ilkley
Menstone
Otley
Pool
Rawden
Weardley
Wigton
Wike
Yeaden

*Staincliffe and Ewcross
Wapentake, East Division.*

Silsden

Staincross Wapentake.

Ardsley
Barnesley
Barugh
Brierley-with-Grims-
thorpe
Carlton
Cawthorne
Chevett
Clayton, West
Cudworth

Darton
Denby
Dodworth
Gunthwaite
Havercroft-with-Cold
Hiendley
Hemsworth
Hiendley, South
Hoyland, High
Kexborough
Monk Bretton
Notton
Roystone
Ryhill
Shafton
Silkstone
Stainborough
Wintersett
Woolley
Worsborough

*Strafforth and Tickhill Wa-
pentake, North Division.*

Billingley
Darfield
Hamphall Stubbs
Hoyland
Houghton, Great
Houghton, Little
Wombwell

Liberty of Ripon.

Aismunderby-with-Bond-
gate
Bishop Monkton
Bishop Thornton
Bishopton
Hewick Bridge
Hewick Copt
Clotherholme
Eavestone
Givendale
Grantley
Ingerthorpe
Markington-with-Waller
thwaite
Newby-with-Mulworth
Nidd-with-Killinghall
Nunwick-with-Howgrave
Ripon, Borough
Sawley
Sharrow
Skelton
Stainley, North, with
Slenningford
Sutton Grange
Westwick
Whitcliffe-with-Thorpe

Borough of Leeds.

Armley
Beeston
Bramley

Chapel Allerton	Middletown	*Newton Hundred, Upper Division.*
Farnley	Rhos Goch	
Headingley-with-Burley	Trelystan	
Holbeck	Uppington	Llandysil
Hunslet		Llanmerewig
Potter Newton	*Cawse Hundred, Upper Division.*	
Wortley		
		Pool Hundred.
WALES.	Castle Caereinion, Upper and Lower	
DENBIGH.	Cyfronydd	Guilsfield
Chirk Hundred.	. *Montgomery Hundred Lower Division.*	*Pool Borough.*
Chirk		
Llansilin	Aston	Cletterwood
	Castlewright	Hope
MONTGOMERY.	Churchstoke	Pool, Lower
	Montgomery	Pool, Middle
Cawse Hundred, Lower Division.		Pool, Upper
	Newton Hundred, Lower Division.	Trewern
Forden		
Leighton	Berriew	

Given under our hands and seal of office, this Twenty-ninth day of January, in the year One thousand eight hundred and forty-five.

(Signed)   GEO. NICHOLLS.

(L.S.)   G. C. LEWIS.

[This Order came into operation on 13th day of March, 1845.]

LETTER RELATING TO THE FOREGOING ORDERS.

Poor Law Commission Office, Somerset House;
SIR,   *January 1st,* 1845.

I AM directed by the Poor Law Commissioners to forward to you a copy of a General Order which they have issued for regulating the proceedings to be taken in the binding of parish apprentices.

The Commissioners were empowered by the 4 and 5 Wm. IV., c. 76, *(the Poor Law Amendment Act)*, to make regulations upon this subject, which were to be enforced by the justices in the indentures which they might allow after the issue of the regulations. But they had not issued any such regulations previous to the passing of the Act of the last Session, which gives a more precise and summary remedy for the enforcing, against the masters, of the regulations which they may prescribe.

That statute having also taken the binding of parish apprentices away from the overseers, and removed the control of the justices over it, has substituted the Board of Guardians in the place of those respective parties. The Commissioners have, therefore, felt it expedient forthwith to prescribe and promulgate the regulations which they think ought to be laid down for the control and guidance of the Guardians upon this subject.

Their object has been to secure a careful attention, on the part of the Guardians who are to bind out the children, to the fitness and propriety of the step which is to affect permanently the future condition of those children, and a due performance afterwards by the masters of the duties which appear naturally to result from the relation of master and apprentice.

I am to call the attention of the Guardians to the fact, that the apprenticeship is a species of relief, and consequently can only be given subject to the regulations which may exist in any particular Union or Parish, with regard to the relief in such Union or Parish generally.

In conclusion, I have to observe, that the Commissioners by no means desire to express any opinion as to the propriety of the Guardians extending the practice of parish apprenticeship. There is no doubt that the compulsory apprenticeship of poor children, which has been abolished by the 13th section of the 7 and 8 Vic., c. 101, has been found productive of great evils and mischief; and there are not wanting authorities of weight against the system of parochial apprenticeship in general.

That system, however, not having been abolished by the Legislature, will doubtless continue to be practised in those districts where it has hitherto prevailed; but the Commissioners do not wish that the Guardians in those parts of the country where the system has not been generally pursued, should infer that they entertain any desire to promote its introduction in consequence of their having issued the order above referred to.

I am, Sir,

Your obedient servant,

To the Clerk of the Guardians.   EDWIN CHADWICK, *Secretary.*

No. 4.

ORDER FOR THE ELECTION OF A DISTRICT AUDITOR.

TO THE GUARDIANS OF THE POOR of the Alcester, Banbury, Chipping Norton, Droitwich, Evesham, Foleshill, Northleach, Pershore, Rugby, Shipston-upon-Stour, Solihull, Southam, Stow-on-the-Wold, Stratford-upon-Avon, Warwick, Witney, Woodstock, and Worcester Unions;

To the Churchwardens and Overseers of the Poor of the several Parishes and Places comprised in the said Unions;

To the Treasurers of the said Unions respectively;

To the Guardians of the Poor of the several Parishes of St. Michael and the Holy Trinity, in the City of Coventry and County of the same City,

To the Churchwardens and Overseers of the Poor of the said last-mentioned Parishes;

To the Clerk or Clerks to the Justices of the Petty Sessions held for the Division or Divisions in which the said Unions and Parishes are situate;

And to all others whom it may concern.

I.—*Creation of District.*

Art. 1.—WE, the Poor Law Commissioners, acting under the authority of an Act passed in the fifth year of the reign of His late Majesty King William the Fourth, intituled "An Act for the Amendment and better Administration of the Laws relating to the Poor in England and Wales," and of an Act passed in the eighth year of the reign of Her present

n

Majesty Queen Victoria, intituled " An Act for the further Amendment
of the Laws relating to the Poor in England," do hereby combine the
following Unions, viz., Alcester, Banbury, Chipping Norton, Droitwich,
Evesham, Foleshill, Northleach, Pershore, Rugby, Shipston-upon-Stour,
Solihull, Southam, Stow-on-the-Wold, Stratford-upon-Avon, Warwick,
Witney, Woodstock, and Worcester Unions, together with the several
Parishes of St. Michael and the Holy Trinity, in the City of Coventry
and County of the same City, into a District for the audit of accounts, to
be termed " The Oxfordshire and Warwickshire Audit District," and do
order and direct that one person shall be appointed as the auditor of the
said district.

II.—*Mode of Election.*

Art. 2.—And we do hereby prescribe the time and manner in which
such auditor shall be elected, as follows ; that is to say,
On some day or days *between the fifth and thirteenth days of June
next,* and on some day *within thirty days* after the happening of any
vacancy in the said office, an Assistant Poor Law Commissioner, to be
determined by the Poor Law Commissioners, shall cause an advertisement
to be inserted in one of the newspapers published in the cities of London
or Westminster, and in two or more newspapers published within the
counties in which the said Unions or some of them are situated, giving
notice of the vacancy, and inviting persons desirous to become candidates
for the office of auditor, to send to him, at some place to be therein
specified, their names in full, their profession or occupation, their age and
residence, within a time *not exceeding fourteen days* from the first
insertion of such notice in such newspapers as aforesaid.
Art. 3.—On the expiration of the said term of fourteen days the
Assistant Poor Law Commissioner shall cause a list to be made of such
persons as may have duly offered themselves as candidates, and may
have forwarded the information hereinbefore required ; and such Assistant Poor Law Commissioner shall send copies of such list, with the
other particulars hereinbefore required, to each of the several chairmen
and vice-chairmen of the Boards of Guardians of the before-mentioned
Unions and Parishes respectively, and to such other persons as may be
qualified to vote at the election of the auditor for the district, and shall
request each elector to return to him in some writing signed by such
elector, on or before a day to be specified by such Assistant Poor Law
Commissioner, being *not less than seven days, nor more than fourteen
days,* after the date of such list, the name of the candidate in such list
for whom such elector votes.
Art. 4.—On the day next after the day specified by such Assistant
Poor Law Commissioner for the return of such names, the said Assistant
Poor Law Commissioner shall examine the Returns then received by
him, and shall cast up the numbers, and shall enter on the said list so
made out by him as aforesaid, against the name of each candidate, the
names of the several electors who shall have voted for such candidate.
Art. 5.—If any candidate shall have obtained the majority of the
votes of the said electors, the Assistant Poor Law Commissioner shall
certify in writing, at the foot of such list, that such candidate hath been
duly elected the auditor for such district.

Art. 6.—If no candidate have received the votes of the majority of the electors, the Assistant Poor Law Commissioner shall again send the names of the two candidates who have received the greatest number of votes to each of the several electors, with a request that each elector will return, in some writing signed by him, the name of one of such two persons to the said Assistant Poor Law Commissioner, on or before a day to be specified, being *not less than seven days, nor more than fourteen days*, after the date of such request.

Art. 7.—On the day next after the day specified for the second return, the Assistant Poor Law Commissioner shall examine the returns then received by him, and shall proceed, as on the former occasion, to cast up the number of the votes, and to enter the names of the persons voting, and to certify in writing that the candidate who then has the greater number of votes is elected the auditor of the district.

Art. 8.—If on the return to the copies of the list first sent out by the said Assistant Poor Law Commissioner, it be found that no candidate has a majority of the votes of the electors, and that the votes are equal in favour of the three candidates who have received the largest number of votes, or in favour of any two of such three candidates, he shall forward on the second occasion the names of all such three candidates, and shall proceed as if the names of the candidates so sent were sent for the first time, except that in the event of there being an equality of votes on the second voting, the election shall be deemed to have failed, and proceedings shall take place as on a new vacancy.

Art. 9.—If only one candidate shall offer himself to the Assistant Poor Law Commissioner, the name and address of such person shall be sent by such Assistant Poor Law Commissioner to all the persons qualified to vote as aforesaid, and such Assistant Poor Law Commissioner shall request such persons to inform him in writing, on or before a day to be specified, being *not less than seven days, nor more than fourteen days*, from the date of such request, whether such persons assent or object to such candidate being elected as an auditor, and if the greater number of the electors then entitled to vote shall signify their assent to the election of such person, but not otherwise, the said Assistant Poor Law Commissioner shall declare the candidate to be duly elected.

Art. 10.—The Assistant Poor Law Commissioner shall cause copies of the list showing the names of the voters who shall have voted for each candidate, or, in case of no contest, of the electors who shall have expressed their assent to the election of the person nominated, with the name of the person elected as auditor duly certified at the foot thereof, to be printed forthwith, and shall transmit to the Guardians of the several Unions and Parishes respectively printed copies thereof, and shall communicate to the person so elected auditor the fact of his having been so elected, and shall advertise the result of the election in some one or more newspaper or newspapers published in the district.

III.— *Continuance in Office.*

Art. 11.—And we do determine that the officer so appointed shall continue in office until he shall die, or resign, or be removed therefrom by the Poor Law Commissioners. And in case of such death, resignation or removal, another auditor shall be appointed in manner aforesaid.

IV.—*Duties of the Auditor.*

Art. 12.—The auditor shall, twice in every year, that is to say, as soon as may be after the Twenty-fifth day of March, and the Twenty-ninth day of September, examine, audit, and allow or disallow, the accounts of the several Unions and Parishes hereinbefore combined, and of the several Parishes comprised in the said Unions, according to the laws in force for the time being for the administration of the relief of the poor.

V.—*Remuneration of Auditor.*

⸋ Art. 13.—And do we regulate the amount of the salary payable to such officer, and the time and mode of payment thereof, and the proportions in which such respective Unions and Parishes shall contribute to such payment, as follows :—

We order that the said auditor shall be paid for the performance of his duties an annual salary of 418*l.*, such sum to be paid by equal periodical payments, to be made after the completion of the audit of the accounts of the several Unions and Parishes so comprised in the said district, and of the Parishes in the said Unions respectively.

Provided nevertheless, that if it shall happen that the person for the time being filling the said office of district auditor shall cease to be such auditor, after having completed the audit of some one or more of the above-mentioned Unions, or of the said Parishes, but before he shall have completed the audit of the whole of them, the Guardians of every Union whose accounts shall have been completely audited, and also of the said Parishes, in the like event of their accounts having been completely audited, shall pay their share of the salary so payable to the said auditor, according to the proportions hereunder set forth.

Art. 14.—And we do hereby order, that the said several Unions and Parishes shall contribute to the said sum of 418*l.* in the manner following ; that is to say,

	£.
The Alcester Union shall contribute the sum of	17
The Banbury Union shall contribute the sum of	37
The Chipping Norton Union shall contribute the sum of .	23
The Droitwich Union shall contribute the sum of . . .	20
The Evesham Union shall contribute the sum of . . .	20
The Foleshill Union shall contribute the sum of	15
The Northleach Union shall contribute the sum of . . .	18
The Pershore Union shall contribute the sum of	22
The Rugby Union shall contribute the sum of	24
The Shipston-upon-Stour Union shall contribute the sum of	26
The Solihull Union shall contribute the sum of	15
The Southam Union shall contribute the sum of	15
The Stow-on-the-Wold Union shall contribute the sum of .	17
The Stratford-upon-Avon Union shall contribute the sum of	24
The Warwick Union shall contribute the sum of	30
The Witney Union shall contribute the sum of	30
The Woodstock Union shall contribute the sum of . . .	25
The Worcester Union shall contribute the sum of . . .	20
The Parishes of Saint Michael and the Holy Trinity, Coventry shall contribute the sum of	20

£418

VI.—*Explanation of Terms.*

Art. 15.—Whenever the majority of electors is spoken of in this Order, it is to be taken to mean the majority of those electors whose assents to, or dissents from, a candidate on any list sent out as aforesaid are received in due form, and within the proper time.

Art. 16.—Whenever any notice or list, or other document is required to be sent, it shall be sufficient if the same be sent by the post, and the date of the delivery of the same to the post-office shall be taken to be the date of sending the same.

Art. 17.—If, by any accident, error, or other cause, a majority of the whole number of votes to be given has not been received on the day appointed for the receipt thereof, the election shall be deemed to have failed.

Art. 18.—The word *parishes* in this Order shall be taken to include all places maintaining their own poor, whether parochial or extra-parochial.

> Given under our hands and seal of office, this Twenty-fourth day of April, in the year One thousand eight hundred and forty-five.

(Signed)

(L.S)   Geo. Nicholls.
        G. C. Lewis.
        Edmund W. Head.

No. 5.

i.—General Orders—Relating to the Election of Guardians.

To the Guardians of the Poor of the several Unions named in the Schedule hereunto annexed ;—

To the Churchwardens and Overseers of the Poor of the several Parishes comprised in the said several Unions ;—

To the Clerk or Clerks to the Justices of the Petty Sessions held for the Division or Divisions in which the said several Parishes are situate ;—

And to all others whom it may concern.

We, the Poor Law Commissioners, do hereby, under the authority of an Act passed in the fifth year of the reign of His late Majesty King William the Fourth, intituled "An Act for the Amendment and better Administration of the Laws relating to the Poor in England and Wales," rescind all such of the provisions contained in any Order or Orders, under the hands and seal of the Poor Law Commissioners, as direct the manner of conducting the election of Guardians of the Poor for the several parishes comprised in the several Unions named in the Schedule hereunto annexed.

And we do hereby order and direct henceforth in regard thereto, with reference to each of the Unions named in the said Schedule, as follows :—

Art. 1.—The Overseers of every parish shall, before the 26th day of March in every year, distinguish in the rate-books, or enter into some other book to be provided for the purpose, the name of every rate-payer in their parish, who has been rated to the relief of the poor for the whole year immediately preceding the said day, and has paid the poor-rates made and assessed upon him for the period of one whole year, except those which have been made or become due within the six months immediately preceding the said day.

Art. 2.—The Clerk to the Board of Guardians shall at every future annual election of Guardians perform the duties hereby imposed upon him, and all other duties suitable to his office which it may be requisite for him to perform in conducting and completing such election; and in case the office of Clerk shall be vacant at any time when any proceeding is to be taken under this Order, or in case the Clerk, from illness or other sufficient cause, shall be unable to discharge such duties, the Guardians shall appoint some person to perform such of the duties imposed by this Order upon the Clerk as shall then remain to be performed, and the person so appointed shall perform such duties.

Art. 3.—The Guardians shall, before or during every such election, appoint a competent number of persons to assist the Clerk in conducting and completing the election in conformity with this Order, but if the Guardians shall not make such appointment within the requisite time, the Clerk shall take such measures for securing the necessary assistance as he shall deem advisable.

Art. 4.—In selecting such persons, the Guardians shall choose such of the paid officers of the Union as may be willing, and as may appear to the Guardians to be able to afford such assistance, without interruption to the proper discharge of their other duties.

Art. 5.—The persons appointed under Articles 3 and 4 shall obey all the directions which may be given by the Clerk for the execution of this Order.

Art. 6.—The overseers of every parish in the Union, and every officer having the custody of the poor-rate books of any such parish, shall attend the Clerk at such times as he shall require their attendance, until the completion of the election of Guardians, and shall, if required by him, produce to him such rate-books, and the registers of owners and proxies, together with the statements of owners, and appointments and statements of proxies, and all books and papers relating to such rates in their possession or power.

Provided that where any register of owners shall have been prepared in any parish containing a population exceeding 2000 persons, it shall not be necessary to produce the statements of owners.

Mode of conducting the Election.

Art. 7.—The Clerk shall prepare and sign a notice which may be in the Form marked (A.), hereunto annexed, and which shall contain the following particulars :—

    1st.—The number of Guardians to be elected for each parish in the Union.

    2nd.—The qualification of Guardians.

    3rd.—The qualification of voters.

    4th.—The persons by whom, and the places in each parish where, the nomination papers in respect of such parish are to be received, and the last day on which they are to be sent.

    5th.—The mode of voting in case of a contest, and the days on which the voting papers will be delivered and collected.

6th.—The time and place for the examination and casting up of
the votes.

And the Clerk shall cause such notice to be published on or before
the 15th day of March, in the following manner :—

1st.—A printed copy of such notice shall be affixed on the principal external gate or door of every Workhouse in the Union,
and shall from time to time be renewed, if necessary, until
the 9th day of April.

2nd.—Printed copies of such notice shall likewise be affixed on
such places in each of the parishes in the Union as are ordinarily made use of for affixing thereon notices of parochial
business.

Art. 8.—Any person entitled to vote in any parish may nominate for
the office of Guardian thereof, himself, if legally qualified, or any other
person or number of persons (not exceeding the number of Guardians
to be elected for such parish) legally qualified to be elected for that
office.

Art. 9.—Every nomination shall be in writing in the Form marked
(B.), hereunto annexed, and be signed by one person only, as the party
nominating, and shall be sent on or before the 26th day of March to
the Clerk, or to such person or persons as may have been appointed to
receive the same, and the Clerk or such person or persons, shall, on the
receipt thereof, mark thereon the date of its receipt, and also a number
according to the order of its receipt ; provided that no nomination sent
after the said 26th day of March shall be valid.

Art. 10.—If the number of the persons nominated for the office of
Guardian for any parish shall be the same as, or less than, the number
of Guardians to be elected for such parish, such persons, if duly qualified,
shall be deemed to be the elected Guardians for such parish, for the
ensuing year, and shall be certified as such by the Clerk under his hand
as hereinafter provided.

Art. 11.—But if the number of the duly qualified persons nominated
for the office of Guardian for any parish shall exceed the number of
Guardians to be elected therein, the Clerk shall cause voting papers, in
the Form marked (C.), hereunto annexed, to be prepared and filled up,
and shall insert therein the names of all the persons nominated, in the
order in which the nomination papers were received, and shall, on the
5th day of April, cause one of such voting papers to be delivered by the
persons appointed for that purpose, to the address in such parish of
each rate-payer, owner, and proxy qualified to vote therein.

Art. 12.—If the Clerk shall consider that any person nominated is
not duly qualified to be a Guardian, he shall state in the voting paper
the fact, that such person has been nominated, but that he considers such
person not to be duly qualified.

Art. 13.—If any person put in nomination for the office of Guardian
shall tender to the officer conducting the election, his refusal, in writing,
to serve such office, and if in consequence of such refusal the number of
persons nominated for the office of Guardian for such parish, shall be
the *same as*, or *less* than, the number of Guardians to be elected for
such parish, all or so many of the remaining candidates as shall be duly

qualified, shall be deemed to be the elected Guardians for such parish for the ensuing year, and shall be certified as such by the Clerk under his hand as hereinafter provided.

Art. 14.—Each voter shall write his initials in the voting paper delivered to him against the name or names of the person or persons (not exceeding the number of Guardians to be elected in the parish) for whom he intends to vote, and shall sign such voting paper ; and when any person votes as a proxy, he shall in like manner write his own initials and sign his own name, and state also in writing, the name of the person for whom he is proxy.

Art. 15.—Provided that if any voter cannot write, he shall affix his mark at the foot of the voting paper in the presence of a witness, who shall attest the affixing thereof, and who shall write the initials of such voter against the name of every candidate for whom the voter intends to vote.

Art. 16.—If the initials of the voter shall be written against the names of more persons than are to be elected Guardians for the parish, or if the voter shall not sign or affix his mark to the voting paper, or if his mark shall not be duly attested, or if a proxy do not sign his own name, and state in writing the name of the person for whom he is proxy, such person shall be omitted in the calculation of votes.

Art. 17.—The Clerk shall cause the voting papers to be collected by the persons appointed for that purpose, on the 7th day of April, in such manner as he shall direct.

Art. 18.—No voting paper shall be received or admitted unless the same shall have been delivered at the address in each parish of the voter, and collected by the persons appointed or employed for that purpose, except as is provided in the following article.

Art. 19.—Provided that every person qualified to vote, who shall not, on the 5th day of April, have received a voting paper, shall, on application before the 8th day of April to the Clerk at his office, be entitled to receive a voting paper, and to fill up the same in the presence of the Clerk, and then and there to deliver the same to him.

Art. 20.—Provided also, that in case any voting paper duly delivered shall not have been collected through the default of the Clerk, or the persons appointed or employed for that purpose, the voter in person may deliver the same to the Clerk before 12 o'clock at noon on the 8th day of April.

Art. 21.—The Clerk shall, on the 9th day of April, and on as many days immediately succeeding as may be necessary, attend at the Board-room of the Guardians of the Union, and ascertain the validity of the votes, by an examination of the rate-books, and the registers of owners and proxies, and such other documents as he may think necessary, and by examining such persons as he may see fit ; and he shall cast up such of the votes as he shall find to be valid, and to have been duly given, collected, or received, and ascertain the number of such votes for each candidate.

Art. 22.—The candidates, to the number of Guardians to be elected for the parish, who being duly qualified, shall have obtained the greatest number of votes shall be deemed to be the elected Guardians for the parish, and shall be certified as such by the Clerk under his hand.

Art. 23.—The Clerk, when he shall have ascertained that any candidate is duly elected as Guardian, shall notify the fact of his having been so elected, by delivering or sending, or causing to be delivered or sent, to him a notice in the Form (D.), hereunto annexed.

Notice of the Election of Guardians.

Art. 24.—The Clerk shall make a list, containing the names of the candidates, together with (in case of a contest) the number of votes given for each, and the names of the elected Guardians according to the Form marked (E.), hereunto annexed, and shall sign and certify the same, and shall deliver such list, together with all the nomination and voting papers which he shall have received, to the Guardians of the Union, at their next meeting, and shall cause copies of such list to be printed, and shall deliver or send, or cause to be delivered or sent, one or more of such copies to the Overseers of each parish, and to the Poor Law Commissioners.

Art. 25.—The Overseers shall affix, or cause to be affixed, copies of such list, at the usual places for affixing in each parish notices of parochial business.

Explanation of Terms.

Art. 26.—Whenever the word "Parish" is used in this Order, it shall be taken to signify any place separately maintaining its own poor.

Art. 27.—Whenever in describing any person or party, matter or thing, the word importing the singular number or the masculine gender only is used in this Order, the same shall be taken to include, and shall be applied to, several persons or parties as well as one person or party, and females as well as males, and several matters or things, as well as one matter or thing respectively, unless there be something in the subject or context repugnant to such construction.

Art. 28.—Whenever in this Order any article is referred to by its number, the article of this Order bearing that number shall be taken to be signified thereby.

Art. 29.—Whenever the day appointed in this Order for the performance of any act shall be a Sunday, or Good Friday, such act shall be performed on the day next following.

Art. 30.—The word "Clerk" shall extend in this Order to the person who may be appointed under Article 2, to act as such in the performance of the duties hereby prescribed.

(A.)

ELECTION of GUARDIANS of the POOR.

———————— UNION. }

I,   Clerk to the Guardians of the Poor of the   Union, with reference to the ensuing Election of Guardians of the Poor for the several Parishes in the said Union, do hereby give notice,—

1. That the number of Guardians of the Poor to be elected for the Parishes in the said Union, is as follows :—

    For the Parish of   One Guardian.
    For the Parish of   Two Guardians.

2. That any person not otherwise disqualified by law who shall be rated to the Poor-rate in any Parish in the Union, in respect of hereditaments of the annual rental of   pounds, is qualified to be nominated for the office of Guardian at the said Election, by any person then qualified to vote.

3. That any Rate-payer who shall have been rated to the Poor-rate in any Parish in the Union for the whole year immediately preceding his voting, and shall have paid the Rates made and assessed on him, for the relief of the poor for one whole year, as well as those due from him at the time of voting, except those which have been made or become due within six months immediately preceding such voting, and that every owner of rateable property situated within the said parish, who shall have given to the Overseers thereof, before the First day of February, the statement in writing required by law, will be entitled according to the Provisions of the 7 and 8 Vict., c. 101, sect. 14, to have the number and proportion of votes at the Election of Guardians for the said Parish, according to the following scale :—

If the property in respect of which he is entitled to vote be rated upon a rateable value of less than £50	He shall have one vote.
If such rateable value amount to £50 and be less than £100	He shall have two votes.
If it amount to £100 and be less than £150	He shall have three votes.
If it amount to £150 and be less than £200	He shall have four votes.
If it amount to £200 and be less than £250	He shall have five votes.
If it amount to or exceed £250 . . .	He shall have six votes.

Any owner of such property who has made such statement may, by writing under his hand, appoint any person to vote as his proxy, but such proxy must, fourteen days previously to the day on which he shall claim to vote, give to one of the Overseers of such Parish, a statement in writing of his own name and address, and also the name and address of the owner appointing him such proxy, and a description of the property as proxy to the owner whereof he claims to vote, and also the original or an attested copy of the writing appointing him such proxy.

4. Nominations of Guardians must be made according to the form below, which is the form prescribed by the Poor Law Commissioners. Such nominations must be sent, on or before the   day of March, to me,

or to Mr.	at	for the Parish of
or to Mr.	at	for the Parish of

who alone are authorized to receive the same. Nominations sent after that day, or sent to any other person, will be invalid.

5. That I shall, if more than the above-mentioned number of Guardians be nominated for any parish, cause Voting Papers to be delivered on the   day of   , at the address in such parish of each Rate-payer, Owner, and Proxy qualified to vote ; and that on the day of   I shall cause such Voting Papers to be collected.

6. That on the   day of   , I shall attend at the Board Room of this Union at the hour of   , and that I shall on that day, and, if necessary, the following days, proceed to ascertain the number of votes given for each candidate.

7. That any person put in nomination for the office of Guardian may at any time during the proceedings in the Election, tender to me in writing his refusal to serve the Office, and the Election, so far as regards that person, will be no further proceeded with.

FORM OF NOMINATION PAPER.

Parish of _____ ⎫
_____ UNION. ⎬ This   day of   184 .

Names of Persons nominated to be Guardians.	Residence of the Persons nominated.	Quality or Calling of Persons nominated.

I, being*   duly qualified to vote in the *Parish*
of   , nominate the above to be Guardian (or
Guardians) for the said *Parish*.

_____ Signature⎫ of Nominator.
_____ Address ⎭

* *Note.*—Only one person is empowered to sign this paper, and after the word *being* must insert (*a rate-payer*) or (*owner of property*), according to his qualification.

Given under my hand, this   day of   18 .
_____ Clerk to the Guardians of the Poor
of the   Union.

(B.)
NOMINATION PAPER.

Parish of _____ ⎫
_____ UNION. ⎬ This   day of   184 .

Names of Persons nominated to be Guardians.	Residence of the Persons nominated.	Quality or Calling of Persons nominated.

I, being*   duly qualified to vote in the *Parish*
of   , nominate the above to be Guardian (or Guardians) for the said *Parish*.

_____ Signature⎫ of Nominator.
_____ Address. ⎭

* *Note.*—Only one person is empowered to sign this Paper, and after the word *being* must insert (*a rate-payer*) or (*owner of property*), according to his qualification.

(C.)

VOTING PAPER.

_____ UNION.

Voting Paper for the *Parish* of

No. of Voting Paper.	Name and Address of Voter.	Number of Votes.	
		As Owner.	As Rate-payer.

Directions to the Voters.

The Voter must write his initials against the Name of every Person for whom he votes, and must sign this Paper.

If the Voter cannot write, he must affix his Mark, but such Mark must be attested by a Witness, and such Witness must write the initials of the Voter against the name of every Person for whom the Voter intends to vote.

If a Proxy vote, he must in like manner write his initials, sign his own name, and state in writing the name of the person for whom he is Proxy; thus, *John Smith* for *Richard Williams.*

This Paper must be carefully preserved by the Voter, as no second Paper will be given. When it is filled up it must be kept ready for delivery to Mr.   , who will call for the same on the day of   . No other person is authorized to receive the Voting Paper.

If the Voting Paper be not ready for the person appointed to collect it when called for, the Vote will be lost. It will also be lost if more than name be returned in the List, with the Initials of the Voter placed against such name, or if the Voting Paper be not signed by the Voter, or if the mark of the Voter be not attested when attestation is required.

Initials of the Voter against the name of the Person for whom he intends to vote.	Names of the Persons nominated as Guardians.	Residence of the Persons nominated.	Qual'ty or Calling of the Persons. nominated.	Names of the Nomina- tors.	Address of the Nominators.	Opinion of the Clerk as to Disqualifica- tion.

I vote for the Persons in the above List against whose names my initials are placed.

Signed _____ [*or the Mark of*] _____

Witness to the Mark _____

or _____ for _____

(D.)

NOTICE to the GUARDIANS ELECTED.

_____,UNION.

Parish of _____

Sir,—I do hereby give you notice, and declare that you have been duly elected a Guardian of the Poor for the *Parish* of
in the　　　　　　　　　Union, and that the next Meeting of the Board of Guardians of the said Union will be held at
on　　　　　　　next, at the hour of

Signed this　　　　　　　day of

_____ Clerk to the Guardians of the Poor of the

　　　　　　Union.

To Mr. _____ of _____

(E.)

_____ UNION.

I do hereby certify, that the election of Guardians of the Poor for the several parishes in the　　　　　　Union was conducted in conformity with the Order of the Poor Law Commissioners, and that the entries contained in the Schedule hereunder written are true.

PARISHES arranged alphabetically	Names of Persons nominated as Guardians.	Residence.	Quality or Calling.	No. of Votes given for each Candidate.	Names of the Guardians elected.

Given under my hand, this　　　　　　day of

_____ Clerk to the Guardians of the Poor of the

Union.

SCHEDULE,

Containing the Names of the UNIONS to which the present Order applies.

Aberaeron	Ampthill	Axbridge
Abergavenny	Andover	Axminster
Aberystwith	Anglesey	Aylesbury
Abingdon	Asaph St.	Aylesford, North
Alban's, St.	Ashbourne	Aylsham
Alcester	Ashby-de-la-Zouch	Bakewell
Alderbury	Ashford, East	Bala
Alnwick	Ashford, West	Banbury
Alresford	Aston	Bangor and Beaumaris
Alton	Atcham	Barnet
Altrincham	Atherstone	Barnstaple
Amersham	Auckland	Barrow-upon-Soar
Amesbury	Austel, St.	Basford

Basingstoke
Bath
Battle
Beaminster
Bedale
Bedford
Bedminster
Belford
Bellingham
Belper
Berkhampstead
Berwick-upon-Tweed
Beverley
Bicester
Bideford
Biggleswade
Billericay
Billesdon
Bingham
Bishop's Stortford
Blaby
Blackburn
Blandford
Blean
Blofield
Blything
Bodmin
Bolton
Bootle
Bosmere and Claydon
Boston
Boughton, Great
Bourn
Brackley
Bradfield
Bradford (Wilts)
Bradford (York)
Braintree
Brampton
Brecknock
Brentford
Bridge
Bridgend and Cowbridge
Bridgnorth
Bridgwater
Bridlington
Bridport
Brixworth
Bromley
Bromsgrove
Bromyard
Buckingham
Builth
Buntingford
Burnley
Burton-upon-Trent
Bury
Caistor
Calne
Cambridge
Camelford
Cardiff
Cardigan
Carlisle

Carmarthen
Carnarvon
Castle Ward
Catherington
Caxton and Arrington
Cerne
Chailey
Chapel-en-le-Frith
Chard
Cheadle
Chelmsford
Cheltenham
Chepstow
Chertsey
Chesterfield
Chester-le-Street
Chesterton
Chippenham
Chipping Norton
Chipping Sodbury
Chorley
Chorlton
Christchurch
Church Stretton
Cirencester
Cleobury Mortimer
Clifton
Clitheroe
Clun
Clutton
Cockermouth
Colchester
Columb, St. Major
Congleton
Conway
Cookham
Corwen
Cosford
Cranbrook
Crediton
Crickhowel
Cricklade and Wootton
   Bassett
Croydon
Cuckfield
Darlington
Dartford
Daventry
Depwade
Derby
Devizes
Dewsbury
Docking
Dolgelly
Doncaster
Dorchester
Dore
Dorking
Dover
Downham
Drayton
Driffield
Droitwich
Droxford

Dudley
Dulverton
Dunmow
Durham
Dursley
Easington
Easingwold
Eastbourne
East Grinstead
Easthampstead
East Redford
Eastry .
East Ward
Eccleshall Bierlow
Edmonton
Elham
Ellesmere
Ely
Epping
Epsom
Erpingham
Eton
Evesham
Faith, St.
Falmouth
Fareham
Faringdon
Faversham
Festiniog
Foleshill
Fordingbridge
Freebridge Lynn
Frome
Fylde
Gainsborough
Garstang
Gateshead
German's St.
Glanford Brigg
Glendale
Glossop
Glouceste
Godstone
Goole
Grantham
Gravesend and Milton
Greenwich
Guildford
Guiltcross
Guisborough
Hackney
Hailsham
Halifax
Halsted
Haltwhistle
Hambledon
Hardingstone
Hartismere
Hartley Wintney
Haslingden
Hastings
Hatfield
Havant
Haverfordwest

Hay
Hayfield
Headington
Helmsley Blackmoor
Helston
Hemel Hempstead
Hendon
Henley
Henstead
Hereford
Hertford
Hexham
Highworth and Swindon
Hinckley
Hitchin
Holbeach
Holborn
Hollingbourn
Holsworthy
Holywell
Honiton
Hoo
Horncastle
Horsham
Houghton-le-Spring
Howden
Hoxne
Huddersfield
Hungerford
Huntingdon
Hursley
Ipswich
Ives, St.
Keighley
Kendal
Kettering
Keynsham
Kidderminster
Kingsbridge
Kingclere
King's Lynn
King's Norton
Kingston-upon-Thames
Kington
Knighton
Lampeter
Lancaster
Lanchester
Langport
Launceston
Ledbury
Leek
Leicester
Leigh
Leighton Buzzard
Leominster
Lewes
Lewisham
Lexden and Winstree
Leyburn
Lichfield
Lincoln
Linton
Liskeard

Llandilo Fawr
Llandovery
Llanelly
Llanfyllin
Llanrwst
Loddon and Clavering
London, City of
London, East
London, West
Longtown
Loughborough
Louth
Ludlow
Luton
Lutterworth
Lymington
Macclesfield
Machynlleth
Madeley
Maidstone
Maldon
Malling
Malmsbury
Malton
Manchester
Mansfield
Market Bosworth
Market Harborough
Marlborough
Martley
Medway
Melksham
Melton Mowbray
Mere
Meridan
Merthyr Tidvil
Midhurst
Mildenhall
Milton
Mitford and Launditch
Monmouth
Morpeth
Nantwich
Narberth
Neath
Neots, St.
Newark
Newbury
Newcastle-in-Emlyn
Newcastle-under-Lyne
Newcastle-upon-Tyne
Newent
New Forest
Newhaven
Newmarket
Newport (Monmouth)
Newport (Salop)
Newport Pagnell
Newton Abbot
Newtown and Llanidloes
Northallerton
Northampton
Northleach
Northwich

North Witchford
Nottingham
Nuneaton
Oakham
Okehampton
Olave's, St.
Ongar
Ormskirk
Orsett
Oundle
Pateley Bridge
Patrington
Pembroke
Penkridge
Penrith
Penzance
Pershore
Peterborough
Petersfield
Petworth
Pewsey
Pickering
Ploinesgate
Plympton, St. Mary
Pocklington
Pont-y-Pool
Poole
Poplar
Portsea Island
Potterspury
Prescot
Presteigne
Preston
Pwllheli
Radford
Reading
Redruth
Reeth
Reigate
Rhayader
Richmond (Surrey)
Richmond (York)
Ringwood
Risbridge
Rochdale
Rochford
Romford
Romney Marsh
Romsey
Ross
Rothbury
Rotherham
Royston
Rugby
Runcorn
Ruthin
Rye
Saffron Walden
Salford
Saviour's St.
Scarborough
Sculcoates
Sedbergh
Sedgefield

Seisdon
Selby
Settle
Sevenoaks
Shaftesbury
Shardlow
Sheffield
Sheppey
Shepton Mallet
Sherborne
Shiffnal
Shipston-upon-Stour
Skipton
Skirlaugh
Sleaford
Solihull
Southam
South Molton
South Shields
South Stoneham
Southwell
Spalding
Spilsby
Stafford
Staines
Stamford
Stepney
Steyning
Stockbridge
Stockport
Stockton
Stokesley
Stone
Stourbridge
Stow
Stow-on-the-Wold
Straud
Stratford-upon-Avon
Stratton
Stroud
Sturminster
Sudbury
Sunderland
Swaffham
Swansea
Tamworth
Taunton
Tavistock
Teesdale

Tenbury
Tendring
Tenterden
Tetbury
Tewkesbury
Thakeham
Thame
Thanet, Isle of
Thetford
Thingoe
Thirsk
Thomas, St.
Thornbury
Thorne
Thrapston
Ticehurst
Tisbury
Tiverton
Todmorden
Tonbridge
Torrington
Totnes
Towcester
Tregaron
Truro
Tynemouth
Uckfield
Ulverston
Uppingham
Upton-upon-Severn
Uttoxeter
Uxbridge
Wakefield
Wallingford
Walsal
Walsingham
Wandsworth and Clapham
Wangford
Wantage
Ware
Wareham and Purbeck
Warminster
Warrington
Warwick
Watford
Wayland
Weardale
Wellingborough

Wellington (Salop)
Wellington (Somerset)
Wells
Welwyn
Wem
Weobly
Westbourne
West Bromwich
Westbury-upon-Severn
Westbury and Whorwelsdown
West Derby
West Firle
West Ham
West Hampnett
West Ward
Weymouth
Wheatenhurst
Whitby
Whitchurch
Whitechapel
Whitehaven
Wigan
Wigton
Williton
Wilton
Wimborne and Cranborne
Wincanton
Winchcombe
Winchester, New
Windsor
Winslow
Wirrall
Wisbeach
Witham
Witney
Woburn
Wokingham
Wolstanton and Burslem
Wolverhampton
Woodbridge
Woodstock
Worcester
Worksop
Wortley
Wrexham
Wycombe
Yeovil
York

Given under our hands and seal of office, this Sixteenth day of January, in the year One thousand eight hundred and forty-five.

         (Signed)   GEO. NICHOLLS.

(*L. S.*)   G. C. LEWIS.

         EDMUND W. HEAD.

[This Order came into operation on the 26th day of February, 1845.]

To THE GUARDIANS OF THE POOR of the several Parishes named
in the Schedule hereunto annexed ;—

To the Churchwardens and Overseers of the Poor of the said several
Parishes ;—

To the Clerk or Clerks to the Justices of the Petty Sessions held for
the Division or Divisions in which the said several Parishes
are situate ;—

And to all others whom it may concern.

We, the Poor Law Commissioners, do hereby, under the authority of
an Act passed in the fifth year of the reign of his late Majesty King
William the Fourth, intituled "An Act for the Amendment and better
Administration of the Laws relating to the Poor in England and Wales,"
rescind all such of the provisions contained in any Order or Orders,
under the hands and seal of the Poor Law Commissioners, as direct the
manner of conducting the election of Guardians of the Poor for the several
Parishes named in the Schedule hereunto annexed.

And we do hereby order and direct henceforth in regard thereto, with
reference to each of the parishes named in the said Schedule, as
follows : —

Art. 1.—The Overseers of the parish shall, before the twenty-sixth
day of March in every year, distinguish in the rate-books, or enter in some
other book to be provided for the purpose, the name of every rate-payer
in the parish, who has been rated to the relief of the poor for the whole
year immediately preceding the said day, and has paid the poor-rates
made and assessed upon him for the period of one whole year, except
those which have been made or become due within the six months immediately preceding the said day.

Art. 2.—The Clerk to the Board of Guardians shall at every future
annual election of Guardians perform the duties hereby imposed upon
him, and all other duties suitable to his office which it may be requisite
for him to perform in conducting and completing such election ; and in
case the office of Clerk shall be vacant at any time when any proceeding
is to be taken under this Order, or in case the Clerk, from illness or
other sufficient cause, shall be unable to discharge such duties, the
Guardians shall appoint some person to perform such of the duties
imposed by this Order upon the Clerk as shall then remain to be performed, and the person so appointed shall perform such duties.

⊁ Art. 3.—The Guardians shall, before or during every such election,
appoint a competent number of persons to assist the Clerk in conducting
and completing the election in conformity with this Order ; but if the
Guardians shall not make such appointment within the requisite time,
the Clerk shall take such measures for securing the necessary assistance
as he shall deem advisable.

Art. 4.—In selecting such persons, the Guardians shall choose such
of the paid officers of the parish as may be willing, and as may appear
to the Guardians to be able to afford such assistance, without interruption
to the proper discharge of their other duties.

Art. 5.—The persons appointed under Articles 3 and 4 shall obey all
the directions which may be given by the Clerk for the execution of
this Order.

Art. 6.—The Overseers of the parish, and every officer having the
custody of the poor-rate books of the parish, shall attend the Clerk at

I

such times as he shall require their attendance, until the completion of the election of Guardians, and shall, if required by him, produce to him such rate-books, and the registers of owners and proxies, together with the statements of owners, and appointments and statements of proxies, and all books and papers relating to such rates in their possession or power.

Provided that where the register of owners shall have been prepared in the parish, it shall not be necessary to produce the statements of owners.

Mode of conducting the Election.

Art. 7.—The Clerk shall prepare and sign a notice, which may be in the Form marked (A), hereunto annexed, and which shall contain the following particulars :—

1st.—The number of Guardians to be elected for the parish.

2d.—The qualification of Guardians.

3d.—The qualification of Voters.

4th.—The persons by whom, and the places in the parish where, the nomination papers in respect of such parish are to be received, and the last day on which they are to be sent.

5th.—The mode of voting in case of a contest, and the days on which the voting papers will be delivered and collected.

6th.—The time and place for the examination and casting up of the votes.

And the Clerk shall cause such notice to be published on or before the fifteenth day of March, in the following manner :—

1st.—A printed copy of such notice shall be affixed on the principal external gate or door of every workhouse in the parish, and shall from time to time be renewed, if necessary, until the ninth day of April.

2d.—Printed copies of such notice shall likewise be affixed on such places in the parish as are ordinarily made use of for affixing thereon notices of parochial business.

Art. 8.—Any person entitled to vote in the parish, may nominate for the office of Guardian thereof, himself, if legally qualified, or any other person or number of persons (not exceeding the number of Guardians to be elected for such parish) legally qualified to be elected for that office.

Art. 9.—Every nomination shall be in writing in the Form marked (B) hereunto annexed, and be signed by one person only, as the party nominating, and shall be sent on or before the twenty-sixth day of March to the Clerk, or to such person or persons as may have been appointed to receive the same and the Clerk, or such person or persons shall, on the receipt thereof, mark thereon the date of its receipt, and also a number according to the order of its receipt; provided that no nomination sent after the said twenty-sixth day of March shall be valid.

Art. 10.—If the number of the persons nominated for the office of Guardian for the parish shall be the same as, or less than, the number of Guardians to be elected for such parish, such persons, if duly qualified, shall be deemed to be the elected Guardians for such parish for the ensuing year, and shall be certified as such by the Clerk under his hand as hereinafter provided.

Art. 11.—But if the number of the duly qualified persons nominated for the office of Guardian for the parish shall exceed the number of Guardians to be elected therein, the Clerk shall cause voting papers, in the Form marked (C), hereunto annexed, to be prepared and filled up, and shall insert therein the names of all the persons nominated, in the order in which the nomination papers were received, and shall on the fifth day of April cause one of such voting papers to be delivered by the persons appointed for that purpose, to the address in such parish of each rate-payer, owner, and proxy qualified to vote therein.

Art. 12.—If the Clerk shall consider that any person nominated is not duly qualified to be a Guardian, he shall state in the voting paper the fact that such person has been nominated, but that he considers such person not to be duly qualified.

Art. 13.—If any person put in nomination for the office of Guardian shall tender to the officer conducting the election his refusal, in writing, to serve such office, and if in consequence of such refusal the number of persons nominated for the office of Guardian for the parish shall be the *same as*, or *less* than, the number of Guardians to be elected for such parish, all or so many of the remaining candidates as shall be duly qualified shall be deemed to be the elected Guardians for such parish for the ensuing year, and shall be certified as such by the Clerk under his hand as hereinafter provided.

Art. 14.—Each voter shall write his initials in the voting paper delivered to him against the name or names of the person or persons (not exceeding the number of Guardians to be elected in the parish) for whom he intends to vote, and shall sign such voting paper; and when any person votes as a proxy, he shall in like manner write his own initials and sign his own name, and state also, in writing, the name of the person for whom he is proxy.

Art. 15.—Provided that if any voter cannot write, he shall affix his mark at the foot of the voting paper in the presence of a witness, who shall attest the affixing thereof, and who shall write the initials of such voter against the name of every candidate for whom the voter intends to vote.

Art. 16.—If the initials of the voter shall be written against the names of more persons than are to be elected Guardians for the parish, or if the voter shall not sign or affix his mark to the voting paper, or if his mark shall not be duly attested, or if a proxy do not sign his own name, and state in writing the name of the person for whom he is proxy, such person shall be omitted in the calculation of votes.

Art. 17.—The Clerk shall cause the voting papers to be collected by the persons appointed for that purpose on the seventh day of April in such manner as he shall direct.

Art. 18.—No voting paper shall be received or admitted unless the same shall have been delivered at the address in the parish of the voter, and collected by the persons appointed or employed for that purpose, except as is provided in the following Article.

Art. 19.—Provided that every person qualified to vote, who shall not on the fifth day of April have received a voting paper, shall, on application before the eighth day of April to the Clerk at his office, be entitled to receive a voting paper, and to fill up the same in the presence of the Clerk, and then and there to deliver the same to him.

(B.)
NOMINATION PAPER.

Parish of_____This_____day of_____184 .

Names of Persons nominated to be Guardians.	Residence of the Persons nominated.	Quality or Calling of Persons nominated.

I being*_____duly qualified to vote in the *Parish* of
nominate the above to be Guardian (*or* Guardians) for the said *Parish.*

_____Signature⎱
_____Address ⎰of Nominator.

* *Note.*—Only one person is empowered to sign this Paper, and after the word
being he must insert (*a rate-payer*) or (*owner of property*) according to his qualification.

(C.)
VOTING PAPER.

Parish of_____Voting Paper for the Parish of .

No. of Voting Paper.	Name and Address of Voter.	Number of Votes.	
		As Owner.	As Rate-payer.

Directions to the Voters.

The Voter must write his initials against the Name of every Person for
whom he votes, and must sign this Paper.

If the Voter cannot write, he must affix his Mark, but such Mark must
be attested by a Witness, and such Witness must write the initials of the
Voter against the Name of every Person for whom the Voter intends
to vote.

If a Proxy vote, he must in like manner write his initials, sign his own
name, and state in writing the name of the person for whom he is Proxy;
thus, *John Smith* for *Richard Williams.*

This Paper must be carefully preserved by the Voter, as no second
Paper will be given. When it is filled up it must be kept ready for delivery
to Mr._____, who will call for the same on the
day of_____. No other person is authorized to receive
the Voting Paper.

If the Voting Paper be not ready for the person appointed to collect
it when called for, the Vote will be lost. It will also be lost if more
than_____name be returned in the List, with the initials of the
Voter placed against such name, or if the Voting Paper be not signed by

the Voter, or if the Mark of the Voter be not attested when attestation is required.

Initials of the Voter against the Name of the Persons for whom he intends to vote.	Names of the Persons nominated as Guardians.	Residence of the Persons nominated.	Quality or Calling of the Persons nominated.	Names of the Nominators.	Address of, the Nominators.	Opinion of the Clerk as to Disqualification.

I vote for the Persons in the above List against whose Names my initials are placed.

Signed_____[*or the mark of*]_____

Witness to the Mark_____

*or*_____for_____

(D.)
NOTICE TO THE GUARDIANS ELECTED.

Parish of_____

Sir,—I do hereby give you notice, and declare, that you have been duly elected a Guardian of the Poor for the Parish of
and that the next meeting of the Board of Guardians of the said Parish will be held at   on   next, at the hour of

Signed this   day of

_____Clerk to the Guardians of the Poor of the Parish of

To Mr._____ of_____

(E.)

Parish of_____

I do hereby certify, that the Election of Guardians of the Poor for the Parish of   was conducted in conformity with the Order of the Poor Law Commissioners, and that the Entries contained in the Schedule hereunder written are true.

Name of PARISH.	Names of Persons nominated as Guardians.	Residence.	Quality or Calling.	No. of Votes given for each Candidate.	Names of the Guardians elected.

Given under my hand, this   day of

_____Clerk to the Guardians of the Poor of the *Parish* of

SCHEDULE

Containing the Names of the PARISHES to which the present Order applies.

Alston and Garrigill	St. George-in-the-East	St. Mary, Lambeth
Bermondsey, St. Mary Magdalen	St. George-the-Martyr, Southwark	St. Mary, Rotherhithe Stoke-upon-Trent
East Stonehouse	St. Giles, Camberwell	Whittlesea, St. Mary
St. Matthew, Bethnal Green	St. Luke, Chelsea	and St. Andrew
	St. Martin-in-the-Fields	Great Yarmouth

Given under our hands and seal of office, this Twenty-fifth day of January, in the year One thousand eight hundred and forty-five.

(*L.S.*)　　(Signed)　　GEO. NICHOLLS.
G. C. LEWIS.

[This Order came into operation on the 9th day of March, 1845.]

LETTER relating to the foregoing ORDERS.

Poor Law Commission Office, Somerset House;
SIR,　　　　　　　　16*th January*, 1845.

I AM directed by the Poor Law Commissioners to transmit to you a copy of a General Order which they have issued to regulate the election of Guardians in parishes now in Union.

The statute of the last Session of Parliament has introduced some alterations in regard to this matter, the most important of which affect the scale of voting, and those alterations have rendered it necessary for the Commissioners to modify some parts of the Orders hitherto in force which regulate the mode and manner of elections of Guardians.

They have, therefore, deemed it advisable to rescind all those Orders, and to issue the present as a General Order, containing the few alterations which appear to them to be requisite.

The plan which the Commissioners established several years back for the conduct of these elections, having worked with success, and having in a satisfactory manner effected the election of the Guardians in the great number of parishes now combined in Unions, has not been departed from in the present Order, and it will be seen, therefore, that it contains little more than verbal alterations, and some few changes in the details.

The Commissioners have, however, thought it expedient to alter the dates on which the several proceedings are to take place, and thus to avail themselves of the provision contained in the seventeenth section of the 7 and 8 Vict., c. 101, which continues the Guardians in office for 40 days after the 25th of March, if a new election do not previously take place.

The Commissioners have not set out in this Order any Forms for the statement of owners of property, for the appointment of proxies, the statements of proxies, and in the register of those statements and appointments, which in the Orders now rescinded appeared as Forms (A.) (B.) (C.) and (D.) At the same time, as the Commissioners believe that it will be convenient if some Forms be suggested for general use, they have reconsidered those formerly prepared with reference to the alterations made by the late statute, and think that Forms to the following effect might be safely used in place of the first three of those Forms.

To the Clerk to the Guardians.

(A.)

OWNER'S STATEMENT.

To the Churchwardens and Overseers of the Poor of the Parish of _____ in the County of _____

This   day of   184 .

I, the undersigned, claim to be entitled to vote, according to the provisions of the statutes of the fifth year of the reign of King William the Fourth and the eighth year of the reign of Her present Majesty, relating to the administration of the laws for the relief of the poor (4 and 5 Wm. IV. c. 76, and 7 and 8 Vic. c. 101), as owner of the property hereinafter described, which is situated in the parish of   that is to say,

I do also state that the interest or estate which I have in such property, and the amount of all the rent-service which I receive or pay in respect thereof, and the names of the Persons from whom I receive or to whom I pay such rent-service, are set forth in the Form hereunder written.

Description of Property.[1]	In respect of which I have an Estate or Interest of.[2]	And in respect of which I receive in Rent-service the sum of[3]			From.[4]	And in respect of which I pay in Rent-service the sum of[5]			To.[6]
		£.	s.	d.		£.	s.	d.	

Signature of Claimant. _____

Address of claimant. _____

* Here insert a clear Statement of the Property, as House, Building , House and   Acres of Land.

[1] Describe the Property by its Name, Situation, or the Name of the Occupier, or any other designation by which it may be identified.

[2] Describe the Estate or Interest, as *an estate in fee simple, a freehold, a term of years,* and also whether it is held by the Claimant solely, or jointly with others.

[3] If the Property is let by the Owner, insert the amount of rent received from each tenant.

[4] Insert name of Tenant or Tenants.

[5] If the Owner is a Lessee paying rent, insert the amount of all the rent he pays.

[6] Insert the name of the Lessor.

(B.)

APPOINTMENT OF PROXY.

To the Churchwardens and Overseers of the Poor of the Parish of _____ in the County of _____

This   day of   184 .

I, the undersigned, being owner of the property hereinafter described, which is situated in the parish of   do hereby appoint   of to vote as my proxy in all cases wherein he may lawfully do so, under the provisions of the statutes of the fifth year of the reign of His late Majesty King William the Fourth, and the eighth year of the reign of Her present Majesty, relating to the administration of the laws for the relief of the poor. And I do hereby state that the description of the said property is as follows, viz.[1] :—

Signature of Owner.
Address of Owner. ·

[1] Describe the property by its name, situation, or the name of the occupier, or any other designation by which it may be identified. It is not necessary here to set out the description of the estate or interest of the owner, nor the statement of the amount of rent received or paid by him.

(C.)

PROXY'S STATEMENT.

To the Churchwardens and Overseers of the Poor of the Parish of
_____ in the County of _____
This _____ day of _____ 184 .

I, the undersigned, having been appointed by
of _____ owner of the property hereinafter described, which is situated in the parish of _____ to vote as his proxy, under the provisions of the statutes of the fifth year of the reign of His late Majesty King William the Fourth, and of the eighth year of the reign of Her present Majesty, relating to the administration of the laws for the relief of the poor, do hereby give you notice, that I am entitled to vote as such proxy. I herewith transmit to you[1] the writing under the hand of the said _____ appointing me such proxy.

The following is a description of the property in respect of which the said _____ is entitled to vote as owner, and in respect of which I am entitled to vote as his proxy, viz.[2] :—

Signature of Proxy.
Address of Proxy.

[1] If the appointment itself be not sent. insert the words *an attested copy of.*
[2] Describe the property by its name, situation, or the name of the occupier, or any other designation by which it may be identified. It is not necessary here to set out the description of the estate or interest of the owner, nor the statement of the amount of rent received or paid by him.

I am to observe that the adoption of these Forms is by no means compulsory upon any owner or proxy, and consequently any Forms which may contain in substance the information herein set forth, which appears to be what is required by the statutes, will be fully available for the purposes of the election.

The form of register of owners and proxies is directed by the General Order as to the duties of overseers, bearing date the 22nd of April, 1842, and addressed to the overseers of all parishes now in Union; and such Order being still in force, it is not necessary to set out the Form in this place.

The Commissioners believe that the general provisions of the former law respecting the election of Guardians are now well known, and they have in their memorandum of the 31st ult., which has been very widely circulated, pointed out the new provisions relative to the claims of owners ; while in the Form of the notice of election, contained in the Order, of which the copy is herewith forwarded, they have set forth at full the new scale of votes for owners and rate-payers.

It does not therefore, appear to them to be necessary to make any further remarks on this subject in the present circular.

I am, Sir
Your obedient servant,
(Signed) EDWIN CHADWICK, *Secretary*.

No. 5.

ii.—GENERAL ORDER—RELATING TO THE EXPENSES OF THE ELECTION OF GUARDIANS.

To THE GUARDIANS OF THE POOR of the several Unions named in the Schedules hereunto annexed ;—

To the Churchwardens and Overseers of the Poor of the several Parishes comprised in the said several Unions ;

To the Clerk or Clerks to the Justices of the Petty Sessions held for the Division or Divisions in which the said several Parishes are situate ;

And to all others whom it may concern.

We, the Poor Law Commissioners, do hereby, under the authority of an Act passed in the fifth year of the reign of His late Majesty King William the Fourth, intituled, "An Act for the Amendment and better Administration of the Laws relating to the Poor in England and Wales," rescind all such of the provisions contained in any Order or Orders under the hands and seal of the Poor Law Commissioners as direct the payment of expenses to be incurred in the election of Guardians of the Poor for the several Parishes comprised in the several Unions named in the Schedules hereunto annexed.

And whereas by a General Order, under the hands and seal of the Poor Law Commissioners, bearing date the 16th day of January instant, addressed to the Guardians of the Poor of the said several Unions, the said Commissioners have prescribed the manner of conducting the future election of Guardians of the Poor for the several parishes comprised in the said Unions ; and it is expedient that provision should be made for the payment of the expenses to be incurred in such elections.

Now therefore, we, the said Poor Law Commissioners, do hereby order and direct henceforth in regard thereto, with reference to each of the said Unions named in the said schedules as follows :—That the expenses of every future election of Guardians of the Poor of the several Parishes comprised in the said Unions shall be defrayed by the Guardians of the said Unions in the manner hereinafter set forth, that is to say :—

Art. 1.—The cost of providing the several Forms marked (A.), (D.), and (E.), contained in the said Order, being the Notice of Election, the Notice to the Guardians elected, and the certificate of the Election, shall be defrayed out of the common fund of the Union.

Art. 2.—The cost of providing the Form marked (C.) contained in the said Order, being the voting payer, shall be defrayed out of the funds in the possession of the said Guardians belonging to the respective parishes to which the voting papers shall relate.

Art. 3.—The compensation which shall be˙paid to the clerk or to the person appointed under the authority of the said recited Order to act as such in the performance of the duties thereby prescribed, shall include the remuneration of the persons who may have been appointed or employed to assist him in conducting and completing the election, and shall, in respect of the several Unions named in the following schedule marked A., be such sum not exceeding *ten pounds*, as the Guardians shall determine, and shall, in respect of the several Unions named in the following schedule marked B., be such sum not exceeding *fifteen pounds*, as the Guardians shall determine, and such sums respectively shall be defrayed out of the common fund of the Unions.

Art. 4.—And in the case of every contested election one farthing per head on the population of the parish in which the contest shall have taken place, if the population shall be more than five hundred, and one halfpenny per head on the population of the parish in which the contest shall have taken place, if the population be not more than five hundred, shall be paid to the said clerk or other person as aforesaid in addition to such compensation, and shall be defrayed out of the funds in the possession of the said Guardians belonging to such parish. And for the purpose of ascertaining the last-mentioned sums, the population of the parish shall be taken to be as stated in the Census which at the time of such election shall have been last made under the authority of any Act of Parliament.

And we do hereby declare, that wherever the word " Parish " is used in this Order, it shall be taken to signify any place in the Union separately maintaining its own poor.

SCHEDULE A.

Containing the Names of the Unions in which the sum is not to exceed Ten Pounds.

Aberaeron	Aston	Berwick-upon-Tweed
Abergavenny	Atherstone	Bideford
Aberystwith	Austel, St.	Biggleswade
Alban's, St.	Axminster	Billericay
Alcester	Aylesford, North	Bishop's Stortford
Alderbury	Bala	Blaby
Alresford	Bangor and Beaumaris	Blackburn
Alton	Barnet	Blean
Amersham	Barrow-upon-Soar	Bodmin
Amesbury	Bath	Bolton
Ampthill	Battle	Bootle
Asaph, St.	Beaminster	Boston
Ashby-de-la-Zouch	Bedale	Brackley
Ashford, East	Bedminster	Bradfield
Ashford, West	Berkhampstead	Bradford (Wilts)

Bradford (York)	Dudley	Holbeach
Braintree	Dulverton	Holborn
Brampton	Dunmow	Hollingbourn
Brentford	Durham	Holsworthy
Bridge	Dursley	Holywell
Bridgnorth	Easington	Honiton
Bridport	Easingwold	Hoo
Bromley	Eastbourne	Horsham
Bromsgrove	East Grinstead	Houghton-le-Spring
Buckingham	Easthampstead	Hoxne
Buntingford	Eastry	Hungerford
Burnley	East Ward	Hursley
Bury	Ecclesall Bierlow	Ipswich
Calne	Edmonton	Ives, St.
Cambridge	Elham	Keighley
Camelford	Ellesmere	Kettering
Cardigan	Ely	Keynsham
Carlisle	Epping	Kidderminster
Carmarthen	Epsom	Kingsbridge
Carnarvon	Eton	Kingsclere
Catherington	Evesham	King's Lynn
Caxton and Arrington	Faith, St.	King's Norton
Cerne	Falmouth	Kingston-upon-Thames
Chailey	Fareham	Kington
Chapel-en-le-Frith	Faversham	Knighton
Cheadle	Festiniog	Lampeter
Cheltenham	Foleshill	Lancaster
Chertsey	Fordingbridge	Lanchester
Chester-le-Street	Frome	Langport
Chippenham	Fylde	Launceston
Chipping Sodbury	Garstang	Ledbury
Chorley	Gateshead	Leek
Chorlton	German's, St.	Leicester
Christchurch	Glossop	Leigh
Church Stretton	Godstone	Leighton Buzzard
Cleobury Mortimer	Goole	Leominster
Clifton	Gravesend and Milton	Lewes
Clun	Greenwich	Lewisham
Clutton	Guildford	Lichfield
Colchester	Guiltcross	Linton
Columb, St. Major	Guisborough	Liskeard
Conway	Hackney	Llandilo Fawr
Cookham	Hailsham	Llandovery
Corwen	Halifax	Llanelly
Cosford	Halsted	Llanfyllin
Cranbrook	Haltwhistle	Llanrwst
Crediton	Hambledon	London, East
Crickhowel	Hardingstone	London, West
Cricklade and Wootton Bassett	Hartley Wintney	Longtown
Croydon	Haslingden	Loughborough
Cuckfield	Hastings	Luton
Dartford	Hatfield	Lymington
Daventry	Havant	Machynlleth
Derby	Hay	Madeley
Devizes	Hayfield	Maidstone
Dewsbury	Headington	Malling
Dolgelly	Helston	Malmsbury
Dore	Hemel Hempstead	Manchester
Dorking	Hendon	Mansfield
Dover	Henley	Market Bosworth
Drayton	Hertford	Marlborough
Droitwich	Highworth and Swinden	Martley
Droxford	Hinckley	Medway
	Hitchin	Melksham

Mere
Meriden
Merthyr Tidvil
Midhurst
Mildenhall
Milton
Neath
Neot's, St.
Newbury
Newcastle-in-Emlyn
Newcastle-under-Lyne
Newcastle-upon-Tyne
Newent
New Forest
Newhaven
Newmarket
Newport (Salop)
Newtown and Llanidloes
Northampton
Northleach
North Witchford
Nottingham
Nuneaton
Oakham
Okehampton
Olave's, St.
Ongar
Ormskirk
Orsett
Pateley Bridge
Patrington
Pembroke
Penkridge
Penzance
Petersfield
Petworth
Pewsey
Pickering
Plympton, St. Mary
Pont-y-pool
Poole
Poplar
Portsea Island
Potterspury
Prescot
Presteigne
Preston
Radford
Reading
Redruth
Reeth
Reigate
Rhayader
Richmond (Surrey)
Ringwood
Risbridge
Rochdale
Rochford
Romford
Romney Marsh

Romsey
Ross
Rotherham
Royston
Ruthin
Rye
Salford
Saviour's, St.
Sculcoates
Sedbergh
Sedgefield
Seisdon
Selby
Sevenoaks
Shaftesbury
Sheffield
Sheppey
Shepton Mallett
Sherborne
Shiffnal
Solihull
Southam
South Molton
South Shields
South Stoneham
Spalding
Stafford
Staines
Stepney
Steyning
Stockbridge
Stockport
Stokesley
Stone
Stourbridge
Stow-on-the-Wold
Strand
Stratton
Stroud
Sturminster
Sunderland
Swansea
Tamworth
Tavistock
Tenbury
Tenterden
Tetbury
Tewkesbury
Thakeham
Thanet, Isle of
Thornbury
Thorne
Thrapston
Ticehurst
Tisbury
Tiverton
Todmorden
Tonbridge
Torrington
Totnes

Towcester
Tregaron
Truro
Tynemouth
Uckfield
Ulverstone
Uptou-upon-Severn
Uttoxeter
Uxbridge
Wakefield
Wallingford
Walsal
Wandsworth and Clap-
    ham
Wangford
Ware
Wareham and Purbeck
Warminster
Warrington
Watford
Wayland
Weardale
Wellingborough
Wellington (Salop)
Wellington (Somerset)
Wells
Welwyn
Wem
Weobly
Westbourne
West Bromwich
Westbury-upon-Severn
Westbury and Whor-
    welsdown
West Derby
West Firle
West Ham
West Ward
Weymouth
Wheatenhurst
Whitby
Whitchurch
Whitechapel
Whitehaven
Wigan
Wilton
Wimborne and Cran-
    borne
Winchcombe
Windsor
Winslow
Wisbeach
Witham
Woburn
Wokingham
Wolstanton and Burslem
Wolverhampton
Worcester
Worksop
Wortley

SCHEDULE B.

Containing the Names of the UNIONS in which the sum is not to exceed Fifteen Pounds.

Abingdon	Depwade	Penrith
Alnwick	Docking	Pershore
Altrincham	Doncaster	Peterborough
Andover	Dorchester	Plomesgate
Anglesey	Downham	Pocklington
Ashbourne	Driffield	Pwllheli
Atcham	East Retford	Richmond (York)
Auckland	Erpingham	Rothbury
Axbridge	Faringdon	Rugby
Aylesbury	Freebridge Lynn	Runcorn
Aylsham	Gainsborough	Saffron Walden
Bakewell	Glanford Brigg	Scarborough
Banbury	Glendale	Settle
Barnstaple	Gloucester	Shardlow
Basford	Grantham	Shipston-upon-Stour
Basingstoke	Hartismere	Skipton
Bedford	Haverfordwest	Skirlaugh
Belford	Helmsley Blackmoor	Sleaford
Bellingham	Henstead	Southwell
Belper	Hereford	Spilsby
Beverley	Hexham	Stamford
Bicester	Horncastle	Stockton
Billesdon	Howden	Stow
Bingham	Huddersfield	Stratford-upon-Avon
Blandford	Huntingdon	Sudbury
Blofield	Kendal	Swaffham
Blything	Lexden and Winstree	Taunton
Bosmere and Claydon	Leyburn	Teesdale
Boughton, Great	Lincoln	Tendring
Bourn	Loddon and Clavering	Thame
Brecknock	London, City of	Thetford
Bridgend and Cowbridge	Louth	Thingoe
Bridgwater	Ludlow	Thirsk
Bridlington	Lutterworth	Thomas, St.
Brixworth	Macclesfield	Uppingham
Bromyard	Maldon	Walsingham
Builth	Malton	Wantage
Burton-upon-Trent	Market Harborough	Warwick
Caistor	Melton Mowbray	West Hampnett
Cardiff	Mitford and Launditch	Wigton
Castle Ward	Monmouth	Williton
Chard	Morpeth	Wincanton
Chelmsford	Nantwich	Winchester, New
Chepstow	Narberth	Wirrall
Chesterfield	Newark	Witney
Chesterton	Newport (Monmouth)	Woodbridge
Chipping Norton	Newport Pagnell	Woodstock
Cirencester	Newton Abbot	Wrexham
Clitheroe	Northallerton	Wycombe
Cockermouth	Northwich	Yeovil
Congleton	Oundle	York
Darlington		

Given under our hands and seal of office, this **Twenty-seventh** day of January, in the year One thousand eight hundred and forty-five.

                    (Signed)   GEO. NICHOLLS.

(*L.S.*)   G. C. LEWIS.

[This Order came into operation on the 10th day of March, 1845.]

No. 6.

GENERAL ORDER requiring Returns from certain Parishes under Local Acts.

To the Guardians of the Poor of the several Unions and
Parishes named in the Schedule hereunto annexed:—

To the Churchwardens and Overseers of the Poor of the said several
Unions and Parishes ;—

To the Clerk or Clerks to the Justices of the Petty Sessions held
for the Division or Divisions in which the said several Unions
and Parishes are situate ;—

And to all others whom it may concern.

In pursuance and exercise of the authorities vested in us by an Act
passed in the fifth year of the reign of His late Majesty King William
the Fourth, intituled " An Act for the Amendment and better Administration of the Laws relating to the Poor in England and Wales," we,
the Poor Law Commissioners, do hereby order, direct, and declare,
with respect to each of the Unions and Parishes named in the Schedule
(B.) hereunto annexed, as follows:—

Art. 1.—That it shall be a duty of the Clerk to the Guardians of
every such Union and Parish to prepare, after every ordinary Meeting
of the Board of Guardians of such Union or Parish, a weekly statement
or weekly statements for the several weeks that may have elapsed since
the last previous meeting of such Board of Guardians, in the Form contained in the Schedule (A.) hereunto annexed, and punctually to transmit the same, as soon as may be after such meeting, to the Assistant
Poor Law Commissioner, who shall be notified by the Poor Law Commissioners from time to time to the said Clerk, as having for the time
the superintendence of such Union or Parish.

Art 2.—And we do hereby order and direct the Clerk to the Guardians of every such Union or Parish to prepare and transmit such statement or statements accordingly.

Art. 3.—Whenever the word " Guardians" is used in this Order, it
shall be taken to include any Governors, Trustees, Directors, Managers,
or Acting Guardians entitled to act in the ordering of relief to the poor
from the Poor-rates under any Local Act of Parliament.

Art. 4.—Whenever the term " Clerk to the Guardians" is used in
this Order, it shall be taken to include any Secretary, or person appointed under any other designation to perform the duties of the office
of Secretary or principal Clerk to a Board of Guardians.

K

SCHEDULE A.

Containing the Form above referred to.

FORM.

—

_____ UNION [*or* PARISH.]

Day of Meeting _____ day of _____ 184 .

Day and Hour to which adjourned _____

RETURN OF THE INDOOR AND OUT-DOOR PAUPERS

_____ Week ended the _____ day of _____

CLASS.	In the House at commencement of the Week.	NUMBERS.				Remaining at the corresponding date last year.
		Admitted	Discharged	Dead.	Remaining	
MEN—						
Able-bodied . .						
Temporarily disabled by sickness or accident . .						
Old and infirm .						
YOUTHS—						
From 7 to 15 years						
BOYS—						
From 2 to 7 years .						
WOMEN—						
Able-bodied . .						
Temporarily disabled . . .						
Old and infirm .						
GIRLS—						
From 7 to 15 years						
From 2 to 7 years.						
INFANTS—						
Born						
Totals . .						

.	In the House at commencement of the week.	Admitted	Discharged	Dead.	Remaining
TRAMPS OR VAGRANTS—					
Men					
Women					
Children under 15 . . .					
Total . . .					
Number in corresponding week of last year . .					

Number of Paupers at any Lunatic Asylum . . {Males
                                                {Females

                                                     Total

Number of Children at any separate Establishment {Boys
                                                  {Girls

                                                     Total

Number of Paupers receiving In-door and Out-door Relief, and the
amount of such Out-door Relief.

	In-door	Out-door.	Total.	Out-relief in		Total.
				Kind.	Money.	
Corresponding week of last year						

(Signed)_____ *Clerk to the Guardians.*

To _____

Assistant Poor Law Commissioner.

Sent this_____day of _____184 .

SCHEDULE B.

Containing the Names of the UNIONS and PARISHES to which the
above Order refers.

St. George, Bloomsbury and St. Giles-in-the-Fields.
St. George, Hanover Square
St. James, Clerkenwell

St. James, Westminster
St. Leonard, Shoreditch
St. Luke, Middlesex
St. Margaret and St. John-the-Evangelist, Westminster.

St. Mary, Islington
St. Mary-le-bone
St. Mary, Newington
St. Pancras

Given under our hands and seal of office, this Eighth day of
February, in the year One thousand eight hundred and
forty-five.

(Signed)   GEO. NICHOLLS.
(*L.S.*)   G. C. LEWIS.
           EDMUND W. HEAD.

[This Order came into effect on the 24th day of March, 1845.]

K 2

No. 7.

ORDERS ISSUED TO THE ROYSTON UNION RELATIVE TO RELIGIOUS
WORSHIP IN THE UNION WORKHOUSE.

TO THE GUARDIANS OF THE POOR of the Royston Union, in the
Counties of Hertford, Cambridge and Essex ;—

To the Master, Matron, Schoolmaster, Schoolmistress, and Porter
of the Workhouse of the said Union ;—

To the Clerk or Clerks to the Justices of the Petty Sessions, held
for the Division or Divisions in which the Parishes and Places
comprised in the said Union are situate ;—

And to all others whom it may concern.

Whereas by an Order, bearing date the First day of February, One
thousand eight hundred and forty-two, the Poor Law Commissioners did
order and direct that no child under the age of sixteen, being a pauper
and an inmate of the workhouse belonging to the Guardians of the poor
of the Royston Union, who should be a member of the Established
Church of England and Ireland, or either of whose parents should be a
member of such Established Church, should be compelled, required, or
permitted to attend the religious service or instruction of any minister
dissenting from the principles of such Established Church, either in
or out of such workhouse.

And whereas by another Order, dated the Fifth day of February, One
thousand eight hundred and forty-two, and addressed to the Guardians
of the poor of the several Unions and of the several parishes under a
Board of Guardians named in the Schedule thereunto annexed, among
which the name of the Royston Union was included, the Poor Law
Commissioners did rescind so much of every Order theretofore issued by
the Poor Law Commissioners to each of the said Unions and Parishes
as related to the government of the workhouse, or the powers and duties
of the officers for such workhouse, except in so far as the said orders, or
any of them, might have authorized the appointment of the then existing
officers, or might have prescribed a dietary for the use of the inmates of
the workhouse, or the times of labour and the intervals for meals.

And whereas the said Order of the First day of February, One thousand eight hundred and forty-two, is deemed to have been rescinded by
the said last recited Order, and it is expedient that the provisions contained therein should be altered, and be in force in the said Union in the
manner hereinafter set forth.

Now, therefore, in pursuance of the powers and authorities given in
and by an Act passed in the fifth year of the reign of His late Majesty
King William the Fourth, intituled "An Act for the Amendment and
better Administration of the Laws relating to the Poor in England and
Wales," we, the Poor Law Commissioners, do hereby order and direct,
that no child under the age of sixteen years, being a pauper, and an inmate of the workhouse belonging to the Guardians of the Poor of the
Royston Union, who shall be a member of the Established Church of
England and Ireland, shall be compelled, required, or permitted to attend
the religious service or instruction of any minister dissenting from the
principles of such Eatablished Church, either in or out of such workhouse.

And we do hereby order and direct that the master, matron, schoolmaster, schoolmistress, and porter of the said workhouse respectively, shall not permit any such child as aforesaid to attend such religious service or instruction as aforesaid.

> Given under our hands and seal of office, this Twentieth day of April, in the year One thousand eight hundred and forty-two.
>
> (Signed)   G. C. Lewis.
> (*L.S.*)   Edmund W. Head.

> To the Guardians of the Poor of the Royston Union, in the Counties of Hertford, Cambridge, and Essex;—
> To the Master, Matron, Schoolmaster, Schoolmistress, and Porter of the Workhouse of the said Union;—
> To the Clerk or Clerks to the Justices of the Petty Sessions held for the Division or Divisions in which the said Union is situate;—
> And to all others whom it may concern.

We, the Poor Law Commissioners, by virtue of the powers and authorities vested in us by an Act passed in the fifth year of the reign of His late Majesty King William the Fourth, intituled " An Act for the Amendment and better Administration of the Laws relating to the Poor in England and Wales," do hereby order and direct, that from and after the date hereof no person being a pauper and an inmate of the workhouse belonging to the Guardians of the Poor of the Royston Union, in the counties of Hertford, Cambridge, and Essex, who shall be a member of the Established Church of England, shall be required or permitted to attend the religious service or instruction of any minister dissenting from the principles of such Established Church, either in or out of such workhouse.

And we do hereby order and direct, that the master, matron, schoolmaster, schoolmistress, and porter of the said workhouse respectively shall not compel, require, or permit any such person as aforesaid to attend such religious service or instruction as aforesaid.

> Given under our hands and seal of office, this Eighteenth day of January, in the year One thousand eight hundred and forty-five.
>
> (Signed)   Geo. Nicholls.
> (*L.S.*)   G. C. Lewis.
>   Edmund W. Head.

No. 8.

CIRCULAR LETTER OF THE COMMISSIONERS RELATING TO THE ACT OF 7 AND 8 VICT., c. 101.

> *Poor Law Commission Office, Somerset House;*
> Sir,   *17th October,* 1844.

The Act passed on the 9th of August, 1844, intituled " An Act for the further Amendment of the Laws relating to the Poor in England," (7 and 8 Vict. c. 101,) having made many important alterations in the

Poor Laws, it has appeared to the Poor Law Commissioners to be desirable that a short and plain statement of the effect of such alterations, so far as they immediately affect the powers and duties of Guardians of the Poor and their paid officers, or the powers and duties of Overseers, should be circulated for the use of those officers. Accordingly, the Poor Law Commissioners have directed the enclosed statement to be forwarded to you for the guidance of the Guardians and their paid officers.

　　　　　I am, Sir,

　　　　　　　Your obedient Servant,

To　　　　　　GEORGE COODE, *Assistant Secretary.*

　The Clerk to the Guardians.

I.—THE OPERATION AND CONSTRUCTION OF THE ACT (7 AND 8 VICT. c. 101) FOR THE FURTHER AMENDMENT OF THE LAWS RELATING TO THE POOR IN ENGLAND.

This Act came into operation on the 10th of August, 1844, the day after it received the Royal Assent. (s. 76.)

It is to be construed as if it and the Poor Law Amendment Act (4 and 5 Wm. IV. c. 76) and the series of Acts amending and extending the latter were one Act. (s. 74.)

II.—RELIEF OF THE POOR.

The duty of relieving the Poor is in no instance diminished, except by the abolition of compulsory apprenticeship, a mode of relief for poor children but rarely resorted to in later times. Even in those instances in which new modes of relief are provided for particular classes of poor, the duty of relieving such poor in the manner required by the previous law is in no case dispensed with, and, in some instances, is expressly retained. Thus, in places where special provision may be made for the relief of houseless poor in asylums, for large districts, the obligation imposed by previous Statutes, or the regulations of the Commissioners upon Guardians, Overseers, Relieving Officers, and Masters of Workhouses of the respective parishes and Unions within those districts, to afford relief in cases of sudden and urgent necessity, or dangerous illness, is expressly retained. (s. 54.) Thus, also, although it is provided that non-resident relief may, in certain cases, be given to widows, it is at the same time expressly provided, that the obligation to afford relief, previously imposed on the places where such widows are resident, shall continue in full force. (s. 26.)

i.—*The Classes of Poor.*

Poor children can no longer be put out as apprentices under the 43 Eliz., or the 8 and 9 Wm. III., c. 30, to parishioners unwilling to receive them : all provisions in those Acts, and in all other Acts, general or local, for this purpose being repealed. (s. 13.)

But poor children may still be bound apprentices to persons willing to take them. Overseers, however, are, after the first day of October, 1844, deprived of the power of binding or assigning apprentices where there is a Board of Guardians, and their powers are transferred to such Guardians. (s. 12.)

The Poor Law Commissioners, in addition to their power to regulate the apprenticing of poor children under the 4 and 5 Wm. IV. c. 76, s. 15, which did not appear to extend to the controlling of the masters, are enabled by the present Act to prescribe the duties of the masters, and the terms and conditions to be inserted in the indentures; for breach of which the masters are made subject to a summary penalty not exceeding twenty pounds. (s. 12.)

Where there are Guardians, they are to execute the indenture of apprenticeship which, as a corporation under the 5 and 6 Vict., c. 57, s. 16, they will do by affixing their common seal; and in this case the allowance of the Justice of the Peace is dispensed with. The Guardians must cause their clerk to register all apprentices bound or assigned by them in the following form, so far as it is applicable to the case. (s. 12.) It is desirable that the clerk should sign his name against each entry.

Form of the Register of Apprentices bound or assigned by the Board of Guardians of the _____ *Union.*

Number,	Date of Indenture.	Name of Apprentice.	Sex.	Age.	His or her Parent's Name.	Their residence.	Name of the Persons to whom bound or assigned, as the case may be.	His or her trade.	His or her residence.	Term of the Apprenticeship or Assignment.	Apprentice or Assignment Fee.	

Where there are no Guardians, the Overseers must still obtain the allowance of the Justices, and must in all other respects conform to the law previously in force.

The provisions of the Act do not extend to apprentices to be bound to the sea service, who must still be bound under the 5 and 6 Wm. IV. c. 19, until the first of January, 1845. After that date they must be bound under the 7 and 8 Vict., c. 112, ss. 32 to 36.

The other provisions relating more particularly to the relief of children are of a local character. The more important of these are the powers for the formation of school districts for the management of orphan or deserted children, or children whose parents consent to their being placed in the district schools. The limit as to the size of these districts is such as to prevent them from being formed in any but a very few extremely populous places, and there only at the discretion of the Poor Law Commissioners. (ss. 40 to 51.) These provisions, therefore, are too partial in operation to interest the great majority of Parishes and Unions. When school districts are formed, however, it will be competent to the Board of Guardians of any Parish or Union, any part of which is within 20 miles from the district school, by arrangement with the district board, to send the children of their respective Parishes or Unions to the district school, upon such terms as are mutually agreed upon. (s. 51.)

The provisions of the Acts 2 Geo. III. c. 22, and 7 Geo. III. c. 39, relating to parish poor children within the city of London, and a certain district in its immediate vicinity, which provisions had for the most part been disregarded in practice, are now repealed. (s. 52.)

The changes in the law of bastardy, which will be hereafter more fully adverted to, make no difference in the legal obligation on parishes to relieve bastard children, whenever their necessities require relief.

Widows in certain cases are made the subject of a provision entirely new to the statute law. The provision is as follows :—

" In the case of any person being a widow—

having a legitimate child dependent on her for support— and no illegitimate child born after the commencement of her widowhood—

and who at the time of her husband's death was resident with him, in some place other than the parish of her legal settlement, and not situate in any Union in which such settlement is comprised—

it shall be lawful for the Guardians of such Parish or Union, if they see fit, to grant relief to such widow, although not residing in such Parish or Union." (s. 26.)

It is to be observed that the widow must have been resident with her husband at the time of his death, not only out of the parish of her settlement, but also out of the Union in which that parish may be comprised. The object of the clause appears to be to avoid the disturbance of those connexions and mode of life, at a distance from the Union, to which the family may have become accustomed, and which existed at the time of the husband's death.

Where all the conditions exist which would enable the Guardians to grant non-resident relief, they are still to use their discretion, as to whether non-resident relief to the widow is in each particular case desirable. The general objections to such relief, such as the difficulty of ascertaining the circumstances of paupers beyond the power of inspection of the Guardians or their Officers, and the further difficulties attendant on the transmission of relief to places where the Guardians have no authority and no official agency, will be weighed by the Guardians.

This power is one intrusted to Boards of Guardians only. Overseers acquire no authority under this provision to administer non-resident relief to the class of widows described.

It must be borne in mind by Guardians and their officers that they are in no wise exempted from their previous obligation to relieve any widow who may be in their Parish or Union requiring relief, by the power thus given to the Guardians of the place of her settlement to afford her non-resident relief. And even when that power is exerted, if notwithstanding the relief sent to her by her parish, she or her children require additional or further relief, the officers of the place where she is, are still bound as heretofore to afford her the relief which the circumstances require. (s. 26.)

Married Women, whose children required and received relief, were not before the passing of this Act liable to any conditions in respect of such relief, and could cast off their children upon the parish, however well such women might be able to maintain their children, or to contribute to their maintenance. Widows, on the other hand, were liable to the like conditions and consequences of relief afforded to themselves and their children as the fathers of legitimate children are. The present Act declares that while the husband of any woman is beyond the seas, (that is, out of Great Britain,) or in custody of the law, or in confinement in any licensed house or asylum as a lunatic or idiot, all relief given to the wife, or to her child or children shall, notwithstanding her coverture, be given to her, in the same manner and subject to the same conditions as if she were a widow. (s. 25.)

Insane Poor, in places where the Poor Laws are administered under Local Acts, are placed under the control of the Guardians and officers appointed under such Local Acts, in the same manner as if they were appointed under the Poor Law Amendment Act. (s. 28.) The Guardians under such Local Acts will therefore exercise all the duties and powers in respect to insane persons as Overseers were previously invested with. The Guardians may contract with a medical man to certify as to the state of insane persons. The officers who, under such Local Act, exercise the functions of relieving officers, must give to the Justices the information heretofore required of Overseers. The officer performing the duties of clerk to the Guardians, must on the 15th of August, in every year, make out two lists of all the insane persons chargeable, and transmit one copy to the Clerk of the Peace of the county, and the other copy to the Poor Law Commissioners. (5 and 6 Vic., c. 57, s. 6.)

Houseless Poor are for the first time particularly provided for by the general law. The asylums for their reception and relief can only be established in the metropolis, and in five other populous cities and towns. (ss. 40 to 55.)

ii.—*Modes of Relief.*

Relief, with the above exception in the case of certain widows, remains subject in all cases to the regulation of the Poor Law Commssioners, and is to be administered by Guardians and their officers, and the Overseers of the Poor, in all respects as before the passing of the Act.

The administration of *Relief in the Workhouse* is freed from some technical difficulties. Relief in a Union workhouse is to be deemed relief in the parish to which the pauper is chargeable. There will, therefore, be no further doubt as to the power of executing an order of removal from the workhouse. (s. 56.) The punishment for offences in the workhouses, or in relation to the property therein, under the 2nd and 5th sections of the 55th Geo. III. c. 137, is in the first case made capable of mitigation, at the discretion of the justices: and in the last case, if the offence be repeated, may be increased. (s. 58.) Persons convicted before justices of any offence in a workhouse, or absconding from any workhouse with parish property, could only be committed to the gaol of the place where the offence was committed; that is to say, of the place where the workhouse was situated. Now they may be committed to the gaol of the place where they were chargeable. (s. 57.)

Emigration.—The Guardians appointed under the Poor Law Amendment Act, are exclusively to apply money raised or borrowed under that Act for the purpose of emigration. (s. 29)

Burial.—Guardians and Overseers have hitherto been without legal authority to provide directly for the burial of paupers dying out of the workhouse. Guardians, and Overseers in places where there are no

Guardians, are now enabled to bury the dead body of any poor person being within their Parish or Union. The churchyard or other consecrated burial-ground belonging to the parish, or place in which the death occurred, is to be the ordinary place of burial, for the bodies, both of persons who have been chargeable in their lifetime, and of those who have not. If, however, a deceased person in his lifetime, or the husband or wife, or next of kin of deceased have otherwise desired, it would appear that the Guardians may have regard to such desire, and may arrange and pay for the burial elsewhere. In any case where the deceased has been chargeable to any other parish than that in which he died, the Guardians are enabled, either in compliance with any desire expressed by the deceased, or by any of his relations, or for any other cause, to direct authoritatively that the body be buried in the churchyard or burial-ground of the parish to which the deceased was so chargeable. (s. 31, see also s. 56.) This latter provision is intended for the benefit of parishes where Union workhouses are situate, upon whom the burden has hitherto fallen of providing ground for the burial of the paupers of other parishes dying in the workhouse.

III.—LIABILITIES OF PERSONS RELIEVED.

Generally the obligations of persons to maintain themselves, of parents to maintain their children, of husbands to maintain their wives, and of such persons, parents, and husbands, to repay the cost of relief to themselves, their children, or wives; of grandfathers and grandmothers to contribute to the maintenance of their grandchildren; and of children to contribute to the maintenance of their parents, remain undiminished.

The estates of *insane persons and idiots* were only liable in a very imperfect manner to the repayment of relief afforded them. Now to the extent to which their property may be more than sufficient to maintain their families, such property is made liable generally to repay the costs incurred by parishes in respect of such persons, and trustees and all other persons in possession of property belonging to insane or idiot persons, are indemnified for any payments they may make to Guardians or Overseers. (s. 27.)

The Fathers of Legitimate Children remain liable for the relief of such children as heretofore, and their liabilities are continued unimpaired in the cases where their wives are made responsible in respect of the same relief. (s. 25.)

The Wife of a man beyond the seas, (that is, out of Great Britain,) or in the custody of the law, or in confinement as a lunatic or idiot, in a licensed house or asylum, is to receive relief for herself and her children in the same manner, and subject to the same conditions, as if she were a widow. (s. 25.) Where widows are obliged to receive relief for their children within the Union or within the workhouse, these married women will be subject to the like condition. Relief may be afforded to such married women or their children as a loan repayable by such married women, notwithstanding the ordinary exemption of married women from similar liabilities.

The Mothers of Bastards, and *the Putative Fathers of Bastards* are the subject of the most considerable change in the policy of the law effected by the present Act. (ss. 1—11.)

The principle of the law for charging the putative fathers of bastard children is wholly different from that of any law which has heretofore been in force in England either before or since the Poor Law Amendment Act. Formerly the remedy was intended exclusively for the parish: now the mother alone can obtain it, and the parish is expressly prohibited from originating any proceedings for obtaining the order or payment under it to themselves. Formerly the chargeability of the child, either in fact or in prospect, was the ground of the remedy: now the actual or probable chargeability of the child is made wholly immaterial.

It is very necessary that Guardians and Overseers should make themselves fully aware of the nature of so much of this change as affects them as officers, inasmuch as their powers for the enforcement of the liabilities of putative fathers are abrogated, and their interference, in the matter in which they were formerly exclusively concerned is now made criminal.

All the pre-existing powers for making orders on putative fathers for the maintenance of bastard children are abrogated from the 10th of August, 1844, (s. 1,) except only in the cases where proceedings before justices were pending on that day, in which cases the proceedings may be continued, and orders made as if the Act had not passed. (s. 9.)

Orders previously made (and apparently orders afterwards made in cases pending on the 10th of August, 1844) remain valid according to their effect. But orders made before the 14th of August, 1834, (the date of the passing of the Poor Law Amendment Act,) which had, as to the time of their operation, no defined limit, are not to remain in force after the 1st of January, 1849, at which date the most recent of such orders will have been in force more than fourteen years and four months. (s. 9.) Orders made since the passing of the Poor Law Amendment Act remain in force only until the child attains the age of seven years, and the last of these orders must expire some time before the 9th of August, 1851.

The parish is deprived of the power to apply for any Order on the putative father.

The mother alone of the bastard is entitled to apply for such an Order.

No officer of any parish or Union may conduct any application to make or enforce any such Order, or in any way interfere in causing such an application to be made, or in procuring evidence to support such application, or in receiving money under such an Order. If he does so he is subject to a penalty of 40s. But after the death of the mother, or when she becomes legally incapable of receiving money under an Order, if a child for whose maintenance an Order has been made, becomes chargeable to a Parish or Union through the neglect of the putative father to make the payments due from him under the Order, in such a case the Guardians, or, if there are no Guardians the Overseers, may so far interfere as is necessary to compel a compliance with the Order; but even in this case they must not receive the money, but it must be paid to some person appointed to have the custody of the child, who is to receive it on the condition that the child is to cease to be chargeable. (s. 7.)

Any officer of a Union or Parish who endeavours to induce any man to contract marriage, by means of threat or promise respecting any application for an Order, or enforcement of an Order, is declared guilty of a misdemeanour. (s. 8.)

The *Mothers of Bastards* remain, as heretofore, liable while unmarried, or in the state of widowhood, to maintain such bastards up to the age of 16, or the previous marriage of their female bastards. (Poor Law Amendment Act, s. 71.) By the recent Act such mothers are expressly subjected to the punishment of idle and disorderly persons under the Vagrant Act, for neglecting to maintain such bastards, and permitting them to become chargeable, and to the punishment of rogues and vagabonds for offending in the same way a second time, or for deserting such children, and so permitting them to become chargeable. (s. 6.)

IV.—POOR-RATES, THEIR ASSESSMENT, COLLECTION, AND APPROPRIATION.

Assessments.—The Act referred to makes no alteration in the law relating to the assessment to the Poor Rate. The Act 7 and 8 Vict., c. 40, continues the exemption of stock in trade for another year.

Collection.—Provisions are made for the better collection of poor's rates, with the view more especially of connecting the Guardians more closely with the operation, and of giving them a better security for the supply of the funds they require for the performance of their duties. On the application of any Board of Guardians, the Poor Law Commissioners can issue an Order for the appointment by such Guardians of a collector of poor's rates, who is to be subject to the laws and regulations applicable to other paid officers appointed by Guardians. When such Order is issued, the powers of all other persons to appoint officers to collect poor's rates in the same parish are to cease. (s. 62.)

As regards the collectors and assistant Overseers heretofore appointed under the Orders of the Poor Law Commissioners, confirmed by the 2nd and 3rd Vic., c. 84, any such collector or assistant Overseer may be appointed by the inhabitants in vestry, of any parish in which he was acting, on the 10th of August, 1844, to discharge all the duties of an assistant Overseer, in addition to the collection of poor's rates. Every collector and assistant Overseer is to obey in all matters relating to the duties of Overseers the directions of the majority of the Overseers, and the Overseers' responsibility for the provision and supply of money for the relief of the poor and other lawful purposes is, notwithstanding the appointment of the assistant Overseers, still retained. (s. 61.)

If the Overseers of any parish neglect to make or collect sufficient rates for the relief of the poor, or to pay such monies to the Guardians, as the Guardians may require, and if in consequence any relief directed by the Guardians be withheld during a period of seven days, every such Overseer is liable to a penalty of 20*l*. (s. 63.)

Appropriation.—The appropriation of the poor's rates is in no instance restricted, though their due appropriation is better secured. On the other hand the appropriation to new or extended purposes is authorized in several instances by the present Act, as in the case of—

The costs and fees for burial of poor persons. (s. 31.)
The providing of district schools. (s. 47.)
The providing of district asylums. (s. 48.)
The payment of the salaries of auditors of districts for schools or asylums. (s. 49.)

The extension of the amount to be expended on workhouses in the Metropolis and Liverpool. (s. 30.)

Expense of recovering balances on accounts, and of the auditor in defending his decisions, (ss. 35, 39,) and, where the court orders it, of the party impugning his decision. (s. 35.)

The apprehension and prosecution of persons under the Vagrant Act, being chargeable, or making their families chargeable. (s. 59.) or disobeying the regulations of the Poor Law Commissioners. (s. 59)

guilty of offence or misbehaviour in workhouses. (*ib.*)

absconding from workhouses with clothes, &c. (*ib.*)

disobeying the lawful and reasonable orders of Justices or Guardians, or district boards. (*ib.*)

obstructing or assaulting officers engaged in administering the Poor Laws. (*ib.*)

unlawfully obtaining or misapplying property applicable to the relief of the poor. (*ib.*)

guilty of any offence directly affecting the administration of the Poor Laws. (*ib.*)

the apprehending and prosecuting of officers employed in the administration of the Poor Laws, for neglect or breach of duty. (*ib.*)

All these payments under s. 59, are to be made by Guardians or district boards, and are to be charged, subject to the approval of the Poor Law Commissioners to the particular Parishes or Unions concerned, or to the common fund of the Union or District. (*ib.*)

The making out, preparing, printing, and collecting the lists of persons to serve on juries. (s. 60.)

The perambulation of parishes, not more than once in three years, and the setting up and maintaining boundary-stones. (s. 60.)

In addition to these new and extended purposes, a new mode of appropriating the poor's rate to the purposes of the county, hundred, police, and other like rates authorized to be levied in counties, and parts of counties, is provided by another Act, the 7 and 8 Vict., c. 33. This Act enables justices after the 1st of October 1844, so soon as any vacancy occurs in the office of high constable, to issue their precepts for the payment of such rates to the Guardians at once, by post or otherwise, without the intervention of the high constable. The Guardians are required to raise and pay such rates. (s. 1.) If they fail to do so, the monies may be levied from the Overseers, with an addition of one shilling in every ten. (s. 2.) The provisions of the whole of this Act should be carefully examined by the Guardians and Overseers.

V.—ACCOUNTS—AUDIT—RECOVERY OF BALANCES.

Important changes are made by the 7 and 8 Vict., c. 101, for the purpose of increasing the efficiency of the Audit, and of the remedies against defaulters.

Accounts.—The Accounts are no longer required by statute to be rendered every quarter of the year; they are to be rendered as often as the Commissioners may direct, but not less than once in every half-year.

(s. 38.)   The subsisting Orders of the Commissioners which remain in force, still require the accounts to be rendered quarterly, and until these are revoked, the accounts must be so rendered.

In order to clear the future accounts from the embarrassment caused by old disputed accounts and by the bringing forward of balances found before the passing of the Act, against officers now out of office, and which, in many cases, are not recoverable from the persons who were originally in default, there is a power given to the auditor, with the consent of the Poor Law Commissioners, to discharge existing officers from responsibility in respect of such balances.   Old balances not so discharged are to be recovered as found by the auditor, (s. 34,) and the persons against whom they were originally struck, may be proceeded against for them, under this Act.

In future the overseers and other officers of parishes are required to make up and balance their books of account, seven clear days before the audit, (s. 33,) of which they will have had notice from the auditor fourteen days before the audit. (*ib.*)   The overseers and other officers are to deposit such books at the house of one of the officers of the parish for such seven days to be inspected, between the hours of eleven and three, by any person liable to be rated to the relief of the poor.   Notice is to be affixed at the usual places for giving notices, stating the place where the books are deposited, and the time and place of audit. (*ib.*)   If any overseer or officer neglect to make up his account, or to give notice of the time and place of audit or inspection, or alter his account, or refuse to allow it to be inspected, he is made liable to forfeit 40*s*. (s. 33.)

It will be observed that all these provisions are in force at once, without any reference to the appointment of a district auditor or any orders of the Commissioners.

Audit.—Every rate-payer is entitled to be present at the audit, and, if he thinks fit, to make any objection. (s. 33.)

The auditor may require any person holding, or accountable for, any money or property relating to the relief of the poor, to produce accounts and vouchers, and to make and sign a declaration with respect to such accounts. (s. 33.)

If any person required by the auditor to attend his audit fails to do so, or to produce his accounts or vouchers, or refuses to make or sign a declaration as to his accounts if required, he is made liable to a penalty of 40*s*., and if he make a false declaration, to the penalties of perjury.

District Auditors.—With the exception of certain places under local Acts, (s. 65,) it is intended that the whole of England and Wales should be comprised in more extensive districts of audit, consisting of combinations of Unions, or of Unions and Parishes.   The Commissioners are enabled from time to time to form and alter such districts.   Thereupon the chairmen and vice-chairmen of Boards of Guardians, or, where there are no Guardians, the overseers, are to elect the auditor of the district, in a manner to be prescribed by the Commissioners. (s. 32.)   But auditors of districts existing at the time of the passing of the Act may be retained. Where districts are altered, the auditor's office is not vacated. (s. 37.)

Such auditor has full power to audit, allow, and disallow of accounts, and is invested with a new and important authority of charging any person accounting with deficiencies and losses, caused by the negligence of such person, or with any sums for which he may be accountable. (s. 32.)

The auditor is to certify on the face of the account the sums which he finds to be due. (*ib.*)

The person from whom any money is so certified to be due, notwithstanding that he may continue in office, and would hitherto have been still entitled to hold the balance, is now bound, within seven days, to pay the money into the hands of the treasurer of the Guardians, where there is such an officer. In the case of a Union, the Guardians are to apply such sum for the benefit of the parishes respectively interested in the money. (*ib.*) The importance of this provision is very great, as rendering the audit operative immediately, and preventing officers from still keeping in their hands the balances found to be due from them. Overseers and other officers leaving office must actually pay over the balances due from them, and the law can no longer be evaded by a mere entry to their credit in their successors' accounts,

If there is no treasurer, the money certified to be due must be paid over within seven days, to the person authorized to receive it. (*ib.*)

If the money be not duly paid, it is to be recovered as certified on the application of the auditor, or any person authorized to receive it, that is, by the treasurer; or, if there is no such treasurer, by the officer succeeding the accountant. The expenses of the recovery, if not obtained from the person accounting, are to be repaid to the auditor by the Guardians. (*ib.*)

If any person refuse to deliver over other property, he is liable to the same penalties and proceedings as overseers who neglect to deliver over the property of the parish to their successors. (*ib.*)

In order to prevent the practice occasionally resorted to by parish-officers, of making up from other rates the sums disallowed in the accounts of poor's rate, it is provided, that if any churchwarden, surveyor of highways, overseer, or other officer of any Parish or Union, wilfully makes any illegal payment from any rate or fund of a Parish or Union, or any unlawful entry in his accounts for the purpose of making up to himself or any other person, any sum disallowed or surcharged in account, the offender, on conviction before two justices, shall forfeit three times the amount of such payment, or of the sum wrongfully entered in the account, in addition to a penalty not exceeding 20*l.* (*ib.*)

Any person aggrieved by the decision of the auditor may require the auditor to state his reasons for his decision, and may have a certiorari in the Court of Queen's Bench, to try the legality of the auditor's decision (s. 35); or in lieu of applying at once for a certiorari, may apply to the Poor Law Commissioners to decide upon the question, which they may do by order under their hands and seal, and this order may then be removed into the Queen's Bench by certiorari. (s. 36.)

In every district for which an auditor is appointed under this Act, the power of justices of the peace, and of all other persons to audit the same accounts, is repealed. (s. 37.)

VI.—Appointment and Election of Parish and Union Officers.

Overseers.—The power to appoint separate Overseers *for townships or villages*, which had not separate overseers appointed before the 10th of August, 1844, is repealed. (s. 22.)

Election of Guardians.—Powers are given for altering the number of Guardians to be elected for a parish, (s. 18,) and for dividing parishes for purposes of election into wards, (ss. 19, 20, 21,) and for adding parishes to Unions, or separating parishes from Unions, and constituting Boards of Guardians for the parishes so separated. (s. 66.)   But nothing is to be done in these matters until orders are issued by the Commissioners for the purpose.

Considerable changes are made in the *constituency* who elect the Guardians.

In the first place as regards the *rate-payers*—in order to vote they are not required to have paid any other parochial rates and assessments besides the rates made for the relief of the poor. (s. 16.)   The periods for which they must have been rated, and have paid their poor's rate remain unchanged.

They are hereafter to have the same number of votes in proportion to the value of property as owners, (s. 14,) namely :—

For less than . . . 50*l*.	1 vote.
For 50*l*. and less than 100*l*.	2 votes.
For 100*l*. ,, 150*l*.	3 votes.
For 150*l*. ,, 200*l*.	4 votes.
For 200*l*. ,, 250*l*.	5 votes.
For 250*l*. and upwards	6 votes.

The votes of *owners of property* are reduced in proportion to their property, and the scale of their voting is identified with that on which rate-payers vote, as just before stated. (s. 14.)

It is necessary that before the 1st of February in each year, owners should make statements containing particulars set forth in the present Act.   Statements of owners once made will remain good while the circumstances described in the statement remain the same.   But no statement will operate during any year unless made before the 1st of February in that year.

The statement must contain—

> a description of the interest or estate the owner has in the property —
>
> a statement of the amount of all rent service (*i. e.* rent not being rent charges, or rents seck, annuities, encumbrances, &c.) which he may receive in respect of the property, and of the persons from whom he receives it—
>
> a like statement of the amount of all rent service he may pay in respect of the same property, and of the persons to whom he pays it. (s. 15.)

Owners may appoint *proxies* as heretofore, but no person can vote as proxy until 14 days after he has made his claim to vote ; and no person can vote as proxy for more than four owners of property, unless he be a steward, bailiff, land-agent, or collector of rents for such owners.   And no appointment of proxy is to remain in force for more than two years, excepting only in the case where an owner appoints his tenant, bailiff, steward, land-agent or collector of rents, in which case the appointment will remain in force while such relation between the owner and the proxy continues.

It is important, in order to prevent the disfranchisement of many owners, that this information should be conveyed to them by any means which the Guardians can resort to for the purpose. An extract from this circular might be affixed to the church-door in every parish about the 1st January next.

The statements of owners are to be *registered* by overseers as heretofore : but in parishes containing a population exceeding 2000 persons they must complete the registry before the 5th of February in each year, and allow any person to inspect it without fee between the 5th and the 10th of February. Any person who has claimed as owner or proxy, and any rate-payer, may object to any other person as not being entitled to vote as an owner, by delivering to the Clerk to the Guardians notice in writing of the grounds of his objection. Provisions are made for revising the registries in such parishes, and the persons whose names are left in the register by the revising officer are to be alone entitled to vote as owners in the year following the then next 25th of March. (s. 15.)

The time for the *annual election* of Guardians is now extended to 40 days after the 25th of March. (s. 17.)

Ex-officio Guardians.—Justices of the Peace residing in extra-parochial places, whose boundary line is included within that of the Union, or for the greater part coincident with it, are to be declared to be *Ex-officio* Guardians of the Union. Every Justice also residing in any Parish in a Union, although that parish is not within his jurisdiction as a Justice, is declared to be an *Ex-officio* Guardian. (s. 24.)

VII.—Districts for Administration of the Poor Laws.

The prohibition of the further division of parishes for the appointment of Overseers, the power to divide parishes into wards for the election of Guardians, the powers to add to Unions or diminish them, the power to combine Parishes and Unions into districts for the maintenance of schools and asylums, and for audit, have been adverted to before.

VIII.—Simplification of Legal Proceedings.

Various provisions are made for avoiding formal and technical difficulties, and occasions for expense, in the conduct of the legal business of Parishes and Unions.

Such is the declaration that the workhouse for all purposes of relief, settlement, and removal, and for the burial of the poor, shall be considered as situated in the parish to which the person relieved or removed, or whose body is to be buried, is or was chargeable. (s. 56.)

The clerk, or any other officer empowered by a Board of Guardians, is enabled to take, resist, and conduct proceedings on behalf of the Board before Justices of the Peace acting singly or in Petty or Special Sessions, although such clerk or officer is not an attorney. (s. 68.) This removes the question which was raised upon this subject in reference to the Act for amending the law relating to attorneys, (6 and 7 Vic. c. 73,) so far only as relates to business before Justices out of Quarter or General Sessions. As regards other business, the right of clerks of Guardians who are not professional men, to act for the Guardians, in legal proceedings, remains on the same footing as before.

Another Act, the 7 and 8 Vic., c. 33, before referred to, contains (s. 7) a provision of great importance to Guardians as regards the enforcement of their orders on Overseers for the payment of the contributions of parishes. Any person may apply to any one Justice acting

L

for a division for a notice of a Special Sessions to be holden. Such Justice may issue such notice, which, being sent by post, a reasonable time before the day for holding the Sessions, to the address of each Justice residing and usually acting within the division, the Special Sessions may thereupon lawfully proceed in the matter.

In all proceedings before Justices in Petty or Special Sessions, or out of Sessions, any Justices may on the request of a party, summon any person to appear as a witness. If the person summoned, having been paid or tendered his expenses, do not appear, he may be brought up by the warrant of one Justice. Any person before Justices in Petty or Special Sessions, or out of Sessions, refusing to give evidence, may be committed to gaol for 14 days, unless he previously submits to be examined. (s. 70.)

The evidence of proceedings of the Guardians and of facts in which they are interested, is, in several matters, made more cheap and easy by 69th sect. of the 7 and 8 Vict., c. 101. The Guardians' certificate of the chargeability of a pauper is made evidence of that fact. Copies of the minutes of the Guardians under their seal, signed by the Chairman, and countersigned by their Clerk, are to be received in evidence, without proof of the seal being that of the Guardians, or the signatures being those of the Chairman and Clerk. (s. 69.)

The Rules, Orders, and Regulations of the Poor Law Commissioners, when printed by the Queen's printer, are to be received in evidence, and taken notice of judicially by all Courts and Judges, when so printed. (s. 71.)

Evidence of the transmission of the Rules, Orders, and regulations of the Poor Law Commissioners to any other person than the Clerk of the Guardians, (or where there are no Guardians,) to the Overseers, is also dispensed with in all civil and criminal proceedings, unless special notice is given that proof of the transmission will be required. (s. 72.)

IX.—SUMMARY OF DUTIES OF GUARDIANS AND THEIR OFFICERS, AND OF OVERSEERS.

It may be well shortly to indicate the powers and duties which Guardians and their officers and Overseers are called on to exercise and perform under the Act, without previous order or intimation from the Poor Law Commissioners. Such powers and duties as depend on some previous act of the Commissioners will be best explained on the occasions when the Commissioners may be called on to act.

The Guardians :—

To abstain from interference on applications in bastardy. Proviso (s. 7)—

After the 1st of October, 1844, to bind apprentices, exclusively of the Overseers, (s. 12,) and to cause their Clerk to keep a register, (*ib*)—

To apply the money raised for the purposes of emigration, (s. 29)—

To bury the bodies of poor persons within their Parish or Union (s. 31)—

To pay various expenses of legal proceedings, (s. 59)—

To put in suit bonds and securities given by Assistant Overseers to Overseers, (s. 61)—

And under the 7 and 8 Vict., c. 33, s. 1, on receipt of the precepts of Justices of the Peace to pay County Rate, Hundred Rate, Police or other like rates.

The Clerk to the Guardians :—

To abstain from interference in applications in bastardy, (s. 7)—

After the 1st October, 1844, to keep a register of children apprenticed or assigned by the Guardians, (s. 12)—

To receive notice of grounds of objection to persons voting as owners, (s. 15)—

And on or before the 20th of February, to send notice of revision of the register of owners, (*ib.*)—

When empowered by Guardians to conduct their legal proceedings before Justices out of Quarter or General Sessions, (s. 68.)

The Auditor.—(Whether he be a district auditor, or an auditor already appointed, and acting under 4 and 5 Wm. IV., c. 76.)—

To send 14 days' notice of audit to Overseers and other officers of parishes, by post or otherwise. (s. 33.)

Such notice may be in the following form :—

To the Overseers of the Parish [or Township, &c.] of

In pursuance of the Act of Parliament 7 and 8 Vic., c. 101, *for the further Amendment of the Laws relating to the Poor in England,*

This is to give you Notice that I shall attend as auditor of the   to audit the accounts of your [Parish, &c.] at   , on   day, the   th day of

You are required by the above-named Act of Parliament to have your rate-books and other accounts, made up and balanced, seven clear days before the day fixed for the audit. You are likewise to deposit them for the inspection of all persons liable to be rated to the relief of the poor at the house of a Churchwarden, Overseer, Collector, or Assistant Overseer, or some other parish-officer: and you are, as soon as such books are ready for inspection, to affix at the usual places of giving parish notices, notice of the time and place of audit, as above notified by me, and of the place where the rate-books and books of account are deposited.

To receive objections of rate-payers at the audit—

On application of Parish Officers or Guardians, and with the consent of the Commissioners, to discharge old or disputed balances, (s. 34)—

To state reasons for his decisions, if required, and to defend them on certiorari, (s. 35)—

To decide on legality of law bills, and where such bills are not taxed, on the reasonableness of the particular items. (s. 39.)

Overseers :—

To abstain from interference in applications in bastardy. Proviso (s. 7)—

To abstain after the first of October, 1844, from apprenticing or assigning poor children, (s. 12)—

Where there are no Guardians, to bury the bodies of poor persons within the parish, (s. 31)—

To receive statements of owners and proxies, (s. 15)—

And where the population exceeds 2000, to keep a register of owners' statements, to allow inspection of it, to publish notice of revision, and to attend the revising officer, (s. 15)—

Seven days before the audit to make up their rate-books and books of account; to deposit them for inspection, and immediately give notice thereof, and of the time and place of audit.

Such notice may be in the following form :—

To the Rate-payers, and persons liable to be rated for the relief of the Poor of the parish [or Township &c.] of
We, the Churchwardens and Overseers of the Parish [Township, &c.] of   ,
Hereby give Notice that the Auditor of the
has notified to us that he will attend to audit the accounts of the officers of this [Parish, &c.]   at
on   day the   th day of
And that the rate-books of the said parish and the book of account of the said officers are deposited at the house of
at   , within the Parish [&c.]
And that the said books will be there open for the inspection of every person liable to be rated to the relief of the poor of the said parish [&c.] until the day of audit, between the hours of 11 in the forenoon and 3 of the afternoon of each day.

}*Churchwardens.*

}*Overseers.*

Under the 7 and 8 Vict., c. 33, if the Guardians fail to pay the County Rate, or any similar rate required by the Justices, the Overseers are to pay the same, with an addition of 1s. in every 10s. (ss. 2, 3.) In certain parishes payment is to be made without a previous precept issuing to Guardians. (s. 5.)

No. 9.

CIRCULAR LETTER of the Commissioners relating to the Audit of the Accounts of Overseers and other Parochial Officers.

Poor Law Commission Office, Somerset House;
Sir,   *8th July,* 1844

I AM directed by the Poor Law Commissioners to transmit to you for your guidance, a copy of a judgment pronounced during the last Term by the Court of Queen's Bench, in a case of "The Queen on the prosecution of the Poor Law Commissioners v. The Governors and Directors of the Poor of St. Andrew Holborn-above-Bars, and St. George-the-Martyr."

You will observe from this decision that it is your duty to inquire into the expenditure by the Overseers, or other Parochial officers, within your district, of the whole of the monies raised by them under the name of the poor-rate, whether the expenditure by them be strictly confined to the relief of the poor or relate to any other object; and that if the accounts of such expenditure have not hitherto been laid before you, you must henceforth require them to be produced.

It is right, at the same time, to notice that these officers are not re-sponsible for the expenditure by other parties of such sums as they are called upon by law to pay out of the poor-rates to such parties for specific application; thus, the Overseers are not answerable for the expenditure by the Guardians of the contributions which they have called for, or by the justices, of the sums paid to the county rate, or for the application of the sums paid to the Police Commissioners, or to the treasurer of the borough where police or borough rates are made.

In these cases you will only require the production of the proper orders upon the Overseers, or other vouchers, by which the amounts paid by them are legally demanded.

I am, Sir,

Your obedient Servant,

W. G. Lumley, *Assistant Secretary.*

To the Auditor of the
Union.

In the Queen's Bench.

Westminster Hall, 8th June, 1844.

The Queen v. the Governors and Directors of St. Andrew, Holborn-above-Bars, and St. George-the-Martyr.

JUDGMENT.

Lord Denman.—In the case of the Queen against the Governors and Directors of St. Andrew Holborn-above-Bars and St. George-the-Martyr, and their collector, there were two questions proposed for our consideration; first, whether the defendants, having accounted to the auditor, under the local Act of the 6th of George the Fourth, were also bound to account to the auditor appointed under the order of the Poor Law Commissioners;—secondly, whether if they were bound to account to the auditor, the account rendered by them as stated in the case is sufficient.

With respect to the first question, the powers of the Auditors under the local Act are so inadequate to the performance of the duties required of the auditor appointed under the order of the Poor Law Commissioners, having no power to disallow any of the items in the account, that we are clearly of opinion that the defendants were bound to account to the latter auditor, although they had already accounted to the auditor under the local Act. This part of the case was indeed scarcely contested on the part of the defendants, and was in effect settled by the decision of this Court in the case of the Alstonefield Union, in the 11 Adolphus and Ellis, p. 558.

With respect to the second question, it was contended on the part of the defendants that they were not bound to render an account to the auditors appointed under the order of the Poor Law Commissioners of *all the money* collected by them under the rate denominated *the poor-rate*, which is partly applicable to other purposes than the relief of the poor, but only so much of the produce of the rate as was raised for and applied to the purposes of the relief of the poor.

The defendants made a rate of 1*s.* 2*d.* in the pound for the relief maintenance, lodging and employment of the poor, which by estimation would produce a sum of upwards of 6000*l.*, but of this not much more than half was applied or intended to be applied to the relief of the poor, the residue was applied and intended to be applied to the police rate and county rate, payment of principal and interest due in respect of debts; contracted under the authority of the local Act, and salaries and expenses attending the carrying of the local Act into effect.

The defendants did account for so much of the money raised under the rate as had been applied and was intended to be applied to the relief and maintenance of the poor, but objected to account for the residue which was raised for and applied to other purposes, and whether they are bound to do so, is in fact the question.

It is not necessary to refer to the local Act, as the question turns entirely on the Poor Law Amendment Act, and applies undoubtedly to every parish, in England, where the poor-rate is in part applicable to the payment of the county rates, police rate, or *any other expenses* than the relief and maintenance of the poor.

, By the 46th section of the Poor Law Amendment Act, the Commissioners may direct the Guardians of any Parish or Union to appoint an officer for the examining, auditing, and allowing or disallowing of accounts in such Parish or Union, or united parishes ; and may define, and specify, and direct the execution of the duties of such officers, and the places or limits within which the same shall be performed.

In pursuance of this power, the Commissioners did direct the Guardians of the Holborn Union, of which the district in question forms a part, to appoint an auditor, whose duties were specified to be, among others, to audit the accounts of the said Union, and of the several parishes comprised therein, at proper times, and to examine whether the expenditure in all cases was such as might lawfully be made, and to strike out such payments and charges as were not authorized by some provision of law or the order of the Commissioners.

By the 47th section of the Poor Law Amendment Act, every person having the collection, receipt or distribution of the monies raised for the relief of the poor, in any Parish or Union, or holding or accountable for any balance relating to the relief of the poor, or the collection or distribution of the poor-rate of any Parish or Union, shall, where the orders of the Commissioners shall have come in force, as often as the said orders shall direct, make, and render to the Guardians, auditor, or such other persons as by virtue of any statute or custom, or of the said orders, may be appointed to examine, audit, allow, or disallow such accounts, a full and distinct account in writing of all monies, matters and things committed ,to their charge ; or received, held, or expended by them on behalf of any such Parish or Union ; and all balances due from any person having the control and distribution of the poor-rate, or accountable for such balances, may be;recovered in the same manner as any penalties are recoverable under the Act.

Two things may be observed in this section ; first, the accounts are to be rendered to a person appointed either by statute, custom, or order of the Poor Law Commissioners, to examine, audit, allow, or disallow such accounts and, secondly, that the account is to be made of *all monies*, matters, and things committed to their charge, or received, held, or expended by them on behalf of the Parish or Union, and the balance may be recovered under the Act.

The auditors under the local Act do not, as already observed, possess the power required for an auditor under this section : they have no power to disallow accounts, but the auditor appointed under the Order of the Commissioners does possess the power, and is therefore the person to whom the accounts should be rendered under the terms of the 47th section.

With respect to the accounts themselves, the terms of the 46th and 47th sections of the Act include *all monies* held by the parties accounting on behalf of the Parish or Union, and would therefore apply to all money raised by the poor-rate. And it is also to be observed, that in the description of the persons who are to account, given in the beginning of the early part of the 47th section, persons holding or accountable for any money or balance relating to the relief of the poor, or the collection or distribution of the poor-rate are mentioned.

It appears to us, therefore, that by the terms of the 46th and 47th sections of the Poor Law Amendment Act, as applied to this case, the defendants were bound to account to the auditor appointed under the order of the Poor Law Commissioners, *not only for so much of the money raised by the poor-rate as was raised for and applied to the relief and maintenance of the poor, but for the whole amount of the money raised by the poor-rate,* and that the auditor may insist on ascertaining the amount of balance of the whole rate in the hands of the accountant.

There is but one rate levied, and that professedly for the relief, maintenance, lodging, and employment of the poor; and even although the inquiry into the mode of disposing of the proceeds of the rate may introduce matters foreign to the direct and avowed object of the rate, this is but a necessary incident in the inquiry, and seems to have been contemplated by the legislature when a remedy is provided for the recovery of the balance in the hands of the accountant, obviously meaning the balance of the whole rate levied for the relief, maintenance, lodging, and employment of the poor.

We are, therefore, of opinion, that the verdict which has been entered for the prosecutors should stand.

No. 10.

CIRCULAR LETTER of the Commissioners relating to Art. 25 of the Workhouse Rules.

Poor Law Commission Office, Somerset House;
Sir,   *31st October,* 1844.

THE Poor Law Commissioners, by Article 25 of their Workhouse Rules have provided that—

" Any person may visit any pauper in the workhouse by permission of
" the master, or (in his absence) of the matron, subject to such condi-
" tions and restrictions as the Board of Guardians may prescribe,
" such interview to take place except where a sick pauper is visited,
" in a room separate from the other inmates of the workhouse, in the
" presence of the master, matron, or porter."

The Commissioners find, from a case which has recently occurred that the master of an Union workhouse understood the purport of the latter clause of this rule (as regards visits to the sick) to be—that although such visits were excepted from the condition that they should take place in a room separate from the other inmates of the workhouse, they are still required to be in the presence of the master, matron, or porter.

The Commissioners think it right to explain that this is an erroneous view of the intent and effect of the Rule. The object of the Commissioners was to allow communication, with as few impediments as possible, between the sick inmates and their friends, especially in dangerous cases, and with this view to except these cases from the conditions which, for the purpose of preventing visits for improper purposes, the Commissioners have thought it right generally to lay down. The exception applies not only to the room in which such visits take place, but also to the presence of the master or other officer.

The meaning of the Rule appears to the Commissioners so obvious,

that if an actual case of misapprehension had not occurred, they would
have thought any explanation on the subject superfluous, especially after
the full explanation afforded in the Instructional Letter appended to
the Workhouse Regulations. As, however, it appears to them of importance that no possibility of a misunderstanding of the Rule in question
should exist on the part of any workhouse officers, they request that the
Board of Guardians will communicate to their officers the real intent of
the Rule as stated in this Letter.

I am, Sir,

Your most obedient Servant,

(Signed)   EDWIN CHADWICK, *Secretary.*

The Clerk to the
Board of Guardians.

No. 11.

REPORT BY RICHARD HALL, ESQ., ASSISTANT POOR LAW COMMIS-
SIONER, ON THE EMPLOYMENT OF THE INMATES OF WORKHOUSES IN
NEEDLEWORK.

GENTLEMEN,   *Dover, 5th April,* 1845.

I FORWARD herewith a tabular statement of the value of the
needlework executed for the trade by inmates of metropolitan workhouses during the year ended the 25th December, 1844.

There are 28 metropolitan workhouses under your regulations.

In 13 of these workhouses such needlework has been discontinued, or
has never been practised.

The value of the work done in the other 15 workhouses during this
year was 683*l.* 1*s.* 0¾*d.*

This sum gives 13*l.* 2*s.* 8*d.* as the average value of the work done
per week, or 9*s.* 4*d.* as the average weekly amount for each metropolitan
workhouse.

The sum of 9*s.* 4*d.* may be taken to represent the earnings of two
needleworkers, or the maintenance of three inmates of a workhouse. If,
therefore, 56 needleworkers are deprived of employment out of the workhouse by reason of the work done in the workhouses, 84 needleworkers
may be maintained in the workhouses by means of the proceeds of that
work.

It cannot be reasonably said that the employment of the inmates of
workhouses in needlework, to the extent to which it is carried, affects
injuriously the class of needleworkers out of the workhouses.

It is more probable that the practice of giving small allowances of
outdoor relief to needleworkers operates to depress the class.

Under the circumstances disclosed by this statement, and by the returns
from which it is drawn up, and which are also submitted for your consideration, you will probably deem it better to leave Boards of Guardians,
for the present, at least, to the exercise of their own discretion in this
matter.

I have the honour to be, Gentlemen,

Your obedient servant,

(Signed)   RICHARD HALL,

Assistant Poor Law Commissioner.

The Poor Law Commissioners.

A Return of Needlework, or Slopwork executed for the Trade, in Unions and Parishes within the limits of the Metropolis, to which the Workhouse Rules have been issued; showing the value of such work during the Year ended the 25th December, 1844.

Name of Union or Parish.	Value of Work done in the Year 1844.	Average Value of Work done per Week.
	£. s. d.	£. s. d.
Bermondsey	14 12 11½	0 5 7½
Bethnal Green	Nil.	Nil.
Camberwell	23 6 8¾	0 8 11¾
Chelsea, St. Luke	16 4 7¼	0 6 3
Clerkenwell, St. James	8 14 0	0 3 4½
Greenwich	38 5 11	0 14 8¾
Hackney	Nil.	Nil.
Holborn	48 2 8	0 18 6¼
Kensington	Nil.	Nil.
Lambeth	Nil.	Nil.
London, City of	Nil.	Nil.
London, East	Nil.	Nil.
London, West	35 12 9	0 13 8½
Poplar	36 12 3½	0 14 1
Rotherhithe	27 8 5	0 10 6½
St. George-in-the-East	Nil.	Nil.
St. George-the-Martyr	17 17 9	0 6 10½
St. Leonard, Shoreditch	7 14 3	Discontinued.
St. Luke, Middlesex	112 2 3	2 3 1½
St. Margaret and St. John, Westminster	42 13 7¾	0 16 5
St. Martin in the Fields	60 18 5	1 3 5¼
St. Olave	37 19 10½	0 14 7¼
St. Saviour	Nil.	Nil.
Stepney	Nil.	Nil.
Strand	154 2 6¼	2 19 3¼
Wandsworth and Clapham	Nil.	Nil.
West Ham	Nil.	Nil.
Whitechapel	0 12 0	Discontinued.
Total	£683. 1*s*. 0¾*d*., or £13. 2*s*. 8*d*. pr. week.	

No. 12.

REPORT from the Board of Guardians of the Honiton Union on the state of the Cottages of Paupers in several Parishes of that Union.

Sirs, *Honiton, 5th April,* 1845.

I am instructed by the Board to forward you copy of a Report of a Committee of the Guardians appointed to inquire into the state of the pauper cottages in the Union.

I am, Sirs, your obedient servant,

The Poor Law Commissioners for England and Wales. (Signed) H. C. Mules.

(Copy)   HONITON UNION, 10 FEBRUARY, 1845.

Report of the Committee appointed to inquire into the state of Pauper Cottages.

Present :—

Bishop Coleridge, Chairman.   Mr. Newbery.
Mr. Gustavus Smith.   Mr. Devenish.

Your Committee have received reports from 11 parishes out of the 28 comprised in the Union, namely, Dunkeswell, Ottery St. Mary, Salcombe, Sidmouth, Up Ottery, Gittisham, Payhembury, Sheldon, Tallaton, Ven Ottery, and Honiton.

Dunkeswell.—The population of this parish is 536. In this parish there are six paupers' cottages, containing 22 rooms, inhabited by 36 persons sleeping in 11 bed-rooms with 14 beds. In one house we find nine persons sleeping in one room, and four of these are married couples, and five children. Four of the cottages have gardens, but half of them are without privies. Rent is generally low in this parish. In half the cases the paupers pay rates.

Gittisham.—Population, 376. In this parish there are 15 paupers' cottages, containing 43 rooms, inhabited by 73 persons sleeping in 23 rooms with 23 beds. Gardens to all the cottages with one exception, and privy to each house; all in good repair. Rent very low. Rates paid by owners. In this parish every able-bodied labourer has an allotment of one quarter of an acre of good land at a rent of 10s. a-year including all expenses, and on a fixed day in each year the rent is readily and cheerfully paid by every tenant.

Ottery St. Mary.—Population, 4185. In this parish there are 83 paupers' cottages, containing 188 rooms, inhabited by 320 persons sleeping in 105 bed-rooms with 139 beds. About half the cottages have gardens and privies. Bed-rooms are generally plastered. Rent is very high; and 15 of the cottages are in a bad state of repair. The floors in many instances are merely the bare earth. In about half of these the rates are paid by the landlords. There are too many families of all ages and sexes sleeping in the same rooms, and in some cases sad instances of great want of cleanliness.

Payhembury.—Population, 545. In this parish there are 13 paupers' cottages, containing 39 rooms, inhabited by 36 persons sleeping in 19 rooms with 23 beds. All the cottages have gardens, and as to privies, either none or in very bad repair, with but two exceptions. Bed-rooms are plastered. with but two exceptions, and in general the cottages are in good repair. The rent is moderate. The rates are paid by the owners. All the cottages are in repair but three.

Salcombe.—Population, 525. In this parish there are 10 paupers' cottages, containing 28 rooms, inhabited by 59 persons sleeping in 16 bed-rooms with 23 beds. Five of the cottages have gardens, and five not. There are no privies. Each cottage has a well. Repair indifferent. Rent moderate. Rates, where any, paid by renter, with but two exceptions.

Sheldon.—Population   . In this parish there are five paupers' cottages, containing 17 rooms, inhabited by 36 persons sleeping in seven bed-rooms with 10 beds. Gardens to all the cottages. No privy to any. None of the bed-rooms are plastered. Three of the cottages are in a bad state of repair, and one particularly so. Occupiers generally pay the rates.

Sidmouth.—Population, 3309. In this parish there are 56 cottages, containing 156 rooms, inhabited by 321 persons sleeping in 106 bed-rooms with 111 beds. Almost all without gardens, and 45 of the cottages have no privies ; in some instances five or six cottages have a common privy, which is very objectionable. This want of privies must be injurious to the health of the neighbourhood. Bed-rooms are plastered. There are 13 cottages in bad repair. Rent is very high, and in many instances exceeds what in the opinion of your Committee, paupers are justified in paying. The rates are paid principally by owners.

Tallaton.—Population, 462. In this parish there are 12 pauper cottages, containing 28 rooms, inhabited by 33 persons sleeping in 15 bedrooms with 20 beds. Most of the cottages have gardens, and about half of them privies. The bed-rooms are plastered with one exception. Repair pretty good. Rent is moderate. The rates are paid by the occupiers.

Up Ottery.—Population, 991. In this parish there are 22 paupers' cottages, containing 68 rooms, inhabited by 102 persons sleeping in 31 bed-rooms with 49 beds. Each cottage has a garden. There are scarcely any privies. Not above one-half of the cottages are plastered. There are 10 cottages out of repair, and in some cases it is very bad indeed. There are two instances in which families, without regard to sex or age occupy the same room. The rents are moderate. About half of the rates are paid by the owners.

Ven Ottery—Population, 134. In this parish there are two pauper cottages, containing four rooms, inhabited by nine persons sleeping in two rooms with five beds. Both cottages have large gardens but no privies, and are in bad repair. Bed-rooms not plastered. Occupiers pay no rent or rates.

Honiton.—Population, 3773. In this parish there are 78 pauper cottages, containing 206 rooms, inhabited by 293 persons sleeping in 107 bed-rooms, and 163 beds. Many of the cottages in this parish are in a bad state of repair, and although many of them have gardens belonging to them they are generally too small to be useful to the occupiers. The privies are, with very few exceptions, exceedingly bad, and in several instances are resorted to by the inmates of several cottages, in common, a habit which, in the opinion of your Committee, is exceedingly objectionable. Although there are instances in which the rent of cottages in this parish appears to your Committee to be too high, it does not generally exceed the average, but it is almost universally in arrear. In more than one instance your Committee found examples, as was before observed in other parishes, in which, without reference to sex, age or relationship, persons were sleeping in the same bed-room, and as might have been expected, the inhabitants of these houses exhibited in the dirty and filthy state of their habitations and persons, the inevitable consequence of the loss of that sense of delicacy which conduces, next to religious culture, more than anything else, to uphold the character and improve the habits of its possessor.

Your Committee would beg to suggest that a copy of this Report be forwarded to the Poor Law Commissioners (in the event of its being adopted by the Board.) In conclusion, your Committee cannot but express their regret that so few of the parishes should have sent in returns, as the sole object of the formation of this Committee has been the improvement of the condition of the dwellings of the poor.

(Signed)   W. H. COLERIDGE, *Chairman.*

No. 13.

LETTER ADDRESSED TO THE COMMISSIONERS BY THOMAS LAW HODGES, ESQ,. RELATIVE TO THE EFFECT OF EMIGRATION ON THE STATE OF THE PARISH OF BENENDEN, IN KENT.

To the Poor Law Commissioners.

GENTLEMEN,

YOUR Eighth Annual Report (1842) contains Mr. Tufnell's report on Kent and Sussex; and in pages 242 and 243 that gentleman makes particular allusion to the Parish of Benenden, in Kent, and to the evidence I gave before the Lords' Committee in 1831. He also refers to a return from the said parish, made in 1835, by Mr. George Lansdell, then assistant overseer, and now the relieving officer of the Cranbrook Union, comprehending the above Parish.

In reading Mr. Tufnell's remarks on the above documents and on the state of this parish, I was forcibly struck with several errors into which he has been led ; and feeling confident that Mr. George Lansdell's report to Sir Francis Head could not really have the meaning which Mr. Tufnell attributes to it, I beg to give you a copy of a letter received from that intelligent relieving officer on this subject :—

SIR   *Benenden, January 31st,* 1843.

My attention having been called to a statement of Mr. Tufnell's in the last Report of the Poor Law Commisioners, in which I am represented to have furnished Sir Francis Head with a return in September, 1835, that although we had then no able-bodied men out of work, we had usually from 50 to 60, I hasten to correct the erroneous conclusion which either Mr. Tufnell or Sir Francis Head have come to. I feel quite satisfied that the question against which I have placed the above numbers referred to the number of able persons receiving relief, and I enclose a list of persons who were usually in receipt of permanent relief, in consequence of having large families. The number you will perceive amounts to 37. These men, I would observe, were all (or nearly all) in constant work throughout the year, and merely received relief in consequence of having larger families than it was then thought they could support by their labour ; and if to the above number you add the persons usually employed on the road (we also used to reckon them as being out of work) and those who were occasionally employed grubbing of roots and in trenching, the number upon an average would very nearly correspond with the return above alluded to. I find in the winter months of 1833 and 1834 we had about 30 or 35 employed on the road, and in trenching, &c ; in the summer, during the years 1832, 1833, 1834, and 1835, we had very few persons out of work.

I have been, perhaps, somewhat lengthy in my explanations, for I not only wish to place before you an exact statement of the facts of the case, but to clear my own character from the charge of having intentionally made an incorrect return.

To show the great advantages which have resulted to this parish from emigration, I have enclosed a statement of the expenditure from Lady-day, 1824, to Lady-day, 1835. I believe in many parishes there was considerable reduction in the rates after 1824, but none that I know of so much as was the case in this parish. I feel that I am perfectly justified in saying that at this time there is not a single parish in this locality in which the agricultural labourers generally are in a more healthy condition or their homes present more appearance of comfort than are to be met with in this parish, and I would ask any impartial person whether this important and pleasing change is not more owing to the extensive system of emigration which has been adopted than to any other circumstance ; it has certainly raised the condition of the labourers from the worst to one of the best parishes in the neighbourhood. Having stated thus much of the advantages of emigration, I feel it right to acquaint you (although I may be accused of some inconsistency) that in the years 1836, 1837, and 1838 I thought it was useless for parishes to expend large sums of money for emigration, finding that so few persons accepted of orders to go into the workhouse, but since those years I have seen quite sufficient to alter my opinion.

I have the honour to be, Sir,

To   Your very obedient servant,

T. L. Hodges, Esq.   GEORGE LANSDELL.

You will observe that in the extract from my evidence, which Mr. Tufnell gives in page 242, I stated in (1831) that "during great part of the years 1825 and 1826 there were from 70 to 80 able-bodied men on the parish books for want of employment; since 56 of them have emigrated, it is a rare circumstance to have any out of work except in severe weather :" and Mr. Lansdell says, in 1835, previously to the provisions of the new Poor Law coming into operation,* usually about 60 able-bodied men, with 360 wives and children, and 12 single able-bodied men, are on the parish. Mr. Lansdell explains this by stating, what I knew must be the real fact when I read Mr. Tufnell's remark upon it, that this number of persons were not out of work, but in consequence of their large families they were receiving assistance from the parish ; and I have been furnished with an extract from the former rate-books, containing the names of those persons so receiving permanent relief in consequence of their large families. Some of them were employed by the parish road surveyor, and were, therefore, classed in our parish books as out of work, that is to say, the parish roads were receiving a far larger degree of repair, both as to space and materials, than hitherto had been the case in consequence of having hands occasionally wanting work, and still more, perhaps, from the farmers, whose residences were along these roads, requiring better roads than their forefathers did, who were content to carry their corn to the neighbouring markets and mills on packhorses instead of in carts and waggons as at present.

Mr. Tufnell also adds a startling remark, " That in spite of the emigration, which mostly took place in 1827 and 1828, in seven or eight years afterwards this parish had reverted to its old state of pauperism, and the number of unemployed labourers was as great as ever." Mr. Lansdell's letter happily shows how entirely at variance with the real condidition of the parish of Benenden is this remark of the Assistant Poor Law Commissioner.

Mr. Tufnell's reasoning on the effect caused by emigration in this parish appears very inconclusive. He says, in page 343, " Since the Union, in which this parish is situated, has been brought into operation, 164 persons have emigrated, or more than previous to the Union, yet the expenditure on the poor in 1841 was 1342*l.*, the population being then 1594, and the departure of these numbers seems to have had comparatively little effect on the population, as the number by the Census of 1821, was 1746 ; in 1831 was 1663 ; in 1841 was 1594." I think it would have been a more prudent course if Mr. Tufnell had paid a visit to this parish, and had examined the former rate-books and had made himself acquainted with other local circumstances, so necessary towards enabling him to form a correct judgment before he expressed so decided an opinion. If he had done so he would have found that the amount of poor-rates expended in 1825, the year before we began to emigrate, was 3184*l.*, whereas the amount expended in 1835, the year before the New Poor Law Act came into operation in this Union, was 1814*l.* 9*s.* The total number of persons who emigrated between 1826 and 1835 was 161 ; from 1836 to 1842, 180 more emigrated. It will appear that the first number itself caused a reduction of upwards of one-third of the whole parish expenditure; and although, by comparing the Census of

---

* The Board of Guardians of the Cranbrook Union did not administer relief till February, 1836.

1821 with that of 1841, there appears a difference now of only 152 persons, can it be doubted that if no emigration had taken place the 341 persons who had gone to the Colonies from this parish would have largely added to the parochial population? and what effect this must have had on the amount of the rates is sufficiently obvious. He would have found also, in looking through the old rate-books, that the total expense, from March, 1826 to May, 1842, to the parish in emigrating these 341 persons has been 1796*l.* 10*s.* 9½*d.*, a sum bearing a very small proportion to the aggregate amount of the annual reduction of the rates, and that from the commencement of this system the amount of our rates has been decreasing, until at the present time it is about half what it was in 1825, before we began to emigrate, notwithstanding the present unfavourable state of the country.

The two concluding sentences of Mr. Tufnell's remarks on the parish of Benenden must be noticed, in order to remove a difficulty in the way of any general adoption of the system of emigration, which his statements may create, unless shown to be unfounded. He says, " The diminution of the numbers here has, however, been greater than elsewhere, under the effect of a similar emigration, owing to the partial adoption of what has been termed the clearing system, that is pulling down the cottages of those who emigrated," and he adds, " but this plan is only practicable where a parish belongs, as in this instance, exclusively to one or two proprietors." Undoubtedly I have taken down some cottages that had become untenanted by persons emigrating; but I believe the number of new ones since built, and old ones enlarged by other persons, has more than equalled those so taken down, and, therefore, little or no effect can be attributed to this cause. Besides, instead of this parish belonging, as Mr. Tufnell intimates, to one or two proprietors, (and I conclude he considers me one of them,) there are 58 proprietors of farms and lands in this parish, beside myself.

It is not my intention to make the occasion of this letter an excuse for offering any information on parochial emigration, or of troubling you with any arguments in its favour, as I have had other opportunities of stating my decided opinions on the subject; and I should not have taken the liberty of troubling you with this letter did I not suppose that, when the subject of emigration and colonization comes, as it inevitably must, to occupy the serious attention of the Government of this country, a reference to the Poor Law Commissioners' Reports would probably be made; and as I believe that from no rural parish has emigration proceeded, with reference to its population, in a greater degree than from the parish in which I live, nor anywhere have its effects on the rates and on the general condition of the population been more carefully watched and recorded, I have felt it a duty to the public to offer these remarks upon the errors of your Assistant Commissioner. In conclusion I will only add, that if the beneficial effects of our parochial emigration were so trifling as Mr. Tufnell considers them, it is not likely that such a failure would be unknown to the rate-payers of the parish; whereas, on the contrary, there is no subject of parochial management marked with such entire unanimity as this, from a consciousness of the benefits which all have received from this source, and on which we confidently rely for further advantages. It is satisfactory to know that the neighbouring parishes have become equally impressed with the necessity as well as the benefits of its adoption.

I am far from considering the condition of the labourers, even in this parish, as being so comfortable as it ought to be and as I well remember it to have formerly been; but I have the strongest conviction that their condition would not have been what it is now, and what Mr Lansdell in his letter truly describes it to be, had not so many of their fellow-labourers possessed the good sense and the spirit to avail themselves of the opportunities offered them of seeking independence among their countrymen who are settled in other parts of the world.

I have the honour to be, Gentlemen,

Your obedient servant,

THOMAS LAW HODGES.

Hemsted, Kent, March 30th, 1843.

IRELAND.

. No. 14.

LETTER FROM THE COMMISSIONERS TO THE BOARD OF GUARDIANS OF THE SOUTH DUBLIN UNION RESPECTING THE PAYMENT OF A CONSIDERATION FOR THE OFFICE OF MEDICAL OFFICER TO THE UNION WORKHOUSE.

Poor Law Commission Office, Dublin,

SIR, *10th April,* 1845.

THE Poor Law Commissioners have received and considered Mr. Gilbert's report and evidence relative to the appointment of Doctor Mayne as Physician to the South Dublin Union.

It apears from the evidence that an agreement was entered into between Doctor Lees and Doctor Mayne that the former should receive 100*l.* on his resignation and 200*l.* on Doctor Mayne's election to the office of physician. This fact is, indeed, admitted by both the parties concerned in the transaction.

The Commissioners are not aware that they have the power, nor are they called upon to take any step with respect to the agreement which is thus proved to have once existed between Doctor Mayne and Doctor Lees. It is distinctly affirmed that the parties renounced such agreement before the election of medical officer.

The Commissioners certainly regret that it ever existed.

They think it desirable shortly to advert to one point suggested by the evidence on this case, and that is, the amount of the salaries fixed for the medical officers of the South Dublin Union workhouse.

The Guardians in January, 1840, proposed a salary of 60*l.* each for the surgeon and physician, and to this the Commissioners assented.

On the 26th June, 1841, the Guardians expressed a wish to raise their salaries to 100*l.* each. The Commissioners dissented from this increase. The Guardians, however, requested the Commissioners to reconsider their refusal, and many inquiries were made as to the nature of the duties performed by the medical officers. Some protests against the increase of salary were received; but after another resolution of the Guardians, and after, on the 18th February, 1842, receiving a deputation of the South Dublin Board, the Commissioners, who were anxious that the remuneration should be sufficient to secure proper medical attendance on the inmates without being extravagant in itself, finally consented to fix the salaries at 100*l.* a year each.

Doctor Lees, the person now charged with making the bargain to receive 300*l.* on the election of Doctor Mayne, was one of the medical officers benefited by this increase of salary.

Now, on reviewing all these circumstances, and considering what has been admitted by Doctor Mayne and Doctor Lees, the Commissioners are inclined to arrive at the conclusion, that if the place is such that the physician elected can afford to pay 300*l.* for the purpose of obtaining the situation, the salary must be too high. It is clear that this payment would be in the nature of a fine on taking possession of an office which was to yield a certain amount of emolument, and that it represents, in fact, the excess of that emolument over and above what would adequately remunerate the person accepting the office for the discharge of his duties from day to day; for if he did not pay this sum to obtain the office, it is clear that he could afford to discharge his duties with equal efficiency for a salary just so much lower in proportion.

According to this view, therefore, the excess is a charge cast on the rate-payers not to pay for the attendance of the poor who are inmates of the workhouse during the time the incoming officer holds office, but in order to benefit some person who ceases to have any duties in connexion with those inmates, and who is paid this sum precisely because he ceases to have such duties.

It would seem necessarily to follow that an amount of salary such as would enable this payment to be made cannot be justified as a fair and proper burthen on the rate-payers of the South Dublin Union.

The Commissioners will be ready to take the subject into consideration as soon as they shall have received the observations of the Guardians of the South Dublin Board on the view of the case laid before them in this letter.

I am, &c.,

(Signed)   ARTHUR MOORE, *Chief Clerk.*

To the Clerk of the Guardians,
  South Dublin Union.

TABLES AND RETURNS.

No. 1.—SUMMARY of RETURNS showing the Pauperism and Expenditure in 585 Unions in England and Wales, under the Poor Law Amendment Act, for the Years 1843 and 1844.

COUNTIES.	Population* in 1841.	Number of Paupers relieved.						Proportion per Cent. of Total Number of Paupers relieved to Population in 1841.
		Quarters ended at Lady-day, 1843.			Quarters ended at Lady-day, 1844.			
		In-door.	Out-door.	Total.	In-door	Out-door.	Total.	
ENGLAND.								
Bedford	112,379	2,484	10,562	13,046	2,190	11,028	13,218	11·8
Berks	190,367	4,682	15,263	19,945	4,821	16,177	20,998	11·0
Buckingham	140,352	2,703	15,755	18,458	3,133	16,346	19,479	13·9
Cambridge	171,848	3,895	15,118	19,013	4,197	16,108	20,305	11·8
Chester	371,331	2,736	24,912	27,648	2,332	21,752	24,084	6·5
Cornwall	340,728	2,688	20,419	23,107	2,789	19,572	22,361	6·6
Cumberland	177,912	2,182	9,045	11,227	2,149	9,208	11,357	6·4
Derby	220,028	2,203	10,636	12,839	1,614	9,727	11,341	5·2
Devon	430,221	4,827	37,033	41,860	4,632	35,567	40,199	9·3
Dorset	167,874	2,508	20,083	22,591	2,313	19,935	22,248	13·3
Durham	325,997	2,229	25,362	27,591	2,181	24,430	26,611	8·2
Essex	320,818	9,149	35,545	44,694	9,075	35,524	44,599	13·9
Gloucester	330,562	4,622	24,751	29,373	4,258	25,442	29,700	9·0
Hereford	110,675	1,430	8,716	10,146	1,424	8,995	10,419	9·4
Hertford	176,173	4,334	13,735	18,069	4,607	14,585	19,192	10·9
Huntingdon	55,573	1,059	4,445	5,504	777	4,832	5,609	10·1
Kent	534,882	11,762	38,128	49,890	10,525	39,588	50,113	9·4
Lancaster	1,207,802	11,612	114,132	125,744	9,892	85,797	95,689	7·9
Leicester	220,232	3,776	23.296	27,072	4,004	20,103	24,107	10·9
Lincoln	356,347	5,315	19,649	24,964	5,429	21,234	26,663	7·5
Middlesex	841,402	20,515	43,815	64,330	21,478	47,101	68,579	8·2
Monmouth	150,222	1,205	8,846	10,051	1,146	8,268	9,414	6·3
Norfolk	343,277	7,817	29,849	37,666	8,105	33,150	41,255	12·0
Northampton	197,197	3,134	17,481	20,615	2,963	18,988	21,951	11·1
Northumberland	265,988	2,246	21,185	23,431	2,370	22,020	24,390	9·2
Nottingham	270,719	3,317	19,149	22,466	2,926	15,645	18,571	6·9
Oxford	141,330	2,699	16,344	19,043	2,763	16,482	19,245	13·6
Rutland	23,150	418	1,510	1,928	521	1,701	2,222	9·6
Salop	191,052	3,526	11,185	14,711	3,932	13,272	17,204	9·0
Somerset	454,446	7,122	46,764	53,886	6,643	46,367	53,010	11·7
Southampton	268,866	5,191	24,558	29,749	5,037	25,403	30,440	11·3
Stafford	442,348	7,851	26,500	34,351	6,225	24,201	30,426	6·9
Suffolk	314,722	7,726	31,763	39,489	6,474	34,266	40,740	12·9
Surrey	512,580	10,478	29,685	40,163	10,582	30,588	41,170	8·0
Sussex	223,435	6,121	25,102	31,223	5,402	24,217	29,619	13·3
Warwick	220,029	2,375	13,481	15,856	2,196	13,307	15,503	7·0
Westmoreland	56,469	1,113	6,157	7,270	794	5,429	6,223	11·0
Wilts	233,246	5,763	30,972	36,735	5,699	30,551	36,250	15·5
Worcester	336,108	3,312	26,372	29,684	3,568	23,787	27,355	8·1
York { East Riding	180,218	1,628	14,639	16,267	1,582	13,710	15,292	8·5
York { North Riding	180,527	1,959	12,783	14,742	2,053	12,909	14,962	8·3
York { West Riding	790,751	5,467	83,214	88,681	4,789	54,138	58,927	7·5
Totals of England	12,569,303	197,179	1,027,939	1,225,118	189,590	971,450	1,161,040	9·2
WALES.								
Anglesey	38,105	..	5,120	5,120	..	5,573	5,573	14·6
Brecon	55,399	506	4,462	4,968	527	5,075	5,602	10·1
Cardigan	75,136	178	6,124	6,302	225	6,375	6,600	8·8
Carmarthen	110,404	934	8,311	9,245	1,249	8,969	10,218	9·3
Carnarvon	86,728	114	8,700	8,814	133	9,368	9,501	11·0
Denbigh	68,483	502	6,785	7,287	550	7,113	7,663	11·2
Flint	64,355	419	4,938	5,357	375	5,159	5,534	8·6
Glamorgan	178,041	757	11,900	12,657	1,206	12,591	13,797	7·7
Merioneth	50,696	176	6,050	6,226	205	6,218	6,423	12·7
Montgomery	59,709	565	7,916	8,481	513	8,653	9,166	15·6
Pembroke	78,563	504	5,333	5,837	552	5,543	6,095	7·7
Radnor	19,554	93	2,394	2,487	95	2,375	2,470	12·6
Totals of Wales	884,173	4,748	78,033	82,781	5,630	83,012	88,642	10·0
Total of 585 Unions in England and Wales	13,453,476	201,927	1,105,972	1,307,899	195,220	1,054,462	1,249,682	9·3

NOTE.—The above results are obtained from the Union Quarterly Abstracts.
* Some of the Unions are composed of Parishes situate in different Counties, which causes the population to differ from that published by the Census Commissioners.

M

No. 1, *(continued)*.—SUMMARY of RETURNS showing the Pauperism and Expenditure in 585 Unions in England and Wales, under the Poor Law Amendment Act, for the Years 1843 and 1844.

COUNTIES.	Expenditure for the Relief and Maintenance of the Poor.					
	Years ended at Lady-day, 1843.					
	In-maintenance.	Out-relief.	Establishment and Salaries.	Workhouse Loans repaid.	Other Charges connected with Relief to the Poor.	Total Expenditure for Relief to the Poor.
ENGLAND.	£.	£.	£.	£.	£.	£.
Bedford	8,829	26,898	7,788	1,649	21	45,185
Berks	18,044	51,071	17,576	5,274	13	91,981
Buckingham	9,971	45,080	11,065	3,191	10	69,317
Cambridge	11,795	47,625	12,951	4,175	47	76,593
Chester	11,562	60,782	17,039	1,358	5	90,746
Cornwall	10,812	55,360	13,446	2,648	53	82,319
Cumberland	6,948	23,302	6,590	888	5	37,733
Derby	6,929	24,184	10,790	2,965	23	44,890
Devon	17,643	122,597	22,106	6,575	114	169,035
Dorset	9,910	53,763	12,565	3,533	45	79,816
Durham	8,718	59,987	9,728	1,968	111	80,512
Essex	28,915	88,230	28,774	6,759	35	152,713
Gloucester	18,297	62,812	19,530	5,371	51	106,061
Hereford	4,718	27,994	7,627	2,200	5	42,474
Hertford	16,886	38,577	14,206	3,850	12	73,531
Huntingdon	3,241	15,523	4,507	1,100	14	24,385
Kent	52,711	93,205	38,781	10,650	1,979	197,276
Lancaster	50,626	178,573	45,961	1,774	90	277,024
Leicester	12,736	60,110	13,090	2,790	2	88,718
Lincoln	17,798	67,294	19,463	4,258	29	108,842
Middlesex	115,618	109,478	68,026	9,577	388	303,087
Monmouth	4,726	20,534	5,015	1,804	11	32,090
Norfolk	24,725	100,828	30,459	6,466	19	162,497
Northampton . . .	11,997	57,349	15,691	4,832	186	90,055
Northumberland . . .	8,796	54,201	8,760	2,586	103	74,446
Nottingham . . .	13,793	50,416	11,982	2,226	83	78,400
Oxford	8,810	50,343	10,810	3,015	3	72,981
Rutland	1,320	4,585	1,750	578	5	8,238
Salop	10,964	29,860	11,956	1,896	186	54,822
Somerset	23,992	118,535	25,186	7,483	542	175,688
Southampton	22,897	71,086	21,358	4,639	48	120,028
Stafford	25,708	54,945	25,871	6,093	295	112,912
Suffolk	21,642	88,453	25,204	5,026	12	140,337
Surrey	54,492	72,760	46,153	7,878	1,246	192,539
Sussex	26,252	65,418	21,800	6,012	432	119,914
Warwick	9,858	39,370	11,380	2,450	173	63,231
Westmoreland	3,684	13,226	2,318	119	7	19,354
Wilts	18,930	85,571	20,394	5,905	88	130,888
Worcester	13,235	56,045	15,584	3,158	1	88,023
York { East Riding . .	6,105	40,889	7,442	916	27	55,379
York { North Riding . .	6,101	40,099	8,210	667	509	55,586
York { West Riding . .	24,365	174,099	24,149	3,847	74	226,534
Totals of England .	795,098	2,600,987	752,951	160,112	7,002	4,316,150
WALES.						
Anglesey	. .	12,506	751	. .	. .	13,257
Brecon	1,195	14,992	2,578	661	. .	19,426
Cardigan	520	16,990	2,223	418	1	20,152
Carmarthen	2,275	26,538	3,878	1,298	14	34,003
Carnarvon	131	22,942	1,998	. .	11	25,082
Denbigh	2,097	16,896	3,642	884	. .	23,519
Flint	1,263	15,069	3,247	915	34	20,528
Glamorgan	2,768	34,817	5,120	666	19	43,390
Merioneth	351	14,918	1,697	467	. .	17,433
Montgomery	2,686	19,682	4,000	879	11	27,258
Pembroke	1,415	16,436	2,985	658	. .	21,494
Radnor	573	6,070	1,078	145	. .	7,866
Totals of Wales . .	15,274	207,856	33,197	6,991	90	273,408
Totals of 585 Unions in England and Wales }	810,372	2,818,843	786,148	167,103	7,092	4,589,558

No. 1, (*continued*).—SUMMARY of RETURNS showing the Pauperism and Expenditure in 585 Unions in England and Wales, under the Poor Law Amendment Act, for the Years 1843 and 1844.

COUNTIES.	Expenditure for the Relief and Maintenance of the Poor. Years ended at Lady-day, 1844.						Decrease per Cent. of Expenditure in 1844 compared with 1843.	Increase per Cent. of Expenditure in 1844 compared with 1843.
	In-maintenance.	Out-relief.	Establishment and Salaries.	Workhouse Loans repaid.	Other Charges connected with Relief to the Poor.	Total Expenditure for Relief to the Poor.		
	£.	£.	£.	£.	£.	£.		
ENGLAND.								
Bedford	7,279	26,049	7,501	1,627	13	42,469	6·0	
Berks	16,633	50,188	16,687	5,445	10	88,913	8·3	
Buckingham	8,563	45,162	10,914	3,257	4	67,900	2·0	
Cambridge	10,743	48,634	11,902	4,054	16	75,349	1·6	
Chester	8,189	56,058	14,411	1,741	14	80,413	11·4	
Cornwall	9,761	52,284	12,145	2,579	11	76,780	6·8	
Cumberland	6,028	22,379	6,193	1,135	22	35,757	5·2	
Derby	5,833	24,150	8,871	2,766	.	41,820	8·0	
Devon	14,534	113,685	20,395	6,702	117	155,433	8·0	
Dorset	8,760	51,970	11,826	3,749	24	76,329	4·4	
Durham	8,089	60,313	9,481	1,898	83	79,863	0·8	
Essex	25,326	86,014	27,458	8,219	29	147,046	3·7	
Gloucester	15,588	62,191	17,403	5,558	111	100,851	4·9	
Hereford	4,588	26,721	7,228	2,506	6	41,049	3·4	
Hertford	14,361	38,532	12,799	4,008	21	69,721	5·2	
Huntingdon	2,941	15,130	3,842	1,078	.	22,991	5·7	
Kent	47,022	91,850	39,594	9,703	1,114	189,283	2·1	
Lancaster	40,320	146,314	41,817	3,011	186	231,648	16·4	
Leicester	10,446	55,643	13,583	2,647	110	82,379	7·1	
Lincoln	16,818	70,601	18,445	3,741	5	109,610		0·7
Middlesex	99,292	108,020	63,858	7,280	743	279,193	7·9	
Monmouth	3,973	20,677	4,910	1,856	5	31,420	2·1	
Norfolk	22,776	100,724	29,630	7,341	115	160,586	1·2	
Northampton	11,118	58,294	13,646	5,672	135	88,865	1·3	
Northumberland	8,718	55,953	8,879	2,483	30	76,063		2·2
Nottingham	11,209	43,859	13,067	6,081	75	74,291	5·2	
Oxford	8,345	50,490	11,022	2,822	56	72,735	0·8	
Rutland	1,382	4,835	1,730	578	.	8,525		3·5
Salop	11,157	34,683	12,122	1,764	4	59,630		8·8
Somerset	20,741	116,171	23,993	6,766	153	167,824	4·5	
Southampton	19,553	69,159	19,754	4,579	26	113,071	5·8	
Stafford	21,794	51,952	23,798	5,492	69	103,105	8·7	
Suffolk	19,255	87,798	24,842	4,702	61	136,658	2·6	
Surrey	54,058	73,655	44,567	19,664	1,167	193,111		0·3
Sussex	22,452	62,432	20,757	6,087	535	112,263	6·4	
Warwick	8,722	38,537	10,094	2,467	20	59,840	5·4	
Westmoreland	2,991	12,724	2,888	115	29	18,747	3·1	
Wilts	16,354	83,741	19,241	6,076	81	125,493	4·1	
Worcester	13,062	55,508	15,086	3,178	62	86,896	1·3	
York { East Riding	5,937	41,329	6,766	899	45	54,976	0·7	
York { North Riding	5,660	40,714	7,809	853	54	55,090	0·9	
York { West Riding	21,356	156,488	26,799	4,013	149	208,805	7·8	
Totals of England	691,726	2,511,410	717,403	176,192	5,510	4,102,241	5·0	
WALES.								
Anglesey	.	12,556	733	.	.	13,289		0·2
Brecon	1,041	16,002	2,618	557	3	20,221		4·1
Cardigan	347	16,393	2,005	427	.	19,172	4·9	
Carmarthen	1,992	25,037	3,702	1,125	10	31,856	6·3	
Carnarvon	146	22,532	2,183	350	11	25,222		0·6
Denbigh	2,096	16,240	3,548	912	.	22,796	3·1	
Flint	1,020	15,125	2,927	913	8	19,993	2·6	
Glamorgan	2,603	35,423	4,842	890	21	43,779		0·9
Merioneth	418	14,678	1,850	813	1	17,760		1·9
Montgomery	2,117	19,425	3,411	916	10	25,879		5·1
Pembroke	1,241	15,846	2,769	658	10	20,524	4·5	
Radnor	506	5,794	994	145	.	7,439	5·4	
Totals of Wales	13,527	215,041	31,582	7,706	74	267,930	2·	
Totals of 585 Unions in England and Wales }	705,253	2,726,451	749,985	183,898	5,584	4,370,171	4·8	

M 2

No. 2. (i.)—COMPARATIVE STATEMENT of the Total Number of Paupers relieved in 585 Unions in the several Counties of England and Wales, during the Quarters ended Lady-day, 1843 and 1844 respectively, and the Total Amount expended for Relief, &c., to the Poor, during each of the Years ended Lady-day, 1843 and 1844, in which the Counties are ranged according to their highest rate of Decrease and lowest rate of Increase in the latter as compared with the former period.

COUNTIES.	Total Number of Paupers relieved. Quarters ended Lady-day.		Decrease per Cent. in 1844, compared with 1843.	Increase per Cent. in 1844, compared with 1843.
	1843	1844		
York, West Riding	88,681	58,927	33·6	..
Lancaster	125,744	95,689	23·9	..
Nottingham	22,466	18,571	17·3	..
Westmoreland	7,270	6,223	14·4	..
Chester	27,648	24,084	12·9	..
Derby	12,839	11,341	11·7	..
Stafford	34,351	30,426	11·4	..
Leicester	27,072	24,107	11·0	..
Worcester	29,684	27,355	7·8	..
Monmouth	10,051	9,414	6·3	..
York, East Riding	16,267	15,292	6·0	..
Sussex	31,223	29,619	5·1	..
Devon	41,860	40,199	4·0	..
Durham	27,591	26,611	3·6	..
Cornwall	23,107	22,361	3·2	..
Warwick	15,856	15,503	2·2	..
Somerset	53,896	53,010	1·6	..
Dorset	22,591	22,248	1·5	..
Wilts	36,735	36,250	1·3	..
Radnor	2,487	2,470	0·7	..
Essex	44,694	44,599	0·2	..
Kent	49,890	50,113	..	0·5
Gloucester	29,373	29,700	..	1·1
Oxford	19,043	19,245	..	1·1
Cumberland	11,227	11,357	..	1·2
Bedford	13,046	13,218	..	1·3
York, North Riding	14,742	14,962	..	1·5
Huntingdon	5,504	5,609	..	1·9
Southampton	29,749	30,440	..	2·3
Surrey	40,163	41,170	..	2·5
Hereford	10,146	10,419	..	2·7
Suffolk	39,489	40,740	..	3·2
Merioneth	6,226	6,423	..	3·2
Flint	5,357	5,534	..	3·3
Northumberland	23,431	24,390	..	4·1
Pembroke	5,837	6,095	..	4·4
Cardigan	6,302	6,660	..	4·7
Denbigh	7,287	7,663	..	5·2
Berks	19,945	20,998	..	5·3
Buckingham	18,458	19,479	..	5·5
Northampton	20,615	21,951	..	6·0
Hertford	18,069	19,192	..	6·2
Middlesex	64,330	68,579	..	6·6
Cambridge	19,013	20,305	..	6·8
Lincoln	24,964	26,663	..	6·8
Carnarvon	8,814	9,501	..	7·8
Montgomery	8,481	9,166	..	8·1
Anglesey	5,120	5,573	..	8·9
Glamorgan	12,657	13,797	..	9·0
Norfolk	37,666	41,255	..	9·5
Carmarthen	9,245	10,218	..	10·5
Brecon	4,968	5,602	..	12·8
Rutland	1,928	2,222	..	15·2
Salop	14,711	17,204	..	17·0
Totals of 585 Unions in England and Wales	1,307,899	1,249,682	4·5	..

NOTE.—The above results were obtained from the Union Quarterly Abstracts.

No. 2 (i.)—*(continued)*.—COMPARATIVE STATEMENT of the Total Number of Paupers relieved in 585 Unions in the several Counties of England and Wales, during the Quarters ended Lady-day, 1843 and 1844 respectively, and the Total Amount expended for Relief, &c., to the Poor, during each of the Years ended Lady-day, 1843 and 1844, in which the Counties are ranged according to their highest rate of Decrease and lowest rate of Increase in the latter as compared with the former period.

COUNTIES.	Total Amount expended for Relief, &c., to the Poor. Years ended Lady-day.		Decrease per Cent. in 1844, compared with 1843.	Increase per Cent. in 1844, compared with 1843.
	1843.	1844.		
Lancaster	277,024	231,648	16·4	..
Chester	90,746	80,413	11·4	..
Stafford	112,912	103,105	8·7	..
Derby	44,890	41,320	8·0	..
Devon	169,035	155,433	8·0	..
Middlesex	303,087	279,193	7·9	..
York, West Riding	226,534	208,805	7·8	..
Leicester	88,718	82,379	7·1	..
Cornwall	82,319	76,730	6·8	..
Sussex	119,914	112,263	6·4	..
Carmarthen	34,003	31,856	6·3	..
Bedford	45,185	42,469	6·0	..
Southampton	120,028	113,071	5·8	..
Huntingdon	24,385	22,991	5·7	..
Warwick	63,231	59,840	5·4	..
Radnor	7,866	7,439	5·4	..
Cumberland	37,733	35,757	5·2	..
Hertford	73,531	69,721	5·2	..
Nottingham	78,400	74,291	5·2	..
Gloucester	106,061	100,851	4·9	..
Cardigan	20,152	19,172	4·9	..
Somerset	175,688	167,824	4·5	..
Pembroke	21,494	20,524	4·5	..
Dorset	79,816	76,329	4·4	..
Kent	197,276	189,283	4·1	..
Wilts	130,888	125,493	4·1	..
Essex	152,713	147,046	3·7	..
Hereford	42,474	41,049	3·4	..
Berks	91,951	88,913	3·3	..
Westmoreland	19,354	18,747	3·1	..
Denbigh	23,519	22,796	3·1	..
Suffolk	140,337	136,658	2·6	..
Flint	20,528	19,993	2·6	..
Monmouth	32,090	31,420	2·1	..
Buckingham	69,317	67,900	2·0	..
Cambridge	76,593	75,349	1·6	..
Northampton	90,055	88,865	1·3	..
Worcester	88,023	86,996	1·3	..
Norfolk	162,497	160,586	1·2	..
York, North Riding	55,586	55,090	0·9	..
Durham	80,512	79,863	0·8	..
York, East Riding	55,379	54,976	0·7	..
Oxford	72,981	72,735	0·3	..
Anglesey	13,257	13,289	..	·2
Surrey	192,539	193,111	..	·3
Carnarvon	25,082	25,222	..	·6
Lincoln	108,842	109,610	..	·7
Glamorgan	43,390	43,779	..	·9
Merioneth	17,433	17,760	..	1·9
Northumberland	74,446	76,063	..	2·2
Rutland	8,238	8,525	..	3·5
Brecon	19,426	20,221	..	4·1
Montgomery	27,253	25,879	..	5·1
Salop	54,822	59,630	..	8·8
Totals of 585 Unions in England and Wales . }	4,589,558	4,370,171	4·8	..

NOTE.—The above results were obtained from the Union Quarterly Abstracts,

No. 2. (ii.)—SUMMARY of RETURNS, showing the Number of Adult Able-bodied Paupers relieved in 585 Unions, under the Poor Law Amendment Act, in the several Counties of England and Wales, during the Quarters ended Lady-day, 1843 and 1844, respectively.

COUNTIES.	Number of Adult Able-bodied Paupers Relieved.						
	Quarter ended Lady-day, 1843.						
	In-door.			Out-door.			Total In-door and Out-door
	On Account of Sickness or Accident.	All other Causes, including Vagrancy.	Total.	On Account of Sickness or Accident.	All other Causes, including Vagrancy.	Total.	
ENGLAND.							
Bedford	179	869	1,048	1,932	1,232	3,164	4,212
Berks	190	1,705	1,895	2,270	997	3,267	5,162
Buckingham	148	1,100	1,248	2,768	1,653	4,421	5,669
Cambridge	126	1,744	1,870	2,505	1,320	3,825	5,695
Chester	79	942	1,021	1,944	5,899	7,843	8,864
Cornwall	179	683	862	2,077	2,595	4,672	5,534
Cumberland	64	699	763	849	1,432	2,281	3,044
Derby	84	758	842	1,437	1,318	2,755	3,597
Devon	375	1,637	2,012	4,502	2,301	6,803	8,815
Dorset	156	726	882	3,232	1,909	5,141	6,023
Durham	109	763	872	1,870	6,870	8,740	9,612
Essex	392	4,728	5,120	6,081	3,419	9,500	14,620
Gloucester	250	1,398	1,648	2,974	3,000	5,974	7,622
Hereford	97	317	414	1,207	517	1,724	2,138
Hertford	208	1,732	1,940	2,568	1,921	4,489	6,429
Huntingdon	12	480	492	700	279	979	1,471
Kent	673	3,896	4,569	4,615	6,119	10,734	15,303
Lancaster	979	3,391	4,370	5,524	30,615	36,139	40,409
Leicester	87	1,523	1,610	3,150	3,412	6,562	8,172
Lincoln	175	2,157	2,332	2,729	2,361	5,090	7,422
Middlesex	971	7,139	8,110	3,131	11,629	14,760	22,870
Monmouth	88	374	462	1,085	1,718	2,803	3,265
Norfolk	149	3,122	3,271	3,399	2,428	5,827	9,098
Northampton	87	1,030	1,117	2,973	1,418	4,391	5,508
Northumberland	144	848	992	1,342	5,546	6,888	7,880
Nottingham	96	1,068	1,164	2,685	2,679	5,364	6,528
Oxford	88	1,002	1,090	3,151	1,359	4,510	5,600
Rutland	4	213	217	165	161	326	543
Salop	147	1,421	1,568	1,611	1,390	3,001	4,569
Somerset	296	2,724	3,020	6,892	3,900	10,792	13,812
Southampton	209	1,573	1,782	4,321	2,170	6,491	8,273
Stafford	268	3,558	3,826	2,850	6,773	9,623	13,449
Suffolk	134	3,335	3,469	4,909	2,458	7,367	10,836
Surrey	673	4,117	4,790	3,421	7,448	10,869	15,659
Sussex	145	2,238	2,383	3,841	1,928	5,769	8,152
Warwick	85	762	847	1,618	1,441	3,059	3,906
Westmoreland	18	556	574	357	1,751	2,108	2,682
Wilts	169	3,461	2,630	4,963	3,277	8,240	10,870
Worcester	226	1,048	1,274	2,792	5,482	8,274	9,548
York { East Riding	55	588	643	1,375	2,882	4,257	4,900
York { North Riding	79	798	877	995	2,480	3,475	4,352
York { West Riding	324	2,004	2,328	4,073	26,495	30,568	32,896
Totals of England	9,017	73,227	82,244	116,883	175,982	292,865	375,109
WALES.							
Anglesey	..	..	..	594	805	1,399	1,399
Brecon	12	284	296	338	477	815	1,111
Cardigan	7	69	76	464	584	1,048	1,124
Carmarthen	19	408	427	912	720	1,632	2,059
Carnarvon	30	26	56	641	1,538	2,179	2,235
Denbigh	24	140	164	1,009	777	1,786	1,950
Flint	23	95	118	490	657	1,147	1,265
Glamorgan	11	92	103	1,151	2,607	3,758	3,861
Merioneth	5	57	62	415	623	1,038	1,100
Montgomery	28	136	164	641	1,079	1,720	1,884
Pembroke	31	129	160	312	482	794	954
Radnor	2	26	28	228	319	547	575
Totals of Wales	192	1,462	1,654	7,195	10,668	17,863	19,517
Totals of 585 Unions in England and Wales	9,209	74,689	83,898	124,078	186,650	310,728	394,626
Estimated for Unions not included and places not in Union	1,679	13,619	15,298	22,626	34,035	56,661	71,959
Estimated Totals of England and Wales	10,888	88,308	99,196	146,704	220,685	367,389	466,585

NOTE.—The above results were obtained from the Union Quarterly Abstracts, an estimate being made for places not under the Poor Law Amendment Act.

No. 2, (ii.)—(*continued*).—SUMMARY of RETURNS, showing the Number of Adult Able-bodied Paupers **relieved in 585 Unions**, under the Poor Law Amendment Act, in the several **Counties of England and Wales**, during the **Quarters** ended Lady-day, 1843 **and** 1844, respectively.

COUNTIES.	In-door. On Account of Sickness or Accident.	In-door. All other Causes, including Vagrancy.	In-door. Total.	Out-door. On Account of Sickness or Accident.	Out-door. All other Causes, including Vagrancy.	Out-door. Total.	Total In-door and Out-door
ENGLAND.							
Bedford	158	760	918	2,271	974	3,245	4,163
Berks	172	1,986	2,158	2,548	1,020	3,568	5,726
Buckingham	154	1,481	1,635	3,172	1,413	4,585	6,220
Cambridge	124	2,093	2,217	2,606	1,380	3,986	6,203
Chester	110	864	974	2,052	4,428	6,480	7,454
Cornwall	230	657	887	1,975	2,382	4,357	5,244
Cumberland	65	745	810	1,021	1,246	2,267	3,077
Derby	83	374	457	1,436	975	2,411	2,868
Devon	376	1,482	1,858	4,466	2,187	6,653	8,511
Dorset	149	666	815	3,267	1,758	5,025	5,840
Durham	112	753	865	2,080	5,618	7,698	8,563
Essex	392	4,628	5,020	6,934	2,680	9,614	14,634
Gloucester	254	1,135	1,389	3,133	3,209	6,342	7,731
Hereford	123	305	428	1,250	525	1,775	2,203
Hertford	229	2,255	2,484	2,981	1,393	4,374	6,858
Huntingdon	41	238	279	754	425	1,179	1,458
Kent	760	3,267	4,027	4,902	6,305	11,207	15,234
Lancaster	1,026	2,485	3,511	5,324	19,930	25,254	28,765
Leicester	85	1,856	1,941	2,959	2,369	5,328	7,269
Lincoln	191	2,210	2,401	3,128	2,072	5,200	7,601
Middlesex	1,023	8,633	9,656	4,050	12,051	16,101	25,757
Monmouth	121	370	491	1,021	1,351	2,372	2,863
Norfolk	176	3,346	3,522	4,243	2,685	6,928	10,450
Northampton	75	1,054	1,129	3,454	1,433	4,887	6,016
Northumberland	152	877	1,029	1,449	5,864	7,313	8,342
Nottingham	111	892	1,003	2,357	1,672	4,029	5,032
Oxford	101	1,059	1,160	3,311	1,265	4,576	5,736
Rutland	5	299	304	245	167	412	716
Salop	148	1,824	1,972	2,173	1,415	3,588	5,560
Somerset	300	2,440	2,740	7,145	3,467	10,612	13,352
Southampton	197	1,589	1,786	4,746	2,213	6,959	8,745
Stafford	300	2,390	2,690	2,944	5,818	8,762	11,452
Suffolk	128	2,636	2,764	5,435	2,465	7,900	10,664
Surrey	736	3,671	4,407	3,844	7,382	11,226	15,633
Sussex	171	1,850	2,021	4,061	1,632	5,693	7,714
Warwick	75	722	797	1,583	1,419	3,002	3,799
Westmoreland	27	294	321	396	1,180	1,576	1,897
Wilts	156	2,497	2,653	5,144	2,886	8,030	10,683
Worcester	249	1,136	1,385	3,284	3,480	6,764	8,149
York { East Riding	45	545	590	1,253	2,257	3,510	4,100
York { North Riding	80	958	1,038	1,070	2,303	3,373	4,411
York { West Riding	299	1,588	1,887	4,313	11,080	15,402	17,289
Totals of England	9,509	70,910	80,419	125,780	137,783	263,563	343,982
WALES.							
Anglesey				682	893	1,575	1,575
Brecon	13	291	304	514	521	1,035	1,339
Cardigan	7	123	130	530	624	1,154	1,284
Carmarthen	35	684	719	1,018	771	1,789	2,508
Carnarvon	16	55	71	702	1,579	2,281	2,352
Denbigh	25	168	193	1,083	731	1,814	2,007
Flint	7	128	135	454	600	1,054	1,189
Glamorgan	16	312	328	1,299	2,390	3,689	4,017
Merioneth	6	50	56	275	556	831	887
Montgomery	29	111	140	943	1,101	2,044	2,184
Pembroke	25	162	187	358	528	886	1,073
Radnor	3	19	22	231	288	519	541
Totals of Wales	182	2,103	2,285	8,089	10,582	18,671	20,956
Totals of 585 Unions in England and Wales	9,691	73,013	82,704	133,869	148,365	282,234	364,938
Estimated for Unions not included and places not in Union	1,767	13,314	15,081	24,411	27,054	51,465	66,546
Estimated Totals of England and Wales	11,458	86,327	97,785	158,280	175,419	333,699	431,484

No. 3.—STATEMENT showing the Average Number of Paupers relieved in the several Unions, &c., in England and Wales, in operation under the Poor Law Amendment Act, during each of the Years ended Lady-day, 1837 to 1844; also, the Proportion per Cent. which the In-door and Out-door Paupers bear to the Total Number Relieved.

Years ended at Lady-day.	No. of Unions in Operation in each Year.	Average Number of Paupers Relieved.					
		In-Door.	Proportion Per Cent. to Total.	Out-Door.	Proportion Per Cent. to Total.	Total.	
1837	204	30,351	11	258,367	89	288,718	
1838	445	78,264	12	568,113	88	646,377	
1839	535	98,755	13	674,788	87	773,543	
1840	567	114,626	13	747,052	87	861,678	
1841	580	136,442	14	814,425	86	950,867	
1842	580	149,461	15	855,283	85	1,004,744	
1843	585	183,974	15	1,010,136	85	1,194,110	
1844	585	179,663	15	997,224	85	1,176,887	

No. 4.—COMPARATIVE STATEMENT of the Amount of Money Levied and Expended in England and Wales during the Ten Years prior and the Ten Years subsequent to the passing of the Poor Law Amendment Act.

Years ended Lady-day.	Total Amount of Money Levied.	Expended in Relief and Maintenance of the Poor.*	Law Charges, Removals, &c.	County Rate.	All other Purposes.	Total Parochial Rates Expended.	Rate per Cent. of Increase or Decrease on Amount Expended in Relief, &c., to the Poor in each Year compared with the preceding.		Average Price of Wheat per Quarter.
							Increase.	Decrease.	
	£.	£.	£.	£.	£.	£.			*s. d.*
1825	6,972,323	5,786,989	..	663,644	548,555	6,999,188	1	..	66 6
1826	6,965,051	5,928,502	..	743,111	503,034	7,174,647	2	..	58 9
1827	7,784,352	6,441,088	..	762,187	600,191	7,803,466	9	..	56 9
1828	7,715,055	6,298,000	..	721,308	651,125	7,670,433	..	2	60 5
1829	7,642,171	6,332,410	..	714,308	566,021	7,612,739	1	..	66 3
1830	8,111,422	6,829,042	..	726,800	605,439	8,161,281	8	..	62 10
1831	8,279,219	6,798,889	..	772,966	767,232	8,339,087	..	..	67 8
1832	8,622,920	7,036,969	..	799,414	847,079	8,683,462	4	..	63 4
1833	8,606,501	6,790,800	254,412	745,270	949,400	8,739,882	..	4	57 3
1834	8,338,079	6,317,255	258,604	691,548	1,021,941	8,289,348	..	7	51 11

Ten Years since the passing of the Poor Law Amendment Act.

1835	7,373,807	5,526,418	202,527	705,711	935,362	7,370,018	..	13	44 2
1836	6,354,538	4,717,630	172,432	699,845	823,213	6,413,120	..	15	39 5
1837†	5,294,566	4,044,741	126,951	604,203	637,043	5,412,938	..	14	52 6
1838	5,186,389	4,123,604	93,982	681,842	569,271‡	5,468,699	2	..	55 3
1839	5,613,938	4,406,907	63,412§	741,407	602,855	5,814,581	7	..	69 4
1840	6,014,605	4,576,965	67,020	855,552	567,889	6,067,426	3	..	68 6
1841	6,351,828	4,760,929	69,942	1,026,035	636,266‖	6,493,172	4	..	65 3
1842	6,552,890	4,911,498	68,051	1,230,718	501,504	6,711,771	3	..	64 0
1843	7,085,595	5,208,027	84,730	1,295,616	446,748	7,035,121	6	..	54 4
1844	6,847,205	4,976,093	105,304	1,356,457	462,263	6,900,117	..	..	51 5

* Under this head is included In-door and Out-door Relief, Establishment Charges, and, since the passing of the Poor Law Amendment Act, in addition thereto, Building and Emigration Loans repaid, and Interest on Money borrowed under Poor Law Amendment Act.
† The year in which the expenditure for relief, &c., to the poor was at the minimum.
‡ Including in this and the following years expenses incurred under the Registration and Parochial Assessments Act.
§ In this and the following years the expense incurred in removal of paupers is included under the head of "Other Purposes."
‖ Including in this and subsequent years expenses incurred under the Vaccination Extension Act.

TOTAL AMOUNT of Money Levied and Expended under the following heads in England and Wales during the Ten Years prior and the Ten Years subsequent to the passing of the Poor Law Amendment Act.

Years.	Amount of Money Levied.	Amount of Money Expended in Relief and Maintenance of the Poor.	Expenditure in Law Charges, Removals, &c.	Expenditure for County Rate.	Expended for all other Purposes.	Total Parochial Rates Expended.
	£.	£.	£.	£.	£.	£.
1825 to 1834	79,037,092	64,559,994	(a)513,016	7,340,556	7,060,017	79,473,533
1835 to 1844	62,675,361	47,252,812	1,054,351	9,197,386	6,182,414	63,686,963
Decrease	16,361,731	17,307,132	..	..	877,603	15,786,570
Increase	..	..	..	1,856,830	..	..

(a) Total of two years only.

Note.—The amount expended for Law, &c., was not distinguished until 1833, previous to which time the expenditure under that head was included partly with Relief, &c., to the Poor, and partly under the head of other Purposes.

** The above results are obtained from the Annual Poor Rate Return received from Clerks to Unions and Overseers of the Poor.

No. 5. TABLE A.—Able-bodied who have received Out-door Relief, on account of being out Resident and

COUNTIES.	Married Men and Widowers having Children.											
	On Account of Want of Work.				On Account of Insufficiency of Earnings.				Other Causes not being Sickness, Accident, or Infirmity.			
	Out-door.				Out-door.				Out-door.			
	Resident.		Non-resident.		Resident.		Non-resident		Resident.		Non-resident	
	A.	C.	A.	C.	A.	C.	A.	C.	A.	C.	A.	C.
ENGLAND.												
Bedford	3	8	·	·	1	6	·	·	5	8	·	·
Berks	61	141	1	6	36	120	4	25	19	46	6	3
Buckingham	112	359	2	5	26	101	·	·	18	40	1	4
Cambridge	16	35	1	4	16	47	·	·	34	82	·	·
Chester	304	900	96	298	76	305	27	111	34	89	2	7
Cornwall	67	185	9	32	159	614	8	33	19	56	4	2
Cumberland	19	46	2	7	91	251	15	65	19	49	2	3
Derby	71	282	7	31	19	79	4	21	9	29	1	1
Devon	23	83	·	·	97	360	·	·	30	101	5	21
Dorset	51	189	9	43	95	356	9	42	65	238	2	8
Durham	429	1,186	14	39	52	123	8	20	14	38	3	12
Essex	18	65	1	3	27	69	1	4	76	204	·	·
Gloucester	132	359	1	3	32	108	·	·	21	75	·	·
Hereford	9	39	·	·	2	8	2	6	2	6	·	·
Hertford	69	204	·	·	9	40	·	·	32	68	1	8
Huntingdon	1	4	·	·	·	·	·	·	2	6	·	·
Kent	289	947	12	37	22	80	1	5	27	102	·	·
Lancaster	1,364	4,724	328	1,082	2,418	9,909	809	3,493	62	231	42	145
Leicester	86	334	·	·	192	807	32	144	21	60	1	1
Lincoln	39	139	·	·	31	107	·	·	30	99	·	·
Middlesex	1,010	3,635	155	493	311	939	186	587	32	94	32	77
Monmouth	64	243	8	29	78	253	9	42	30	86	·	·
Norfolk	76	285	1	6	171	458	17	34	28	82	1	3
Northampton	34	98	1	5	24	70	·	·	4	18	2	8
Northumberland	428	926	17	56	26	68	7	24	3	6	·	·
Nottingham	113	473	15	60	24	95	1	3	6	12	·	·
Oxford	24	62	2	8	11	52	·	·	6	16	·	·
Rutland	16	42	·	·	1	7	·	·	·	·	·	·
Salop	92	312	16	49	67	191	8	24	52	151	11	35
Somerset	73	255	8	27	54	228	·	·	24	62	1	2
Southampton	121	414	27	32	61	174	10	35	41	154	23	30
Stafford	257	918	11	44	6	16	1	8	6	4	·	·
Suffolk	196	699	6	24	30	151	·	·	25	66	9	12
Surrey	1,096	3,017	53	154	287	863	28	73	20	75	2	8
Sussex	48	182	2	10	13	53	1	2	34	85	·	·
Warwick	100	326	1	4	47	211	1	4	42	178	1	5
Westmoreland	163	297	8	9	43	180	6	28	4	11	·	·
Wilts	71	219	5	19	48	190	7	37	86	139	·	·
Worcester	297	829	29	49	120	495	·	37	123	286	·	·
York { East Riding	146	364	18	61	170	568	37	126	17	60	1	6
York { North Riding	63	195	16	55	81	266	23	78	20	71	3	7
York { West Riding	991	3,105	243	790	553	2,011	261	884	159	476	42	144
Totals of England	8,642	26,523	1,125	3,574	5,627	21,029	1,532	5,990	1,246	3,759	198	547
WALES.												
Anglesey	27	86	6	20	54	195	3	3	20	52	2	2
Breeon	14	27	·	·	36	128	9	26	2	·	·	·
Cardigan	14	43	2	4	34	138	·	·	·	·	·	·
Carmarthen	3	7	·	·	20	44	3	12	86	287	5	20
Carnarvon	121	320	14	36	84	286	18	56	29	67	6	13
Denbigh	21	73	2	5	139	217	56	83	·	·	·	·
Flint	5	16	·	·	24	92	·	·	23	73	·	·
Glamorgan	231	518	19	48	425	830	17	56	186	232	·	·
Merioneth	6	22	3	11	88	342	5	21	·	·	·	·
Montgomery	79	331	15	57	67	303	·	·	26	100	6	25
Pembroke	·	·	·	·	8	35	·	·	17	56	4	17
Radnor	9	44	·	·	14	62	5	30	2	4	·	·
Totals of Wales	530	1,487	61	181	993	2,675	116	287	391	871	23	77
Totals of 585 Unions in England and Wales.	9,172	28,010	1,186	3,755	6,620	23,704	1,648	6,277	1,637	4,630	221	624

of Work, and other Causes during the Quarter ended Lady-day, 1844, distinguishing the Non-resident.

Married Men and Widowers without Children, and Single Men.						Single Women, having an Illegitimate Child or Children.											
On Account of Want of Work.		On Account of Insufficiency of Earnings.		Other Causes not being Sickness, Accident, or Infirmity.		On Account of Want of Work.				On Account of Insufficiency of Earnings.				Other Causes, not being Sickness, Accident, or Infirmity.			
Out-door.		Out-door.		Out-door.		Out-door.				Out-door.				Out-door.			
R.	N.R.	R.	N.R.	R.	N.R.	Resident.		Non-resident.		Resident.		Non-resident.		Resident.		Non-resident.	
A.	A.	A.	A.	A.	A.	A.	C.	A.	C.	A.	C.	A.	C.	A.	C.	A.	C.
26	·	11	·	3	·	·	·	·	·	2	5	·	·	4	4	·	·
31	1	5	·	2	·	3	3	·	·	13	16	·	·	2	2	1	3
24	·	1	·	12	·	3	3	·	·	11	13	·	·	5	7	·	·
2	·	1	·	16	·	3	5	·	·	3	3	1	2	1	1	·	·
101	14	11	8	·	1	47	66	3	4	214	260	89	50	5	7	2	3
14	·	8	·	3	·	6	9	·	·	95	111	6	7	34	42	·	·
4	·	2	·	4	·	·	·	·	·	6	11	1	3	·	·	·	·
11	3	3	·	2	3	1	4	·	·	3	5	·	·	·	·	·	·
3	·	7	·	9	·	·	·	·	·	44	50	10	12	17	18	·	·
30	·	4	4	18	·	19	28	·	·	31	36	3	3	·	·	·	·
146	5	5	·	10	6	27	37	·	·	20	31	9	11	3	3	·	·
5	·	1	·	16	·	3	5	·	·	13	13	1	1	9	10	·	·
19	·	8	2	5	·	2	7	·	·	10	18	·	·	·	·	·	·
·	·	3	·	8	·	7	10	·	·	6	14	·	·	·	·	·	·
16	·	·	·	·	·	1	1	·	·	1	1	·	·	6	5	·	·
2	·	·	·	·	·	1	1	·	·	·	·	·	·	·	·	·	·
148	5	7	1	21	·	64	90	1	2	25	34	1	1	2	2	·	·
311	28	156	33	90	31	229	330	31	48	220	1,388	179	276	32	45	9	10
19	5	56	7	2	·	8	8	·	·	20	22	5	5	·	·	·	·
8	·	7	·	2	3	2	2	·	·	2	4	·	·	·	·	5	·
411	74	65	33	40	48	62	85	21	28	49	81	44	75	12	15	34	39
205	·	11	·	·	·	2	2	·	·	13	14	·	·	21	2	·	·
44	1	5	·	7	·	1	1	·	·	5	10	·	·	3	8	·	·
6	·	4	·	2	·	·	·	·	·	2	2	·	·	2	3	·	·
128	11	8	·	1	·	130	164	10	11	40	50	7	10	16	16	2	2
11	1	10	·	3	·	2	3	·	·	1	1	·	·	4	4	·	·
6	·	7	·	4	·	·	·	·	·	1	1	·	·	1	1	·	·
6	2	·	·	·	·	3	5	·	·	4	5	·	·	24	33	3	3
14	5	12	4	11	1	20	27	1	3	6	9	·	·	2	3	·	·
29	·	3	·	25	·	4	8	·	·	31	43	·	·	2	1	·	·
16	1	15	·	15	·	25	44	1	2	26	45	1	1	·	·	·	·
50	4	·	·	2	·	10	10	2	4	·	·	1	1	·	·	·	·
37	6	·	·	6	4	10	11	·	·	2	2	·	·	·	·	·	·
608	25	45	4	10	1	145	220	13	21	87	163	19	30	3	13	1	7
24	1	10	2	19	·	1	1	·	·	3	4	·	·	2	2	·	·
17	·	2	·	12	·	·	·	·	·	8	9	·	·	3	3	·	·
82	·	10	1	·	·	40	43	6	8	23	32	7	18	1	·	1	3
88	7	18	2	10	2	1	3	·	·	8	7	8	8	7	8	3	1
102	·	7	·	5	·	6	7	·	·	23	30	7	7	1	2	3	5
36	8	31	15	10	3	1	3	·	·	79	112	34	35	·	·	1	1
21	7	42	20	6	1	24	50	14	22	45	53	26	47	6	13	1	1
594	115	116	49	31	15	115	141	23	25	1,089	1,279	123	171	27	78	38	·
3,389	**329**	**716**	**285**	**437**	**119**	**1,035**	**1,425**	**126**	**187**	**2,963**	**3,974**	**531**	**773**	**241**	**351**	**91**	**68**
4	2	26	·	6	·	25	30	3	3	103	115	12	14	10	11	·	·
·	·	·	·	·	·	·	·	·	·	12	11	·	·	·	·	·	·
2	·	4	2	50	9	6	6	4	4	89	96	·	·	·	·	·	·
1	·	·	5	·	·	1	1	·	·	13	17	·	·	1	1	1	1
9	3	37	·	·	·	62	64	4	4	126	145	12	12	9	18	·	·
6	·	46	17	·	·	·	·	·	·	20	20	4	4	·	·	·	·
13	2	·	·	6	·	·	·	·	·	·	·	·	·	3	3	·	·
100	6	41	2	33	9	·	·	·	·	76	117	7	10	5	7	·	·
1	1	5	·	6	·	·	·	·	·	7	7	·	4	·	·	·	·
·	·	·	·	·	·	100	116	·	·	129	194	·	·	18	19	·	·
·	·	·	·	·	·	·	·	·	·	4	9	·	·	3	3	·	·
3	·	5	·	·	·	·	·	·	·	30	43	7	10	·	·	·	·
139	**14**	**164**	**26**	**101**	**18**	**194**	**217**	**11**	**11**	**609**	**784**	**49**	**54**	**44**	**62**	**1**	**1**
3,528	**343**	**880**	**261**	**538**	**137**	**1,229**	**1,642**	**137**	**198**	**3,592**	**4,758**	**573**	**827**	**285**	**413**	**92**	**69**

No. 5, (continued). TABLE A.—Able-bodied who have received Out-door Relief on account the Resident and

COUNTIES.	Women, not having a Child or Children whose Husbands have deserted them.						Other Able-bodied W							
	On Account of Want of Work. Out-door.		On account of Insufficiency of Earnings. Out-door.		Other Causes not being Sickness, Accident, or Infirmity. Out-door.		[On Account] of Want of Work. Out-door.				On Account of Insufficiency of Earnings. Out-door.			
	R.	N.R.	R.	N.R.	R.	N.R.	Resident.		Non-resident.		Resident.		Non-resident.	
	A.	A.	A.	A.	A.	A.	A.	C.	A.	C.	A.	C.	A.	C.
ENGLAND.														
Bedford	•	•	•	•	3	•	•	•	•	•	•	•	•	•
Berks	20	•	13	•	1	•	5	1	•	•	1	4	•	•
Buckingham	25	•	29	•	18	3	10	30	1	•	11	38	•	•
Cambridge	3	•	12	1	9	•	•	•	•	•	11	19	•	•
Chester	26	5	12	•	19	2	3	5	1	1	7	19	•	•
Cornwall	11	•	45	1	11	•	3	2	•	•	6	1	•	•
Cumberland	7	3	•	4	6	2	8	2	•	•	2	1	2	•
Derby	6	•	•	•	5	1	4	•	•	•	1	•	•	•
Devon	•	•	18	•	12	2	•	•	•	•	94	115	3	•
Dorset	31	•	18	•	9	•	20	11	•	•	70	35	5	•
Durham	20	•	16	•	4	•	1	3	1	1	12	6	4	•
Essex	2	•	32	6	33	•	3	•	•	•	1	3	•	•
Gloucester	12	•	80	13	2	•	7	7	•	•	6	13	•	•
Hereford	2	•	5	•	3	•	•	•	•	•	•	•	•	•
Hertford	16	•	20	•	2	•	1	•	•	•	3	10	•	•
Huntingdon	•	•	•	•	•	•	1	•	•	•	•	•	•	•
Kent	106	•	30	4	8	•	30	113	2	•	3	3	•	•
Lancaster	258	29	229	55	40	27	32	2	3	•	26	32	2	3
Leicester	3	2	12	6	•	•	•	•	•	•	5	•	•	•
Lincoln	8	•	5	•	1	•	2	3	•	•	5	•	•	•
Middlesex	212	63	107	187	101	33	111	54	7	2	25	35	7	•
Monmouth	6	•	1	•	•	•	•	•	•	•	5	11	•	•
Norfolk	23	•	1	•	9	•	5	11	•	•	5	13	•	•
Northampton	•	•	24	3	4	•	•	•	•	•	10	17	•	•
Northumberland	95	6	23	8	1	•	4	•	•	•	31	57	16	•
Nottingham	4	2	•	•	3	•	9	4	•	•	•	•	•	•
Oxford	4	1	15	•	9	•	•	•	•	•	1	2	•	•
Rutland	8	•	4	•	1	•	6	3	•	•	3	5	•	•
Salop	7	•	17	8	11	1	•	•	•	•	3	3	•	•
Somerset	25	3	10	•	10	•	1	•	•	•	7	20	2	•
Southampton	28	6	58	1	17	•	1	2	•	•	21	4	28	•
Stafford	11	•	10	•	1	•	3	5	3	•	4	•	•	•
Suffolk	5	•	33	•	•	•	•	•	•	•	•	•	•	•
Surrey	487	46	215	22	22	4	68	116	3	2	75	128	16	•
Sussex	2	•	3	2	5	•	2	•	•	•	9	9	•	•
Warwick	7	•	3	•	4	•	5	9	2	•	3	7	1	•
Westmoreland	3	1	5	2	•	•	•	•	•	•	•	•	•	•
Wilts	67	1	25	3	18	•	7	16	•	•	25	37	•	•
Worcester	6	•	32	3	8	•	2	•	•	•	3	2	•	•
York { East Riding	11	6	45	5	9	2	•	•	•	•	9	18	6	•
York { North Riding	27	10	72	29	6	•	5	5	•	•	54	109	14	•
York { West Riding	110	43	177	30	50	16	30	43	7	15	51	105	7	•
Totals of England	1,704	227	1,456	393	475	93	393	447	27	22	612	364	114	•
WALES.														
Anglesey	10	•	80	8	34	4	•	•	•	•	6	•	•	•
Brecon	•	•	•	•	•	•	•	•	•	•	•	•	•	•
Cardigan	•	•	•	•	•	•	•	•	•	•	•	•	•	•
Carmarthen	•	•	4	•	85	4	1	•	•	•	7	•	•	•
Carnarvon	66	11	17	•	17	5	3	3	•	•	1	1	•	•
Denbigh	2	•	18	2	•	•	•	•	•	•	•	•	•	•
Flint	20	•	15	•	36	6	•	•	•	•	•	•	•	•
Glamorgan	7	•	4	4	54	5	15	•	•	•	22	26	11	•
Merioneth	•	•	7	•	•	•	•	•	•	•	41	26	5	•
Montgomery	•	•	2	•	•	•	•	•	•	•	3	9	•	•
Pembroke	•	•	3	•	•	•	•	•	•	•	•	•	•	•
Radnor	4	•	12	1	•	•	•	•	•	•	•	•	•	•
Totals of Wales	109	11	162	15	226	24	19	3	•	•	80	36	16	19
Totals of 585 Unions in England and Wales	1,813	238	1,618	408	701	117	412	450	27	22	692	900	130	191

of being out of Work, and other Causes during the Quarter ended Lady-day, 1844, distinguishing and Non-resident

Table headings:
- **Included in Table B.** — Other Causes not being Sickness, Accident, or Infirmity. (Out-door): Resident (A., C.), Non-resident (A., C.)
- **Wives of Married Men above mentioned.**: On Account of Want of Work (Out-door) R., N.R.; On Account of Insufficiency of Earnings (Out-door) R., N.R.; Other Causes not being Sickness, Accident, or Infirmity (Out-door) R., N.R.
- **Totals of the Six Classes.**: Resident (A., C.), Non-resident (A., C.)
- **Grand Total Adults and Children**

Other Res. A.	Other Res. C.	Other N.R. A.	Other N.R. C.	Want Work R.A.	Want Work N.R.A.	Insuff. R.A.	Insuff. N.R.A.	Other Causes R.A.	Other Causes N.R.A.	Tot. Res. A.	Tot. Res. C.	Tot. N.R. A.	Tot. N.R. C.	Grand Total
				2		27	2	2		51	31			82
				16	1	12		8		271	337	16	37	661
				109	1	18		9		427	553	9	9	998
				7	1	64	25	20		179	218	4	6	407
2	4			327	98	154	7	23	2	1,281	1,670	323	477	3,751
	6			55	5	17	14	13		715	1,094	40	74	1,853
8				19	2	21	4	13	2	217	360	49	80	706
8	19	3	3	71	1	72		10	1	238	404	25	53	720
7	4			16		21	5	16	11	489	741	29	46	1,305
1	5			28	6	72		35		600	925	43	103	1,671
27	19	2		444	10	53	7	7		1,264	1,431	67	85	2,847
10	36			14		12		54		352	391	10	8	761
1	4			105	1	14		9		459	587	15	3	1,064
34	22			7		1	1	1		51	77	5	6	139
				69		7		23	1	287	329	3	8	627
3						2		2		10	13			28
1	2			255	13	11	1	27		1,085	1,388	44	46	2,563
9	15	8	1	1,303	265	2,291	623	70	32	9,835	16,665	2,527	5,061	34,088
4	12	2	4	67		152	18	13	1	651	1,231	77	150	2,109
42	29			40		28		22		272	883	7	3	665
88	141	15	16	995	159	285	215	42	22	3,958	4,480	1,380	1,311	11,129
1	1			100	8	68	7	23		608	612	32	71	1,323
3	3			72	1	75	2	3		534	871	25	43	1,473
1				34	1	15		5		173	217	5	5	400
6	10	3	9	430	21	22	2	1	2	1,394	1,297	114	155	2,960
				103	15	27	1	1		317	588	34	63	1,002
1	2			21	2	9		3		125	137	6	8	276
1		1		23		1				77	71	2		150
9	6			73	6	61	7	43	7	520	729	80	113	1,442
8	5			65	8	41		22		434	693	19	32	1,108
2	3			99	18	48	3	22	8	633	943	127	99	1,702
9	4			210	13	6		21		574	956	35	52	1,617
32	95	3	5	172	6	6		21		536	933	38	36	1,546
2	2			1,159	54	228	16	17	2	4,599	4,690	316	333	9,938
1	6			46	1	6	26	41	1	254	338	10	12	614
8	17			95		40	1	2		430	749	8	14	1,201
4				163	2	22	5	2		510	553	39	66	1,168
7	17	4	5	77	7	36	7	30		574	635	50	65	1,324
82	210	18	55	297	6	113	9	11	2	1,160	1,651	66	98	2,975
56	112	11	21	166	25	181	44	17	2	935	1,142	210	243	2,530
				54	13	66	33	22	1	696	970	229	283	2,178
				1,097	213	480	213	115	32	5,889	7,351	1,442	2,094	16,776
478	**811**	**70**	**119**	**8,505**	**983**	**4,861**	**1,298**	**819**	**127**	**43,667**	**59,194**	**7,560**	**11,451**	**121,872**
				29	7	63	1	21		518	499	48	42	1,097
				6		34	6	1		105	166	15	26	312
						26				171	283	6	8	468
11		1				11	3	48	4	346	357	32	33	768
16	51			120	10	99	23	22	6	838	955	117	121	2,031
				13	2	109	36			374	320	119	92	905
31	51			4		4		27		211	235	8	8	454
154	382	10	20	117	8	216	10	90	4	1,776	2,086	112	134	4,108
						62	3	21		248	397	17	51	713
				80	7	58		20	6	577	1,072	34	82	1,765
						7		14		56	106	8	17	187
1				7		15	4	2		104	153	17	40	314
213	**484**	**11**	**20**	**376**	**34**	**704**	**86**	**266**	**24**	**5,324**	**6,619**	**533**	**646**	**13,122**
691	**1,295**	**81**	**139**	**8,881**	**1,017**	**5,565**	**1,384**	**1,085**	**151**	**48,991**	**65,813**	**8,093**	**12,097**	**134,994**

No. 5, (*continued*). TABLE A.—COMPARATIVE STATEMENT of the Number of Able-bodied Persons who have received Out-door Relief, on account of being out of Work and other causes (*not being Sickness, Accident, or Infirmity*) during the Quarters ended Lady-day, 1843 and 1844, in 585 Unions, in the several Counties of England and Wales.

Description of Paupers.	Quarters ended Lady-day.	On Account of Want of Work.		On Account of Insufficiency of Earnings.		Other Causes, not being Sickness, Accident, or Infirmity.		Total.		Grand Total.
		Adults.	Children.	Adults.	Children.	Adults.	Children.	Adults.	Children.	
Married men and widowers having children	1843	20,752	62,465	11,325	40,542	2,229	6,073	34,306	109,070	143,376
	1844	10,858	31,765	8,268	29,981	1,858	5,254	20,484	67,000	87,484
Married men and widowers without children, and single men	1843	7,553	..	1,483	..	1,023	..	10,059	..	10,059
	1844	3,871	..	1,141	..	675	..	5,687	..	5,687
Single women having an illegitimate child or children	1843	1,336	1,732	3,596	4,945	439	583	5,361	7,210	12,571
	1844	1,366	1,840	4,165	5,585	377	482	5,908	7,907	13,815
Women not having a child or children, whose husbands have deserted them	1843	2,821	..	2,350	..	869	..	6,040	..	6,040
	1844	2,051	..	2,026	..	818	..	4,895	..	4,895
Other able-bodied women not included in Table B	1843	650	700	873	1,096	752	1,362	2,275	3,158	5,433
	1844	439	472	822	1,091	772	1,434	2,033	2,997	5,030
Wives of married men above mentioned	1843	20,998	..	9,777	..	1,406	..	32,181	..	32,181
	1844	9,898	..	6,949	..	1,236	..	18,083	..	18,083
Totals of 585 Unions	1843	54,110	64,887	29,394	46,583	6,718	7,968	90,222	119,438	209,660
	1844	27,983	34,077	23,371	36,657	5,736	7,170	57,090	77,994	134,994

No. 5, (*continued*). TABLE B.—SUMMARY, showing the Number of Widows having a Child or Children under 16 dependent on them, who have received Out-door Relief during the Quarter ended Lady-day, 1844.

COUNTIES.	Widows having a Child or Children.							
	On Account of Sickness, Accident, or Infirmity.				On Account of Want of Work.			
	Out-door.				Out-door.			
	Resident.		Non-resident.		Resident.		Non-resident.	
	A.	C.	A.	C.	A.	C.	A.	C.
ENGLAND.								
Bedford	6	9						
Berks	60	130	6	9	60	136	6	17
Buckingham	127	241	3	13	30	53	1	3
Cambridge	28	53	11	25	99	179	19	37
Chester	62	143	9	20	23	65	6	14
Cornwall	37	85	6	10	69	164	6	11
Cumberland	41	95	24	65	41	103	4	8
Derby	26	105	6	29	36	183	10	48
Devon	186	386	12	34	27	65	15	56
Dorset	154	441	16	41	19	39		
Durham	83	130	23	53	18	43	7	15
Essex	17	40	2	4	1	4		
Gloucester	46	129	9	20	33	109	1	
Hereford	17	35	5	10				
Hertford	65	173	2	5	1	2		
Huntingdon	5	11	4	10	4	6		
Kent	54	126	9	17	164	401	11	41
Lancaster	296	539	52	106	287	672	64	194
Leicester	134	346	42	130	34	109	3	11
Lincoln	82	129	5	10	20	45		
Middlesex	76	160	38	97	153	309	60	154
Monmouth	7	12	1	3				
Norfolk	152	313	9	17	167	549	11	35
Northampton	9	10	1	1			1	4
Northumberland	100	267	35	80	111	276	21	39
Nottingham	15	35	10	33	16	40	2	3
Oxford	37	96	1	4	12	17		
Rutland	3	7			5	14		
Salop	38	107	13	27	16	41	6	18
Somerset	144	310	19	24	6	14		
Southampton	105	234	12	25	48	120	2	2
Stafford	68	158	15	39	7	9	2	10
Suffolk	58	139	2	5	90	281	23	56
Surrey	162	378	27	66	193	414	33	82
Sussex	55	135	13	32	4	5		
Warwick	40	55	5	10	4	11		
Westmoreland	12	10	7	8				
Wilts	60	117	6	14	47	115	4	9
Worcester	192	347	27	45	79	210	2	6
York ⎧ East Riding	18	32	6	6	6	9	5	12
⎨ North Riding	47	117	7	14	19	56	3	13
⎩ West Riding	82	187	29	61	126	281	76	153
Totals of England	2,996	6,572	529	1,222	2,075	5,149	404	1,051
WALES.								
Anglesey	19	36	5	9	13	21	3	6
Brecon	9	16	6	16				
Cardigan	8	13						
Carmarthen	8	11	7	22				
Carnarvon	40	61	15	27	31	53	2	7
Denbigh	75	198	10	21	2	6	2	8
Flint	27	49			72	148		
Glamorgan	138	305	53	135	3	7		
Merioneth	16	19	4	9				
Montgomery	24	17			19	23		
Pembroke	26	30						
Radnor	13	15	2	6	11	19		
Totals of Wales	403	770	102	245	151	279	7	21
Totals of 585 Unions in England and Wales.	3,399	7,342	631	1,467	2,226	5,428	411	1,072

No. 5, (*continued*). TABLE B.—SUMMARY, showing the Number of Widows having a
ended

	Widows having a Child or Children.						
	On Account of Insufficiency of Earnings.				Other Causes.		
COUNTIES.	Out-door.				Out-door.		
	Resident.		Non-Resident.		Resident.		Non-Residen
	A.	C.	A.	C.	A.	C.	A.
ENGLAND.							
Bedford	347	989	17	52	.	.	.
Berks	392	1,124	51	156	.	.	.
Buckingham	572	1,454	29	77	8	21	.
Cambridge	436	1,135	21	57	103	213	4
Chester	636	1,648	266	711	6	21	1
Cornwall	899	2,352	93	216	8	11	4
Cumberland	356	821	135	408	9	25	10
Derby	267	776	57	161	10	17	3
Devon	778	1,732	79	216	98	182	16
Dorset	512	1,305	55	158	20	47	.
Durham	965	2,465	386	1,019	45	43	13
Essex	1,164	3,082	86	256	6	13	.
Gloucester	817	2,437	180	514	17	19	.
Hereford	271	723	50	129	3	14	1
Hertford	401	1,071	31	103	50	117	1
Huntingdon	166	444	13	38	.	.	.
Kent	1,111	3,102	229	607	3	9	.
Lancaster	1,891	5,661	656	2,107	16	39	1
Leicester	727	1,758	75	217	8	26	3
Lincoln	911	2,278	55	145	.	.	.
Middlesex	1,137	3,021	620	1,756	27	68	19
Monmouth	320	835	46	157	23	37	21
Norfolk	799	2,189	99	246	144	377	16
Northampton	808	1,940	44	118	.	.	.
Northumberland	551	1,407	317	780	42	108	13
Nottingham	471	1,422	67	185	3	8	1
Oxford	530	1,308	34	88	.	.	.
Rutland	43	95	11	27	.	.	.
Salop	255	624	104	309	.	139	20
Somerset	1,327	3,551	156	408	2	1	1
Southampton	821	1,966	94	270	9	21	.
Stafford	709	2,110	91	290	1	1	1
Suffolk	963	2,554	63	176	32	98	4
Surrey	918	2,490	159	454	59	193	8
Sussex	584	1,726	131	389	.	.	.
Warwick	438	1,193	44	131	8	21	1
Westmoreland	124	313	52	162	.	.	.
Wilts	907	2,546	152	411	2	4	1
Worcester	774	2,178	109	309	25	68	9
York { East Riding	390	943	171	465	.	.	3
North Riding	302	759	153	349	7	26	8
West Riding	1,627	4,118	555	1,577	78	227	14
Totals of England	28,417	75,645	5,836	16,404	955	2,214	197
WALES.							
Anglesey	181	301	50	111	43	56	8
Brecon	117	286	29	75	5	13	.
Cardigan	256	773	24	52	.	.	.
Carmarthen	455	1,108	80	219	1	.	.
Carnarvon	380	1,108	110	217	12	23	9
Denbigh	140	320	77	199	9	35	3
Flint	223	436	32	91	8	27	.
Glamorgan	409	1,005	50	152	34	66	2
Merioneth	178	349	62	161	.	.	.
Montgomery	196	508	15	35	17	39	.
Pembroke	196	496	46	117	70	182	25
Radnor	59	150	30	65	2	6	.
Totals of Wales	2,790	6,840	605	1,494	201	447	47
Totals of 585 Unions in } England and Wales . }	31,207	82,485			1,156	2,661	

have deserted them, or who are Transported, having a Child or Children under 16 dependent during the Quarter ended Lady-day, 1844.

Wives (whose Husbands have deserted them) having a Child or Children.

On account of Sickness, Accident, or Infirmity.				On account of Want of Work.				On account of Insufficiency of Earnings.				Other Causes.			
Out-door.				Out-door.				Out-door.				Out-door.			
Resident.		Non-Resident.		Resident.		Non-Resident.		Resident.		Non-Resident.		Resident.		Non-Resident.	
A.	C.	A.	C.	A.	C.	A.	C.	A.	C.	A.	C.	A.	C.	A.	C.
1	2	.	.	3	6	1	1	21	59	1	1	1	3	1	3
1	3	.	.	.	.	.	.	12	31	1	4	.	.	.	.
13	20	3	6	18	32	1	2	47	140	1	4	15	29	1	3
9	20	3	6	7	17	.	.	54	111	3	9	1	3	4	6
10	28	1	1	24	50	2	10	51	140	29	65	5	16	1	.
12	30	.	.	3	4	.	.	79	221	6	22	1	6	.	.
2	8	1	5	.	.	2	6	28	80	12	31	.	.	.	.
48	77	3	9	11	33	5	17	16	52	1	2	15	33	1	3
21	64	9	17	2	3	1	5	106	291	9	23	.	.	.	.
27	75	1	5	12	29	3	7	37	115	4	12	8	22	1	2
1	7	2	2	1	4	.	.	60	132	14	29	14	30	2	2
1	4	1	3	.	.	.	.	35	99	.	.	3	5	1	2
9	27	1	3	.	.	.	.	59	180	6	13	1	2	.	.
1	1	.	.	.	.	.	.	16	42	1	3	3	10	.	.
10	29	1	2	10	22	.	.	7	20	.	3	.	.	.	.
118	207	10	18	90	202	11	23	13	31	.	.	3	7	.	.
12	34	2	7	3	9	.	.	69	204	8	17	2	5	2	6
6	19	.	.	3	13	.	.	307	861	67	222	.	.	.	.
7	20	4	12	7	17	4	14	91	263	6	22	.	.	.	.
2	8	.	.	.	.	.	.	44	132	.	6	4	7	1	1
18	60	.	.	12	44	.	.	49	126	25	73	6	20	.	.
.	.	1	2	3	8	.	.	37	98	.	.	10	36	.	.
25	76	16	34	71	171	6	15	155	274	26	65	16	44	.	.
9	26	.	.	1	6	.	.	21	57	.	.	.	.	.	.
.	.	.	.	2	9	.	.	71	156	32	81	.	.	.	.
1	1	.	.	.	.	.	.	43	141	7	24	.	.	.	.
7	19	3	7	5	20	.	.	37	109	5	15	.	.	.	.
11	22	.	.	5	8	2	8	4	10	.	.	4	13	5	15
16	26	.	.	6	17	2	3	23	55	4	11	8	22	1	4
21	50	.	4	11	32	2	3	131	347	4	9	6	22	4	16
3	6	1	4	.	.	1	2	75	187	2	5	.	.	1	.
25	85	6	12	23	62	1	3	28	83	8	22	4	10	1	4
8	17	.	.	4	8	.	.	38	123	.	.	.	.	.	.
.	.	.	.	.	.	.	.	45	143	1	3	3	7	.	.
6	14	1	1	38	128	2	5	47	158	11	31	1	4	.	.
11	20	1	2	12	53	.	.	24	54	.	.	6	15	.	.
2	4	.	.	1	2	.	.	17	50	3	12	.	.	.	.
2	4	.	.	5	8	2	3	61	157	9	26	.	.	.	.
.	.	.	.	.	.	.	.	68	191	1	3	.	.	.	.
.	.	.	.	.	.	.	.	59	150	16	56	.	.	.	.
.	.	.	.	.	.	.	.	19	42	6	10	.	.	.	.
9	19	5	13	40	92	15	39	216	496	60	149	18	50	4	12
485	**1,132**	**76**	**171**	**433**	**1,109**	**61**	**168**	**2,420**	**6,416**	**392**	**1,080**	**158**	**421**	**31**	**81**
.	.	.	.	1	2	.	.	10	27	2	4	1	1	.	.
5	14	.	.	.	.	.	.	12	23	9	25	.	.	.	.
.	.	.	.	.	.	.	.	18	61	.	.	.	.	.	.
2	6	.	.	2	5	.	.	15	39	2	3	2	3	1	2
11	36	.	.	7	19	.	.	21	51	9	27	1	2	3	11
2	5	.	.	.	.	.	.	22	51	2	5	5	18	.	.
4	6	.	.	.	.	.	.	3	10	.	.	.	.	.	.
17	62	2	6	.	.	.	.	51	121	.	.	4	10	.	.
11	22	4	9	.	.	.	.	20	20	2	4	.	.	.	.
3	7	.	.	3	8	.	.	31	123	3	7	3	7	.	.
3	11	.	.	.	.	.	.	3	6	2	4	6	21	.	.
1	1	.	.	.	.	.	.	4	11	1	5	.	.	.	.
59	**170**	**6**	**15**	**13**	**34**	**.**	**.**	**210**	**542**	**32**	**84**	**22**	**62**	**4**	**13**
544	**1,302**	**82**	**186**	**446**	**1,143**	**61**	**163**	**2,630**	**6,958**	**424**	**1,164**	**180**	**483**	**35**	**94**

No. 5, (*continued.*) TABLE B.—SUMMARY of the Number of Women whose Husbands
dependent on them, who have received Out-

COUNTIES.	Resident.		Non-Resident.		On account of Want of Work.			
					Resident.		Non-Resident.	
	A.	C.	A.		A.	C.	A.	C.
ENGLAND.								
Bedford	.				.	.	.	
Berks	5				3	8		
Buckingham	4				1	3		
Cambridge	1				9	24		13
Chester	7				4	10		5
Cornwall	7				4	9		.
Cumberland	.				1	4		
Derby	3				1	6		
Devon	36				1	5		30
Dorset	3				1	4		
Durham	14				6	14		.
Essex	.				.	.		
Gloucester	2				1	2		.
Hereford	6				.	.		
Hertford	6				.	.		
Huntingdon . . .	2				.	.		
Kent	7	13			9	29		
Lancaster	33	61			41	77		4
Leicester	6				1	3		
Lincoln	3				1	4		
Middlesex	20				5	11		1
Monmouth	.				.	.		
Norfolk	13				4	15		2
Northampton . . .	2				.	.		1
Northumberland . . .	23				26	66		
Nottingham	.				.	.		
Oxford	.				3	10		
Rutland	.				.	.		
Salop	1				.	.		4
Somerset	4				.	.		
Southampton	19				1	6		4
Stafford	13				2	5		.
Suffolk	4				1	1		.
Surrey	10				25	59		6
Sussex	2				.	.		
Warwick	2				.	.		
Westmoreland	.				.	.		
Wilts	5				8	25		4
Worcester	22				16	74		
York { East Riding . .	.				.	.		
{ North Riding .	2				2	8		.
{ West Riding .	13				10	28		26
Totals of England . .	300	672	33	87	187	510	37	104
WALES.								
Anglesey					.	.	.	.
Brecon					.	.	.	.
Cardigan					.	.	.	.
Carmarthen					2	2	.	.
Carnarvon					.	.	.	.
Denbigh					10	33	.	.
Flint					.	.	.	.
Glamorgan					1	3	.	.
Meriogeth					.	.	.	.
Montgomery					.	.	.	.
Pembroke					.	.	.	.
Radnor				.	.	.	.	.
Totals of Wales . . .		73		3	13	35	.	.
Totals of 585 Unions in } England and Wales . }	325	745	34	90	200	545	37	104

have deserted them, or who are Transported, having a Child or Children under 16 door Relief during the Quarter ended Lady-day, 1844.

than Desertion.) having a Child, or Children.

On account of Insufficiency of Earnings. Out-door.				Other Causes. Out-door.				Totals of the three Classes.				Grand Total Adults and Children
Resident.		Non-Resident.		Resident.		Non-Resident.		Resident.		Non-Resident.		
A.	C.	A.	C.	A.	C.	A.	C.	A.	C.	A.	C.	
36	91	.	.	.	.	.	.	410	1,148	18	53	1,629
16	54	2	7	.	.	.	.	553	1,507	68	197	2,325
56	159	3	6	23	57	.	.	869	2,147	39	109	3,164
52	155	2	7	4	12	.	.	837	1,965	71	168	3,041
44	137	7	22	21	73	5	11	871	2,296	335	873	4,375
29	89	1	2	12	37	2	3	1,183	3,074	123	283	4,663
9	31	6	27	1	3	.	.	502	1,202	191	562	2,457
10	30	1	5	.	.	.	.	371	1,192	83	268	1,914
34	98	1	6	20	42	.	.	1,360	3,093	154	438	4,955
30	82	2	6	3	8	.	.	802	2,124	87	239	3,252
51	124	2	4	5	11	3	9	1,294	3,126	453	1,178	6,051
56	153	1	2	4	14	.	.	1,297	3,435	91	264	5,087
50	158	4	11	5	16	1	2	1,035	3,074	205	567	4,881
17	52	.	.	.	.	.	.	832	894	56	143	1,425
13	37	.	.	2	5	.	.	557	1,480	36	118	2,191
16	48	.	.	.	.	.	.	207	544	17	48	816
65	193	8	20	7	25	.	.	1,512	4,160	268	708	6,648
171	518	30	88	14	35	5	20	3,256	8,877	904	2,811	15,848
47	159	1	2	.	.	.	.	1,063	2,726	132	402	4,323
27	78	3	12	.	.	.	.	1,097	2,707	66	173	4,043
51	157	20	50	9	26	3	6	1,545	3,933	798	2,224	8,555
9	24	.	.	1	3	.	.	405	1,037	68	187	1,697
38	99	5	18	9	12	.	.	1,521	4,002	167	420	6,110
39	116	.	.	11	28	1	3	893	2,164	48	128	3,233
109	290	3	12	.	.	.	.	1,145	2,907	443	1,068	5,563
31	98	.	.	6	20	.	.	595	1,796	87	248	2,726
29	63	.	.	.	.	.	.	650	1,612	40	107	2,409
1	2	1	2	2	6	.	.	59	135	12	29	235
24	66	1	6	6	20	1	5	457	1,107	158	459	2,181
132	362	4	12	20	66	1	3	1,790	4,713	189	471	7,163
64	155	3	6	3	12	1	.	1,167	2,784	114	308	4,373
46	155	17	59	2	2	1	4	914	2,652	144	455	4,165
81	232	4	6	.	.	.	.	1,270	3,442	102	280	5,094
58	171	10	24	17	62	1	2	1,539	4,089	248	680	6,556
21	75	3	11	12	45	4	12	737	2,172	163	479	3,551
29	96	2	7	1	4	.	.	549	1,445	52	153	2,199
31	83	12	35	.	.	.	.	185	460	74	217	936
62	198	6	14	6	18	1	4	1,208	3,352	183	490	5,233
36	107	1	6	2	8	.	.	1,237	3,282	152	392	5,063
24	73	9	33	11	29	1	2	511	1,242	212	581	2,546
13	35	4	12	.	.	.	.	418	1,056	183	425	2,082
180	475	56	157	15	40	2	4	2,414	6,039	829	2,229	11,511
1,937	5,578	235	697	254	739	32	90	40,617	106,157	7,863	21,632	176,269
.	.	.	.	1	1	.	.	269	445	68	141	923
10	41	.	.	.	.	.	.	160	401	44	116	721
16	45	1	4	.	.	.	.	299	896	25	56	1,276
7	20	.	.	5	21	1	2	499	1,215	91	248	2,053
21	71	.	.	.	.	1	3	521	1,420	149	320	2,410
5	20	.	.	.	.	.	.	287	731	94	245	1,357
2	3	.	.	.	.	.	.	339	679	32	91	1,141
14	31	.	.	.	.	.	.	676	1,625	108	302	2,711
1	3	.	.	1	3	.	.	228	418	72	183	901
4	11	.	.	.	.	.	.	300	743	18	42	1,103
.	.	.	.	3	10	.	.	308	758	73	185	1,324
2	6	2	6	.	.	.	.	93	210	35	82	420
82	251	3	10	10	35	2	5	3,979	9,541	809	2,011	16,340
2,019	5,829	238	707	264	774	34	95	44,596	115,698	8,672	23,643	192,609

No. 5, (*continued.*) TABLE B.—COMPARATIVE STATEMENT of the Number of Widows, and Women whose Husbands have deserted them, or who are Transported, having a Child or Children under 16 dependent on them, who have received Out-door Relief during the Quarters ended Lady-day 1843 and 1844, in 585 Unions in the several Counties of England and Wales.

Description of Paupers.	Quarters ended Lady-day.	On Account of Sickness, Accident, or Infirmity.		On Account of Want of Work.		On Account of Insufficiency of Earnings.		Other Causes.		Total.		Grand Total.
		Adults.	Children.	Adults.	Children.	Adults.	Children.	Adults.	Children.	Adults.	Children.	
Widows having a child or children	1843	3,532	6,102	3,245	7,896	36,521	95,937	1,698	4,000	44,996	115,935	160,931
	1844	4,030	8,809	2,637	6,500	37,648	100,353	1,400	3,259	45,715	118,951	164,666
Wives whose husbands have deserted them, &c., having a child or children.	1843	550	1,299	599	1,540	3,332	8,710	281	713	4,762	12,262	17,024
	1844	626	1,488	507	1,311	3,054	8,122	215	577	4,402	11,498	15,900
Wives whose husbands are absent from them, from any other cause than desertion, having a child or children	1843	389	932	260	724	2,503	6,987	363	961	3,515	9,604	13,119
	1844	359	835	237	652	2,257	6,536	298	869	3,151	8,892	12,043
Totals of 585 Unions	1843	4,471	10,333	4,104	10,160	42,356	111,634	2,342	5,674	53,273	137,801	191,074
	1844	5,015	11,132	3,391	8,463	42,959	115,041	1,913	4,705	53,268	139,341	192,609

No. 5, (*continued.*) TABLE C.—AGED and INFIRM Out-door Paupers, partially or wholly disabled, relieved during the Quarter ended Lady-day, 1844, distinguishing the Resident and Non-Resident.

UNIONS.	Out-door Resident.				Out-door Non-Resident.			
	Wholly Unable to Work.		Partially Able to Work.		Wholly Unable to Work.		Partially Able to Work.	
	Males.	Females	Males.	Females	Males.	Females	Males.	Females
ENGLAND.								
Bedford	692	1,009	169	861	30	109	5	37
Berks	1,315	1,878	509	719	100	140	32	62
Buckingham	913	1,522	533	1,556	61	136	23	45
Cambridge	951	1,662	369	897	81	185	13	52
Chester	860	1,542	554	1,138	295	485	170	362
Cornwall	1,379	2,807	632	1,464	208	415	56	128
Cumberland	338	702	282	738	151	263	104	282
Derby	559	973	299	618	128	234	52	100
Devon	3,041	5,235	2,146	3,587	261	470	177	320
Dorset	1,367	2,579	538	998	111	264	58	108
Durham	1,055	2,479	400	1,334	338	840	113	364
Essex	2,296	3,516	495	990	155	332	23	46
Gloucester	1,648	3,071	936	1,691	247	521	73	168
Hereford	593	941	424	849	165	345	41	80
Hertford	865	1,796	196	486	72	172	16	23
Huntingdon	417	825	77	263	15	37	3	8
Kent	2,056	3,387	960	1,891	314	805	109	235
Lancaster	1,842	3,402	2,116	4,128	502	854	584	1,038
Leicester	1,058	1,511	687	1,118	134	231	85	126
Lincoln	1,572	2,866	645	1,546	141	344	37	106
Middlesex	994	2,386	668	2,022	310	995	185	796
Monmouth	518	891	207	439	55	96	20	37
Norfolk	2,479	4,240	846	1,356	438	975	165	317
Northampton	1,419	2,438	376	1,087	88	210	12	58
Northumberland	846	1,864	349	1,422	465	973	148	593
Nottingham	895	1,411	448	1,060	163	273	58	141
Oxford	1,345	1,996	352	572	76	166	13	31
Rutland	93	183	48	140	13	25	3	9
Salop	658	1,195	456	907	220	356	135	242
Somerset	3,256	6,112	1,710	3,208	283	595	102	197
Southampton	1,606	2,880	638	1,205	191	310	30	89
Stafford	1,073	2,208	596	1,125	239	496	63	138
Suffolk	2,740	4,476	882	1,604	169	367	30	66
Surrey	1,076	1,979	695	1,443	135	307	55	186
Sussex	1,232	1,551	934	876	222	334	108	181
Warwick	855	1,246	495	1,070	109	265	58	133
Westmoreland	1,111	166	211	353	32	55	60	136
Wilts	2,241	3,777	811	1,577	228	448	84	163
Worcester	1,219	2,149	749	1,334	187	340	116	232
York { East Riding	515	1,045	414	981	140	293	110	349
North Riding	736	1,466	418	976	251	587	114	309
West Riding	2,037	4,003	1,307	2,628	659	1,261	478	920
Totals of England	53,763	93,355	26,577	54,317	8,182	15,899	3,921	9,013
WALES.								
Anglesey	294	595	161	379	37	71	25	59
Brecon	249	505	226	487	63	99	51	151
Cardigan	469	1,069	232	771	60	98	20	88
Carmarthen	566	1,062	421	1,230	73	257	71	226
Carnarvon	418	599	445	1,017	120	153	88	209
Denbigh	344	616	223	658	59	116	45	169
Flint	319	770	223	547	31	60	29	71
Glamorgan	766	1,228	242	805	105	213	42	120
Merioneth	238	406	389	905	74	161	146	287
Montgomery	375	759	371	673	71	161	62	123
Pembroke	406	1,002	256	667	56	156	22	83
Radnor	101	212	102	165	23	43	17	38
Totals of Wales	4,545	8,813	3,291	8,304	772	1,588	618	1,624
Totals of 585 Unions in England and Wales	58,308	102,168	29,868	62,621	8,954	17,487	4,539	10,637

No. 6, (*continued*.) TABLE C.—AGED and INFIRM Out-door Paupers, partially or wholly disabled, relieved during the Quarter ended Lady-day, 1844, distinguishing the Resident and Non-Resident.

UNIONS.	Totals.				Grand Total.
	Resident.		Non-Resident.		
	Males.	Females.	Males.	Females.	
ENGLAND.					
Bedford	861	1,870	35	146	2,912
Berks	1,824	2,597	132	202	4,755
Buckingham	1,446	3,078	84	181	4,789
Cambridge	1,320	2,559	94	237	4,210
Chester	1,414	2,680	465	847	5,406
Cornwall	2,011	4,271	264	543	7,089
Cumberland	620	1,440	255	545	2,860
Derby	858	1,591	180	334	2,963
Devon	5,187	8,822	438	790	15,237
Dorset	1,905	3,577	169	372	6,023
Durham	1,455	3,813	451	1,204	6,923
Essex	2,791	4,506	178	378	7,853
Gloucester	2,584	4,762	320	689	8,355
Hereford	1,017	1,790	206	425	3,438
Hertford	1,061	2,272	88	195	3,616
Huntingdon	494	1,088	18	45	1,645
Kent	3,016	5,278	423	1,040	9,757
Lancaster	3,958	7,530	1,085	1,892	14,465
Leicester	1,745	2,629	219	357	4,950
Lincoln	2,217	4,412	178	450	7,257
Middlesex	1,662	4,408	495	1,791	8,356
Monmouth	725	1,330	75	133	2,263
Norfolk	3,325	5,596	603	1,292	10,816
Northampton	1,795	3,525	100	268	5,688
Northumberland	1,195	3,286	613	1,566	6,660
Nottingham	1,343	2,471	221	414	4,449
Oxford	1,697	2,568	89	197	4,551
Rutland	143	323	16	34	516
Salop	1,114	2,102	355	598	4,169
Somerset	4,966	9,320	385	792	15,463
Southampton	2,244	4,085	221	399	6,949
Stafford	1,669	3,833	302	634	5,938
Suffolk	3,622	6,080	199	433	10,334
Surrey	1,771	3,422	190	493	5,876
Sussex	2,166	2,427	330	515	5,438
Warwick	1,350	2,316	167	898	4,231
Westmoreland	1,322	519	92	191	1,124
Wilts	3,052	5,354	312	611	9,329
Worcester	1,968	3,543	303	572	6,386
York { East Riding	929	2,026	250	632	3,837
North Riding	1,154	2,442	365	896	4,857
West Riding	3,344	6,631	1,137	2,181	13,293
Totals of England	80,340	147,672	12,103	24,912	265,027
WALES.					
Anglesey	455	974	62	130	1,621
Brecon	475	992	114	250	1,831
Cardigan	701	1,840	80	186	2,807
Carmarthen	987	2,292	144	483	3,906
Carnarvon	863	1,606	208	362	3,039
Denbigh	567	1,274	104	285	2,230
Flint	542	1,317	60	131	2,050
Glamorgan	1,008	2,033	147	333	3,521
Merioneth	627	1,311	220	448	2,606
Montgomery	746	1,432	133	284	2,595
Pembroke	662	1,669	78	239	2,648
Radnor	203	377	40	81	701
Totals of Wales	7,836	17,117	1,390	3,212	29,555
Totals of 585 Unions in England and Wales	88,176	164,789	13,493	28,124	294,582

No. 5, (*continued.*) TABLE C.—Comparative Statement of the Number of Aged and Infirm Out-door Paupers, partially or wholly disabled, relieved during the Quarters ended Lady-day, 1843 and 1844, in 585 Unions in the several Counties of England and Wales.

	Quarters ended Lady-day.	Wholly Unable to Work.		Partially Able to Work.		Total.		Grand Total.
		Males.	Females.	Males.	Females.	Males.	Females.	
Totals of 585 Unions . . .	1843	64,246	117,806	34,716	74,306	98,962	192,112	291,074
Totals of 585 Unions . . .	1844	67,262	119,655	34,407	73,258	101,669	192,913	294,582

No. 6, (i.)—AMOUNT of Money expended for County and Police Rate in each County in England and Wales during the Years ended Lady-day 1840, 1841 and 1842, as shown in the Annual Poor Rate Return; also the Amount received by the County Treasurers for County and Police Rate, for the Years ended Michaelmas 1840, 1841, and 1842.

COUNTIES.	*Payments by Overseers—Years ended Lady-day			Total of the Three Years.	†Receipts by County Treasurers—Years ended Michaelmas.			Total of the Three Years.
	1840	1841	1842		1840	1841	1842	
ENGLAND.	£.	£.	£.	£.	£.	£.	£.	£.
Bedford	5,296	9,701	8,448	23,445	4,869	8,323	9,334	22,526
Berks	11,987	11,373	11,428	34,788	8,780	9,579	8,610	26,969
Buckingham	8,305	10,344	12,309	30,958	8,613	11,925	10,600	31,138
Cambridge	10,361	8,496	17,402	36,259	6,482	4,864	12,299	23,645
Chester	11,641	20,724	25,262	57,627	10,261	16,071	20,712	47,044
Cornwall	13,442	11,270	11,531	36,243	10,067	10,428	11,159	31,654
Cumberland	6,879	8,694	10,828	26,401	9,777	8,984	11,486	30,247
Derby	14,021	16,955	16,069	47,045	15,206	15,206	14,256	44,668
Devon	16,357	17,346	19,318	53,021	17,288	15,310	16,267	48,865
Dorset	11,266	8,763	11,688	31,717	8,408	8,903	8,972	26,283
Durham	14,347	19,641	16,006	49,994	17,683	15,243	14,514	47,440
Essex	18,449	32,520	29,927	80,896	19,371	28,744	30,771	78,886
Gloucester	30,263	38,204	39,469	107,936	22,603	33,935	31,449	87,989
Hereford	6,146	5,992	7,007	19,145	5,108	5,610	6,317	17,035
Hertford	12,286	9,171	16,902	38,359	6,482	11,685	13,360	31,527
Huntingdon	5,165	4,929	4,933	15,027	4,662	4,659	4,368	13,689
Kent	29,964	33,126	39,877	102,967	17,566	17,747	18,035	53,348
Lancaster	100,761	132,570	152,520	385,851	45,860	71,860	60,947	178,667
Leicester	16,080	21,619	20,356	58,055	15,945	20,753	18,349	55,047
Lincoln	25,285	26,737	30,152	82,174	25,862	28,303	31,185	85,350
Middlesex	94,652	102,136	222,106	418,894	83,516	90,848	87,715	262,079
Monmouth	8,860	12,764	8,817	30,441	9,513	10,398	7,563	27,474
Norfolk	20,546	29,747	25,655	75,948	28,200	26,400	27,000	81,600
Northampton	10,051	12,942	17,203	40,196	8,042	11,805	15,256	35,103
Northumberland	8,095	8,765	6,124	22,984	7,836	8,821	6,053	22,710
Nottingham	20,329	20,413	18,307	59,049	12,892	8,595	11,460	32,947
Oxford	8,324	9,617	8,480	26,421	8,154	8,119	7,943	24,216
Rutland	876	1,050	1,010	2,936	1,144	1,095	1,343	3,582
Salop	11,988	15,832	16,725	44,545	11,130	14,938	15,348	41,416
Somerset	23,788	25,801	21,728	71,317	14,651	18,371	21,533	54,555
Southampton	23,572	30,046	27,548	81,166	16,637	22,647	21,485	60,769
Stafford	15,028	18,271	19,330	52,629	17,236	20,918	17,796	55,950
Suffolk	21,776	26,861	25,740	74,377	16,428	19,709	17,595	53,732
Surrey	37,195	44,960	68,591	150,746	27,803	27,803	32,544	88,150
Sussex	10,561	16,378	20,999	47,938	12,491	19,437	14,094	46,022
Warwick	14,975	31,567	44,796	91,338	16,581	16,534	12,977	46,092
Westmoreland	3,094	3,929	3,450	10,473	3,984	3,131	2,846	9,961
Wilts	14,808	24,713	23,460	62,981	20,896	24,868	22,939	68,703
Worcester	27,832	23,992	26,132	77,956	23,551	21,320	18,380	63,251
York { East Riding	8,511	9,790	12,348	30,649	6,803	6,005	9,285	22,093
{ North Riding	4,538	6,190	7,897	18,625	7,500	12,500	12,000	32,000
{ West Riding	54,654	50,966	54,735	160,355	40,189	41,454	49,593	131,236
Totals of England	812,354	974,905	1,182,613	2,969,872	676,072	783,848	785,738	2,245,658
WALES.								
Anglesey	1,941	1,167	1,525	4,633	1,964	1,178	1,571	4,713
Brecon	2,837	2,975	3,043	8,855	2,832	3,402	3,282	9,516
Cardigan	2,627	2,767	2,559	7,953	2,302	2,630	1,689	6,621
Carmarthen	5,123	5,603	4,971	15,697	4,204	4,159	4,094	12,457
Carnarvon	3,996	4,079	2,936	11,001	4,290	3,343	2,400	10,033
Denbigh	4,589	6,272	6,167	17,027	4,714	6,769	6,474	17,957
Flint	3,054	3,207	2,492	8,753	3,200	2,700	2,650	8,550
Glamorgan	5,496	5,413	8,273	19,182	5,395	8,705	9,153	23,253
Merioneth	1,588	1,298	1,599	4,485	1,447	1,449	1,558	4,454
Montgomery	6,517	10,887	8,137	25,541	4,840	6,936	5,910	17,686
Pembroke	3,189	4,484	3,384	11,057	2,250	4,483	916	7,649
Radnor	2,252	2,978	3,019	8,249	2,310	2,970	2,640	7,920
Totals of Wales	43,198	51,130	48,105	142,433	39,748	48,724	42,337	130,809
Totals of England and Wales	855,552	1,026,035	1,230,718	3,112,305	715,820	832,572	828,075	2,376,467

* Taken from Annual Poor Rate Return.
† See Parliamentary Papers, No. 434, Sess. 1842, and No. 76, Sess. 1844.

No. 6, (ii.)*—SUMMARY of COUNTY TREASURERS' RETURNS for the Years ended Michaelmas, 1840 to 1842.

RECEIPTS.

Years ended Michaelmas.	Balance in hand.	Country Rate.	Allowance from the Treasury.	Police Rate, (if any.)	Other Receipts.	Total.
	£.	£.	£.	£.	£.	£.
1840	75,879	679,292	100,907	36,536	68,216	960,830
1841	80,232	679,324	96,429	153,246	69,181	1,078,412
1842	111,854	703,526	114,734	124,549	83,100	1,137,763
Total	267,965	2,062,142	312,070	314,331	220,497	3,177,005

DISBURSEMENTS.

Years ended Michaelmas.	Balance due to Treasurer.	Gaol.	House of Correction.	Prosecution of Prisoners.	Conveyance of Prisoners to Gaol.	Conveyance of Transports.	Vagrants.	Maintenance of Pauper Lunatics.	Shire Hall, Judges' Lodgings, &c.	County Bridges.	Clerk of the Peace.	Treasurer.	Coroners.	Inspectors of Weights and Measures.	Incidental Expenses.	Expenses of Rural Police, (if any.)	Other Expenses (if any.)	Total Disbursements.
	£.	£.	£.	£.	£.	£.	£.	£.	£.	£.	£.	£.	£.	£.	£.	£.	£.	£.
1840	10,875	138,896	126,114	169,047	25,266	9,217	5,137	8,866	26,865	61,558	34,515	7,118	45,960	11,505	92,815	75,575	41,697	881,118
1841	6,931	133,146	132,735	173,615	23,249	8,954	7,442	10,116	23,714	63,907	35,316	7,179	47,786	10,730	94,670	136,664	55,974	955,198
1842	4,625	149,648	140,411	203,759	26,516	9,819	7,201	10,913	26,451	64,092	36,407	7,369	48,893	11,282	97,220	147,400	64,043	1,051,428
Total	22,431	421,690	399,260	546,421	75,031	27,990	19,780	29,895	77,030	189,557	106,238	21,666	142,641	33,517	274,705	359,639	161,714	2,887,744

* See Parliamentary Papers, No. 434, Sess. 1842, and No. 76, Sess. 1844.

No. 7.—ABSTRACT of Returns showing the Number of Pauper Lunatics and Idiots chargeable to Parishes comprised in each Union in England and Wales, in the Month of August, 1844 ; distinguishing the Number of each Sex, whether Dangerous to themselves or others, where Maintained, and the Average Weekly Cost per Head for Maintenance, Clothing, &c.

Number of Lunatics and Idiots Chargeable to Parishes in each Union, in the Month of August, 1844.

COUNTIES.	Population in 1841.	Number of Lunatics and Idiots.										Proportion per Cent. to Population.	Where Maintained.							
		Lunatics.			Idiots.			Grand Total Lunatics and Idiots.					In County Lunatic Asylum.			In Licensed House.				
		M.	F.	Total.	M.	F.	Total.						M.	F.	Total.	M.	F.	Total.		Total.
ENGLAND.																				
Bedford	112,379	37	42	79	29	37	76		155			1·10	34	27	61					117
Berks	190,367	61	67	128	62	84	146		274			1·10	6	1	7	56	61	117		
Buckingham	140,282	33	47	80	34	37	71		151			1·10	4	7	11	25	22	47		
Cambridge	171,848	27	32	59	44	36	80		139			8·100	19	16	35	8	11	19		
Chester	371,331	61	67	128	77	101	178		306			8·100	57	65	122		1	1		
Cornwall	340,738	62	97	159	95	85	180		339			1·20	59	67	126					
Cumberland	177,912	46	40	86	36	48	84		170			9·100	3	4	7	32	22	54		
Derby	220,028	37	30	67	53	55	108		175			8·100	2	3	5	30	12	42		
Devon	430,291	108	135	243	158	146	304		547			1·10	9	9	18	61	63	124		
Dorset	167,874	52	74	·126	31	48	79		205			1·10	45	55	100	8	11	19		
Durham	325,997	55	66	121	80	68	148		269			8·100		4	4	57	47	104		
Essex	390,818	72	107	179	85	92	177		356			1·10	·7	5	12	53	72	125		
Gloucester	330,582	103	127	230	72	103	175		405			1·10	72	94	166	15	10	28		
Hereford	110,675	23	83	56	40	46	86		142			1·10		1	1	13	15	28		
Hertford	176,173	40	64	104	76	80	156		260			1·10	·33	37	70	5	15	20		
Huntingdon	55,573	16	14	30	12	16	28		58			1·10	13	13	26	1	2	3		
Kent	534,882	115	193	308	107	121	228		536			1·10	100	130	230	19	45	64		
Lancaster	1,634,283	336	353	689	259	270	529		1,218			7·100	238	223	461	61	76	137		
Leicester	220,232	71	75	146	90	78	168		314			1·10	54	48	102	1	1	2		
Lincoln	366,347	85	78	163	65	73	138		381			9·00	38	32	70	18	18	36		
Middlesex	841,408	295	473	768	130	136	266		1,034			1·10	180	246	426	117	196	313		
Monmouth	150,222	37	38	75	26	38	64		139			9·100	7	5	12	20	16	36		
Norfolk	343,577	86	104	190	113	130	243		433			1·10	82	77	169	3	4	6		
Northampton	197,197	56	68	124	71	94	165		289			1·10	57	47	104	5	4	9		
Northumberland	265,985	65	74	139	95	97	192		331			1·10	8	2	5	60	59	119		
Nottingham	270,719	63	85	148	68	74	142		290			1·10	58	60	118		1	1		
Oxford	141,330	32	54	86	64	49	113		199			1·20				31	35	66		
Rutland	23,160	9	8	17	8	7	15		32			1·10					1	1		
Salop	191,032	49	57	106	58	94	152		258			1·10	·7	10	19	23	23	46		
Somerset	454,446	89	161	250	150	187	337		587			1·10	9	22	29	71	90	161		
Southampton	289,655	87	143	230	105	101	206		496			1·10	1		1	72	109	181		
Stafford	442,349	88	94	183	129	139	268		451			1·10	87	64	151	5	11	16		
Suffolk	314,723	109	117	226	91	90	181		407			1·10	97	101	198	7	14	21		

	Population								Prop.						
Surrey	512,580	156	234	390	92	94	198	576	1:10	151	177	328	13	43	56
Sussex	223,435	56	56	112	82	90	181	293	1:10	7	7	14	45	42	87
Warwick	220,029	47	68	115	59	87	146	261	1:10	8	12	20	36	42	78
Westmoreland	56,469	7	21	28	10	15	53	53	9:100	.	3	.	5	10	15
Wilts	238,246	89	107	196	88	88	176	372	1:10	3	2	5	85	87	172
Worcester	336,108	62	98	154	90	96	166	320	1:10	15	18	33	37	41	74
York { East Riding	190,218	48	68	116	40	33	73	189	1:10	6	10	16	37	46	83
North Riding	190,527	35	42	77	33	43	78	153	9:100	9	5	14	20	22	42
West Riding	790,751	175	185	360	169	201	370	730	9:100	137	141	278	3	5	8
Totals	**13,026,664**	**3,181**	**4,090**	**7,271**	**3,271**	**3,611**	**6,882**	**14,159**	**1:10**	**1,720**	**1,854**	**3,574**	**1,156**	**1,402**	**2,559**
WALES.															
Anglesey	38,105	5	14	19	17	19	36	55	1:10	.	.	.	1	.	2
Brecon	55,399	6	13	19	25	22	47	66	1:10	1	1	2	1	1	1
Cardigan	75,136	17	25	42	35	50	85	127	2:10	1	.	2	5	1	16
Carmarthen	110,404	34	45	79	38	60	98	177	1:10	4	1	5	2	1	4
Carnarvon	96,728	30	20	50	39	64	103	153	2:10	1	1	2	1	3	.
Denbigh	68,483	5	8	13	36	32	68	81	9:100	.	3	4	.	.	4
Flint	64,355	4	8	12	23	21	43	55	9:100	1	.	4	15	11	26
Glamorgan	178,041	36	36	72	31	54	85	157	1:10	1	1	4	.	.	.
Merioneth	60,696	10	7	17	37	30	67	84	2:10	3	.	4	2	.	2
Montgomery	66,709	12	9	21	37	57	96	117	1:10	.	.	3	.	.	.
Pembroke	78,563	12	16	28	31	38	69	97	2:100	3	.	15	.	.	.
Radnor	19,554	4	3	7	15	8	23	30	1:10	11	4	.	1	.	1
Totals	**994,173**	**175**	**204**	**379**	**365**	**456**	**820**	**1,199**	**1:10**	**25**	**12**	**37**	**28**	**27**	**55**
Totals of 589 Unions in England and Wales	13,910,837	3,356	4,294	7,650	3,636	4,066	7,702	15,382	1:10	1,745	1,866	3,611	1,184	1,430	2,614
Totals of Places under Local Acts	1,574,371	443	643	1,086	229	229	458	1,544	1:10	258	355	613	185	199	334
Estimated for other Places not in Union	421,533	103	134	237	105	117	222	459	1:10	.	.	.	.	.	.
Estimated Totals for England and Wales	15,906,741	3,902	5,071	8,973	3,970	4,412	8,382	17,355	1:10	2,003	2,221	4,224	1,319	1,629	2,948
Estimated Totals for England and Wales in 1843	. .	3,646	4,626	8,272	4,028	4,464	8,492	16,764	.	.	.	.	.	.	.
Increase in 1844 compared with 1843	. .	256	445	701	. .	. .	. .	591	.	.	.	.	.	.	.
Decrease in 1844 compared with 1843	. .	. .	. .	. .	58	52	110	. .	.	.	.	.	.	.	.

Note.—Some of the Unions have Parishes situate in more than one County, which causes the population of Counties to differ from that published in the Census for 1841

No. 7, (*continued.*)—ABSTRACT of Returns showing the Number of Pauper Lunatics and Idiots chargeable to Parishes comprised in each Union in England and Wales, in the Month of August, 1844; distinguishing the Number of each Sex, whether Dangerous to themselves or others, where Maintained, and the average Weekly Cost per Head for Maintenance, Clothing, &c.

COUNTIES.	Number of Lunatics and Idiots chargeable to Parishes in each Union, in the Month of August, 1844. Where maintained. In Union Workhouse. M.	F.	Total.	With their Friends or elsewhere. M.	F.	Total.	Ages. 0 to 5	5 to 10	10 to 20	20 to 30	30 to 40	40 to 50	50 to 60	60 to 70	70 and upwards	Dangerous to themselves or others.	Of Dirty Habits.	Average Weekly Cost per Head of Maintenance and Clothing. In County Lunatic Asylum. s. d.	Licensed House. s. d.	Elsewhere. s. d.	Average. s. d.
ENGLAND.																					
Bedford	26	30	56	16	22	38	.	.	8	26	32	33	26	20	10	31	23	7 1	.	2 6¾	4 4
Berks	32	41	73	29	48	77	.	1	31	66	45	55	44	23	9	93	42	8 4½	8 5	2 6¼	5 2½
Buckingham	15	20	35	24	34	58	.	1	9	23	35	35	23	17	8	36	21	9 7	9 8	2 10½	5 6
Cambridge	14	14	28	29	28	57	.	.	9	30	30	31	22	12	5	26	29	9 3½	8 6	2 9¼	5 2½
Chester	34	31	65	47	71	118	.	1	22	64	72	71	39	28	9	73	34	4 11½	7 0	2 3¾	3 4¼
Cornwall	54	73	127	44	42	86	.	1	18	53	70	75	62	40	20	94	73	5 11¾	.	2 0¾	3 6
Cumberland	27	32	59	18	32	50	.	.	9	40	44	44	16	13	3	36	23	8 0	8 0½	2 4¼	4 5
Derby	21	30	51	36	41	77	1	.	9	34	43	47	21	16	5	35	31	7 9¾	9 6¼	2 5¼	4 3½
Devon	69	86	155	122	128	250	.	1	31	101	114	112	89	71	28	99	95	8 5¾	9 4	2 8¼	4 4½
Dorset	13	37	50	17	19	36	.	1	4	29	35	49	41	29	17	56	28	7 0	7 3	2 5½	5 1½
Durham	37	39	76	41	44	85	.	.	13	59	68	52	42	25	10	80	32	7 4½	7 8½	2 5¼	4 6½
Essex	43	67	110	53	56	109	.	2	34	87	71	58	60	30	14	59	57	8 11¼	9 4¼	3 0¼	5 5¼
Gloucester	44	69	113	42	58	100	.	.	18	83	94	82	58	41	29	147	61	9 0¾	8 6	2 6	5 6¾
Hereford	5	9	14	45	54	99	.	2	11	25	21	40	21	15	7	24	23	12 0	10 5	2 7½	4 2¼
Hertford	36	37	73	42	55	97	.	.	21	62	53	47	46	25	6	56	31	8 2	9 3¾	2 8	4 7½
Huntingdon	11	6	17	3	9	12	.	.	3	11	10	18	9	6	1	12	10	9 4½	9 0	3 0	6 1½
Kent	67	75	142	39	61	100	.	2	21	89	137	119	91	52	25	156	115	8 1	8 10½	2 8	5 8¾
Lancaster	179	190	369	112	139	251	.	6	70	259	309	264	172	116	22	345	146	5 6¼	7 7¼	2 3¾	4 1½
Leicester	54	56	110	51	49	100	1	2	10	63	67	65	55	33	18	62	57	9 3¾	6 9	2 5¼	4 8¾
Lincoln	53	47	100	40	55	95	1	.	19	63	53	69	61	24	11	67	43	11 1	10 4¼	2 11¼	5 8¾
Middlesex	117	149	266	13	16	29	.	2	39	196	251	244	158	99	45	234	156	7 7	9 5¼	3 1	6 11¼
Monmouth	10	24	34	26	31	57	1	1	9	27	20	27	22	24	8	36	26	9 1	8 4	2 7¾	4 8
Norfolk	59	55	114	55	99	154	1	.	30	86	89	84	70	46	27	118	87	5 10½	9 4	2 4¾	3 9½
Northampton	31	43	74	41	61	102	.	.	17	55	61	78	38	27	13	63	58	9 10¼	9 1½	3 1¼	5 8½
Northumberland	59	57	116	37	54	91	.	.	17	56	78	76	60	27	17	75	50	8 0	8 2	2 7	4 8
Nottingham	43	73	116	24	31	55	.	.	8	65	67	65	57	22	6	85	54	8 0¼	9 0	2 7	4 10
Oxford	27	41	68	38	27	65	.	1	15	41	39	39	38	14	11	28	22	.	8 9½	2 7½	4 8

Rutland																						
Salop																						
Somerset																						
Southampton																						
Stafford																						
Suffolk																						
Surrey																						
Sussex																						
Warwick																						
Westmoreland																						
Wilts																						
Worcester																						
York {East Riding}																						
York {North Riding}																						
York {West Riding}																						
Totals	1,819	2,261	4,080	1,748	2,192	3,940	6	40	818	2,828	3,117	3,046	2,272	1,430	596	3,544	2,390					

WALES.

Anglesey																						
Brecon																						
Cardigan																						
Carmarthen																						
Carnarvon																						
Denbigh																						
Flint																						
Glamorgan																						
Merioneth																						
Montgomery																						
Pembroke																						
Radnor																						
Totals	43	48	91	450	566	1,016		56	69	224	261	213	204	156	55	94	200					

Totals of 589 Unions in England and Wales	1,862	2,309	4,171	2,198	2,758	4,956	6	47	887	3,052	3,378	3,259	2,476	1,586	651	3,638	2,690					
Totals of Places under Local Acts	226	283	509	47	41	88	2	9	91	273	355	353	246	141	74	283	229					
Estimated for other Places not in Union																						
Estimated Totals for England and Wales	2,088	2,592	4,680	2,245	2,799	5,044	8	56	978	3,335	3,733	3,612	2,722	1,727	725	4,031	2,819					

NOTE.—Some of the Unions have Parishes situate in more than one County, which causes the population of Counties to differ from that published in the Census for 1841.

No. 8.—VACCINATION EXTENSION ACT.—ABSTRACT of Returns from 542 Unions and Parishes under Boards of Guardians in England and Wales, of the Number of Persons Vaccinated in such Unions and Parishes in the Year ended 29th September, 1844.

COUNTIES.	Number of Unions or Places from which Returns have been received.	Numbers of Vacci-nators.	Number of Vacci-nation Stations (including the Vacci-nators' Residences.)	Number of Persons Vaccinated.			
				At the Residences of the Vaccina-tors.	At the Out-stations.	At the Residences of the Parties.	Total.
ENGLAND.							
Bedford	5	24	111	745	1,463	1,868	4,076
Berks	12	45	113	1,323	789	2,157	4,745
Buckingham	4	21	84	115	119	148	935
Cambridge	8	40	99	1,216	1,148	3,369	6,711
Chester	10	46	137	4,506	1,975	1,995	8,476
Cornwall	12	57	193	1,238	1,364	3,315	5,951
Cumberland	8	32	86	923	686	1,774	3,442
Derby	7	38	101	1,374	783	1,876	4,401
Devon	19	144	397	3,696	3,082	2,676	9,454
Dorset	9	30	113	214	312	1,123	1,654
Durham	12	51	103	1,481	560	2,596	4,882
Essex	14	111	244	2,558	1,948	4,749	9,426
Gloucester	14	55	144	2,318	3,212	1,945	7,475
Hereford	7	22	95	482	915	504	1,901
Hertford	10	38	111	1,548	777	1,324	4,797
Huntingdon	3	13	44	1,575	1,271	710	3,556
Kent	28	109	245	6,263	1,327	3,364	10,944
Lancaster	20	106	275	15,977	8,454	5,335	30,012
Leicester	8	31	118	1,014	590	481	2,560
Lincoln	13	82	183	1,698	889	4,378	6,965
Middlesex	27	158	189	15,691	1,816	8,195	25,202
Monmouth	5	24	85	1,479	1,383	376	3,238
Norfolk	21	114	338	1,710	928	1,881	5,609
Northampton	8	28	95	893	1,099	429	2,626
Northumberland	13	76	187	1,982	869	2,946	5,797
Nottingham	9	51	129	2,051	952	1,995	4,998
Oxford	8	29	77	497	1,185	1,078	3,393
Rutland	2	8	36	217	357	182	756
Salop	12	51	125	1,354	1,482	1,049	4,291
Somerset	17	109	350	3,313	2,130	4,965	11,163
Southampton	20	68	154	2,784	874	1,411	5,069
Stafford	14	62	150	3,621	1,509	1,372	6,502
Suffolk	17	86	305	1,722	2,418	3,428	8,026
Surrey	16	86	120	5,078	1,120	3,003	9,740
Sussex	19	75	193	2,454	1,886	2,127	6,467
Warwick	10	37	106	920	1,431	1,583	3,934
Westmoreland	2	8	20	16	25	186	227
Wilts	18	66	194	624	991	2,061	3,676
Worcester	11	62	126	2,664	1,102	3,352	8,213
York { East Riding	10	58	143	2,044	824	1,917	4,785
{ North Riding	12	54	165	551	395	2,294	3,240
{ West Riding	17	102	309	5,864	4,448	4,284	14,738
Totals of England	509	2,507	6,592	107,793	60,355	95,297	274,053
WALES.							
Anglesey	1	5	13	496	682	52	1,230
Brecknock	3	8	38	192	20	273	485
Cardigan	3	5	26	271	290	235	796
Carmarthen	5	15	68	352	560	527	1,439
Carnarvon	3	7	29	480	522	402	1,404
Denbigh	3	12	44	195	778	979	1,952
Flint	2	8	30	270	411	719	1,400
Glamorgan	4	19	74	2,896	1,195	1,029	5,050
Merioneth	2	6	37	149	238	138	525
Montgomery	2	7	47	449	489	157	1,095
Pembroke	3	12	61	150	64	655	869
Radnor	2	3	16	45	. .	. .	155
Totals of Wales	33	107	483	5,875	5,249	5,166	16,400
Totals of England and Wales	542	2,614	7,705	113,668	65,604	100,463	290,453

Note.—The total numbers Vaccinated in each County do not in all cases comprise the numbers in the three preceding columns, owing to several Unions not distinguishing the places where the parties were vaccinated. As regards the number of Births, it is also to be noted that they have been estimated from the best available data for those Unions, the Returns for which were defective in this respect. Nor do the columns relating to Small Pox show the actual extent of the prevalence of that disease, only so far as came within the knowledge of the Clerks and Public Vaccinators of the Unions from which Returns have been received.

No. 8, (*continued.*)—VACCINATION EXTENSION ACT.—ABSTRACT of Returns from 542 Unions and Parishes under Boards of Guardians in England and Wales, of the Number of Persons Vaccinated in such Unions and Parishes in the Year ended 29th September, 1844.

COUNTIES.	Number of the preceding cases which, on inspection, proved to have been successfully Vaccinated.				Number of Births during the Year.	Number of cases of Small Pox attended by the Vaccinators.	Number of such cases where the parties were known to have been previously Vaccinated.	Number of Unions or Places from which Returns have not been received, or from which the Returns are defective.
	At the Residences of the Vaccinators.	At the Out-stations.	At the Residences of the Parties.	Total.				
ENGLAND.								
Bedford	705	1,394	1,768	3,867	3,483	25	14	1
Berks	1,311	769	2,046	4,609	5,789	68	33	..
Buckingham	139	119	118	880	2,054	8	1	3
Cambridge	1,135	1,170	2,855	6,196	5,122	59	29	1
Chester	4,240	1,896	1,893	8,029	12,305	94	27	..
Cornwall	1,149	1,312	3,154	5,637	11,435	15	8	1
Cumberland	869	658	1,688	3,273	5,196	7	2	1
Derby	1,262	752	1,321	4,903	7,107	59	25	2
Devon	3,618	2,978	2,482	9,078	15,254	68	17	1
Dorset	184	306	1,097	1,589	3,558	10	..	3
Durham	1,422	573	2,533	4,729	10,912	36	2	2
Essex	2,437	1,791	4,601	8,985	8,444	117	49	3
Gloucester	2,233	2,825	1,752	6,810	10,333	169	61	3
Hereford	456	895	476	1,814	3,187	21	4	1
Hertford	1,533	923	1,116	4,719	4,345	102	45	3
Huntingdon	1,499	1,239	692	3,430	2,045	18	..	..
Kent	6,020	1,199	3,234	10,511	17,127	100	44	..
Lancaster	16,140	8,131	4,788	29,305	53,597	201	55	6
Leicester	956	570	476	2,487	6,326	31	6	2
Lincoln	1,627	868	4,339	6,834	10,463	21	1	2
Middlesex	14,914	1,218	7,485	23,694	46,910	948	285	3
Monmouth	1,426	1,280	855	3,061	4,945	37	24	..
Norfolk	1,703	853	1,829	5,360	12,053	62	15	1
Northampton	854	1,081	414	2,535	4,495	71	6	4
Northumberland	1,873	870	2,742	5,574	8,872	13	4	..
Nottingham	2,020	874	1,950	4,844	9,015	22	5	..
Oxford	433	1,149	1,074	3,299	4,256	133	34	1
Rutland	217	357	181	755	751	8	3	..
Salop	1,327	1,403	1,030	4,166	5,144	21	6	3
Somerset	3,227	2,042	4,759	10,783	14,174	94	22	..
Southampton	2,737	847	1,297	4,881	7,571	162	52	7
Stafford	3,574	1,487	1,295	6,356	10,962	15	8	2
Suffolk	1,730	2,233	3,257	7,778	10,502	53	24	..
Surrey	4,974	1,104	2,816	9,428	14,727	365	153	4
Sussex	2,520	1,746	1,823	6,089	7,719	87	37	4
Warwick	875	1,346	1,433	3,703	10,015	72	9	3
Westmoreland	15	25	175	215	592	..	..	1
Wilts	608	964	1,982	3,554	7,359	39	32	..
Worcester	2,562	1,065	3,068	7,599	10,667	19	3	2
York { East Riding	1,962	794	1,854	4,610	7,024	110	45	..
York { North Riding	507	368	2,215	3,090	4,984	57	15	2
York { West Riding	5,790	4,354	4,142	14,428	27,396	181	64	9
Totals of England	**104,780**	**57,818**	**89,605**	**252,775**	**428,187**	**3,798**	**1,269**	**82**
WALES.								
Anglesey	496	682	52	1,230	1,011	5	..	..
Brecknock	185	18	268	471	1,617	1	..	1
Cardigan	213	285	188	686	1,305	..	..	2
Carmarthen	328	510	492	1,330	3,652	21	1	..
Carnarvon	470	516	364	1,350	2,083	19	..	1
Denbigh	194	775	945	1,914	1,942	2	..	..
Flint	254	396	710	1,360	1,724	66	1	1
Glamorgan	2,641	1,111	984	4,736	5,752	35	8	1
Merioneth	147	229	127	503	719	..	..	2
Montgomery	238	468	130	836	1,238	6	3	3
Pembroke	141	64	642	847	2,605	..	..	1
Radnor	44	..	..	154	400	1	1	1
Totals of Wales	**5,351**	**5,054**	**4,902**	**15,417**	**24,048**	**156**	**14**	**11**
Totals of England and Wales	**110,131**	**62,872**	**94,507**	**278,192**	**452,235**	**3,954**	**1,283**	**93**

No. 9.—LIST of UNIONS for which Workhouses have been ordered by the Poor Law Commissioners to be provided or adapted, with the Sums authorized to be expended, &c.—(*Continued from the Tenth Annual Report, App. B, No.* 8.)

I.—Workhouses ordered to be Built.

Union or Parish.	Counties in which situate.	Number of Paupers to be provided for.	Amount authorized to be Expended.	Additional Amount authorized to be Expended on Work-houses previously ordered to be built.	
			£.	£.	*s.*
Alnwick	Northumberland .	..	..	200	0
Blean	Kent	..	..	250	0
Bromley	Ditto	..	..	3,700	0
Carnarvon . . .	Carnarvon & Anglesey	..	..	500	0
Chard	Somerset, Dorset, & Devon.	..	..	330	0
Clifton	Gloucester . . .	1,180	20,000	. .	
Clun	Salop & Montgomery	..	..	1,500	0
St. Columb Major .	Cornwall	..	..	602	10
Cranbrook . . .	Kent	..	..	194	0
Doncaster . . .	York & Nottingham	..	..	320	0
Droitwich . . .	Worcester . . .	..	..	150	0
Eton	Buckingham . . .	..	..	1,000	0
Hereford	Hereford	..	..	250	0
Highworth & Swindon	Wilts and Berks .	480	7,220	. .	
Hinckley . . .	Leicester & Warwick	..	..	650	0
Holbeach . . .	Lincoln	..	..	350	0
Kingsbridge . . .	Devon	..	..	200	0
Manchester . . .	Lancaster . . .	..	..	11,500	0
Melksham . . .	Wilts	..	..	200	0
Newport	Monmouth & Glamorgan.	..	..	200	0
Newbury . . .	Berks & Southampton.	..	.. .	400	0
Prescot . . .	Lancaster . . .	..	..	650	0.
Rye	Sussex and Kent .	..	..	2,500	0
Saffron Walden .	Essex	..	..	200	0
Skipton	York	..	..	150	0
Wigton . . .	Cumberland . . .	..	..	150	0
Wolverhampton . .	Stafford	..	..	700	0

II.—Workhouses ordered to be Altered and Enlarged.

Union or Parish.	Counties in which situate.	Amount authorized to be Expended.	Amount authorized to be Expended in addition to that previously ordered.		
		£.	£.	*s.*	*d.*
Alton	Southampton	..	1,200	0	0
Aston	Warwick	..	1,550	0	0
Berkhampstead . .	Hertford and Buckingham	2,210	. .		
Bolton	Lancaster	..	620	0	0
Chorley	Ditto	700	. .		
St. Faith's . . .	Norfolk	..	125	0	0
Hackney . . .	Middlesex	..	2,550	0	0
Manchester . . .	Lancaster	..	2,500	0	0
Midhurst . . .	Sussex and Southampton	..	131	0	6
Monmouth . . .	Monmouth, Hereford, and Gloucester.	..	350	0	0
Ongar	Essex	..	550	0	0
Poplar	Middlesex	..	1,000	0	0
Reigate	Surrey	..	2,400	0	0
Shoreditch, St. Leonard	Middlesex	..	284	10	0
Strand	Ditto	..	1,200	0	0
Weardale . . .	Durham	..	105	9	4¼
Westbury-upon-Severn	Gloucester	..	1,200	0	0

No. 10.

LIST of UNIONS in which PARISH PROPERTY has been Sold, and the Produce appropriated under Orders of the Commissioners.

(i.)—Parochial Property ordered to be Sold, and the Purposes to which the Produce has been directed to be applied.—(*In continuation of List in Tenth Annual Report, Appendix B., No. 9, i.*)

UNION.	PARISH.	Amount of Purchase Money.	Sums directed to be applied by Orders of the Commissioners.	Purposes to which the Sums have been directed to be applied.
		£. s. d.	£. s. d.	£. s. d.
Abingdon	Appleford	124 0 0		
,, ...	Clifton Hampden	256 0 0	252 2 0	{ 72 12 0 towards cost of Union workhouse.
				179 10 0 investment.
,, ...	Steventon	*225 0 0	215 6 0	Towards cost of Union workhouse.
Alcester	Aston Cantlow .	76 10 0		
,, ...	Feckenham . . .	70 0 0		
Alresford	Rockley	65 10 0		
		190 0 0		
Alton	Bentworth . . .	{ 126 0 0 }	296 3 3	{ 103 11 3 Vide 10 Report.
		Vide 9 Rep.		192 12 0 Liquidation of parochial debts.
Altrincham . . {	Ashton-upon-Mer-sey.	} 30 0 0		
Auckland	West Auckland .	12 10 0		
Axbridge	Churchill	22 0 0	10 0 9	Towards cost of Union workhouse.
,, ...	Weare	122 0 0		
Bakewell	Matlock	241 0 0		
Banbury	Banbury	1310 0 0		
Bangor and Beau-maris	} Bangor	500 0 0	496 5 0	{ 37 9 1 towards cost of Union workhouse.
				458 15 11 investment.
Basford	Beeston	192 0 0		
Bedford	Yielden	20 0 0	18 12 0	Expenses of valuation.
Belper	Belper	192 0 0		
,, ...	Ripley	197 10 8	†205 18 1	Towards cost of Union workhouse.
Bicester	Heyford, Upper .	67 0 0		
Bishop's Stortford	Sawbridgeworth .	80 17 0		
Blofield	Blofield	125 0 0	120 0 0	Expenses of emigration.
Bridgnorth . . .	{ St. Mary Mag-dalene . . . }	315 0 0		
Bridlington . . .	Bridlington . . .	210 0 0		
Brixworth	Holcot	64 0 0	45 14 10	Towards cost of Union workhouse.
Bromley	Bromley	1137 7 0		
,, ...	Cudham	211 0 0		
		42 0 0		
Caistor	Waltham	{ 32 0 0 }	59 6 11	Towards cost of Union workhouse.
		Vide 8 Rep.		
Cardiff	Porthkerry . . .	40 0 0		
Carmarthen . .	Abergwilly . . .	170 0 0	170 0 0	{ 5 18 0 liquidation of outstanding claim.
				164 2 0 investment.
Caxton and Ar-rington . . . }	Kingston	126 0 0		
,,	Toft	49 7 0		
Cerne	Cerne Abbas . .	110 0 0		
Chailey	Wivelsfield . . .	182 0 0	172 15 6	{ 159 16 7 payment of cost of action of eject-ment.
				12 18 11 towards cost of Union work
Chard	Dowlish Wake .	40 0 0		
Chelmsford . . .	Writtle	580 0 0	543 8 11	Towards cost of Union workhouse.
Chesterton . . .	Dry Drayton . .	65 2 0		
Columb Major, St.	Newlyn	40 0 0		
Cosford	Brent Eleigh . .	‡22 11 7	22 11 7	Expenses of valuation.
,, ...	Cockfield	69 0 0		
Cuckfield	Clayton	100 0 0	93 13 2	{ 43 0 0 expenses of valuation.
				50 13 2 towards cost of Union workhouse.
,, ...	Keymer	270 0 0		
Depwade	Hapton	30 0 0		

* No conveyance; the property having been purchased by the Great Western Railway Company, under their Act of Parliament.

† Partly produced by the sale of materials.　　　‡ This amount was produced by the sale of materials.

O

No. 10, i. (*continued.*)—Parochial Property ordered to be Sold. and the Purposes to which the Produce has been directed to be applied.—(*In continuation of List in Tenth Annual Report, Appendix B. No. 9.*)

UNION.	PARISH.	Amount of Purchase Money.	Sums directed to be applied by Orders of the Commissioners.	Purposes to which the Sums have been directed to be applied.
		£. s. d.	£. s. d.	£. s. d.
Doncaster	Misson	248 0 0		
Downham . . .	{ West Dereham, Crimplesham, and Boughton }	250 0 0	250 0 0	Liquidation of outstanding claim.
,, ...	Marham	60 0 0	43 16 4	Towards cost of Union workhouse.
,, ...	Stoke Ferry . . .	190 0 0	177 19 10	{ 116 9 3 liquidation of outstanding claim. 61 10 7 towards cost of Union workhouse.
Driffield	Frodlingham, North	127 0 0		
Droxford	Bishop's Waltham	66 0 0	59 1 10	Expenses of valuation.
	Droxford	119 0 0	108 0 6	Towards cost of Union workhouse.
Dulverton	Hawkridge . . .	15 0 0		
Ecclesall Bierlow	Ecclesall Bierlow	1,200 0 0		
Elham	Postling	100 0 0	100 0 0	{ 77 6 4 towards cost of Union workhouse. 22 13 8 investment.
Freebridge Lynn	Castleacre . . .	122 0 0	109 11 3	Investment.
Godstone	Crowhurst . . .	116 0 0		
Grantham . . .	Ancaster	40 0 0		
Guildford	Send and Ripley .	240 0 0	215 5 2	Investment.
Guisborough. . .	Lofthouse	48 0 0	42 13 5	Towards cost of Union workhouse.
Hailsham	Chiddingly . . .	{ 120 0 0 39 0 0 Vide 8 Rep.	159 0 0	{ 130 0 0 liquidation of outstanding claim. 29 0 0 towards cost of Union workhouse.
,, ...	Hellingly . . .	{ 99 0 0 753 0 0 Vide 10 Rep	817 9 1	{ 714 0 8 Vide 10 Report. 103 8 5 liquidation of outstanding claims.
Hinckley	Sharnford	64 0 0		
Highworth and Swindon . .	Swindon	135 0 0		
,, ...	Wanborough . .	{ 65 0 0 243 0 0 Vide 6 Rep.	294 16 7	{ 229 16 7 Vide 6 Report. 65 0 0 expenses of valuation.
,, ...	Wroughton . . .	122 0 0	113 15 0	Liquidation of outstanding claim.
Holywell	Llanasa	160 0 0		
Keynsham . . .	Keynsham . . .	1 18 0		
Kingsbridge . . .	Stokefleming . . .	112 0 0		
Launceston . . .	{ St. Mary Magdalen. }	401 0 0		
Leicester	St. Nicholas . . .	100 0 0		
Liskeard	Menheniot . . .	40 0 0		
Lutterworth . . .	Misterton . . .	39 0 0		
Malmesbury . .	{ Malmesbury, Saint Paul. }	571 0 0	538 17 0	Investment.
Market Bosworth	Ratby	{ 60 0 0 250 0 0 Vide 10 Rep	298 0 0	{ 208 2 10 towards cost of Union workhouse. 89 17 2 investment.
Martley	Lulsley	19 0 0		
Midhurst	Rogate	{ 42 10 0 90 0 0 Vide 4 Rep.	99 18 10	{ 74 18 6 towards cost of Union workhouse. 25 0 4 liquidation of outstanding claim.
Newent	Kempley	14 0 0		
North Witchford	Benwick	{ 46 0 0 318 0 0 Vide 10 Rep	356 6 8	{ 230 9 6 towards cost of Union workhouse. 125 17 2 investment.
Pershore	Bishampton . . .	48 0 0	29 12 6	Towards cost of Union workhouse.
Peterborough . .	Maxey	236 0 0	216 0 0	{ Discharge of mortgage debt without the Commissioners' order.
Petworth	Rudgwick . . .	160 0 0		
Pickering	{ Thornton and Ellerburn. }	285 0 0	285 0 0	Liquidation of outstanding claim.
Plympton Saint Mary . .	Yealmpton . .	150 0 0		
Potterspury . . .	Cosgrove	29 0 0	20 0 0	Towards cost of Union workhouse.
,, . .	{ Stony Stratford, St. Giles. }	502 0 0		
Rye	Iden	285 0 0		
Saffron Walden .	Wimbish	45 0 0	41 0 0	Ditto.
Settle	{ Burton in Lonsdale. }	{ 28 0 0 90 0 0 Vide 8 Rep.	103 8 6	Investment.

UNION.	PARISH.	Amount of Purchase Money.	Sums directed to be applied by Orders of the Commissioners.	Purposes to which the Sums have been directed to be applied.
		£. s. d.	£. s. d.	£. s. d.
Shaftesbury . . .	{ Cann, otherwise Shaston St. Rumbold. }	30 0 0		
,, ...	Fontmell Magna	100 0 0	94 15 0	Towards cost of Union workhouse.
Shepton Mallet .	Shepton Mallet .	876 0 0	876 0 0	{ 149 3 6 expenses of emigration. 330 10 9 towards cost of Union workhouse, 396 5 9 investment. }
Skirlaugh	Atwick	34 7 0		
Sleaford	Martin	60 0 0		
Spalding	Surfleet	130 0 0	113 0 8	Towards cost of Union workhouse.
Sturminster . . .	Marnhull	{ 141 0 0 50 0 0 Vide 9 Rep. }	156 3 10	Ditto.
Sudbury . . .	Long Melford . .	35 0 0	27 1 6	Ditto.
Tamworth	Tamworth . . .	140 0 0		
,, ...	Wigginton . . .	155 0 0		
,, ...	Wilnecote . . .	80 0 0		
Thame	Crowell . . .	95 0 0		
Thingoe	Bradfield Combust	55 0 0		
,, ...	Timworth	60 0 0		
Thomas, St. . .	Brampford Speke	40 0 0		
Thornbury . . .	{ Hinton . . . Hamfallow, and Breadstone. }	350 0 0		
Thrapston . . .	{ Chelveston-cum-Caldecot }	15 0 0		
Tisbury	Semley	770 0 0		
Tonbridge . . .	Brenchley . . .	62 7 0		
,, . . .	Pembury . . .	680 0 0	638 13 11	Liquidation of outstanding claims.
Wayland	Watton	89 0 0		
Wellington, Somerset . .	Fitzhead	33 0 0		
Wells	Baltonsborough .	179 0 0		
,, ...	Dinder	60 0 0		
,, ...	Rodney Stoke . .	54 0 0		
,, ...	{ St. Cuthbert Out-Parish. }	{ 91 0 0 750 0 0 Vide 6 Rep. }	733 17 0	{ 161 0 0 Vide 6 Report. 572 17 0 expenses of valuation. }
Westbury and Whorwellsdown }	Bradley, North .	74 0 0		
Westfirle	Chalvington . . .	{ 120 0 0 105 0 0 Vide 10 Rep. }	221 3 8	{ 49 7 9 Vide 10 Report. 159 0 0 liquidation of outstanding claim. 12 15 11 towards cost of Union Workhouse. }
Williton	Treborough . . .	25 0 0		
Wimborne and Cranborne . . }	Farnham	12 0 0		
Winchcomb . . .	Woodmancote . .	{ *11 10 0 125 0 0 Vide 4 Rep. }	114 18 10	{ 60 6 2 towards cost of Union workhouse. 54 12 8 investment. }
Winchester, New	Sparsholt	20 10 0		
Windsor	Thorpe	{ 20 0 0 42 0 0 Vide 8 Rep. }	62 0 0	Towards cost of Union workhouse.
Wisbeach	Elm	250 0 0		
,, ...	{ Tilney Saint Lawrence. }	400 0 0	373 9 5	Investment.
Wycombe . . .	Marlow, Little . .	138 0 0		
Yeovil	{ Hardington Mandeville. }	35 10 0	20 19 8	Towards cost of Union workhouse.
,, ...	{ Stoke-under-Hamden. }	{ 15 0 0 149 10 0 Vide 7 & 8 Rep. }	156 2 5	Ditto.
,, ...	Yeovil	530 0 0	505 3 11	Ditto.

No. 10, ii.—Statement showing the Purposes to which the Produce has been directed to be applied of such part of the Property in the former Reports as was not previously applied.—(*In continuation of List in Tenth Annual Report, Appendix B. No. 9.*)

UNION.	PARISH.	Amount of Purchase Money.	Sums directed to be applied by Orders of the Commissioners.	Purposes to which the Sums have been directed to be applied.
		£. s. d.	£. s. d.	£. s. d.
Alderbury	Nunton and Bodenham.	*20 0 0 Vide 5 Rep.	15 0 0	Towards cost of Union workhouse.
Alresford	Kilmeston	40 0 0 Vide 4 Rep.	39 11 8	Ditto.
,, ...	Tisted, West . . .	40 0 0 Vide 4 Rep.	28 15 0	Ditto.
Alton	Farringdon . . .	68 0 0 Vide 9 Rep.	53 10 4	Ditto.
Ashby-de-la-Zouch	Snareston	188 0 0 Vide 9 & 10 Rep	188 0 0	Liquidation of outstanding claims.
Aylsham	Skeyton	65 0 0 Vide 8 Rep.	60 17 6	Investment.
Bakewell	Tansley	45 0 0 Vide 10 Rep.	45 0 0	Liquidation of outstanding claim.
Barrow-upon-Soar	Birstall	260 0 0 Vide 7 Rep.	253 2 6	19 1 6¼ towards cost of incorporation property. 90 18 9 towards cost of Union workhouse. 143 2 2¼ investment.
,, . . .	Syston.	323 0 0 Vide 5 Rep.	303 15 3	200 0 0 Vide 5 Report. 38 0 0 expenses of valuation. 65 15 3 towards cost of Union workhouse.
Battle.	Battle.	1446 0 0 Vide 9 & 10 Rep	1363 10 4	1263 10 4 Vide 9 Report. 100 0 0 outstanding claim.
Billericay	Childerditch . . .	160 0 0 Vide 10 Rep.	153 9 11	Investment.
Bishop's Stortford	Braughen	183 15 0 Vide 4 Rep.	170 1 3	Towards cost of Union workhouse.
,, . . .	Henham	124 0 0 Vide 6 Rep.	105 3 4	Ditto.
,, . . .	Stansted Mount Fitchet.	227 0 0 Vide 4 Rep.	213 4 3	Ditto.
Bodmin	Cardingham . . .	61 0 0 Vide 7 Rep.	58 14 0	Investment.
,, . . .	Egloshayle. . . .	15 0 0 Vide 8 Rep.	11 18 6	Ditto.
,, . . .	Lostwithiel . . .	246 0 0 Vide 7 Rep.	243 15 6	Ditto.
,, . . .	St. Mabyn . . .	75 0 0 Vide 10 Rep.	68 4 2	Ditto.
Bourn	Aslackby	549 0 0 Vide 9 Rep.	490 5 0	296 8 5 towards cost of Union workhouse. 193 16 7 investment.
,, . . .	Billingborough .	458 0 0 Vide 8 Rep.	397 17 4	373 8 1¼ towards cost of Union workhouse. 24 9 2¾ investment.
,, . . .	Careby	80 0 0 Vide 4 Rep.	78 9 9	39 8 9 Vide 4 Report. 2 15 5 towards cost of Union workhouse. 36 5 7 investment.
,, . . .	Castle Bytham .	250 0 0 Vide 4 Rep.	220 2 1¼	209 9 6 Vide 4 Report. 10 12 7¼ towards cost of Union workhouse.
,, . . .	Dowsby	206 0 0 Vide 8 Rep.	186 3 10	132 1 0¼ ditto 51 7 5 liquidation of outstanding claim. 2 15 4¾ investment.
,, . . .	Falkingham . . .	300 0 0 Vide 4 Rep.	270 7 3¼	217 7 0 Vide 4 Report. 17 0 1¼ toward cost of Union workhouse. 36 0 2 investment.
,, . . .	Hacconby	40 0 0 Vide 4 Rep.	37 17 1	Towards cost of Union workhouse.
,, . . .	Langtoft	72 0 0 Vide 9 Rep.	55 18 6	Ditto.
,, . . .	Laughton	50 0 0 Vide 7 Rep.	44 7 6	21 10 1¼ ditto. 22 17 4½ investment.
,, . . .	Manthorpe. . . .	72 0 0 Vide 4 Rep.	62 6 2	39 18 10½ towards cost of Union workhouse. 22 7 3½ investment.
,, . . .	Toft-cum-Lound .	†135 0 0 Vide 5 & 6 Rep.	112 1 7	93 9 7½ towards cost of Union workhouse. 18 11 11½ investment.
Bradfield	Tilehurst	598 18 9 Vide 10 Rep.	572 9 10	299 4 2 towards cost of Union workhouse. 273 5 8 investment.

* Reported as £400 in 5th Report.

† Of this amount £35 was reported in the 6th Report under the head of "Witham-on-the-Hill."

UNION.	PARISH.	Amount of Purchase Money.	Sums directed to be applied by Orders of the Commissioners.	Purposes to which the Sums have been directed to be applied.
		£. s. d.	£. s. d.	£. s. d.
Brentford	Isleworth	692 8 0 Vide 8 Rep.	*1132 15 11	Towards cost of Union workhouse.
Bridgend and Cowbridge..	Cowbridge....	80 0 0 Vide 5 Rep.	80 0 0	Towards cost of Union workhouse.
Bridgwater ...	Chedzoy.....	47 0 0 Vide 10 Rep.	44 0 1	Ditto.
,, ...	Thurloxton ...	40 0 0 Vide 10 Rep.	25 8 3½	Ditto.
Bridlington ...	Carnaby.....	12 10 0 Vide 5 Rep.	11 14 0	Investment.
,, ...	Dringhoe, Upton, & Brough	22 10 0 10 0 0 Vide 10 Rep.	21 0 0	Ditto.
,, ...	Reighton	10 0 0 Vide 10 Rep.	8 14 6	Ditto.
,, ...	Thwing	6 0 0 Vide 6 Rep.	5 0 0	Ditto.
Caistor	Clee.......	100 0 0 Vide 10 Rep.	96 2 8	{ 41 10 11 towards cost of Union workhouse. 54 11 9 investment.
Caxton and Arrington ...	Caxton	262 10 0 Vide 8 Rep.	236 7 0	Towards cost of Union workhouse.
,, ...	Elsworth	96 0 0 Vide 8 Rep.	85 0 0	Ditto.
,, ...	Hardwick	52 0 0 Vide 5 Rep.	52 0 0	Ditto.
Chailey	Ditchling	266 0 0 Vide 9 Rep.	256 18 8	{ 151 3 1 expenses of valuation. 49 0 7 towards cost of Union workhouse. 56 15 0 investment.
,, ..	Westmeston & East Chiltington	152 0 0 Vide 4 Rep.	137 4 1	{ 57 7 6 Vide 6 Report. 79 16 7 expenses of valuation.
Chesterton....	Oakington	268 16 0 Vide 10 Rep.	251 8 6	{ 134 12 7 Vide 10 Report. 116 15 11 purchase of fire-engine.
Church Stretton .	Wistantow ...	72 0 0 Vide 4 Rep.	62 6 8	{ 22 0 0 liquidation of outstanding claim. 40 6 8 towards cost of Union workhouse.
Congleton	Biddulph	320 0 0 Vide 10 Rep.	302 10 0	Liquidation of outstanding claim.
,,	Oddrode.....	176 0 0 Vide 5 Rep.	168 1 6	Towards cost of Union workhouse.
Cosford	Milden	180 0 0 Vide 5 Rep.	167 3 1	{ 20 0 0 expenses of valuation. 147 3 1 investment.
,, ...	Monks Eleigh ..	55 0 0 Vide 7 Rep.	47 3 10	Expenses of valuation.
Cranbrook....	Cranbrook....	313 0 0 Vide 7&10 Rep	280 12 3	Towards cost of Union workhouse.
,,	Goudhurst....	384 0 0 Vide 7 & 9 Rep	345 18 10	{ 237 0 0 ditto. 108 18 10 investment.
,,	Sandhurst	195 0 0 Vide 9 Rep.	173 15 4	{ 87 0 0 towards cost of Union workhouse. 86 15 4 investment.
Crickhowel ...	Llanguttock ...	400 0 0 Vide 4 Rep.	379 9 9	{ 166 5 0 Vide 4 Report. 213 4 0 investment.
Doncaster	Armthorpe....	123 0 0 Vide 10 Rep.	80 9 10	{ 26 7 6 towards cost of Union workhouse. 54 2 4 investment.
,, ...	Awkley	153 0 0 Vide 9 Rep.	133 8 0	{ 25 2 0 towards cost of Union workhouse. 108 6 0 investment.
,, ..	Cantley	184 0 0 Vide 9 Rep.	177 0 0	{ 38 19 3 towards cost of Union workhouse. 138 0 9 investment.
,, ...	Owston	15 0 0 Vide 6 Rep.	15 0 0	Towards cost of Union workhouse.
Dorking.....	Effingham ...	260 0 0 Vide 4 Rep.	249 5 11	{ 128 8 3 ditto. 120 17 8 investment.
,, ...	Newdigate....	262 0 0 Vide 6 Rep.	237 7 0	{ 186 19 7 towards cost of Union workhouse. 50 7 5 investment.
,, ...	Ockley	553 0 0 Vide 4 & 9 Rep.	524 13 0	{ 385 5 2 Vide 9 Report. 139 7 10 investment.
,, ...	Wotton	312 0 0 Vide 4 Rep.	307 3 2	{ 200 0 0 Vide 5 Report. 107 3 2 towards cost of Union workhouse.
Dulverton	Dulverton	72 0 0 Vide 5 Rep.	63 18 10	Expenses of valuation.

* Partly produced by the sale of materials.

No. 10, ii. (*continued*).—Statement showing the Purposes to which the Produce has been directed to be applied of such part of the Property in the former Reports as was not previously applied.—(*In continuation of List in Tenth Annual Report, Appendix B. No. 9.*)

UNION.	PARISH.	Amount of Purchase Money.	Sums directed to be applied by Orders of the Commissioners.	Purposes to which the Sums have been directed to be applied.
		£. s. d.	£. s. d.	£. s. d.
Easthampstead .	Binfield	864 0 0 Vide 9 & 10 Rep	804 16 0	{ 772 1 3 towards cost of Union workhouse. { 32 14 9 investment.
,, . . .	Easthampstead .	600 0 0 Vide 8 Rep.	520 13 4	{ 255 10 6 towards cost of Union workhouse. { 43 0 0 expenses of valuation. { 222 2 10 investment.
,, . . .	Warfield	250 0 0 Vide 9 Rep.	229 16 0	Towards cost of Union workhouse.
Honiton	Buckerell	{ 50 0 0 } Vide 6 Rep {	45 15 0	Ditto.
,, . . .	Dunkeswell . .	{ 22 0 0 } Vide 9 Rep {	17 12 4	Ditto.
,, . . .	Sheldon . .	{ 42 0 0 } Vide 4 Rep {	36 17 4	Ditto.
Horsham	Ifield	878 0 0 Vide 7 Rep.	627 10 10	{ 442 12 4 Vide 7 Report. { 184 18 6 expenses of plan.
Hinckley	Stoney Stanton . .	269 0 0 Vide 7 & 9 Rep	250 14 3	{ 167 3 4 Vide 7 Report. { 83 10 11 towards cost of Union workhouse.
Kendal	Lambrigg . . .	205 13 0 Vide 9 Rep.	205 13 0	Investment.
,, . . .	Preston Patrick . .	29 0 0 Vide 7 Rep.	29 0 0	Ditto.
Kingsbridge . . .	Slapton	100 0 0 Vide 10 Rep.	102 4 6	Ditto.
Lutterworth . . .	Leire	171 9 3 Vide 10 Rep.	157 19 0	Liquidation of outstanding claim.
Malton	Norton	246 0 0 Vide Rep.	24 15 10½	Towards cost of Union Workhouse.
Mansfield	Hucknall under } Huthwaite. }	166 0 0 Vide 7 Rep.	121 5 0	{ 62 15 0 Vide 7 Report. { 22 6 0 towards cost of Union workhouse { 36 4 0 liquidation of outstanding claim.
,, ...	Mansfield	845 0 0 Vide 4 Rep.	834 15 6	Towards cost of Union workhouse.
Martley	Alfrick	142 0 0 Vide 10 Rep.	112 13 0	Investment.
,, . . .	Areley Kings . .	185 0 0 Vide 10 Rep.	151 4 8	{ 45 18 9 Vide 10 Report. { 92 0 0 expenses of plan and valuation. { 13 5 11 towards cost of Union workhouse.
,, . . .	Lulsley	129 0 0 Vide 10 Rep.	118 11 8	Investment.
,, . . .	Wichingford . . .	50 0 0 Vide 10 Rep.	28 3 0	Ditto.
,, . . .	Witley, Little . .	55 0 0 Vide 9 Rep.	35 1 0	Ditto.
Midhurst	Lurgashall . . .	35 0 0 Vide 6 Rep.	30 1 10	Liquidation of parochial debt.
,, . . .	*Harting	555 0 0 Vide 4 Rep.	555 0 0	Towards cost of Union workhouse.
,, . . .	Midhurst . . .	280 0 0 Vide 4 Rep.	280 0 0	Ditto.
,, . . .	North Chapel . .	233 0 0 Vide 4 Rep.	222 3 10	Ditto.
North Witchford .	Doddington . . .	68 0 0 Vide 10 Rep.	60 9 8	Ditto.
Pembroke	Lamphey	70 0 0 Vide 10 Rep.	66 8 4	Ditto.
Potterspury . . .	Paulerspury . . .	179 0 0 Vide 6 Rep.	143 8 6	{ 116 10 6 Vide 6 Report. { 26 18 0 towards cost of Union workhouse
Redruth	Phillack	160 0 0 Vide 10 Rep.	154 14 6	Ditto.
Romsey	Mitchelmersh . .	45 0 0 Vide 10 Rep.	45 0 0	Towards cost of Union workhouse.
,, ...	Romsey Infra . .	255 0 0 Vide 4 & 5 Rep.	†244 1 2	{ 113 16 2 ditto. { 130 5 0 investment.
,, ...	West Wellow . . .	318 5 6 Vide 9 Rep.	316 6 4	{ 12 15 0 Vide 9 Report. { 26 12 8 towards cost of Union workhouse { 276 18 8 investment.
Royston	Melbourn	370 2 0 Vide 10 Rep.	360 2 2	{ 336 3 4 towards cost of Union workhouse. { 23 18 10 investment.
Settle	Bentham	77 0 0 Vide 8 Rep.	66 4 5	Investment.

* Reported as "Harling" in 4th Report.　　　　† The present appropriation in lieu of that mentioned in 4th Report.

No. 10, ii. (*continued*).—Statement showing the purposes to which the Produce has been directed to be applied of such part of the Property in the former Reports as was not previously applied. — (*In continuation of List in Tenth Annual Report, Appendix B. No. 9.*)

UNION.	PARISH.	Amount of Purchase Money.	Sums directed to be applied by Orders of the Commissioners.	Purposes to which the Sums have been directed to be applied.
		£. s. d.	£. s. d.	£. s. d.
Sheffield . . . . ,	Handsworth . . ,	289 0 0 Vide 6 Rep.	101 12 5	Towards cost of Union workhouse.
Shepton Mallet .	{ Stoke Lane, otherwise Stoke St. Michael. }	113 0 0 Vide 10 Rep.	113 0 0	{ 73 12 10　Vide 10 Report. *59 7 2　towards cost of Union workhouse.
Sherborne	Trent	164 0 0 Vide 8 & 9 Rep.	151 11 5	{ 91 14 2　expenses of valuation. 59 17 3　investment.
Shipston-on-Stour	Whichford	130 0 0 Vide 10 Rep.	109 8 8	{ 67 4 0　towards cost of Union workhouse. 42 4 8　investment.
South Stoneham .	Hound	314 0 0 Vide 10 Rep.	307 14 0	Liquidation of outstanding claims.
Stafford	Seighford	87 0 0 Vide 10 Rep.	83 13 0	{ 20 0 0　payment of claim in respect of the property. 63 13 0　defence of action of ejectment.
Stow	Woolpit	100 0 0 Vide 10 Rep.	100 0 0	{ 48 3 9　Vide 10 Report. *51 16 3　cost of engine-house, and purchase of fire-engine.
Sunderland . . .	Bishop Wearmouth	2100 0 0 Vide 10 Rep.	2095 8 0	{ 867 3 8　Vide 10 Report. 1228 4 4　investment.
Tetbury	Shipton Moyne .	85 0 0 Vide 4 Rep.	85 0 0	Towards cost of Union workhouse.
Thomas, St. . . .	Topsham	60 0 0 Vide 10 Rep.	60 0 0	Ditto.
Thornbury . . .	Ham and Stone .	187 10 0 Vide 7 & 9 Rep.	176 19 1	Liquidation of outstanding claim.
,, . . .	Titherington . .	78 0 0 Vide 7 Rep.	63 14 10	Ditto.
Thrapston . . .	Ringstead	227 0 0 Vide 5 Rep.	205 19 7	Towards cost of Union workhouse.
,, . . .	Thrapston . . .	549 0 0 Vide 4 Rep.	515 16 3	{ 298 4 5　ditto. 46 0 0　valuation. 171 11 10　investment.
,, . . .	Twywell	140 0 0 Vide 5 Rep.	116 15 2	{ 61 0 6　towards cost of Union workhouse. 55 14 8　investment.
Tiverton	Cadbury . . .	100 0 0 Vide 9 Rep.	97 3 4	{ 53 9 6¼　towards cost of Union workhouse. 43 13 9¾　investment.
,, . . .	Cullompton . . .	1035 0 0 Vide 8 Rep.	1030 2 8	{ 379 11 9¾　towards cost of Union workhouse. 150 10 10¼　investment.
,, . . .	Uplowman . . .	50 0 0 Vide 4 Rep.	45 11 10	Towards cost of Union workhouse.
,, . . .	Willand	68 0 0 Vide 5 Rep.	64 12 2	{ 54 5 11¼　ditto. 10 6 2¾　investment.
Torrington . . .	Alverdiscott . .	60 0 0 Vide 7 Rep.	57 2 0	{ 50 2 0¼　Vide 8 Report. 6 19 11¼　expenses of valuation.
Uckfield . .	Maresfield . . .	542 0 0 Vide 9 & 10 Rep.	515 10 7	{ 90 10 7　Vide 9 Report. 425 0 0　towards cost of Union workhouse.
,, . . .	Waldron	260 0 0 Vide 10 Rep.	253 10 0	Liquidation of outstanding claims.
Wantage	Blewbury	42 0 0 Vide 7 Rep.	35 5 8	Towards cost of Union workhouse.
,, . .	Braxted, Great .	250 0 0 Vide 4 Rep.	238 12 7	Ditto.
,, . .	Hampstead Norris	179 0 0 Vide 8 Rep.	155 18 6	Ditto.
,, . .	Sparsholt	195 0 0 Vide 4 Rep.	133 2 9	{ 112 10 0　liquidation of outstanding claims. 20 12 9　towards cost of Union workhouse.
,, . . .	Upton	19 10 0 Vide 6 Rep.	18 1 2	Ditto.
Watford	Abbots Langley .	325 0 0 Vide 5 Rep.	330 8 10	Ditto.
Wem	Ightfield	112 10 0 Vide 10 Rep.	88 17 8	Liquidation of outstanding claims.
Westbury-upon Severn. }	Blaisdon	54 0 0 Vide 9 Rep.	48 5 4	Investment.

* The investment mentioned in 10th Report rescinded.

No. 10, ii. (*continued.*)—Statement showing the Purposes to which the Produce has been directed to be applied of such part of the Property in the former Reports as was not previously applied.— (*In continuation of List in Tenth Annual Report, Appendix B. No. ii.*)

UNION.	PARISH.	Amount of Purchase Money.	Sums directed to be applied by Orders of the Commissioners.	Purposes to which the Sums have been directed to be applied.
		£. s. d.	£. s. d.	£. s. d.
Westbury-upon Severn.	Westbury-upon Severn.	1200 0 0 Vide 4 Rep.	1200 0 0	{ 1073 5 8 Vide 4 Report. { 126 14 4 expenses of valuation. 38 0 0 liquidation of mortgage debt without the Commissioners' order.
Winchcombe ..	Alderton	*175 0 0 Vide 4 Rep.	150 16 0	100 0 0 towards cost of Union workhouse. 22 16 0 investment.
,, ...	Backford	‾104 10 0 Vide 5 Rep.	88 0 0	Towards cost of Union workhouse.
,, ...	Bishop's Cleeve .	†96 0 0 Vide 4 Rep.	76 10 7	Ditto.
,, ...	Bishop's Cleeve and Woodmancote.	†225 0 0 Vide 4 Rep.	} 225 0 0	{ ‡ Liquidation of mortgage debt without the Commissioners' order.
,, ...	Gotherington ..	112 0 0 Vide 4 Rep.	98 9 8	
,, ...	Southam	†63 0 0 Vide 4 Rep.	53 10 0	
Winchcombe....	Stanley Pontlarge	20 0 0 Vide 6 Rep.	16 0 0	
Witham	Coggleshall, Great	496 0 0 Vide 5 Rep.	379 8 10	
,, ...	Coggleshall, Little	34 0 0 Vide 4 Rep.	24 16 8	
,, ...	Fairsted	65 0 0 Vide 4 Rep.	55 3 6	
,, ...	Feering	114 0 0 Vide 4 Rep.	106 0 0	⎬ Towards cost of Union workhouse.
,, ...	Inworth.....	156 0 0 Vide 6 Rep.	78 4 6	
,, ...	Kelvedon	275 0 0 Vide 4 Rep.	253 12 9½	
,, ...	Rivenhall....	300 0 0 Vide 4 Rep.	285 15 6	
,, ...	Wickham Bishop.	120 0 0 Vide 4 Rep.	24 17 10	
,, ...	Witham.....	232 0 0 Vide 4 Rep.	213 0 6	
.....	Petherton, South	80 0 0 Vide 9 Rep.	70 2 6	

* Reported as 137*l.* in 4th Report.
† These three amounts were reported in 4th Report as one sum (348*l.*) under the head of "Bishop's Cleeve."
‡ Reported in 4th Report as "the liquidation of debt incurred previous to the passing of the Poor Law Amendment Act."

No. 10, iii.—Statement of the Appropriation of such of the Sums of Money paid in respect of the Property of Dissolved Incorporations as have been directed by the Poor Law Commissioners to be appropriated since the date of their Tenth Annual Report.

BARROW-UPON-SOAR.

Names of the Disincorporated Parishes.	Names of the Unions in which the Parishes are now included.	Shares in the Incorporation Property, and Sums received in respect thereof.	Sums Appropriated and Reported in the Commissioners' former Reports.	Sums directed to be Appropriated by the Commissioners, and not yet Reported.	The Purposes to which the Appropriation has been directed to be made.
		£. s. d.	£. s. d.	£. s. d.	£. s. d.
Barrow-upon-Soar	Barrow-upon-Soar.	154 8 10	..	154 8 10	Towards purchase of Incorporation property.
Barkby	,, ,,	52 7 1	..	39 19 3¼	Ditto.
Beeby.	,, ,,	25 19 6	..	25 19 6	21 17 4½ ditto. 4 1 10¾ towards cost of Union workhouse.
Belgrave	,, ,,	89 17 6	..	89 17 6	86 0 11½ towards purchase of Incorporation property. 3 16 6½ towards cost of Union workhouse.
Cossington . . .	,, ,,	37 13 9	..	37 13 9	Towards purchase of Incorporation property.
Croxton, South .	,, ,,	42 3 8	..	42 3 8	35 15 3½ ditto. 6 8 4½ towards cost of Union workhouse.
Hathern	Loughborough .	80 2 1	..	80 2 1	Ditto.
Keyham.	Billesdon . . .	27 18 10	..	..	
Long Whatton. .	Loughborough	55 15 2	..	55 15 2	Ditto.
Mountsorrel, North.	Barrow-upon-Soar.	55 0 11	.	49 4 6¼	Towards purchase of Incorporation property.
Mountsorrel, South.	,, ,,	38 11 6	..	38 11 6	Ditto.
Queniborough .	,, ,,	64 4 3	..	38 1 7¼	Ditto.
Quorndon	,, ,,	102 17 4	..	99 6 0¼	Ditto.
Rearsby	,, ,,	52 0 4	..	52 0 4	Ditto.
Rothley	,, ,,	85 9 6	..	83 10 4¼	Ditto.
Seagrave	,, ,,	42 11 6	..	42 11 6	40 16 3¼ ditto. 1 15 2¾ towards discharge of parochial debt.
Sileby	,, ,,	171 12 3	..	99 13 10¾	Towards purchase of Incorporation property.
Swithland . . .	,, ,,	36 19 11	..	36 19 11	Ditto.
Syston	,, ,,	108 8 10	..	108 8 10	Ditto.
Thrussington . .	Barrow-upon-Soar.	47 7 8	..	34 5 10¼	Towards purchase of Incorporation property.
Thurcaston . . .	,, ,,	44 9 10	..	32 16 5	Ditto.
Thurmaston, South	,, ,,	80 6 0	..	80 6 0	56 3 4 ditto. 24 2 8 towards discharge of parochial debt.
Thurnby.	Billesdon . . .	15 5 8	..	..	
Ulverscroft. . . .	Barrow-upon-Soar.	11 16 6	..	11 16 6	7 19 11 towards purchase of Incorporation property. 3 16 7 towards cost of Union workhouse.
Wimeswould . .	Loughborough.	50 19 3	..	50 19 3	Ditto.
		1,574 4 8*	..	..	

* Reported in the 9th Report as 1483*l.* 9*s.* 5*d.* only

No. 10, iii. (*continued*).—Statement of the Appropriation of such of the Sums of Money paid in respect of the Property of Dissolved Incorporations as have been directed by the Poor Law Commissioners to be appropriated since the date of their Tenth Annual Report.

CLAYPOLE.

Names of the Disincorporated Parishes.	Names of the Unions in which the Parishes are now included.	Shares in the Incorporation Property, and sums received in respect thereof.	Sums Appropriated and Reported in the Commissioners' former Reports.	Sums directed to be Appropriated by the Commissioners, and not yet Reported.	The Purposes to which the Appropriation has been directed to be made.
		£. s. d	£. s. d.	£. s. d.	£. s. d.
Baruby	Newark . . .	18 14 6 Vide 6 Rep.	. .	18 14 6	
Broughton . . .	,, . . .	78 18 2¼ Vide 6 Rep.	. .	78 18 2¼	
Benuington . . .	,, . . .	124 18 3 Vide 6 Rep.	. .	124 18 3	
Claypole	,, . . .	75 15 11¼ Vide 6 Rep.	. .	75 15 11¼	
Coddington . . .	,, . . .	61 17 8¼ Vide 6 Rep.	. .	61 17 8¼	
Doddington . . .	,, . . .	32 18 4¼ Vide 6 Rep.	. .	32 18 4¼	⎬ Paid to the credit of the parishes.
Fulbeck	,, . . .	86 10 5¼ Vide 6 Rep.	. .	86 10 5¼	
Marston	,, . . .	59 19 4¼ Vide 6 Rep.	. .	59 19 4¼	
Sedgebrook . . .	,, . . .	62 4 3¼ Vide 6 Rep.	. .	62 4 3¼	
Stubton	,, . . .	47 11 1 Vide 6 Rep.	. .	47 11 1	
Westborough . .	,, . . .	16 17 8¼ Vide 6 Rep.	. .	16 17 8¼	

EASTBOURNE.

Trotton	Midhurst . . .	*259 9 0¼ Vide 9 Rep.	180 0 0	79 3 6¼	Investment.

EASTRY.

Ham	Eastry	9 18 9 Vide 7 Rep.	5 7 1¼	4 11 7¼	⎰ 1 7 10 towards cost of Union workhouse. ⎱ 3 3 9¼ expenses of valuation.
Tilmanstone . .	,, ,,	30 17 2¼ Vide 6 Rep.	. .	30 17 2¼	Towards cost of Union workhouse.

MARTIN.

Sutton	Eastry	52 10 11¼ Vide 6 & 8 Rep.	44 9 4	2 15 8¼	Towards cost of Union workhouse.

ONGAR.

Abbot's Roothing	Ongar	210 15 7¼ Vide 6 Rep.	. .	204 2 8¼	⎰ Towards liquidation of parochial debts.
Bobbingworth . .	,, . . .	345 13 3¼ Vide 6 Rep.	. .	336 10 4¼	⎰ 303 17 2¼ ditto. ⎱ 32 13 2¼ towards cost of Union workhouse.
Greenstead . . .	,, . . .	49 7 0¼ Vide 6 Rep.	. .	47 7 8¼	⎰ Towards liquidation of parochial debt.
Laver, Little . .	,, . . .	198 9 8¼ Vide 6 Rep.	. .	192 15 0¼	Ditto.
Stapleford Abbots	,, . . .	388 2 0¼ Vide 6 Rep.	. .	377 7 5¼	⎰ 367 12 0 ditto. ⎱ 9 15 5¼ towards cost of Union workhouse.
Stapleford Tawney	,, . . .	228 9 5¼ Vide 6 Rep.	. .	228 9 5¼	⎰ 215 2 5 towards liquidation of parochial debt. ⎱ 13 7 0¼ towards cost of Union workhouse.
Stondon Massey .	,, . . .	53 18 11¼ Vide 6 Rep.	. .	51 7 11¼	⎰ Towards liquidation of parochial debt.
Shelley	,, . . .	155 9 6¼ Vide 6 Rep.	. .	151 2 0¼	⎰ 147 2 0 ditto. ⎱ 4 0 0¼ towards cost of Union workhouse.

* Part of this sum was produced by interest on the purchase money.

No. 10, iii. (*continued*).—Statement of the Appropriation of such of the Sums of Money paid in respect of the Property of Dissolved Incorporations as have been directed by the Poor Law Commissioners to be appropriated since the date of their Tenth Annual Report.

RIVER.					
Names of the Disincorporated Parishes.	Names of the Unions in which the Parishes are now included.	Shares in the Incorporation Property, and Sums received in respect thereof.	Sums Appropriated and Reported in the Commissioners' former Reports.	Sums directed to be Appropriated by the Commissioners, and not yet Reported.	The Purposes to which the Appropriation has been directed to be made.
		£. s. d.	£. s. d.	£. s. d.	£. s. d.
Eythorne	Eastry	*25 6 5 Vide 10 Rep.	. .	25 6 5	Towards cost of Union workhouse.
ROSLISTON.					
Croxall	Tamworth . .	53 6 4 Vide 9 Rep.	. .	53 6 4	{ Towards liquidation of outstanding claim.

* Reported as 24*l.* 16*s.* 7¼*d.* in 10th Report.

No. 11.—Union formed under the Poor Law Amendment Act, with particulars of Population, Average Poor Rates, and Number of Guardians.—(*In continuation of List in Seventh Annual Report, Appendix E., No.* 6.)

ASHBOURNE UNION.							
DERBYSHIRE AND STAFFORDSHIRE.	Population in 1841.	Averages for the Years ended 25th March, 1842, 43, and 44.	Number of Elected Guardians	DERBYSHIRE AND STAFFORDSHIRE.	Population in 1841.	Averages for the Years ended 25th March, 1842, 43, and 44.	Number of Elected Guardians
		£.				£.	
Alkmonton	102	7	1	Ilam	244	57	1
Ashbourne	2,158	661	2	Kirk Ireton	714	160	1
Atlow	156	39	1	Kniveton	326	92	1
Ballidon	92	53	1	Lea Hall	22	. .	1
Bentley Fenny . . .	343	51	1	Longford	568	252	1
Bentley Hungry . . .	83	3	1	Mappleton	204	83	1
Biggin	149	71	1	Mayfield	847	86	1
Blore with Swinescoe. .	273	80	1	Mercaston	138	51	1
Bonsall	1,496	285	2	Middleton by Wirksworth	1,031	168	1
Bradbourne	175	114	1				
Bradley	271	131	1	Newton Grange	39	5	1
Brailsford	756	237	1	Offcote and Underwood .	344	145	1
Brassington	776	242	1	Okeover	67	30	1
Callow	112	63	1	Osmaston	271	103	1
Calton in Blore . . .	60	12	1	Parwich	533	121	1
Calton in Mayfield . .	88	50	1	Prestwood	68	36	1
Calton in Waterfall . .	71	12	1	Ramshorn	142	44	1
Calwich	131	36	1	Rodsley	207	47	1
Carsington	235	138	1	Shirley	390	114	1
Clifton and Compton .	839	144	1	Snelston	399	84	1
Eaton and Alsop . . .	67	10	1	Stanton	393	94	1
Edlaston and Wyaston .	214	50	1	Sturston	662	154	1
Eliastone	351	115	1	Stydd	40	14	1
Hartington Town Quarter . . . . }	486	84	1	Thorpe	196	35	1
				Tissington	427	138	1
Hartington Nether Quarter . . . . }	475	81	1	Waterfall	446	97	1
				Woodhouses	25	5	1
Hognaston	272	97	1	Wootton	223	87	1
Hollington	289	107	1	Yeaveley	239	55	1
Hopton	83	38	1	Yeldersley	211	67	1
Hulland	204	51	1				
Hulland Ward	355	49	1	Total	20,658	5,567	63
Hulland Ward Intacks .	57	18	1				
Ible	93	14	1				

[Declared to take effect from the 4th day of January, 1845.]

No. 12.—STATEMENT of the Number of Poor Persons who have Emigrated, and of the Sums which the Poor Law Commissioners have authorized to be raised or borrowed, from the 1st January to the 31st December, 1844.—(*In continuation of Statement in* 10th *Annual Report, Appendix B. No.* 10.)

COUNTY.	PARISH.	Amount authorized to be raised or borrowed.	Number of Poor Persons, who have Emigrated.						To what part Emigrated.
			Males.			Females.			
			Adult Persons above 14 Years of Age.	Children between 7 and 14 Years of Age.	Children under 7 Years of Age.	Adult Persons above 14 Years of Age.	Children between 7 and 14 Years of Age.	Children under 7 Years of Age.	
		£. s. d.							
Bedford ...	Bletsoe	80 0 0	8	.	3	3	.	4	South Australia.
,, ...	Bromham	10 0 0	1	.	.	1	.	1	Ditto.
,, ...	Ridgmont	40 0 0	1	1	.	1	.	3	Canada.
,, ...	Riseley	121 0 0	10	1	4	5	.	.	South Australia.
,, ...	Wilshamstead	40 10 0	3	.	1	2	.	1	Canada.
Berks ...	Newbury	●	2	.	.	2	.	.	South Australia.
			2	1	.	1	.	.	Ditto.
Bucks...	Bow Brickhill	90 0 0 {	1	1	.	1	2	1	Canada.
,, ...	Bradwell	50 0 0	3	2	1	3	3	2	South Australia.
,, ...	Buckingham	100 0 0	4	.	.	.	.	.	Canada.
,, ...	Cheddington	80 0 0	2	1	2	2	2	3	Ditto.
,, ...	Fenny Stratford	50 0 0	2	1	2	1	2	1	Ditto.
,, ...	Linford, Great	50 0 0	14	4	3	6	.	5	Ditto.
,, ...	Loughton	40 0 0	2	2	.	4	.	2	South Australia.
,, ...	Olney	100 0 0	2	4	3	4	1	1	Canada.
,, ...	Thornborough	300 0 0 {	13	3	5	8	4	5	South Australia.
			1	2	1	1	1	1	Canada.
,, ...	Water Eaton	16 0 0	2	.	.	.	.	.	Ditto.
,, ...	Weston Underwood	35 0 0	1	1	1	1	1	.	Ditto.
,, ...	Winslow	80 0 0	5	.	1	4	1	.	South Australia.
Cambridge..	Abington, Little	90 0 0	1	1	1	3	3	2	Canada.
,,	Borough Green	22 0 0	1	.	1	1	.	.	Ditto.
,,	Kirtling	60 0 0	7	1	.	1	.	2	Ditto.
,,	Wisbeach, St. Peter	35 0 0	1	.	.	.	3	.	Ditto.
Cornwall ..	Lezant	15 0 0	1	.	.	4	1	2	South Australia.
,,	Petherwin, North.	10 0 0	1	.	.	1	.	3	Ditto.
Derby	Chapel-en le-Frith	10 0 0	2	.	1	2	1	3	Ditto.
Devon ...	Lewtrenchard	40 0 0							
,, ...	Whitchurch	20 0 0							
Dorset. ...	Hawkchurch	30 0 0	.	1	2	1	2	.	Canada.
,, ...	Stockland	15 0 0	2	.	2	2	3	.	Ditto.
Essex	Clavering	25 0 0							
,, ...	Harlow	10 0 0	.	.	.	1	.	.	Ditto.
,, ...	Wimbish	60 0 0	3	2	3	3	.	.	Ditto.
Hertford...	Baldock	25 0 0							
,,	Hitchin	30 0 0	1	1	2	1	2	.	Ditto.
,,	Layston	26 0 0	1	.	1	1	1	.	Ditto.
Kent	Gondhurst	200 0 0	4	3	3	2	4	2	Ditto.
,, ...	Hawkhurst	●	.	1	.	.	.	.	Ditto.
,, ...	Tenterden	20 0 0	2	.	.	.	.	.	Ditto.
,, ...	Wittersham	●	1	.	1	2	2	1	South Australia.
Lincoln ...	Grantham	30 0 0	3	2	1	1	2	1	Canada.
,, ...	Thurlby	40 0 0	1	.	1	1	.	.	Ditto.
Norfolk ...	Blofield	250 0 0	15	1	2	8	3	7	Ditto.
,, ...	Diss	38 0 0	1	3	.	1	1	.	Ditto.
,, ...	Gunthorpe	125 0 0	3	1	3	3	1	.	Ditto.
,, ...	Holt	40 0 0 {	.	.	1	2	2	1	Ditto.
			1	.	1	1	.	.	South Australia.
,, ...	Letheringsett	35 0 0	1	1	1	2	.	2	Ditto.
Northampton	Brackley, St. Peter	200 0 0	10	6	5	4	2	7	Canada.
,,	Buckby, Long	37 0 0	1	1	2	1	2	.	Ditto.
,,	Marston St. Lawrence	100 0 0	3	1	5	4	3	3	Ditto.
,,	Paulerspury	50 0 0							
,,	Woodford	120 0 0	7	2	2	5	2	3	Ditto.
Nottingham	Ratcliffe-upon-Trent	●	4	1	2	4	5	5	South Australia.
Oxford ...	Aston Rowant	100 0 0	3	1	1	4	1	2	Ditto.
,, ...	Chesterton	50 0 0	2	1	3	3	2	2	Ditto.
,, ...	Sydenham	50 0 0	17	3	1	10	4	2	Ditto.

● Vide 10th Report, Appendix B. No. 10.

No. 12, (*continued.*)—Statement of the Number of Poor Persons who have Emigrated, and of the Sums which the Poor Law Commissioners have authorized to be raised or borrowed, from the 1st January to the 31st December, 1844.—(*In continuation of Statement in* 10th *Annual Report, Appendix B., No.* 10.)

COUNTY.	PARISH.	Amount authorized to be raised or borrowed.	Males. Adult Persons above 14 Years of Age.	Children between 7 and 14 Years of Age.	Children under 7 Years of Age.	Females. Adult Persons above 14 Years of Age.	Children between 7 and 14 Years of Age.	Children under 7 Years of Age.	To what part Emigrated.
		£. s. d.							
Somerset	Ditcheat	100 0 0	1	2	.	1	.	1	Canada.
,,	Selworthy	35 0 0	1	2	1	1	.	1	Ditto.
,,	Shepton Mallet	220 0 0	16	.	.	.	.	.	Ditto.
,,	Wincanton	100 0 0	1	2	.	1	1	.	South Australia.
Southampton	Chawton	50 0 0	.	.	.	.	.	.	
,,	Longparish	36 0 0	1	.	.	2	2	.	Canada.
Suffolk	Blythburgh	20 0 0	2	.	.	.	.	.	Ditto.
,,	Bramfield	5 0 0	2	.	.	.	.	.	South Australia.
,,	Brundish	25 0 0	1	1	1	1	1	1	Ditto.
,,	Claydon	10 0 0	1	.	.	.	.	.	Canada.
,,	Cookley	50 0 0	4	1	.	.	1	.	South Australia.
,,	Debenham	10 0 0	1	.	.	.	.	.	Canada.
,,	Frostenden	10 0 0	1	.	1	1	.	.	South Australia.
,,	Halesworth	15 0 0	1	.	1	1	.	1	Ditto.
									Canada.
,,	Hemingstone	35 0 0							
,,	Middleton	20 0 0							
,,	Otley	45 0 0	4	2	4	5	2	1	Ditto.
,,	Peasenhall	10 10 0							
,,	Stradbroke	30 0 0	1	.	.	1	.	1	Ditto.
,,	Thorndon, All Saints	300 0 0	10	4	6	9	6	4	Ditto.
,,	Westleton	60 0 0	6	1	.	1	.	2	South Australia.
,,	Wetheringsett-cum-Brockford	35 0 0	1	1	1	1	.	1	Canada.
,,	Wickham Skeith	65 0 0	3	.	.	.	.	.	Ditto.
,,	Wisset	6 0 0	2	.	.	.	.	.	South Australia.
,,	Wrentham	13 0 0	3	.	.	.	.	.	Ditto.
Surrey	Banstead	30 0 0	.	.	.	.	1	.	Ditto.
,,	Chiddingfold	100 0 0	4	.	1	1	2	2	Ditto.
,,	Cranley	10 0 0	.	.	.	1	.	.	Canada.
,,	Hascomb	40 0 0	1	1	.	1	2	1	Ditto.
,,	Witley	60 0 0	3	1	1	2	2	.	Ditto.
Sussex	Chailey	35 0 0	5	.	.	2	1	.	Ditto.
,,	Cuckfield	100 0 0	6	3	2	4	4	2	Ditto.
,,	Dallington	45 0 0	2	2	1	1	1	2	Ditto.
,,	Glynde	50 0 0	2	1	1	1	1	3	Ditto.
,,	Graffham	30 0 0	1	.	.	1	3	2	Ditto.
,,	Grinsted, West	30 0 0	1	1	.	1	3	.	Ditto.
,,	Hailsham	100 0 0	1	1	5	4	.	.	Ditto.
			3	.	.	2	2	.	South Australia.
			2	6	.	.	.	.	Canada.
			1	.	.	1	.	.	South Australia.
,,	Herstmonceux	*	1	.	.	1	.	.	Canada.
									South Australia.
,,	Horsted Keynes	130 10 0	2	1	1	2	.	2	Canada.
,,	Laughton	†	1	.	.	.	.	.	Ditto.
,,	Lurgashall	15 0 0	2	2	.	2	1	3	South Australia.
,,	Petworth	50 0 0	9	3	.	3	.	.	Canada.
,,	Ringmer	10 0 0	1	.	.	.	.	.	Ditto.
,,	Rogate	7 0 0	.	.	.	.	.	.	
,,	Salehurst	†	2	.	.	.	.	1	Ditto.
,,	Shermanbury	15 0 0	1	.	1	1	.	1	South Australia.
,,	Street	30 0 0	1	1	2	1	1	1	Canada.
,,	Tillington	165 0 0	7	4	4	8	4	5	Ditto.
,,	Twineham	75 0 0	4	2	2	2	.	2	Ditto.
,,	Wartling	56 0 0	1	.	.	.	.	.	Ditto.
,,	Wivelsfield	37 0 0	3	.	.	1	1	.	Ditto.
Warwick	Prior's Hardwick	35 0 0	1	3	1	1	.	.	South Australia.
,,	Solihull	25 0 0	2	.	.	1	2	.	Canada.
Wilts	Christian Malford	*	4	1	1	1	2	.	South Australia.
,,	Collingbourn Ducis	65 0 0	.	.	.	.	.	.	
,,	Purton	150 0 0	10	.	.	2	1	1	Canada.
Worcester	Kidderminster Borough	50 0 0	.	.	.	.	.	.	

* Vide 10th Annual Report, Appendix B., No. 10.   † Vide 8th Annual Report, Appendix E., No. 7.

No. 13.—**IRELAND.**—SUMMARY of AUDITED UNION ACCOUNTS for the Half-years ended respectively 25th March and 29th September, 1844, showing the RECEIPTS and EXPENDITURE of UNIONS in IRELAND, and the Balances in those Half-years.

(i.)—Half-year ended 25th March, 1844.—100 Unions.

UNIONS.	CHARGE.						
	Balances in favour of Unions at the close of last Half-year.	RECEIPTS. Amount of Poor-Rate Collected.	RECEIPTS. Repayment of Relief by way of Loan.	RECEIPTS. Other Receipts.	RECEIPTS. Total Receipts in the Half-year.	Balances against Unions at close of this Half-year.	TOTAL.
	£. s. d.	£. s. d.	£. s. d.	£. s. d.	£. s. d.	£. s. d.	£. s. d.
Abbeyleix	.	2,126 14 2	.	.	2,126 14 2	211 6 8¼	2,338 0 10¼
Antrim	.	2,483 5 4	0 6 0	.	2,483 11 4	1 2 10	2,484 14 2
Ardee	914 6 11¼	743 1 1	.	.	743 1 1	106 18 8¼	1,764 6 8½
Armagh	1,765 0 7	1,719 19 10	.	.	1,719 19 10	629 19 6	4,114 19 11
Athy	.	1,414 19 8¾	.	.	1,414 19 8¾	148 3 5½	1,563 3 2¼
Bailieborough	70 1 9	1,383 13 3	.	.	1,383 13 3	448 7 1	1,902 2 1
Ballina	.	2,512 15 11	.	12 0 0	2,524 15 11	93 15 0	2,618 10 11
Ballinasloe	816 3 11	802 14 3¾	.	.	802 14 3¾	1,419 1 8¾	3,037 19 11½
Ballinrobe	6 14 2¼	793 13 6	.	.	793 13 6	943 3 9¾	1,743 11 6
Ballycastle	133 14 1	599 3 5	.	.	599 3 5	57 0 7¼	789 18 1¼
Ballymena	.	3,196 15 4	.	.	3,196 15 4	.	3,196 15 4
Ballymoney	1,719 12 2¼	330 6 3¾	.	.	330 6 3¾	.	2,049 18 6
Ballyshannon	11 18 8¾	197 9 6	6 9 6	.	203 19 0	123 16 4¼	339 14 1
Baltinglass	494 16 5	1,533 11 3¾	.	.	1,533 11 3¾	114 12 10	2,143 0 6¾
Banbridge	344 14 1	1,150 10 4	.	29 19 6	1,180 9 10	328 12 3¾	1,853 16 2¾
Bandon	820 4 0½	1,663 5 7	.	.	1,663 5 7	345 2 0½	2,828 11 8
Belfast	2,407 7 10¾	891 13 7	0 6 10	.	892 0 5	552 16 6¾	3,852 4 10½
Callan	159 12 10½	719 2 8	.	.	719 2 8	230 3 0¾	1,108 18 7¼
Carrickmacross	.	1,690 2 8	.	.	1,690 2 8	12 5 3¾	1,702 7 11¾
Carrick-on-Shannon	.	600 6 10	.	.	600 6 10	1,592 2 6½	2,192 9 4½
Carrick-on-Suir	11 8 6½	1,315 16 8	.	.	1,315 16 8	369 8 7¼	1,696 13 9¾
Cashel	244 15 6¾	1,482 13 2	.	.	1,482 13 2	846 14 6¼	2,574 3 3
Castlebar	.	57 14 2	.	.	57 14 2	1,753 19 7	1,811 13 9
Castleblayney	.	1,125 17 8	5 9 3	.	1,131 6 11	711 7 10¼	1,842 14 9¼
Castlederg	405 10 11½	300 13 6	3 2 10	.	303 16 4	2 8 8¼	711 15 11¾
Celbridge	335 4 11	383 6 10¾	.	.	383 6 10¾	229 8 8	948 0 5¾
Clogheen	76 2 3½	849 6 7	.	.	849 6 7	472 16 4¼	1,398 5 2¾
Clones	649 4 4½	222 2 4	.	6 13 11	228 16 3	99 16 4¼	977 16 11¾
Clonmel	277 16 1	1,608 5 2	.	.	1,608 5 2	.	1,886 1 3
Coleraine	688 13 9¾	723 18 7	.	.	723 18 7	236 13 7¼	1,649 6 0
Cookstown	707 3 8¼	341 9 9½	.	.	341 9 9½	130 12 9½	1,179 6 3¼
Cootehill	323 17 11¼	824 0 7	.	29 15 2	853 15 9	1,002 16 2	2,180 9 10¼
Cork	.	8,511 10 7	.	422 0 7	8,933 11 2	7,801 3 1	16,734 14 3
Donegal	0 15 10	984 17 6	.	.	984 17 6	.	985 13 4
Downpatrick	543 9 1¾	2,699 15 8	.	.	2,699 15 8	8 6 0½	3,251 10 10¼
Drogheda	840 11 5½	1,550 10 0	.	.	1,550 10 0	459 4 6¼	2,850 5 11¾
Dublin, North	3,430 10 7¼	5,958 18 7	10 4 2¼	688 0 5¾	6,657 3 3	318 13 0½	10,406 6 10¾
Dublin, South	708 2 9¼	10,222 6 10¼	1 7 7¾	105 17 4	10,329 11 10	2,101 17 8¼	13,139 12 3½
Dundalk	204 7 6½	1,518 17 7	.	.	1,518 17 7	861 7 6	2,584 12 7½
Dungannon	615 19 10½	1,610 3 9	.	.	1,610 3 9	17 14 9¾	2,243 18 5¼
Dunmanway	366 13 11	333 13 9	.	.	333 13 9	.	700 7 8
Dunshaughlin	64 1 9½	1,218 3 7	.	.	1,218 3 7	381 1 3¼	1,663 6 7¾
Ennis	89 9 5½	937 18 3	.	.	937 18 3	549 1 2¼	1,576 8 10¾
Ennistymon	135 7 0¼	474 8 4	.	.	474 8 4	194 16 6¼	804 11 10½
Fermoy	283 10 3½	1,232 14 0½	.	.	1,232 14 0½	1,867 9 8¼	3,383 14 0¼
Galway	7 4 1	1,922 6 11	.	350 0 0	2,272 6 11	806 0 6	3,085 11 6
Gorey	529 7 11	545 12 1	.	.	545 12 1	705 2 6	1,780 2 6
Gort	.	153 10 11	.	.	153 10 11	1,337 6 8	1,490 17 7
Gortin	168 9 6¾	528 10 0	.	.	528 10 0	127 17 1¼	824 16 8
Granard	73 9 5½	1,411 2 4	.	.	1,411 2 4	642 19 4	2,127 11 1½
Inishowen	.	1,629 15 0	.	.	1,629 15 0	.	1,629 15 0

No. 13.—Ireland, (*continued*).—Summary of Audited Union Accounts for the Half-years end respectively 25th March and 29th September, 1844, showing the Receipts and Expenditure Unions in Ireland, and the Balances in those Half-Years.

(i.)—Half-year ended 25th March, 1844.—100 Unions.

UNIONS.	CHARGE.						
	Balances in favour of Unions at the close of last Half-year.	RECEIPTS.				Balances against Unions at close of this Half-year.	TOTAL.
		Amount of Poor Rate Collected.	Repayment of Relief by way of Loan.	Other Receipts.	Total Receipts in the Half-year.		
	£. s. d.	£. s. d.	£. s. d.	£. s. d.	£. s. d.	£. s. d.	£. s. d.
Kells	561 19 0¼	792 5 1	.	.	792 5 1	415 3 6¼	1,769 7 7
Kilkeel	153 11 7¼	634 8 6	.	.	634 8 6	40 10 11¼	828 11 1
Kilkenny	464 17 0¼	2,397 17 4	.	41 9 4¼	2,439 6 8¾	2,190 7 0¼	5,094 10 9
Kilmallock	585 18 4¼	525 13 6	.	.	525 13 6	1,396 10 6¼	2,508 2 5
Kilrush	51 14 11¼	1,139 10 7	.	.	1,139 10 7	85 19 10¾	1,277 5 5
Kinsale	321 9 5¼	919 0 3¼	.	9 6 1	928 6 4¼	325 14 6	1,575 10 8
Larne	733 14 0¼	294 15 0	0 13 0	.	295 8 0	180 19 10	1,210 1 10
Limerick	94 12 4¼	2,270 0 1¼	0 3 6	.	2,270 3 7¼	3,301 14 7¾	5,666 10 8
Lisburn	1,285 4 5¼	857 1 10	.	3 0 0	860 1 10	469 15 1¼	2,615 1 4
Lismore	111 3 6	454 13 7	.	.	454 13 7	131 10 1¼	697 7 [illegible]
Lisnashea	406 7 2¼	153 16 4	.	289 18 1	443 14 5	63 18 9¼	914 0 5
Londonderry	507 4 7¼	1,687 12 5	4 10 8	.	1,692 3 1	26 0 0¼	2,226 7 9
Longford	381 6 5	990 0 0	.	.	990 0 0	1,004 11 1¼	2,375 17 6
Loughrea	11 5 1	502 13 10	.	.	502 13 10	1,430 8 9¼	1,944 7 8
Lurgan	281 10 10¼	1,196 0 0	2 16 0	.	1,198 16 0	595 8 4¼	2,075 15 [illegible]
Macroom	349 8 2	101 17 5	.	.	101 17 5	160 6 6¼	611 12 1
Magherafelt	1,569 6 0¼	760 2 9	9 13 9	.	769 16 6	.	2,339 2 6
Mallow	339 3 3¼	234 4 8¼	0 11 10	3 3 3	237 19 9¼	482 6 4¼	1,059 9 5
Midleton	538 10 3¼	752 13 2¼	.	.	752 13 2¼	1,321 18 4¼	2,613 1 10
Monaghan	535 5 11¼	867 13 10¼	.	0 2 0	867 15 10¼	313 6 0	1,716 7 9
Mullingar	657 1 10¼	921 11 11	.	.	921 11 11	452 3 10¼	2,030 17 8
Naas	1,369 18 1¼	689 12 4	.	.	689 12 4	2,146 18 3¼	4,156 8 9
Navan	278 7 10¼	1,184 3 2	.	.	1,184 3 2	721 1 5¼	2,183 12 6
Nenagh	201 19 5¼	2,212 16 11¼	.	1 5 0	2,214 1 11¼	803 1 7¼	3,219 3 0
Newcastle	82 8 11¼	932 12 0¼	.	.	932 12 0¼	947 19 0¼	1,963 0 0
New Ross	664 5 8	860 17 2	0 8 9	0 2 4	861 8 3	756 0 4¼	2,281 14 8
Newry	708 16 2	635 2 4	.	.	635 2 4	677 8 1	2,021 6 7
Newtownards	675 2 2	259 5 1	.	1 0 0	260 5 1	693 19 4	1,629 6 7
Newtown Limavady	326 14 6	518 6 11	.	.	518 6 11	115 9 9¼	960 11 2
Oldcastle	205 18 6¼	392 5 0	.	.	392 5 0	618 5 8¼	1,216 9 3
Omagh	490 11 6¼	965 5 6	.	.	965 5 6	218 12 3¼	1,674 9 4
Parsonstown	400 15 7	734 1 2	.	.	734 1 2	807 18 9¼	1,942 15 6
Rathdown	574 0 7¼	467 7 6	.	.	467 7 6	1,574 15 6	2,616 3 7
Rathdrum	672 18 9¼	1,065 16 10	.	.	1,065 16 10	883 7 4¼	2,622 3 0
Rathkeale	266 14 0¼	400 6 7¼	.	1 0 0	401 6 7¼	498 17 4¼	1,166 18 0
Roscommon	.	1,493 6 3	.	.	1,493 6 3	121 5 3¼	1,616 11 6
Roscrea	348 12 2¼	1,355 11 10	.	16 0 9	1,371 12 7	322 1 2	2,042 5 11
Scariff	.	1,880 7 0	.	.	1,880 7 0	416 13 8	2,297 0 8
Shillelagh	60 12 5	1,449 7 3¼	0 1 2	.	1,449 8 5¼	190 13 11	1,700 14 9
Skibbereen	7 11 11¼	1,402 14 11¼	.	.	1,402 14 11¼	1,609 1 0	3,019 7 11
Sligo	472 2 6	1,488 10 10	.	.	1,488 10 10	682 9 0¼	2,643 2 4
Strabane	1,486 1 5¼	287 11 4	.	.	287 11 4	56 9 9¼	1,830 2 7
Thurles	334 10 10	542 2 9	.	11 18 9	554 1 6	614 12 5¼	1,503 4 9
Tipperary	207 19 6¼	1,374 8 2	.	9 17 7¼	1,384 5 9¼	1,403 9 4	2,995 14 7
Tralee	.	3,813 4 7	.	.	3,813 4 7	8 1 11¼	3,821 6 6
Trim	421 16 6¼	357 19 9	.	.	357 19 9	648 13 3¼	1,428 9 6
Tullamore	281 5 6¼	1,477 8 7	.	.	1,477 8 7	599 7 11¼	2,358 2 0
Waterford	85 15 5¼	1,929 19 10¼	0 17 6	0 4 2	1,931 1 6¼	2,679 1 3	4,695 18 2
Wexford	48 16 7¼	503 2 2	.	.	503 2 2	1,267 2 5	1,819 1 2
Totals	42,060 8 5¼	128,312 11 8	47 2 5	2,032 14 5	130,392 8 6	67,866 7 3¼	240,319 4

No. 13.—Ireland, (*continued*).—Summary of Audited Union Accounts for the Half-Years of Unions in Ireland, and the

i.—Half-year ended 25th

UNIONS.	DISCHARGE.					
		EXPENDITURE.				
	Balances against Unions at close of last Half-year.	Maintenance and Clothing. On account of Electoral Division Paupers.	Maintenance and Clothing. On account of Union Paupers.	Maintenance and Clothing. Total for Maintenance and Clothing.	Establishment Charges.	Repayment of Workhouse Loans.
	£. s. d.	£. s. d.	£. s. d.	£. s. d.	£. s. d.	£. s. d.
Abbeyleix	817 8 8	611 15 4¼	161 15 10	773 11 2¼	365 15 7	.
Antrim	.	331 14 11	12 2 11	343 17 10	1,251 5 0	.
Ardee	256 6 0¼	553 11 8¼	73 16 1	627 7 9¼	258 0 3¼	.
Armagh	501 4 6¼	691 17 3¼	67 3 10	759 1 1¼	305 17 8	.
Athy	.	210 7 9	14 1 0	224 8 9	613 18 10	.
Bailieborough	984 7 8	471 6 1	2 8 2	473 14 3	261 6 1½	.
Ballina	.	193 4 1½	30 19 6	224 3 7½	874 4 6	.
Ballinasloe	1,248 6 6¼	473 3 1¼	33 6 8½	506 9 10¾	368 5 9	.
Ballinrobe	1,.29 1 2¼	99 19 5¼	7 13 11	107 13 4¼	191 3 3	.
Ballycastle	118 15 9¼	159 6 9¾	0 11 8¼	159 18 6	122 10 2¼	.
Ballymena	.	162 0 1¼	1 9 6¾	163 9 8	873 5 7	.
Ballymoney	.	292 6 9½	21 8 10½	313 15 8	573 15 9	.
Ballyshannon	127 19 6¼	67 14 5¼	2 12 0	70 6 5¼	128 17 4½	.
Baltinglass	269 14 8	631 3 5½	28 1 3½	659 4 9	365 8 4	340 0 0
Banbridge	500 17 11	452 14 8¼	11 1 10	463 16 6¼	304 6 8¼	.
Bandon	433 14 5¼	423 6 6¾	128 11 11¼	551 18 6	620 3 10	.
Belfast	267 4 3¼	1,545 19 0¼	167 6 3	1,713 5 3¼	385 4 10	600 0 0
Callan	235 10 4	337 7 4	95 18 11¼	433 6 3¼	261 3 0	.
Carrickmacross	868 9 11	65 1 7	10 16 7	75 18 2	276 0 8¾	.
Carrick-on-Shannon	1,455 19 2	469 4 7¼	23 12 2	492 16 9¼	209 8 0¼	.
Carrick-on-Suir	748 18 3¼	467 10 2¼	35 16 6¼	503 6 9½	282 4 6¼	.
Cashel	1,079 10 1¾	639 7 2½	162 7 2½	801 14 5	400 7 11	.
Castlebar	1,512 2 1¼	142 17 5½	4 12 10¼	147 10 3¾	143 8 3¾	.
Castleblayney	754 5 4¼	549 6 6¾	16 17 7¼	566 4 2	451 17 1¼	.
Castlederg	68 7 1¾	88 14 5¼	.	88 14 5¼	114 17 1	.
Celbridge	171 6 9	256 0 6¼	30 2 9½	286 3 4¾	223 8 5	.
Clogheen	347 7 11¼	445 18 9¼	9 11 6¼	455 10 3½	423 5 10	.
Clones	2 15 4¾	528 2 9½	28 14 11½	556 17 9	217 11 1	.
Clonmel	28 18 6	565 2 7	132 10 4	697 12 11	195 16 5	115 0 0
Coleraine	36 14 5	581 4 2¼	14 18 10¾	596 3 1	356 2 3¼	.
Cookstown	32 11 7	294 18 6	37 16 9¾	332 15 3¾	34 6 8¼	315 0 0
Cootehill	566 7 0¾	911 15 2½	8 18 7½	920 13 10	374 15 2¼	.
Cork	5,131 13 6¼	2,629 7 8	2087 5 0¼	4,716 12 8¼	1,108 0 7¼	.
Donegal	236 9 5¼	42 1 6½	0 10 4¼	42 11 11¾	256 19 7¼	.
Downpatrick	387 15 11¾	748 14 1¼	73 2 1½	821 16 3¾	501 5 10	.
Drogheda	1,185 15 10¾	508 19 0¼	49 0 11	557 19 11¼	266 10 0	.
Dublin, North	724 6 0¼	4,034 9 0	302 18 3	4,337 7 3	1,210 6 2¼	.
Dublin, South	2,021 19 1¼	4,199 18 6	354 5 11¾	4,554 4 5¾	1,803 5 10	800 0 0
Dundalk	878 4 11¼	712 4 0¼	30 5 10½	742 9 10¾	271 0 9	.
Dungannon	206 15 9	542 5 10¼	33 3 5¼	575 9 4½	227 9 3	.
Dunmanway	.	22 19 7	202 1 8	225 1 3	196 0 0	.
Dunshaughlin	622 10 2¾	661 1 3¼	51 4 10	712 6 1¼	227 15 1	.
Ennis	443 15 9¼	648 17 10	83 15 7	732 13 5	.	.
Ennistymon	206 4 1¾	0 1 5¼	261 4 3	261 5 8¼	160 10 5¼	.
Fermoy	1,750 14 2¼	937 3 2	281 18 7	1,219 1 9	344 19 1	.
Galway	2,168 13 11	281 12 7	21 4 2	302 16 9	243 19 4	.
Gorey	331 19 0¾	587 17 6¼	168 16 10	756 14 4¼	241 17 2	.
Gort	1,086 15 7	212 14 9½	10 14 0¼	223 8 10¾	175 13 10¾	.
Gortin	134 10 7¼	125 8 1¼	3 9 11½	128 18 0¾	121 9 2	180 0 0
Granard	924 10 8	656 4 10¼	9 2 1½	665 6 11¾	199 13 4	.
Inishowen	.	42 9 0¼	3 7 2	45 16 2¼	394 5 10	.

EXPENDITURE.

Vaccination Expenses. £. s. d.	Expense of Valuing or revising Valuations. £. s. d.	Collector's Poundage, or other Remuneration. £. s. d.	Funerals, Election, Law, and other Expenses. £. s. d.	Total Expenditure in the Half-year. £. s. d.
10 11 6	10 0 0	68 2 10	17 9 6	1,245 10 7½
123 5 0	228 5 0	38 8 1	61 12 9	2,046 13 8
27 15 0	.	.	6 17 11	920 1 0
17 2 0	.	.	9 0 11	1,091 1 8½
32 0 0	204 3 0	.	97 14 7	1,172 5 2
1 16 0	3 9 2	36 2 9	32 19 6	809 7 9½
354 14 0	500 0 0	11 1 6	252 14 11	2,216 18 6½
0 18 0	.	27 14 4	5 5 8½	908 13 8
1 1 2½	.	39 13 8	36 8 0	375 19 5½
3 9 0	.	33 5 5	1 19 10	321 2 11½
262 0 0	342 0 0	54 8 2	66 4 6	1,761 7 11
12 9 10	62 12 9	.	15 12 9	978 6 9
.	.	3 3 9	9 7 0	211 14 6¼
.	12 10 0	64 4 0¼	6 10 6	1,447 17 7¾
86 10 0	15 3 3	10 0 5	10 4 9½	890 1 8
.	150 0 0	104 18 3	28 3 8	1,455 4 3
24 16 6	.	7 9 10	29 4 10½	2,760 1 4
0 18 0	.	8 4 2	7 1 2	710 12 7½
4 7 0	.	2 3 2	1 7 2	339 16 2¼
10 0 0	.	.	24 5 5	736 10 2¼
.	.	14 13 9	6 7 2	806 12 2¼
.	3 2 6	39 8 4	11 5 0	1,255 18 2
4 10 5	.	1 8 10	2 13 9	299 11 7½
.	.	22 6 6	26 10 4½	1,066 18 1¼
.	.	1 4 0	69 2 1	273 17 7½
.	.	36 8 4½	0 15 6	546 15 7¾
53 15 0	.	46 7 0	12 8 6	991 6 7½
1 8 0	.	18 15 3	29 10 10½	824 2 11½
.	.	30 18 8	1 12 0	1,041 0 0
26 15 6	.	35 19 10	9 12 6	1,024 13 2½
.	.	72 13 0	2 8 4	757 3 4½
.	.	.	7 13 0	1,303 2 0½
.	56 17 0	134 8 0	5,587 2 5	11,603 0 8½
12 8 0	.	.	5 17 4	317 16 10¼
69 7 10	33 2 6	.	15 1 10	1,440 14 3½
56 4 0	.	7 10 0	55 18 7	944 2 6½
.	70 0 0	284 15 7½	78 17 5	5,981 6 6
26 4 0	.	267 17 1	41 8 2½	7,492 19 7½
48 12 0	43 0 0	19 11 6	49 8 0	1,176 2 1¼
.	.	14 7 6	4 2 2½	821 8 3¾
13 16 0	2 6 8	8 13 3	5 1 0	450 18 2
12 4 0	.	30 16 6	4 17 9	987 19 5½
.	30 0 0	43 7 8	11 4 4	819 5 5
.	.	.	3 8 8	425 4 10
.	.	.	9 6 5½	1,573 7 3½
.	50 0 0	80 4 7	7 5 1	684 5 9
1 9 6	13 17 6	33 15 1	12 12 6	1,060 6 1½
3 3 6	.	.	1 15 9	404 2 0
.	.	52 3 9	7 18 6	490 9 5¼
13 5 0	.	20 10 8	3 6 3	902 1 9¼
11 2 0	192 7 5	.	69 17 8	713 8 8½

No. 13.—Ireland, (*continued*).—Summary of Audited Union Accounts for the Half-years ended
of Unions in Ireland, and the
I.—Half-year ended 25th

DISCHARGE.

EXPENDITURE.

UNIONS.	Balance against Unions at close of last Half-year.	Maintenance and Clothing. On account of Electoral Division Paupers.	On account of Union Paupers.	Total for Maintenance and Clothing.	Establishment Charges.	Repayment of Workhouse Loans.
	£. s. d.	£. s. d.	£. s. d.	£. s. d.	£. s. d.	£. s. d.
Kells	273 5 6¼	539 0 5¼	49 3 9¾	588 4 3¼	249 16 0¼	.
Kilkeel	117 1 1¼	130 18 7¼	14 6 1¼	145 4 8¾	202 1 10	.
Kilkenny	2,599 6 6¼	1,475 4 11	146 7 8	1,621 12 7	570 16 0¼	.
Kilmallock	737 13 4¼	1,032 4 8¼	83 13 3	1,115 17 11¼	309 19 0	.
Kilrush	372 17 4¼	272 13 8	30 9 10	303 3 6	152 9 4¼	.
Kinsale	298 15 7	289 12 1¼	56 9 9	346 1 10¼	217 0 4	.
Larne	31 13 1¼	405 10 5¼	4 6 10¾	409 17 4	132 7 3	290 0 0
Limerick	3,050 3 4¾	1,129 0 1¼	767 7 5	1,896 7 6¼	651 11 3¼	.
Lisburn	505 7 3¼	636 19 9	24 14 0	661 13 9	367 9 11¾	.
Lismore	85 3 5	190 6 0¼	26 13 7	216 19 7¼	262 11 7	.
Lisnashea	13 1 1¼	260 3 6¼	10 2 11¼	270 6 6¼	319 19 1	.
Londonderry	75 17 3	497 17 8¼	42 15 8	540 13 4¼	350 14 3¾	.
Longford	809 19 0¼	868 18 1	23 8 2¼	892 6 3¼	354 0 6	.
Loughrea	1,371 5 0¼	307 4 10¼	13 0 6¼	320 5 5	220 1 3¼	.
Lurgan	516 1 9¼	553 2 1¼	11 15 9	564 17 10¼	431 13 7	.
Macroom	.	317 10 2	22 7 1¼	339 17 8¼	122 1 5	.
Magherafelt	.	359 11 3¼	37 9 10	397 1 1¼	277 3 11¾	405 0 0
Mallow	105 1 10¼	401 12 9¼	76 10 2¼	478 3 0	216 14 6	.
Midleton	618 2 6¼	771 7 2¼	57 4 4¼	828 11 7	409 19 6¼	.
Monaghan	396 13 6¼	427 16 8¼	54 16 0	482 12 8¼	298 10 8¼	.
Mullingar	301 15 3	972 14 7¾	54 5 8	1,027 0 3¾	197 6 11	.
Naas	1,692 0 3¼	859 6 6¼	21 5 0	880 11 6¼	224 7 2	.
Navan	545 13 6¼	642 17 11¼	32 19 3	675 17 2¼	320 13 10	.
Nenagh	1,410 0 6¼	813 7 2	59 2 3¼	872 9 5¼	324 0 9¾	495 0 0
Newcastle	630 5 11	816 1 4¼	118 14 0	934 15 4¼	364 4 5¼	.
New Ross	298 0 7¾	900 2 1¼	59 18 4	960 0 5¼	272 15 0	.
Newry	266 12 1	949 11 3	33 18 6	983 9 9	178 1 1	.
Newtownards	385 13 4¾	327 4 11¾	64 10 1¾	391 15 1¼	319 5 5	335 0 0
Newtown Limavady	98 10 1¼	189 1 1¼	12 1 3¼	201 2 5	255 19 4¼	.
Oldcastle	334 18 5¼	480 3 2¼	20 10 6¾	500 13 9¼	223 14 10¾	.
Omagh	303 10 4	372 14 8	81 12 1¼	454 6 9¼	261 14 2¼	.
Parsonstown	888 6 5	388 10 11¾	21 18 4¾	410 9 4¾	255 10 0	.
Rathdown	379 7 2¼	912 13 10¾	139 13 2¼	1,052 7 1¼	542 16 10	490 0 0
Rathdrum	543 11 3¼	762 7 10	87 4 4¼	849 12 2¼	288 19 0	415 0 0
Rathkeale	167 8 1	437 2 9	47 3 8	484 6 5	281 0 9¼	.
Roscommon	.	105 12 8	20 12 3¾	126 4 11¼	793 14 1	.
Roscrea	573 18 4¼	603 7 2¼	79 19 9	683 6 11¼	292 18 3¼	.
Scariff	1,885 10 1¾	77 1 9¼	26 10 11¼	103 12 9	227 17 1	.
Shillelagh	627 11 7¼	496 12 3	55 11 4¼	552 3 7¼	281 1 7¼	.
Skibbereen	2,144 2 9¾	471 16 8	36 17 6	508 14 2	252 0 0	.
Sligo	997 4 6¾	643 14 8¾	63 13 8¼	707 8 5¼	405 18 10¼	.
Strabane	81 10 6	401 2 1¾	21 7 7	422 9 8¾	243 1 6¾	.
Thurles	428 14 0¼	496 15 5¼	6 7 11¾	503 3 5	387 16 0	.
Tipperary	1,335 2 8	821 18 3¼	116 5 1	938 3 4¼	345 15 0	.
Tralee	.	51 9 7	3 14 9¾	55 4 4¾	914 14 6¼	.
Trim	615 1 11¾	298 13 9¾	42 14 7¼	341 8 5¼	231 14 6¾	.
Tullamore	1,041 2 7	679 14 6	20 13 11¼	700 8 5¼	208 18 6¼	.
Waterford	1,963 12 10¼	1,539 9 3	157 18 6	1,697 7 9	793 2 8¾	.
Wexford	576 6 10¾	667 17 9¼	86 10 3	754 8 0¼	404 5 1¼	.
Totals	63,650 1 8	39,354 15 7¼	8,551 16 8	67,906 12 3¾	35,923 18 1¼	4,770 0 0

respectively 25th March and 29th September, 1844, showing the Receipts and Expenditure Balances in those Half-years.

March, 1844.—100 Unions.

DISCHARGE.						
EXPENDITURE.					Balances in favour of Unions at the close of this Half-year.	TOTAL.
Vaccination Expenses.	Expense of Valuing or revising Valuations.	Collector's Poundage, or other Remuneration.	Funerals, Election, Law, and other Expenses.	Total Expenditure in the Half-year.		
£. s. d.	£. s. d.	£. s. d.	£. s. d.	£. s. d.	£. s. d.	£. s. d.
			8 0 6	846 0 10	650 1 3¼	1,769 7 7¾
28 18 0	6 6 0	3 17 10	5 6 7	391 14 11½	319 14 11½	828 11 1
			9 7 10	2,201 16 5½	293 7 9½	5,094 10 9½
4 14 0		13 14 7	17 3 0½	1,461 8 6¾	309 0 6	2,508 2 5½
	30 0 0	28 9 8	29 5 4	543 7 10½	361 0 2½	1,277 5 5½
	21 7 5	37 1 1	274 15 9½	896 6 5¾	380 8 2¼	1,575 10 3¼
19 19 0		42 6 6	2 12 8½	897 2 9½	281 5 11¼	1,210 1 10½
			67 15 0	2,615 13 10	0 13 5½	5,666 10 8¼
7 6 0	16 0 0	47 13 8	8 5 10	1,108 9 2¼	1,001 4 10½	2,615 1 4¼
11 3 6		37 14 1	7 12 0	536 0 9½	76 3 0½	697 7 2¼
1 13 0			1 7 6	593 6 1¼	307 13 2¼	914 0 5
43 0 0	9 0 0	63 11 10	5 10 6	1,012 10 0	1,137 0 6	2,225 7 9
17 0 0			16 6 6	1,279 13 3¼	286 5 2¼	2,375 17 6¼
5 5 0		18 17 0	0 15 6	565 4 2½	7 18 5¼	1,944 7 8¼
			11 16 3½	1,008 7 9	551 5 9¼	2,075 15 3¼
2 5 0	20 0 0	30 12 3	0 3 0	514 18 11½	96 13 2¼	611 12 1¾
25 13 0		41 14 10	5 0 3	1,151 13 2¼	1,187 9 4¼	2,339 2 6½
		56 4 8	9 18 0	761 0 2	193 7 5	1,059 9 5½
12 10 2	20 0 0	136 19 0½	49 16 3	1,457 16 7	537 2 9¼	2,612 1 10¾
23 1 6		54 8 8	6 17 0	865 10 6¼	454 3 8¼	1,716 7 9¾
	35 0 0		4 19 9	1,264 6 11½	464 15 5½	2,030 17 8¾
13 3 0		15 19 6	7 14 9	1,141 15 11½	1,322 12 6½	4,156 8 9
0 3 6		41 15 3	6 1 11½	1,044 11 9	593 7 3½	2,182 18 6½
1 9 6	0 15 11	21 9 10½	7 19 4	1,723 4 10½	85 17 8	3,219 3 0¾
		22 16 7	4 17 11	1,326 14 4	5 19 9½	1,963 0 0½
18 11 0		15 10 11	8 3 1	1,275 0 5½	708 13 2	2,281 14 2½
78 15 6	22 7 6	33 7 1	14 2 3	1,310 3 2	444 11 4	2,021 6 7
		38 5 11	16 10 11½	1,100 17 5½	142 15 9	1,629 6 7
5 12 0		28 19 6	3 14 6	495 7 9½	366 13 8¼	960 11 2½
17 10 2		8 3 4	5 14 0	755 16 2½	125 14 7½	1,216 9 8
	10 15 0	17 14 8	6 19 9	751 10 5	619 8 7½	1,674 9 4½
21 3 0		39 19 2	2 9 9	729 11 3½	324 17 10½	1,942 15 6¾
13 5 0		48 17 9	50 16 1	2,188 2 9½	48 13 8¼	2,616 3 7¾
32 17 6	15 0 0	120 13 0	28 8 2	1,750 9 10½	328 1 10¾	2,622 3 0
	25 0 0	69 19 11	15 14 1	876 1 2½	123 8 8½	1,166 18 0
155 10 0	256 0 0	31 2 8	118 0 7	1,480 12 3½	135 19 3	1,616 11 6½
18 9 0		29 12 8	83 19 3½	1,108 6 2½	360 1 4½	2,042 5 11½
		3 5 0		334 14 10	76 15 8¼	2,297 0 8
4 16 0	21 15 0	6 8 3	4 15 3½	870 19 9¼	202 8 4¼	1,709 14 9¼
	11 5 0		23 6 6	795 5 8	79 19 5½	3,019 7 11¼
35 19 0			24 19 6	1,174 5 9½	471 11 11¼	2,643 2 4¼
		43 16 9	23 16 6	733 4 6½	1,065 7 6¾	1,838 2 7¾
			22 18 8	853 18 1	220 12 8	1,503 4 9½
		28 17 0	6 14 1½	1,319 9 6	341 2 5¾	2,995 14 7¾
288 14 6	515 0 0	94 10 5	158 17 8	2,027 1 6½	1,794 5 0½	3,821 6 6½
3 10 0	13 4 0		1 13 5	591 10 5	221 17 8	1,428 9 6¾
		43 2 6	20 10 9	967 0 3	349 10 9¼	2,358 2 0¾
73 11 7	15 0 0	97 6 4½	35 10 8	2,711 19 0½	20 6 8¾	4,695 18 2¼
15 14 0	12 10 0	29 1 6¼	8 3 11½	1,224 2 8¼	10 11 7¾	1,819 1 2¼
2,329 0 2½	3,101 2 7	3,373 6 1½	8,130 2 9	125,533 17 1	49,185 5 6¾	240,319 4 8¼

P 2

UNIONS.	CHARGE.				
	Balances in favour of Unions at the close of last Half-year.	RECEIPTS.			
		Amount of Poor-Rate Collected.	Repayment of Relief by way of Loan.	Other Receipts.	Total Receipts in the Half-year.
	£. s. d.	£. s. d.	£. s. d.	£. s. d.	£. s. d.
Abbeyleix	275 1 6¾	1,022 12 10	.	.	1,022 12 10
Antrim	438 0 6	81 14 2	.	.	81 14 2
Ardee	587 19 9	1,726 3 0	.	.	1,726 3 0
Armagh	2,522 13 8¼	584 10 0	.	.	584 10 0
Athy	390 18 0¼	567 16 11¾	.	.	567 16 11¾
Bailieborough	108 6 7½	461 19 2	.	.	461 19 2
Ballina	401 12 4¼	1,104 15 0	.	.	1,104 15 0
Ballinasloe	880 19 9	933 17 5¼	.	.	933 17 5¼
Ballinrobe	38 10 10¼	434 7 9¼	.	.	434 7 9¼
Ballycastle	349 19 4¼	815 14 0	.	.	815 14 0
Ballymena	1,435 7 5	.	.	.	.
Ballymoney	1,071 11 9	606 18 5	.	.	606 18 5
Ballyshannon	.	877 9 9	.	.	877 9 9
Baltinglass	425 8 2½	1,026 13 5	.	.	1,026 13 5
Banbridge	462 16 7½	954 2 6	.	8 7 0	962 9 6
Bandon	939 12 11½	1,358 8 11	.	.	1,358 8 11
Belfast	824 19 2¼	5,304 5 5½	.	0 14 6	5,304 19 11½
Boyle	438 19 10¼	562 18 11¾	.	.	562 18 11¾
Callan	162 15 8	1,196 17 0	.	.	1,196 17 0
Carrickmacross	474 1 9¾	88 11 7	.	.	88 11 7
Carrick-on-Shannon	.	1,606 3 0	.	0 4 3	1,606 7 3
Carrick-on-Suir	141 3 3½	666 14 10	.	.	666 14 10
Castlebar	.	99 3 6	1 2 9	.	100 6 3
Castleblayney	21 11 3½	861 15 0	.	.	861 15 0
Castlederg	369 11 2½	138 0 0	2 18 9	.	140 18 9
Celbridge	229 18 1	865 6 0	.	.	865 6 0
Clogheen	59 10 8¾	974 16 6½	.	.	974 16 6½
Clogher	.	2,084 13 5	.	.	2,084 13 5
Clones	150 18 7½	1,817 0 10	.	0 4 10	1,817 5 8
Clonmel	816 2 9	1,062 16 3	.	.	1,062 16 3
Coleraine	587 18 4¾	1,352 12 5	4 7 0	.	1,356 19 5
Cookstown	389 11 4	977 0 0	.	.	977 0 0
Cootehill	311 0 9¾	1,693 19 2	.	.	1,693 19 2
Cork	.	11,865 0 11	.	2 18 2	11,867 19 1
Donegal	431 7 0	103 8 1	.	.	103 8 1
Downpatrick	1,423 0 7½	1,481 15 3	.	2 19 6	1,484 14 9
Drogheda	720 7 7	297 4 1	.	.	297 4 1
Dublin, North	3,700 13 4¼	3,049 13 11	.	216 8 7	3,266 2 6
Dublin, South	3,624 13 6¼	3,845 15 6	4 0 11¾	1010 10 7	4,860 7 0¾
Dundalk	530 5 6½	2,071 8 8	.	.	2,071 8 8
Dungannon	1,215 14 4½	612 1 4	.	.	612 1 4
Dungarvan	1,452 7 2½	684 9 6	.	.	684 9 6
Dunmanway	249 9 6	591 6 0	.	.	591 6 0
Dunshaughlin	52 16 11½	1,091 15 3	.	.	1,091 15 3
Ennis	313 7 8¼	1,222 19 2	.	.	1,222 19 2
Enniscorthy	169 18 2½	2,367 6 0	.	.	2,367 6 0
Ennistymon	173 2 10¾	657 7 10	.	0 5 0	657 12 10
Fermoy	59 12 6½	3,458 18 3	.	27 11 5	3,486 9 8
Galway	232 11 10	757 9 5	.	.	757 9 5
Gorey	387 17 4	1,179 1 8	.	.	1,179 1 8
Gort	.	812 13 6	.	.	812 13 6
Gortin	199 16 6¼	487 18 8	.	.	487 18 8
Granard	300 18 7½	760 6 6	.	.	760 6 6
Inishowen	916 6 8¼	33 0 0	.	.	33 0 0

CHARGE.

UNIONS.	Balances in favour of Unions at the close of last Half-year.	RECEIPTS.				Balances against Unions at close of this Half-year.	TOTAL.
		Amount of Poor-Rate Collected.	Repayment of Relief by way of Loan.	Other Receipts.	Total Receipts in the Half-year.		
	£. s. d.	£. s. d.	£. s. d.	£. s. d.	£. s. d.	£. s. d.	£. s. d.
Kanturk	.	1,502 5 8	.	.	1,502 5 8	243 9 9	1,745 15 5
Kells	650 1 3½	526 0 11	.	.	526 0 11	601 16 5½	1,777 18 8
Kilkeel	319 14 11¼	118 0 9	.	.	118 0 9	167 14 9½	605 10 5¾
Kilkenny	293 7 9½	797 7 2	.	.	797 7 2	3,429 10 8	4,520 5 7¼
Kilmallock	309 0 6	1,480 13 5	.	.	1,480 13 5	1,131 13 1¼	2,921 7 0¾
Kilrush	361 0 2½	120 9 4	.	.	120 9 4	209 0 2	690 9 8½
Kinsale	380 8 2¾	841 18 3	.	4 0 0	845 18 3	256 3 8½	1,482 10 2
Larne	281 5 11¾	250 0 0	.	.	250 0 0	478 10 6¾	1,009 16 6½
Lisburn	1,001 4 10½	1,381 11 5	.	.	1,381 11 5	233 4 0¾	2,616 0 4
Lismore	76 3 0½	59 9 8	.	.	59 9 8	385 2 4	520 15 0½
Lisnaskea	307 13 2½	1,627 17 10	.	168 15 6	1,796 13 4	.	2,104 6 6½
Londonderry	1,137 0 6	571 12 1	0 12 8	.	572 4 9	81 1 6½	1,790 6 9½
Longford	286 5 2¾	351 16 0	.	.	351 16 0	2,288 8 4½	2,926 9 7½
Loughrea	7 18 5¾	132 9 7	.	0 1 9	132 11 4	1,906 15 5½	2,047 5 3
Lurgan	551 5 9½	1,705 15 0	6 6 6	22 9 10½	1,734 11 4½	203 7 1½	2,489 4 3
Macroom	96 13 2½	1,396 1 9¾	.	.	1,396 1 9¾	179 16 11½	1,672 11 11¾
Magherafelt	1,187 9 4½	95 2 6	5 12 10	.	100 15 4	243 12 0	1,531 16 8½
Mallow	193 7 6	52 11 7½	.	.	52 11 7½	1,022 7 11½	1,268 7 0½
Midleton	537 2 9½	2,557 18 4¾	.	.	2,557 18 4¾	202 12 0	3,297 13 2½
Monaghan	454 3 8½	1,410 15 0	.	.	1,410 15 0	71 5 0½	1,936 3 8
Mullingar	464 15 5½	1,043 11 6	.	0 19 9	1,044 11 3	593 2 6	2,102 9 2
Naas	1,322 12 6½	1,322 14 7	.	0 3 6½	1,322 18 1½	2,031 2 4½	4,676 13 0½
Navan	593 7 3½	1,042 12 11	.	.	1,042 12 11	818 8 8½	2,454 8 10¾
Nenagh	85 17 8	1,427 19 10	.	7 16 6	1,435 16 4	693 0 3	2,214 14 3
Newcastle	5 19 9½	1,359 0 4	.	.	1,359 0 4	906 18 8½	2,271 18 9½
New Ross	708 13 2	2,433 1 5	0 6 3	.	2,433 7 8	278 14 11¾	3,420 15 9¾
Newry	444 11 4	1,343 8 9	.	.	1,343 8 9	615 4 8	2,403 4 9
Newtownards	142 15 9	2,566 9 7	.	.	2,566 9 7	187 18 3½	2,897 3 7½
Newtown Limavady	366 13 3¾	878 13 7	.	.	878 13 7	1 7 3½	1,246 14 2½
Oldcastle	125 14 7½	1,309 1 8	.	.	1,309 1 8	305 8 7¾	1,740 4 11
Omagh	619 8 7½	1,246 3 5	.	1 0 0	1,247 3 5	71 17 3	1,938 9 3½
Parsonstown	324 17 10½	1,037 0 0	.	.	1,037 0 0	597 14 2½	1,959 12 1
Rathdown	48 13 8½	1,404 14 9	.	.	1,404 14 9	2,329 15 11¾	3,783 4 5
Rathdrum	328 1 10½	2,268 3 6	.	.	2,268 3 6	557 12 4¾	3,153 17 9
Rathkeale	123 8 8½	1,942 15 5	.	0 0 6	1,942 15 11	127 17 7¾	2,194 2 3½
Roscommon	185 19 3	264 12 8	.	.	264 12 8	497 17 9	898 9 8
Roscrea	360 1 4½	1,197 18 4	.	15 6 6	1,213 4 10	124 18 8	1,698 4 10½
Scariff	76 15 8¾	265 2 3½	.	.	265 2 3	573 8 1½	915 6 1
Shillelagh	202 3 4½	762 10 3	1 10 10	.	764 1 1½	195 6 9	1,161 11 2½
Skibbereen	79 19 5½	1,734 5 2	1 5 0	.	1,735 10 2	1,002 16 3½	2,818 5 10¾
Sligo	471 11 11¾	1,207 16 4	.	.	1,207 16 4	777 1 11½	2,456 10 3½
Strabane	1,065 7 6¾	979 19 11	.	.	979 19 11	14 7 3½	2,059 14 9½
Stranorlar	.	1,052 0 10	.	.	1,052 0 10	.	1,052 0 10
Thurles	220 12 8	894 8 10	.	1 2 6	895 11 4	606 16 9	1,723 0 9
Tipperary	341 2 5¾	1,052 6 8	.	.	1,052 6 8	1,703 2 9	3,096 11 10¾
Tralee	1,794 5 0	138 5 2	.	1 0 0	139 5 2	19 10 3¾	1,953 0 5¾
Trim	221 17 2	583 10 1	.	.	583 10 1	668 3 11½	1,473 11 2½
Tullamore	349 19 2¾	907 10 8	.	.	907 10 8	842 13 10	2,100 3 8¾
Waterford	20 6 3¾	3,925 4 1	0 17 6	0 4 0	3,926 5 7	2,018 6 6	5,964 18 4¾
Wexford	117 6 10½	2,435 3 8	0 9 3	.	2,435 12 11	259 12 1½	2,812 11 11
TOTALS	51,075 16 7¾	128,346 19 5	29 10 3¾	1,493 4 3	129,869 13 11¾	60,627 19 1	241,573 9 8½

No. 13.—Ireland, (*continued*).—Summary of Audited Union Accounts for the Half-years of Unions in Ireland, and the

ii.—Half-Year ended 29th

UNIONS.	Balances against Unions at close of last Half-year.	Maintenance and Clothing. On account of Electoral Division Paupers.	Maintenance and Clothing. On account of Union Paupers.	Maintenance and Clothing. Total for Maintenance and Clothing.	Establishment Charges.	Repayment of Workhouse Loans.
	£. s. d.	£. s. d.	£. s. d.	£. s. d.	£. s. d.	£. s. d.
Abbeyleix	211 6 8½	700 1 10½	149 4 5	849 6 3½	353 18 5	
Antrim	1 2 10	473 4 6	20 9 2½	493 13 8½	795 3 9	
Ardee	106 18 8½	768 2 0½	78 16 10	846 18 10½	437 12 5½	
Armagh	629 19 6	772 17 5	68 9 8	841 7 1	461 16 8	
Athy	148 8 5½	818 10 8	76 19 2½	895 9 10½	188 19 5½	
Bailieborough	448 7 1	459 0 7½	1 7 11½	460 8 7	253 13 0	
Ballina	93 15 0	553 13 9	61 4 7	614 18 4	296 16 9	
Ballinasloe	1,419 1 8½	418 6 2½	39 1 4	457 7 6½	362 19 1½	
Ballinrobe	943 3 9½	107 18 4½	17 8 11½	125 7 4½	428 12 1½	
Ballycastle	57 0 7½	109 3 11½	4 11 2	113 15 1½	120 9 3½	265 0 0
Ballymena	.	322 9 5½	6 10 9½	329 0 3	570 17 6	
Ballymoney	.	318 17 8	20 17 3	339 14 11	405 17 11	35 0 0
Ballyshannon	123 16 4½	112 8 11½	4 3 7	116 11 6½	226 7 7	
Baltinglass	114 12 10	670 6 8	42 1 0	712 7 8	330 13 3½	50 0 0
Banbridge	328 12 3½	621 6 1½	16 5 8	637 11 9½	327 4 8½	
Bandon	345 2 0½	592 12 5½	169 17 5½	762 9 10½	492 11 4	
Belfast	552 16 6½	1,638 9 4	164 10 9½	1,803 0 1½	788 11 7½	
Boyle	643 5 7	580 14 11½	15 1 6½	595 16 6	309 16 5½	
Callan	230 3 0½	394 11 4½	90 4 9½	484 16 2	267 2 2½	
Carrickmacross	12 5 3½	163 9 2½	27 2 10½	190 12 1	229 13 10	
Carrick-on-Shannon	1,592 2 6½	453 17 4½	32 1 1	485 18 5½	249 12 9½	
Carrick-on-Suir	369 8 7½	552 19 7½	45 2 3	598 1 10½	160 14 10	
Castlebar	1,753 19 7	185 14 6	2 3 10	187 18 4	.	393 0 0
Castleblayney	711 7 10½	766 10 3½	23 17 1	790 7 4½	164 14 0	
Castlederg	2 8 8½	86 9 3	.	86 9 3	97 18 11½	
Celbridge	229 8 8	287 10 3½	48 4 4	335 14 7½	244 5 7	
Clogheen	472 16 4½	536 1 11½	11 6 10½	547 8 9½	269 11 9½	
Clogher	.	192 0 10½	22 19 9½	215 0 8	338 7 3½	
Clones	99 16 4½	640 2 4½	37 5 2½	677 7 7½	224 16 3½	363 0 0
Clonmel	.	949 7 10	205 14 1½	1,155 1 11½	345 15 4½	80 0 0
Coleraine	236 13 7½	521 4 1½	13 18 11½	535 3 0½	478 1 5½	450 0 0
Cookstown	130 12 9½	289 8 0½	48 8 3½	337 16 3½	275 14 9½	
Cootehill	1,002 16 2	796 1 0	6 1 6½	802 2 6½	367 0 5½	
Cork	7,801 3 1	4,685 19 6	3,179 11 0	7,865 10 6	831 6 8½	
Donegal	.	86 6 7½	1 10 11	87 17 6½	154 10 2½	
Downpatrick	8 6 0½	768 2 10	67 16 9½	835 19 7½	409 4 6	65 0 0
Drogheda	459 4 6½	478 18 8½	52 15 6½	531 14 3	268 10 5	
Dublin, North	318 13 0½	4,414 5 8½	322 14 1½	4,736 19 10½	1,154 19 3	800 0 0
Dublin, South	2,101 17 8½	4,151 10 3½	388 2 11½	4,539 13 3½	1,369 16 6½	
Dundalk	861 7 6	973 11 7	39 16 11	1,013 8 6	508 4 10½	
Dungannon	17 14 9½	476 8 0½	40 6 2½	516 14 3	241 16 0	437 10 0
Dungarvan	.	56 7 9½	3 3 4½	59 11 1½	304 12 1½	
Dunmanway	.	.	398 8 3½	398 8 3½	255 5 0	
Dunshaughlin	381 1 3½	779 6 3½	67 9 5	846 15 8½	295 8 1½	
Ennis	549 1 2½	650 19 11½	94 16 8½	745 16 7½	4 7 1½	
Enniscorthy	444 18 2½	696 7 0½	120 4 11	816 11 11½	546 4 5½	
Ennistymon	194 16 6½	.	357 9 11	357 9 11	114 1 2½	
Fermoy	1,867 9 8½	874 7 4½	188 1 5	1,062 8 9½	607 17 8	
Galway	806 0 6	464 3 3	41 10 0	505 13 3	292 19 5	
Gorey	705 2 6	495 6 9½	182 0 3½	677 7 0½	240 15 1½	
Gort	1,337 6 8	235 15 8	27 10 0	263 5 8	182 11 9½	
Gortin	127 17 1½	120 7 3	5 9 10	125 17 1	124 18 10	
Granard	642 19 4	742 17 9	27 19 4½	770 17 1½	238 10 10½	
Inishowen	.	89 8 3½	7 3 5	96 11 8½	127 6 11½	

ended respectively 25th March and 29th September, 1844, showing the Receipts and Expenditure Balances in those Half-years.

September, 1844.—104 Unions.

DISCHARGE.

EXPENDITURE.								
Vaccination Expenses.	Expense of Valuing or revising Valuations.	Collector's Poundage, or other Remuneration.	Amount expended on Emigration.	Funerals, Election, Law, and other Expenses.	Total Expenditure in the Half-year.	Balances in favour of Unions at close of this Half-year.	TOTAL.
£. s. d.	£. s. d.	£. s. d.	£. s. d.	£. s. d.	£. s. d	£. s. d.	£. s. d.
40 4 0	10 0 0	3 16 8	.	39 7 6	1,296 12 10¼	79 3 10	1,587 3 4¼
29 14 0	15 0 0	9 14 2	.	17 15 0	1,361 0 7¼	.	1,362 8 5¼
30 0 0	25 0 0	25 3 2	.	16 10 8	1,381 5 2	830 18 4	2,319 2 2¼
49 16 6	18 15 0	22 8 6	.	19 5 10	1,413 9 7	1,843 17 1¼	3,357 6 2¼
10 16 0	.	.	.	24 19 6	1,120 4 10	179 9 3	1,447 17 6¼
10 9 0	.	23 5 2	.	3 6 2	751 1 11	61 16 4¼	1,281 5 4¼
.	100 0 0	.	.	111 15 8	1,113 10 9	618 11 1	1,825 16 10
0 19 0	.	31 9 6	.	16 13 0¼	869 8 2¼	681 6 10	2,969 16 9
2 9 0	.	23 4 10	.	43 15 9¼	623 9 1¼	.	1,586 12 11
.	.	0 8 5	.	11 10 1	511 2 11	663 13 9¼	1,231 17 4¼
.	.	.	.	12 9 4	912 7 1	613 8 8¼	1,523 16 9¼
9 6 0	1 10 0	1 2 8	.	22 19 11	815 11 5	862 18 9	1,678 10 2
.	.	6 8 1	.	23 16 1	373 3 3¼	380 10 1	877 9 9
13 18 0	12 10 0	33 12 1	.	12 17 9	1,165 18 9¼	314 10 6¼	1,595 2 2
.	.	66 10 9	.	23 17 8¼	1,055 5 0	541 15 10	1,925 13 1¼
.	.	91 19 7	.	19 9 4	1,366 10 1¼	835 5 4¼	2,546 17 7
32 9 6	21 17 6	13 5 0	.	84 11 10¼	2,693 15 8	3,064 15 2	6,311 7 4¼
4 13 2¼	.	36 11 4	.	24 17 11	971 15 4¼	327 5 4¼	1,914 6 4¼
0 19 0	.	59 3 10	.	17 1 8	829 2 10¼	895 19 1	1,455 5 [illegible]
1 12 0	.	23 1 8	.	15 6 9	465 5 11	170 17 6¼	648 8 9¼
30 10 0	.	.	.	136 19 9	903 1 0¼	7 2 9	2,502 6 4¼
.	.	12 19 5	.	3 13 6	775 9 7¼	189 0 0¼	1,333 18 3¼
.	.	14 14 6¼	.	17 13 6	615 6 4¼	.	2,369 5 11
19 4 0	.	48 4 7	.	12 8 0	1,034 17 11¼	67 19 3¼	1,814 5 1¼
9 17 0	0 18 1	11 17 4	.	22 0 9	229 1 4¼	279 10 3	511 0 4
31 9 0	.	12 1 5	.	1 16 0	625 6 7¼	376 19 0¼	1,231 14 4¼
.	.	5 0 0	.	15 12 1	837 12 8¼	143 3 0	1,433 12 1
82 4 10	218 0 0	43 7 2	.	49 2 10	1,446 2 9¼	638 10 7¼	2,084 13 5
.	.	2 4 0	.	17 9 11¼	1,286 17 10¼	581 10 0¼	1,963 4 3¼
.	45 18 5	56 18 8	.	37 11 0	1,671 5 5	256 18 5	1,928 3 10
16 16 0	10 0 0	62 1 3	.	30 8 7	1,582 10 4	313 5 2¼	2,132 9 2
118 12 0	.	.	.	13 19 9	746 2 10¼	521 5 4¼	1,898 1 0¼
26 9 0	27 2 0	78 4 2	.	25 8 11	1,326 7 1	642 4 9¼	2,971 8 0¼
.	50 0 0	.	.	505 1 4	9,301 18 6¼	62 11 0¼	17,165 12 8
22 11 0	.	41 8 3¼	.	49 17 10¼	356 4 10¼	181 10 3¼	537 15 2
.	10 0 0	64 11 1	.	42 9 10¼	1,427 5 1	1,482 6 8¼	2,917 17 10¼
4 12 0	.	69 6 8	.	23 5 4	897 8 8	442 13 0¼	1,799 6 2¼
21 1 0	30 0 0	185 0 0	.	100 0 8	7,028 0 9¼	756 11 9¼	8,103 5 7¼
40 13 6	.	203 5 8	.	181 5 11	6,334 14 10¼	1,145 8 5¼	9,532 1 0¼
53 8 0	.	38 14 2	.	37 0 11	1,650 16 5¼	621 12 2¼	3,133 16 2¼
.	.	.	84 13 11	17 15 1	1,318 9 3	571 16 9¼	1,908 0 10¼
.	.	30 0 0	.	8 8 7	402 11 10	1,734 4 10¼	2,136 16 8¼
.	.	.	.	15 12 0	669 5 3¼	171 10 2¼	840 15 6
10 0 0	.	25 9 1	.	19 5 6	1,196 18 5	79 8 0	1,657 7 8¼
.	30 0 0	16 19 8	.	31 17 9	829 1 2¼	264 14 2¼	1,642 16 7
16 11 0	15 0 0	90 0 0	.	16 19 4	1,500 6 9	659 10 8¼	2,604 16 1¼
.	.	15 8 2	.	23 2 3	510 1 6¼	301 10 8¼	1,006 8 9¼
.	.	.	5 0 0	21 1 8	1,696 7 8¼	430 5 2¼	4,014 [illegible] 7
29 14 0	.	114 18 6	.	37 1 0	980 6 2	130 7 9	1,916 14 5
41 17 2	.	69 0 0	.	11 16 6	1,040 15 10	261 9 0¼	2,007 7 4¼
4 1 0	.	.	.	10 1 10	460 0 3¼	7 15 6¼	1,805 8 6
.	.	25 15 7	.	61 16 10	838 8 4	290 8 0¼	[illegible] 8 5¼
21 9 0	.	.	.	19 11 9	1,030 8 9¼	130 13 3¼	1,824 1 5
.	2 18 1	.	.	32 5 8	259 2 5¼	690 8 10¼	945 6 3¼

No. 13.—Ireland, (*continued*).—Summary of Audited Union Accounts for the Half-year ... of Unions in Ireland, and ...

ii.—Half-year ended 29th ...

UNIONS.	DISCHARGE.																	
	Balance against Unions at close of this Half-year.			EXPENDITURE.														
				Maintenance and Clothing.									Establishment Charges.			Repayment of Workhouse Loans.		
				On account of Electoral Division Paupers.			On account of Union Paupers.			Total for Maintenance and Clothing.*								
	£.	s.	d.	£.	s.	d.	£.	s.	d.	£.	s.	d.	£.	s.	d.	£.	s.	d.
Kanturk . .		.		206	1	6	17	19	9	224	1	3	472	18	4		.	
Kells . .	415	3	6¼	643	12	0¼	49	18	5½	693	10	6¼	120	10	3½		.	
Kilkeel . .	40	10	11½	133	12	3¼	34	10	10½	168	3	2¼	123	15	8		.	
Kilkenny .	2,190	7	0½	1,538	19	1	151	14	6¼	1,690	13	7½	346	1	0¾		.	
Kilmallock .	1,396	10	6¼	710	7	3	104	0	4	814	7	7	274	4	5¾		.	
Kilrush . .	85	19	10¾	279	15	4½	30	13	2½	310	8	6¼	160	19	3¾		.	
Kinsale . .	325	14	6	387	9	8½	74	15	3¼	462	4	11¾	191	11	0½		.	
Larne . .	180	19	10	431	14	7½	8	13	9	440	8	4½	219	10	6		.	
Lisburn . .	469	15	1½	702	18	9¾	24	17	11	727	16	8¾	166	0	5		.	
Lismore . .	131	10	1¾	252	8	2	30	19	4¾	282	17	6¾	68	13	7½		.	
Lisnaskea .	63	18	9¾	264	11	7	34	1	8¾	298	13	3¾	289	13	2		.	
Londonderry.	26	0	0½	519	14	3½	42	0	4½	561	14	8	360	9	5¾		.	
Longford .	1,004	11	1¾	1,352	4	11½	89	7	3½	1,441	12	3	310	12	3		.	
Loughrea .	1,430	8	9½	289	13	10½	15	1	8	304	15	6¼	229	14	8½		.	
Lurgan . .	595	8	4¾	595	11	7½	9	18	2¾	605	9	10	772	18	8½		.	
Macroom .	160	6	6¾	459	13	1¾	40	16	6	500	9	7¾	325	16	6½		.	
Magherafelt .		.		400	0	9½	56	17	11¾	456	18	9½	308	8	5	57	10	0
Mallow . .	492	6	4½	389	10	4	73	18	11	463	9	3	232	3	7		.	
Midleton .	1,321	18	4¾	833	6	5½	63	12	8¾	896	19	1½	436	19	2		.	
Monaghan .	313	6	0	445	17	7½	47	18	1¾	493	15	9¼	218	9	0	75	0	0
Mullingar .	452	3	10½	922	17	8½	60	1	6½	982	19	3½	412	8	4		.	
Naas . .	2,146	18	3½	945	9	2	35	10	4	980	19	6	276	1	11		.	
Navan . .	721	1	5¾	650	1	9¾	43	14	0	693	15	9¾	217	3	0¾		.	
Nenagh . .	803	1	7½	845	19	6½	72	12	10¾	918	12	5	414	12	11½		.	
Newcastle .	947	19	0½	785	11	5	129	12	2½	915	3	7½	391	9	10¾		.	
New Ross .	756	0	4¾	937	0	9½	53	1	0	990	1	9½	442	8	9	126	13	4
Newry . .	677	8	1	973	5	2	50	4	10	1,023	10	0	275	1	2		.	
Newtownards.	693	19	4	467	14	9½	85	13	6	553	8	3½	321	7	9½	52	10	0
Newtown Limavady }	115	9	9½	181	7	0½	17	13	4½	199	0	5	201	9	3½		.	
Oldcastle .	618	5	8½	529	5	8½	18	18	3	548	3	11½	187	7	11		.	
Omagh . .	218	12	3½	290	13	9½	79	5	9¾	369	19	7½	241	19	9½	395	0	0
Parsonstown .	807	18	9¾	392	9	1	28	12	10¾	421	1	11¾	279	19	1¾		.	
Rathdown .	1,574	15	6	940	14	2	123	7	9¾	1,064	1	11¾	544	13	7½	480	0	0
Rathdrum .	883	7	4½	1,006	8	9½	109	9	3½	1,115	18	0½	502	14	8½		.	
Rathkeale .	498	17	4½	537	17	7½	86	17	0	624	14	7½	299	3	9½	485	0	0
Roscommon .	121	5	3½	364	19	11½	31	9	6½	396	9	6	279	10	10		.	
Roscrea . .	322	1	2	612	2	4½	75	1	8	687	4	0½	349	6	2		.	
Scariff . .	416	13	8	123	3	5½	98	7	9½	221	11	2¾	205	17	4½		.	
Skillelagh .	190	13	11	473	5	5½	42	19	0¾	516	4	6½	259	6	0½		.	
Skibbereen .	1,609	1	0	570	1	4½	48	1	0½	618	2	4½	259	9	8		.	
Sligo . .	682	9	0½	800	3	3½	91	12	2	891	15	5¾	339	5	5½		.	
Strabane . .	56	9	9½	373	9	9¾	16	13	0½	390	2	10¼	238	9	11½		.	
Stranorlar .		.		32	12	7	1	5	6	33	18	1	514	6	3		.	
Thurles . .	614	12	5	520	11	1½	29	1	9	549	12	10½	230	3	7		.	
Tipperary .	1,403	9	4	829	13	10	165	0	2	994	14	0	272	9	2		.	
Tralee . .	8	1	11½	272	5	6	64	12	10	336	18	4	292	16	4¾		.	
Trim . .	648	13	3½	378	9	5	56	7	0	434	16	5	237	17	2¼		.	
Tullamore .	599	7	11½	763	3	2½	48	7	7	811	10	9½	278	16	4		.	
Waterford .	2,679	1	3	2,043	15	11	244	6	9	2,288	2	8	602	13	7		.	
Wexford . .	1,020	17	7¾	706	13	2½	83	13	1½	790	6	4	337	3	2½		.	
Totals .	64,561	17	7¾	68,202	14	4¾	10,278	13	8	78,481	8	0¾	34,963	1	3¾	4584	3	4

ended respectively 25th March and 29th September, 1844, showing the Receipts and Expenditure Balances in those Half-years.

September, 1844.—104 Unions.

DISCHARGE.							
EXPENDITURE.						Balances in favour of Unions at the close of this Half-year.	TOTAL.
Vaccination Expenses.	Expense of Valuing or revising Valuations.	Collector's Poundage, or other Remuneration.	Amount expended on Emigration.	Funerals, Election, Law, and other Expenses.	Total Expenditure in the Half-year.		
£. s. d.	£. s. d.	£. s. d.	£. s. d.	£. s. d.	£. s. d.	£. s. d.	£. s. d.
165 6 0	440 0 0	.	.	326 14 7	1,629 0 2	116 15 3	1,745 15 5
.	.	7 18 9	.	5 10 9	827 10 3¼	535 4 10	1,777 18 8
.	.	16 5 3	.	9 2 1	317 6 2¼	247 13 4	605 10 5¼
.	.	137 15 2	.	37 5 11	2,211 15 9¼	118 2 10	4,520 5 7¼
6 12 0	.	.	.	27 0 3	1,122 4 3¼	402 12 2¼	2,921 7 0¼
.	.	1 15 2	.	28 14 0	501 17 0¼	102 12 9¼	690 9 8¼
.	13 9 2	30 17 1	.	22 5 10	720 8 1¼	436 7 6¼	1,482 10 2
.	.	15 7 0		3 13 6	678 19 4¼	149 17 4	1,009 16 6½
26 5 0	17 0 0	8 6 4	.	22 2 9½	967 11 3¼	1,178 13 11½	2,616 0 4
14 1 0	.	.	.	.	365 12 2¼	23 12 8½	520 13 0¼
4 18 0	12 0 0	.	.	8 19 5	614 3 10¼	1,426 3 10	2,104 6 6¼
34 3 0	.	.	.	4 8 3	960 15 4¼	803 11 4¼	1,790 6 9¼
5 10 0	100 0 0	.	.	16 18 0	1,874 12 6	47 5 11¼	2,926 9 7¼
.	20 0 0	5 11 3	.	54 5 0	614 6 5¼	2 9 11¼	2,047 5 3
37 16 6	.	31 10 0	.	66 17 4½	1,514 12 5¼	379 3 5	2,489 4 3
25 0 0	7 10 0	.	.	194 8 4	1,053 4 6	459 0 11	1,672 11 11¼
.	6 15 0	26 18 5	.	16 12 9	873 3 4¼	658 13 4	1,531 16 8¼
.	.	14 19 1	.	22 4 8	732 16 7	53 4 1¼	1,268 7 0¼
8 7 0	.	.	.	118 16 10	1,461 2 1¼	514 12 8	3,297 13 2¼
49 8 0	.	.	.	5 3 11	841 16 8¼	781 1 0¼	1,936 3 8¼
9 10 0	14 4 4	27 5 8	.	14 16 7½	1,461 4 2¼	189 1 1	2,102 9 2½
57 17 6	.	42 14 1¼	.	33 9 6½	1,391 2 6¼	1,138 12 2¼	4,676 13 0¼
34 5 0	50 0 0	.	.	16 5 9	1,011 9 7¼	721 17 9¼	2,454 8 10¼
.	.	.	.	36 14 4	1,369 19 8¼	41 12 10¼	2,214 14 3
.	.	.	.	17 6 3	1,323 19 9	.	2,271 18 9¼
22 9 0	.	77 2 1	.	4 11 9	1,663 6 8¼	1,001 8 9	3,420 15 9¼
57 9 6	6 10 0	2 6 4	.	12 1 5	1,376 18 5	348 18 3	2,403 4 9
48 7 6	.	48 13 0	.	29 4 8½	1,053 11 2¼	1,149 13 0¼	2,897 3 7¼
.	.	.	12 0 0	3 9 7½	415 19 4	715 5 1¼	1,246 14 2½
17 1 3	.	27 4 10	.	24 12 11	804 10 10¼	317 8 4¼	1,740 4 11
.	.	43 0 11	.	9 11 9	1,039 12 0¼	660 4 10¼	1,938 9 3¼
25 7 0	.	.	.	8 9 5	734 17 6¼	416 15 8¼	1,939 13 1
37 19 0	15 0 0	52 13 5¼	.	14 0 10	2,208 8 11	.	3,783 4 5
29 11 8	15 0 0	6 7 6	.	31 15 3	1,701 7 1¼	569 3 2¼	3,153 17 9
.	25 0 0	.	.	23 6 4	1,457 4 9	238 0 2	2,194 2 3¼
10 12 6	.	9 2 6¼	.	23 7 8	719 3 0¼	58 1 4	898 9 8
3 13 0	.	34 18 2	.	37 19 10	1,113 1 2¼	263 2 6	1,698 4 10¼
.	.	.	.	50 0 0	477 8 7¼	21 3 9¼	915 6 1
23 19 0	.	13 18 7	.	21 15 3	835 3 5	135 13 10¼	1,161 11 2¼
.	25 0 0	91 9 3	.	28 16 0	1,022 17 3¼	186 7 7¼	2,818 5 10¼
67 12 6	25 0 0	.	.	6 11 0	1,330 4 4¼	423 16 10¼	2,456 10 3¼
.	8 0 0	9 5 3	.	16 3 4	662 1 4¼	1,341 3 7	2,059 14 9¼
20 7 0	154 18 5	1 0 0	.	87 8 6	811 18 3	240 2 7	1,052 0 10
.	.	.	.	21 2 3	800 18 8¼	307 9 7¼	1,723 0 9
.	.	43 16 7	.	34 19 2	1,345 18 11	347 3 7¼	3,096 11 10¼
32 3 6	22 1 4	.	.	11 12 1¼	695 11 8¼	1,249 6 10	1,953 0 5¼
3 15 6	17 10 0	21 5 10	.	14 12 9	729 17 8¼	95 0 2¼	1,473 11 2¼
.	.	.	.	24 1 9	1,114 8 10¼	386 6 10¼	2,100 3 8¼
	68 9 1	143 9 1¼	.	29 3 8	3,131 18 1¼	153 19 0¼	5,964 18 4½
37 6 0	12 10 0	61 7 6¼	.	19 11 6	1,258 4 7	533 9 8¼	2,812 11 11
1,754 17 7¼	1,720 6 5	2,867 18 8¼	101 13 11	3,910 15 0¼	128,404 4 4¼	48,607 7 8¼	241,573 9 8½

No. 14.—IRELAND.—Tables abstracted from the Union Accounts, which have been
i.—Showing the Particulars included under the head of Establishment Charges for the
the Date of opening the Workhouse

UNIONS.	Date of First Admission of Paupers.	No. of Paupers for which the Workhouse is calculated.	Salaries and Rations of Officers.	Proportion of Fuel, &c., Debited to Establishment.	Repairs, Improvements, and Additional Building.	Furniture, Utensils, and Implements of Work.
			£. s. d.	£. s. d.	£. s. d.	£. s. d.
Abbeyleix	6 June, 1842	500	276 7 1	11 13 0	15 3 4	34 1 8½
Antrim	19 Sept. 1843	700	283 11 5	26 14 0	9 8 10	699 9 3
Ardee	13 May, 1842	600	194 1 0	1 5 3	15 11 2	9 5 6
Armagh	4 Jan. ,,	1,000	206 5 6½	15 9 0½	19 3 8	21 14 1
Athy	9 Jan. 1844	600	225 2 4	8 10 10	46 14 4	216 6 4
Bailieborough . . .	20 June, 1842	600	179 18 3½	12 15 3	6 5 6	14 18 9
Ballina	3 Nov. 1843	1,200	311 10 8	13 1 6½	3 16 8	384 19 9
Ballinasloe	1 Jan. 1842	1,000	255 1 1½	16 14 3½	17 10 0	17 13 11
Ballinrobe.	26 May, ,,	800	141 19 8½	7 7 0	2 19 2	6 11 11
Ballycastle	3 Jan. 1843	300	111 14 5	11 13 7½	67 12 7	8 2 3½
Ballymena	17 Nov. ,,	900	215 1 7	23 5 8	67 1 0	428 3 4
Ballymoney	6 Mar. ,,	700	174 13 2	17 11 0	239 0 3	44 17 3
Ballyshannon . . .	6 May, ,,	500	86 16 6	7 18 7½	14 2 1	6 15 4
Baltinglass	28 Oct. 1841	500	208 7 0	16 0 2	35 11 3	25 17 5
Banbridge.	22 June, ,,	800	201 3 2	8 10 0	33 11 8	5 14 11
Bandon	17 Nov. ,,	900	204 18 7	3 0 0	103 10 3½	14 14 5½
Belfast	11 May, ,,	1,000	374 10 8	16 10 0	1,043 8 8	155 17 0
Callan	25 Mar. 1842	600	160 5 2½	17 4 1½	3 16 3½	17 15 3
Carrickmacross . .	11 Feb. 1843	500	216 19 6½	7 17 6	6 2 6	7 15 0
Carrick-ou-Shannon	21 July, 1842	800	131 8 0½	27 5 7	1 6 10	16 15 5
Carrick-on-Suir . .	8 July, ,,	500	148 18 4	11 6 3	4 12 3	15 2 7½
Cashel	23 Jan. ,,	700	208 4 6	11 10 9	53 14 8	20 13 10
Castlebar	22 Oct. ,,	700	110 18 8½	5 7 4½	3 17 2½	
Castleblayney . . .	15 Dec. ,,	800	279 11 3½	9 13 8	2 4 7	22 18 4½
Castlederg	2 Mar. 1841	200	100 7 9	6 10 6		
Celbridge	9 June, ,,	400	186 14 9	.	33 0 4½	11 5 6
Clogheen	29 June, 1842	500	191 17 8½	20 10 1½	21 10 0	65 3 5
Clones	23 Feb. 1843	600	129 18 6½	17 4 10½	8 12 4	19 7 8
Clonmel.	1 Jan. 1841	600	89 6 11	10 12 9	40 2 4	14 1 8
Coleraine. . . . :	19 April, 1842	700	189 15 2	24 10 1	50 13 2	59 11 11
Cookstown. . . .	31 May, ,,	600	151 8 6	8 6 7	62 13 0	18 17 6
Cootehill	2 Dec. ,,	800	172 11 11	21 5 0	38 6 0	114 18 5
Cork	1 Mar. 1840	2,000	539 15 1	20 0 0	136 0 0	56 6 6
Donegal.	21 May, 1843	500	156 3 11½	.	0 15 0	63 11 10
Downpatrick. . . .	17 Sept. 1842	1,000	218 2 6	6 17 6	154 15 8	33 3 5
Drogheda	16 Dec. 1841	800	232 11 7	5 2 1	14 2 4	4 3 4
Dublin, North . . .	4 May, 1840	2,000	657 0 8½	5 0 0	204 9 9½	92 17 11
Dublin, South . . .	24 April, ,,	2,000	796 4 7	5 10 4	347 4 7½	213 18 10
Dundalk	14 Mar. 1842	800	165 8 0	8 0 9	30 13 10	20 19 7
Dungannon	23 June, ,,	800	182 17 8	13 17 0	35 14 1	10 15 3
Dunmanway	2 Oct. 1841	400	105 16 0	3 6 5	40 0 5	0 16 8
Dunshaughlin . . .	17 May, ,,	400	156 8 0	23 10 9	4 4 4	27 13 6
Ennis	15 Dec. ,,	800	188 7 2½	.	4 17 0	0 7 9
Ennistymon	5 Sept. 1842	600	173 7 8	7 10 11	14 9 6	16 19 9
Fermoy	6 July, 1841	900	187 13 6	38 4 2	25 19 10	33 3 3
Galway	2 Mar. 1842	1,000	165 7 1	8 11 3	6 11 7	28 17 3
Gorey	22 Jan. ,,	500	134 4 5½	19 15 6½	13 18 0	16 11 4
Gort	11 Dec. 1841	500	120 16 2½	10 0 3	5 3 3	3 2 10
Gortin	19 Feb. 1842	200	77 12 11	3 2 6	14 12 0	8 0 9
Granard	30 Sept. ,,	600	137 2 1½	.	14 14 9	30 12 1
Inishowen	2 Oct. 1843	600	95 15 3½	6 11 9	0 6 4	170 10 9
Kells	23 May, 1842	600	176 0 9½	20 19 8½	7 17 1	34 7 0
Kilkeel	1 Sept. 1841	300	161 14 6	4 10 0	2 3 4	24 17 8½
Kilkenny	21 April, 1842	1,300	219 19 5	28 15 11	203 17 2½	18 5 6½
Kilmallock	29 Mar. 1841	800	223 13 7	8 17 0	6 10 4	17 3 4
Kilrush	9 July, 1842	800	143 11 9	8 18 3	9 3 3	4 14 9½
Kinsale	4 Dec. 1841	500	133 4 3	3 7 0	38 6 11	8 11 6

Audited for the Half-years ended respectively 25th March and 29th September, 1844.

Half-year ended 25th March, in 100 Unions, the Accounts of which have been Audited; also in each Union, and its Capacity.

Printing, Stationery, Advertising, and Postage. £. s. d.	Drugs, and Medical or Surgical Appliances. £. s. d.	Rent. £. s. d.	Insurance. £. s. d.	Other Charges. £. s. d.	Amount Debited to Establishment. £. s. d.	Credits Deducted. £. s. d.	Amount of Establishment Charges Apportioned. £. s. d.
17 2 10	.	.	3 15 0	8 16 0½	366 19 0	1 3 5	365 15 7
143 11 0	49 17 0	9 16 8	5 15 11	36 19 8	1,267 3 9	15 18 9	1,251 5 0
13 4 6¼	.	22 0 10	.	2 12 0	258 0 3¼	.	258 0 3¼
22 7 1	12 12 9	.	6 0 0	32 13 6	836 6 2	30 8 6	805 17 8
74 7 7	22 11 0	.	4 19 4	16 11 4	615 3 1	1 4 3	613 18 10
17 18 3	12 19 8	.	4 19 0	12 7 5	262 2 1½	0 16 0	261 6 1½
111 15 1	0 9 1	.	16 14 2	31 17 6½	874 4 6	.	874 4 6
25 17 7	14 7 6	5 6 10	7 10 0	8 4 6	368 5 9	.	368 5 9
12 13 1	.	.	.	22 17 9½	194 8 8½	3 5 5¼	191 3 3
26 0 10	16 17 3	.	3 0 0	44 5 11½	289 7 4½	166 17 2	122 10 2½
100 1 11	31 6 10	.	6 2 6	29 13 2	900 16 0	27 10 5	873 5 7
14 18 4	0 2 8	.	4 10 0	92 11 4	688 4 0	14 8 3	673 15 9
6 5 4	0 18 1	.	.	6 1 5	128 17 4½	.	128 17 4½
25 19 5	7 14 0	35 5 4	3 15 0	25 8 10	383 18 5	18 10 1	365 8 4
33 6 7	12 4 5	.	.	12 15 6½	307 6 3½	2 19 7	304 6 8½
26 15 10	35 18 2	.	5 0 0	226 8 6	620 3 10	.	620 3 10
31 9 1	38 14 10	29 14 8	0 15 0	40 6 1	1,729 6 0	1,344 1 2	385 4 10
24 19 7	15 1 7	.	.	23 1 2½	267 0 3	5 17 3	261 3 0
11 14 0	2 1 5½	.	3 0 0	20 9 10½	276 0 8½	.	276 0 8½
18 16 3	.	.	.	13 15 11	209 8 0½	.	209 8 0½
30 18 7	.	47 14 0	4 17 6	20 14 3	284 3 9½	1 19 3	282 4 6½
61 4 6	8 5 4	.	4 10 0	32 4 4	400 7 11	.	400 7 11
15 1 9	.	.	7 4 9	6 10 11	149 0 9	5 12 5½	143 8 3½
32 2 8½	85 5 9	.	4 10 0	47 12 9	483 16 1½	31 19 0½	451 17 1½
4 14 11	.	.	2 5 0	16 17 4½	130 15 6½	15 18 5½	114 17 1
4 7 5	.	.	.	2 16 3	238 4 3½	14 15 10½	223 8 5
25 5 4½	85 1 8	.	4 10 0	9 7 6½	423 5 10	.	423 5 10
18 2 9	9 12 10	.	3 15 0	18 17 1	217 11 1	.	217 11 1
26 15 7	12 6 11	.	0 7 6	2 2 9	195 16 5	.	195 16 5
36 12 6	12 9 2	.	.	16 10 8	390 2 8	34 0 4½	356 2 3½
20 4 1	.	18 1 7	.	25 17 3	305 8 6	271 1 9½	34 6 8½
7 4 11	.	.	7 10 0	13 3 9	375 0 0	0 4 9½	374 15 2½
120 17 8	139 16 0	70 3 1	19 1 3	6 7 0½	1,108 0 7½	.	1,108 0 7½
8 10 11½	28 10 10½	.	.	.	257 12 7½	0 13 0	256 19 7½
48 18 8	2 10 6½	.	.	40 18 5	505 6 8½	4 0 10½	501 5 10
21 18 10	1 19 0	.	4 10 0	.	286 7 2	19 17 2	266 10 0
93 15 2½	87 3 1	.	.	69 19 6	1,210 6 2½	.	1,210 6 2½
193 15 2	159 17 11	.	.	124 10 10½	1,840 19 4	37 13 6	1,803 5 10
19 0 4½	11 8 7	.	.	28 0 6	283 11 7½	12 10 10½	271 0 9
20 10 1	.	.	.	5 8 0	269 2 6	41 13 3	227 9 3
7 13 11	.	.	2 15 6	39 2 1	199 10 0	3 10 0	196 0 0
8 8 6	.	.	2 5 0	8 3 4	230 13 5	2 18 4	227 15 1
43 5 3	9 3 10	26 0 0	5 0 0	18 18 7½	295 19 8½	295 19 8½	.
41 1 0	1 9 4	.	.	6 10 2	261 8 4	100 17 10½	160 10 5½
13 19 0	.	.	.	45 19 4	344 19 1	.	344 19 1
16 11 5	.	.	7 10 0	37 9 5	270 11 0	26 11 8	243 19 4
18 10 5	5 19 7	.	4 10 0	30 9 10	252 19 2	11 2 0	241 17 2
22 9 10½	0 9 0	.	5 5 0	28 6 11¼	195 13 4¼	19 19 6	175 13 10¼
10 5 4	5 9 6	.	1 10 0	8 12 10	129 5 10	7 16 8	121 [illegible] 2
2 3 4	.	.	4 10 0	10 11 0½	199 13 4	.	199 13 4
92 3 1	18 12 3	.	3 0 0	34 15 7	421 15 0¾	27 9 2¾	394 5 10
14 8 9	17 17 5	.	.	2 13 8½	274 4 5½	24 8 5	249 16 0½
14 17 9½	7 6 6	.	.	10 16 11	226 6 9	24 4 11	202 1 10
37 18 4	48 19 9	.	.	14 0 7	570 16 9	0 0 8½	570 16 0½
35 3 6	33 15 6	.	.	7 18 5½	333 1 8½	23 2 8½	309 19 0
5 12 3½	0 19 6	.	3 15 0	11 10 3¼	188 5 1¼	35 15 9	152 9 4¼
7 19 1	.	.	.	5 11 7	217 0 4	.	217 0 4

No. 14.—Ireland, (*continued*).—Tables abstracted from the Union Accounts, which have

i.—Showing the Particulars included under the head of Establishment Charges for the

the Date of opening the Workhouse

UNIONS.	Date of First Admission of Paupers.		No. of Paupers for which the Workhouse is calculated.	Salaries and Rations of Officers. £. s. d.	Proportion of Fuel, &c., Debited to Establishment. £. s. d.	Repairs, Improvements, and Additional Building. £. s. d.	Furniture, Utensils, and Implements of Work. £. s. d.
Larne	4 Jan.	1843	400	149 10 0	4 11 6	40 19 2	11 0 7½
Limerick	20 May,	1841	1,600	365 11 8	27 8 10	99 14 11½	67 16 1
Lisburn	11 Feb.	,,	800	174 14 6¼	12 12 5	179 7 1	15 14 2
Lismore	18 May,	1842	500	163 19 0¼	7 15 10¾	37 5 0	3 18 4
Lisnaskea	25 Feb.	1843	500	128 18 3¼	9 12 9	140 10 9	16 5 7½
Londonderry	10 Nov.	1840	800	231 2 8	27 1 8	67 14 6	27 10 8
Longford	24 Mar.	1842	1,000	175 1 0	13 6 6	25 6 3	39 9 9
Loughrea	26 Feb.	,,	800	166 19 6	9 14 6¼	1 13 3	0 9 11
Lurgan	22 Feb.	1841	800	178 9 5	11 4 11	125 12 2	33 9 6
Macroom	13 May,	1843	600	67 6 6	15 12 8¼	0 18 2	22 2 0
Magherafelt	11 Mar.	1842	900	180 0 3¼	38 0 2¼	28 18 5	21 7 1
Mallow	2 Aug.	,,	700	147 11 3	18 5 4	10 17 6	4 5 5
Midleton	21 Aug.	1841	800	212 2 10	7 2 6	96 10 0	28 6 11
Monaghan	25 May,	1842	900	175 11 1¼	9 17 11	25 7 9	14 5 8
Mullingar	8 Dec.	,,	800	139 5 5	19 16 11	14 4 7	16 3 8
Naas	4 Aug.	1841	550	157 18 3	20 0 0	12 0 1¼	24 18 0¼
Navan	4 May,	1842	500	146 8 10¼	12 5 2¼	110 11 0¼	48 11 2
Nenagh	28 April,	,,	1,000	180 5 4¾	13 10 3¼	43 3 3	5 2 10
Newcastle	15 Mar.	1841	550	200 17 5¼	24 19 9¼	116 18 10	5 3 1
New Ross	6 July,	1842	900	156 0 3	5 12 0	28 0 10	43 18 2
Newry	16 Dec.	1841	1,000	122 0 0	15 0 0	21 13 4	18 18 7
Newtownards	4 Jan.	1842	600	212 15 0	52 11 7	5 11 6	86 0 0
Newtown Limavady	15 Mar.	,,	600	167 5 0	14 7 0	5 2 9	18 15 10
Oldcastle	12 Aug.	,,	600	136 3 3¼	15 4 6	11 0 11	35 7 3
Omagh	24 Aug.	1841	800	176 18 5	19 2 10	23 15 3	16 7 4
Parsonstown	2 April,	1842	800	175 5 9¼	1 11 11	24 5 11½	14 15 4
Rathdown	12 Oct.	1841	600	303 6 5	32 0 3¼	72 3 0¼	37 10 9
Rathdrum	8 Mar.	1842	600	190 14 3	21 12 0	19 2 6	4 4 10
Rathkeale	26 July,	1841	660	159 4 11¼	7 11 7	30 13 10	3 10 5
Roscommon	4 Nov.	1843	900	356 0 11	21 13 3	4 2 7	200 10 7
Roscrea	7 May,	1842	700	186 19 2	3 17 0	30 17 11	37 6 0
Scariff	11 May,	,,	600	116 17 11	2 7 7	63 11 7	12 11 0
Shillelagh	18 Feb.	,,	400	188 11 1½	14 16 0¼	16 17 8	15 6 6
Skibbereen	19 Mar.	,,	800	166 1 4	11 9 0	12 12 8	8 11 9
Sligo	17 Dec.	1841	1,200	221 11 11¼	14 0 0	22 1 1	13 2 0
Strabane	18 Nov.	,,	800	181 11 10	13 8 8	14 16 3	23 3 1
Thurles	7 Nov.	1842	700	277 2 11¼	9 0 6¼	11 1 6	8 9 7
Tipperary	3 July,	1841	700	184 4 2	14 11 10	25 18 3	31 18 11
Tralee	1 Feb.	1844	1,000	285 4 3¼	•	11 3 0¼	297 7 9
Trim	11 Oct.	1841	500	152 2 10¼	16 8 4¼	0 14 6	11 7 2
Tullamore	9 June,	1842	700	121 5 10	6 0 0	2 11 1	52 3 6¼
Waterford	20 April,	1841	900	353 1 10	20 0 0	40 6 10¼	29 11 5
Wexford	25 July,	1842	600	188 7 6	16 15 0	32 19 1¼	19 9 3
TOTALS			74,460	19,788 13 2¼	1,329 14 5¼	5,127 9 3¼	4,883 9 1

been Audited for the Half-years ended respectively 25th March and 29th September, 1844.

Half-year ended 25th March, in 100 Unions, the Accounts of which have been Audited; also in each Union, and its Capacity.

Printing, Stationery, Advertising, and Postage.	Drugs, and Medical or Surgical Appliances.	Rent.	Insurance.	Other Charges.	Amount Debited to Establishment.	Credits Deducted.	Amount of Establishment Charges Apportioned.
£. s. d.	£. s. d.	£. s. d.	£. s. d.	£. s. d.	£. s. d.	£. s. d.	£. s. d.
7 11 3½	.	.	4 10 0	18 19 1	237 1 8	104 14 5	132 7 3
94 15 10	.	.	.	100 16 3	756 3 7½	104 12 4	651 11 3½
37 8 7	20 0 8	.	4 10 0	37 11 10	481 19 3¾	114 9 4	367 9 11¾
14 2 8	0 6 8	30 0 0	.	5 17 10	263 5 5½	0 13 10½	262 11 7
15 17 2	0 5 8	.	5 0 0	7 5 8	323 15 11	3 16 10	319 19 1
21 15 0	10 9 7	4 0 0	5 5 0	25 11 10½	420 10 11½	69 16 7¾	350 14 3¾
30 8 5	18 1 2	35 6 6	6 16 6	10 4 5	334 0 6	.	354 0 6
7 2 2	28 9 5	.	6 0 0	4 19 10	225 8 7½	5 7 4	220 1 3½
23 8 1	16 19 10	.	.	56 18 9	446 2 8	14 9 1	431 13 7
6 4 6	1 11 0½	.	.	8 6 6	122 1 5	.	122 1 5
19 19 9	.	.	3 16 3	22 8 4½	314 10 5	37 6 5½	277 3 11¾
10 9 6	17 16 9	.	4 10 0	12 6 8	226 2 5	9 7 11	216 14 6
26 6 0	21 6 0	.	.	18 5 3½	409 19 6½	.	409 19 6½
34 11 2	25 12 6	.	4 10 0	33 0 0	322 16 1½	24 5 4¾	298 10 8½
26 9 5	7 14 5	.	6 15 0	24 13 3	255 2 3	57 15 4	197 6 11
10 17 1	.	4 0 0	.	0 15 0	230 8 6	6 1 4	224 7 2
11 13 3	.	.	6 0 0	5 10 7½	341 0 2	20 6 4	320 18 10
38 0 0	18 1 0	25 0 0	6 0 0	39 0 6	368 3 3½	44 2 6	324 0 9½
22 13 7½	.	.	.	16 17 9	387 10 6½	23 6 1	364 4 5½
5 14 2	8 6 4	43 6 3	5 5 0	3 7 0	299 10 0	26 15 0	272 15 0
12 19 5	1 3 7	.	6 0 0	15 6 2	213 1 1	35 0 0	178 1 1
29 8 6	1 12 6	.	4 10 0	4 10 3	396 14 4	77 8 11	319 5 5
11 15 8	14 11 6	.	.	27 17 3½	259 15 0½	3 15 8	255 19 4½
19 16 2	11 3 0	.	.	6 17 2	235 12 3½	11 17 5	223 14 10½
22 12 2	1 4 9	15 0 0	3 15 0	3 5 10	282 1 7	20 7 4½	261 14 2½
24 6 7	.	4 7 8	6 0 0	4 16 9	255 10 0	.	253 10 0
61 3 6½	28 13 8	.	.	21 1 3	555 18 11½	13 2 1½	542 16 10
3 10 6	.	.	4 12 8	45 2 3	288 19 0	.	288 19 0
24 1 1	8 6 9½	.	.	80 14 8½	314 3 4	33 2 6½	381 0 9½
126 4 8	48 10 4	24 6 4	6 0 0	6 13 1	794 1 9	0 7 8	793 14 1
31 14 5½	7 13 8	.	.	10 10 10	308 19 0½	16 0 9	292 18 3½
14 15 7	4 1 5	.	9 0 0	9 19 8½	233 4 9½	5 7 8½	227 17 1
9 7 11	23 10 6	.	4 10 0	17 11 0½	290 10 9½	9 9 2	281 1 7½
28 10 3	14 4 0	.	.	10 11 0	252 0 0	.	252 0 0
28 0 5	9 19 9	61 13 6	14 10 0	24 13 2	409 11 10½	3 13 0	406 18 10½
14 0 10	4 0 10	.	5 5 0	6 0 0½	262 6 6½	19 4 11½	243 1 6½
20 4 9	.	.	4 0 0	9 15 5	339 14 9	11 18 9	327 16 0
88 14 0	14 15 2	25 4 0	.	26 15 11½	361 17 3½	16 2 3½	345 15 0
136 8 8	.	98 18 11	26 13 8	58 18 7½	914 14 6½	.	914 14 6½
16 17 7	17 9 8	.	.	24 12 7	239 12 8½	7 18 2	231 14 6½
31 19 8	4 10 7	.	.	16 17 7	235 8 3½	32 9 9	202 18 6½
61 12 4	138 13 11	.	.	162 6 9½	805 13 2½	12 10 6	793 2 8½
39 1 4½	33 14 10½	29 8 0	.	55 14 8½	415 9 10	11 4 8½	404 5 1½
3,234 10 11	1,651 7 8	664 14 2	342 11 1	2,636 9 4½	39,660 19 2½	3,737 6 1	35,923 13 1½

No. 14.—Ireland, (*continued*).—Tables abstracted from the Union Accounts which have been
ii.—Showing the Particulars included under the head of Establishment Charges,
have been Audited; also the Date of opening

UNIONS.	Date of First Admission of Paupers.		No. of Paupers for which the Workhouse is calculated.	Salaries and Rations of Officers.	Proportion of Fuel, &c., Debited to Establishment.	Repairs, Improvements, and Additional Building.	Furniture, Utensils, and Implements of Work.
				£. s. d.	£. s. d.	£. s. d.	£. s. d.
Abbeyleix	6 June,	1842	500	225 11 5	4 12 3	22 8 5	61 2 6
Antrim	19 Sept.	1843	700	212 14 0	16 16 8	180 1 10	290 9 0
Ardee	13 May,	1842	600	251 7 7	0 8 3	56 11 9	14 3 4
Armagh	4 Jan.	,,	1,000	252 19 11¼	14 3 0	27 4 5	89 8 7
Athy	9 Jan.	1844	600	77 2 10¼	3 16 0	18 17 3	129 2 6
Bailieborough	20 June,	1842	600	169 10 11½	9 14 7½	0 7 6	19 1 8
Ballina	3 Nov.	1843	1,200	115 1 1	13 14 0	14 6 11	60 7 3
Ballinasloe	1 Jan.	1842	1,000	263 12 3¼	19 18 7½	7 18 10	17 4 2
Ballinrobe	26 May,	,,	800	143 12 7	9 0 10	226 15 0¼	5 8 2
Ballycastle	3 Jan.	1843	300	115 16 3½	6 15 7	41 0 1	23 5 3
Ballymena	17 Nov.	,,	900	207 10 0	17 7 10	289 19 8	40 5 0
Ballymoney	6 Mar.	,,	700	176 8 10	15 6 2	155 12 5	12 15 0
Ballyshannon	6 May,	,,	500	90 8 10	7 12 1	3 5 7	5 16 2
Baltinglass	28 Oct.	1841	500	193 11 0½	15 15 3	37 0 9	25 3 9
Banbridge	22 June	,,	800	198 10 8	6 8 9	47 2 5	10 14 5
Bandon	17 Nov.	,,	900	207 3 3	2 0 0	33 1 2	18 9 5
Belfast	11 May,	,,	1,000	364 2 4	8 10 0	272 14 4	116 1 7
Boyle	31 Dec.	,,	700	173 11 6	1 12 8	52 8 10	24 13 11½
Callan	25 Mar.	1842	600	158 19 0	13 8 6½	38 14 5½	1 15 7
Carrickmacross	11 Feb.	1843	500	147 2 11½	9 3 8½	16 5 11	2 0 0
Carrick-on-Shannon	21 July,	1842	800	132 19 4	6 18 2	20 14 6	6 0 5
Carrick-on-Suir	8 July,	,,	500	129 4 3	0 4 7	5 11 8½	10 15 0
Castlebar	22 Oct.	,,	700	113 11 6½	3 19 8½	2 12 1	3 2 2½
Castleblayney	15 Dec.	,,	800	34 9 4	6 3 4	4 15 6½	76 5 6
Castlederg	2 Mar.	1841	200	100 3 9½	4 15 3½	1 5 7	.
Celbridge	9 June	,,	400	172 1 5½	.	20 9 7	30 16 3
Clogheen	29 June,	1842	500	208 7 9	12 11 0	16 14 9½	23 8 2½
Clogher	9 Mar.	1844	500	232 6 10½	13 18 9	154 9 3	296 7 5
Clones	23 Feb.	1843	600	136 19 11½	9 2 2	8 16 6	24 14 9
Clonmel	1 Jan.	1841	600	258 19 0	8 15 11	8 16 5	12 5 8
Coleraine	19 April,	1842	700	202 9 1½	15 17 1	175 15 5	32 10 10
Cookstown	31 May,	,,	600	165 2 6	5 14 1½	90 4 11	6 19 8
Cootehill	2 Dec.	,,	800	189 12 0½	9 0 0	33 19 11	51 7 10
Cork	1 Mar.	1840	2,000	432 0 5	15 0 0	44 4 11	110 3 1½
Donegal	21 May,	1843	500	108 14 7½	.	11 6 9	9 7 3
Downpatrick	17 Sept.	1842	1,000	258 19 10	.	90 13 5	25 10 6
Drogheda	16 Dec.	1841	800	203 17 5	.	9 3 7	27 6 6
Dublin, North	4 May,	1840	2,000	663 6 2	.	116 10 11½	72 19 6
Dublin, South	24 April,	,,	2,000	760 3 7	21 6 9	186 15 1½	220 1 11
Dundalk	14 Mar.	1842	800	290 8 9½	12 1 0½	22 2 7	95 3 4
Dungannon	23 June,	,,	800	190 0 10	10 16 0	17 17 7	16 10 0
Dungarvan	4 July,	1844	600	133 10 1	3 17 9	5 17 0	127 2 2
Dunmanway	2 Oct.	1841	400	119 15 0	5 0 0	11 5 1	5 6 9
Dunshaughlin	17 May,	,,	400	216 16 5	1 5 0	33 0 7	14 9 8½
Ennis	15 Dec.	,,	800	198 16 4¼	9 3 3½	45 16 9	24 6 0
Enniscorthy	11 Nov.	1842	600	317 15 4½	7 17 7½	70 3 7	33 10 6
Ennistymon	5 Sept.	,,	600	58 16 10¼	7 3 0	16 14 3	3 2 10
Fermoy	6 July,	1841	900	250 3 0	53 13 1	94 15 7	56 18 8
Galway	2 Mar.	1842	1,000	167 9 5	7 3 5	36 2 0	35 15 8
Gorey	22 Jan.	,,	500	242 0 5	10 16 5	24 10 1	7 12 4
Gort	11 Dec.	1841	500	122 13 0	4 0 11	2 13 4	7 8 1½
Gortin	19 Feb.	1842	200	93 18 5	3 0 0	11 18 2	4 5 10
Granard	30 Sept.	,,	600	139 11 1	.	21 13 7	58 8 5
Inishowen	2 Oct.	1843	600	104 10 7	2 2 10½	.	2 1 1
Kanturk	18 July,	1844	800	228 3 6	3 4 6	19 17 2	58 5 4
Kells	23 May,	1842	600	87 7 7½	10 0 0	18 12 9	3 13 0
Kilkeel	1 Sept.	1841	300	125 7 6	3 0 0	9 14 9½	4 19 3
Kilkenny	21 April,	1842	1,300	206 13 4½	17 11 7	28 7 2½	8 8 0

Audited for the Half-years ended respectively 25th March and 29th September, 1844.

for the Half-year ended 29th September, 1844, in 104 Unions, the Accounts of which the Workhouse in each Union, and its Capacity.

Printing, Stationery, Advertising, and Postage.	Drugs and Medical, or Surgical Appliances.	Rent.	Insurance.	Other Charges.	Amount Debited to Establishment.	Credits Deducted.	Amount of Establishment Charges Apportioned.
£. s. d.	£. s. d.	£. s. d.	£. s. d.	£. s. d.	£. s. d.	£. s. d.	£. s. d.
16 4 4	16 12 5	.	.	7 12 1	853 18 5	.	853 18 5
59 16 4	23 5 10	2 9 2	.	14 0 7	799 13 5	4 9 8	795 3 9
21 16 8¼	68 13 4	11 18 8	4 10 0	8 2 10	437 12 5¼	.	437 12 5¼
46 13 9	13 17 5½	.	.	40 18 6	485 5 8	23 9 0	461 16 8
6 9 3	.	.	4 10 0	59 10 11	299 3 9¼	110 9 4	188 19 5¼
25 1 8	15 13 1	.	4 19 0	9 19 9	254 3 3	0 15 3	253 18 0
40 19 4	31 0 0	.	.	18 10 9	288 19 4	2 2 7	286 16 9
21 1 6	13 3 10	5 6 11	.	33 4 2¼	881 5 4¼	18 6 3¼	862 19 1¼
6 18 9¼	.	.	.	36 16 8¼	428 12 1¼	.	428 12 1¼
6 16 8	1 0 6	.	.	23 1 1½	217 15 5¼	97 6 2¼	120 9 3¼
24 2 3	.	.	.	13 2 8	592 7 5	21 9 11	570 17 6
14 18 8	23 15 0	.	.	28 19 7	427 15 8	21 17 9	405 17 11
53 14 2	27 14 11	13 9 0	2 5 0	22 6 10	226 7 7	.	226 7 7
44 2 6	0 11 9	.	.	16 18 0	832 3 0¼	1 9 8¼	830 13 3¼
31 15 8	13 18 7	.	4 10 0	30 3 6¼	342 19 0¼	15 14 3¾	327 4 8¼
21 9 0	6 19 5	29 13 4	.	208 5 9	527 1 4	34 10 0	492 11 4
40 8 1	1 6 10	.	4 12 8	23 10 11¼	831 6 4¼	92 14 9	738 11 7¼
18 4 1¼	8 19 2	15 0 0	.	19 12 10½	314 3 1¼	4 6 8	309 16 5¼
9 0 5¼	.	.	6 5 0	49 13 1	277 16 1¼	10 13 11	267 2 2¼
22 19 2	23 15 0	.	.	11 3 5	232 10 2	2 16 4	229 13 10
9 19 0	0 5 10	21 2 8	6 0 0	52 3 9¼	256 2 8¼	6 10 10¼	249 12 9¼
6 8 8	0 11 10¼	.	.	26 8 9	179 4 10	18 10 0	160 14 10
12 17 6	.	.	.	5 16 3¼	141 19 4	141 19 4	.
14 9 0¼	1 6 11	.	.	49 0 4	186 10 0	21 16 0	164 14 0
7 6 0	.	.	.	19 0 7	132 11 2¼	34 12 3	97 18 11¼
15 8 1	.	.	4 7 6	15 12 7	258 15 5¼	14 9 10¼	244 5 7
5 10 0	10 7 5	18 1 6	4 10 0	5 11 3	305 1 11	35 10 1¼	269 11 9¼
113 17 3	26 13 8	.	3 15 0	6 18 3	848 6 5¼	9 19 2	838 7 3¼
9 19 9	12 13 10	.	.	22 9 4	224 16 3¼	.	224 16 3¼
22 10 0	16 6 2	23 13 1	1 19 4	10 10 5¼	363 16 0¼	18 0 8	345 15 4¼
26 5 3	18 17 2	.	3 15 0	15 7 2	490 17 0¼	12 15 7¼	478 1 5¼
5 11 6	.	.	5 0 0	7 9 8	286 2 4¼	10 7 7	275 14 9¼
18 9 9	41 14 3	.	7 10 0	16 8 8	368 2 5¼	1 1 11¼	367 0 5¼
105 18 0	109 4 8	53 13 10	.	29 14 3	899 19 2¼	18 13 6	881 6 8¼
14 18 0	.	.	3 15 0	9 10 7	157 12 2¼	3 2 0¼	154 10 2¼
11 0 9	3 14 5	.	6 0 0	25 14 1	421 13 0	12 8 6	409 4 6
7 11 2	12 9 8	.	.	8 2 1	268 10 5	.	268 10 5
58 12 5	105 0 10	72 0 10	25 0 0	41 8 6¼	1,154 19 8	.	1,154 19 3
85 10 2	84 5 11	.	12 0 0	17 19 3¼	1,388 2 9	18 6 2¼	1,369 16 6¼
51 8 1	19 5 5	.	4 10 0	22 8 0	517 7 3¼	9 2 4¼	508 4 10¼
8 16 9	.	.	2 11 0	6 0 11	252 13 1	10 17 1	241 16 0
12 16 2	.	.	4 11 6	16 17 5¼	304 12 1¼	.	304 12 1¼
10 12 9	5 19 10	.	.	97 5 7	255 5 0	.	255 5 0
16 17 7	14 2 5	.	.	5 5 5	301 17 1¼	6 9 0	295 8 1¼
35 2 10	14 9 1¼	.	.	55 1 4	382 15 8¼	378 8 6¼	4 7 1¼
71 8 10	32 1 0	.	4 10 0	16 19 6¼	554 6 5¼	9 2 0	545 4 5¼
14 19 6	.	.	4 10 0	16 4 2	121 10 7¼	7 9 5	114 1 2¼
26 3 0	100 0 0	.	10 14 2	15 16 7	607 17 8	.	607 17 8
25 5 8	5 17 10	.	.	15 5 10	292 19 5	.	292 19 5
25 0 3	1 5 4	22 12 8	.	26 7 10¼	360 5 4¼	119 10 3	240 15 1¼
13 4 6	13 10 11	.	.	19 1 0¼	182 11 9¼	.	182 11 9¼
9 11 11	.	.	.	2 12 4	125 6 8	0 7 10	124 18 10
11 8 2	0 10 0	.	4 10 0	2 18 2	238 19 5	0 8 6¼	228 10 10¼
12 7 2	.	.	.	17 6 11¼	138 8 8¼	11 1 9	127 6 11¼
110 4 0	19 14 3	.	9 13 1	23 16 6	472 18 4	.	472 18 4
6 8 7	3 10 9	.	7 8 6	27 6 6	164 7 8¼	43 17 5	120 10 3¼
14 11 2	0 15 8¼	.	3 15 0	8 14 10¼	170 18 3¼	47 2 7½	123 15 8
77 10 10¼	.	.	7 10 0	22 14 9	368 15 9¼	22 14 9	346 1 0¼

No. 14.—Ireland, (continued).—Tables abstracted from the Union Accounts which have

ii.—Showing the Particulars included under the head of Establish
have been Audited; also the Date of ope

UNIONS.	Date of First Admission of Paupers.	No. of Paupers for which the Workhouse is calculated.	Salaries and Rations of Officers.	Proportion of Fuel, &c., Debited to Establishment.	Repairs, Improvements, and Additional Building.	
			£. s. d.	£. s. d.	£ s. d.	
Kilmallock	29 Mar. 1841	800	206 1 3½	9 15 7½	13 1 2	
Kilrush	9 July, 1842	800	150 0 2	2 10 0	12 5 10	2 19
Kinsale	4 Dec. 1841	500	103 19 3	1 3 0	13 7 7½	7 8
Larne	4 Jan. 1843	400	150 19 9	3 2 10	42 7 6	
Lisburn	11 Feb. 1841	800	182 11 5	7 15 7	87 2 5	45 12
Lismore	18 May, 1842	500	68 12 2½	5 18 6½	1 11 9	
Lisnaskea	25 Feb. 1843	500	131 18 3	•	83 9 1	
Londonderry	10 Nov. 1840	800	234 6 9	18 0 1	102 6 4	
Longford	24 Mar. 1842	1,000	202 0 3	0 9 3	15 5 4	
Loughrea	26 Feb. ,,	800	158 18 0½	7 1 3½	8 14 7½	
Lurgan	22 Feb. 1841	800	181 5 7½	9 7 5½	475 3 0	
Macroom	13 May, 1843	600	197 7 5½	7 4 6	0 11 9	
Magherafelt	11 Mar. 1842	900	190 6 9	19 3 11	52 16 5	
Mallow	2 Aug. ,,	700	143 16 2	6 17 0	5 14 9	
Midleton	21 Aug. 1841	800	271 13 7	3 1 8	74 2 2	
Monaghan	25 May, 1842	900	187 13 0¾	9 17 11½	9 13 8	
Mullingar	8 Dec. ,,	800	129 2 3	•	212 0 3	
Naas	4 Aug. 1841	550	186 2 10½	13 6 6	8 18 2	
Navan	4 May, 1842	500	170 2 1½	•	19 7 1	
Nenagh	28 April, ,,	1,000	220 15 3½	•	15 17 9	
Newcastle	15 Mar. 1841	550	207 16 10	14 2 6	50 10 11½	
New Ross	6 July, 1842	900	303 7 5	5 12 0	7 15 10	
Newry	16 Dec. 1841	1,000	205 10 0	10 0 0	10 3 9	
Newtownards	4 Jan. 1842	600	262 14 11	10 0 0	9 3 7	
Newtown Limavady	15 Mar. ,,	600	175 12 2	5 10 0	3 3 8	
Oldcastle	12 Aug. ,,	600	150 1 6½	11 17 7	5 12 11	
Omagh	24 Aug. 1841	800	170 18 3	12 16 6	23 0 4	
Parsonstown	2 April, 1842	800	190 9 6½	1 1 2	19 17 2	27 8
Rathdown	12 Oct. 1841	600	255 12 3	1 3 4	36 0 10	
Rathdrum	8 Mar. 1842	600	242 19 0	10 0 0	23 4 11	
Rathkeale	26 July, 1841	600	169 10 2½	7 19 1	83 17 5	
Roscommon	4 Nov. 1843	900	184 2 8	•	13 1 0	
Roscrea	7 May, 1842	700	213 7 6	3 4 10	26 0 1	
Scariff	11 May, ,,	600	112 15 8	1 17 3	56 0 0	
Shillelagh	18 Feb. ,,	400	207 0 5	11 6 8	11 12 2½	
Skibbereen	19 Mar. ,,	800	171 7 9	6 1 7	6 6 8	
Sligo	17 Dec. 1841	1,200	236 10 11½	3 16 9½	19 8 6	
Strabane	18 Nov. ,,	800	189 13 3	10 1 7½	19 19 11	
Stranorlar	3 May, 1844	400	190 9 3	•	30 0 0	
Thurles	7 Nov. 1842	700	144 19 0	8 7 8	5 15 6	
Tipperary	3 July, 1841	700	210 17 1	13 12 3	37 10 11	
Tralee	1 Feb. 1844	1,000	165 18 7½	0 4 0	•	
Trim	11 Oct. 1841	500	156 5 7	12 9 10½	23 4 0	
Tullamore	9 June, 1842	700	193 17 8	6 0 0	1 7 10	
Waterford	20 April, 1841	900	305 13 9½	10 0 0	24 16 0	125 16
Wexford	25 July, 1842	600	187 15 4¼	9 10 5½	47 8 0	28 5
Totals		75,760	20,213 18 3½	812 8 5½	4,894 14 3½	4,027 16

Audited for the Half-years ended respectively 25th March and 29th September, 1844.

Charges, for the Half-year ended 29th September, 1844, in 104 Unions, the Accounts of which the Workhouse in each Union, and its Capacity.

Printing, Stationery, Advertising, and Postage.	Drugs and Medical, or Surgical Appliances.	Rent.	Insurance.	Other Charges.	Amount Debited to Establishment.	Credits Deducted.	Amount of Establishment Charges Apportioned.
£. s. d.	£. s. d.	£. s. d.	£. s. d.	£. s. d.	£. s. d.	£. s. d.	£. s. d.
·	·	·	7 1 0	44 7 8	285 8 9	11 4 3¼	274 4 5¾
2 4 11	0 9 6	·	·	14 9 8½	184 18 6½	23 19 3	160 19 3½
83 19 9	·	16 4 1½	6 0 0	9 10 4½	191 11 0½	·	191 11 0½
15 0 2	·	·	·	20 14 3	232 4 6	12 14 0	219 10 6
32 4 11	24 0 5	·	·	36 11 5	415 18 2	249 17 9	166 0 5
2 19 11	·	·	6 5 0	1 8 10½	86 16 3¾	18 2 7¼	68 13 7½
20 16 11	12 6 10	·	·	9 6 4	289 13 2	·	289 18 2
12 18 1	11 8 10	·	·	17 11 6	417 16 5	57 6 11½	360 9 5½
27 19 1	11 12 11	·	·	17 17 8	312 12 3	2 0 0	310 12 3
18 1 1	6 1 6	19 0 4½	·	14 11 5	246 12 9½	16 18 1¼	229 14 8¼
84 14 11	23 4 7	·	4 10 0	49 0 0	780 15 10¼	7 17 2	772 18 8¼
20 1 9	12 0 4½	·	1 10 0	13 7 6½	325 16 6½	·	325 16 6½
17 4 8	0 9 1	·	2 15 0	24 4 5	326 7 5	17 19 0	308 8 5
20 3 7	13 10 5	·	·	27 16 2	232 3 7	·	232 3 7
16 6 6	18 2 8	·	8 0 0	41 19 9	437 7 4	0 8 2	436 19 2
14 19 10	·	·	·	8 1 7	243 1 4	24 12 4	218 9 0
25 11 2	9 3 11	·	·	32 4 4	418 2 5	5 14 1	412 8 4
21 14 2	1 17 1	22 12 7	5 0 0	2 6 0	291 3 9¾	15 1 10¾	276 1 11
24 10 6	·	·	·	13 1 7	246 11 8½	29 8 8	217 3 0½
64 1 6½	33 16 5	25 6 6	·	71 8 10½	444 8 11½	29 16 0	414 12 11½
31 16 0½	33 9 9	·	6 0 0	1 11 11	397 10 5½	6 0 7	391 9 10½
24 3 0	0 16 8	21 13 1	·	27 5 8½	458 4 6¾	15 15 9¾	442 8 9
28 18 6	·	·	·	17 12 6	304 3 11	29 2 9	275 1 2
27 10 0	5 4 6	10 0 0	·	8 4 10	350 8 4	29 0 6½	321 7 9½
3 19 6	·	·	3 15 0	9 8 6½	216 8 0½	14 18 9	201 9 3½
11 18 7	5 7 6	·	5 5 0	15 3 2	215 16 7½	28 8 8½	187 7 11
13 8 11	6 13 0	15 0 0	·	4 5 5	254 15 8	12 15 10½	241 19 9½
11 0 2	9 6 6	·	·	31 6 8	290 9 3¼	10 10 1½	279 19 1¾
62 8 5½	19 7 3	·	3 15 0	26 12 5	544 13 7½	·	544 13 7½
89 6 4	22 2 8	16 7 0	·	56 14 0½	502 14 8½	·	502 14 8½
24 7 4	13 12 1½	·	6 12 0	17 9 3	332 8 9½	33 4 11¾	299 3 9½
19 11 10	7 12 2	24 6 4	·	11 2 8	279 10 10	·	279 10 10
34 4 1	23 12 8	·	3 12 0	16 11 9	357 6 2	8 0 0	349 6 2
·	·	·	·	38 15 11	209 8 10	3 11 5½	205 17 4½
3 2 7	19 7 4	·	·	7 6 2½	286 9 6	27 3 5½	259 6 0½
28 8 9	15 5 0	·	4 0 0	·	259 9 8	· [illegible]	259 9 8
41 13 9	4 15 5	·	·	40 13 7½	359 11 5¼	0 5 11¾	359 5 5½
7 0 4	2 17 4	·	·	7 10 11	261 12 10½	23 2 11	238 9 11½
70 1 1	28 10 9	4 7 6	4 7 6	28 0 2	526 18 3	12 12 0	514 6 3
29 12 11	·	·	·	4 13 11	231 6 1	1 2 6	230 3 7
6 7 3	·	·	7 10 0	16 19 0	307 10 1	35 0 11	272 9 2
31 2 4½	5 2 3	32 17 6	·	15 1 9½	292 17 4¾	0 1 0	292 16 4¾
15 13 2	1 8 0	·	4 10 0	29 0 6	256 4 9½	18 7 7	237 17 2½
23 15 9½	9 14 9	·	10 2 6	4 7 8½	278 17 2½	0 0 10½	278 16 4
59 0 9	1 16 8	·	5 5 0	141 11 4	673 19 11½	71 6 4½	602 13 7
10 10 9	16 7 9	29 8 0	5 5 0	12 11 11	347 2 8	9 19 5½	337 3 2½
2,723 3 2½	1,395 16 10¾	521 17 2	290 6 4	2,534 5 2½	37,404 0 2¼	2,420 18 10¼	34,983 1 3¾

No.15.— IRELAND.—TABLES abstracted from the Union Accounts which have been Audited for the Half-years ended respectively 25th March and 29th September, 1844.

i.—Showing the Expenditure for Provisions, Necessaries, and Clothing of Paupers, in the Half-year ended 25th March, 1844, in 100 Unions, the Accounts of which have been Audited: also the Number of Paupers Relieved in the Half-year, and the average Weekly Cost per Head.

UNIONS.	Cost of Provisions Consumed.			Cost of Necessaries Consumed.			Cost of Clothing.			Total Cost of Provisions, Necessaries, and Clothing.			Total Number of Paupers Relieved.	Collective Number of Days for all Paupers Relieved in the Half-year.	Average Number of Days of Relief to each Pauper.	Average Weekly Cost per Head.		
	£.	s.	d.	£.	s.	d.	£.	s.	d.	£.	s.	d.				Provisions and Necessaries. s. d.	Clothing. d.	TOTAL. s. d.
Abbeyleix	621	15	7¼	108	4	0¾	43	11	7	773	11	2¼	795	73,215	92	1 4¼	1	1 5¼
Antrim	217	7	1	73	1	3½	53	9	5½	343	17	10	390	25,667	78	1 6¼	3¼	1 10¼
Ardee	444	12	3	84	14	10	98	12	8½	627	7	9½	514	47,057	92	1 7¼	3¾	1 10¾
Armagh	519	14	10¼	92	9	6	146	12	6	759	1	1½	740	70,378	95	1 2¼	3¾	1 6¼
Athy	144	4	4½	49	9	6	30	14	10¼	224	8	9	371	14,757	40	1 10¼	3¼	2 1¾
Ballieborough	317	8	1¾	96	18	10¾	59	7	2¼	473	14	3	454	56,989	126	1 0¼	1¾	1 1¾
Ballina	149	15	0	42	4	4½	32	4	2	224	3	7½	303	15,460	51	1 8½	3½	2 0¼
Ballinasloe	349	13	9	59	13	6¾	96	6	5	505	13	8½	435	46,234	106	1 2¾	3¾	1 6¾
Ballinrobe	65	2	6¾	22	18	5½	19	12	4	107	13	4½	69	9,416	136	1 3½	3¾	1 7¼
Ballycastle	100	0	10¼	16	8	11¾	43	8	7¼	159	18	6	118	13,898	118	1 2	4¼	1 7¼
Ballymena	94	6	0	39	12	5	29	11	3	163	9	8	237	14,190	60	1 3¼	3¼	1 7¼
Ballymoney	185	8	7¾	61	11	11½	66	9	1½	313	8	10¾	268	31,899	119	1 1	3½	1 4¾
Ballyshannon	47	13	0	12	12	11½	10	0	6	70	6	5¼	63	4,812	76	1 4½	3¾	1 8
Balinglass	484	7	1¾	70	0	0¾	104	17	7	659	4	9	414	50,342	122	1 6¼	4	1 10
Banbridge	318	13	8¾	99	19	9	45	3	0½	463	16	6¼	386	43,846	112	1 3¼	4¼	1 6½
Bandon	374	4	3	64	6	6½	113	3	1½	551	18	5	608	54,815	89	1 2	3¼	1 5½
Belfast	1,135	4	3	251	15	7	326	5	6¼	1,713	5	3¼	1,774	156,611	88	1 3	2¾	1 6¼
Callan	243	0	2	98	8	11½	91	11	7½	433	0	9	313	29,306	94	1 7	5¼	2 0¼
Carrickmacross	46	0	10¾	16	5	5½	13	11	9½	75	18	2	109	4,349	40	1 6¼	6¼	1 1
Carrick-on-Shannon	333	3	11¾	111	0	4½	48	12	8½	492	16	9½	375	46,677	124	1 4	4¾	1 5¼
Carrick-on-Suir	369	9	0	68	18	7½	64	10					466	31,180	69	1 1¼		1 3

	£	
Cashel	92 13	13,643
Castlebar	387 5	48,300
Castleblayney	55	10,873
Castlederg	184 16	21,424
Calbridge	324 17	34,407
Clogheen	372 2	47,634
Clones	522	83,735
Clonmel	325 15	50,364
Coleraine	213 14	28,378
Cookstown	560 19	86,341
Cootehill	3,884 5	332,305
Cork		
Donegal	27 14	2,957
Downpatrick	569 16	75,384
Drogheda	443 4	60,028
Dublin, North	3,295 10	310,600
Dublin, South	3,450 19	349,414
Dundalk	513 1	67,202
Dungannon	366 15	52,848
Dunmanway	209 17	31,534
Dunshaughlin	456 17	55,673
Ennis	533 14	65,941
Enniskymon	179 0	28,297
Fermoy	883 8	96,505
Galway	224 7	36,562
Gorey	572 6	55,722
Gort	144 18	21,350
Gortin	74 6	10,565
Granard	361 7	62,946

No. 15.—IRELAND, (*continued.*)—Tables abstracted from the Union Accounts which have been Audited for the Half-years ended respectively 25th March and 29th September, 1844.

i.—Showing the Expenditure for Provisions, Necessaries, and Clothing of Paupers, in the Half-year ended 25th March, 1844, in 100 Unions, the Accounts of which have been audited: also the Number of Paupers Relieved in the Half-Year, and the Average Weekly Cost per Head.

UNIONS.	Cost of Provisions Consumed. (£ s. d.)	Cost of Necessaries Consumed. (£ s. d.)	Cost of Clothing. (£ s. d.)	Total Cost of Provisions, Necessaries, and Clothing. (£ s. d.)	Total Number of Paupers Relieved.	Collective Number of Days for all Paupers Relieved in the Half-year.	Average Number of Days of Relief to each Pauper.	Average Weekly Cost per Head: Provisions and Necessaries. (s. d.)	Clothing. (d.)	Total. (s. d.)
Inishowen	24 16 9¼	10 15 10	10 3 7	45 16 2¼	73	4,886	67	1 0½	3¼	1 3¾
Kells	393 6 1½	97 18 6¼	96 19 7½	588 4 3¾	531	46,552	88	1 4¼	3¼	1 8
Kilkeel	114 4 1¼	24 0 4¼	8 12 1	146 16 7½	192	16,519	86	1 2	1	1 3
Kilkenny	1,279 10 0½	164 18 3	177 4 8	1,621 12 11½	1,488	114,912	77	1 9	0½	1 9½
Kilmallock	841 1 6¼	109 4 1	165 12 3¼	1,115 17 11½	1,023	79,495	78	1 8	3¼	1 11¼
Kilrush	197 16 4¼	42 19 5¼	62 7 7½	303 3 6	283	29,943	105	1 1½	3¼	1 5
Kinsale	221 3 6¼	44 16 11	80 1 5	346 1 10¼	402	28,873	72	1 1	4¼	1 5¼
Larne	275 10 11	54 10 5¼	79 15 11½	409 17 4	346	38,303	111	1 2¼	3¼	1 6
Limerick	1,301 15 11	226 14 10	367 16 9¼	1,896 7 6¾	1,709	176,563	103	1 2¾	3¾	1 6½
Lisburn	480 6 0½	108 4 2¼	72 16 0¼	661 6 3	557	69,889	125	1 2¼	1¼	1 3¾
Lismore	149 11 6	24 10 2¼	42 17 11	216 19 7¼	167	18,017	108	1 2¼	4	1 6¼
Limnakee	166 6 3	41 7 3¼	62 13 0	270 6 6¼	297	30,072	101	0 11½	3¼	1 3½
Londonderry	327 5 6	99 15 2¼	113 12 8	540 13 4½	536	54,544	102	1 1¼	2¾	1 4¼
Longford	610 18 2	123 10 10½	157 17 3	892 6 3¾	761	83,950	110	1 1½	2¾	1 4
Loughrea	212 8 4½	46 17 7½	60 19 5	320 5 5	233	29,266	126	1 1¾	3¾	1 5
Lurgan	394 3 7	71 19 4¼	105 16 6	571 19 5¼	621	50,796	82	1 3½	2¾	1 6¼
Macroom	240 11 7	35 3 7½	64 2 1	339 17 3¾	404	30,770	76	1 3	3¼	1 6¼
Magherafelt	221 5 4	106 0 11½	69 14 10	397 1 1¾	360	33,476	93	1 4½	3¼	1 8
Mallow	359 15 11¼	50 16 8¼	96 11 4	478 3 0	563	46,352	82	1 1¾	3¼	1 5¼
Midleton	604 14 7¼	111 7 2¼	187 5 4½	682 11 7	714	61,089	86	1 7¾	3¼	1 10½
Monaghan	372 18 1¼	59 7 2¼	121 7 0¼	451 15 8¼	869	38,582	110	1 3¾	4¼	1 9

Naas	639	172	69	880	532	66,815	125
Navan	461	107	107	675	616	51,483	84
Nenagh	684	96	91	872	805	77,449	96
Newcastle	691	78	164	934	748	69,206	92
New Ross	732	90	136	960	762	65,407	86
Newry	600	122	260	983	809	83,320	103
Newtownards	267	47	76	391	450	35,686	79
Newtown Limavady	118	45	36	200	175	17,754	101
Oldcastle	325	76	99	500	422	47,537	113
Omagh	266	82	105	454	501	50,500	101
Parsonstown	267	63	79	410	343	38,245	112
Rathdown	776	139	136	1,052	863	65,426	76
Rathkeale	565	133	151	849	670	72,567	108
Roscommon	346	43	94	484	398	45,393	114
Roscrea	68	38	19	126	181	9,143	50
	472	101	108	683	541	52,096	96
Shillelagh	63	20	20	103	96	9,854	103
	392	55	104	552	387	50,174	130
Sligo	413	44	50	508	454	48,836	107
Strabane	464	119	1	707	483	59,377	123
	264	70	86	422	372	41,720	112
Thurles	354	68	80	503	313	38,666	124
Tipperary	627	142	167	937	774	80,367	104
Tralee	36	10	7	55	137	3,690	27
Trim	235	56	49	341	292	32,287	110
Tullamore	509	80	110	700	478	52,390	111
Waterford	1,327	124	242	1,695	1,279	116,598	91
Wexford	563	81	109	754	555	52,568	95
TOTALS	48,374	8,368	11,164	67,907	58,202	5,649,329	97

No. 15.—Ireland, (*continued.*)—Tables abstracted from the Union Accounts which have been Audited for the Half-years ended respectively 25th March and 29th September, 1844.

ii.—Showing the Expenditure for Provisions, Necessaries, and Clothing of Paupers, in the Half-year ended the 29th September, 1844, in 104 Unions, the Accounts of which have been Audited: also the Number of Paupers relieved in the Half-year, and the average Weekly Cost per Head.

UNIONS.	Cost of Provisions Consumed.	Cost of Necessaries Consumed.	Cost of Clothing.	Total Cost of Provisions, Necessaries, and Clothing.	Total Number of Paupers Relieved.	Collective Number of Days for all Paupers Relieved in the Half-year.	Average Number of Days of Relief to each Pauper.	Average Weekly Cost per Head. Provisions and Necessaries.	Average Weekly Cost per Head. Clothing.	Average Weekly Cost per Head. Total.
	£. s. d.	£. s. d.	£. s. d.	£. s. d.				s. d.	d.	s. d.
Abbeyleix	717 6 2¼	84 14 11	47 5 2	849 6 3¼	869	79,398	91	1 5	1	1 6
Antrim	347 3 0	60 8 4¾	86 2 3½	493 13 8¼	405	41,335	102	1 4½	3½	1 8
Ardee	625 15 0¼	84 6 9¾	136 17 0½	846 18 10½	757	65,689	87	1 6	3½	1 9½
Armagh	680 16 6	60 13 10½	99 16 8½	841 7 1	971	83,863	86	1 2¼	2	1 4¼
Athy	707 9 3½	58 18 6¾	129 2 0	895 9 10¼	646	61,968	96	1 8¾	3½	2 0¼
Bailieborough	394 14 5	65 14 2	..	460 8 7	713	61,461	86	1 0½	..	1 0½
Ballina	462 15 9	48 13 4	103 9 3	614 18 4	600	49,662	83	1 5¼	3½	1 8¾
Ballinasloe	377 0 4⅛	33 15 2½	46 12 0	457 7 6⅝	463	44,736	96	1 3¾	1¾	1 5½
Ballinrobe	85 17 1¾	17 11 10	21 18 4½	125 7 4¾	76	10,521	138	1 4¼	3½	1 8
Ballycastle	75 9 0	15 4 8½	23 1 5	113 15 1½	124	11,074	89	0 11½	3½	1 3
Ballymena	205 0 8	60 9 2	63 10 5	329 0 3	342	30,490	89	1 2¼	3½	1 6
Ballymoney	226 13 7	35 2 3	77 19 1	339 14 11	311	37,418	120	0 11¾	3½	1 3¼
Ballyshannon	76 7 6¾	22 8 9¾	17 15 2	116 11 6½	98	8,524	87	1 3	3½	1 6½
Baltinglass	530 15 9¾	69 10 7¾	112 1 2½	712 7 8	444	53,789	121	1 6¾	3½	1 10¼
Banbridge	407 12 10	74 1 2	155 17 9¾	637 11 9¾	425	49,885	117	1 4 1/16	5 1/16	1 9 7/16
Bandon	568 0 11¼	40 12 3¼	142 1 8¼	770 14 10¾	788	68,200	87	1 3	3½	1 6½
Belfast	1,240 1 8¼	228 10 6¾	334 7 10½	1,803 0 1¾	1,642	160,509	98	1 3¼	3½	1 6¾
Boyle	434 2 7½	74 10 4	87 3 6½	595 16 6	365	41,845	114	1 8½	3½	2 0
Callan	326 2 4¾	87 6 11½	71 6 10	484 16 2	412	34,244	83	1 8¼	3½	1 11¾
Carrickmacross	127 11 1¼	23 0 5	40 0 6¾	190 12 1	206	12,609	62	1 7¾	5¼	2 1
Carrick-on-Shannon	367 2 0¾	64 7 9¼	54 8 7¾	485 18 5¾	464	52,255	113	1 1¾	1¾	1 3½
Carrick-on-Suir	463 6 1	54 17 0	79 18 9½	598 1 10½	513	38,371	75	1 10¾	3½	2 2½

Castlebar	126	17	3	25	17	4	35	3	9	187	18	4	156	16,890	108	1	3	1	6¾
Castleblayney	500	2	6¼	82	1	0	208	3	10¼	790	7	4¼	649	66,022	103	1	2¼	1	8
Castlederg	55	6	1½	14	9	0	16	11	7	86	9	4	80	16,595	90	0	2½	2	0½
Cahbridge	230	14	1¼	57	5	11¼	47	14	7	335	14	7½	304	22,910	75	1	9	1	7¾
Clogheen	420	3	9	69	4	1¼	58	0	11	547	8	0	342	44,091	130	1	5½	1	1½
Clogher	124	19	11	57	11	0	32	8	11	215	0	7	162	15,574	96	1	4	1	9¾
Clones	468	5	2	85	10	4	123	12	1½	677	7	7½	556	59,381	107	1	2¼	1	7¾
Clonmel	906	19	1	69	19	2½	178	3	8	1,155	1	11½	964	94,643	98	1	2¼	1	6
Coleraine	344	13	0	91	13	4	108	10	8	535	3	0	469	52,093	111	1	2¾	1	9¾
Cookstown	223	14	0	47	6	0½	66	18	3¼	337	16	3½	292	30,797	105	1	2¾	1	4
Cootehill	642	9	5½	114	6	2¼	45	6	10½	802	2	6½	1,018	104,761	103	1	0½	1	10½
Cork	6,341	11	3¾	301	1	3½	1,222	17	11	7,805	10	6	5,214	360,201	69	1	6¼	1	5¾
Donegal	59	5	9¼	15	8	7¼	13	3	1¾	87	17	6¼	91	6,315	78	1	3¾	1	9¾
Downpatrick	605	3	2¼	77	16	3¼	153	0	2	835	19	7¾	705	73,444	104	1	3½	1	7
Drogheda	433	6	1¼	39	9	0	58	19	1½	531	14	3	742	56,599	76	1	11¾	1	3¾
Dublin, North	3,735	17	5¼	341	6	7	659	15	10¼	4,736	19	10½	3,055	316,700	104	2	1	1	3½
Dublin, South	3,538	8	7¼	263	17	3½	737	7	4¼	4,539	13	3¼	3,384	353,937	105	1	9¾	1	3½
Dundalk	761	8	1¼	68	3	4½	153	17	8	1,013	8	6	1,048	88,246	84	1	6	1	7¾
Dungannon	344	5	8	71	3	4½	101	5	0	516	14	3	552	48,490	88	1	3¾	1	6
Dungarvan	45	9	7½	4	11	1½	9	10	5	59	11	1¼	139	4,570	33	1	6½	1	9¾
Dunmanway	241	15	8¾	84	10	0	72	2	7	398	8	3¾	428	40,934	96	1	7	1	4
Dunshaughlin	595	19	2¼	122	19	4½	127	17	2	846	15	8½	623	61,372	98	1	7	1	10¼
Ennis	545	0	8¼	58	8	10¼	142	7	0¼	745	16	7¼	671	74,023	110	1	2	1	5½
Enniscorthy	633	6	1½	57	17	11¼	125	7	10¼	816	11	11¾	779	60,189	77	1	7½	1	10½
Ennistymon	256	10	6	20	4	11	80	14	6	357	9	11	385	38,748	100	0	0	1	3¼
Fermoy	797	17	3¼	80	4	10¾	184	6	7¾	1,062	8	9½	1,432	88,479	62	1	4½	1	8½
Galway	372	4	7	35	17	7	97	11	1	505	13	3	680	46,827	65	1	2¼	1	6
Gorey	487	2	3½	84	15	2	105	9	7	677	7	0½	526	50,630	96	1	7	1	10½
Gort	186	9	1½	23	2	0½	53	14	3	263	6	8	227	25,782	113	1	1½	1	5
Gortin	77	12	10	24	19	10	23	4	5	125	17	1	107	11,146	104	1	2	1	5¾
Granard	519	10	1	106	13	2	143	13	10¼	770	17	1¼	668	69,453	104	1	4	1	7¾

No. 15.—IRELAND, (*continued.*)—Tables abstracted from the Union Accounts which have been Audited for the Half-years ended respectively 25th March and 29th September, 1844.

ii.—Showing the Expenditure for Provisions, Necessaries, and Clothing of Paupers, in the Half-year ended the 29th September, 1844, in 104 Unions the Accounts of which have been Audited: also the Number of Paupers relieved in the Half-year, and the average Weekly Cost per Head.

UNIONS.	Cost of Provisions Consumed.	Cost of Necessaries Consumed.	Cost of Clothing.	Total Cost of Provisions, Necessaries, and Clothing.	Total Number of Paupers Relieved.	Collective Number of Days for all Paupers Relieved in the Half-year.	Average Number of Days of Relief to each Pauper.	Average Weekly Cost per Head.		
	£. s. d.	£. s. d.	£. s. d.	£. s. d.				Provisions and Necessaries. s. d.	Clothing. d.	TOTAL.
Inishowen	64 13 11½	12 1 6¼	19 16 3	96 11 8¾	84	9,510	113	1 1¼	3¾	3¾
Kanturk	102 14 4½	9 12 5¾	111 14 5	224 1 3	272	10,677	39	1 5¼	3½	
Kells	568 10 2	92 9 9¾	32 10 6¼	693 10 6¼	689	62,458	90	1 5¼	0¾	
Kilkeel	129 18 10¾	21 15 10	17 9 2	169 4 10¾	206	16,760	81	1 3	1¼	
Kilkenny	1,570 9 3	120 4 4¾		1,690 13 7¼	1,514	126,468	83	1 10¼	::	
Kilmallock	682 0 8¾	61 15 10	70 11 0¼	814 7 7	888	67,729	76	1 6¼	1¼	
Kilrush	212 11 3¾	35 1 6	62 15 9¾	310 8 6¼	289	30,139	104	1 1½	3¾	
Kinsale	346 17 4¾	66 2 4	49 5 3	462 4 11¼	481	37,123	77	1 3¼	4¼	
Larne	309 18 4	41 13 7½	88 16 5	440 8 4½	384	42,634	111	1 2	3¼	
Lisburn	518 3 3	63 10 1¼	146 3 4	727 16 8¼	563	70,160	125	1 2	3¼	
Lismore	213 8 2¼	20 19 6	48 9 10¼	282 17 6¼	214	23,277	108	1 4¼	3¼	
Lisnaskea	192 2 10¼	33 17 9¾	72 12 7¾	298 13 3¼	376	34,863	92	0 10¼	2¾	
Londonderry	377 18 10¼	65 14 8¼	118 1 1¼	561 14 8	635	56,667	89	1	2	
Longford	1,153 12 9	113 3 5	174 16 1	1,441 12 3	1,129	192,835	109	1 3¼	2	
Loughrea	278 18 5	25 17 1¼		304 15 6¼	328	35,744	109	1 2¼	::	
Lurgan	476 15 9	70 0 10¾	59 18 2¼	606 14 10	614	57,514	93	1 4	1¼	
Macroom	373 8 7	33 13 0¼	93 8 0	500 9 7¼	538	44,839	83	1 2	3¼	
Magherafelt	314 13 2¼	63 2 5¾	79 3 1	456 18 9¼	409	37,994	93	1 4¼	3¼	
Mallow	341 12 6	38 6 5	89 10 5	463 9 3	628	42,970	69	1 2¼	3½	
Middleton	754 11 6	64 18 6¾	76 15 6¼			73,702	78	1 4¼	1¼	
Monaghan	331 6 6	64 9 7	97 19 9¾			47,655	96	1 4¼	2½	
Mullingar						77,440	112			

Naas	803 11 1¼	99 1 0	78 7 4¾	980 19 6	646	75,235	116	1 8	1¾	1 9¾
Navan	498 16 5¼	78 4 2½	116 15 2	693 15 9¾	738	56,065	76	1 5½	3½	1 9
Nenagh	756 0 9¼	72 13 0½	89 18 7	918 12 5	990	87,721	89	1 3¼	0¼	1 4 17/42
Newcastle . . .	694 18 2 23/28	53 14 8⅝	166 10 8 13/16	915 3 7 17/28	892	79,936	89	1 3¼	3½	1 7
New Ross . . .	785 2 10½	69 13 6	135 5 5½	990 1 10	668	64,931	97	1 8¼	3½	1 11¾
Newry	743 10 8	80 6 9	199 12 7	,023 10 0	983	95,823	96	1 2¼	3½	1 6
Newtownards . .	407 16 9¾	55 6 4	90 1½	553 8 3½	561	43,323	76	1 5¼	3½	1 9¼
Newtown Limavady.	113 16 3½	45 18 6½	39 5	199 0 5	252	18,855	75	1 2¾	3½	1 5¾
Oldcastle. . . .	427 6 6½	59 0 8½	61 16 8¼	548 3 11½	572	59,361	104	1 1¾	1¾	1 3½
Omagh	220 11 4½	63 11 11¾	85 16 3	369 19 7¼	486	41,190	85	0 11½	3½	1 3
Parsonstown . . .	303 0 9¼	40 19 2½	77 2 0	421 1 11¾	369	37,008	100	1 3¼	3½	1 6¾
Rathdown . . .	836 10 10½	89 6 9¾	138 4 3½	,064 1 11¾	867	66,343	76	1 11¼	3½	2 2¾
Rathdrum . . .	662 10 0	123 19 0½	329 9 0	1,115 18 0½	658	79,068	120	1 4½	7	1 11¼
Rathkeale . . .	472 9 2¼	30 14 9	121 10 8¼	624 14 7½	632	58,519	92	1 2½	3½	1 6
Roscommon . . .	301 17 11	30 3 2	64 8 5	396 9 6	464	30,922	66	1 5½	3½	1 9
Roscrea	490 17 6	79 7 8½	116 18 10	687 4 0½	588	56,132	95	1 5	3½	1 8½
Scariff	155 8 0	21 2 11¼	45 0 3½	221 11 2¾	217	21,607	99	1 2	3½	1 5½
Shillelagh . . .	413 14 10¼	50 3 4	52 6 4¼	516 4 6¾	454	50,225	110	1 3½	1¾	1 5¼
Skibbereen . . .	530 14 4¾	26 16 8	60 11 4¾	618 2 4½	556	58,145	104	1 3¾	1¾	1 5½
Sligo	648 5 7	95 4 1½	148 5 9	891 15 5¼	604	71,178	108	1 5½	3½	1 9
Strabane	255 17 6¼	55 7 11	78 17 5	390 2 10¼	380	37,858	99	1 2	3½	1 5½
Stranorlar . . .	21 17 1½	5 10 10½	6 10 1	33 18 1	52	3,122	60	1 2¾	3½	1 6¼
Thurles	410 12 6½	48 19 8	90 0 8½	549 12 10½	375	43,215	115	1 6	3½	1 9½
Tipperary . . .	721 8 6	101 15 6	171 10 0	994 14 0	844	82,320	97	1 4¾	3½	1 8¼
Tralee	248 1 4	26 4 11	62 12 1	336 18 4	424	30,050	71	1 4¼	3½	1 7¾
Trim	310 6 4¼	44 3 6¾	80 6 6	434 16 5	350	38,596	110	1 3½	3½	1 7
Tullamore . . .	631 11 11½	51 15 0½	128 3 9½	811 10 9½	521	61,531	115	1 6¾	3½	1 10¼
Waterford . . .	1,852 6 5	102 11 11	333 4 4	2,288 2 8	1,748	159,948	92	1 8½	3½	2 0
Wexford	614 3 9½	62 14 6½	113 8 0	790 6 4	643	54,432	84	1 9	3½	2 0½
TOTALS . . .	59,460 17 4¾	6,928 13 7¾	12,102 7 10	78,491 18 10½	67,951	6,284,350	92½	1 5¾	3¼	1 9

No. 16.—An Account of the Expenditure upon the Relief of the Poor, and the Total Number of Paupers Relieved in each Union in Ireland, during the Year ended on the 1st of January, 1845; (in pursuance of Section 123 of the Irish Poor Relief Act.)

i.—Unions, the Workhouses of which were opened prior to 1844.—(*In continuation of Return in Annual Report for* 1844, *Appendix B. No.* 14.)

UNIONS.	Expenditure of the Union from 1st January, to 31st December, 1844, inclusive.	Total Number of Paupers relieved.			
		Remaining on 1st January 1844.	Admitted and Born in the Workhouse in the Year 1844.	Discharged and Died in the Workhouse in the Year 1844.	Remaining on 1st January 1845.
	£. s. d.				
Abbeyleix . . .	2,791 11 11	396	812	796	412
Antrim . . .	2,767 11 9	137	432	320	249
Ardee . . .	2,462 16 2¼	266	820	674	412
Armagh . . .	2,534 12 6	404	946	865	485
Athlone . . .	(See Note * at foot.)				
Bailieborough .	1,691 4 11	299	551	567	283
Ballina . .	2,214 16 6	66	753	519	300
Ballinasloe .	1,650 5 4	262	365	408	219
Ballinrobe. .	1,311 2 4½	50	70	34	86
Ballycastle .	1,068 9 5	85	125	127	83
Ballymena .	2,507 1 8	113	409	308	214
Ballymoney .	1,551 15 7	184	224	221	187
Bally\hannon .	593 8 11	20	129	81	68
Balrothery .	1,561 16 6¼	208	505	466	247
Baltinglass .	2,617 8 5¼	277	308	281	304
Banbridge .	2,039 9 11	251	235	246	240
Bandon . .	3,030 4 8	296	786	692	390
Belfast . .	6,089 16 8	884	1,617	1,637	864
Boyle . . .	1,612 15 0	274	212	261	225
Callan . . .	1,361 11 2¼	159	452	404	207
Carrickmacross .	796 12 10	26	280	219	87
Carrick-on-Shannon	1,697 15 1	250	384	286	348
Carrick-on-Suir .	1,750 17 5	158	645	549	254
Cashel . .	2,057 4 5	401	979	863	517
Castlebar . .	408 1 0	72	142	120	94
Castleblayney .	2,127 11 9¼	260	536	503	293
Castlederg .	420 17 0	63	55	48	70
Cavan . .	3,140 19 5	541	543	532	552
Celbridge . .	1,158 13 0	127	306	289	144
Clogheen . .	2,077 3 11	184	212	159	237
Clones . . .	2,040 16 11	276	591	545	322
Clonmel . .	2,793 4 6	454	890	845	499
Coleraine . .	2,551 7 2	297	290	317	270
Cookstown . .	1,412 16 11	159	229	227	161
Cootehill . .	2,371 2 8	505	825	848	482
Cork . . .	13,858 16 5	1,783 †	5,780	5,679	1,884
Donegal . .	621 6 8	11	153	81	83
Downpatrick . .	2,421 14 8	425	569	658	336
Drogheda . . .	1,714 3 1	338	824	865	297

* The number of workhouses open prior to 1844 was 106. No return of the expenditure in the year 1844 could be obtained from Athlone Union: the number of paupers relieved in the workhouse of that Union in the year 1844 was 949.

† The number of paupers in the workhouse on the 1st of January, 1844, as given above, is 9 less than appeared by the Return in the Annual Report for 1844. The discrepancy has been explained by the clerk, and the above number is correct.

No. 16. *(continued).*—An Account of the Expenditure upon the Relief of the Poor, and the Total Number of Paupers Relieved in each Union in Ireland, during the Year ended on the 1st of January, 1845; (in pursuance of Section 123 of the Irish Poor Relief Act.)

i.—Unions, the Workhouses of which were opened prior to 1844.—(*In continuation of Return in Annual Report for* 1844, *Appendix B. No.* 14.)

UNIONS.	Expenditure of the Union from 1st January to 31st December, 1844, inclusive.			Total Number of Paupers Relieved.			
				Remaining on 1st January 1844.	Admitted and Born in the Workhouse in the Year 1844.	Discharged and Died in the Workhouse in the Year 1844.	Remaining on 1st January 1845.
	£.	*s.*	*d.*				
Dublin, North .	13,087	16	0¼*	1,709	2,502	2,369	1,842
Dublin, South . .	13,232	1	9†	1,923	2,639	2,538	2,024
Dundalk . . .	2,898	19	10¼	363	1,085	1,002	446
Dungannon . .	2,195	6	9	290	473	475	288
Dunmanway . .	1,137	7	3	165	411	371	205
Dunshaughlin .	2,047	10	8	311	575	583	303
Edenderry . .	2,152	1	2	343	490	506	327
Ennis	2,570	17	0	362	532	461	433
Enniscorthy . .	3,118	1	9	375	735	783	327
Ennistymon .	1,184	0	8½	163	332	246	249
Fermoy . . .	3,617	10	1	559	1,873	1,946	486
Galway . . .	2,017	18	6	193	1,421	1,212	402
Gorey . . .	2,087	11	6	349	430	508	271
Gort	951	17	3¾	123	178	132	169
Gortin	627	18	8	63	77	64	76
Granard . . .	1,980	0	5¾	340	563	508	395
Inishowen . .	480	2	5	25	96	54	67
Kells	1,772	14	7	251	732	612	371
Kilkeel . . .	629	6	0	88	203	204	87
Kilkenny . . .	4,280	12	1	634	1,633	1,589	728
Kilmallock . .	2,496	10	5	440	980	977	443
Kilrush . . .	958	5	11	176	252	251	177
Kinsale . . .	1,494	15	2	167	534	494	207
Larne	1,614	4	11	208	284	253	239
Limerick . . .	6,795	5	2	930	1,891	1,685	1,136
Lisburn . . .	2,559	18	3	394	301	354	341
Lismore . . .	831	1	4	98	204	163	139
Lisnaskea . . .	1,196	14	0½	177	342	325	194
Londonderry . .	1,890	0	3	293	599	560	332
Longford . . .	3,175	4	5	460	1,019	793	686
Loughrea . . .	1,159	9	0¼	169 ‡	247	239	177
Lurgan . . .	2,326	2	7	290	648	680	258
Macroom . . .	1,598	7	8	159	556	502	213
Magherafelt . .	1,883	6	0	188	364	342	210
Mallow . . .	1,357	13	0	268	752	752	268

* This sum includes £415 12*s.* 10*d.* chargeable to Government for the support of paupers who were formerly inmates of the House of Industry, now altered to the workhouse of the North Dublin Union. The number of such inmates remaining on the 1st of January, 1845, was 93.

† This sum includes £384 5*s.* chargeable to Government for the support of paupers who were formerly inmates of the House of Industry. The number of such inmates remaining on the 1st of January, 1845, was 85.

‡ The number of paupers in the workhouse on the 1st of January, 1844, as given above, is one less than appeared by the Return in the Annual Report for 1844. The discrepancy has been explained by the clerk, and the above number is correct.

No. 16, (*continued.*)—An Account of the Expenditure upon the Relief of the Poor, and the Total Number of Paupers Relieved in each Union in Ireland, during the Year ended on the 1st of January, 1845; (in pursuance of Section 123 of the Irish Poor Relief Act.)

i.—Unions, the Workhouses of which were opened prior to 1844.—(*In continuation of Return in Annual Report for* 1844, *Appendix B. No.* 14.)

UNIONS.	Expenditure of the Union from 1st January to 31st December, 1844, inclusive.			Total Number of Paupers Relieved.			
				Remaining on 1st January 1844	Admitted and Born in the Workhouse in the Year 1844.	Discharged and died in the Workhouse in the Year 1844.	Remaining on 1st January 1845.
	£.	s.	d.				
Manorhamilton .	1,020	3	9	109	226	178	157
Midleton . . .	3,008	12	5	339	1,003	975	367
Mohill	700	3	2	142	328	280	190
Monaghan . .	1,438	17	8¾	212	476	413	275
Mullingar . . .	2,742	15	5½	427	526	496	457
Naas	2,592	6	10	375	480	418	437
Navan	2,333	18	8½	284	848	786	346
Nenagh . . .	3,690	8	7	457	872	852	477
Newcastle . . .	2,566	19	0	369	836	809	396
New Ross . . .	3,258	8	7	356	671	640	387
Newry	1,948	8	5	479	830	849	460
Newtownards . .	2,130	4	6	219	628	595	252
Newtown Limavady	839	5	8	100	243	233	110
Oldcastle . . .	1,626	16	5	263	490	374	379
Omagh . . .	1,904	2	5½	289	524	497	316
Parsonstown . .	1,379	3	4½	212	257	276	193
Rathdown . . .	3,620	1	4¾	358	895	848	405
Rathdrum . . .	3,359	16	2	414	557	491	480
Rathkeale . . .	2,262	5	7¼	253	600	497	356
Roscommon . .	1,388	7	8	42	673	446	269
Roscrea . . .	2,132	0	9	299*	614	586	327
Scariff	880	4	2	54	236	120	170
Shillelagh . . .	1,691	6	6¾	299	266	322	243
Skibbereen . .	1,761	4	10	264	464	427	301
Sligo	2,500	5	9¾	332	443	358	417
Strabane . . .	1,425	10	2¾	231	312	307	236
Thurles . . .	1,747	18	6	219	272	214	277
Tipperary . . .	2,960	6	2	407	757	672	492
Trim	1,355	4	7	173	288	278	183
Tullamore . . .	2,246	15	2	296	417	382	331
Waterford . . .	5,937	16	8½	620†	1,711	1,537	794
Wexford . . .	2,731	5	0	292	644	636	300
Totals 105 Unions‡	251,467	1	6	33,192	68,374	63,865	37,701

* The number of paupers in the workhouse on the 1st of January, 1844, as given above, is two more than appeared by the Return in the Annual Report for 1844. The discrepancy has been explained by the clerk, and the above number is correct.

† The number of paupers in the workhouse on the 1st of January, 1844, as given above, is four more than appeared by the Return in the Annual Report for 1844. The discrepancy has been explained by the clerk, and the above number is correct.

‡ The number of workhouses open prior to 1844 was 106. No Return of the expenditure in the year 1844 could be obtained from Athlone Union: the number of paupers relieved in the workhouse of that Union in the year 1844 was 949.

No. 16, (*continued.*)—An Account of the Expenditure upon the Relief of the Poor, and the Total Number of Paupers Relieved in each Union in Ireland, during the Year ended on the 1st of January, 1845 ; (in pursuance of Section 123 of the Irish Poor Relief Act.)

ii.—UNIONS, the WORKHOUSES of which were opened in 1844.

UNIONS.	Date of Declaration of Union.	Date from which the Workhouse was declared fit for the Reception of Paupers.	Date on which Paupers were first admitted into the Workhouse.	Expenditure from the commencement of the Union to the 31st December, 1844, inclusive.	Total Number of Paupers Relieved.		
					Admitted and Born in the Workhouse.	Discharged and Died in the Workhouse.	Remaining on 1st January, 1845.
				£. s. d.			
Athy	23 Jan. 1841	20 Nov. 1843	21 Mar. 1844	3,399 0 6	790	480	310
Carlow . . .	21 Sept. 1840	16 Sept 1844	18 Nov. ,,	1,696 13 7¼	211	19	192
Clogher . .	24 April 1841	9 Mar. ,,	9 Mar. ,,	1,756 0 8	244	110	134
Dungarvan .	8 April 1839	27 Dec. 1841	4 July ,,	4,089 16 4	252	101	151
Kanturk. . .	1 Jan. 1840	16 May 1842	18 July ,,	2,203 10 5	643	235	408
Stranorlar. .	21 Dec. ,,	16 Mar. 1844	3 May ,,	951 19 10	87	34	53
Tralee. . . .	6 April ,,	1 Sept. 1842	1 Feb. ,,	3,965 11 9	616	390	226
Seven Unions	. . . .	. . . .	. . . .	18,062 13 1¼	2,843	1,369	1,474

No. 17.—STATEMENT of PROGRESS, showing the Declaration and Opening of WORKHOUSES, &c., of UNIONS in IRELAND.

(*In continuation of the Table in the Annual Report for 1844, Appendix B. No. 12.*)

NAME OF UNION.	Date of First Rate being made.	Date of Workhouse being declared fit for the Reception of Destitute Poor.	Date of First Admission of Paupers.
Bantry . . .	16 July 1844	19 August 1844	24 April 1845
Cahirciveen. .	—	19 August 1844	
Carlow . . .	29 January 1844	16 Sept. 1844	18 Nov. 1844
Castlerea . .	11 June 1842	6 October 1842	
Clifden . . .			
Clogher . . .	28 October 1843	9 March 1844	9 March 1844
Dunfanaghy .	30 January 1844	15 March ,,	—
Dungarvan . .	17 Nov. 1842	27 Dec. 1841	4 July 1844
Enniskillen . .	—	19 March 1844	—
Glenties . . .			
Kanturk . .	16 April 1844	16 May 1842	18 July 1844
Kenmare . .	15 June ,,	19 August 1844	
Killarney . .	17 August ,,	2 Nov. ,,	5 April 1845
Letterkenny .	8 March ,,	16 Dec. ,,	14 March ,,
Listowel . .	7 February ,,	17 August ,,	13 February ,,
Lowtherstown .	2 April 1845	28 October ,,	—
Milford . . .			
Mountmelick .	19 January 1842	31 August 1844	3 January 1845
Stranorlar . .	21 Dec. 1843	16 March ,,	3 May 1844
Swineford . .	19 Dec. ,,	30 Nov. 1842	—
Tuam . . .	24 October 1842	15 August ,,	—
Westport . .	28 Sept. ,,	15 Nov. ,,	—

No. 18.—TABLE, showing the Amount of Building Loan, the Net Annual Value of Rateable Property, and the Proportion per £. of Loan to Net Value, for each Union in Ireland.

NAMES OF UNIONS.	Sum Borrowed for Building the Workhouse. £.	Net Annual Value of the Property Rated in the Union. £.	Proportion per £. of Loan to Net Value. s. d.	NAMES OF UNIONS.	Sum Borrowed for Building the Workhouse. £.	Net Annual Value of the Property Rated in the Union. £.	Proportion per £. of Loan to Net Value. s. d.
Abbeyleix	7,850	67,232	2 4	Fermoy	7,100	154,788	0 11
Antrim	7,600	100,667	1 6				
Ardee	7,500	93,134	1 7¼				
Armagh	14,000	175,999	1 7	Galway	12,500	101,831	2 5½
Athlone	10,900	109,036	2 0	Glenties*			
Athy	7,000	102,992	1 4½	Gorey	7,500	93,658	1 7½
				Gort	6,850	53,067	2 7
Bailieborough	8,000	52,027	3 3½	Gortin	3,600	15,763	4 6½
Ballina	12,000	96,236	2 6	Granard	7,500	90,040	1 8
Ballinasloe	10,600	134,329	1 4½				
Ballinrobe	8,400	83,217	1 11½				
Ballycastle	5,700	39,150	2 10½	Inishowen	7,600	36,928	4 1½
Ballymena	9,000	97,403	1 10				
Ballymoney	9,200	73,042	2 6				
Ballyshannon	6,400	51,435	2 5½	Kanturk	9,300	106,538	1 9½
Balrothery	7,000	90,702	1 6¼	Kells	8,650	124,194	1 4½
Baltinglass	7,800	91,787	1 8½	Kenmare	6,550	24,862	5 3½
Banbridge	10,000	123,712	1 7¼	Kilkeel	6,300	36,770	3 5
Bandon	8,850	136,078	1 3½	Kilkenny	13,400	242,002	1 1½
Bantry	7,750	41,725	3 8¼	Killarney	9,700	85,581	2 3½
Belfast	13,500	261,252	1 0½	Kilmallock	10,800	176,717	1 2½
Boyle	9,300	81,227	2 3¼	Kilrush	9,350	58,867	3 2
				Kinsale	8,150	74,043	2 2½
Cahirciveen	6,700	27,699	4 10				
Callan	7,950	84,456	1 10½	Larne	7,800	66,629	2 4½
Carlow	11,500	176,384	1 3½	Letterkenny	7,400	31,808	4 7½
Carrickmacross	7,200	46,323	3 1	Limerick	15,600	212,905	1 5½
Carrick-on-Shannon	9,600	61,450	3 1½	Lisburn	9,300	134,368	1 4½
Carrick-on-Suir	7,300	89,957	1 7½	Lismore	7,700	64,460	2 4½
Cashel	8,000	130,782	1 2½	Lisnaskea	8,100	46,919	3 5½
Castlebar	8,050	50,932	3 2	Listowel	8,700	93,457	1 9½
Castleblaney	8,100	65,470	2 5½	Londonderry	10,100	109,414	1 10
Castlederg	3,450	21,761	3 2	Longford	9,950	124,496	1 7
Castlerea	11,000	114,349	1 11	Loughrea	8,700	91,149	1 10½
Cavan	13,400	125,490	2 1½	Lowtherstown	7,300	39,793	3 8
Celbridge	6,900	130,233	1 0½	Lurgan	8,550	92,281	1 10½
Clifden*							
Clogheen	7,150	62,506	2 3½				
Clogher	6,300	42,291	2 11½	Macroom	8,300	93,863	1 9½
Clones	7,750	55,105	2 9½	Magherafelt	9,250	75,189	2 5½
Clonmel	2,900	91,037	0 7½	Mallow	9,500	143,019	1 3½
Coleraine	9,650	76,897	2 6	Manor Hamilton	6,900	47,284	2 11
Cookstown	7,000	56,606	2 5½	Midleton	9,350	163,144	1 1½
Cootehill	8,900	82,845	2 1½	Milford*			
Cork	21,000	372,383	1 1½	Mohill	8,650	57,777	3 0
				Monaghan	10,200	94,533	2 1½
Donegal	7,550	32,073	4 8½	Mountmellick	8,300	90,044	1 9½
Downpatrick	12,300	167,582	1 5½	Mullingar	9,400	189,561	0 11½
Drogheda	9,850	129,444	1 6				
Dublin, North	8,000	384,550	0 5	Naas	9,000	134,671	1 4
Dublin, South	10,000	563,954	0 4½	Navan	7,300	111,135	1 3½
Dundalk	9,100	102,655	1 9½	Nenagh	10,400	136,587	1 6½
Dunfanaghy	5,000	10,657	9 4½	Newcastle	10,150	113,215	1 9½
Dungannon	9,150	90,035	2 0½	New Ross	9,700	109,816	1 9
Dungarvan	10,100	93,719	2 1½	Newry	12,450	134,086	1 10½
Dunmanway	6,750	43,488	3 1½	Newtownards	7,750	118,483	1 3½
Dunshaughlin	6,750	118,077	1 1½	Newtown Lima-vady	8,000	63,560	2 5½
Edenderry	7,950	98,932	1 7½				
Ennis	8,600	100,899	1 8½				
Enniscorthy	7,550	126,797	1 2½	Oldcastle	8,150	79,941	2 0½
Enniskillen	11,200	97,359	2 3½	Omagh	9,050	75,378	2 4½
Ennistymon	8,400	67,486	2 5½				

* Valuation not completed in 3 Unions.

No. 18, (*continued.*)—Table, showing the Amount of Building Loan, the Net Annual Value of Rateable Property, and the Proportion per £. of Loan to Net Value, for each Union in Ireland.

NAMES OF UNIONS.	Sum Borrowed for Building the Work-house.	Net Annual Value of the Property Rated in the Union.	Proportion per £. of Loan to Net Value.	NAMES OF UNIONS.	Sum Borrowed for Building the Work-house.	Net Annual Value of the Property Rated in the Union.	Proportion per £. of Loan to Net Value.
	£.	£.	s. d.		£.	£.	s. d.
Parsonstown . . .	9,400	107,123	1 9¼	Thurles	8,550	110,998	1 6½
				Tipperary	8,150	148,725	1 1
				Tralee.	10,450	113,575	1 10
Rathdown	9,600	173,937	1 1¼				
Rathdrum	8,300	154,407	1 0¾				
Rathkeale	9,700	137,160	1 4¾	Trim	8,750	100,930	1 8¾
Roscommon . . .	9,350	86,666	2 1¾	Tuam	8,500	86,236	1 11½
Roscrea	9,400	102,178	1 10	Tullamore	8,350	86,339	1 11¼
Scariff.	8,650	44,970	3 10				
Shillelagh	7,300	64,204	2 3¼	Waterford	11,350	199,341	1 1½
				Westport	9,800	38,875	5 0½
				Wexford.	6,900	113,740	1 2½
Skibbereen . . .	9,400	97,923	1 11				
Sligo	13,250	144,047	1 10				
Strabane.	9,750	81,828	2 4½	Total 127* Unions	1,122,850	13,204,234	1 8½
Stranorlar	6,700	29,422	4 6½				
Swineford	8,400	45,966	3 7¾				

* Valuation not completed in 3 Unions.

Note.—The Average Proportion per £. of the Building Loan to the Net Annual Value is calculated upon 127 Unions; the Valuation in the three remaining Unions (*viz.*, Clifden, Glenties, and Milford), not being completed. The Building Loans for these three Unions amount to £18,100, making the total amount of the Building Loans for 130 Unions £1,140,350.

No. 19.—RETURN OF VACCINATION ARRANGEMENTS in the UNIONS in IRELAND.

UNIONS.	Number of Vaccination Districts into which the Union is divided.	Number of Medical Men under Contract to Vaccinate.	Number of Electoral Divisions included in Contracts.	Number of Electoral Divisions not included in Contracts.	Rate of Payment for each successful Case.	Number of Cases successfully Vaccinated in the Year ended April, 1845.	Observations.—Causes stated where no Contracts exist.
Abbeyleix	10	8	All.	..	1s.........	1,247	Medical dispensaries being established in each of the districts in which there are no contracts.
Antrim	8	2	3 & parts of 2.	14 and parts of 2.	In 1 district, 1s. each successful case under 200; 6d. per case above that number; in the other, 6d. each successful case throughout.	596	
Ardee		4	All.	..	1s. under 200; 6d. above.	722	
Armagh		9	All.	..	1s.....	1,341	
Athlone		.	..	..	.....	...	No return received.
Athy		5	All.	..	1s. under 200; 6d. above.	743	
Ballieborough		5	All.	..	Ditto.	385	
Ballina		None.	[None.	..	1s. under 200, and 6d. above that number (up to Dec., 1844.)	2,604*	*This was the number of successful cases at end of year 1844, prior to which Contracts discontinued from December, 1844. The Board of Guardians having advertised for tenders from competent persons, to vaccinate at 3d. each case, the majority of the former contractors rejected the terms, and vaccination dropped or ceased.
Ballinasloe		None.	None.	..	1s. under 200, and 6d. above that number.	19 in one district.	The contract in the district for which the return of cases was made expired in November, 1844. Competent persons cannot be got to contract at the rate of payment the Guardians propose to give.
Ballinrobe		1	13	1s. under 200	49	No contracts for 13 divisions, the remuneration being considered too small.
Ballycastle		2 Vaccination Districts.	2 Vaccination Districts.	64....	204 in 1 district; no return received for other districts.	The Island of Rathlin not contracted for, and she would not be sufficient inducement for a vaccinator to reside in the Island.
Ballymena		None.	..	.....	....	The Guardians having been informed that medical men were in the habit of vaccinating free of expense in the families which they attended, determined for this and other reasons not to renew the contracts.

Union					Rate	Number	Remarks
Ballyshannon	5	None.	None.	.	under 200, and 6d. above.	...	Contracts not renewed since August, 1842. The Guardians declined to renew the contracts, not thinking it necessary.
Balrothery	None.	None.	None.	.	...	...	The Dispensary doctors vaccinating gratuitously.
Ballinglass	7	4	10	1	1s.	1,323	The medical gentleman residing in the vacant division refused the rate of remuneration offered.
Banbridge	7	None.	None.	.	1s. under 200; 6d. above.	941 (for 5 divisions), the number not ascertained in 2 other divisions.	The contracts which expired 25th March, 1845, not yet renewed.
Bandon	6	4	16	7	Ditto	1,241	Contracts could not be obtained for some divisions.
Bantry	10	4	All.	.	6d.	505*	*This number is for one division; as regards the other divisions, on application to the medical gentleman for a return of cases, they stated that scarlatina, measles, and hooping cough being prevalent, they did not like to introduce another disease for a little time among the children.
Belfast	7	6	All.	.	1s. under 200; 6d. above.	1,434	In 1 district for which the contract had expired in 1842, the vaccinator appears to be acting, return of cases being made.
Boyle	7	2	9	7	Ditto.	338	
Cahirciveen	4	None.	None.	.	...	...	Guardians not willing to renew contracts.
Callan	7	1	All.	.	1s. under 200; 6d. above.	25	The medical gentleman refused to contract for the remuneration proposed to be given, and the medical officer of the workhouse has contracted to vaccinate in the whole Union.
Carlow	8	8	All.	.	1 district, 10d.; the rest, 1s.	1,652	Of these cases, 880 were returned by one vaccinator, for which he would not accept payment, not having made the required entries in his certificate book.
Carrickmacross	4	3	All.	.	1s.	382	A larger number could not be done in consequence of the prejudice which exists in those parts of the country against vaccination under the Irish Poor Relief Act; but the vaccinating officer states that he has reason to think that that prejudice is wearing away.
Carrick-on-Shannon	8	None.	None.	.	1s. under 200; 6d. above.	375	Resolution of the Guardians, 28th Sept., 1844:—"Resolved that, according as the contracts for vaccination terminate, we in future direct that any person in the Union who wishes to have their children vaccinated, do attend with them at the workhouse, where the operation will be performed."
Carrick-on-Suir	6	3	All.	.	1s. 6d.	230	There has not been any regular return kept by the medical men of the number of cases vaccinated, nor has there been any return made by them except by one.
Cashel	6	5	16	1	1s.	13 in one district.	
Castlebar	4	4	All.	.	1s. under 200; 6d. above.	13	

R

No. 19.—Vaccination Arrangements in the Unions in Ireland—*continued.*

UNIONS.	Number of Vaccination Districts into which the Union is Divided.	Number of Medical Men under Contract to Vaccinate.	Number of Electoral Divisions included in Contracts.	Number of Electoral Divisions not included in Contracts.	Rate of Payment for each successful Case.	Number of Cases successfully Vaccinated in the Year ended April, 1845.	Observations.—Causes stated, where no Contracts exist.
Castleblayney	5	5	All.	..	1s. under 100; 6d. above.	625	...
Castlederg	3	2	All.	..	1s.	20	...
Castlerea	6	None.	None.	..	....	..	Contracts discontinued. The Guardians considered that they had no control over the vaccinator's returns.
Cavan	10	6	13	10	1s. under 200; 6d. above.	407	...
Celbridge	10	8	All.	..	1s.	775	...
Cliften	5	None.	None.	..	...	..	No contract, the Guardians having no funds to pay; a rate not yet made in this Union.
Clogheen	5	None.	None.	..	...	..	The Guardians decline entering into any new contracts; the dispensary doctors acting gratuitously.
Clogher	4	4	All.	..	1s. under 200, and 6d. above, except in one district, where it was 5d. per case, and one, 6d.	675	...
Clones	4	4	All.	.	1s. under 100; 6d. above.	162	...
Clonmel	4	2	5	5	1s. under 200; 6d. above.	532 for two divisions; no return for other divisions.	One of the vaccinators did not renew his contract, and the other medical man made no contract, but undertook to vaccinate gratis in his dispensary district, comprising three divisions of the Union.
Coleraine	6	6	All.	.	1s. under 200; 6d. above in all but one district, where the rate is 10d. instead of the 1s.	1,089*	*Exclusive of one district for which no return received.
Cookstown	4	None.	..	.	No rate is fixed at present 1s. for each successfu case was paid under the former contracts.	..	The clerk cannot state any particular reason why the Board has not entered into contracts, further than having paid 118l. 12s. for vaccination in one year, they considered the expenses too heavy to continue it. The number of cases returned in the year ended April 1844 was 1221.
Cootehill	.	.	.	.	1s. under 200; 6d. above,	627	The medical practitioners still continue to vaccinate at the rates of payment mentioned although contracts have not been renewed with them.

Union					Rate of payment	No. vaccinated	Remarks
Cork	..	..	..	..	..	..	No arrangements for vaccination made by the Guardians in this Union.
Donegal . .	5	3	6	5	1s. under 200; 6d. above.	451	Two vaccination districts vacant, one contractor having died, and another resigned.
Downpatrick . .	12	13	All.	..	1s. under 200; 6d. above, except two districts, where it is 6d. for every case.	1,167	
Drogheda . .	12	None.	None.	..	1s. . . .	..	The Board of Guardians passed a resolution not to contract for any district in which there was a dispensary, in consequence of which no contract now exists.
Dublin, North .	8	4	6	3	1s. . . .	478	The medical officers of the dispensaries of three districts objected to contract, and a Dublin gentleman who contracted in March 1841, resigned in August 1842, stating that it would not pay his expenses.
Dublin, South . .	5	5	All.	..	1s. under 200; 6d. above.	1,299	
Dundalk	7	.	..	..	Ditto	1,597 in six districts : for one district no return.	
Dunfanaghy . .	4	2	All.	..	Ditto	56	
Dungannon . . .	6	None.	None.	..	Ditto	1,059	
Dungarvan . .	.	6	All.	..	1s.	496	
Dunmanway . .	2	2	All.	..	1s. under 200; 6d. above.	149	The medical gentlemen do not attend to enter into contract, but continue to vaccinate.
Dunshaughlin . .	6	1	2	10	Ditto	429	
Edenderry . . .	6	5	All.	..	1s. under 200; 6d. above.	406	
Ennis	6	None.	None.	..	. . .	..	No contracts have ever been entered into, though advertised for by the Board of Guardians at different periods; the medical gentlemen not being satisfied with the remuneration proposed.
Enniscorthy . .	4	4	All.	.	1s. under 200; 6d. above.	840	Repeated application made to the vaccinators to attend and renew their contracts; their general answer is, that they have to attend their dispensaries the day on which the Guardians meet. There has not been a successful case returned by the vaccinators for the last year up to April; the reason assigned by some of them for not having returned a successful case of vaccination in the last year is, that they vaccinated a number of children whose parents did not bring them back to the dispensaries after being vaccinated, and consequently they could not certify as to the cases being successful. One vaccinated upwards of 30 children, who were not brought back to him; the country people disliking to have the lymph taken off their children, which accounts for their not returning with them.
Enniskillen . . .	3	None.	None.	..	..	..	

UNIONS.	Number of Vaccination Districts into which the Union is Divided.	Number of Medical Men under Contract to Vaccinate.	Number of Electoral Divisions Included in Contracts.	Number of Electoral Divisions not included in Contracts.	Rate of Payment for each successful Case.	Number of Cases successfully Vaccinated in the Year ended April, 1845.	Observations.—Causes stated, where no Contracts exist.
Ennistymon	5	None.	None.	...	1s. ...	...	The medical men have refused to accept the compensation offered.
Fermoy	10	None.	None.	...	...	...	In consequence of a resolution of the Board of Guardians adopted on the 30th April, 1841.
Galway	6	5	All.	...	1s. under 200; 6d. above.	433	
Glenties	11	1	7	4	Ditto ...	No return received.	
Gorey	7	5	All.	...	Ditto ...	846	
Gort	2	2	All.	...	6d. ...	208	
Gortin	None.	None.	None.	...	...	...	No contracts have ever been entered into in this Union.
Granard	4	4	All.	...	6d. ...	1,042	The Guardians have not yet renewed the contracts, which expired December, 1844.
Inishowen	5	..	..	...	...	1,085	In consequence of the several medical officers attending dispensaries in this Union being stationed at ...
Kanturk	13	None.	None.	...	...	...	...
Kells	4	None.	None.	*	...	...	...
Kenmare	7	3	5	2	1s. under 200; 6d. above.	366	
Kilkeel	4	3	7	3*	Ditto ...	378	No contract ...
Kilkenny	None.	None.	None.	-	...	...	...
Killarney	12	7.	10	2	1s. under 200; 6d. above.	1,259	Vaccination did not accept the proposition for removal of ...
Kilmallock	4	None.	None.	•	Ditto ...	1,103	...

Union							Remarks
Kilrush	7	None.	None.	..	..	..	No vaccination contract has been entered into in any of the districts, the medical practitioners having refused to vaccinate for less than 2s. 6d. each successful case.
Kinsale	None.	None.	None.	..	..	..	There has been no contract entered into in this Union for vaccinating purposes, for although the Guardians have repeatedly advertised in the two Cork papers having the widest circulation in the county, no tenders have been received.
Larne	5	5	All.	..	1s. under 200; 6d. above.	413	
Letterkenny	3	3	All.	..	Ditto.	178	Contracts never entered into for vaccination in the Union.
Limerick	:	:	:	..	..	..	
Lisburn	7	7	All.	..	1s. under 200; 6d. above.	628	
Lismore	4	1	All.	..	Ditto.	1,267	
Lismasken	5	5	All.	..	Ditto.	165	
Listowel	9	None.	None.	..	..	..	Since the year 1843 the Guardians have not entered into any contract, considering that the several dispensaries in the vicinity accomplish the desired object.
Londonderry	7	7	All.	..	1s.	950	
Longford	5	5	All.	..	4 districts, 1s. under 200, 6d. above, (half-yearly); 1 district 6d.	1,359	
Loughrea	5	None.	None.	..	..	98*	*One return of 98 cases was made for 4 months in last year. The contracts made in 1840 have not been renewed yearly, and only one of the persons appointed in 1840 carrying it into effect, but not making monthly returns.
Lowthersfown	4	3	8, and part of 1. All.	Part of 1.	1s. under 200; 6d. above. 6d.	43	The contractor for the vacant district died, and no other appointed as yet.
Lurgan	Entire Union. 7	5	All.	..	..	1,657	
Macroom	7	1	All.	..	Ditto.	890	
Magheralelt	7	7	All.	..	1s. under 200; 6d. above.	500	
Mallow	2	None.	None.	..	1s.	..	Guardians consider that sufficient provision has been made at the different dispensaries of the Union for vaccination.
Manor Hamilton	3	3	All.	..	..	836	Medical men not willing to contract on the terms allowed.
Midleton	7	5	5 Vaccination Districts. All.	..	1s. under 200; 6d. above.	335	
Milford	6	5	2 Vaccination Districts.	..	Ditto.	..	Number vaccinated since the arrangements were made for carrying the Act into effect, 1848.

No. 19.—Vaccination Arrangements in the Unions in Ireland—*continued.*

UNIONS.	Number of Vaccination Districts into which the Union is divided.	Number of Medical Men under Contract to Vaccinate.	Number of Electoral Divisions included in Contracts.	Number of Electoral Divisions not included in Contracts.	Rate of Payment for each successful case.	Number of Cases successfully Vaccinated in the Year ended April, 1845.	Observations.—Causes stated, where no Contracts exist.
Mohill	3	3	All.	..	Ditto	397	
Monaghan	6	5	All.	..	Ditto	1,316	
Mountmellick	8	7	15	1	Ditto	535	One vacant, owing to the vaccinator not having yet signed his contract.
Mullingar	10	4	21	5	Ditto	220	The medical practitioners refuse to contract on the terms offered by the Guardians.
Naas	7	5	All.	..	Ditto	922	
Navan	4	1	All.	..	..	908	
Nenagh	8	1	All.	..	1s. under 900; 6d. above.	40	Cause of some districts being vacant, the remuneration offered by the Guardians of 1s. for each successful case being considered too low.
Newcastle	6	3	7, and part of 1.	5, and part of 1.	1s.	531	
New Ross	11	None.	..	..	1s. under 200; 6d. above.	449	
Newry	10	10	All.	..	Ditto	1,519	
Newtownards	7	7	All.	..	Ditto	1,195	
Newtown Limavady.	5	None.	None.	..	..	..	The reason contracts have not been entered into in consequence of dispensaries being established in the five districts of the Union, where all children are vaccinated without any charge to their parents. The Guardians, therefore, consider it would be waste of the funds intrusted to them to pay for what has always been performed by the medical officers of the dispensaries without any charge.
Oldcastle	6	5	All.	..	9d. under 200; 4d. above.	888	
Omagh	None.	None.	None.	..	..	..	The Guardians believe that the dispensary doctors render the introduction of the Vaccination Extension Act unnecessary

Union					Rate	Number	Remarks
Rathdown	11	10	9, and part of 1.	Part of 1.	1s. . . .	799	One doctor refuses to renew his contract, because the Guardians would not pay him for all the cases he returned as successful.
Rathdrum	8	8	All.	.	1s. . . .	906	
Bathkeale	8	None.	None.	.		. .	The medical gentlemen have refused to contract on the terms proposed.
Roscommon	6	None.	None.	.		425 for one district; no return for others.	The Guardians, by a minute dated 25th June, 1844, expressed their intention to cease paying for vaccination.
Roscrea	3	None.	None.	.		. .	Contracts have expired, and not since renewed.
Scariff	3	None.	None.	.		. .	Contracts for vaccination have never been entered into by the Board of Guardians.
Shillelagh	8	5	All.	.	1s. under 200; 6d. above.	742	Cause stated for there being no contracts, want of funds.
Skibbereen	8	None.	None.	.		. .	
Sligo	8	7	All.	.	1s. under 200; 6d. above (half-yearly).	2,610	
Strabane	.	.	. .	.		. .	The entire Union being comprehended in dispensary districts, no contracts were ever entered into by the Guardians. The Act not in operation in this Union.
Stranorlar	.	.	. .	3		. .	
Swineford	6	4	9	3	1s. under 200; 6d. above.	494	
Thurles	6	None.	None.	.		. .	The Guardians refuse to enter into contracts.
Tipperary	3	None.	None.	.		. .	The only arrangement made was to divide the Union into districts, for which tenders were received and accepted on the 22nd October, 1842, but no steps have been since taken for entering into contracts.
Tralee	6	5	All.	.	1s. under 200; 6d. above.	1,820	
Trim	4	3	8, and part of 1.	2, and part of 1.	6d. under 200; 3d. above.	287	
Tuam	5	None.	None.	.		. .	No existing contracts. It is understood that the vaccinators still continue to vaccinate in their several districts, but they have never furnished returns of cases.
Tullamore	5	None.	None.	.		. .	Contracts never entered into by the Guardians. Advertisements were several times posted inviting tenders, and tenders were received, but the Guardians declined making any contracts.
Waterford	4	4	All.	.	1s. . . .	818	
Westport	6	5	8	2	1s. under 200; 6d. above.	333	
Wexford	7	4	All.	.	Ditto. . . .	1,027	Vaccination performed gratuitously at the dispensary in one district not contracted for.

No. 20.—PAUPER FEVER PATIENTS—IRELAND.

RETURN giving the NAMES of the UNIONS in IRELAND in which the Provisions of the Act 6 & 7 Vic. c. 92, have been acted on in respect of Fever Patients; specifying the cases in which the Poor Law Commissioners have sanctioned—1st, the Appropriation of a part of the Workhouse for a Fever Hospital; or, 2ndly, the Building of a Fever Ward, its distance from the nearest point of the Workhouse, the number it is calculated to contain, the cost of it, and in what manner the money is obtained; or, 3rdly, the Hiring of a House, the number it will contain, and the rent thereof. Also a Return of the number of Fever Patients relieved under the 15th and of those relieved under the 16th clause of the above-named Act, and the average weekly cost of each.

I.—Cases in which the Poor Law Commissioners have sanctioned the appropriation of a part of the Workhouse for a Fever Hospital.
The Poor Law Commissioners have not sanctioned the appropriation of part of the Workhouse for a Fever Hospital in any case.

ABSTRACTS OF RETURNS FROM CLERKS OF UNIONS.

II.—Cases in which the Poor Law Commissioners have sanctioned the building of a Fever Ward.

NAME OF UNION.	Distance of Fever Ward from the nearest point of the Workhouse.	Number which the Fever Ward is calculated to contain.	Estimated Cost of Building.	The manner in which the Money is obtained.	OBSERVATIONS.
	Feet.		£. s. d.		
Antrim	48	40	520 0 0	By loan from the Ulster Bank.	
Ardee	..	40	759 14 11	By rate.	See also Table III.
Armagh	96	40 beds, and capable of extension for 60.	600 0 0	Part provided for out of loan from Exchequer Bill Loan Commissioners.	
Athlone	150	48	..	...	The building was abandoned for want of funds, through the Board of Guardians agreed to the amount, £350, for the purpose of erecting it.
Ballycastle	About 168	40	Not yet ascertained.	By loan from the Belfast Banking Company.	The site has been chosen and plans approved, and the other necessary arrangements are in progress.
Ballymoney	..	..	..	...	Until the building is completed a house has been hired.—See Return, No. III. (p. 260.)
Ballyshany	51	40	397 0 0	By loan from the Bank of Ireland.	

			£ s. d.		
Carrick-on-Shannon	...	...	...	...	The arrangements for building not yet entered into by the Guardians.
Cashel	90	24	400 0 0	By loan from treasurer.	Contract not yet entered into.
Dundalk	121	44	442 12 3	Raised by rate.	
Dungannon	45	48	473 0 0	By loan from the Belfast Banking Company.	
Ennistymon	132	30	299 0 0	Part out of the workhouse loan from Exchequer Bill Loan Commissioners.	
Galway	...	100	140 0 0	By loan from treasurer.	Temporary accommodation provided adjoining the Hospital in the hospital yards of the Workhouse.—*See* Table IV. (p. 252.)
Kanturk	190	44	360 0 0	Union funds.	
Kilkeel	96	40	378 15 0	By loan from Belfast Banking Company.	
Larne	72	40	573 0 0	By loan from Belfast Banking Company.	
Limerick	123	96	693 0 0	By rate.	
Longford	135	64	700 0 0		
Lurgan	114	40	Not finally ascertained.	From rates, out of which part has been paid.	
Macroom	...	...		...	The subject of Fever Hospital accommodation referred by the Board of Guardians to a committee, who have not yet reported.
Magherafelt	174	40	596 0 0	By loan from a private person.	*See also* Table III. (p. 250.)
New Ross	120	48	446 0 0	Part from loan from Exchequer Bill Loan Commissioners; part from the rates.	
Newtownards	...	60		...	The site and other arrangements for the building are not yet finally decided upon, the matter being now in progress; meantime a house has been hired.—*See* Table III. (p. 230.)
Roscommon	...	...		...	The Commissioners supplied the necessary plans, specification, and working drawings for a Fever Ward in June, 1844, and also sanctioned the borrowing of money for its erection. Subsequently a contractor was engaged to execute the building for £593; the work, however, has not been commenced, inasmuch as the Guardians were unable to obtain a loan for the purpose.
Skibbereen	About 72	44	350 0 0	Not yet obtained.	
Tullamore	90	40	309 0 0	By loan from Bank of Ireland.	

No. 20.—**Fever Patients, Ireland**—*continued.*

II.—*continued.*

Under consideration.

NAME of UNION.	Distance of Fever Ward from the nearest point of the Work-house.	Number which the Fever Ward is calculated to contain.	Estimated Cost of Building.			OBSERVATIONS.
	Feet.		£.	s.	d.	
Ballinasloe . .	150	60	800	0	0	The arrangements not finally concluded.
Drogheda . .	..	..	800	0	0	Since sanctioned.
Kilmallock . .	180	22	270	0	0	Since sanctioned.
Mountmellick .	90	44	211	0	0	Since sanctioned.
Naas . . .	..	44	..			Since sanctioned; the particulars required not finally ascertained.

III.—Cases in which the Poor Law Commissioners have sanctioned the Hiring of a House.

NAME of UNION.	Number that such House will contain.	Rent of House.	OBSERVATIONS.
Abbeyleix . .	50	£2 per annum .	A fever hospital, recently built by the Abbeyleix Loan Fund Trustees, was offered by them at this rental, being half the ground-rent to which it was liable.
Ardee . . .	12	£5 13 0 per annum.	A contract for building a fever hospital for 40 patients has since been agreed upon by the Guardians.—*See* Table II. (p. 248.)
Balrothery . .	24	£10 per annum.	*See* Table II. (p. 248.)
Bandon . . .	..	. .	A house was hired during the prevalence of fever in a part of the Union, and has since been closed.—*See* Table IV. (p. 251.)
Coleraine . .	..	. .	Hiring was sanctioned on the 18th December, 1843, but was not acted on; it not being considered necessary.
Cootehill . .	..	£6 per annum .	House hired by the Guardians, but abandoned before the arrangements completed.
Magherafelt .	4	Nil.	See also Table II. (p. 248)
Midleton . .	32	£25 per annum.	
Newtownards .	40	£20 per annum .	*See* also Table II. (p. 248.)

No. 20.—Fever Patients, Ireland—continued.

IV.—A Return of the Number of Fever Patients relieved under the 15th and 16th Sections of the Irish Poor Law Amendment Act, respectively; and the average Weekly Cost of each.

UNIONS.	Patients sent by the Guardians to a Fever Hospital not under their own management, in pursuance of Section 15 of 6 & 7 Vict. c. 92.		Patients relieved by the Guardians in any House Hired or Rented for Fever Patients under Section 16.		Patients relieved by the Guardians in a Ward or Fever Hospital built for the purpose in connexion with the Workhouse (Class II., p. 246).		OBSERVATIONS.
	Number up to 17 April, 1845.	Average Weekly Cost of each.	Number up to 17 April, 1845.	Average Weekly Cost of each.	Number up to 17 April, 1845.	Average Weekly Cost of each.	
		s. d.		s. d.		s. d.	
Abbeyleix	..	..	727	2 9¾	..	..	
Ardee	..	..	198	2 4	..	..	
Athy	9	..	..	..	..	..	No charge.
Ballina	16	*	..	..	..	..	*£1. for each patient sent to hospital.
Balrothery	..	..	109	2 10	..	..	
Baltinglass	9	2 6	..	..	..	..	"No fever ward or hospital on the workhouse lands;—when fever was prevalent in the workhouse, the upper part of the probationary ward was converted into an hospital for the time being, and the infirmary used as a fever hospital, and 18 paupers treated therein at the average cost of 1s. 9d. per week each.
Bandon	2	5 0	12	*	..	..	*The entire sum for maintaining the patients from the 19th Jan. to the 21st March, 1845, was 12l. 1s. 1d. The house is now closed.
Belfast	..	..	..	..	733	3 4	The Guardians erected temporary accommodation for the relief of fever patients, the new building (Return II., p. 248) not being yet provided.
Callan	3	3 7	..	..	..	..	
Carlow	2*	5 10	..	..	..	..	*For one of these two cases no payment was made; for the other, 5s. 10d a week was paid. "The fever patients sent from the workhouse to the fever hospital in the town of Carlow from the three Queen's County Electoral Divisions, are charged at the rate of 10d. per head per diem; those from the County of Carlow Electoral Divisions are received gratuitously."
Carrickmacross	21	1 11½	..	..	..	..	"There is a fever hospital erected convenient to the workhouse, but not under the management of the Guardians, or in any way connected with or supported by the Union funds, and into which hospital the Guardians have the privilege of removing or sending any fever patients belonging to the workhouse."
Carrick-on-Suir	49	..	..	..	..	..	
Clones	124	2 2	..	..	..	..	The average weekly cost of each is stated at 10s. 10d. under arrangements made with the governors of the fever hospital.

No. 20.—*Fever Patients, Ireland—continued.*

IV.—A Return of the Number of Fever Patients relieved under the 15th and 16th Sections of the Irish Poor Law Amendment Act, respectively; and the average Weekly Cost of each.

UNIONS.	Patients sent by the Guardians to a Fever Hospital not under their own management, in pursuance of Section 15 of 6 & 7 Vict. c. 92.		Patients relieved by the Guardians in any Work House hired or Rented for Fever Patients (Class III., p. 250), under Section 16.		Patients relieved by the Guardians in a Ward or Fever Hospital built for the purpose in connexion with the Workhouse (Class III., p. 249).		Observations.
	Number up to 17 April, 1845.	Average Weekly Cost of each.	Number up to 17 April, 1845.	Average Weekly Cost of each.	Number up to 17 April, 1845.	Average Weekly Cost of each.	
		s. d.		*s. d.*		*s. d.*	
Cork	..	..	..	..	207	2 3	It may be necessary to state, that the cases here referred to were all of a mild character; but, if a serious epidemic should break out, it is the intention to send such cases to the Cork Fever Hospital.
Drogheda	..	..	21	4 0	..	..	
Dublin, North	44	..	..	..	..	..	No charge has been made.
Dublin, South	35	..	..	..	..	..	"When any inmate of the workhouse is attacked with fever, a notification is made to the governor of the fever hospital, Cork street, who remove the patient. No charge has been made by that establishment against the Guardians under the Act."
Dungarvan	2	10 0	..	..	..	..	
Donabaughlin	4	..	..	..	..	..	No arrangement made with the hospital as to cost.
Ennis	68	..	..	..	..	..	"Fever patients are received and maintained from the workhouse in the County Fever Hospital, and no charge made as yet for them." Cost not as yet ascertained by the Guardians.
Enniscorthy	6	..	..	..	..	..	
Galway	..	..	..	..	1,096	2 8¼	Relieved in temporary accommodation erected adjoining the hospital in the hospital yards of the workhouse.—See Table II. (p. 249.)
Gorey	2	7 6	..	..	..	..	
Gortin	2	2 4	..	..	..	..	
Kells	37	3 9¼	..	..	..	..	
Kilrush	29	3 8¼	..	..	..	..	
Kinsale	1	..	..	..	..	..	"No charge made, or agreement entered into, between the Guardians and fever hospital committee."
Lisburn	4	3 9	..	..	..	..	..have also been relieved by the Guardians in detached wards in hospital of workhouse, at a cost of 2s. a week for each.
Lismore	8	..	..	..	..	..	"The Lismore District Fever Hospital being very convenient to the workhouse, the Guardians have sent such paupers as have been attacked with fever to that establishment, for which they have been charged 1l. 1s. 1½d. per head. The Guardians also paid for only four patients as yet. The 4l. paid is for the four above

District						Remarks
Longford			169		2 3	
Loughrea						From a former Return it appears that 19 fever patients were relieved under the 15th section, up to 1st March, 1844.
Magherafelt		8		1 4¼		
Mallow	2	5 0				The rule at Town Hospital is to pay 10s. on admission; the aggregate number of days which the patients remain in being calculated on that sum makes the stated average weekly cost of each.
Midleton		191		1 10		From a former Return it also appeared that 1 fever patient had been relieved under the 15th section, up to 1st March, 1844.
Naas	14	*				*£2 for each patient, per agreement, without reference to time in hospital.
Navan	23					The Governors of the County Fever Hospital decline making any charge for those sent.
Newcastle	39					£1 10s. for each patient, without regard to the time in hospital.
Newry	3					No weekly cost chargeable against the union. The cost of maintenance in the Newry Fever Hospital is defrayed by private subscription and Grand Jury aid; and the admissions were obtained by subscribers' tickets.
Newtownards		266		3 6		4 children in small-pox and 2 female attendants also sent to Rathdown Fever Hospital.
Rathdown	11	5 10				
Rathdrum	4	5 0				
Roscrea	88	5 6¼				
Shillelagh	6	10 6				
Sligo	3					The Guardians have not paid the cost of any patients sent to fever hospital.
Strabane	1	3 9¼				
Tralee	19	2 6				
Trim	5					Since the passing of the Act 6 & 7 Vict. c. 92, five persons have been removed from the workhouse to the fever hospital in the town of Trim by direction of the medical officer. No charge has as yet been made for their maintenance. The fever hospital referred to is maintained at the public expense.
Waterford	169					94 of these were not charged for. 75 who had lived out of the hospital district, but within the union, charged for at £1 11s. 5d. each, without reference to time in hospital.
Wexford	21	7 0				

The Returns from the following Unions also state that **Fever Patients have been relieved** by the Guardians in Wards connected with the Workhouse, or appropriated by them to the purpose, as follows; namely :—

UNIONS.	Number relieved up to 17 April, 1845.	Average Weekly Cost per Head.	OBSERVATIONS.
Athlone	143	*s. d.* 1 5	No ward or hospital built for the purpose since the Amendment Act; and the Clerk's return states, that from necessity the wards over the lunatic cells were used for the purpose of relieving fever patients.—*See* Table II. (p. 248.)
Ballinaslow	102	1 3¼	The idiot wards attached to the workhouse, used by the Guardians as fever wards.
Cashel	431	1 6	Fever ward not yet built.—*See* previous part of Return, No II. (p. 249.)
Cavan	281	1 9	The Guardians made temporary arrangements for the treatment of these cases in a part of the workhouse.
Cootehill	388	1 3¼	These cases appear to have been treated within the wards of the workhouse.—*See* also Table III. (p. 250.)
Dunmanway	136	1 9	These appear to be cases that have occurred and been provided for within the workhouse buildings. A former Return stated that 5 had been relieved under the 16th section, up to 1st March, 1844; and that a room was appropriated for the use of fever patients in the hospital of the workhouse.
Fermoy	80	2 6	No fever ward or fever hospital has been built or hired by the Guardians of the Fermoy Union, but a portion of the workhouse hospital has been appropriated for fever patients. The number of fever patients relieved since the passing of the Irish Poor Law Amendment Act to the 17th of April, 1845, is 80; the average weekly cost per head is 2s. 6d.
Gort	281	2 6	Relieved in the workhouse infirmary, appropriated by the Guardians to the purpose.
Lurgan	431	1 11¼	New fever ward since built, (Table II. p. 249).—Note by Clerk of Guardians: "I beg to state, in reference to the number of fever patients relieved in connexion with this workhouse, that no fever hospital being within from ten to fourteen miles of Lurgan, the Guardians admitted all cases of fever that were sent in by the Wardens since the opening of the house, and the idiot wards were prepared for that purpose.
Mohill	21	1 2¼	In a former Return it was stated that 12 patients were relieved, up to 1st March, 1844. The cases were treated in the workhouse.
Nenagh	27	2 1	In a former Return it was stated that 30 patients had been relieved under the 16th section, up to 1st March, 1844; all of whom were treated in a part of the workhouse infirmary set apart by the medical attendant for the purpose. An arrangement has recently been made by the Guardians with the committee of the Nenagh Fever Hospital for the admission and treatment of fever patients from the workhouse in that hospital.
Roscommon	112	1 9	Relieved in the lunatic wards, which were appropriated by the Guardians for the reception of fever cases.

APPENDIX C.

ENGLAND AND WALES.

———————

No. I.

AN ACCOUNT of the Money Levied and Expended for the Relief and Maintenance of the Poor in each Union, and for Parishes not united under the Poor Law Amendment Act, in *England* and *Wales*, for the Year ended on the 25th March, 1844: distinguishing the Money Expended for the Relief of the Poor; Law Charges; Payments under the Vaccination, Registration, and Parochial Assessments Acts; Payments for or towards the County Rates; and the Money Expended for all other Purposes; also distinguishing the Amount Expended in Medical Relief;—with Summary of such Account; and Comparative Statement of Expenditure for the Year 1844 and the Years 1843 and 1834.

the Year ended 25th March, 1844.

ments on Account Registration Act.	Outlay for Register Offices, Books, and Forms, and other incidental Expenses.	Payments under the Parochial Assessments Act (for Surveys, Valuations, &c,) and Loans repaid under the same.	Payments for or towards the County Rate.	Payments for or towards the County and Local Police Forces.	Money expended for all other Purposes.	Total Parochial Rates, &c., expended.	Medical Relief.	COUNTIES.
£.	£.	£.	£.	£.	£.	£.	£.	ENGLAND.
362	10	233	9,916	..	937	52,496	1,709	Bedford.
483	155	653	16,302	156	3,661	97,208	3,719	Berks.
490	53	486	11,151	3	4,484	93,756	2,742	Buckingham.
503	44	..	16,127	2,672	3,406	94,821	2,747	Cambridge.
1,255	49	404	12,056	3,379	6,970	111,743	2,430	Chester.
1,003	52	233	8,982	..	7,310	96,036	2,356	Cornwall.
531	48	..	6,581	..	1,649	45,008	1,071	Cumberland.
817	91	342	15,977	137	5,351	83,783	1,460	Derby.
1,639	184	1,051	20,711	135	10,666	220,678	5,987	Devon.
521	103	374	10,622	18	3,260	95,885	3,232	Dorset.
1,084	145	60	17,346	2,763	5,975	109,740	1,848	Durham.
1,057	199	1,821	34,992	4,457	6,388	211,001	7,892	Essex.
1,281	113	520	39,432	2,249	10,531	191,264	4,405	Gloucester.
348	35	298	9,955	440	1,757	56,718	2,019	Hereford.
460	50	335	17,571	2,375	2,717	84,696	3,623	Hertford.
196	22	21	4,751	..	1,048	30,761	1,118	Huntingdon.
1,712	299	1,617	34,136	8,099	14,763	257,684	7,687	Kent.
6,036	379	1,656	141,979	5,224	27,088	521,900	6,622	Lancaster.
658	66	204	20,994	710	4,287	107,257	2,634	Leicester.
1,093	163	356	30,898	58	7,693	156,501	3,932	Lincoln.
5,145	514	1,323	93,828	149,042	53,987	779,064	13,955	Middlesex.
446	88	191	12,272	126	3,321	45,243	1,091	Monmouth.
1,211	78	585	26,720	213	7,064	227,415	6,122	Norfolk.
514	90	365	18,381	540	4,445	113,736	3,051	Northampton.
747	228	43	9,236	187	4,127	87,482	1,501	Northumberland.
743	99	117	20,051	1,547	5,010	93,654	2,638	Nottingham.
521	31	209	11,411	301	2,779	95,159	2,961	Oxford.
59	17	..	1,421	..	331	9,667	317	Rutland.
660	81	669	16,376	2,058	5,410	97,295	2,956	Salop.
1,295	69	726	26,464	..	6,718	196,645	6,512	Somerset.
954	164	1,505	29,838	984	7,288	180,616	5,789	Southampton.
1,598	77	793	33,295	5,561	10,688	170,173	3,689	Stafford.
941	249	1,296	29,203	1,160	5,923	176,229	5,132	Suffolk.
1,886	303	3,463	41,092	34,039	18,074	302,627	6,950	Surrey.
931	162	2,005	18,937	1,763	8,588	177,361	6,100	Sussex.
1,295	110	715	51,378	3,845	11,213	176,093	3,043	Warwick.
153	..	..	2,542	..	827	22,967	589	Westmorland.
766	160	1,465	19,878	3,158	6,390	169,580	4,814	Wilts.
667	90	778	21,004	2,250	5,472	98,876	3,504	Worcester.
712	359	36	14,768	2	4,559	96,856	1,674	York, East Riding.
614	227	265	7,099	60	2,958	75,902	1,750	,, North Riding.
3,701	434	2,199	63,278	1,134	31,351	421,757	5,826	,, West Riding.
17,306	5,889	29,454	1,054,951	240,845	342,514	6,538,333	159,217	Totals of England.
								WALES.
106	18	..	1,538	..	1,551	21,143	261	Anglesey.
203	9	..	4,739	..	1,304	25,506	646	Brecon.
193	4	..	4,274	..	834	22,848	407	Cardigan.
333	13	56	9,479	298	1,365	43,609	830	Carmarthen.
225	40	..	2,839	5	1,861	28,482	676	Carnarvon.
254	14	117	6,713	84	1,992	40,107	642	Denbigh.
185	20	..	3,555	110	1,845	25,479	486	Flint.
495	60	78	7,400	3,692	2,868	56,923	749	Glamorgan.
92	19	50	1,307	..	511	17,140	473	Merioneth.
191	7	214	7,046	187	1,026	38,061	874	Montgomery.
247	66	114	4,838	..	1,135	29,271	752	Pembroke.
83	22	..	2,357	..	300	13,315	244	Radnor.
2,607	292	629	56,285	4,376	16,592	361,784	7,040	Totals of Wales.
49,913	6,181	30,083	1,111,236	245,221	359,106	6,900,117	166,257	{ Totals of England and Wales.

Unions and Overseers of the Poor, being a complete Return for England and Wales.

S

No. 1.—COMPARATIVE STATEMENT of EXPENDITURE for the RELIEF of the POOR, &c. during the Year ended 25th March, 1844, with the preceding Years.

COUNTIES.	Expended for the Relief and Maintenance of the Poor during the Years ended 25th March.			Decrease or Increase (marked*) in 1844 compared with 1834.	1844 compared with 1843.		Decrease per Cent. in 1844, compared with 1834.	1844 compared with 1843.		Expended in Law Charges, &c., during the years ended 25th March.		Decrease in 1844 compared with 1834.	Decrease per Cent. in 1844 compared with 1834.
	1834	1843	1844		Increase.	Decrease.		Increase per Cent.	Decrease per Cent.	1834	1844		
	£.	£.	£.	£.	£.	£.				£.	£.	£.	
ENGLAND.													
Bedford	77,819	43,965	40,736	37,083		2,529	48		6	1,366	199	1,067	89
Berks	100,183	77,357	74,524	25,959		3,133	26		4	3,458	1,353	2,105	61
Buckingham	124,200	77,627	75,730	48,470		1,897	39		2	3,140	1,299	1,841	59
Cambridge	96,497	71,900	70,319	26,178		1,581	27		2	3,427	1,344	2,083	61
Chester	92,640	93,362	84,305	8,335		9,057	9		10	8,570	2,986	5,584	65
Cornwall	93,037	80,333	74,962	18,075		5,371	19		7	4,182	2,966	1,216	29
Cumberland	43,067	37,660	35,513	7,554		2,047	18		5	2,316	456	1,860	80
Derby	72,721	61,705	57,743	14,978		3,962	21		6	4,163	2,992	1,171	28
Devon	210,825	194,605	181,054	29,771		13,451	14		7	7,507	4,795	2,712	36
Dorset	84,293	53,657	73,031	5,242		4,606	6		5	2,835	1,636	890	30
Durham	79,399	73,143	60,564	1,165*	1,421		1*			5,946	1,473	3,706	72
Essex	239,946	164,865	159,817	80,129		5,048	33		3	6,893	1,805	5,083	74
Gloucester	161,449	134,143	134,511	26,938		3,632	17		3	7,064	2,236	4,828	68
Hereford	56,683	43,968	42,755	13,928		1,113	25		5	2,345	962	1,383	57
Hertford	85,799	63,673	60,505	25,294		3,168	29		6	2,057		1,602	78
Huntingdon	35,844	25,816	24,135	11,709		1,681	33		6	1,146		671	59
Kent	343,678	200,515	193,642	150,236		6,873	44		3	15,340		12,689	83
Lancaster	253,403	361,771	329,664	76,259*	2,229	32,107	30*		9	15,776		7,631	48
Leicester	100,857	85,256	78,974	21,883		6,282	22		7	5,472		4,987	78
Lincoln	161,074	110,708	112,930	48,144			30		1	8,674		5,791	67
Middlesex	582,412	490,748	456,768	183,644		33,900	32		7	20,497		12,625	61
Monmouth	27,626	28,432	28,082	436*		376	2*		1	2,667	2,161		
Norfolk	306,787	188,964	189,105	117,682	141		38			9,535		7,374	77
Northampton	140,179	90,724	89,081	59,098		2,643	37		3	3,811	1,087	2,294	67
Northumberland	71,983	69,829	71,383		1,554					4,631	1,142	3,409	75
Nottingham	66,030	73,717	69,404			3,313			5*	3,399	1,411		

Westmoreland	22,283	19,309	18,702	3,581	607	16			510	682	172*	34*
Wilts	173,925	142,639	136,084	37,841	6,555	22		3	3,687	1,418	2,169	60
Worcester	81,612	68,424	66,522	15,090	1,902	23		5	3,781	1,837	1,944	51
York, East Riding	91,111	74,886	74,154	16,957	732	19		3	4,049	1,932	2,117	52
,, North Riding	75,810	63,116	61,801	14,009	1,315	18		1 2	3,015	2,556	459	15
,, West Riding	251,821	332,320	305,758	53,937*	26,562	21*		8	13,436	12,853	583	4
Totals of England	6,029,371	4,925,347	4,699,891	1,329,480 *Decrease, after deducting Increase.*	225,456 *Decrease, after deducting Increase.*	22		5	243,346	101,346	142,000 *Decrease, after deducting Increase.*	58
WALES.												
Anglesey	15,542	17,781	17,452	1,910*		12*		2	1,441	438	1,003	70
Brecon	18,974	18,279	18,974		329			.5	737	228	309	69
Cardigan	18,625	18,064	17,099	1,526	695	8	4	6	688	424	264	88
Carmarthen	33,755	33,547	31,446	2,309	985	7			1,850	506	1,344	73
Carnarvon	20,135	22,717	22,897	2,761*	2,101	14*	1	.3	1,367	516	851	62
Denbigh	33,136	31,299	30,388	2,748	180	8		.1	1,440	500	940	65
Flint	19,566	19,600	19,559	7	911	4*			1,853	123	1,730	93
Glamorgan	40,306	14,965	41,726	1,420*	41	1			1,939	238	1,701	88
Merioneth	14,977	14,850	14,850	127	399	15		.3	708	265	443	63
Montgomery	34,201	30,035	28,986	5,215	15	12		5	1,315	365	949	72
Pembroke	25,593	23,732	22,638	2,955	1,049	22		4	1,444	200	1,244	86
Radnor	13,072	10,636	10,167	2,885	1,094				476	154	322	68
					439							
Totals of Wales	287,883	282,680	276,202	11,681 *Decrease, after deducting Increase.*	6,478 *Decrease, after deducting Increase.*	21		4	15,258	3,938	11,300	74
Totals of England and Wales	6,317,254	5,208,027	4,976,093	1,341,161	231,934	21		4	258,604	105,304	153,300	59

* Increase.

No. 1—(*continued*).—Comparative Statement of Expenditure for the Relief of the Poor, &c., during the Year ended 25th March, 1844, with the preceding Years.

COUNTIES.	Expended for purposes other than the Relief of the Poor, during the Years ended 25th March.		Decrease in 1844 compared with 1835.	Decrease per Cent. in 1844 compared with 1835.	Total Expenditure for the Relief of the Poor, Law Charges, and other Purposes (exclusive of County Rates, Payments under the Registration, Parochial Assessment, and Vaccination Acts,) during the Years ended 25th March.		Decrease in 1844 compared with 1834.	Decrease per Cent. in 1844 compared with 1834.	Ratio of Expenditure per head to Population.						
									Population 1831.	1834		Population 1841.	1844		Decrease in the Rate per head in 1844 compared with 1834.
	1835	1844			1834	1844				Expenditure for the Relief of the Poor only.	Rate per head.		Expenditure for the Relief of the Poor only.	Rate per head.	
	£.	£.	£.		£.	£.	£.			£.	*s. d.*		£.	*s. d.*	*s. d.*
ENGLAND.															
Bedford	5,864	937	4,927	84	85,549	41,872	43,677	51	95,483	77,819	16 4	107,936	40,736	7 7	8 9
Berks	11,597	3,661	7,936	68	115,238	79,238	36,000	31	145,389	100,183	13 9	161,147	74,224	7 9	6 0
Buckingham	12,543	4,484	8,059	64	139,883	81,613	58,370	42	146,529	124,200	16 11	155,983	75,730	9 9	7 2
Cambridge	10,561	3,406	7,155	68	110,485	75,069	35,416	32	143,955	96,497	13 5	164,459	70,319	8 7	5 10
Chester	17,229	6,970	10,259	60	118,439	94,261	24,178	20	334,381	92,640	5 6	393,660	84,305	4 3	1 3
Cornwall	11,914	7,310	4,604	39	109,133	85,239	23,993	22	300,938	93,037	6 2	341,279	74,902	4 5	1 9
Cumberland	5,130	1,649	3,481	68	50,513	37,618	12,893	26	169,691	43,067	5 1	178,038	35,513	4 1	1 0
Derby	13,318	5,351	8,467	61	90,702	66,086	24,616	27	237,170	72,721	6 1	272,217	57,743	4 3	1 11
Devon	18,052	10,666	7,386	41	226,384	196,515	29,869	17	494,478	210,825	8 6	533,460	181,034	6 9	1 9
Dorset	6,990	3,260	3,730	53	93,927	84,146	9,781	10	159,252	84,923	10 7	175,043	79,051	9 0	1 7
Durham	9,167	5,975	3,192	35	93,811	88,018	5,793	6	253,910	78,399	6 3	324,284	90,564	5 6	0 9
Essex	23,716	6,388	17,328	73	270,660	168,010	102,550	38	317,507	239,946	15 1	344,979	129,017	9 3	5 10
Gloucester	21,634	10,581	11,053	51	190,147	147,328	42,819	23	387,019	161,449	8 4	431,383	134,311	6 5	2 1
Hereford	5,481	1,757	3,724	68	64,498	45,474	18,935	30	111,211	56,683	10 2	113,878	41,788	7 8	1 4
Hertford	12,197	2,717	9,470	78	100,043	63,677	36,366	36	143,341	84,729	12 0	157,207	60,668	7 8	4 6
Huntingdon	3,968	1,048	2,920	74	40,939	25,639	15,300	37	53,192	33,844	13 0	58,549	24,180	7 6	5 7
Kent	45,885	14,763	31,122	68	405,108	211,037	194,046	48	479,155	343,878	14 3	549,337	199,844	7 3	0 2*
Lancaster	64,488	27,088	37,800	58	384,897	364,897	30,828*	—	1,336,854	253,403	3 8	1,667,054	329,064	3 11	0 3
Leicester	12,691	4,257	7,804	65	118,488	84,446	33,974	—	197,003	100,657	10 3	215,867	170,064	7 4	2 11
Lincoln	25,556	7,663	18,163	70	195,066	123,506	72,098	—	317,465	161,974	10 2	362,602	115,469	5 10	3 11
Middlesex	60,710	69,987	*221	1	862,668	624,754	138,795	—	1,358,330	592,132	8 7	1,576,636			2 9
Monmouth	2,856	3,221	405*	16*	81,888	31,817	31,222	—				134,355			1 6

	£	£		£	£		£		£	£		£	£	s. d.	s. d.	s. d.
Southampton	22,251	14,963	67	232,263	146,782	85,481	37	314,280	203,466	12 11	385,004	137,102	7 9	5 3	4 2*
Stafford	20,829	10,141	49	148,225	127,883	20,330	14	410,512	120,513	5 10	510,594	113,834	4 6	1 9	
Suffolk	19,775	13,855	70	273,030	143,032	129,978	48	296,317	245,509	16 7	315,073	133,820	8 8	6 10	1 9
Surrey	42,812	24,738	58	313,175	221,134	92,041	29	486,334	261,501	10 9	585,678	199,207	9 11	5 11	9
Sussex	30,937	22,349	72	295,436	153,324	70,670	46	272,340	246,628	18 1	299,753	141,906	5 5	4 5	1 1
Warwick	22,092	10,879	49	186,186	115,516	132,112	38	336,610	153,199	9 5	401,715	101,589	5 1	5 6	5
Westmoreland	2,037	827	59	94,530	20,211	4,619	19	55,041	22,283	8 1	56,454	18,702	10 8	5 10	1 0
Wilts	15,888	6,390	60	193,400	143,892	49,508	26	240,156	173,925	4 6	238,733	136,094	6 8	6 1	1 6
Worcester	10,480	5,472	43	95,982	78,831	22,161	23	211,365	81,612	9 8	233,336	66,522	6 4	4 2	6
York, East Riding	10,081	4,539	55	105,341	80,645	34,596	23	204,253	91,111	7 11	233,257	74,154	6 1	2 2	11
", North Riding	7,888	4,930	63	86,713	67,315	19,398	22	190,756	75,810	7 11	204,122	61,801	6 8	2 7	1 10
", West Riding	39,675	31,351	21	304,932	349,962	45,030*	15*	976,360	251,821	7 5	1,154,101	305,758	5 5	4 0	2*
Totals of England	732,046	342,514	54	7,024,763	5,143,751	1,831,012	27	13,091,005	6,029,371	9 3	14,996,138	4,699,991	6 3	3 0	
		Decrease, after deducting Increase.				Decrease, after deducting Increase.									
WALES.															
Anglesey	2,003	1,531	23	18,936	19,441	455*	2*	48,325	15,542	6 5	20,891	17,432	6 10	0 5*
Brecon	1,639	1,304	20	21,350	20,506	844	4	47,763	18,974	7 11	55,603	18,974	6 10	1 9
Cardigan	1,905	834	56	21,218	18,357	2,861	13	64,780	18,625	5 8	64,766	17,099	5 11	1 9
Carmarthen	2,594	1,363	47	38,199	33,317	4,882	13	100,740	30,136	9 8	106,328	31,446	5 8	1 5
Carnarvon	2,149	1,861	13	23,652	25,274	1,622*	7*	66,448	33,136	6 1	81,093	22,897	5 5	0 1
Denbigh	3,981	1,992	50	38,537	32,880	5,677	15	83,629	33,136	7 1	86,966	30,388	5 10	1 8
Flint	2,442	1,845	24	23,861	21,627	2,334	10	60,012	19,566	6 4	66,966	19,539	4 10	0 6
Glamorgan	4,228	2,868	32	46,473	44,832	1,641	4	125,612	40,306	6 4	171,188	41,726	7 7	1 1
Merioneth	830	511	43	16,575	15,626	949	6	35,315	14,977	10 3	39,332	14,830	7 8	1 0
Montgomery	2,162	1,026	53	37,678	30,378	7,300	19	66,482	34,901	8 8	66,219	28,986	5 5	1 1
Pembroke	2,327	1,135	51	29,364	23,973	5,391	18	81,425	25,503	6 3	88,044	22,638	8 8	1 7
Radnor	593	300	49	14,141	10,641	3,500	25	24,651	13,072	10 7	25,356	10,137	5 0	
Totals of Wales	26,913	16,592	38	330,034	296,732	33,302	10	806,182	287,883	7 2	911,603	276,202	6 1	1 1
		Decrease, after deducting Increase.				Decrease, after deducting Increase.									
Totals of England and Wales	778,969	359,106	54	7,354,817	5,440,503	1,914,314	26	13,897,187	6,317,254	9 1	15,906,741	4,976,093	6 3	2 10	

* Increase.

I.—UNIONS AND SINGLE PARISH

NAMES OF UNIONS.	Amount levied by Assessment.	Received from all other Sources, in Aid of Poor Rate.	Total Amount Received for the Relief, &c., of the Poor.	Amount Expended in Relief, &c., of the Poor.	Amount Expended in Law Charges.	Payments under the... Amount of Fees Paid to the Vaccinators.	Outlay for Regist... Books
	£. s.	£. s.	£. s.	£. s.	£. s.	£. s.	£. s.
A.							
Aberayron . . .	4,457 14	12 16	4,470 10	3,730 14	22 15	8 1	..
Abergavenny . .	11,010 10	534 11	11,545 1	7,421 5	..	107 10	..
Aberystwith . . .	6,315 19	49 4	6,365 3	4,358 2	73 10	5 9	..
Abingdon . . .	10,739 4	156 14	10,895 18	7,878 8	34 10	12 6	..
Albans, St. . . .	5,912 18	8 19	5,921 17	3,873 5	4 19	..	..
Alcester	8,219 16	47 6	8,267 2	5,142 10	..	..	..
Alderbury . . .	7,345 4	42 18	7,388 2	6,879 14	25 8	7 6	..
Alnwick . . .	7,051 8	57 13	7,109 1	5,599 3	65 14	40 6	i.
Alresford. . . .	5,121 16	59 0	5,180 16	4,140 19	7 4	17 3	..
Alston-with-Garrigill	1,493 5	26 13	1,519 18	1,214 3	15 11	7 17	..
Alton.	6,252 10	102 2	6,354 12	4,776 15	24 16	9 16	..
Altrincham . . .	12,159 0	375 14	12,534 14	9,446 13	221 9	37 19	1 8
Amersham . . .	10,731 3	30 4	10,761 7	7,798 17	43 18	4 16	..
Amesbury . . .	4,994 7	13 18	5,008 5	3,909 17	13 17	9 12	..
Ampthill. . . .	8,293 8	89 4	8,382 12	6,045 12	43 5	17 8	..
Andover	10,446 0	382 13	10,828 13	8,256 19	40 4	25 9	..
Anglesey. . . .	15,901 7	123 9	16,024 16	13,290 8	262 7	24 4	0 5
Asaph, St. . . .	11,646 13	36 2	11,682 15	8,815 6	7 0	10 15	..
Ashby-de-la-Zouch .	10,141 5	92 8	10,233 13	7,729 0	178 3	4 10	..
Ashford, East . .	6,932 8	57 15	6,990 3	5,848 17	..	15 14	..
Ashford, West . .	7,183 17	234 1	7,417 18	5,696 6	64 10	7 13	..
Ashton-under-Lyne .	15,667 2½	542 18	16,210 0	10,065 6	672 0	12 2	..
Aston.	7,370 8	194 16	7,565 4	5,209 9	443 18	11 0	..
Atcham	7,508 11	21 2	7,529 13	4,423 5	48 3	10 9	0 1
Atherstone . . .	6,324 7	105 13	6,430 0	4,698 19	294 8	10 16	..
Auckland . . .	5,863 17	250 6	6,114 3	3,755 14	..	2 6	..
Austell, St. . . .	10,007 15	55 5	10,063 0	7,764 3	549 17	32 1	..
Axbridge . . .	13,221 13	205 8	13,427 1	10,645 1	31 10	19 2	..
Axminster . . .	11,476 4	94 12	11,570 16	9,568 4	514 12	24 7	0 6
Aylesbury . . .	13,866 3	125 0	13,991 3	12,581 16	23 8	..	..
Aylesham . . .	11,679 15	149 11	11,829 6	9,832 6	..	11 13	..
B.							
Bakewell. . . .	9,186 9	401 5	9,587 14	6,968 13	223 4	52 10	de
Bala	2,829 13	40 16	2,870 9	2,535 14	99 16	29 18	de
Banbury. . . .	18,155 5	354 3	18,509 8	14,149 4	182 4	..	..
Bangor & Beaumaris	9,339 9	28 10	9,367 19	6,365 12	160 17	48 12	..
Barnet	9,864 5	133 8	9,997 13	6,392 2	8 16	15 6	..
Barnstaple . . .	13,031 12	60 4	13,091 16	10,252 5	133 18	78 1	..
Barrow-on-Soar . .	9,279 6	23 6	9,302 12	7,369 12	49 14	25 12	..
Basford	18,534 2	1,393 17	19,927 19	15,692 9	314 2	105 16	..
Basingstoke . . .	13,153 11	115 9	13,269 0	9,787 15	178 17	11 18	..
Bath	27,173 17	229 14	27,403 11	13,211 11	189 0	45 10	..
Battle.	9,788 12	122 9	9,911 1	8,068 8	67 5	17 3	..
Beaminster . . .	9,556 7	95 5	9,651 12	8,202 17	123 7	8 11	..
Bedale	3,957 10	14 12	3,972 2	3,252 8	34 16	46 18	..
Bedford	14,862 8	130 15	14,993 3	11,268 1	2 6	20 0	..
Bedminster . . .	15,365 6	160 4	15,525 10	10,537 6	211 19	42 6	..

UNDER THE POOR LAW AMENDMENT ACT.

Payments on Account of the Registration Act.		Payments under the Parochial Assessments Act (for Surveys, Valuations, &c.), and Loans repaid under the same.	Payments for or towards the County Rate.	Payments for or towards the County and Local Police Forces.	Money Expended for all other Purposes.	Total Parochial Rates, &c., Expended.	Medical Relief.
Fees to Clergymen and Registrars.	Outlay for Register Offices, Books Forms, and other Incidental Expenses.						
£. s.	£. s.	£. s.	£. s.	£. s.	£. s.	£. s.	£. s.
33 5	..	..	569 14	..	132 8	4,496 17	65 10
174 10	10 0	..	2,758 2	..	1,360 1	11,831 8	246 10
62 19	2 13	..	1,633 2	..	286 7	6,422 2	105 9
65 17	..	153 1	1,432 8	..	252 3	9,828 13	457 5
38 8	..	..	2,155 9	..	103 1	6,175 2	165 5
53 6	10 0	..	1,507 8	..	954 15	7,667 14	262 16
36 2	20 0	..	1,022 1	..	117 10	8,108 1	293 2
49 10	25 14	..	1,077 12	..	218 18	7,076 17	144 2
21 0	..	..	781 13	..	121 17	5,089 16	164 2
25 10	41 8	..	125 0	..	94 17	1,524 6	17 0
37 5	..	44 16	1,154 12	..	192 8	6,240 8	257 10
93 13	10 11	..	1,388 5	..	429 0	11,628 18	296 12
58 8	..	153 8	874 3	..	199 19	9,133 9	437 4
22 4	..	226 18	1,067 1	..	32 15	5,282 4	188 10
51 10	3 11	..	1,522 14	..	97 14	7,781 14	273 9
46 7	..	86 0	1,605 5	340 0	278 5	10,678 9	473 7
75 6	16 1	..	1,186 16	..	845 7	15,700 14	260 15
53 5	..	73 6	1,621 1	..	484 18	11,065 11	251 13
79 0	..	100 0	1,635 19	..	959 18	10,686 10	228 15
35 2	..	..	741 1	..	330 17	6,971 11	289 0
38 0	63 16	52 15	645 11	..	229 5	6,797 16	276 12
375 9	11 19	15 18	3,021 14	406 5	1,206 11	15,787 4	245 5
158 14	25 0	187 13	491 8	31 6	545 10	7,103 18	247 10
57 5	18 5	..	2,441 8	..	573 18	7,573 4	288 15
30 13	9 17	13 4	617 1	14 17	148 3	5,837 18	160 7
72 12	11 12	..	1,456 6	..	387 16	5,686 6	94 0
99 10	..	..	638 17	..	920 9	10,004 17	180 12
94 0	14 14	134 13	2,588 15	..	288 8	13,816 3	521 0
56 16	20 2	21 5	1,118 9	..	421 1	11,745 2	480 13
70 9	..	..	1,894 6	..	345 3	14,915 2	536 0
58 3	..	..	1,708 8	..	478 0	12,088 10	331 3
80 13	..	..	1,599 0	..	417 2	9,341 2	214 13
16 17	0 16	..	255 9	..	84 6	3,022 16	60 0
91 10	25 0	..	3,033 6	..	772 12	18,253 16	467 1
85 18	14 7	..	642 13	4 19	990 11	8,313 9	119 7
53 5	25 0	..	1,212 16	2,169 12	394 11	10,271 8	461 0
96 15	..	..	1,479 11	..	486 12	12,527 2	412 11
59 16	..	..	1,440 15	317 1	207 17	9,470 7	282 3
183 0	20 18	..	2,072 13	785 7	2,035 11	21,209 16	662 10
46 14	10 0	10 10	2,109 9	..	333 2	12,488 5	467 10
199 18	3 7	45 12	4,939 19	..	1,489 9	20,124 6	409 0
35 9	20 18	153 11	685 14	270 0	295 1	9,613 9	263 2
45 3	..	162 14	909 18	..	386 13	9,839 3	361 6
24 8	2 19	..	357 8	..	53 1	3,774 8	109 2
109 17	2 0	122 17	3,287 5	..	277 17	15,090 3	331 4
104 7	6 15	..	1,052 10	..	800 2	12,755 5	307 10

NAMES OF UNIONS.	Amount levied by Assessment.	Received from all other Sources, in Aid of Poor Rate.	Total Amount Received for the Relief, &c., of the Poor.	Amount Expended in Relief, &c., of the Poor.		Amount of Fees paid to the Vaccinators.	Outlay for Register and Certificate Books.
	£. s.	£. s.	£. s.	£. s.	£. s.	£. s.	£. s.
Belford . . .	2,454 0	38 0	2,492 0	1,951 9	24 4	9 1	..
Bellingham . .	3,064 19	29 14	3,094 13	2,489 13	0 8	0 15	..
Belper . . .	10,270 16	86 9	10,357 5	6,864 18	87 8	52 12	..
Berkhampstead .	5,773 10	122 0	5,895 10	4,020 10	27 1	11 13	..
Bermondsey . .	19,044 12	1,011 2	20,055 14	13,782 0	164 3	76 2	..
Berwick-upon-Tweed	7,516 11	393 11	7,910 2	6,725 2	93 8	20 16	..
Bethnal Green . .	19,905 13	640 17	20,546 10	11,870 7	80 15	23 4	..
Beverley . . .	8,497 2	185 1	8,682 3	5,850 3	171 18	18 15	..
Bicester . . .	7,941 7	35 18	7,980 5	6,278 13	69 12	24 15	..
Bideford . . .	7,243 9	27 0	7,270 9	5,832 13	84 8	0 6	..
Biggleswade . .	11,266 15	130 7	11,397 2	8,229 1	63 12	10 19	..
Billericay . . .	7,891 6	158 7	8,049 13	5,881 6	177 16	15 2	..
Billesdon . . .	4,753 19	80 16	4,834 15	2,977 13	74 3	10 5	..
Bingham . . .	4,741 13	8 5	4,749 18	2,798 19	43 6	..	..
Bishop's Stortford .	14,080 2	125 1	14,205 3	10,738 19	35 6	24 3	..
Blaby	6,887 19	37 11	6,925 10	5,398 6	24 3	32 13	0 16
Blackburn . . .	19,164 15	448 1	19,612 16	11,387 8	323 6	37 14	..
Blandford . . .	7,189 6	137 3	7,326 9	6,338 12	181 3	..	..
Blean	6,567 4	33 19	6,601 3	4,300 2	95 17	10 15	..
Blofield . . .	6,072 6	49 10	6,121 16	5,522 0	32 14	3 2	..
Blything . . .	11,951 14	441 13	12,393 7	8,266 15	26 1	13 2	..
Bodmin . . .	8,768 8	254 0	9,022 8	6,726 3	87 0	45 8	..
Bolton . . .	28,677 18	2,508 17	31,186 15	20,263 17	577 10	114 4	..
Bootle . . .	1,649 19	189 4	1,839 3	1,349 8	1 14	10 17	..
Bosmere and Claydon	9,742 17	162 4	9,905 1	8,015 2	67 0	31 1	..
Boston . . .	17,572 6	196 12	17,768 18	11,096 14	299 11	50 7	..
Boughton, Great .	12,067 1	50 19	12,118 0	9,466 16	151 16	25 12	..
Bourn	7,927 10	472 8	8,399 18	6,284 13	193 4	18 1	..
Brackley . . .	8,412 10	47 10	8,460 0	7,002 2	28 16	..	..
Bradfield . . .	10,903 19	193 2	11,097 1	8,523 1	612 12	77 14	..
Bradford (Wilts) .	9,681 17	58 15	9,740 12	8,868 4	78 10	9 9	..
Bradford (Yorkshire)	28,201 13	600 9	28,802 2	19,858 2	1436 1	63 16	2 10
Braintree . . .	10,759 1	86 16	10,845 17	9,240 5	38 2	3 10	..
Brampton . . .	2,386 9	19 2	2,405 11	1,966 2	6 11	..	..
Brecknock . . .	12,258 9	89 11	12,348 0	8,972 11	47 1	26 10	..
Brentford . . .	19,149 1	131 9	19,280 10	13,630 19	358 6	126 2	..
Bridge . . .	6,050 15	42 2	6,092 17	4,321 10	40 18	27 13	..
Bridgend & Cowbridge	9,140 18	95 11	9,236 9	7,029 4	70 7	34 9	..
Bridgnorth . . .	5,964 4	78 5	6,042 9	4,021 17	135 5	9 0	..
Bridgwater . . .	14,310 17	302 13	14,613 10	11,825 3	228 11	22 6	..
Bridlington . . .	5,381 13	190 16	5,572 9	4,417 18	50 3	11 1	..
Bridport . . .	8,258 9	60 19	8,319 8	6,870 10	100 13	1 9	..
Brixworth . . .	9,709 6	41 4	9,750 10	7,833 6	..	12 7	..
Bromley . . .	8,042 15	238 6	8,281 1	4,904 16	188 8	8 16	..
Bromsgrove . . .	9,480 7	60 17	9,541 4	6,774 0	214 12	16 16	..
Bromyard . . .	5,514 8	144 19	5,659 7	4,389 10	67 19	7 16	1 ..
Buckingham. . .	9,654 4	114 10	9,768 14	7,714 2	5 15	..	..
Builth . . .	5,161 13	14 18	5,176 11	4,131 2	70 6	1 13	..
Buntingford . . .	4,241 15	15 0	4,256 15	3,426 8	102 4	..	..
Burnley . . .	16,244 10	266 1	16,510 11	10,931 11	432 4	13 12	..
Burton-upon-Trent .	10,407 13	355 2	10,762 15	7,662 5	52 18	15 17	4 ..
Bury (Lancashire) .	22,050 11	105 15	22,156 6	12,400 14	1162 18	75 9	4 ..
Bury St. Edmund's .	5,973 10	32 18	6,006 8	4,444 3	65 13	..	..

| Payments on Account of the Registration Act. | | Payments under the Parochial Assessments Act (for Surveys, Valuations, &c.), and Loans repaid under the same. | Payments for or towards the County Rate. | Payments for or towards the County and Local Police Forces. | Money Expended for all other Purposes. | Total Parochial Rates, &c., Expended. | Medical Relief. |
Fees to Clergymen and Registrars.	Outlay for Register Offices, Books Forms, and other Incidental Expenses.						
£. s.	£. s.	£. s.	£. s.	£. s.	£. s.	£. s.	£. s.
18 0	0 8	..	476 19	..	92 19	2,573 0	52 18
17 9	4 11	..	547 3	..	65 16	3,125 15	39 16
143 17	18 9	122 19	2,028 12	118 18	567 10	10,005 3	265 15
35 13	2 10	..	1,014 11	..	163 12	5,275 4	208 0
131 18	..	26 0	1,262 12	1,490 17	162 17	17,096 9	287 0
61 17	25 13	..	1,209 17	..	285 8	8,422 1	126 10
253 8	10 17	..	1,369 14	2,348 18	1,217 10	17,174 13	240 2
55 7	10 19	..	2,280 5	..	143 11	8,530 18	205 4
47 9	..	..	1,278 12	300 0	228 17	8,227 18	261 4
55 10	22 18	32 17	828 3	..	196 5	7,053 0	267 2
69 8	3 4	..	1,813 12	..	223 12	10,413 8	416 4
42 12	12 15	..	1,881 16	467 7	..	8,478 14	271 0
16 15	5 0	..	1,538 16	..	136 11	4,759 3	100 12
44 4	5 0	..	1,328 3	601 17	128 0	4,949 9	156 6
62 14	19 10	100 0	1,162 10	1,006 9	599 7	13,748 18	665 11
40 1	2 8	..	1,342 3	..	103 2	6,943 12	248 11
266 9	..	110 9	4,606 5	..	1,160 7	17,891 18	395 17
39 7	8 0	61 0	684 19	17 17	203 3	7,534 1	332 5
39 19	6 9	..	1,232 18	..	175 0	5,861 0	153 3
27 14	..	304 15	998 17	..	270 14	7,159 16	159 0
71 9	..	30 0	2,957 9	..	786 4	12,151 0	300 0
58 14	6 18	30 0	966 2	..	368 3	8,288 8	176 18
373 11	22 6	407 7	3,795 10	3,153 5	2,014 9	30,721 19	297 0
15 16	..	..	325 1	..	91 11	1,794 7	53 0
46 1	..	10 10	1,529 7	..	196 0	9,895 1	357 0
104 7	34 10	63 9	4,683 9	..	1,033 14	17,366 1	391 2
47 2	1 11	..	1,515 7	433 11	444 19	12,086 14	184 0
55 15	2 16	..	1,450 19	..	306 14	8,312 2	251 5
41 5	..	232 16	943 8	351 4	159 13	8,759 4	287 10
45 12	2 11	14 14	1,570 18	73 8	196 2	11,116 12	375 19
34 13	20 17	79 16	477 17	323 1	1,993 7	11,885 14	232 7
482 0	77 19	10 10	3,369 0	240 0	2,155 0	27,694 18	468 1
52 12	13 1	137 17	638 9	495 1	184 18	10,803 15	390 17
29 19	..	..	496 2	..	50 9	2,549 3	51 10
68 9	..	..	2,547 2	..	661 18	12,323 11	283 6.
104 1	24 14	110 0	2,108 13	2,809 5	509 6	19,781 6	524 1
31 8	1 18	88 13	808 1	..	147 15	5,467 16	168 16
48 15	..	..	1,312 8	323 18	180 11	8,999 12	157 10
42 14	..	83 12	1,648 17	..	196 13	6,137 18	211 18
92 9	5 15	..	2,141 5	..	655 13	14,971 2	576 10
42 7	12 2	..	980 10	..	65 18	5,579 19	129 7
45 14	..	52 11	704 3	..	215 8	7,990 8	260 17
46 13	20 0	..	1,645 18	..	326 10	9,884 14	306 10
44 16	10 0	..	876 5	1,608 12	478 0	8,119 13	289 1
68 10	3 3	57 11	1,362 19	758 6	356 8	9,612 5	257 10
35 17	..	..	1,028 12	..	94 11	5,625 15	150 4
52 11	16 10	..	1,706 16	2 10	222 4	9,720 8	277 9
25 3	9 18	..	918 16	..	119 0	5,275 18	80 0
20 3	..	..	839 7	..	29 9	4,417 11	108 7
180 9	15 9	220 1	3,554 19	..	1,052 1	16,430 6	280 9
88 19	4 16	100 0	2,236 18	171 14	576 17	10,914 14	371 16
285 19	20 18	137 18	5,312 4	..	1,358 18	20,759 8	224 3
39 8	20 0	..	799 19	..	220 3	5,589 6	160 0

	£.	s.	£.	s.	£.	s.	£.	s.	£.	s.	£.	s.	£.	
Caistor	10,526	15	209	2	10,735	17	7,423	17	179	17	38	5	••	
Calne	6,598	4	113	7	6,711	11	5,297	18	••		25	4	••	
Camberwell	13,172	13	307	19	13,480	12	6,505	14	479	5	42	13	••	
Cambridge	16,126	1	3,797	0	19,923	1	9,211	8	126	14	69	2	0	15
Camelford	3,565	0	12	3	3,577	3	2,636	7	89	18	4	4	••	
Cardiff	16,510	15	108	6	16,619	1	11,921	11	46	14	52	13	••	
Cardigan	6,816	3	64	0	6,880	3	5,576	18	105	13	13	10	••	
Carlisle	7,012	0	8	16	7,020	16	5,939	2	••		24	18	••	
Carmarthen	16,181	12	129	12	16,311	4	11,628	9	312	3	65	4	••	
Carnarvon	9,555	19	52	18	9,608	17	7,599	0	191	4	40	1	••	
Castle Ward	5,439	8	51	16	5,491	4	4,048	9	31	10	41	4	••	
Catherington	1,678	11	19	9	1,698	0	1,302	8	••		••		••	
Caxton and Arrington	6,521	2	21	6	6,542	8	5,373	4	123	7	26	6	••	
Cerne	4,031	2	48	16	4,079	18	3,353	17	21	10	11	0	••	
Chailey	6,424	17	154	16	6,579	13	4,642	19	105	14	15	16	••	
Chapel-en-le-Frith	5,009	19	18	10	5,028	9	2,404	0	1853	14	26	3	••	
Chard	11,271	3	39	3	11,310	6	9,282	17	118	2	44	8	••	
Cheadle	5,811	12	118	18	5,930	10	3,985	8	136	12	5	0	••	
Chelmsford	20,720	9	455	9	21,175	18	15,477	16	155	7	37	17	•:	
Chelsea	15,919	7	571	1	16,490	8	10,204	13	40	2	52	10	••	
Cheltenham	15,706	15	299	7	16,006	2	8,198	18	348	19	10	11	••	
Chepstow	8,418	7	107	3	8,525	10	6,004	8	63	0	18	12	••	
Chertsey	7,660	19	76	19	7,737	18	6,042	14	13	9	6	8	••	
Chesterfield	12,097	8	517	17	12,615	5	9,253	3	146	19	60	13	1	10
Chester-le-Street	7,016	1	126	1	7,142	2	4,805	3	177	17	18	15	••	
Chesterton	10,876	7	203	13	11,080	0	9,876	12	294	13	67	17	••	
Chippenham	11,456	12	236	2	11,692	14	8,483	14	356	14	34	2	••	
Chipping Norton	9,129	13	43	5	9,172	18	7,172	3	312	12	0	7	••	
Chipping Sodbury	9,417	5	104	2	9,521	7	6,272	7	55	3	14	11	••	
Chorley	14,079	10	71	4	14,150	14	8,639	4	152	11	23	12	••	
Chorlton	29,277	0	231	3	29,508	3	11,079	16			98	17	••	
Christchurch	4,067	9	31	0	4,098	9	3,313	8	16	13	41	14	••	
Church Stretton	2,821	2	55	11	2,876	13	2,520	16	22	3	2	14	••	
Cirencester	10,587	4	40	13	10,627	17	6,656	5	58	18	24	2	••	
Cleobury Mortimer	3,295	2	45	12	3,340	14	2,626	7	••		21	3	••	
Clifton	26,882	0	569	5	27,451	5	16,252	17	142	18	46	0	0	12
Clitheroe	10,877	5	251	0	11,128	5	7,477	1	360	8	12	7	••	
Clun	4,831	7	51	4	4,882	11	3,470	0	102	16	••		••	
Clutton	11,564	18	106	6	11,671	4	9,653	14	134	5	86	6	••	
Cockermouth	9,470	8	188	2	9,658	10	7,404	15	121	16	33	3	••	
Colchester	9,163	10	132	12	9,296	2	7,668	17	24	13	5	12	••	
Columb St. Major	6,327	9	22	10	6,349	19	4,605	11	129	5	35	14	••	
Congleton	8,533	18	886	5	9,420	3	6,428	18	137	4	38	3	4	0
Conway	6,295	19	8	17	6,304	16	4,817	18	248	8	23	17	••	
Cookham	5,198	19	30	15	5,229	14	3,640	17	88	18	10	14	••	
Corwen	5,756	0	6	0	5,762	0	4,526	19	78	13	13	0	••	
Cosford	8,020	11	122	1	8,142	12	5,352	2	95	5	15	15	••	
Cranbrook	7,997	1	456	5	8,453	6	7,647	0	92	1	8	14	0	12
Crediton	11,652	4	51	8	11,703	12	10,026	17	46	14	3	15	••	
Crickhowell	4,260	8	222	2	4,482	10	3,329	7	102	18	8	1	••	
Cricklade & Wootton Bassett	7,740	13	215	5	7,955	18	6,104	16	61	3	••		••	
Croydon	15,076	17	150	3	15,227	0	9,901	3	212	0	39	11	6	10
Cuckfield	9,707	7	148	18	9,856	5	7,784	5	59	6	14	12	••	

Payments on Account of the Registration Act.		Payments under the Parochial Assessments Act (for Surveys, Valuations, &c.), and Loans repaid under the same.	Payments for or towards the County Rate.	Payments for or towards the County and Local Police Forces.	Money Expended for all other Purposes.	Total Parochial Rates, &c., Expended.	Medical Relief.
Fees to Clergymen and Registrars.	Outlay for Register Officers, Books, Forms, and other Incidental Expenses.						
£. s.	£. s.	£. s.	£. s.	£. s.	£. s.	£. s.	£. s.
73 10	25 0	32 11	2,345 1	..	882 18	11,000 19	240 0
27 2	1 13	23 8	577 1	494 1	73 18	6,520 5	220 0
114 4	5 17	..	2,775 12	3,323 8	1,007 1	14,253 14	428 7
92 18	4 8	..	4,596 19	..	1,176 0	15,278 4	240 16
26 13	..	..	352 5	..	195 9	3,304 16	77 5
91 2	..	9 3	2,212 5	1,070 10	558 10	15,962 8	254 12
59 5	3 5	..	1,049 8	..	315 7	7,123 6	141 5
114 15	..	..	1,096 2	..	145 19	7,320 16	281 5
104 0	..	..	3,995 9	..	547 4	16,652 9	273 11
83 3	10 0	..	836 19	..	811 5	9,571 12	184 8
36 13	23 8	..	1,088 9	..	184 19	5,454 12	91 0
7 17	6 0	..	208 0	..	17 9	1,541 14	59 16
28 6	1 8	..	689 5	..	267 17	6,509 13	265 8
22 13	19 15	..	537 6	..	260 19	4,227 0	183 10
23 15	4 13	..	593 14	254 8	232 15	5,873 14	199 7
30 10	..	..	689 5	6 19	60 10	5,071 1	76 5
79 15	..	11 0	1,527 18	..	407 16	11,471 16	344 0
53 0	..	180 11	751 17	171 0	331 15	5,615 3	172 10
92 6	21 7	238 11	3,220 2	..	889 14	20,133 0	1128 0
139 13	..	..	1,746 12	2,996 7	3 14	15,183 11	337 4
111 10	35 1	21 0	5,218 15	..	1,276 18	15,221 12	264 18
49 19	..	..	1,771 2	440 17	433 18	8,781 16	243 10
42 6	..	100 15	821 5	..	411 16	7,438 13	320 10
119 11	27 2	41 6	2,305 0	..	669 17	12,625 1	285 6
59 18	2 13	..	1,495 0	..	465 13	7,024 19	60 0
62 13	13 12	..	1,637 12	..	338 13	12,291 12	266 19
59 19	13 6	181 7	2,262 15	..	466 16	11,858 13	362 15
45 11	5 10	38 1	1,410 3	..	205 12	9,189 19	309 2
54 12	2 7	72 0	2,596 8	..	276 13	9,344 1	234 5
129 8	41 17	..	3,413 15	..	507 18	12,908 5	201 7
342 12	1 7	..	17,220 2	..	1,635 8	30,377 12	264 3
14 10	..	329 0	512 13	205 1	78 19	4,511 18	145 18
20 7	..	..	535 15	..	67 6	3,169 1	122 0
61 10	..	..	2,485 1	..	235 8	9,521 4	333 5
26 4	5 7	..	717 12	259 18	87 18	3,744 9	125 15
182 15	11 17	..	8,962 1	..	1,554 1	27,153 1	358 0
64 16	..	..	2,289 19	..	473 15	10,678 6	134 10
34 12	..	233 18	874 5	266 14	112 5	5,094 10	161 10
76 1	..	10 0	1,133 15	..	413 9	11,507 10	366 13
99 19	..	..	1,287 2	..	492 0	9,438 15	201 1
56 13	18 11	..	1,105 13	..	222 15	9,102 14	254 18
49 13	15 2	..	912 15	..	302 7	6,050 7	192 15
76 18	9 8	..	764 2	546 12	559 8	8,564 13	225 10
28 19	5 0	..	522 18	43 19	318 6	6,009 5	100 0
35 10	10 0	..	1,224 14	84 10	246 13	5,341 16	155 0
30 13	..	..	799 15	..	141 2	5,590 2	126 1
52 11	12 0	141 8	1,555 14	187 0	229 8	7,641 3	247 0
38 17	6 5	64 0	526 14	..	701 4	9,085 10	292 10
60 17	20 10	188 3	1,141 6	..	284 17	11,772 19	355 16
73 19	..	..	728 19	..	448 11	4,691 15	103 1
30 5	12 3	37 5	759 13	711 7	688 8	8,405 0	209 11
78 0	9 10	..	1,951 13	2,620 17	668 12	15,487 16	513 15
40 14	4 11	162 19	741 8	293 8	385 11	9,486 14	297 10

or UNIONS.	Amount levied by Assessment.	Received from all other Sources, in Aid of Poor Rate.	Total Amount Received for the Relief, &c., of the Poor.	Amount Expended in Relief, &c., of the Poor.	Amount Expended in Law Charges.	Payments under the Vaccination Extension Act.	
						Amount of Fees Paid to the Vaccinators.	Outlay for Register and Certificate Books.
	£. s.	£. s.	£. s.	£. s.	£. s.	£. s.	£. s.
D.							
ɔn	8,722 4	248 2	8,970 6	5,753 19	192 1	37 19	..
•	9,515 17	167 14	9,703 11	6,525 4	75 5	19 10	8 13
'	11,636 3	174 15	11,810 18	9,261 9	75 3	7 17	..
•	19,329 13	428 4	19,757 17	13,131 6	35 5	4 10	3 11
•	7,010 14	136 2	7,146 16	4,164 8	35 19	34 2	..
•	13,048 12	277 7	13,325 19	10,996 0	31 16	0 16	..
y	16,174 13	2,053 8	18,228 1	13,114 17	343 12	87 6	..
•	10,088 5	81 1	10,169 6	8,352 14	2 14	5 14	..
•	6,765 19	54 7	6,820 6	5,672 11	69 13	10 12	..
ʳ.	14,209 1	196 9	14,404 10	9,905 5	473 1	..	..
er	8,232 5	55 0	8,287 5	6,734 18	346 0	4 8	..
•	4,870 8	19 5	4,889 13	3,987 16	46 4	5 18	..
•	7,946 1	5 17	7,951 18	6,937 0	223 0	..	..
•	11,247 13	185 19	11,433 12	7,692 8	121 15	18 9	..
n	8,908 6	97 6	9,005 12	7,101 18	92 16	19 12	..
•	7,193 8	191 2	7,384 10	5,766 2	46 13	27 13	..
h	9,418 0	53 3	9,476 3	6,148 14	149 4	7 0	..
•	6,951 10	9 11	6,961 1	5,588 19	27 11	30 12	..
•	25,690 16	1,411 14	27,102 10	16,603 13	634 3	223 2	..
n	2,770 16	59 2	2,829 18	2,377 13	23 1	13 2	..
•	15,127 10	53 2	15,180 12	12,608 9	20 1	33 15	..
•	6,137 0	237 18	6,374 18	4,540 15	72 0	6 16	..
•	10,409 2	42 14	10,451 16	8,521 18	84 7	8 3	..
E.							
m	3,178 13	67 7	3,246 0	1,739 4	58 1	34 5	..
old	3,093 11	60 5	3,153 16	2,920 6	142 15	17 4	..
ʾne	5,725 19	37 1	5,763 0	4,456 4	90 5	7 8	0 6
nstead	8,198 9	208 19	8,407 8	6,637 8	106 6	10 8	..
mpstead	3,057 12	111 9	3,169 1	2,751 9	26 1	..	..
tford	8,784 14	67 15	8,852 9	5,826 2	170 19	9 18	..
•	12,044 0	120 19	12,164 19	9,239 3	7 8	51 10	2 5
nehouse	2,978 19	40 15	3,019 14	2,201 13	263 1	4 14	..
ɪrd	4,499 13	115 16	4,615 9	3,841 12	159 0	10 7	..
. Bierlow	17,033 13	446 15	17,480 8	13,970 12	31 19	43 16	..
ɔn	28,761 14	828 15	29,590 9	17,122 5	292 10	113 19	..
ʿ.	7,478 2	94 9	7,572 11	5,270 4	19 16	25 10	..
ʾe	6,559 2	66 17	6,625 19	4,700 8	77 8	26 6	0 3
•	10,034 18	100 7	10,135 5	7,259 11	69 3	..	..
•	8,961 13	240 10	9,202 3	5,970 11	25 8	16 0	..
•	13,064 14	149 10	13,214 4	8,413 18	218 0	11 13	..
am	12,501 11	359 14	12,861 5	10,045 2	76 14	20 8	..
•	9,660 10	215 4	9,875 14	6,941 17	713 7	37 6	..
ı.	7,788 12	58 6	7,846 18	4,705 6	175 13	..	..
F.							
ɪ.	9,432 4	23 18	9,456 2	7,408 10	1 0	11 14	..
h	5,441 19	43 4	5,485 3	4,767 4	233 14	25 10	..
ı.	6,752 5	95 8	6,847 13	5,090 17	123 16	28 16	..
ɔn	8,660 8	205 0	8,865 8	6,854 1	222 4	34 3	..

Fees to Clergymen and Registrars.	Outlay for Register Officers, Books, Forms, and other Incidental Expenses.	Payments under the Parochial Assessments Act (for Surveys, Valuations, &c.), and other Loans repaid under the same.	Payments for or towards the County Rate.	Payments for or towards the County and Local Police Forces.	Money Expended for all other Purposes.	Total Parochial Rates, &c., Expended.	Medical Relief.
£ s.	£ s.	£ s.	£ s.	£ s.	£ s.	£ s.	£ s.
66 17	13 15	..	2,170 1	..	424 14	8,659 6	223 9
71 0	..	..	2,358 9	166 14	816 2	10,040 17	364 5
62 9	..	..	1,986 9	..	898 18	12,292 5	246 3
75 18	4 11	42 10	2,419 5	..	684 14	16,431 10	434 17
121 6	14 0	..	1,602 10	..	179 9	6,151 14	107 2
74 14	20 0	..	2,007 3	..	231 5	13,361 14	458 10
213 14	..	89 10	1,896 5	..	983 5	16,718 9	334 10
52 9	5 0	..	1,362 3	..	249 2	10,029 16	281 0
34 15	18 6	20 0	513 13	..	157 12	6,497 2	143 12
111 6	20 0	163 5	2,464 15	..	470 17	13,608 9	262 15
52 11	..	..	1,106 13	..	211 1	8,455 11	295 5
26 16	3 2	..	839 18	..	84 16	4,994 10	205 0
26 2	8 8	234 0	548 2	..	243 5	8,219 17	201 16
86 18	3 13	..	2,484 4	..	322 13	10,730 0	243 5
63 11	1 12	..	1,274 5	..	420 17	8,974 11	347 5
51 15	8 2	..	1,579 19	..	166 4	7,646 8	177 18
45 2	3 2	..	1,424 1	680 5	291 1	8,748 9	333 16
27 15	1 3	371 15	954 4	..	229 13	7,231 12	277 5
321 6	20 7	30 0	4,119 15	..	4,291 9	26,243 15	347 11
15 16	..	..	346 2	..	110 11	2,886 5	154 6
62 14	3 1	446 17	1,953 16	..	384 19	15,513 12	611 8
101 3	6 7	..	1,387 19	..	477 5	6,592 5	57 0
48 6	..	..	655 8	606 4	200 7	10,124 13	255 10
65 9	..	..	881 2	..	457 16	3,235 17	22 8
28 17	2 2	..	68 10	..	63 19	3,243 13	116 10
21 0	..	2 2	705 19	183 10	374 2	5,840 16	280 19
46 7	15 0	458 14	583 1	186 5	194 10	8,237 19	398 10
..	..	..	513 1	..	227 18	3,518 9	100 0
59 17	10 0	..	2,604 3	..	436 10	9,117 9	239 10
67 6	4 3	164 8	1,965 18	..	562 18	12,064 19	330 15
38 18	11 5	..	136 15	..	382 11	3,033 17	64 16
34 3	..	..	768 19	..	95 4	4,909 5	110 17
101 15	..	262 14	1,564 18	..	1,943 5	17,918 19	204 3
125 3	31 8	..	3,471 0	5,927 0	1,892 18	28,976 3	680 15
64 2	2 3	5 12	1,584 13	..	258 13	7,230 13	248 17
45 13	..	..	1,178 2	232 8	402 15	6,663 3	190 9
72 16	..	..	1,907 11	955 1	274 6	10,538 8	394 2
43 16	..	94 5	2,342 6	..	227 15	8,720 1	476 8
41 8	18 0	946 19	1,134 17	1,113 9	401 14	12,299 18	346 5
61 2	7 16	..	1,611 11	..	549 6	12,371 19	350 10
52 0	25 11	222 2	1,297 1	..	778 6	10,067 10	337 11
41 13	..	..	1,859 12	..	183 5	6,965 9	253 10
32 6	1 13	128 10	1,029 12	..	172 7	8,785 12	214 10
62 6	4 6	..	580 0	..	464 17	6,137 17	102 0
33 17	..	..	1,272 19	..	333 10	6,883 15	287 15
43 4	14 6	..	1,992 2	..	176 17	9,341 17	448 14

NAMES OF UNIONS.	Amount levied by Assessment.		Received from all other Sources, in Aid of Poor Rate.		Total Amount Received for the Relief, &c., of the Poor.		Amount Expended in Relief, &c., of the Poor.		Amount Expended in Law Charges.		Payments under the Vaccination Extension Act.			
											Amount of Fees Paid to the Vaccinators.		Outlay for Register and Certificate Books.	
	£.	s.	£.	s.	£.	s.	£.	s.	£.	s.	£.	s.	£.	s.
Faversham	9,632	15	364	17	9,997	12	7,129	1	..		15	6	..	
Festiniog	5,850	19	9	8	5,860	7	5,054	1	79	3	..		..	
Flegg, East and West	4,304	19	57	2	4,362	1	3,056	13	270	18	13	12	..	
Foleshill	4,873	17	24	0	4,897	17	3,215	8	375	10	..		..	
Fordingbridge	4,324	1	82	4	4,406	5	3,537	13	138	12	3	9	..	
Forehoe	6,339	4	131	2	6,470	6	5,606	10	184	10	3	12	..	
Freebridge Lynn	6,501	1	59	10	6,560	11	4,863	18	225	0	5	17	..	
Frome	16,398	8	125	1	16,523	9	13,586	3	523	6	19	1	..	
Fylde, The	6,239	15	247	3	6,486	18	4,124	13	225	14	17	10	..	

G.

NAMES OF UNIONS.	Amount levied by Assessment.		Received from all other Sources.		Total Amount Received.		Amount Expended in Relief.		Amount Expended in Law Charges.		Amount of Fees Paid to the Vaccinators.		Outlay for Register and Certificate Books.	
Gainsborough	9,842	1	211	11	10,053	12	7,031	11	123	18	32	12	..	
Garstang	6,953	19	254	12	7,208	11	5,083	2	124	1	..		..	
Gateshead	13,633	18	270	12	13,904	10	9,837	12	241	12	42	7	..	
George, St., in-the-East	20,247	13	849	6	21,096	19	13,426	10	..		71	7	..	
George, St., the-Martyr	17,488	10	617	18	18,106	8	9,053	19	75	3	74	7	..	
Germans, St.	6,177	4	66	13	6,243	17	5,372	1	49	0	22	0	..	
Glanford Brigg	12,077	13	145	4	12,222	17	8,984	1	431	12	19	16	..	
Glendale	5,241	10	11	12	5,253	2	4,205	19	35	12	22	12	3	8
Glossop	2,399	3	280	2	2,679	5	1,287	14	102	14	1	0	..	
Gloucester	9,177	2	330	14	9,507	16	7,193	9	91	18	24	18	..	
Godstone	5,875	15	185	0	6,060	15	4,440	10	113	14	..		..	
Goole	4,931	6	69	10	5,000	16	3,546	4	307	10	27	8	..	
Grantham	8,795	5	116	6	8,911	11	6,154	3	167	4	44	15	0	19
Gravesend and Milton	5,252	3	100	3	5,352	6	3,327	14	194	0	1	6	..	
Greenwich	33,317	13	100	19	33,418	12	21,481	17	411	15	120	1	..	
Guildford	15,694	4	903	6	16,597	10	12,598	11	129	6	88	6	..	
Guiltcross	7,529	6	193	6	7,722	12	6,875	10	..		13	12	..	
Guisborough	4,705	13	79	17	4,785	10	3,647	9	71	13	14	9	..	

H.

NAMES OF UNIONS.	Amount levied by Assessment.		Received from all other Sources.		Total Amount Received.		Amount Expended in Relief.		Amount Expended in Law Charges.		Amount of Fees Paid to the Vaccinators.		Outlay for Register and Certificate Books.	
Hackney	20,247	4	752	7	20,999	11	12,793	8	83	13	51	8	..	
Hailsham	11,796	8	185	3	11,981	11	9,592	16	109	17	0	15	..	
Halifax	25,477	2	1,907	6	27,384	8	18,386	5	927	14	137	8	..	
Halsted	10,734	1	67	11	10,801	12	8,696	18	163	5	5	12	..	
Haltwhistle	1,851	8	5	5	1,856	13	1,334	16	43	12	6	2	..	
Hambledon	7,399	11	14	2	7,413	13	6,424	2	43	6	14	8	..	
Hardingstone	5,413	3	15	1	5,428	4	4,387	10	..		..		..	
Hartismere	10,660	1	591	18	11,251	19	9,576	3	211	0	10	2	..	
Hartley Wintney	5,625	18	56	8	5,682	6	4,643	6	5	15	17	15	..	
Haslingden	8,985	15	152	11	9,138	6	5,534	3	73	8	53	15	..	
Hastings	7,311	10	249	19	7,561	9	5,506	19	308	3	3	4	..	
Hatfield	3,064	8	177	9	3,241	17	2,222	16	..		10	14	..	
Havant	3,561	1	41	6	3,602	7	2,773	15	38	1	..		..	
Haverfordwest	11,387	16	29	13	11,417	9	9,034	5	46	2	5	13	..	
Hay	4,676	12	22	2	4,698	14	3,786	6	5	1	4	16	..	
Hayfield	3,520	4	97	19	3,618	3	2,195	1	66	11	..		..	
Headington	7,046	17	308	10	7,355	7	5,900	11	51	2	2	15	..	
Helmsley	3,307	16	116	18	3,424	14	2,966	1	301	1	32	16	..	
on	7,798	16	456	10	8,255	6	6,331	6	646	19	67	19	..	
Helst Ihempstead	5,748	12	38	4	5,786	16	3,552	6	..		4	4	..	
Ieme														

Payments on Account of the Registration Act.		Payments under the Parochial Assessments Act (for Surveys, Valuations, &c.), and Loans repaid under the same.	Payments for or towards the County Rate.	Payments for or towards the County and Local Police Forces.	Money Expended for all other Purposes.	Total Parochial Rates, &c., Expended.	Medical Relief.
Fees to Clergymen and Registrars.	Outlay for Register Offices, Books, Forms, and other Incidental Expenses.						
£. s.	£. s.	£. s.	£. s.	£. s.	£. s.	£. s.	£. s.
47 1	7 14	366 3	1,537 4	..	778 4	9,880 13	228 10
27 2	..	30 2	441 8	..	240 12	5,872 8	143 11
44 3	..	..	694 5	..	84 6	4,163 17	100 11
28 1	..	25 0	1,099 11	..	176 15	4,920 5	171 19
21 13	1 13	266 2	636 4	..	201 13	4,806 19	151 10
42 7	2 6	..	1,065 5	..	148 18	7,053 8	224 5
42 5	..	..	1,164 1	..	243 17	6,544 18	242 2
77 4	8 0	7 12	1,120 13	..	393 2	15,735 1	417 11
54 16	5 0	..	1,598 2	626 10	280 7	6,932 12	155 13
80 6	7 1	..	1,990 14	..	456 16	9,722 18	190 8
38 8	1 19	..	1,542 4	..	119 9	6,909 3	103 0
130 1	..	..	1,093 2	768 4	779 1	12,891 19	198 1
155 18	22 6	..	1,975 8	3,385 8	1,684 14	20,721 11	351 4
169 18	24 0	..	877 16	2,633 6	4,290 18	17,199 7	290 0
50 4	2 8	7 6	717 2	..	205 3	6,425 4	186 12
80 3	4 18	..	2,535 4	..	620 15	12,676 9	292 8
35 1	4 9	..	832 7	..	159 10	5,298 18	97 0
44 3	2 1	..	459 5	..	321 10	2,218 7	25 0
92 11	..	..	1,603 6	..	466 14	9,472 16	300 0
41 1	14 0	104 13	749 6	..	301 7	5,764 11	236 8
36 9	12 0	..	989 13	..	189 17	5,109 1	123 17
60 8	27 18	..	1,634 12	..	587 12	8,677 11	270 15
42 17	15 0	..	1,408 14	..	349 3	5,338 14	121 16
250 9	46 10	60 0	1,976 2	4,983 2	3,373 1	32,702 17	415 6
63 19	3 5	351 17	1,712 10	..	647 12	15,595 6	598 17
35 19	..	..	1,001 17	..	171 2	8,098 0	263 17
33 10	8 0	..	720 17	..	164 10	4,660 8	105 0
125 16	8 0	..	2,293 16	3,936 19	1,060 0	20,353 0	378 0
41 16	1 15	..	1,079 9	..	627 17	11,454 5	443 11
355 11	42 18	49 10	3,471 0	..	1,666 2	25,036 8	524 7
51 14	12 19	38 6	1,168 7	..	274 12	10,411 13	496 11
14 15	4 9	..	334 3	..	36 15	1,774 12	32 0
31 0	10 3	169 5	702 3	..	494 7	7,888 14	305 11
28 7	..	..	878 7	..	214 13	5,508 17	132 13
53 3	..	..	1,408 5	..	400 19	11,659 12	408 15
32 7	11 6	..	1,044 5	..	151 16	5,906 10	269 10
112 2	..	..	2,604 9	..	205 6	8,583 3	97 0
49 11	..	..	1,513 15	72 9	456 0	7,910 1	121 11
15 6	0 16	..	936 14	..	68 11	3,254 17	103 12
20 2	..	..	537 0	..	59 17	3,428 15	154 10
94 11	36 0	80 5	2,067 2	..	352 14	11,716 12	331 2
32 19	..	..	1,099 12	..	56 5	4,984 19	179 6
28 5	5 1	20 0	387 19	20 0	283 16	3,006 13	59 0
46 13	..	..	632 15	..	414 5	7,048 1	175 1
34 10	5 1	..	32 0	..	71 0	3,442 9	134 0
100 13	8 0	..	530 6	..	890 2	8,575 5	265 5
36 18	..	51 16	1,154 2	..	154 10	4,953 16	178 1

NAMES OF UNIONS.	Amount levied by Assessment.		Received from all other Sources, in Aid of Poor Rate.		Total Amount Received for the Relief, &c., of the Poor.		Amount Expended in Relief, &c., of the Poor.		Amount of Fees Paid to the Vaccinators.		Outlay for Register and Certificate Books.	
	£.	s.	£.	s.	£.	s.	£.	s.	£.	s.	£.	s.
Hendon	12,497	1	175	5	12,672	6	7,017	12	64	8	28	11	
Henley	9,635	5	116	5	9,751	10	8,443	6	50	13	16	16	
Henstead . . .	7,600	11	213	16	7,814	7	6,602	13	1	19	25	6	
Hereford . . .	10,928	15	199	19	11,128	14	8,403	2	155	18	6	0	
Hertford . . .	7,356	12	101	16	7,458	8	5,812	0	65	18	. .	
Hexham	9,558	5	90	16	9,649	1	8,134	16	60	16	37	19	
Highworth & Swindon	9,613	15	183	12	9,797	7	7,693	3	28	7	29	15	
Hinckley . . .	7,028	9	4	2	7,032	11	6,752	13	64	12	15	0	
Hitchin . . .	11,609	3	166	7	11,775	10	8,885	19	12	4	28	19	
Holbeach . . .	9,987	3	111	18	10,099	1	6,482	7	50	12	32	7	
Holborn* . . .	3.298	8	228	19	3,527	7	8,650	12	. .	9	12	
Hollingbourn . .	10,389	11	201	2	10,590	13	9,441	14	242	12	16	14	
Holsworthy . .	4,072	17	76	11	4,149	8	3,426	1	. .	9	7	
Holywell . . .	14,469	1	330	11	14,799	12	11,269	1	49	18	53	16	
Honiton . . .	11,428	6	38	15	11,467	1	9,833	8	434	16	1	1	
Hoo	1,677	5	0	3	1,677	8	1,277	8	. .	5	5	
Horncastle . .	11,332	9	195	8	11,527	17	9,184	14	300	16	24	1	
Horsham	8,333	10	17	9	8,350	19	7,171	16	20	1	5	6	
Houghton-le-Spring	5,640	17	112	9	5,753	6	3,664	1	166	4	19	14	
Howden . . .	5,925	11	116	7	6,041	18	4,768	15	247	13	25	3	
Hoxne	10,018	1	108	3	10,126	4	7,849	19	3	2	3	0	
Huddersfield . . .	26,158	3	1,928	12	28,086	15	19,307	11	1226	5	150	2	
Hungerford . . .	14,619	15	58	19	14,678	14	8,562	17	95	2	0	16	
Huntingdon . . .	10,005	12	133	9	10,139	1	7,554	8	139	6	8	19	
Hursley . . .	1,319	14	7	15	1,327	9	958	13	. .	. .	

I.

	£.	s.	£.	s.	£.	s.	£.	s.	£.	s.	£.	s.
Ipswich	14,665	18	719	5	15,385	3	11,153	10	41	5	8	11	
Ives, St.	9,343	3	15	6	9,358	9	7,586	9	190	7	23	18	

K.

	£.	s.	£.	s.	£.	s.	£.	s.	£.	s.	£.	s.
Keighley. . . .	9,724	14	100	9	9,825	3	7,370	11	495	3	26	13	
Kendal . . .	14,180	3	829	6	15,009	9	12,293	7	507	9	39	8	
Kensington . .	40,106	17	643	2	40,749	19	17,080	6	556	15	94	18	
Kettering . . .	10,819	18	109	18	10,929	16	9,025	15	311	9	10	5	
Keynsham . .	10,535	1	171	19	10,707	0	8,281	8	48	4	36	17	
Kidderminster . .	14,475	11	177	1	14,652	12	8,625	7	249	11	41	8	
Kingsbridge . .	10,902	4	113	9	11,015	13	9,163	13	81	12	10	14	
Kingsclere . .	5,054	16	1	6	5,056	2	4,409	7	75	14	18	4	
King's Lynn . .	7,362	7	822	8	8,184	15	7,877	0	177	16	12	15	
King's Norton . .	11,210	13	27	19	11,238	12	4,542	16	145	10	3	14	
Kingston-on-Thames	16,971	2	189	10	17,160	12	8,397	7	254	17	33	18	
Kington . . .	6,536	9	43	16	6,580	5	4,592	1	209	3	44	9	
Knighton . . .	4,648	13	17	5	4,665	18	3,600	0	. .	2	12	

L.

	£.	s.	£.	s.	£.	s.	£.	s.	£.	s.	£.	s.
Lambeth	56,725	2	1,262	18	57,988	0	33,256	19	665	19	85	1	. . 3
Lampeter. . . .	4,173	18	46	5	4,220	3	3,351	7	40	12	. .	. .

* Holborn Union.—The Governors and Directors of the Parishes of St. Andrew and St. Geo[...]
to the Auditor; the Clerk of the Union consequ[...]

Payments on Account of the Registration Act.		Payments under the Parochial Assessments Act (for Surveys, Valuations, &c.), and Loans repaid under the same.	Payments for or towards the County Rate.		Payments for or towards the County and Local Police Forces.		Money Expended for all other Purposes.		Total Parochial Rates, &c., Expended.		Medical Relief.	
Fees to Clergymen and Registrars.	Outlay for Register Offices, Books, Forms, and other Incidental Expenses.											
£. s.	£. s.	£. s.	£.	s.	£.	s.	£.	s.	£.	s.	£.	s.
39 8	..	..	1,381	9	2,372	1	383	14	11,287	3	294	7
51 15	..	..	1,097	8	..		199	1	9,858	19	362	5
30 15	1 18	..	1,120	9	..		205	19	7,988	19	227	0
79 7	7 17	53 12	2,285	9	..		382	9	11,373	14	370	3
40 2	..	..	1,251	0	..		562	7	7,731	7	327	5
82 16	19 10	..	1,453	2	..		268	6	10,057	5	128	0
50 11	12 2	..	1,674	2	..		371	14	9,859	14	342	13
47 2	10 0	..	784	14	116	9	155	5	7,945	15	150	6
63 3	..	..	2,573	13	..		270	16	11,834	14	405	10
62 1	22 15	207 12	2,458	4	..		707	14	10,023	12	258	11
124 14	..	..	1,169	4	..		199	18	10,154	0	300	0
43 9	20 0	115 16	755	16	..		147	3	10,783	4	337	0
35 4	..	..	473	16	..		146	4	4,090	12	110	12
119 1	20 0	..	1,442	10	..		1,260	5	14,214	11	234	14
61 16	4 14	95 12	1,264	5	..		527	16	12,223	8	485	4
8 19	..	..	363	1	..		74	4	1,728	17	80	0
71 13	1 14	..	1,593	9	..		409	17	11,586	4	274	10
34 11	..	97 10	501	11	90	12	437	15	8,359	2	320	10
48 4	..	..	666	6	380	15	310	19	5,256	3	104	0
44 18	7 10	..	1,117	15	..		121	19	6,333	13	147	10
50 13	2 8	108 0	1,440	4	..		312	14	9,770	0	309	16
353 6	..	424 10	3,219	7	..		3,556	14	28,237	15	422	0
66 18	..	296 14	1,767	6	..		310	18	11,100	11	429	2
61 13	3 0	21 1	1,733	9	..		418	16	9,940	12	472	9
7 17	..	..	317	8	..		35	12	1,319	12	75	0
77 6	20 0	155 12	3,149	6	..		1,197	9	15,802	19	277	0
69 15	17 12	..	1,384	17	..		304	3	9,577	1	289	8
77 6	4 16	..	1,249	0	..		333	8	9,556	17	130	13
99 12	..	..	1,292	8	..		687	16	14,920	0	402	11
214 13	11 15	..	5,771	13	10,342	15	2,847	10	36,920	5	577	5
57 5	2 15	..	1,368	12	..		164	5	10,940	6	361	12
62 7	3 9	..	1,417	5	..		396	3	10,245	13	282	0
84 5	..	306 17	2,886	6	..		993	16	13,187	10	345	4
64 3	..	41 4	995	5	..		354	15	10,711	6	271	0
31 11	2 13	..	763	4	..		54	7	5,355	0	202	0
60 2	2 17	..	29	7	..		446	17	8,606	14	173	8
63 0	16 0	94 11	2,721	9	2,206	1	885	6	10,678	7	223	2
63 11	..	..	1,743	8	2,464	6	795	10	13,752	17	294	10
39 16	..	..	1,177	14	383	8	126	9	6,573	0	338	15
31 7	..	..	881	14	..		234	7	4,750	0	144	5
419 6	24 0	548 2	11,567	12	7,818	1	3,701	18	58,086	18	847	8
25 18	..	56 0	660	6	..		105	12	4,239	15	60	0

e Martyr, appointed under the 6 Geo. IV., c. 175, refuse to submit their accounts as not the means of furnishing a complete Return.

T

NAMES OF UNIONS.	Amount levied by Assessment.	Received from all other Sources, in Aid of Poor Rate.	Total Amount Received for the Relief, &c., of the Poor.	Amount Expended in Relief, &c., of the Poor.	Amount Expended in Law Charges.	Payments under the Vaccination Extension Amount of Fees paid to the Vaccinators.	Outl
	£. s.	£. s.	£. s.	£. s.	£. s.	£. s.	£.
Lancaster	9,391 6	2,139 16	11,531 2	8,202 1	39 3	17 19	.
Lanchester	3,508 9	7 11	3,516 0	2,385 15	19 3	19 8	.
Langport	6,392 8	253 11	6,645 19	4,948 16	40 2	25 11	.
Launceston	6,371 10	17 9	6,388 19	5,146 12	238 4	2 11	.
Ledbury	5,349 3	114 17	5,464 0	4,492 18	35 1	. .	.
Leek	7,878 4	224 13	8,102 17	4,657 8	245 3	20 15	.
Leicester	23,533 1	1,256 7	24,789 8	18,837 19	168 0	23 15	.
Leigh	8,686 19	555 18	9,242 17	5,798 6	204 19	16 2	0
Leighton-Buzzard	7,195 4	78 18	7,274 2	5,458 7	9 5	4 1	.
Leominster	7,121 10	49 3	7,170 13	5,785 15	211 16	44 13	.
Lewes	5,267 16	167 10	5,435 6	4,282 4	141 10	4 4	.
Lewisham	10,100 2	2,868 19	12,969 1	5,167 9	175 13	22 3	.
Lexden and Winstree	11,318 15	21 4	11,339 19	8,089 17	228 6	38 10	.
Leyburn	4,848 14	67 0	4,915 14	3,542 16	32 14	56 2	.
Lichfield	9,792 6	189 12	9,981 18	7,156 15	332 15	26 3	.
Lincoln	8,156 10	352 7	8,508 17	7,682 0	207 16	25 9	0
Linton	10,024 9	77 3	10,101 12	8,216 17	83 10	85 4	.
Liskeard	11,364 11	264 9	11,629 0	9,112 6	131 2	7 2	0
Liverpool	68,017 13	52 16	68,070 9	50,678 2	827 0	384 18	2
Llandilo Fawr	7,720 18	30 12	7,751 10	5,490 2	20 15	18 2	.
Llandovery	5,964 15	29 15	5,994 10	4,301 18	32 10	1 4	.
Llanelly	6,875 12	137 2	7,012 14	5,031 1	45 11	28 18	.
Llanfyllin	9,782 5	10 7	9,792 12	7,062 19	97 2	6 5	.
Llanrwst	5,834 0	6 12	5,840 12	4,397 4	9 0	9 16	.
Loddon and Clavering	7,689 4	168 15	7,857 19	5,706 16	30 6	28 11	.
London, City of	52,963 0	3,815 10	56,778 10	51,180 9	839 10	. .	.
,, East	17,714 10	1,962 4	19,676 14	16,140 7	238 4	23 19	5
,, West	10,658 1	840 0	11,498 1	14,033 18	107 4	2 12	.
Longtown	3,515 8	30 14	3,546 2	2,949 10	16 15	20 9	.
Loughborough	9,822 9	55 15	9,878 4	6,890 5	51 13	5 9	.
Louth	14,179 10	256 0	14,435 10	11,244 2	220 11	11 5	.
Ludlow	8,670 7	43 18	8,714 5	6,537 15	1 4	43 11	.
Luton	8,196 4	68 5	8,264 9	5,978 16	68 14	24 0	.
Lutterworth	8,363 11	199 4	8,562 15	6,285 15	37 8	. .	.
Lymington	5,355 14	104 10	5,460 4	4,234 11	104 18	7 2	.

M.

Macclesfield	13,754 2	1,038 19	14,793 1	10,096 4	258 14	54 12	.
Machynlleth	7,306 1	50 8	7,356 9	5,972 9	202 13	18 16	.
Madeley	8,851 6	553 9	9,404 15	6,911 7	541 2	40 0	.
Maidstone	13,373 13	160 17	13,534 10	11,979 14	57 7	64 15	.
Maldon	13,935 0	188 10	14,123 10	9,614 10	220 16	30 9	.
Malling	10,731 14	130 8	10,862 2	9,372 5	76 11	111 13	.
Malmsbury	9,299 15	86 12	9,386 7	6,550 11	260 9	7 4	.
Malton	8,400 19	169 7	8,570 6	6,773 12	187 10	32 3	.
Manchester	103,862 8	10,211 9	114,073 17	58,461 14	634 17	274 5	.
Mansfield	10,165 2	418 12	10,583 14	7,108 18	397 18	22 3	.
Market Bosworth	7,459 10	67 8	7,526 18	5,849 6	142 3	17 12	.
Market Drayton	5,883 19	72 17	5,956 16	3,567 1	45 16	8 16	.
Market Harborough	10,661 13	296 10	10,958 3	8,208 11	. .	13 4	.
Marlborough	6,509 18	45 12	6,555 10	5,458 11	0 19	3 6	.

Payments on Account of the Registration Act.		Payments under the Parochial Assessments Act (for Surveys, Valuations, &c.), and Loans repaid under the same.	Payments for or towards the County Rate.	Payments for or towards the County and Local Police Forces.	Money Expended for all other Purposes.	Total Parochial Rates, &c., Expended.	Medical Relief.
Fees to Clergymen and Registrars.	Outlay for Register Offices Books Forms, and other Incidental Expenses.						
£. s.	£. s.	£. s.	£. s.	£. s.	£. s.	£. s.	£. s.
75 19	3 15	51 0	1,625 12	500 0	531 6	11,046 15	147 0
35 5	..	..	948 9	..	175 16	3,583 16	54 13
58 3	8 6	..	1,162 6	..	184 15	6,427 19	273 0
53 0	..	..	680 12	..	307 8	6,428 7	182 2
37 13	1 16	..	964 13	..	131 0	5,663 1	286 19
65 6	15 0	..	708 11	330 17	717 7	6,760 7	205 3
175 19	3 2	..	3,825 11	..	1,632 16	24,667 2	325 19
88 18	5 3	28 10	2,213 0	..	136 16	8,491 19	140 18
51 14	..	212 10	952 2	..	123 3	6,811 2	260 0
47 14	11 13	..	1,143 9	..	154 11	7,399 11	191 10
27 18	5 11	..	826 14	..	227 10	5,515 11	141 14
62 17	..	..	2,740 14	1,289 15	864 12	10,323 3	219 0
66 1	25 0	152 13	2,217 9	..	153 0	10,970 16	508 16
29 6	5 0	61 5	467 6	..	62 6	4,256 15	143 0
63 9	..	..	1,248 18	..	702 12	9,530 12	318 12
110 10	7 18	42 0	1,538 2	..	573 5	10,187 11	274 10
51 5	7 15	..	899 12	..	188 0	9,532 8	277 0
82 9	3 14	..	1,398 14	..	298 19	11,034 7	189 0
856 8	69 9	210 0	8,522 17	..	528 1	62,079 13	344 6
58 11	..	..	1,665 8	..	223 16	7,476 14	133 13
53 10	2 15	..	1,590 7	..	160 8	6,142 12	142 10
71 18	9 19	..	919 15	304 17	227 7	6,639 6	119 10
52 1	..	16 0	2,386 4	1 16	175 7	9,797 14	259 0
34 13	6 10	..	617 13	..	287 9	5,362 5	77 10
43 8	5 0	71 19	1,724 2	..	267 5	7,877 7	242 0
..	151 8	..	..	..	2,427 10	54,598 17	525 0
134 9	9 7	..	..	..	2,552 7	19,103 18	544 4
117 18	19 5	..	..	..	497 11	14,778 8	298 0
27 6	2 0	..	326 3	..	58 7	3,400 10	79 16
74 8	4 0	..	1,453 14	305 14	255 11	9,040 14	205 16
91 3	15 0	..	2,353 3	..	371 0	14,306 4	471 3
51 6	3 14	4 0	1,620 6	..	298 11	8,561 7	370 10
58 17	..	..	1,351 10	..	181 0	7,662 17	225 15
30 19	12 11	90 11	2,032 17	..	298 10	8,788 11	289 0
26 17	12 6	..	721 6	..	168 13	5,275 13	212 0
192 5	..	..	1,923 11	..	729 10	13,254 16	281 10
35 1	2 9	..	758 12	..	178 15	7,168 15	117 3
77 7	..	106 19	907 7	..	459 4	9,043 6	177 3
102 13	15 0	78 15	664 7	50 13	863 3	13,876 7	504 0
60 4	34 7	..	2,085 2	1,187 19	495 17	13,729 7	639 16
60 14	3 1	164 11	816 18	..	405 5	11,010 18	420 16
41 11	1 9	208 18	1,864 2	..	217 0	9,151 4	255 12
75 10	7 15	..	1,445 13	..	694 1	9,216 4	229 10
776 13	58 4	..	35,323 18	..	4,328 15	99,858 6	453 16
90 7	4 3	96 16	1,483 0	..	551 16	9,755 1	253 18
41 15	3 12	..	563 5	..	165 7	7,783 0	168 0
38 17	3 14	..	989 3	314 6	535 6	5,502 19	129 14
34 7	5 0	..	2,184 11	..	672 5	11,117 18	363 14
27 3	..	..	725 19	..	98 4	6,314 2	150 0

T 2

NAMES OF UNIONS.	Amount levied by Assessment.		Received from all other Sources, in Aid of Poor Rate.		Total Amount Received for the Relief, &c., of the Poor.		Amount Expended in Relief, &c., of the Poor.		Amount Expended in Law Charges.		Payments under the Vaccination Extension Act		
											Amount of Fees Paid to the Vaccinators.		Outlay for Register and Certified Books.
	£.	s.	£.	s.	£.	s.	£.	s.	£.	s.	£.	s.	£.
Martin-in-the-Fields, St.	22,013	9	638	0	22,651	9	10,919	4	302	5	18	1	..
Martley	6,792	1	121	9	6,913	10	4,864	6	39	17	7	10	..
Medway	11,571	11	1,867	12	13,439	3	8,471	12	228	2	54	15	1 1
Melksham	12,896	18	247	14	13,144	12	11,697	14	207	11	21	0	..
Melton Mowbray	8,813	2	188	7	9,001	9	5,125	10	157	9	26	1	3 1
Mere	6,801	12	29	6	6,830	18	5,622	8	61	4	4	14	..
Meriden	6,381	17	126	8	6,508	5	4,349	16	81	1	14	2	..
Merthyr Tydfil	16,989	12	763	1	17,752	13	9,040	5	..		81	13	..
Midhurst	7,527	11	46	2	7,573	13	6,631	15	239	3	9	8	..
Mildenhall	5,222	14	102	1	5,324	15	3,751	1	22	2	2	8	..
Milton	5,978	1	154	7	6,132	8	4,569	6	58	16	15	17	..
Mitford & Launditch	16,029	11	160	5	16,189	16	12,144	7	34	19	9	9	..
Monmouth	8,222	10	210	8	8,432	18	5,709	10	79	9	27	0	..
Morpeth	6,297	9	24	19	6,322	8	4,820	15	185	10	12	3	..
Mutford and Lothingland	6,304	4	86	14	6,390	18	4,288	11	..		14	0	..

N.

NAMES OF UNIONS.													
Nantwich	15,033	12	480	8	15,514	0	11,040	18	777	6	26	18	7 1
Narberth	7,948	13	79	11	8,028	4	6,030	1	103	11	2	8	.. ..
Neath	9,185	3	29	6	9,214	9	7,386	14	70	9	36	17	.. ..
Neot's, St.	9,396	10	185	0	9,581	10	7,182	12	23	19	98	3	.. ..
Newark	7,953	15	307	6	8,261	1	8,525	12	215	10	27	10	.. ..
Newbury	16,033	14	188	3	16,221	17	12,337	9	317	17	20	8	.. ..
Newcastle-in-Emlyn	6,302	5	168	12	6,470	17	5,262	2	75	9	2	1	.. ..
Newcastle-under-Lyne	6,734	11	246	15	6,981	6	4,249	17	72	4	31	12	..
Newcastle-upon-Tyne	25,199	12	1,163	13	26,363	5	22,884	14	307	10	77	9	.. ..
Newent	6,268	7	83	18	6,352	5	4,652	13	70	14	7	9	.. ..
New Forest	7,221	11	91	9	7,313	0	6,465	4	72	9	12	18	.. ..
Newhaven	3,327	0	66	16	3,393	16	2,539	1	16	17	..		.. ..
Newmarket	15,545	14	63	12	15,609	6	13,301	9	568	16	65	10	..
Newport (Monmouth)	15,279	6	141	4	15,420	10	8,311	0	213	12	101	3	.. .(
Newport (Salop)	7,209	4	181	11	7,390	15	4,657	5	233	7	9	10	.. ..
Newport Pagnell	12,275	11	174	15	12,450	6	9,534	5	116	0	15	7	.. ..
Newton Abbott	15,807	9	162	9	15,969	18	13,183	19	448	12	32	15	.. .(
Newtown and Llanidloes	17,355	19	120	14	17,476	13	12,856	10	130	16	2	0	.. ..
Northallerton	5,505	6	75	12	5,580	18	4,915	6	124	8	19	4	2 15
Northampton	13,952	2	148	17	14,100	19	8,166	1	28	7	24	18	.. ..
North Aylesford	7,212	4	231	5	7,443	9	5,644	19	189	18	18	2	.. ..
Northleach	6,420	3	46	14	6,466	17	4,148	16	0	7	..		.. ..
Northwich	10,814	14	294	4	11,108	18	8,591	7	346	0	27	5	.. ..
North Witchford	8,178	7	21	9	8,199	16	5,415	9	4	1	1	14	.. ..
Nottingham	21,832	6	382	15	22,215	1	21,689	15	31	8	42	0	.. ..
Nuneaton	6,657	8	115	18	6,773	6	4,704	0	48	2	..		.. ..

O.

NAMES OF UNIONS.													
Oakham	5,646	3	37	14	5,683	17	4,316	5	40	8	28	4	.. ..
Okehampton	8,216	9	107	11	8,324	0	6,859	17	152	19	..		.. ..
Olave, St.	11,715	1	738	18	12,453	19	7,452	6	172	12	30	2	.. ..
Oldham	15,227	8	1,259	3	16,486	11	10,354	15	141	5	60	6	.. ..

Payments on Account of the Registration Act.		Payments under the Parochial Assessments Act (for Surveys, Valuations, &c.), and Loans repaid under the same.	Payments for or towards the County Rate.	Payments for or towards the County and Local Police Forces.	Money Expended for all other Purposes.	Total Parochial Rates, &c., Expended.	Medical Relief.
Fees to Clergymen and Registrars.	Outlay for Register Offices, Books Forms, and other Incidental Expenses.						
£. s.	£. s.	£. s.	£. s.	£. s.	£. s.	£. s.	£. s.
89 12	7 10	..	3,516 13	6,048 14	1,130 7	22,032 6	336 10
32 16	..	51 0	1,069 15	660 14	107 3	6,833 1	226 10
116 5	7 12	..	1,739 3	..	969 9	11,588 9	136 10
57 0	..	64 9	427 13	410 2	354 11	13,240 0	244 16
57 10	3 4	..	3,180 1	..	262 6	8,815 2	241 18
20 8	..	..	700 15	..	115 13	6,525 2	206 10
31 6	18 14	74 8	1,470 1	201 0	236 19	6,477 7	199 9
182 10	..	64 15	1,374 6	2,030 17	1,219 17	13,994 3	152 0
39 10	7 10	161 13	510 3	..	431 2	8,030 4	322 3
31 1	11 17	272 6	930 9	..	169 3	5,190 7	156 10
26 10	8 8	208 1	713 5	..	292 4	5,892 7	185 9
86 12	..	..	2,404 15	..	521 16	15,201 18	444 14
88 4	..	..	2,141 13	222 18	350 1	8,618 15	234 0
41 9	10 4	..	962 15	..	314 16	6,347 12	77 0
47 0	2 11	..	1,358 16	..	260 15	5,971 13	118 0
104 15	39 12	46 4	897 17	738 11	663 15	14,343 9	331 6
62 18	..	..	1,612 17	..	438 2	8,249 17	184 0
97 2	..	..	1,563 2	..	152 1	9,306 5	184 12
55 13	..	..	1,310 16	..	178 7	8,849 10	356 8
78 19	25 18	..	2,769 7	..	704 17	12,347 13	264 18
56 1	35 14	341 19	2,125 6	..	463 15	15,698 9	428 14
54 19	..	..	1,101 17	..	202 14	6,699 2	160 10
70 16	2 12	..	1,987 12	165 16	317 1	6,897 10	116 10
240 8	41 4	..	74 0	..	1,898 10	25,523 15	357 0
34 7	..	23 6	1,532 13	..	326 11	6,647 13	205 8
39 3	12 0	..	763 5	..	172 19	7,537 18	335 0
16 10	2 0	..	658 11	23 1	206 1	3,462 1	124 10
85 8	..	26 5	1,844 18	..	537 17	16,430 3	361 12
111 5	8 6	16 13	4,445 10	100 0	747 18	14,055 7	231 10
39 14	..	..	1,432 0	..	404 6	6,776 2	174 10
71 12	10 1	..	1,876 2	..	784 18	12,408 5	260 10
120 15	..	169 10	1,563 3	..	873 9	16,392 3	352 18
94 5	..	125 14	2,096 12	..	416 3	15,722 0	374 18
34 18	7 4	..	501 16	60 0	150 6	5,815 17	138.16
84 7	36 8	..	3,084 5	..	769 15	12,194 1	192 17
49 8	..	..	827 15	..	496 5	7,226 7	273 0
28 1	..	155 12	1,599 7	..	72 6	6,004 9	192 2
96 15	..	..	632 17	..	1,039 1	10,733 5	341 12
49 14	8 19	..	1,550 2	775 1	51 16	7,856 16	245 5
173 16	9 19	..	5,085 8	..	271 6	27,303 12	485 12
38 5	..	138 12	672 11	105 16	399 12	6,106 18	166 5
29 10	11 15	..	893 6	..	115 0	5,434 8	135 14
60 13	4 2	105 0	818 1	..	347 16	8,348 8	184 19
83 16	6 13	3 0	1,325 0	1,814 6	1,002 16	11,890 11	183 0
279 19	5 7	0 3	3,261 18	287 8	399 3	14,790 4	583 10

NAMES OF UNIONS.	Amount levied by Assessment.	Received from all other Sources, in Aid of Poor Rate.	Total Amount Received for the Relief &c., of the Poor.	Amount Expended in Relief, &c., of the Poor.	Amount Expended in Law Charges.	Payments under the Vaccination Extension Act.	
						Amount of Fees Paid to the Vaccinators.	Outlay for Registers and Certificate Books.
	£. s.	£. s.	£. s.	£. s.	£. s.	£. s.	£.
Ongar	7,877 7	94 18	7,972 5	5,897 13	64 6	14 6	5 1
Ormskirk. . . .	9,573 19	86 13	9,660 12	5,309 2	24 7	61 7	..
Orsett	6,701 0	31 11	6,732 11	4,645 6	22 1	16 16	..
Oundle	8,309 12	131 17	8,441 9	6,778 1	140 2	29 8	..

P.

NAMES OF UNIONS.	Amount levied by Assessment.	Received from all other Sources, in Aid of Poor Rate.	Total Amount Received for the Relief &c., of the Poor.	Amount Expended in Relief, &c., of the Poor.	Amount Expended in Law Charges.	Amount of Fees Paid to the Vaccinators.	Outlay for Registers and Certificate Books.
Pateley Bridge . .	3,888 18	148 2	4,037 0	2,975 10	27 4	15 18	..
Patrington . . .	4,480 11	70 10	4,551 1	3,255 9	7 12	14 15	..
Pembroke . . .	6,773 1	45 10	6,818 11	5,368 8	..	17 1	..
Penkridge . . .	6,127 15	127 1	6,254 16	4,188 11	59 15	40 2	1 .
Penrith . . .	7,367 4	78 6	7,445 10	5,513 13	60 19	4 10	8 .
Penzance . . .	6,281 8	435 12	6,717 0	4,898 15	188 14	79 14	13 1
Pershore]. . . .	6,798 5	163 17	6,962 2	4,010 14	286 5	22 0	..
Peterborough . .	13,084 3	235 8	13,319 11	9,344 17	276 16	31 2	..
Petersfield . . .	5,265 6	40 6	5,305 12	4,498 19	33 5	7 5	..
Petworth	5,703 10	168 19	5,872 9	5,468 10	16 10	6 1	..
Pewsey	7,366 8	23 11	7,389 19	5,449 11	2 2	34 10	..
Pickering . . .	3,175 4	36 13	3,211 17	2,924 9	7 9	27 12	..
Plomesgate . . .	11,882 12	604 17	12,487 9	9,367 13	47 0	4 18	..
Plympton, St. Mary	9,546 0	72 7	9,618 7	7,155 4	118 11	12 9	0 .
Pocklington . . .	6,684 2	342 6	7,026 8	5,648 8	229 5	38 6	2 1
Pontypool . . .	7,037 10	166 0	7,203 10	4,328 2	97 19	29 16	30 .
Poole (Dorset) . .	6,590 0	21 4	6,611 4	4,583 13	92 0	..	..
Poplar	19,496 8	2,039 6	21,535 14	11,621 0	347 6	52 11	..
Portsea Island . .	21,890 7	548 10	22,438 17	17,397 4	308 8	35 15	..
Potterspury . . .	5,362 8	130 3	5,492 11	4,325 3	28 0	..	..
Prescot	12,375 17	299 15	12,675 12	7,152 8	34 7	65 0	..
Presteigne . . .	1,687 2	19 1	1,706 3	1,167 13	81 3	..	..
Preston	23,748 15	1,076 11	24,825 6	16,785 9	672 11	56 1	8 8
Pwllheli . . .	8,195 14	..	8,195 14	6,398 18	193 19	..	..

R.

NAMES OF UNIONS.	Amount levied by Assessment.	Received from all other Sources, in Aid of Poor Rate.	Total Amount Received for the Relief &c., of the Poor.	Amount Expended in Relief, &c., of the Poor.	Amount Expended in Law Charges.	Amount of Fees Paid to the Vaccinators.	Outlay for Registers and Certificate Books.
Radford	4,658 12	292 5	4,950 17	3,497 0	11 10	44 12	..
Reading	8,032 2	751 3	8,783 5	4,898 19	182 6	23 15	..
Redruth	7,802 8	82 8	7,884 16	5,256 12	289 5	87 14	..
Reeth	3,100 11	21 2	3,121 13	2,905 4	36 2	7 11	..
Reigate	9,672 16	266 13	9,939 9	7,265 19	28 14	28 6	..
Rhayader . . .	3,408 9	32 19	3,441 8	2,677 11	29 1	..	..
Richmond (Surrey) .	7,701 9	881 9	8,582 18	4,406 1	237 11	14 10	..
Richmond (Yorkshire)	4,667 2	74 6	4,741 8	4,157 1	207 19	2 15	..
Ringwood . . .	2,755 9	39 11	2,795 0	2,326 16	..	1 9	..
Risbridge . . .	10,154 17	167 7	10,322 4	9,608 5	195 16	41 14	..
Rochdale . . .	14,852 10	778 5	15,630 15	10,329 12	233 17	..	..
Rochford . . .	7,947 10	151 9	8,098 19	5,006 6	166 6	..	..
Romford	13,455 2	124 0	13,579 2	9,770 1	100 16	43 5	..
Romney Marsh . .	3,737 9	112 9	3,849 18	3,067 12	23 16	..	..
Romsey	4,578 6	318 6	4,896 12	3,812 1	28 1	..	..
Ross	8,777 12	23 16	8,801 8	6,481 19	106 17	31 12	3 .
Rothbury . . .	3,739 0	48 11	3,787 11	3,056 17	14 2	28 8	..
Rotherham . . .	12,984 9	740 5	13,724 14	10,842 19	223 3	11 7	..
Rotherhithe . . .	9,015 3	1,361 16	10,376 19	6,482 18	19 19	26 13	..

Payments on Account of the Registration Act.		Payments under the Parochial Assessments Act (for Surveys, Valuations, &c.), and Loans repaid under the same.	Payments for or towards the County Rate.	Payments for or towards the County and Local Police Forces.	Money Expended for all other Purposes.	Total Parochial Rates, &c., Expended.	Medical Relief.
Fees to Clergymen and Registrars.	Outlay for Register Offices, Books, Forms, and other Incidental Expenses.						
£. s.	£. s.	£. s.	£. s.	£. s.	£. s.	£. s.	£. s.
31 17	2 6	63 8	1,673 17	..	225 11	7,979 2	488 16
107 9	5 0	..	4,069 8	..	148 15	9,733 8	237 1
34 6	..	..	1,447 11	..	136 4	6,302 4	299 15
54 8	..	..	1,441 4	..	188 12	8,631 15	298 2
24 19	..	..	466 17	..	225 10	3,735 18	72 6
24 7	..	..	1,167 2	..	212 15	4,682 0	123 10
62 17	27 15	33 10	1,214 14	..	191 1	6,915 6	236 12
46 18	12 4	75 4	1,017 13	231 17	167 2	5,840 6	203 18
53 12	2 5	..	1,091 3	..	252 19	6,987 6	142 5
156 2	0 8	30 0	489 2	..	838 10	6,694 1	192 4
34 16	8 8	286 10	1,953 16	..	88 6	6,690 15	293 16
84 19	..	..	2,909 17	..	609 19	13,257 10	336 8
23 10	10 11	..	628 10	..	111 5	5,313 5	196 0
30 5	6 10	112 10	418 2	..	131 4	6,189 12	198 15
37 2	17 9	..	1,391 19	..	95 15	7,028 8	307 2
32 9	2 4	..	..	..	114 9	3,108 12	88 10
64 8	22 2	124 7	1,501 16	599 13	266 0	11,997 17	422 0
52 3	2 9	117 17	1,275 11	..	350 7	9,085 5	273 12
40 6	20 16	..	978 17	..	320 3	7,278 16	180 15
68 14	69 11	174 15	1,846 15	..	641 12	7,287 4	135 0
33 15	30 0	..	1,866 1	..	143 14	6,749 3	160 0
106 18	14 7	544 3	2,368 13	3,943 7	2,536 16	21,535 1	367 11
178 2	27 16	..	3,362 3	..	382 0	21,691 8	370 13
33 0	1 17	..	564 3	..	226 17	5,179 0	126 16
148 15	6 0	..	4,857 7	..	407 14	12,671 11	182 10
12 1	5 13	..	331 5	57 1	27 1	1,681 17	50 0
257 5	58 11	41 7	4,827 1	..	875 0	23,581 13	594 14
42 6	10 0	..	956 6	..	368 15	7,970 4	271 16
85 13	19 9	18 2	775 19	9 3	293 17	4,755 5	149 1
61 3	41 19	..	2,751 6	..	806 7	8,765 15	187 0
113 4	10 16	165 4	280 9	..	757 5	6,960 9	184 1
22 4	1 13	7 8	168 14	..	104 2	3,252 18	48 0
40 2	..	51 5	969 19	..	284 12	8,668 17	351 15
21 3	11 5	..	604 9	..	49 7	3,392 16	50 0
35 19	22 5	243 9	999 2	1,562 4	488 6	8,009 7	167 10
38 13	7 7	85 0	581 7	..	106 6	5,186 8	103 0
15 13	5 8	..	407 13	..	32 17	2,789 16	133 15
57 4	..	..	1,367 2	..	204 15	11,474 16	103 16
246 16	22 5	66 5	4,138 18	..	635 7	15,673 0	64 5
44 2	..	..	1,912 19	..	359 15	7,489 8	399 0
73 1	..	493 7	1,492 12	1,519 9	350 15	13,848 6	425 17
18 18	..	..	377 15	..	248 12	3,736 13	221 1
35 3	3 17	..	671 4	221 12	315 3	5,087 1	246 12
40 8	9 16	222 12	1,257 6	31 13	326 9	8,511 12	313 10
16 2	1 15	..	628 17	..	77 9	3,853 10	95 5
92 13	10 0	89 19	1,694 6	..	611 2	13,575 9	186 15
59 7	47 19	500 0	813 10	1,195 7	995 18	10,141 11	150 0

NAMES OF UNIONS.	Amount levied by Assessment.	Received from all other Sources, in Aid of Poor Rate.	Total Amount Received for the Relief, &c., of the Poor.	Amount Expended in Relief, &c., of the Poor.	Amount Expended in Law Charges.	Payments under the Vaccination Extension Act	
						Amount of Fees Paid to the Vaccinators.	Outlay for Register and Certified Books.
	£. s.	£. s.	£. s.	£. s.	£. s.	£. s.	£. s.
Royston	8,743 5	121 2	8,864 7	6,706 15	..	106 5	..
Rugby	10,356 8	426 17	10,783 5	6,139 7	120 13	31 18	..
Runcorn	8,376 9	273 16	8,650 5	6,035 13	187 5	13 19	..
Ruthin	10,038 0	61 14	10,099 14	7,815 14	160 18	3 9	..
Rye	9,733 4	524 3	10,257 7	7,539 19	270 3	3 19	..

S.

NAMES OF UNIONS.	Amount levied by Assessment.	Received from all other Sources, in Aid of Poor Rate.	Total Amount Received for the Relief, &c., of the Poor.	Amount Expended in Relief, &c., of the Poor.	Amount Expended in Law Charges.	Amount of Fees Paid to the Vaccinators.	Outlay for Register and Certified Books.
Saffron Walden . .	14,040 13	296 7	14,337 0	11,280 7	80 15	26 0	..
Salford	16,906 1	1,409 1	18,315 2	9,052 16	260 9	92 8	..
Samford . . .	5,530 6	63 1	5,593 7	4,223 17	81 9	2 9	0 11
Saviour's, St. . .	16,106 8	1,945 0	18,051 8	11,783 0	208 18	57 6	2 19
Scarborough . .	5,859 16	175 19	6,035 15	4,971 8	156 5	..	..
Sculcoates . . .	11,841 13	800 6	12,641 19	10,124 10	161 5	42 0	..
Sedbergh . . .	2,324 8	67 18	2,392 6	1,912 0	20 0	2 8	..
Sedgefield . . .	2,976 16	32 10	3,009 6	1,871 0	75 3	..	..
Seisdon . . .	3,935 5	21 6	3,956 11	2,038 5	61 10	8 11	..
Selby	6,772 9	84 17	6,857 6	5,501 6	89 3	24 10	1 1
Settle	9,039 10	128 3	9,167 13	6,531 11	..	12 10	..
Sevenoaks . . .	10,820 13	140 3	10,960 16	9,496 2	19 9	13 6	..
Shaftesbury . . .	7,387 4	60 19	7,448 3	6,227 9	77 12	..	..
Shardlow . . .	11,322 0	105 3	11,427 3	8,041 0	200 1	10 2	..
Sheffield	38,806 11	9,260 4	48,066 15	33,707 6	205 8	46 6	..
Sheppy	3,870 9	95 14	3,966 3	3,097 19	..	7 4	..
Shepton-Mallet . .	14,528 0	218 4	14,746 4	13,106 4	96 14	20 13	..
Sherborne . . .	6,563 2	45 13	6,608 15	5,895 4	185 6	9 10	..
Shiffnal	6,458 2	52 0	6,510 2	4,564 13	115 2	16 0	..
Shipston-on-Stour .	10,793 12	113 12	10,907 4	7,803 4	104 3	6 5	..
Skipton	13,023 9	434 12	13,458 1	8,587 3	298 17	11 18	..
Skirlaugh . . .	4,485 3	115 10	4,600 13	3,741 14	8 9	8 19	..
Sleaford . . .	8,514 11	137 10	8,652 1	6,935 16	72 12	9 4	..
Solihull	4,730 16	53 13	4,784 9	3,264 19	173 13	12 10	..
Southam . . .	4,948 5	229 8	5,177 13	3,416 1	83 13	29 3	..
South Molton . .	9,124 12	92 7	9,216 19	7,499 5	68 14	11 5	..
South Shields . .	10,128 4	108 18	10,237 2	8,074 12	79 14	49 10	..
South Stoneham .	4,683 10	156 3	4,839 13	3,608 19	55 5	9 1	..
Southwell . . .	9,112 6	236 9	9,348 15	5,633 15	131 18	40 16	..
Spalding	10,380 7	121 17	10,502 4	6,126 1	134 10	17 2	..
Spilsby	13,841 4	400 0	14,241 4	10,085 4	366 13	58 4	..
Stafford	6,496 18	213 16	6,710 14	4,448 4	49 0	73 8	..
Staines	10,212 8	706 10	10,918 18	7,368 7	113 15	20 18	..
Stamford	7,658 10	90 14	7,749 4	5,187 9	30 17	7 1	..
Stepney	32,115 14	2,000 0	34,115 14	20,089 0	289 18	72 12	..
Steyning	6,058 1	199 10	6,257 11	4,894 19	67 9	6 11	..
Stockbridge . . .	4,184 12	41 13	4,226 5	3,042 17	13 18	5 19	..
Stockport	21,815 6	2,440 8	24,255 14	16,114 11	583 0	60 18	..
Stockton	9,047 12	146 17	9,194 9	5,786 18	125 1	31 8	..
Stokesley	4,051 19	91 4	4,143 3	3,493 18	119 6	3 17	13 4
Stoke-upon-Trent .	15,423 0	3,245 3	18,668 3	10,102 19	355 10	110 1	..
Stone	8,128 1	215 1	8,343 2	4,825 2	10 3	32 3	..
Stourbridge . . .	13,163 7	605 12	13,768 19	9,343 19	401 6	36 4	0 4
Stow	9,730 12	192 18	9,923 10	8,035 19	111 18	30 12	..
Stow-on-the-Wold .	5,315 18	57 0	5,372 18	3,777 8	72 8	4 10	..

Payments on Account of the Registration Act.		Payments under the Parochial Assessments Act (for Surveys, Valuations, &c.), and Loans repaid under the same.	Payments for or towards the County Rate.	Payments for or towards the County and Local Police Forces.	Money Expended for all other Purposes.	Total Parochial Rates, &c., Expended.	Medical Relief.
Fees to Clergymen and Registrars.	Outlay for Register Offices, Books Forms, and other Incidental Expenses.						
£. s.	£. s.	£. s.	£. s.	£. s.	£. s.	£. s.	£. s.
62 15	..	..	1,465 10	..	196 12	8,537 17	303 18
59 0	2 4	110 11	2,455 12	1,161 12	539 17	10,620 14	279 0
80 6	..	..	542 14	551 18	618 7	8,030 2	166 4
50 8	2 3	..	1,519 14	..	346 16	9,899 2	230 5
33 10	..	96 0	728 4	283 12	960 12	9,915 19	217 5
56 16	23 2	..	1,724 15	..	382 4	13,573 19	402 18
259 7	2 12	..	4,314 9	..	1,448 18	15,430 19	181 7
37 9	2 2	11 1	879 8	373 1	76 10	5,687 17	252 0
128 9	30 6	..	4,994 3	..	793 16	17,998 17	236 2
66 13	142 10	..	152 4	..	188 1	5,676 11	162 10
123 4	269 1	..	949 2	..	893 13	12,562 15	196 15
18 16	0 9	..	454 15	..	36 14	2,445 2	48 19
23 16	0 15	..	884 10	..	154 15	3,009 19	36 10
43 14	1 12	..	861 18	..	316 17	3,332 7	142 0
44 17	9 5	36 3	946 8	4 11	238 13	6,896 3	126 11
42 9	..	..	1,955 6	..	227 13	8,769 9	185 2
61 5	..	155 17	920 6	..	373 16	11,070 9	505 5
41 19	11 0	39 5	675 12	..	230 8	7,303 5	210 0
98 11	15 3	44 10	2,574 13	..	943 1	11,927 1	281 11
307 15	20 16	39 16	4,739 18	..	7,383 7	46,450 12*	191 12
38 9	15 18	..	465 16	..	106 1	3,731 7	160 13
52 9	..	25 0	1,091 17	..	281 5	14,677 3	430 0
41 0	1 16	..	757 14	..	248 2	7,138 12	242 0
28 3	17 6	45 0	899 16	280 11	180 0	6,146 11	162 0
60 11	9 12	..	2,005 19	..	452 15	10,442 9	357 5
87 10	14 0	..	2,457 14	..	1,309 17	12,766 19	132 18
33 12	..	..	930 8	..	52 5	4,775 7	154 17
70 6	3 9	10 19	1,266 1	..	256 18	8,625 5	245 13
32 6	..	53 5	1,202 7	..	258 0	4,997 0	105 15
34 9	..	..	1,179 16	396 8	264 14	5,404 4	117 10
59 1	16 14	30 16	1,064 14	..	395 8	9,145 17	397 0
102 7	87 13	..	919 12	277 15	545 0	10,136 3	162 0
51 0	13 3	19 19	1,422 3	..	229 0	5,408 10	166 0
43 8	..	..	2,920 5	..	678 14	9,448 16	251 18
70 10	3 7	..	2,663 1	..	675 5	9,689 16	284 11
86 8	..	..	2,403 8	57 19	437 14	13,495 14	317 11
60 9	2 13	120 16	976 6	186 0	507 13	6,424 9	216 10
44 11	16 15	40 0	876 18	1,524 3	365 9	10,370 16	338 8
50 7	26 10	..	2,187 7	..	273 3	7,762 14	190 0
293 18	51 15	..	3,212 8	5,433 13	4,830 19	34,274 3	466 10
41 5	6 19	156 17	824 19	74 0	468 13	6,541 12	183 10
21 13	5 2	22 11	809 15	..	67 17	3,989 12	218 12
275 7	..	342 1	2,162 4	410 6	1,025 14	20,974 1	344 12
100 4	..	..	2,341 10	..	509 16	8,894 17	227 5
23 5	1 2	..	452 8	..	81 15	4,176 14	97 4
181 17	..	141 8	3,728 10	2,241 3	275 14	17,137 2	245 9
66 15	..	..	3,008 7	..	522 12	8,465 2	168 9
156 6	11 11	..	2,839 15	..	521 13	13,310 0	301 0
61 7	20 0	..	1,604 9	..	216 17	10,081 2	389 0
27 8	..	..	1,290 6	..	95 7	5,267 7	164 4

NAMES of UNIONS.	Amount levied by Assessment.	Received from all other Sources, in Aid of Poor Rate.	Total Amount Received for the Relief, &c., of the Poor.	Amount Expended in Relief, &c., of the Poor.	Amount Expended in Law Charges.	Payments under the Vaccination Extension Act	
						Amount of Fees paid to the Vaccinators.	Outlay for English and Certified Books.
	£. s.	£. s.	£. s.	£. s.	£. s.	£. s.	£. s.
Strand . . .	24,571 11	518 3	25,089 14	13,793 7	222 11	46 2	..
Stratford-on-Avon .	11,388 2	137 8	11,525 10	7,221 14	313 2	21 8	..
Stratton . .	4,280 15	21 3	4,301 18	3,438 11	71 7	..	..
Stroud . . .	18,765 7	172 17	18,938 4	13,410 2	166 9	55 9	..
Sturminster . .	7,228 1	398 11	7,626 12	5,807 6	203 2	14 6	..
Sudbury . . .	20,923 0	239 9	21,162 9	16,163 14	131 3	35 14	..
Sunderland . .	22,754 6	1,064 12	23,818 18	18,233 16	110 13	24 2	..
Swaffham . .	9,130 8	11 11	9,141 19	7,622 18	18 3	21 16	..
Swansea . . .	10,834 15	301 12	11,136 7	8,256 15	93 9	60 10	8 18

T.

Tamworth . .	6,994 16	73 17	7,068 13	5,472 7	78 14	15 6	..
Taunton . . .	13,935 2	141 11	14,076 13	11,603 6	44 17	37 14	0 0
Tavistock . .	9,360 2	168 14	9,528 16	7,448 12	68 8	36 16	..
Teesdale . . .	7,026 11	122 1	7,148 12	5,518 8	80 0	5 8	..
Tenbury . . .	3,700 10	15 14	3,716 4	2,463 15	69 19	47 6	..
Tendring . . .	14,076 11	250 3	14,326 14	9,557 7	7 17	35 12	..
Tenterden . .	7,075 6	131 17	7,207 3	5,789 16	20 9	7 17	..
Tetbury . . .	2,689 11	36 19	2,726 10	1,558 13	116 17	..	..
Tewkesbury . .	7,703 5	67 1	7,770 6	4,921 9	6 12	19 5	..
Thakeham . .	4,527 3	5 14	4,532 17	3,689 1	52 4	9 6	..
Thame . . .	14,431 7	94 11	14,525 18	12,543 19	132 4	4 5	..
Thanet, Isle of .	11,179 19	57 18	11,235 17	7,400 18	35 8	63 8	..
Thetford . . .	9,309 12	82 13	9,392 7	6,659 5	161 1	10 2	..
Thingoe . . .	11,867 10	206 10	12,074 0	9,305 14	76 16	40 4	..
Thirsk . . .	5,143 2	188 0	5,331 2	3,832 9	290 1	6 4	..
Thomas, St. . .	21,324 10	163 4	21,487 14	17,594 17	789 10	32 19	10 18
Thornbury . .	9,222 4	173 11	9,395 15	6,020 15	220 10	7 16	..
Thorne . . .	6,031 16	123 16	6,155 12	4,099 12	121 10	32 2	..
Thrapstone . .	7,352 12	86 12	7,439 4	6,240 17	124 17	8 5	..
Ticehurst . . .	8,440 16	234 11	8,675 7	6,036 9	88 4	13 6	..
Tisbury . . .	7,342 9	124 15	7,467 4	5,700 17	62 11	24 11	..
Tiverton . . .	20,498 16	71 3	20,569 19	16,970 9	216 5	11 7	..
Todmorden . .	8,967 10	454 16	9,422 6	7,231 2	356 18	..	..
Tonbridge . .	12,507 8	35 11	12,542 19	10,886 16	80 12	9 1	..
Torrington . .	8,220 5	40 18	8,261 3	7,070 5	191 15	11 4	..
Totnes . . .	13,557 11	89 17	13,647 8	11,192 16	397 15	29 3	..
Towcester . .	7,385 15	111 19	7,497 14	5,877 4	80 17	..	..
Tregaron . . .	2,992 15	1 17	2,994 12	2,145 14	170 19	..	..
Truro . . .	11,899 18	251 7	12,151 5	9,170 8	262 2	103 10	..
Tunstead and Happing	7,777 15	9 6	7,787 1	5,976 2	43 16	0 14	..
Tynemouth . .	12,850 1	144 5	12,994 6	10,783 4	392 7	107 5	..

U.

Uckfield . . .	8,722 9	144 19	8,867 8	7,012 1	..	54 2	2 4
Ulverstone . .	10,474 4	540 11	11,014 15	7,498 2	41 2	30 4	1 10
Uppingham . .	5,547 18	203 18	5,751 16	4,212 6	42 1	4 13	..
Upton-on-Severn .	7,786 10	247 0	8,033 10	4,673 18	63 6	6 10	..
Uttoxeter . .	4,881 8	12 12	4,894 0	3,415 12	56 15	15 4	..
Uxbridge . .	9,644 18	54 5	9,699 3	5,907 14	186 17	28 1	..

Payments on Account of the Registration Act.		Payments under the Parochial Assessments Act (for Surveys, Valuations, &c)., and Loans repaid under the same.	Payments for or towards the County Rate.	Payments for or towards the County and Local Police Forces.	Money Expended for all other Purposes.	Total Parochial Rates, &c., Expended.	Medical Relief.
Fees to Clergymen and Registrars.	Outlay for Register Offices, Books, Forms, and other Incidental Expenses.						
£. s.	£. s.	£. s.	£. s.	£. s.	£. s.	£. s.	£. s.
130 10	7 12	72 11	9,030 18	..	675 8	23,978 19	374 10
63 11	18 1	..	2,072 19	..	1,142 4	10,852 19	266 13
29 8	0 10	..	541 2	..	105 2	4,186 0	115 5
110 1	9 1	48 0	2,285 7	..	804 3	16,888 12	459 0
30 3	1 16	..	744 9	..	306 10	7,107 12	209 8
83 15	27 6	37 19	3,157 3	..	518 12	20,155 6	592 2
187 17	..	28 10	1,426 4	712 2	982 19	21,706 3	359 9
37 7	5 0	..	1,197 11	..	171 5	9,074 0	253 10
96 6	60 4	4 0	1,351,19	286 0	843 10	11,061 11	190 11
33 12	10 0	..	1,237 19	..	316 1	7,163 19	241 0
101 19	5 8	64 1	1,790 12	..	390 11	14,038 14	547 1
77 4	10 15	84 15	1,165 13	134 13	589 9	9,616 5	200 13
61 16	7 0	31 10	1,094 15	398 8	148 0	7,345 5	159 5
22 6	..	70 10	1,035 13	..	42 13	3,752 2	132 17
77 9	25 0	150 17	2,704 12	..	444 12	13,003 6	402 4
32 17	..	..	701 16	..	411 3	6,963 18	246 0
17 9	1 16	22 17	541 4	323 14	93 3	2,675 13	113 3
46 4	5 9	41 13	2,375 9	..	143 17	7,559 19	295 17
20 4	21 3	..	337 1	..	173 10	4,302 9	173 10
49 14	0 5	76 17	1,391 6	..	553 11	14,752 1	504 10
80 5	0 8	38 8	2,105 7	..	124 15	9,848 17	263 10
54 13	26 0	..	1,824 15	..	327 4	9,063 0	295 19
51 14	..	124 16	1,842 18	..	201 17	11,643 19	370 10
41 12	9 4	111 8	650 5	..	178 11	5,119 14	112 1
128 18	22 5	121 9	2,504 2	..	883 11	22,088 7	649 1
44 12	..	..	2,641 13	..	396 10	9,331 16	196 0
47 18	30 6	..	1,270 7	..	245 14	5,847 9	121 2
33 11	10 0	..	993 6	..	182 1	7,592 17	230 16
49 12	2 18	437 15	915 15	8 15	806 0	8,358 14	322 5
33 9	..	..	563 14	516 7	180 19	7,082 8	212 15
97 16	..	..	1,867 14	..	703 19	19,867 10	511 18
99 7	9 16	344 9	969 3	..	476 4	9,486 19	83 3
69 14	3 14	36 8	1,227 8	..	325 19	12,639 12	517 17
49 3	..	25 1	846 2	..	176 17	8,370 7	156 17
89 17	4 7	39 0	1,483 13	..	602 16	13,839 7	293 19
36 19	4 10	..	964 3	..	225 12	7,189 5	260 11
33 10	..	..	547 6	..	161 11	3,059 0	35 0
126 7	..	..	929 0	..	1,656 7	12,247 14	812 7
45 14	..	..	1,427 0	..	140 17	7,634 3	245 11
179 15	56 6	45 0	1,587 15	187 4	775 5	14,114 1	260 13
52 1	15 0	148 18	1,191 5	..	496 2	8,971 17	487 17
71 13	10 9	25 0	2,955 18	..	298 18	10,932 16	327 14
35 1	..	..	1,027 1	151 6	273 2	5,745 10	180 18
45 9	..	..	2,205 14	..	254 19	7,249 16	231 17
33 13	11 11	103 19	1,109 6	..	161 1	4,907 1	126 19
70 12	10 0	27 0	2,820 6	..	437 15	9,488 5	298 4

NAMES OF UNIONS.	Amount levied by Assessment.		Received from all other Sources, in Aid of Poor Rate.		Total Amount Received for the Relief, &c., of the Poor.		Amount Expended in Relief, &c., of the Poor.		Amount Expended in Law Charges.		Payments under the Vaccination Extension Act			
											Amount of Fees Paid to the Vaccinators.		Outlay for Register and Certificate Books.	
	£.	s.	£.	s.	£.	s.	£.	s.	£.	s.	£.	s.	£.	s.
Wakefield . . .	17,097	13	2,732	13	19,830	6	15,264	17*	805	15	76	7	..	
Wallingford . . .	8,992	5	31	16	9,024	1	8,327	3	73	3	11	6	..	
Walsall . . .	10,364	16	141	9	10,506	5	7,679	7	150	12	27	4	..	
Walsingham . .	14,810	2	27	2	14,837	4	11,171	18	90	1	37	8	..	
Wandsworth and Clapham . . .	21,227	17	173	19	21,401	16	14,017	13	119	8	32	4	5	1(
Waugford . . .	8,127	2	115	17	8,242	19	6,030	7	88	8	36	1	..	
Wantage . . .	11,763	2	144	18	11,908	0	9,453	6	38	6	15	13	..	
Ware	10,548	18	85	3	10,634	1	7,586	7	68	17	..		0	1:
Wareham & Purbeck	8,960		48	14	9,009	2	8,073	14	67	12	17	4	..	
Warminster . . .	14,492	9	189	19	14,682	8	11,457	16	29	13	23	6	..	
Warrington . . .	13,620	9	1,268	19	14,889	8	8,536	13	212	14	16	11	..	
Warwick	17,356	19	231	19	17,588	18	12,121	18	378	14	24	8	..	
Watford . . .	9,658	1	76	13	9,734	14	5,823	19	20	15	22	7	..	
Wayland . . .	6,515	3	139	5	6,654	8	5,917	11	..		5	4	..	
Weardale . . .	4,517	17	46	4	4,564	1	3,742	15	101	7	17	6	..	
Wellingborough . .	10,039	9	20	8	10,059	17	8,378	0	133	5	1	18	..	
Wellington (Salop) .	10,998	3	1,042	10	12,040	13	7,757	19	674	5	34	6	..	
Wellington (Somerset)	11,647	3	215	4	11,862	7	10,479	13	14	3	23	4	..	
Wells	9,587	11	43	8	9,630	19	7,078	19	178	18	6	7	..	
Welwyn . . .	1,199	19	98	10	1,298	9	783	1	..		1	16	..	
Wem	5,056	3	14	8	5,070	11	3,647	8	245	2	9	6	..	
Weobly . . .	4,108	0	45	15	4,153	15	2,902	3	109	19	10	8	..	
Westbourne . . .	4,050	5	76	7	4,126	12	2,932	13	20	0	8	11	..	
West Bromwich . .	17,925	5	317	8	18,242	13	13,264	19	496	19	49	15	..	
Westbury-on-Severn .	4,711	11	46	17	4,758	8	3,217	14	5	3	1	0	..	
Westbury and Whorwelldown . . .	10,580	3	191	18	10,772	1	7,831	18	106	7	1	16	1	1(
West Derby . . .	21,382	0	716	4	22,098	13	8,855	8	311	15	118	13	..	
West Firle . . .	2,792	19	44	11	2,837	10	2,220	8	10	0	8	17	..	
West Ham . . .	15,630	18	359	18	15,990	16	11,325	10	176	15	91	18	..	
West Hampnett . .	6,932	16	154	9	7,087	5	5,437	7	26	1	12	6	12	(
West Ward . . .	2,858	17	18	13	2,877	10	2,563	11	15	12	11	2	..	
Weymouth . . .	8,626	6	444	1	9,070	7	6,791	15	286	18	16	0	..	
Wheatenhurst . .	4,145	10	14	7	4,159	17	2,574	4	121	7	27	9	0	1(
Whitby	5,521	14	359	8	5,881	2	4,617	12	51	8	29	16	..	
Whitchurch (Hants)	3,207	11	67	11	3,275	2	2,611	5	33	1	4	2	..	
Whitechapel . .	28,200	7	2,293	5	30,493	12	16,967	8	195	5	122	17	..	
Whitehaven . . .	6,831	2	186	13	7,017	15	5,340	12	224	7	66	16	..	
Whittlesey . . .	2,539	18	23	12	2,563	10	1,938	8	3	6	7	5	..	
Wigan	17,733	0	239	0	17,972	0	11,726	2	310	16	62	12	..	
Wight (Incorporation of the Isle of) .	17,237	8	47	14	17,285	2	12,557	13	11	13	..		..	
Wigton	5,200	10	139	5	5,339	15	3,844	1	8	11	44	5	1	'
Williton	10,539	14	105	14	10,645	8	9,701	0	158	1	40	14	..	'
Wilton	7,508	3	600	16	8,108	19	6,870	15	17	8	14	18	..	'
Wimborne and Cranborne	7,527	14	235	17	7,763	11	6,947	3	39	2	6	2	..	:
Wincanton . . .	12,851	4	751	10	13,602	14	11,467	1	165	0	9	11	..	(

* In the Wakefield Union, the amount under the 4th Column includes about £2,500 the Union, and payme

Fees to Clergymen and Registrars.	Outlay for Register Offices, Books, Forms, and other Incidental Expenses.	Payments under the Parochial Assessments Act (for Surveys, Valuations, &c.), and Loans repaid under the same.	Payments for or towards the County Rate.	Payments for or towards the County and Local Police Forces.	Money Expended for all other Purposes.	Total Parochial Rates, &c., Expended.	Medical Relief.
£. s.	£. s.	£. s.	£. s.	£. s.	£. s.	£. s.	£. s.
145 10	..	365 10	1,952 4	..	1,659 5	20,269 8	298 6
49 10	40 10	..	1,411 0	..	155 18	10,068 10	367 2
106 6	7 16	..	807 11	..	835 15	9,614 11	222 15
62 18	19 4	..	1,671 6	..	361 13	13,414 8	337 0
102 1	19 19	70 11	3,202 19	4,526 5	456 7	22,553 5	515 10
40 1	27 14	..	1,505 7	..	370 7	8,098 5	213 9
48 5	..	..	2,096 4	..	266 14	11,918 8	285 0
44 18	2 13	233 2	2,010 12	..	239 14	10,186 16	351 5
47 9	..	..	702 10	..	267 3	9,175 12	336 11
54 4	10 0	100 0	1,292 3	..	323 13	13,290 15	449 2
114 15	..	..	2,889 16	..	2,180 7	13,950 16	252 11
109 13	25 0	..	4,081 8	..	1,125 12	17,866 13	354 8
57 8	..	..	2,841 0	..	252 11	9,018 0	334 10
30 1	..	37 8	1,022 3	..	242 14	7,255 1	270 10
34 17	..	..	396 0	225 15	124 13	4,642 13	90 1
62 12	3 11	69 6	1,610 9	..	198 12	10,457 13	271 9
53 9	4 17	200 0	1,079 2	..	1,482 0	11,285 18	189 10
57 17	3 17	202 12	1,134 3	..	333 11	12,237 16	318 11
62 6	2 10	55 13	1,960 19	..	189 6	9,534 18	295 0
6 3	0 4	..	120 5	110 8	1 13	1,023 10	43 10
29 5	1 0	..	855 2	281 0	200 4	5,268 7	189 5
24 19	..	13 11	868 17	..	152 19	4,082 16	162 15
20 14	..	..	496 13	..	186 5	3,664 16	163 0
173 13	10 0	..	2,873 0	..	485 1	17,353 7	318 6
28 12	..	43 10	1,036 17	..	79 13	4,412 9	159 0
47 13	15 0	282 19	1,094 16	..	313 17	9,696 2	259 19
320 9	20 15	..	7,205 2	..	4,199 4	21,031 6	229 18
8 19	8 14	..	435 8	..	42 1	2,734 7	89 17
69 11	..	..	3,827 8	..	366 2	15,857 4	480 12
48 10	16 9	..	923 7	..	335 2	6,811 10	519 0
19 17	3 16	..	480 10	..	44 2	3,138 10	75 15
55 6	10 17	37 4	809 15	..	317 3	8,324 18	311 10
25 18	6 18	51 0	1,125 16	..	189 3	4,122 5	133 9
57 3	..	..	558 11	..	352 18	5,667 8	116 3
21 16	4 19	..	606 13	..	209 8	3,491 9	140 14
257 11	51 0	..	2,745 0	4,979 14	3,292 17	28,611 12	450 0
94 19	0 11	..	826 16	..	271 14	6,825 15	127 5
26 11	8 0	..	264 5	352 7	97 8	2,697 10	72 0
242 12	24 16	..	5,539 16	..	474 14	18,331 8	298 13
..	1 6	237 3	3,275 9	214 15	529 10	16,827 9	..
68 14	1 16	..	1,007 17	..	190 14	5,167 3	137 10
54 5	..	25 0	1,128 12	..	213 12	11,321 4	450 3
29 19	15 0	112 15	599 16	564 1	75 4	8,299 16	320 1
48 18	20 1	..	893 1	..	365 15	8,320 2	328 17
65 16	4 2	139 10	1,398 5	..	197 6	13,446 11	422 10

to Pensioners by way of Loan, and to Paupers on account of Townships out of
on account of Bastardy.

NAMES of UNIONS.	Amount levied by Assessment.	Received from all other Sources, in Aid of Poor Rate.	Total Amount Received for the Relief, &c., of the Poor.	Amount Expended in Relief, &c., of the Poor.	Amount Expended in Law Charges.	Payments under the Vaccination, &c. Act.	
						Amount of Fees Paid to the Vaccinators.	Outlay for Register and Certificate Books.
	£. s.	£. s.	£. s.	£. s.	£. s.	£. s.	£. s.
Winchcombe . .	4,885 8	21 12	4,907 0	3,333 14	..	..	..
Winchester (New) .	11,075 6	159 5	11,234 11	7,168 16	641 18	11 16	..
Windsor	8,366 4	374 6	8,740 10	6,602 4	..	30 11	..
Winslow	6,177 5	156 12	6,333 17	5,587 19	..	..	..
Wirrall	5,060 8	42 7	5,102 15	2,634 15	140 1	23 9	..
Wisbeach . . .	18,222 0	522 14	18,744 14	14,573 8	311 11	..	..
Witham	7,118 1	226 1	7,344 2	5,483 19	25 1	0 16	..
Witney	12,458 9	285 17	12,744 6	10,918 15	262 7	..	..
Woburn	6,136 14	41 8	6,178 2	5,207 12	12 13	2 9	..
Wokingham . . .	8,802 3	76 15	8,878 18	7,724 0	162 18	10 18	..
Wolstanton & Burslem	16,162 14	119 0	16,281 14	9,140 15	268 18	54 7	..
Wolverhampton . .	14,224 3	472 0	14,696 3	9,928 10	294 19	177 14	..
Woodbridge . . .	13,710 19	96 4	13,807 3	11,204 2	43 10	6 9	..
Woodstock . . .	8,752 17	53 14	8,806 11	6,967 5	128 4	..	0 15
Worcester . . .	9,338 1	557 6	9,895 7	6,240 11	63 0	12 7	0 15
Worksop	8,246 14	44 8	8,291 2	5,380 1	236 7	35 9	..
Wortley	10,345 1	1,453 12	11,798 13	7,457 12	543 8	33 13	1 6
Wrexham . . .	15,485 0	182 10	15,667 10	10,577 2	136 0	20 18	1 6
Wycombe . . .	22,173 13	270 10	22,444 3	17,697 6	339 11	..	..
Y.							
Yarmouth (Great) .	9,080 15	256 3	9,336 18	8,752 0	194 10	14 16	..
Yeovil	11,009 16	57 10	11,067 6	9,208 3	..	17 13	..
York	15,990 4	299 18	16,290 2	11,600 2	717 7	85 19	7 12

Payments on Account of the Registration Act.		Payments under the Parochial Assessments Act (for Surveys, Valuations, &c.), and Loans repaid under the same.	Payments for or towards the County Rate.	Payments for or towards the County and Local Police Forces.	Money Expended for all other Purposes.	Total Parochial Rates, &c., Expended.	Medical Relief.
Fees to Clergymen and Registrars.	Outlay for Register Offices, Books Forms, and other Incidental Expenses.						
£. s.	£. s.	£. s.	£. s.	£. s.	£. s.	£. s.	£. s.
28 6	..	..	832 19	745 8	113 16	5,054 3	153 0
70 15	..	..	2,163 13	..	331 16	10,388 14	317 6
61 17	..	..	453 18	..	1,035 8	8,183 18	205 2
24 9	1 10	7 13	751 11	..	157 12	6,530 14	236 9
110 1	14 19	..	493 1	577 4	719 17	4,713 7	127 10
28 15	..	..	2,116 2	802 16	931 18	18,764 10	623 6
70 9	..	..	1,395 19	..	723 9	7,699 13	214 16
69 8	..	0 11	1,659 4	..	196 2	13,108 7	525 19
36 6	1 15	..	1,220 1	..	83 8	6,564 4	202 10
33 17	10 10	5 2	1,176 15	..	240 0	9,364 0	264 16
117 4	..	37 14	2,865 8	1,667 10	644 9	14,796 5	230 9
230 1	..	..	3,615 3	..	920 10	15,166 17	354 19
71 4	12 4	244 2	2,400 4	..	279 6	14,261 1	455 0
34 18	..	93 8	1,133 7	..	201 14	8,558 16	286 5
60 2	15 12	..	3,123 3	..	436 13	9,952 3	200 10
49 5	..	22 15	1,789 11	..	408 4	7,921 12	174 0
71 7	..	..	1,230 6	..	2,575 17	11,913 9	115 5
133 1	1 17	44 3	3,009 2	..	1,036 0	14,959 9	324 0
107 9	..	..	1,537 7	..	1,863 2	21,544 15	657 0
74 13	..	..	..	..	208 18	9,244 17	82 5
95 14	..	..	1,490 3	..	227 13	11,039 6	397 0
138 7	8 4	25 18	2,916 12	..	532 8	16,032 9	225 5

NAMES OF COUNTIES, PARISHES, &c.	Amount levied by Assessment.	Received from all other Sources, in Aid of Poor Rate.	Total Amount Received for the Relief, &c., of the Poor.	Amount Expended in Relief, &c., of the Poor.	Amount Expended in Law Charges.	Amount of Fees Paid to the Vaccinator
CHESTER, CITY.	£. s.	£. s.	£. s.	£. s.	£. s.	£.
UNITED PARISHES. { Baptist, St. John · · Bridget, St. · · · Martin, St. · · · Mary-on-the-Hill, St. · · Michael, St. · · · Olave, St. · · · · Peter, St. · · · · Trinity, the Holy · · }	9,146 13	10 0	9,156 13	5,967 2	62 19	28
Total · · ·	9,146 13	10 0	9,156 13	5,967 2	62 19	28
DERBY.						
Appletree Hundred.						
Alkmonton · · · · ·	32 14	··	32 14	5 3	··	··
Atlow · · · · · ·	76 1	0 1	76 2	27 6	··	··
Bentley, Hungay · · ·	33 3	··	33 3	2 15	··	··
Biggin · · · · · ·	97 12	0 12	98 4	89 10	··	··
Brailsford · · · · ·	392 11	··	392 11	298 7	··	··
Cubley · · · · · ·	210 1	··	210 1	160 13	··	··
Edlaston and Wyaston · ·	80 0	··	80 0	38 17	··	··
Hollington · · · · ·	146 15	8 11	155 6	103 8	··	4
Hulland · · · · ·	60 19	12 7	73 6	41 14	0 7	··
Hulland Ward · · ·	70 17	··	70 17	42 12	7 2	··
Hulland Ward Intacks · ·	29 2	2 12	31 14	16 6	··	··
Longford · · · ·	251 17	5 18	257 15	265 3	··	··
Marston Montgomery · · ·	170 0	110 0	280 0	242 3	··	··
Mercaston · · · · ·	73 8	··	73 8	63 4	··	··
Norbury and Roston · ·	250 0	1 15	251 15	152 15	··	··
Osmaston · · · · ·	137 18	5 0	142 18	101 7	··	··
Rodsley · · · · ·	49 11	··	49 11	49 11	··	··
Shirley · · · · ·	135 0	··	135 0	80 16	··	0 10
Snelston · · · · ·	154 3	3 4	157 7	79 10	··	··
Sturston · · · · ·	203 10	··	203 10	117 6	8 16	··
Stydd · · · · ·	23 4	··	23 4	12 0	··	··
Yeaveley · · · · ·	82 17	6 18	89 15	55 19	··	0
Yeldersley · · · · ·	120 2	5 14	125 16	62 18	··	··
High Peake Hundred.						
Blackwell · · · · ·	37 14	··	37 14	21 6	··	··
Rowland · · · · ·	8 9	··	8 9	7 16	··	··
Wormhill · · · · ·	226 4	··	226 4	79 10	56 11	1
Youlgrave · · · · ·	335 8	10 2	345 10	293 7	··	··
Morleston and Litchurch Hundred.						
Clifton and Compton · · ·	258 0	··	258 0	157 8	13 14	7

POOR LAW AMENDMENT ACT.

Vac- Act.	Payments on Account of the Registration Act.		Payments under the Parochial Assessments Act (for Surveys, Valuations, &c.), and Loans repaid under the same.	Payments for or towards the County Rate.	Payments for or towards the County and Local Police Forces.	Money Expended for all other Purposes.	Total Parochial Rates, &c., Expended.	Medical Relief.
	Fees to Clergymen and Registrars.	Outlay for Register Offices, Books Forms, and other Incidental Expenses.						
s.	£. *s.*	£. *s.*	£. *s.*	£. *s.*	£. *s.*	£. *s.*	£. *s.*	£. *s.*
4	83 2	..	..	2,783 17	..	779 8	9,709 17	130 14
4	83 2	..	..	2,783 17	..	779 8	9,709 17	130 14
	0 3	..	..	14 6	..	6 12	26 4	..
	0 10	..	..	31 6	..	8 2	67 4	5 0
	0 2	..	..	21 3	..	5 13	29 13	..
	0 9	..	..	13 1	..	7 16	110 16	5 6
	1 5	..	..	113 10	..	..	413 2	..
	0 9	..	..	43 14	..	5 5	210 1	8 0
3	..	0 6	..	31 3	4 4	6 18	81 8	..
	..	..	..	26 3	..	12 13	147 7	..
	0 13	..	..	17 1	..	13 3	72 18	5 10
	..	0 18	..	24 12	..	2 16	78 0	..
	..	..	..	7 11	..	11 7	35 4	..
	1 13	..	..	..	..	6 0	272 16	8 0
	1 12	..	..	47 12	..	17 14	309 1	5 5
	0 5	..	..	..	..	..	63 9	3 0
	0 17	..	..	61 4	..	24 18	239 14	7 16
	..	0 16	..	25 0	..	15 15	142 18	4 10
	0 6	..	..	20 0	..	..	69 17	3 0
	1 1	..	..	40 0	..	3 0	125 13	..
	..	..	..	44 6	..	56 5	180 1	10 15
	..	1 15	..	38 5	..	14 7	180 9	..
	..	..	..	7 19	..	..	19 19	..
	0 11	..	..	20 7	..	6 6	83 12	5 9
	..	0 10	..	27 7	..	20 18	111 13	4 4
	..	..	..	13 8	..	3 0	37 14	..
	0 5	..	..	5 12	..	4 0	17 13	..
	..	..	..	65 0	..	4 12	206 13	..
	4 8	..	..	46 4	..	5 5	349 4	1 11
	..	2 6	..	45 8	5 11	26 9	258 0	..

U

NAMES OF COUNTIES, PARISHES, &c.	Amount levied by Assessment.		Received from all other Sources, in Aid of Poor Rate.		Total Amount Received for the Relief, &c., of the Poor.		Amount Expended in Relief, &c., of the Poor.		Amount Expended in Law Charges.		Amount Paid the Vaccine
	£.	s.	£.	s.	£.	s.	£.	s.	£.	s.	£.
DERBY—*continued*.											
Repton and Gresley Hundred.											
Catton	No Levy.		..		..		..		..		..
Wirksworth Hundred.											
Ashborne	831	7	32	9	863	16	684	16	15	9	..
Ballidon	72	13	..		72	13	35	4	..		..
Bentley, Fenny	77	11	14	10	92	1	50	0	..		..
Bonsall	438	12	5	15	444	7	236	3	71	0	..
Bradbourne	212	12	..		212	12	165	7	..		..
Brassington	349	11	30	6	379	17	209	18	..		..
Callow	87	10	0	2	87	12	61	1	0	6	..
Carsington	152	13	2	0	154	13	135	7	..		..
Eaton and Alsop . . .	70	13	6	4	76	17	12	5	..		..
Elton	156	8	4	2	160	10	69	17	..		1
Hartington, Town Quarter .	161	3	4	17	166	0	102	15	..		..
Hartington, Nether Quarter .	192	0	..		192	0	183	13	..		..
Hognaston	126	10	5	14	132	4	80	16	9	1	..
Hopton	60	4	..		60	4	37	9	..		..
Ible	19	10	5	13	25	3	15	7	..		..
Kirk Ireton	189	2	6	0	195	2	147	18	..		1
Kniveton	153	0	..		153	0	66	8	..		..
Mappleton	114	8	2	9	116	17	85	2	..		..
Middleton by Wirksworth .	215	13	19	17	235	10	168	9	3	11	..
Offcoat and Underwood . .	230	1	3	12	233	13	117	9	..		6
Parwick	169	11	..		169	11	85	10	11	4	2
Thorpe	98	12	..		98	12	32	8	..		..
Tissington, with the extra-parochial place of Lea. . .	157	11	..		157	11	132	9	..		5
Total	8,083	15	316	4	8,399	19	5,484	1	197	1	29 1
DEVON.											
United Parishes of the City of Exeter	8,750	0	234	6	8,984	6	6,769	7	304	6	29
Plymouth	11,000	0	614	2	11,614	2	10,207	0	221	3	75
Stoke Damerell	9,262	8	..		9,262	8	7,639	16	304	4	..
Total	29,012	8	848	8	29,860	16	24,616	3	829	13	104
GLOUCESTER.											
United Parishes of the City of Bristol	25,993	18	3,073	18	29,067	16	22,021	2	472	2	42 1
KENT.											
United Parishes of the City of Canterbury	6,668	4	305	3	6,973	7	4,568	17	132	1	12 1

r the Vaccination Act. Outlay for Register and Certificate Books.	Payments on Account of the Registration Act. Fees to Clergymen and Registrars.	Outlay for Register Offices, Books Forms, and other Incidental Expenses.	Payments under the Parochial Assessments Act (for Surveys, Valuations, &c.), and Loans repaid under the same.	Payments for or towards the County Rate.	Payments for or towards the County and Local Police Forces.	Money Expended for all other Purposes.	Total Parochial Rates, &c., Expended.	Medical Relief.
£. s.	£. s.	£. s.	£. s.	£. s.	£. s.	£. s.	£. s.	£. s.
..	..	..	..	29 6	..	..	29 6	..
..	5 19	..	..	63 7	..	41 11	811 2	12 0
..	..	..	..	37 9	..	..	72 13	0 10
..	1 1	..	..	26 4	..	20 7	97 12	4 0
..	5 3	..	..	52 2	..	46 4	410 12	5 9
..	..	0 14	..	46 10	..	..	212 11	..
..	2 2	..	..	81 14	..	86 2	379 16	..
..	0 8	..	..	21 3	0 9	10 14	94 1	1 19
..	..	1 3	..	27 18	..	12 14	177 2	8 12
..	0 2	..	..	26 14	..	33 3	72 4	..
..	1 8	..	..	39 0	..	48 15	160 10	..
..	1 3	..	..	51 11	..	15 18	171 7	7 4
..	0 5	..	..	45 16	..	74 11	204 0	..
..	0 7	..	..	37 2	..	3 16	131 0	0 10
..	0 1	..	..	18 3	..	6 1	62 0	..
0 1	0 16	..	..	5 14	0 12	2 18	24 12	..
..	..	1 7	..	35 17	..	8 12	194 10	5 11
..	0 8	..	..	43 11	..	..	111 6	5 0
..	..	3 2	..	27 3	..	5 18	118 11	4 10
..	1 0	..	..	22 7	..	30 7	227 16	6 4
..	..	0 8	..	69 5	..	40 0	232 17	6 3
..	1 0	..	..	57 14	..	11 19	169 11	..
..				40 17	..	..	73 13	..
..	1 0	..	..	68 2	..	..	206 11	..
1 4	35 12	13 5	..	1,825 11	10 16	788 4	8,385 6	144 18
..	176 18	7 12	..	..	..	800 13	8,088 4	220 0
..	152 5	15 8	..	..	..	943 6	11,614 2	178 0
..	119 4	10 0	..	627 3	..	1,209 8	9,909 15	120 0
..	448 7	33 0	..	627 3	..	2,953 7	29,612 1	518 0
..	231 12	41 13	49 7	..	..	3,677 4	26,535 16	587 14
..	81 9	27 10	17 12	1,570 15	..	536 4	6,947 2	95 4

NAMES of COUNTIES, PARISHES, &c.	Amount levied by Assessment.		Received from all other Sources, in Aid of Poor Rate.		Total Amount Received for the Relief, &c., of the Poor.		Amount Expended in Relief, &c., of the Poor.		Amount Expended in Law Charges.		Amount of Fees paid to the Vaccinators
LANCASTER.	£.	s.	£.	s.	£.	s.	£.	s.	£.	s.	£.
Lonsdale Hundred.											
Arkholm-with-Cawood	219	6	6	17	226	3	131	14	25	12	..
Bare	57	2	1	5	58	7	26	1	0	15	..
Bolton-by-the-Sands	458	11	52	10	511	1	335	15	9	0	..
Borwick	195	14	0	11	196	5	208	18	3	4	..
Burrow-with-Burrow	296	18	..		296	18	188	11	65	0	..
Cansfield, or Cantsfield	83	13	..		83	13	43	3	..		2
Caton	520	9	100	13	621	2	452	9	2	12	..
Claughton	86	6	..		86	6	41	2	1	12	..
Dalton-with-Hutton	119	0	4	8	123	8	55	3	1	14	..
Farleton	103	2	..		103	2	24	16	..		..
Gressingham	207	3	9	14	216	17	150	17	18	10	..
Halton-with-Aughton	486	14	28	3	514	17	404	0	1	1	..
Heysham	395	5	14	6	409	11	133	9	4	10	..
Hornby	230	18	..		230	18	139	8	..		..
Ireby	78	7	..		78	7	58	7	..		..
Kellet, Nether	226	16	28	18	255	14	190	16	2	17	..
Kellet, Over	331	2	11	9	342	11	245	5	12	15	..
Leck	163	1	3	0	166	1	98	3	3	15	..
Melling-with-Wrayton	118	15	..		118	15	76	18	..		..
Poulton	153	17	7	3	161	0	101	10	1	9	..
Quernmoor	295	3	7	3	302	6	229	13	1	12	..
Roberindale	152	13	0	9	153	2	111	13	..		..
Slyne-with-Hest	176	8	60	6	236	14	155	19	..		..
Tatham, Lower End	245	13	0	10	246	3	179	11	..		..
Tatham, Upper End	277	13	0	10	278	3	167	3	..		..
Torrisholme	114	11	7	11	122	2	76	0	1	3	..
Tunstal	107	4	..		107	4	64	8	..		..
Wennington	89	3	9	0	98	3	87	14	0	19	..
Whittington	324	19	3	18	328	17	210	8	..		..
Wray-with-Botton	338	19	47	11	386	10	315	2	1	13	..
Salford Hundred.											
Clifton	530	16	10	9	541	5	290	7	..		..
Worsley	1,728	7	65	5	1,793	12	1,302	5	..		..
Total	8,913	8	481	9	9,394	17	6,296	8	159	13	2 6
LEICESTER.											
Sparkenhoe Hundred.											
Higham-on-the-Hill & Lindley	368	3	..		368	3	255	16	..		..
Ratcliffe Culey	192	13	..		192	13	120	18	..		..
Sibson, Wellesborough, and Temple Hall	104	19	65	0	169	19	178	19	8	0	..
Stapleton	205	8	15	6	220	14	141	11	19	18	..
Stoke Golding	507	8	3	5	510	13	468	19	..		..
Sutton Cheney	112	5	30	2	142	7	49	8	1	2	..
Witherley	270	19	5	4	276	3	221	15	..		1 17
Totals	1,761	15	118	17	1,880	12	1,437	6	29	0	1 7

Outlay for Register and Certificate Books.	Payments on Account of the Registration Act.		Payments under the Parochial Assessments Act (for Surveys, Valuations, &c.), and Loans repaid under the same.	Payments for or towards the County Rate.	Payments for or towards the County and Local Police Forces.	Money Expended for all other Purposes.	Total Parochial Rates, &c., Expended.	Medical Relief.
	Fees to Clergymen and Registrars.	Outlay for Register Offices, Books Forms, and other Incidental Expenses.						
£. s.	£. s.	£. s.	£. s.	£. s.	£. s.	£. s.	£. s.	£. s.
..	0 15	..	..	..	59 5	7 17	225 3	..
..	..	0 12	..	..	16 1	16 13	60 2	0 15
..	1 8	0 2	..	68 10	..	0 19	415 14	6 16
..	..	..	..	25 13	..	2 0	239 15	..
..	..	0 9	..	35 7	7 10	..	296 17	1 0
..	..	..	..	29 3	..	6 0	80 12	..
..	7 11	..	..	108 0	..	14 3	584 15	4 15
..	0 2	0 1	..	26 12	..	4 19	74 8	1 13
..	..	0 7	..	34 16	..	15 8	107 8	3 0
..	0 2	..	7 5	20 12	..	3 11	56 6	..
..	0 14	0 1	..	39 6	..	..	209 8	..
..	1 16	0 7	..	94 1	..	11 18	513 3	39 5
..	3 12	..	..	73 15	8 5	116 14	340 5	..
..	0 15	..	..	41 15	..	50 12	232 10	0 15
..	0 13	..	..	21 0	..	18 5	98 5	0 10
..	0 7	1 0	..	49 16	..	..	244 16	..
..	1 11	..	..	59 16	..	7 1	326 8	3 1
..	0 16	..	..	47 10	..	5 18	156 2	..
..	..	1 11	..	..	27 7	8 8	114 4	..
..	..	1 15	..	..	47 9	19 19	172 2	2 3
..	1 13	..	..	105 10	..	3 1	341 9	1 2
..	0 15	..	..	35 1	5 15	1 9	154 13	0 5
..	..	1 4	0 1	11 0	53 15	14 15	236 14	0 6
..	1 8	..	..	48 0	2 8	16 16	248 3	3 5
..	1 5	..	..	53 0	..	9 19	231 7	0 7
..	..	1 5	..	..	32 19	13 0	124 7	1 10
..	..	..	6 0	24 15	5 17	..	101 0	..
..	0 11	..	..	23 14	..	..	112 18	..
..	2 0	..	..	84 16	12 8	7 1	316 13	0 4
..	2 1	..	..	65 19	•	8 17	393 12	1 5
..	2 8	..	..	150 9	..	48 6	491 10	8 0
..	26 13	1 0	..	264 12	197 5	186 1	1,977 16	40 10
..	58 16	9 14	13 6	1,642 8	476 4	619 10	9,278 5	102 8
..	1 5	..	..	74 13	16 12	19 11	367 17	8 10
..	0 18	..	..	35 16	7 19	9 0	174 11	5 0
..	..	..	..	80 17	..	..	267 16	..
..	0 6	..	..	42 6	9 8	6 2	219 11	4 4
..	..	..	..	58 4	..	..	527 3	..
..	0 16	..	..	51 10	..	4 15	107 11	5 0
..	..	1 18	..	57 14	..	..	283 4	6 18
..	3 5	1 18	..	401 0	33 19	39 8	1,947 13	29 12

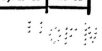

NAMES OF COUNTIES, PARISHES, &c.	Amount levied by Assessment.	Received from all other Sources, in Aid of Poor Rate.	Total Amount Received for the Relief, &c., of the Poor.	Amount Expended in Relief, &c., of the Poor.	Amount Expended in Law Charges.

MIDDLESEX.

Ossulston Hund., Finsbury Division

	£. s.	£. s.	£. s.	£. s.	£. s.
James, St. and St. John, Clerk-enwell	24,114 12	2,441 16	26,556 8	12,065 12	1616 7
Luke, St.	23,233 0	1,636 2	24,869 2	13,558 0	102 13
Mary, St., Islington	18,985 6	3,839 15	22,825 1	7,033 15	128 17
Sepulchre, St.	2,508 4	44 15	2,553 19	1,695 3	22 4

Ossulston Hund., Holborn Division.

Giles-in-the-Fields, St. and St. George, Bloomsbury.	25,032 7	777 8	25,809 15	14,506 9	
Mary-le-bone, St.	93,564 2	2,636 17	96,200 19		
Pancras, St.	54,829 14	1,429 8	56,259 2	23,806 18	

Ossulston Hundred, Tower Division.

Leonard, St., Shoreditch.	24,072 14	3,585 19	27,658 13	19,058 2	

Westminster, City and Liberty.

George, St., Hanover Square.	42,136 12	1,478 18	43,615 10	16,664 2	
James, St.	20,382 9	1,196 5	21,578 14	11,114 4	
Margaret, St. and St. John the Evangelist	19,271 0	79 17	19,350 17	10,735 9	
Totals	348,130 0	19,147 0			

NORFOLK.

Holt Hundred.

Brinton	223 19	1 10	225 9	180 5	
Melton Constable and Burgh Parva	184 11	..	184 11	129 19	
United Parishes of the City of Norwich	26,004 10	149 16	26,154 6	24,379 6	
Totals	26,413 0	151 6			271 18

OXFORD.

United Parishes of the City of Oxford	5,193 11	1,405 5	6,598 16	5,698 2	944 2

SALOP.

Bradford, North, Hundred, Whitchurch Division.

Whitchurch.	2,619 11	37 13	2,657 4	1,710 19	20 13

* The amount paid for Salaries to Officers, &c., included in this

After the Vac- tension Act. Outlay for Register and Certificate Books.	Payments on Account of the Registration Act.		Payments under the Parochial Assessments Act (for Survey, Valuations, &c.), and Loans repaid under the same.	Payments for or towards the County Rate.	Payments for or towards the County and Local Police Forces.	Money Expended for all other Purposes.	Total Parochial Rates, &c., Expended.	Medical Relief.
	Fees to Clergymen and Registrars.	Outlay for Register Offices, Books, Forms, and other Incidental Expenses.						
£. s.	£. s.	£. s.	£. s.	£. s.	£. s.	£. s.	£. s.	£. s.
0 6	179 8	11 13	..	2,527 17	6,981 15	2,477 12	25,880 13	264 18
..	188 6	11 17	..	1,908 18	3,274 3	4,445 4	23,663 15	102 17
0 5	154 8	..	28 19	3,076 11	5,294 16	6,188 8	21,947 0	291 18
16 13	..	..	..	199 12	342 3	269 19	2,550 3	63 0
..	170 12	10 15	..	3,476 19	5,998 12	339 0	24,664 6	1,207 12
..	437 17	..	..	15,330 6	27,192 18	4,799 10	93,689 16	1,633 16
..	667 10	..	..	6,821 16	13,984 0	9,239 15	55,486 6	928 4
..	335 14	..	500 0	2,558 8	4,360 9	136 18	27,110 10	412 18
..	179 4	13 3	..	8,694 19	14,819 18	337 5	41,076 0	701 0
2 9	98 17	8 9	..	3,863 13	5,987 1	1,115 5	22,263 17	350 0
0 12	182 2	10 0	..	2,387 12	4,083 6	1,901 7	19,392 0	317 10
20 5	2,593 18	65 17	528 19	50,846 11	92,319 1	31,250 3	357,724 6	6,273 13
..	..	..	..	30 16	..	5 9	225 9	5 0
..	..	..	..	55 0	..	34 15	219 14	10 0
1 12	171 10	..	..	..	..	238 7	25,053 14	586 3
1 12	171 10	..	..	85 16	..	278 11	25,498 17	601 3
..	79 9	..	..	..	..	68 6	6,789 19	70 0
..	20 2	..	..	274 18	84 17	245 2	2,359 16	65 0

have been inserted in Column 4, under the head of Relief to the Poor.

NAMES OF COUNTIES, PARISHES, &c.	Amount levied by Assessment.	Received from all other Sources, in Aid of Poor Rate.	Total Amount Received for the Relief, &c., of the Poor.	Amount Expended in Relief, &c., of the Poor.	Amount Expended in Law Charges.	
SALOP—*continued.*	£. *s.*	£. *s.*	£. *s.*	£. *s.*	£. *s.*	£
Chirbury Hundred.						
Brompton and Riston . . .	138 5	..	138 5	91 18	..	
Chirbury	1,123 12	10 15	1,134 7	782 10	22 14	
Worthen	1,594 5	46 4	1,640 9	1,478 13	42 4	
Oswestry Hundred.						
*Felton, West	344 3	0 3	344 6	154 9	..	
Kinnerley	670 3	..	670 3	511 2	..	
Knockin	103 6	..	103 6	59 17	..	
Llanyblodwell	420 5	..	420 5	..	..	
Llanymynech and Trefneual .	135 9	7 15	143 4	74 12	..	
Martin's, St.	486 14	..	486 14	348 13	..	
*Oswestry (Parish) . . .	1,142 18	..	1,142 18	789	..	
*Oswestry (Town) . . .	1,142 7	..	1,142 7	789 13	*...	15
Ruyton-of-the-Eleven-Towns .	394 3	..	394 3	262 3	..	15
Soughton	92 0	..	92 0	53 13	..	5
Syllatin	389 13	..	389 13	264 1	..	
Whittington	586 13	..	586 13	203 13	..	
Shrewsbury Town.						
Alkmond, St.	592 7	28 4	620 11	531 6	1 14	
Chad, St	2,188 9	430 1	2,618 10	2,210 0	33 18	
Holy Cross and St. Giles . .	679 19	74 14	754 13	445 1	1 11	
Julian, St.	499 1	94 9	593 10	494 5	0 9	
Mary, St.	1,145 6	88 8	1,233 14	1,071 17	..	
Meole Brace	542 16	..	542 16	399 19	..	
Totals . . .	17,031 5	818 6	17,849 11	12,727 17	123 3	25
SOUTHAMPTON.						
Alton Hundred, North Division.						
Bramshott	457 0	0 18	457 18	394 12	8 2	
Duckenfield	129 19	11 13	141 12	122 16	..	
Kingsley	229 9	..	229 9	176 1	..	
Bishop's Sutton Hundred.						
Headley	764 3	8 0	772 3	510 15	1 16	
Crondall Hundred, Basingstoke Division.						
Aldershott	304 10	53 14	358 4	349 18	..	
Cove	234 2	4 18	239 0	149 2	..	
Farnborough	225 16	..	225 16	132 18	..	
Hawley	523 18	11 10	535 8	379 2	..	
Long Sutton	244 7	6 11	250 18	208 17	9 5	
Yateley	249 15	39 19	289 14	193 13	..	

* No Returns have been received from the Parishes of West Felton, &c.

Outlay for Register and Certificate Books.	Fees to Clergymen and Registrars.	Outlay for Register Offices, Books, Forms, and other Incidental Expenses.	Payments under the Parochial Assessments Act (for Surveys, Valuations, &c.), and Loans repaid under the same.	Payments for or towards the County Rate.	Payments for or towards the County and Local Police Forces.	Money Expended for all other Purposes.	Total Parochial Rates, &c., Expended.	Medical Relief.
£ s.	£ s.	£ s.	£ s.	£ s.	£ s.	£ s.	£ s.	£ s.
..	0 13	..	..	39 17	..	5 13	138 1	2 6
..	3 14	0 3	..	152 13	46 19	10 19	1,021 10	22 6
..	4 5	..	..	188 9	..	18 15	1,732 6	38 15
..	0 4	..	..	94 17	34 10	40 15	324 15	..
..	..	..	..	97 5	40 10	22 19	671 16	..
..	..	..	..	25 8	8 9	5 10	99 4	..
..	2 16	..	..	89 13	..	..	92 9	..
..	..	..	..	38 1	11 14	3 0	127 7	..
..	7 7	..	..	90 3	37 11	2 19	486 13	24 9
..	..	..	..	169 19	63 0	114 14	1,142 6	..
..	..	..	..	186 19	68 0	74 16	1,119 8	..
..	..	..	..	70 12	23 10	..	371 5	..
..	..	..	..	19 3	5 18	7 0	90 14	5 0
..	..	..	..	82 9	25 7	2 16	374 13	10 0
..	0 7	..	..	191 13	59 0	132 0	586 13	17 10
..	4 17	..	..	53 9	17 16	111 19	721 1	21 12
..	36 3	21 5	..	..	..	189 8	2,490 14	114 18
..	4 8	..	..	186 5	..	122 2	759 7	21 3
..	12 17	..	..	..	..	11 17	519 8	20 1
..	20 4	0 11	..	43 1	..	..	1,205 13	52 7
..	..	4 5	..	57 17	43 4	11 0	516 5	47 13
..	117 17	26 4	..	2,222 11	575 5	1,133 4	16,951 4	463 0
..	3 12	..	..	83 18	..	16 5	506 9	25 0
..	0 6	..	..	3 6	..	1 13	128 1	9 15
..	2 1	..	..	29 8	11 19	10 0	229 9	10 0
..	5 16	..	..	26 19	8 19	122 1	676 6	..
..	1 14	..	..	44 2	..	23 10	419 4	..
..	2 1	..	..	43 0	..	20 14	214 17	12 17
..	..	0 15	..	63 6	..	27 11	224 10	10 10
..	..	2 8	..	97 5	..	29 0	507 15	19 19
..	..	0 13	..	43 14	..	..	262 9	23 8
..	1 8	0 1	..	58 2	..	33 0	286 4	13 0

and Oswestry Township; last year's Return is therefore inserted.

NAMES OF COUNTIES, PARISHES, &c.	Amount levied by Assessment.	Received from all other Sources in Aid of Poor Rate.	Total Amount Received for the Relief, &c. of the Poor.	Amount Expended in Relief, &c. of the Poor.	Amount Expended in Law Charges.
	£. s.	£. s.	£. s.	£. s.	£. s.
SOUTHAMPTON—*continued.*					
Fawley Hundred, Fawley Division.					
Avington	103 14	..	103 14	63 18	..
Overton Hundred, Kingsclere Division.					
Laverstoke	No Levy.				
Alverstoke Parish and Gosport Town	3,301 0	260 13	3,561 13	2,518 7	52 16
United Parishes of the Town and County of the Town of Southampton	12,574 3	117 13	12,691 16	7,627 17	286 11
Totals . . .	19,341 16	515 9	19,857 5	12,827 16	358 10
STAFFORD.					
Offlow, North, Hundred.					
Haselour	45 1	..	45 1	22 6	7 12
Pirehill, South, Hundred.					
Ronton Abbey	15 11	..	15 11	5 17	..
Totmanslow, North, Hundred.					
Alstonefield	325 11	9 14	335 5	221 3	..
Blore with Swincoe . . .	109 18	..	109 18	83 11	..
Calton in Blore	25 16	..	25 16	14 1	..
Grindon Town and Parish .	194 18	19 2	214 0	153 4	..
Ilam, Casterton, and Throwley	114 14	..	114 14	74 13	..
Okeover	49 3	..	49 3	37 12	..
Totmanslow, South Hundred.					
Butterton	160 5	14 6	174 11	126 15	..
Calton-in-Mayfield . . .	51 11	0 6	51 17	33 8	..
Calton-in-Waterfall . . .	24 15	..	24 15	9 14	..
Culwick	..	..	..	33 6	..
Ellastone	125 14	7 19	133 13	108 16	1 2
Mayfield	165 4	31 12	196 16	88 9	..
Prestwood	27 5	14 4	41 9	41 14	..
Ramshorn, or Ramsor . .	91 6	..	91 6	69 15	2 6
Stanton	115 6	..	115 6	85 13	..
Waterfall	137 17	5 4	143 1	98 4	2 0
Wetton	246 12	1 17	248 9	170 15	29 0
Woodhouses	9 18	..	9 18	4 19	..
Wotton	114 18	..	114 18	95 18	..
Totals . . .	2,151 3	104 4	2,255 7	1,579 13	42 0

er the Vac-cination Act. / Outlay for Register and Certificate Books.	Payments on Account of the Registration Act.		Payments under the Parochial Assessments Act (for Surveys, Valuations, &c.), and Loans repaid under the same.	Payments for or towards the County Rate.	Payments for or towards the County and Local Police Forces.	Money Expended for all other Purposes.	Total Parochial Rates, &c., Expended.	Medical Relief.
	Fees to Clergymen and Registrars.	Outlay for Register Offices, Books, Forms, and other Incidental Expenses.						
£. s.	£. s.	£. s.	£. s.	£. s.	£. s.	£. s.	£. s.	£. s.
..	..	..	..	32 15	..	..	96 13	10 0
..	44 17	..	..	435 19	..	497 6	3,561 13	184 15
..	72 1	25 0	66 9	2,404 0	..	1,856 7	12,419 7	147 7
..	133 16	28 17	66 9	3,365 14	20 18	2,637 7	19,532 17	466 11
..	..	..	..	14 10	..	0 13	45 1	..
..	..	..	..	7 14	2 14	..	16 5	..
..	1 1	..	15 0	37 8	8 10	25 17	308 19	8 8
..	1 1	..	..	25 6	..	..	109 18	..
..	..	..	..	5 12	..	4 17	24 10	..
..	..	..	..	38 7	8 14	12 14	213 7	3 5
..	1 1	..	..	35 17	..	1 6	112 17	..
..	0 2	..	..	11 19	2 14	4 13	57 0	2 4
..	0 19	..	..	17 8	3 18	25 11	174 11	..
..	..	..	..	4 9	..	13 17	51 17	..
0 7	..	..	..	6 18	..	6 6	23 5	..
..	..	0 18	..	17 9	..	8 1	62 14	..
..	..	0 15	..	16 5	..	..	127 13	6 6
..	2 10	..	11 15	36 2	8 4	52 14	200 17	6 2
..	..	..	..	6 5	1 8	..	49 7	..
..	..	..	..	16 11	..	..	88 12	..
..	..	0 13	..	22 7	..	5 7	114 0	4 0
..	0 14	..	..	22 6	5 1	8 7	137 0	4 16
..	1 4	..	..	29 9	6 14	11 7	248 9	2 17
..	..	..	..	2 12	0 12	3 16	11 19	..
..	..	0 5	..	18 15	..	..	114 18	4 13
0 7	8 12	2 11	26 15	393 9	48 9	185 6	2,292 19	42 11

NAMES of COUNTIES, PARISHES, &c.	Amount levied by Assessment.	Received from all other Sources, in Aid of Poor Rate.	Total Amount Received for the Relief, &c., of the Poor.	Amount Expended in Relief, &c., of the Poor.	
	£. *s.*	£. *s.*	£. *s.*	£. *s.*	£. *s.*
SURREY.					
Brixton Hundred, East Division.					
Mary, St., Newington. . .	22,256 19	807 11	23,064 10	15,496 13	344 13
Farnham Hundred.					
Farnham	3,374 8	..	3,374 8	3,006 9	58 1
Frensham	719 3	72 2	791 5	640 16	18 10
Seal and Tongham. . . .	243 14	11 18	255 12	198 19	1 14
Godalming Hundred, First Division.					
Puttenham	311 11	2 0	313 11	238 12	3 19
Godley Hundred, First Division.					
Frimley	875 14	15 2	890 16	781 11	40 15
Woking Hundred, First Division.					
Ash and Normanby . . .	612 1	73 6	685 7	546 1	20 0
Totals	28,393 10	981 19	29,375		487 12
SUSSEX.					
Rape of Arundel, Arundel Hundred.					
Arundel	1,249 16	385 6	1,635 2	1,253 7	49 9
Avesford Hundred.					
Climping	143 3	..	143 3	89 9	1 9
Ford	73 6	..	73 6	36 15	1 8
South Stoke and Offham . .	154 7	..	154 7	125 0	1 6
Tortington	54 6	..	54 6	31 14	2 2
Bury Hundred.					
Bignor	149 16	10 18	160 14	149 10	1 11
Bury and West Burton . .	386 0	5 6	391 6	362 19	1 10
Coates	28 4	..	28 4	13 12	..
Fittleworth	497 12	..	497 12	428 1	..
Houghton	53 0	..	53 0	62 19	..

* No Return has been received from the parish of H

	Payments on Account of the Registration Act.		Payments under the Parochial Assessments Act (for Surveys, Valuations, &c.), and Loans repaid under the same.	Payments for or towards the County Rate.	Payments for or towards the County and Local Police Forces.	Money Expended for all other Purposes.	Total Parochial Rates, &c., Expended.	Medical Relief.
	Fees to Clergymen and Registrars.	Outlay for Register Offices, Books Forms, and other Incidental Expenses.						
s.	£. *s.*	£. *s.*	£. *s.*	£. *s.*	£. *s.*	£. *s.*	£. *s.*	£. *s.*
	.178 19	16 3	..	2,456 17	4,025 11	576 0	23,120 9	371 3
	20 15	..	..	311 14	..	123 5	3,520 4	130 0
	3 12	0 11	65 11	44 4	..	70 5	843 9	74 16
	1 6	..	..	32 13	2 5	16 5	255 11	16 3
	0 14	..	..	42 17	..	14 0	300 2	..
	..	..	..	67 4	..	..	889 10	62 17
	1 10	..	47 13	38 6	..	22 19	676 9	20 10
	206 16	16 14	113 4	2,993 15	4,027 16	822 14	29,605 14	675 9
	9 10	..	..	112 5	..	35 1	1,459 12	36 11
	..	0 7	..	27 19	..	..	119 4	..
	..	..	..	9 2	..	..	47 5	5 0
	..	..	..	11 0	..	..	137 6	4 0
	0 5	..	..	8 1	..	..	42 2	..
	..	0 12	..	7 13	..	..	159 6	6 15
	2 9	..	..	24 7	..	..	391 5	..
	0 11	..	..	3 17	..	3 10	21 10	4 6
	2 5	..	..	13 19	..	15 7	459 12	17 17
	..	..	..	11 13	..	..	74 12	..

NAMES of COUNTIES, PARISHES, &c.	Amount levied by Assessment.	Received from all other Sources, in Aid of Poor Rate.	Total Amount Received for the Relief, &c., of the Poor.	Amount Expended in Relief, &c., of the Poor.	Amount Expended in Law Charges.	
	£. s.	£. s.	£. s.	£. s.	£. s.	
Sussex—*continued.*						
Poling Hundred.						
Angmering	553 16	20 14	579 10	487 8	..	
Burpham	98 19	..	98 19	118 11	5 5	
Ferring	69 5	32 1	101 6	104 16	2 6	
Goring	378 2	..	378 2	363 11	31 9	
Kingston	No poor.	..	..	..	..	
Leominster	268 15	..	268 15	224 13	6 15	
Littlehampton	632 14	15 17	648 11	433 7	50 2	..
North Stoke	No levy.					
Poling	56 9	..	56 9	95 8	1 10	..
Preston, East	120 5	1 19	122 4	101 4	1 7	..
Rustington	176 7	3 17	180 4	144 12	18 13	..
Warningcamp	46 16	..	46 16	35 4	1 10	..
Rotherbridge Hundred.						
Barlavington	142 0	..	142 0	89 17	..	..
Burton	107 14	..	107 14	174 12	..	..
Duncton	105 11	4 17	110 8	109 19	0 13	..
Egdean	131 3	..	131 3	75 19	1 9	..
Sutton	297 0	51 18	348 18	350 0	..	..
Westeaswrith Hundred.						
Amberley	244 7	...	244 7	168 3	1 9	..
*Greatham	82 19	..	82 19	52 10	..	..
Rackham	60 0	..	60 0	64 0	..	1
Wiggenholt	35 14	..	35 14	25 19	..	..
Rape of Bramber, Brightford Hundred.						
Broadwater	1,426 4	77 10	1,503 14	1,239 10	35 14	..
Clapham	248 16	..	248 16	188 4	2 2	..
Durrington	113 10	4 17	118 7	84 8	1 15	..
Heene	84 10	0 6	84 16	68 10	3 13	0 1
Lancing	272 9	..	272 9	232 6	..	..
Patching Hundred.						
Patching	12 4	..	128 4	112 17	..	..
Tarring Hundred.						
West Tarring	415 4	7 0	422 4	363 8	8 3	..
Rape of Chichester, Aldwick Hundred.						
Slindon	160 9	..	160 9	192 15	1 5	..
Southberstead	1,041 0	3 2	1,044 2	935 9	2 13	3

* No Return has been received from the parish of Greatham

Outlay for register and certificate Books.	Payments on Account of the Registration Act.		Payments under the Parochial Assessments Act (for Surveys, Valuations, &c.), and Loans repaid under the same.	Payments for or towards the County Rate.	Payments for or towards the County and Local Police Forces.	Money Expended for all other Purposes.	Total Parochial Rates, &c., Expended.	Medical Relief.
	Fees to Clergymen and Registrars.	Outlay for Register Offices, Books Forms. and other Incidental Expenses.						
£. s.	£. s.	£. s.	£. s.	£. s.	£. s.	£. s.	£. s.	£. s.
..	..	2 15	..	60 7	..	13 14	564 4	23 2
..	0 14	..	7 1	16 8	..	2 18	150 17	6 0
..	1 0	..	..	17 12	2 0	..	127 14	8 0
..	0 17	..	..	36 16	..	..	432 13	18 0
..	..	..	..	7 16	..	..	7 16	..
..	1 8	..	..	46 6	..	..	279 2	11 10
..	10 8	..	42 11	54 18	..	43 15	635 1	32 6
..	..	0 14	..	13 4	..	..	110 16	4 12
..	0 19	..	5 17	10 7	..	0 11	120 5	..
..	1 4	..	..	27 1	..	6 14	198 4	8 0
0 6	..	0 5	..	8 2	..	3 15	49 2	..
..	0 10	..	5 3	10 19	..	1 13	108 2	7 2
..	..	..	..	3 1	..	..	177 13	..
..	..	0 18	..	10 3	..	16 3	136 16	5 0
..	0 7	0 1	..	5 15	..	7 12	91 3	7 10
..	1 2	..	..	12 2	..	..	363 4	..
..	2 9	..	..	24 16	..	..	196 17	10 0
..	0 3	..	..	5 10	..	..	58 3	..
..	..	..	..	9 0	..	..	74 1	..
..	0 2	..	..	9 15	..	..	35 16	..
..	11 17	..	..	230 14	..	218 10	1,736 5	77 7
..	..	..	..	16 18	..	..	207 4	7 0
..	..	1 12	..	14 0	0 2	2 14	104 11	..
..	0 7	..	..	12 15	..	14 5	100 6	5 17
..	..	..	..	29 11	..	..	261 17	..
0 17	..	..	..	10 8	..	..	124 2	4 4
..	1 14	..	..	26 1	..	14 11	413 17	20 0
..	2 1	0 1	..	21 7	..	0 18	218 7	13 3
..	7 19	..	..	118 10	21 6	10 10	1,099 17	48 11

ar ended 25th March, 1839, which Return is therefore inserted.

NAMES of COUNTIES, PARISHES, &c.	Amount levied by Assessment.	Received from all other Sources, in Aid of Poor Rate.	Total Amount Received for the Relief, &c., of the Poor.	Amount Expended in Relief, &c., of the Poor.	Amount Expended in Law Charges.	Amount of Fees Paid to the Vaccinat
	£. s.	£. s.	£. s.	£. s.	£ s.	£.
Sussex—*continued.*						
Eastbourne Hundred.						
Heyshott	329 0	..	329 0	266 2	2 1	..
Rape of Lewes, Whalesbone Hundred.						
Brighthelmstone	22,644 3	1,788 18	24,433 1	18,650 0	681 17	2
City of Chichester.						
United Parishes	2,779 12	140 19	2,920 11	2,407 2	95 1	4 1
Totals	36,045 7	2,555 5	38,600 12	30,512 10	1,015 7	12 1
WARWICK.						
Camlingford Hundred, Atherstone Division.						
Hartshill	296 12	29 13	326 5	237 17	..	..
Knightlow Hundred, Kirby Division.						
Bedworth	1,450 9	81 7	1,531 16	1,063 13	35 16	..
Brinklow	381 13	35 7	417 0	300 3	12 18	..
Pailton	284 16	12 10	297 6	193 16	..	..
Wolvey	630 16	..	630 16	465 16	1 12	..
Town of Birmingham . . .	63,663 7	3,585 8	67,248 15	28,733 2	270 17	81
United Parishes of the City of Coventry	7,934 14	1,579 17	9,514 11	8,290 7	151 10	16 1
Totals . . .	74,642 7	5,324 2	79,966 9	39,284 14	472 13	97 1
WILTS.						
Kinwardstone Hundred.						
Brimslade and South Savernake (Extra-parochial) . .	130 8	..	130 8	92 3	..	..
Selkley Hundred.						
Savernake, North (Extra-parochial)	93 15	..	93 15	47 3	..	..
New Sarum City.						
United Parishes	5,458 4	279 2	5,737 6	4,628 7	35 1	0 1
Totals . . .	5,682 7	279 2	5,961 9	4,767 13	35 1	0.1

to Vac-tion Act. Outlay for Register and Certificate Books.	Payments on Account of the Registration Act.		Payments under the Parochial Assessments Act (for Surveys, Valuations, &c.), and Loans repaid under the same.	Payments for or towards the County Rate.	Payments for or towards the County and Local Police Force	Money Expended for all other Purposes.	Total Parochial Rates, &c., Expended.	Medical Relief.
	Fees to Clergymen and Registrars.	Outlay for Register Offices, Books, Forms, and other Incidental Expenses.						
£. s.	£. s.	£. s.	£. s.	£. s.	£. s.	£. s.	£. s.	£. s.
..	0 16	..	..	8 19	..	19 7	297 5	8 0
..	169 8	..	..	3,281 5	..	730 15	23,515 14	346 6
..	26 15	15 0	..	..	..	53 0	2,601 17	85 8
1 3	257 0	22 5	60 12	4,390 2	23 8	1,215 3	37,510 5	831 7
..	4 7	..	..	47 19	..	36 2	326 5	..
..	17 1	..	..	146 7	73 4	141 11	1,477 12	51 4
..	3 9	..	..	47 0	23 10	7 10	394 10	12 0
..	..	..	..	46 17	23 4	27 7	291 4	10 15
..	5 8	..	..	85 3	42 12	14 2	614 13	18 18
..	490 3	..	..	34,276 0	..	4,229 1	68,080 5	410 0
..	113 10	..	158 17	1,173 2	..	201 12	10,105 15	208 18
..	633 18	..	158 17	35,822 8	162 10	4,657 5	81,290 4	711 5
..	..	..	..	18 2	16 1	..	126 6	9 7
..	..	..	..	13 10	12 18	..	73 11	4 4
..	33 7	1 12	..	..	..	497 2	5,196 1	87 1
..	33 7	1 12	..	31 12	28 19	497 2	5,395 18	100 12

x

NAMES OF COUNTIES, PARISHES, &c.	Amount levied by Assessment.	Received from all other Sources, in Aid of Poor Rate.	Total Amount Received for the Relief, &c., of the Poor.	Amount Expended in Relief, &c., of the Poor.	Amount Expended in Law Charges.
YORK, EAST RIDING.	£. *s.*	£. *s.*	£. *s.*	£. *s.*	
Ouse and Derwent Wapentake.					
Menthorpe-cum-Bowthorpe .	81 6	55 3	136 9	..	
Kingston-upon-Hull.					
United Parishes	18,085 14	115 3	18,200 17	14,436 13	
The Liberty of St. Peter of York.					
Helperby	220 0	3 11	223 11	179 14	
Ainsty of the City of York.					
Acaster Selby	127 16	7 3	134 19	111 14	
Acomb	267 12	5 1	272 13	200 19	
Angram	8 11	..	8 11	8 11	
Appleton Roebuck . . .	305 1	..	305 1	192 12	
Askham Bryan	191 5	..	191 5	127 12	
Bickerton	90 17	..	90 17	68 16	
Bilborough	107 8	1 0	108 8	60 3	
Bilton	210 14	..	210 14	169 9	
Bolton Percy	196 7	..	196 7	117 10	
Catterton	51 2	..	51 2	45 0	
Colton	60 5	..	60 5	30 1	
Helaugh	99 16	..	99 16	37 8	
Hessay	82 1	..	82 1	51 4	
Hutton	78 19	..	78 19	26 9	
Knapton	70 1	13 11	83 12	38 17	
Long Marston	290 10	..	290 10	225 10	
Moor Monkton	202 0	..	202 0	144 13	
Oxton	30 18	..	30 18	14 4	
Poppleton, Nether . . .	172 8	..	172 8	100 13	
Poppleton, Upper . . .	71 19	5 17	77 16	69 18	
Rufforth	181 5	..	181 5	85 8	
Steeton	73 12	..	73 12	45 13	
Tadcaster, East	213 12	..	213 12	177 9	
Thorp Arch	247 10	1 15	249 5	151 7	
Tockwith	298 13	..	298 13	227 8	
Walton	118 5	..	118 5	80 2	
Wighill	182 17	..	182 17	103 11	
Wilstrop	64 15	..	64 15	41 8	
Totals	22,482 19	208 4		17,369 16	
YORK, NORTH RIDING.					
Allertonshire Wapentake.					
Hutton Conyers (Extra-Parochial)	124 10	5 18	130 8	100 13	..
Norton Conyers	18 5	..	18 5	0 6	..

Outlay for Register and Certificate Books. (or the Vaccination Act.)	Payments on Account of the Registration Act.		Payments under the Parochial Assessments Act (for Surveys, Valuations, &c.), and Loans repaid under the same.	Payments for or towards the County Rate.	Payments for or towards the County and Local Police Forces.	Money Expended for all other Purposes.	Total Parochial Rates, &c., Expended.	Medical Relief.
	Fees to Clergymen and Registrars.	Outlay for Register Offices, Books, Forms, and other Incidental Expenses.						
£. s.	£. s.	£. s.	£. s.	£. s.	£. s.	£. s.	£. s.	£. s.
..	..	..	..	23 12	..	2 4	25 16	..
2 0	125 16	17 15	..	..	..	1,988 2	16,953 4	100 0
..	1 17	..	..	..	..	14 8	223 4	..
..	0 10	..	..	42 8	..	..	156 10	1 19
..	2 5	..	..	80 18	..	3 8	292 5	4 3
..	..	..	..	..	..	..	8 11	..
..	2 8	..	..	77 15	..	1 6	277 3	1 1
..	1 5	..	..	56 3	..	..	191 5	..
..	..	..	..	22 1	..	..	90 17	3 5
..	0 8	0 3	..	39 8	..	2 0	105 9	0 15
..	0 14	0 2	..	51 5	..	..	244 1	..
..	..	0 17	..	70 12	..	7 18	196 17	0 5
..	..	..	..	12 2	..	..	57 2	..
..	0 9	..	..	29 15	..	..	60 5	1 17
..	0 10	..	..	72 12	..	1 4	111 14	..
..	0 2	..	..	26 15	..	4 0	82 1	..
..	0 3	..	..	33 18	..	..	60 10	..
..	0 3	..	..	25 6	..	9 1	73 7	..
..	1 11	..	..	66 5	..	..	307 2	..
..	0 2	..	..	57 5	..	..	202 0	6 12
..	0 3	..	..	17 4	..	0 19	32 10	..
..	..	..	..	71 15	..	..	173 8	1 0
..	..	0 6	..	..	..	2 9	72 13	..
..	0 18	..	..	57 19	..	1 18	173 12	1 8
..	0 6	..	..	27 12	..	..	73 11	..
..	3 7	0 3	..	28 12	..	1 8	221 2	1 6
..	0 14	..	10 10	50 11	..	1 16	226 14	7 1
..	1 9	0 1	..	44 15	..	..	284 7	..
..	..	1 8	..	37 19	..	..	119 9	..
..	..	0 18	..	59 11	..	3 10	169 3	2 6
..	..	0 4	..	23 3	..	..	64 15	..
2 0	145 0	21 17	10 10	1,207 1	..	2,045 11	21,330 7	132 18
..	..	0 2	..	25 18	..	..	126 13	3 15
..	0 2	..	..	11 10	..	5 18	17 16	..

NAMES of COUNTIES, PARISHES, &c.	Amount levied by Assessment.	Received from all other Sources, in Aid of Poor Rate.	Total Amount Received for the Relief, &c., of the Poor.	Amount Expended in Relief, &c., of the Poor.	Amount Expended in Law Charges.	A͟m͟
York, North Riding—*continued.*	£. s.	£. s.	£. s.	£. s.	£. s.	£.
Bulmer Wapentake.						
Shipton	170 0	. .	170 0	110 0	60 0	
Skelton	110 0	. .	110 0	. .	. .	
Tollerton	241 15	26 3	267 18	210 0	40 7	4
Youlton	37 0	. .	37 0	36 8	. .	
Hallikeld Wapentake.						
Asenby	106 0	. .	106 0	85 13	. .	
Baldersby	99 16	8 6	108 2	72 5	. .	
Cundall and Leckby . . .	162 0	. .	162 0	34 13	. .	
Dishforth	296 19	10 0	306 19	151 5	127 12	
Humberton and Milby . .	17 8	. .	17 8	17 8	. .	
Kirkby Hill, or Kirkby-on-the} Moor . . . .}	118 10	. .	118 10	37 5	55 12	
Langthorpe	180 0	. .	180 0	35 0	130 0	
Marton-le-Moor	98 16	. .	98 16	41 16	. .	
Melmerby	152 19	. .	152 19	101 14	. .	
Middleton Quernhow . . .	55 16	. .	55 16	34 14	. .	
Norton-le-Clay	65 15	. .	65 15	51 5	. .	
Rainton-with-Newby . . .	60 8	. .	60 8	57 0	8 6	
Sutton-cum-Howgrave. . .	24 19	3 6	28 5	20 5	. .	
Tanfield, East	7 9	. .	7 9	. .	. .	
Tanfield, West	308 10	18 0	326 10	180 10	68 10	
Thornton Bridge	14 4	. .	14 4	14 4	. .	
Wath	51 8	. .	51 8	26 7	. .	
Hang, West, Wapentake.						
Abbotside, Higher . . .	247 14	0 16	248 10	157 6	1 0	
Abbotside, Lower . . .	218 14	. .	218 14	148 14	. .	
Askrigg	465 1	0 12	465 13	366 16	24 15	
Aysgarth	154 14	11 9	166 3	126 6	1 19	
Bainbridge	523 13	63 3	586 16	448 16	1 6	
Bishop Dale	37 18	. .	37 18	15 0	. .	
Burton and Walden . . .	238 12	11 8	250 0	215 8	. .	
Carperby	194 16	. .	194 16	192 4	. .	
Hawes	788 16	20 10	809 6	653 13	0 10	
Newbiggen	79 4	0 7	79 11	74 2	. .	
Thoralby	180 0	18 1	198 1	161 7	1 6	
Thornton Rust	41 16	. .	41 16	37 14	3 12	
Langbaurgh Liberty, West Division.						
Picton	26 13	. .	26 13	27 1	0 8	
Totals . . .	5,719 18	197 19	5,917 17	4,042 18	525 3	. . . 5

the Vaccination Act. Outlay for Register and Certificate Books.	Payments on Account of the Registration Act. Fees to Clergymen and Registrars.	Outlay for Register Offices, Books, Forms, and other Incidental Expenses.	Payments under the Parochial Assessments Act (for Surveys, Valuations, &c.), and Loans repaid under the same.	Payments for or towards the County Rate.	Payments for or towards the County and Local Police Forces.	Money Expended for all other Purposes.	Total Parochial Rates, &c., Expended.	Medical Relief.
£. s.	£. s.	£. s.	£. s.	£. s.	£. s.	£. s.	£. s.	£. s.
..	..	..	..	..	..	..	170 0	..
..	0 16	..	..	95 10	..	..	96 6	..
..	1 13	..	..	..	..	7 15	264 10	5 5
0 1	..	..	..	10 19	..	..	47 8	..
0 17	..	..	..	18 11	..	..	106 0	..
0 17	..	..	..	23 6	..	0 10	96 18	0 6
..	..	0 15	..	46 16	..	79 16	162 0	..
..	1 6	..	..	26 16	..	..	306 19	1 17
..	..	..	..	14 4	..	..	31 12	..
..	0 7	..	..	19 6	..	3 18	116 8	2 10
..	..	0 17	..	19 1	..	..	184 18	..
..	..	0 5	..	52 0	..	4 15	98 16	..
..	1 14	..	..	17 8	..	12 4	133 0	..
..	..	0 7	..	21 17	..	..	56 18	..
..	0 7	..	..	14 1	..	..	65 13	..
..	..	1 4	..	21 10	..	1 14	89 14	1 17
..	..	0 7	..	7 10	..	..	28 2	..
..	..	..	..	12 13	..	..	12 13	..
..	1 12	..	..	41 15	..	26 15	319 2	5 0
..	0 4	..	..	..	..	..	14 8	..
..	0 12	..	..	11 16	..	9 8	48 3	..
..	1 13	..	..	29 2	..	..	189 1	..
..	1 7	0 6	..	13 18	..	31 14	195 19	3 0
..	2 4	..	..	28 9	..	31 18	454 2	0 17
..	3 5	1 4	..	..	..	5 14	138 8	..
..	..	2 5	..	37 13	..	38 6	528 6	6 0
..	..	0 7	..	13 15	..	6 12	35 14	..
..	..	1 10	..	..	..	20 18	237 16	..
..	0 15	0 6	..	..	..	..	193 5	2 9
..	6 2	0 13	..	61 19	..	54 19	777 16	10 0
..	..	0 14	..	12 2	..	..	86 18	..
..	..	0 15	..	17 18	..	2 13	183 19	..
..	0 9	..	..	..	..	0 10	42 5	..
..	..	..	..	..	..	0 8	27 17	3 12
1 15	24 8	11 17	..	727 3	..	346 5	5,685 3	46 8

NAMES OF COUNTIES, PARISHES, &c.	Amount levied by Assessment.	Received from all other Sources, in Aid of Poor Rate.	Total Amount Received for the Relief, &c. of the Poor.	Amount Expended in Relief, &c., of the Poor.	Amount Expended in Law Charges.	Am of Fo Pa th Vancl
YORK, WEST RIDING.	£. s.	£. s.	£. s.	£. s.	£. s.	£.
Agbrigg Wapentake.						
Ackton	80 13	. .	80 13	53 4	4 12	0
Altofts	364 15	77 2	441 17	121 12	98 18	.
Crofton	216 2	5 15	221 17	161 12	15 0	.
Lofthouse and_Carlton . .	535 1	42 1	577 2	474 3	20 18	.
Methley	632 9	29 3	661 12	511 8	8 11	3
Middleton	536 14	. .	536 14	405 18	29 10	.
Normanton and Woodhouse .	146 5	22 1	168 6	89 4	1 1	.
Rothwell with Rothwell, High,} and Royds Green . . . }	1,409 16	12 3	1,421 19	657 13	90 14	6
Saddleworth with Quick . .	4,647 2	1,089 10	5,736 12	4,353 15	67 2	20
Snydale	101 10	. .	101 10	78 11	. .	.
Whitwood	218 3	16 15	234 18	137 18	22 10	0
Barkston Ash, Wapentake Lower Division.						
Birken	190 1	. .	190 1	151 16	2 0	.
Burton Salmon	144 15	2 2	146 17	59 2	. .	.
Byrome-cum-Poole . . .	25 8	23 14	49 2	25 8	. .	.
Haddesley, West . . .	266 8	6 9	272 17	210 1	23 0	.
Hambleton	214 6	44 12	258 18	152 8	6 4	.
Hilham	150 0	. .	150 0	100 13	22 14	.
Monk Fryston	118 13	. .	118 13	55 12	. .	.
Ryther and Ozendike . . .	250 11	0 4	250 15	158 4	0 18	.
Sutton	46 18	. .	46 18	12 4	. .	.
Barkston Ash Wapentake, Upper Division.						
Barkston Ash	96 4	. .	96 4	66 12	1 15	.
Bramham	468 15	12 8	481 3	251 4	26 15	.
Brotherton	613 10	. .	613 10	370 1	13 1	.
Clifford-cum-Boston . . .	338 19	21 15	360 14	301 4	. .	3
Fairburn	190 8	22 8	212 16	170 2	. .	.
Fenton-cum-Biggin . . .	198 5	18 11	216 16	146 11	. .	.
Grimston	56 13	. .	56 13	24 18	2 13	.
Huddlestone and Lumby . .	143 1	2 12	145 13	148 7	. .	.
Kirkby Wharf and Milford .	113 11	. .	113 11	74 16	3 17	.
Kirk Fenton	196 2	13 10	209 12	167 14	. .	.
Lead	65 2	. .	65 2	44 2	. .	.
Ledsham	106 15	8 10	115 5	55 5	4 16	.
Ledstone	176 2	8 11	184 13	85 16	. .	.
Lotherton-with-Abberford .	143 15	12 7	156 2	94 9	7 2	.
Micklefield	205 17	43 17	249 14	110 14	103 8	.
Micklethwaite	49 11	. .	49 11	25 7	. .	.
Milford, South	388 18	27 14	416 12	269 18	92 19	.
Newthorpe	52 19	. .	52 19	33 1	4 13	.
Newton Kyme and Foulston .	109 18	. .	109 18	50 19	. .	0
Saxton and Scarthingwell .	208 6	6 10	214 16	147 9	. .	.
Sherburn	613 0	29 7	642 7	387 5	86 11	.
Sutton-with-Hazlewood . .	134 19	. .	134 19	78 1	. .	.
Tadcaster West (part of) .	431 1	5 0	436 1	364 15	. .	.
Towton	86 4	6 0	92 4	56 19	. .	.
Ulleskelf	180 0	. .	180 0	116 19	11 13	.

(Vac- Act)	Payments on Account of the Registration Act.		Payments under the Parochial Assessments Act (for Surveys, Valuations, &c.), and Loans repaid under the same.	Payments for or towards the County Rate.	Payments for or towards the County and Local Police Forces.	Money Expended for all other Purposes.	Total Parochial Rates, &c., Expended.	Medical Relief.
	Fees to Clergymen and Registrars.	Outlay for Register Offices, Books, Forms, and other Incidental Expenses.						
£. s.	£. s.	£. s.	£. s.	£. s.	£. s.	£. s.	£. s.	£. s.
0 9	0 10	3 19	..	18 12	..	1 17	83 10	5 0
..	1 4	0 2	..	51 4	..	23 0	296 0	3 3
..	0 10	..	..	43 6	..	0 11	220 19	..
..	..	5 14	..	91 5	11 8	10 12	614 0	..
0 5	..	4 18	..	164 18	..	24 18	718 10	16 19
..	3 16	0 8	..	80 1	..	20 12	540 5	11 8
..	0 17	0 2	..	42 3	..	6 5	139 12	..
..	11 17	..	..	166 11	..	25 2	958 15	18 7
..	50 19	11 6	86 0	717 9	29 12	252 4	5,588 18	100 9
..	..	..	..	39 3	..	..	117 14	..
..	1 9	..	..	39 17	..	10 18	213 0	5 5
..	0 2	..	..	45 16	..	10 0	209 14	8 7
..	0 9	..	16 15	19 3	..	11 10	106 19	0 15
..	..	..	..	23 14	..	..	49 2	..
..	..	..	..	29 16	..	10 0	272 17	7 10
..	2 13	..	..	44 17	..	13 0	219 2	7 17
..	0 15	..	..	25 18	..	..	150 0	..
..	..	..	..	31 12	..	19 18	107 2	3 0
..	1 9	..	..	67 12	..	14 16	242 19	..
..	0 8	..	..	18 8	..	11 17	42 17	..
..	1 0	..	..	26 13	..	5 18	101 18	2 0
..	4 6	..	85 16	74 14	..	33 6	476 1	..
..	8 6	..	..	67 11	..	27 15	486 14	17 8
..	4 7	..	1 15	44 17	..	5 5	360 14	4 10
..	..	1 7	..	40 2	..	..	211 11	4 1
..	0 10	..	..	32 2	..	2 6	181 9	4 18
..	0 4	..	..	28 18	..	..	56 13	..
..	0 13	..	..	21 2	..	5 7	175 9	..
..	0 3	..	..	34 15	..	..	113 11	..
..	1 12	..	..	42 2	..	0 17	212 5	6 2
..	..	0 4	..	19 19	0 17	..	65 2	..
..	1 5	..	..	37 1	..	4 5	102 12	..
..	..	0 18	..	52 16	..	22 13	162 3	1 10
..	2 4	..	..	25 10	..	9 4	138 9	1 6
..	1 10	..	..	27 14	..	3 11	246 17	10 9
..	..	..	..	18 12	..	..	43 19	..
..	2 1	..	..	59 6	..	..	424 4	..
..	0 7	..	..	6 7	..	5 12	50 0	..
..	0 15	..	..	47 7	2 11	2 4	104 9	..
..	..	..	..	56 6	..	10 11	214 6	5 13
..	4 5	..	..	124 11	..	24 13	627 5	15 16
..	..	..	..	56 2	..	..	134 3	..
6 3	0 5	..	..	79 10	..	2 10	453 3	1 9
..	0 10	..	..	20 0	6 0	7 17	91 6	..
..	2 3	0 3	..	42 8	..	5 0	189 0	..

Claro Wapentake, Lower Division.

	£ s.	£ s.	£ s.	£ s.	£ s.	£
Aldborough	242 6	4 17	247 3	113 12	2 5	
Aldfield	79 4	17 0	96 4	49 19	0 10	
Arkendale	178 4	2 0	180 4	119 9	..	
Azerley	515 8	20 11	535 19	397 1	1 17	
Bilton and Harrogate . . .	997 2	428 3	1,425 5	982 18	49 2	
Birtswith	252 7	..	252 7	186 19	0 6	
Blubberhouses	43 16	..	43 16	23 15	30 9	
Boroughbridge	291 2	22 1	313 3	285 12	..	
Brearton	129 4	15 3	144 7	96 18	2 13	
Burton Leonard	271 13	0 6	271 19	240 8	3 12	
Clifton-with-Norwood . . .	311 5	..	311 5	220 14	36 19	
Cliut	162 4	..	162 4	149 13	31 17	2 11
Copgrove	82 9	..	82 9	38 0	..	0
Farnham	91 18	..	91 18	42 15	24 15	..
Fellixcliffe	191 15	..	191 15	125 2	6 14	..
Ferrensby	63 6	0 1	63 7	35 4	11 11	..
Fewston	611 19	11 0	622 19	533 4	59 3	..
Grewelthorpe	203 18	..	203 18	129 11	1 3	..
Hampsthwaite	270 4	..	270 4	171 15	3 7	..
Haverah Park (Extra-Parochial)	65 0	2 5	67 5	41 18	..	2 10
Killinghall	356 2	18 14	374 16	271 15	8 6	4 4
Kirby Hall	40 19	..	40 19	25 9	..	..
Kirkby Malzeard . . .	371 7	9 7	380 14	277 6	..	4 11
Knaresborough	2,283 18	..	2,283 18	1,997 9	90 8	..
Laverton	280 2	..	280 2	222 19	13 16	..
Lindrick (Extra-Parochial) . .	34 16	..	34 16	7 0	..	..
Milby	93 8	6 17	100 5	52 7	8 2	..
Minskip	158 13	1 4	159 17	103 7	2 12	..
Ouseburn, Great . . .	156 13	..	156 13	115 0	..	..
Pannall	650 2	46 4	696 6	484 10	49 15	..
Rocliffe	119 18	10 12	130 10	82 16	2 2	0 11
Scotton	113 1	..	113 1	93 13	..	..
Scriven-with-Tentergate . .	1,051 2	1 0	1,052 2	603 3	44 9	..
Skelding	52 17	..	52 17	44 9	..	..
Stainley, South, and Clayton.	182 10	14 18	197 8	150 6	0 5	..
Staveley	199 6	..	199 6	167 15	3 10	5
Studley Roger	61 2	0 4	61 6	24 19	3 14	..
Thornville, Old. . . .	29 16	..	29 16	20 18	..	..
Timble, Great	91 13	..	91 13	42 15	..	..
Winksley	91 2	..	91 2	67 4	13 18	..

Claro Wapentake, Upper Division.

	£ s.	£ s.	£ s.	£ s.	£ s.	£
Allerton Mauliverer-with-Hopperton . . . . . }	157 14	4 1	161 15	78 19	8 7	..
Askwith	152 4	..	152 4	105 14	..	..
Beamsley-in-Skipton . . .	98 18	..	98 18	78 11	..	..
Castley	61 4	..	61 4	43 15	..	..
Cattall	65 5	..	65 5	36 18	..	..
Clareton	..	3 0	3 0	6 10	..	..
Coueythorpe	24 5	..	24 5	14 1	..	..
Cowthorpe	88 18	..	88 18	31 9	30 15	..
Deighton, North	143 8	3 18	147 6	96 6	31 4	..
Denton	136 6	..	136 6	97 13	..	..
Dunkswick	149 15	6 4	155 19	121 17	0 5	..

or the Vaccination Act. Outlay for Register and Certificate Books.	Payments on Account of the Registration Act. Fees to Clergymen and Registrars.	Outlay for Register Offices, Books, Forms, and other Incidental Expenses.	Payments under the Parochial Assessments Act (for Surveys, Valuations, &c.), and Loans repaid under the same.	Payments for or towards the County Rate.	Payments for or towards the County and Local Police Forces.	Money Expended for all other Purposes.	Total Parochial Rates, &c., Expended.	Medical Relief.
£. s.	£. s.	£. s.	£. s.	£. s.	£. s.	£. s.	£. s.	£. s.
..	1 0	0 4	3 13	86 13	13 8	1 11	222 6	6 7
..	1 5	..	..	24 6	..	2 1	78 1	..
..	0 13	..	..	43 14	..	4 1	167 17	0 15
..	1 7	..	..	66 4	..	3 18	470 7	8 5
..	9 11	0 4	..	148 2	..	235 7	1,425 4	25 0
..	1 3	..	..	25 5	..	10 12	224 5	2 0
..	..	0 3	..	6 4	..	2 19	63 10	0 15
..	2 8	..	..	25 3	..	..	313 3	4 5
..	1 7	..	..	36 1	..	4 0	140 19	..
..	2 0	..	..	40 4	..	..	286 4	3 0
..	1 2	..	..	33 16	..	8 3	300 14	..
..	1 7	..	..	39 12	..	..	225 4	..
..	..	0 9	..	20 10	..	..	59 5	..
..	..	0 9	..	23 8	..	..	91 7	..
..	0 13	..	..	36 2	..	3 17	172 8	..
..	..	0 3	..	14 3	..	..	61 1	..
..	3 11	..	..	21 16	..	3 2	620 16	9 11
..	..	1 6	..	66 3	..	..	198 3	4 0
..	1 9	..	..	26 0	..	26 19	229 10	2 10
0 3	..	..	..	18 4	..	..	62 19	..
..	1 8	..	..	57 3	..	16 3	358 15	4 0
..	..	0 1	..	15 9	..	..	40 19	..
..	2 18	..	4 10	46 16	..	50 8	386 17	6 10
..	17 2	..	..	178 19	..	..	2,283 18	52 12
..	1 7	..	..	27 16	..	13 5	279 3	1 16
..	..	..	..	27 16	..	..	34 16	..
..	..	0 2	..	28 14	4 2	..	93 7	..
..	..	0 15	..	42 19	6 0	..	155 13	0 19
..	1 6	..	..	40 7	..	..	156 13	10 16
..	..	3 17	5 0	88 6	11 11	10 16	653 15	..
..	..	0 8	..	38 11	6 0	..	130 10	..
..	..	0 17	..	18 11	..	..	113 1	1 11
..	5 12	0 3	..	93 19	..	95 8	842 14	19 7
..	..	..	..	7 14	..	0 4	52 7	..
..	1 4	..	..	45 13	..	..	197 8	..
..	0 16	..	..	16 6	..	5 6	199 6	..
..	0 4	..	..	23 11	..	4 8	56 16	..
..	..	..	..	8 18	..	..	29 16	..
..	..	0 14	..	16 19	..	..	60 8	..
..	..	0 14	..	9 6	..	..	91 2	..
..	..	1 0	..	59 6	..	..	147 12	2 2
..	..	1 1	..	30 12	..	12 7	149 14	0 4
..	..	..	..	16 3	..	..	94 14	2 5
..	0 3	..	..	14 8	..	3 1	61 7	..
..	0 10	..	..	27 17	..	..	65 5	..
..	..	..	..	10 4	..	..	16 14	..
..	..	0 5	..	10 0	..	..	24 6	0 9
..	..	0 8	..	25 2	..	..	87 14	..
..	0 14	..	..	34 12	..	3 17	166 13	12 6
..	0 7	..	..	..	31 8	9 17	139 5	3 4
..	0 14	..	0 10	36 12	3 15	..	163 13	5 3

NAMES OF COUNTIES, PARISHES, &c.	Amount levied by Assessment.		Received from all other Sources. in Aid of Poor Rate.		Total Amount Received for the Relief, &c., of the Poor.		Amount Expended in Relief, &c., of the Poor.		Amount Expended in Law Charges.		Amount of Fees Paid to the Vaccinators	
	£.	s.	£.	s.	£.	s.	£.	s.	£.	s.	£.	s.
Dunsforth, Low	58	0	2	2	60	2	54	7	..		..	
Dunsforth, High, with Branton Green	70	5	..		70	5	44	10	1	16	..	
Farnley	100	4	..		100	4	51	10	3	0	..	
Flaxby	31	12	22	2	53	14	28	8	8	11	..	
Follifoot	181	17	22	6	204	3	128	19	27	0	..	
Goldsborough	91	17	23	10	115	7	72	13	3	2	..	
Greenhammerton	241	2	..		241	2	127	3	..		3	3
Hunsingore	114	12	..		114	12	78	14	..		..	
Kirkby-with-Netherby	119	18	8	16	128	14	74	13	1	7	..	
Kirk Deighton	199	8	..		199	8	101	3	34	12	..	
Kirkby Overblows	232	9	18	14	251	3	159	9	14	9	..	
Kirkhammerton	126	12	7	13	134	5	102	12	..		..	
Leathley	304	16	4	7	309	3	219	19	39	12	..	
Lindley	128	16	0	8	129	4	106	4	2	4	..	
Linton	86	0	5	12	91	12	51	11	..		0	10
Marton and Grafton	179	7	..		179	7	120	9	..		..	
Middleton	72	9	..		72	9	40	19	..		..	
Nesfield and Langbar	100	0	..		100	0	70	0	..		..	
Newhall and Clifton	141	5	..		141	5	79	9	1	8	..	
Nun Monkton	186	18	9	15	196	13	121	12	8	3	..	
Ouseburn, Little	114	3	24	0	138	3	112	2	..		..	
Plumpton	169	10	3	5	172	15	137	4	..		..	
Ribston, Little	62	10	..		62	10	60	15	..		..	
Rigton	189	0	10	17	199	17	131	9	..		..	
Ripley	110	0	..		110	0	110	0	..		..	
Sicklinghall	177	16	..		177	16	140	7	..		..	
Spofforth and Stockhill	877	0	..		877	0	828	3	50	0	..	
Stainburn	120	2	..		120	2	73	16	2	2	..	
Thorpe Green, or Underwood	224	8	..		224	8	181	12	..		..	
Timble, Little	48	6	..		48	6	37	13	..		..	
Walsford and Great Ribston	80	0	..		80	0	29	17	..		..	
Weeton	157	10	..		157	10	72	6	45	14	..	
Weston	76	3	..		76	3	47	19	..		..	
Wetherby	472	7	..		472	7	358	7	4	12	..	
Whixby	192	11	21	6	213	17	106	19	7	3	..	
Widdington	28	19	..		28	19	14	5	..		..	
Morley Wapentake.												
Churwell	421	15	..		421	15	315	13	8	15	..	
Eccleshill	873	9	8	17	882	6	582	18	99	9	5	3
Gildersome	620	7	1	1	621	8	518	18	..		..	
Osgoldcross Wapentake, Lower Division.												
Balne	260	7	8	17	269	4	164	6	1	15	..	
Beaghall	379	18	0	13	380	11	276	2	3	17	..	
Cridling Stubbs	105	10	..		105	10	45	19	9	15	..	
Eggborough	140	15	0	5	141	0	103	1	..		..	
Heck	105	4	..		105	4	81	9	..		..	
Hensall	102	5	10	1	112	6	80	0	..		..	
Kellington	116	17	..		116	17	83	9	..		0	16
Smeaton, Little	89	13	..		89	13	83	3	3	6	..	
Stubbs Waldon	100	7	..		100	7	62	16	..		..	
Whitley	182	13	10	9	193	2	157	15	..		..	
Womersley	322	3	3	2	325	5	220	2	5	11	..	

Vaccination Act. Outlay for Register and Certificate Books.	Payments on Account of the Registration Act.		Payments under the Parochial Assessments Act (for Surveys, Valuations, &c.), and Loans repaid under the same.	Payments for or towards the County Rate.	Payments for or towards the County and Local Police Forces.	Money Expended for all other Purposes.	Total Parochial Rates, &c., Expended.	Medical Relief.
	Fees to Clergymen and Registrars.	Outlay for Register Offices, Books Forms, and other Incidental Expenses.						
£. s.	£. s.	£. s.	£. s.	£. s.	£. s.	£. s.	£. s.	£. s.
..	..	0 7	..	27 11	2 5	..	84 10	3 10
..	0 13	..	..	20 14	..	4 12	72 5	..
..	0 8	..	..	43 7	..	..	98 5	..
..	..	0 3	..	16 12	..	..	53 14	..
..	1 15	..	..	31 12	..	14 17	204 3	..
..	0 15	..	..	36 3	..	..	112 13	..
..	1 12	..	..	56 3	..	53 1	241 2	..
..	0 10	..	..	35 8	..	..	114 12	..
..	0 2	..	..	36 10	4 1	1 10	118 3	0 15
..	0 18	..	..	58 18	..	3 7	198 18	0 5
..	1 1	..	..	57 3	..	27 5	259 7	6 5
..	..	1 6	..	29 16	..	..	133 14	..
..	0 19	..	..	48 13	..	..	309 3	2 6
..	0 6	..	..	20 17	..	..	129 11	..
..	0 19	..	..	26 13	3 9	8 10	91 12	3 3
..	..	1 9	..	57 9	..	..	179 7	5 0
..	..	0 9	..	31 1	..	..	72 9	..
..	..	..	..	30 0	..	..	100 0	..
..	0 4	..	..	37 19	3 18	11 3	134 1	..
..	..	1 2	..	47 19	..	17 17	196 13	1 13
..	..	..	..	37 15	..	..	149 17	..
..	1 0	..	..	43 6	..	..	181 10	3 10
..	0 13	..	..	15 16	..	30 6	107 10	..
..	1 3	..	..	49 4	..	8 10	190 6	4 0
..	..	..	..	44 0	..	..	154 0	..
..	..	0 8	..	35 12	..	..	176 7	2 6
..	2 17	..	..	90 0	..	..	971 0	..
..	0 7	..	..	40 10	..	4 7	121 2	..
..	..	0 7	..	42 9	..	..	224 8	..
..	0 3	..	..	6 3	..	..	43 19	..
..	..	0 16	..	49 7	..	..	80 0	..
0 15	0 11	..	..	38 4	..	..	157 10	3 14
..	..	0 7	..	22 3	..	5 13	76 2	..
..	4 14	..	..	84 17	..	..	452 10	8 14
..	1 19	..	..	65 1	..	6 19	188 1	2 3
..	..	..	..	13 9	..	1 4	28 18	..
..	..	4 6	48 5	44 16	..	..	421 15	4 15
..	6 11	..	..	102 3	..	47 2	843 6	23 16
..	..	6 17	..	64 3	..	20 0	609 18	..
..	..	0 17	..	39 5	..	63 1	269 4	6 0
..	..	1 13	..	44 15	..	8 10	334 17	5 7
..	0 8	..	..	16 9	..	15 15	88 6	1 13
..	1 2	..	..	27 1	..	2 5	133 9	5 0
..	0 8	..	..	23 16	..	..	105 13	5 0
..	..	0 13	..	19 12	..	10 14	110 19	1 7
..	..	1 1	..	35 8	..	..	120 14	..
..	..	0 6	..	18 19	..	..	105 14	..
..	..	0 6	..	25 12	..	12 7	101 1	..
..	0 16	..	..	20 10	..	26 0	205 1	6 0
..	..	1 5	..	75 19	..	14 19	317 16	7 0

NAMES OF COUNTIES, PARISHES, &c.	Amount levied by Assessment.		Received from all other Sources, in Aid of Poor Rate.		Total Amount Received for the Relief, &c., of the Poor.		Amount Expended in Relief, &c. of the Poor.		Amount Expended in Law Charges.		Payments claimed. Amount of Vac. Paid to the Vaccinators.	
	£.	s.	£.	s.	£.	s.	£.	s.	£.	s.	£.	s.
Osgoldcross Wapentake, Upper Division.												
Ackworth	575	14	142	7	718	1	344	14	130	16	..	
Badsworth	256	2	6	4	262	6	140	0	65	0	5	0
Carleton	83	12	4	3	87	15	54	5	..		..	
Castleford	293	12	57	13	351	5	249	4	14	11	3	1
Darrington	191	0	14	12	205	12	106	9	13	0	..	
Elmsall, North	296	3	2	7	298	10	222	8	3	5	..	
Elmsall, South	319	6	2	3	321	9	169	12	86	13	..	
Featherstone	160	13	..		160	13	117	6	..		1	0
Ferry Frystone	388	3	..		388	3	228	17	17	0	..	
Hardwick, East	99	15	14	0	113	15	102	9	..		..	
Hardwick, West	52	1	..		52	1	26	14	2	6	0	15
Hessle	87	5	..		87	5	43	14	1	14	0	11
Hilltop	44	15	..		44	15	22	13	6	8	0	5
Houghton Glass	143	11	2	0	145	11	111	3	10	13	1	8
Kirkby, South	273	1	4	0	277	1	167	12	12	11	..	
Kirksmeaton	152	8	..		152	8	112	11	..		..	
Knottingley	2,013	14	181	2	2,194	16	1,903	19	140	17	3	15
Monkhill	7	15	0	2	7	17	3	18	..		..	
Nostell, Huntwick, and Foulby	201	0	4	19	205	19	205	9	1	1	..	
Pontefract	1,913	4	284	9	2,197	13	2,000	12	73	6	..	
Pontefract Park (Extra-Parochial)	74	9	..		74	9	33	19	0	11	..	
Purston Jaglin	113	16	..		113	16	72	19	3	16	0	18
Skelbrooke	60	12	..		60	12	29	14	..		..	
Stapleton	86	17	..		86	17	81	1	..		..	
Tanshelf	201	13	8	12	210	5	157	12	..		..	
Thorp Audlin	140	7	..		140	7	85	15	21	4	..	
Upton	107	15	..		107	15	70	9	..		..	
Skyrack Wapentake, Lower Division.												
Abberford	200	3	4	17	205	0	134	5	4	12	..	
Allerton Bywater	248	16	2	1	250	17	176	11	..		..	
Austhorpe	208	1	..		208	1	144	5	..		..	
Bardsey-with-Rigton	200	0	3	11	203	11	118	12	10	0	1	5
Barwick-in-Elmet	394	14	125	10	520	4	344	1	43	14	..	
Collingham	132	1	1	5	133	6	96	11	..		0	10
Garforth, West	262	2	4	16	266	18	196	11	3	18	..	
Guiseley	356	0	..		356	0	274	0	..		..	
Keswick, East	125	3	4	14	129	17	81	12	2	18	0	12
Kippax	514	14	14	10	529	4	320	11	..		..	
Parlington	75	0	..		75	0	33	8	..		..	
Preston, Great and Little	252	10	41	2	293	12	250	3	..		..	
Roundhay	404	0	..		404	0	292	19	6	7	..	
Scarcroft	44	9	2	8	46	17	10	19	0	6	..	
Seacroft	326	14	1	0	327	14	215	15	..		2	6
Shadwell	90	6	..		90	6	46	5	..		..	
Sturton Grange	29	13	..		29	13	16	5	..		..	
Swillington	450	9	..		450	9	294	0	14	17	4	8
Temple Newsham	740	15	2	2	742	17	481	11	25	3	6	3
Thorner	235	1	..		235	1	166	12	..		2	8
Wothersome	9	17	..		9	17	3	5	..		..	

Outlay for Register and Certificate Books. (Vaccination Act)	Fees to Clergymen and Registrars.	Outlay for Register Offices, Books Forms, and other Incidental Expenses.	Payments under the Parochial Assessments Act (for Surveys, Valuations, &c.), and Loans repaid under the same.	Payments for or towards the County Rate.	Payments for or towards the County and Local Police Forces.	Money Expended for all other Purposes.	Total Parochial Rates, &c., Expended.	Medical Relief.
£. s.	£. s.	£. s.	£. s.	£. s.	£. s.	£. s.	£. s.	£. s.
..	3 18	..	40 11	137 7	11 18	48 17	718 1	14 17
..	0 12	..	..	38 1	..	..	248 13	5 0
..	..	..	..	42 7	..	..	96 12	3 6
..	5 2	..	..	33 18	..	59 12	365 8	8 8
..	1 5	..	..	74 10	..	10 0	205 4	7 0
..	0 12	..	..	55 16	..	11 11	293 12	6 1
..	1 4	..	..	36 16	7 19	20 10	322 14	7 15
..	0 8	..	..	39 10	..	..	158 4	3 0
..	..	3 10	..	83 14	..	50 18	383 19	4 4
..	..	0 2	..	15 15	..	..	118 6	4 0
..	..	1 0	..	15 12	..	1 18	48 5	1 0
3 6	0 8	0 17	..	22 5	..	1 5	74 0	2 5
..	0 12	0 16	..	7 10	..	4 13	42 17	1 10
..	0 18	..	..	32 13	..	..	156 15	0 2
..	..	2 4	..	66 1	..	21 7	269 15	5 0
..	0 18	..	..	37 7	..	..	150 16	5 0
..	18 19	..	..	136 11	..	21 0	2,225 1	49 9
..	0 4	..	..	2 10	..	2 11	9 3	..
..	..	..	..	8 14	..	..	215 4	..
..	14 16	2 7	..	..	..	..	2,091 1	40 0
..	..	..	..	23 10	..	15 9	73 9	..
..	0 8	..	..	28 11	1 5	..	107 17	4 1
..	0 9	..	..	26 2	..	2 0	58 5	..
..	0 1	..	..	16 4	..	..	97 6	6 0
..	..	1 4	..	24 5	..	19 17	202 18	..
..	1 9	..	..	35 2	..	..	143 10	3 0
..	..	0 13	..	22 17	..	9 7	103 6	..
..	2 4	..	..	37 13	..	12 13	191 7	5 0
..	1 13	..	..	48 14	..	10 13	237 11	1 17
..	0 6	..	..	35 13	..	4 17	185 1	1 1
..	0 10	..	..	60 8	..	9 0	199 15	..
..	5 10	0 5	..	125 5	..	17 14	536 9	..
..	..	..	..	30 18	..	..	127 19	..
..	4 15	..	..	45 18	..	14 14	265 16	..
..	8 0	..	..	60 0	..	8 17	350 17	..
..	1 0	..	..	29 2	..	13 16	129 0	..
..	4 5	..	..	59 2	..	14 16	398 14	9 10
..	..	..	..	31 3	..	6 4	70 15	..
..	0 17	..	..	26 2	..	16 10	293 12	9 13
..	1 5	..	..	71 9	2 11	..	374 11	..
..	0 16	..	..	15 16	..	17 12	45 9	..
..	4 0	..	..	57 16	..	15 17	295 14	..
..	..	..	..	38 6	..	27 13	112 4	..
..	0 5	..	..	13 8	..	..	29 18	..
..	2 6	..	..	89 16	..	41 16	447 3	7 9
..	5 9	..	..	92 14	..	46 6	657 6	7 1
..	3 0	..	..	48 9	4 0	10 12	235 1	..
..	..	..	..	6 5	..	0 7	9 17	..

NAMES OF COUNTIES, PARISHES, &c.	Amount levied by Assessment.	Received from all other Sources, in Aid of Poor Rate.	Total Amount Received for the Relief, &c., of the Poor.	Amount Expended in Relief, &c., of the Poor.	Amount Expended in Law Charges.
	£. s.	£. s.	£. s.	£. s.	£. s.
YORK, WEST RIDING—*continued.*					
Skyrack Wapentake, Upper Division.					
Addle-cum-Eccup	549 4	1 11	550 15	331 8	3 19
Allwoodley	61 0	3 0	64 0	32 2	..
Arthington	234 1	4 0	238 1	126 0	..
Baildon	627 7	34 15	662 2	501 12	71 10
Bramhope	136 3	..	136 3	100 2	3 9
Burleigh-in-Wharfdale . .	557 19	..	557 19	432 10	12 3
Carlton	90 5	..	90 5	45 0	..
Esholt	147 14	..	147 14	64 16	..
Harewood	275 5	15 16	291 1	138 9	..
Hawksworth	132 5	..	132 5	69 19	2 15
Horsforth	1,386 10	..	1,386 10	1,138 15	29 1
Ilkley	102 17	3 0	105 17	52 1	11 12
Menstone	88 2	..	88 2	53 2	0 11
Otley	904 0	11 18	915 18	684 3	64 16
Poole	126 1	..	126 1	70 12	18 18
Rawden	566 3	13 17	580 0	342 2	31 16
Weardley	79 3	..	79 3	40 2	..
Wigton	110 11	..	110 11	71 17	1 2
Wike	58 11	..	58 11	30 4	..
Yeaden	652 16	..	652 16	626 15	6 12
Staincliffe and Ewcross Wapentake, East Division.					
Silsden	948 10	..	948 10	760 16	..
Staincross Wapentake.					
Ardsley	466 15	9 0	475 15	337 9	54 6
Barnesley	3,632 4	86 7	3,718 11	2,279 8	89 1
Barugh	270 5	25 15	296 0	182 17	6 11
Brierley-cum-Grimsthorpe .	320 6	1 1	321 7	223 12	1 8
Carlton	326 10	..	326 10	219 19	..
Cawthorne	779 1	25 3	804 4	474 17	46 10
Chevett	72 12	4 0	76 12	35 19	..
Clayton, West	232 5	18 10	250 15	225 9	1 0
Cudworth	261 12	43 1	304 13	231 19	1 18
Darton	454 19	70 10	525 9	423 19	17 0
Denby	436 0	21 2	457 2	348 17	2 15
Dodworth	477 15	19 1	496 16	437 4	..
Gunthwaite	42 19	12 19	55 18	28 17	..
Havercroft-with-Cold-Hiendley	65 4	39 18	105 2	63 3	..
Hemsworth	563 4	6 11	569 15	341 7	94 11
Hiendley, South	164 12	4 0	168 12	111 17	2 0
Hoyland, High	101 19	5 13	107 12	91 0	..
Kexborough	262 12	10 14	273 6	180 7	14 5
Monk Bretton	647 8	2 0	649 8	491 1	22 5
Notton	265 1	22 17	287 18	231 12	2 10
Royston	323 3	24 17	348 0	281 0	..
Ryhill	60 7	6 17	67 4	38 8	..
Shafton	130 17	..	130 17	80 1	..
Silkstone	393 12	1 14	395 6	264 9	30 0
Stainborough	145 19	..	145 19	66 11	..
Wintersett	118 11	..	118 11	54 0	4 17
Woolley	397 9	14 9	411 18	291 10	11 5
Worsborough	767 6	113 7	880 13	478 3	15 0

er the Vac-nsion Act. Outlay for Register and Certificate Books.	Payments on Account of the Registration Act. Fees to Clergymen and Registrars.	Outlay for Register Offices, Books Forms, and other Incidental Expenses.	Payments under the Parochial Assessments Act (for Surveys, Valuations, &c.), and Loans repaid under the same.	Payments for or towards the County Rate.	Payments for or towards the County and Local Police Forces.	Money Expended for all other Purposes.	Total Parochial Rates, &c., Expended.	Medical Relief.
£. s.	£. s.	£. s.	£. s.	£. s.	£. s.	£. s.	£. s.	£. s.
..	..	1 7	4 4	107 1	2 9	4 1	454 18	9 9
..	0 3	..	..	20 4	..	11 12	64 1	0 14
..	..	1 3	..	80 10	..	8 1	215 14	4 11
..	10 19	0 4	..	76 18	..	18 7	680 13	0 11
..	0 15	..	..	31 17	..	..	136 3	4 14
..	..	8 13	..	83 11	..	21 1	557 18	2 13
..	0 16	..	..	25 19	..	13 12	85 7	..
..	1 2	..	10 3	37 14	5 12	22 5	141 12	..
..	1 15	..	..	107 3	..	43 13	291 0	4 7
..	..	0 15	..	47 16	..	8 17	130 2	..
0 10	8 17	..	..	130 16	1 8	..	1,317 1	10 17
..	1 14	0 4	..	43 16	..	63 4	172 11	5 17
..	0 8	..	..	29 17	..	..	84 10	1 10
..	12 18	..	..	109 17	17 19	75 6	964 19	15 3
..	..	3 7	..	31 7	..	2 10	126 14	..
..	..	5 7	..	94 2	13 2	15 0	501 9	5 10
..	0 8	..	..	20 14	1 0	15 16	78 0	..
..	..	0 6	..	22 16	..	..	96 1	..
..	0 9	..	..	15 13	..	12 4	58 10	..
..	10 6	..	..	86 12	..	..	730 5	15 4
..	9 10	..	..	159 14	..	5 10	940 0	3 9
..	3 18	..	..	54 12	..	20 9	470 14	5 5
..	43 14	..	..	392 14	160 11	276 1	3,241 9	44 4
..	5 12	0 4	..	48 6	..	13 2	256 12	5 5
..	1 3	..	..	56 15	..	28 8	311 6	5 0
..	..	0 18	..	70 5	..	..	291 2	5 5
..	5 5	..	..	166 14	..	110 18	804 4	10 7
..	0 5	..	..	25 5	..	5 15	67 4	..
..	3 17	0 5	2 10	42 2	..	13 0	289 17	2 9
..	..	1 12	..	60 8	..	20 0	320 17	5 0
..	5 9	0 7	20 2	41 3	..	21 16	529 16	8 0
..	5 6	..	..	56 1	..	41 16	454 15	3 19
..	3 14	0 5	..	52 15	..	3 13	497 11	5 0
..	..	..	..	18 8	..	3 9	50 14	..
..	..	0 8	..	32 4	..	..	95 15	1 8
..	2 12	0 9	..	136 13	..	60 8	636 0	12 0
..	1 8	..	..	30 12	..	20 12	166 9	4 0
..	1 4	0 1	..	23 14	..	1 12	118 1	..
..	1 18	..	..	49 0	..	7 15	253 5	4 4
..	6 2	1 2	..	75 12	..	53 6	649 8	8 0
..	0 12	..	..	60 5	..	1 1	296 0	..
..	1 18	..	..	35 16	..	..	318 14	..
..	0 8	..	..	15 6	..	18 3	72 5	..
..	..	0 14	..	20 1	..	26 13	127 9	..
..	6 13	0 7	..	41 19	..	37 3	380 11	6 6
..	..	0 18	..	47 8	4 14	25 2	144 13	2 6
..	..	0 6	..	22 16	..	23 6	105 5	..
..	1 17	..	..	52 13	..	4 9	361 14	..
..	..	27 14	..	212 2	..	39 17	772 16	..

NAMES of COUNTIES, PARISHES, &c.	Amount levied by Assessment.	Received from all other Sources, in Aid of Poor Rate.	Total Amount Received for the Relief, &c., of the Poor.	Amount Expended in Relief, &c., of the Poor.	Amount Expended in Law Charges.
	£. s.	£. s.	£. s.	£. s.	£. s.
YORK, WEST RIDING—*continued.*					
Strafforth and Tickhill Wapentake, North Division,					
Billingley	104 14	12 2	116 16	99 5	..
Darfield	476 15	..	476 15	249 10	5 10
Hamphall Stubbs	10 19	..	10 19	5 7	..
Houghton, Great	247 15	9 2	256 17	196 8	..
Houghton, Little	68 17	..	68 17	19 14	..
Wombwell	561 4	34 17	596 1	462 7	1 11
Liberty of Ripon.					
Aismunderby-with-Bondgate .	250 10	25 0	275 10	183 4	12 18
Bishop Monkton	260 6	..	260 6	183 2	20 11
Bishop Thornton	280 9	28 5	308 14	230 8	10 0
Bishopton	30 16	1 6	32 2	24 2	..
Bridge Hewick	58 12	..	58 12	39 9	..
Clotherholme	No Levy.				
Copt Hewick	82 4	..	82 4	49 15	14 4
Eavestone	48 5	..	48 5	33 15	..
Givendale	21 1	..	21 1	..	..
Grantley	150 12	..	150 12	118 10	..
Ingerthorpe	63 17	..	63 17	44 19	..
Markington-with-Wallerthwaite	387 15	3 7	391 2	237 7	4 4
Newby-with-Mulwith . . .	47 2	..	47 2	28 0	..
Nidd-with-Killinghall . . .	70 12	..	70 12	47 2	..
Nunwick-with-Howgrave . .	44 4	0 10	44 14	13 5	0 11
Ripon Borough	1,772 10	153 2	1,925 12	1,275 14	155 15
Sawley	190 7	19 13	210 0	202 6	..
Sharrow.	36 16	16 0	52 16	19 7	..
Skelton	114 6	10 3	124 9	69 10	1 14
Stainley, North, with Slenning-ford.. . . . . . .}	257 11	..	257 11	101 11	..
Sutton Grange	85 14	..	85 14	85 14	..
Westwick	19 13	..	19 13	8 6	..
Whitcliffe-with-Thorpe . .	73 15	3 0	76 15	38 7	..
Borough of Leeds.					
Armley	1,464 19	144 11	1,609 10	1,013 3	66 17
Beeston	848 10	78 5	926 15	537 2	132 16
Bramley	2,838 18	687 10	3,526 8	2,398 16	130 0
Chapel Allerton	936 4	49 18	986 2	599 19	..
Farnley	986 18	..	986 18	541 4	27 19
Headington-with-Burley . .	1,354 0	65 16	1,419 16	700 6	41 5
Holbeck	5,081 18	206 3	5,288 1	3,210 17	240 0
Hunslett	4,213 19	248 9	4,462 8	2,835 12	129 0
Leeds	36,486 11	431 10	36,918 1	25,674 1	597 12
Potter Newton	468 14	42 11	511 5	244 4	2 16
Wortley	1,863 13	1,278 7	3,142 0	2,204 0	98 19
Totals	133,916 18	7,650 18	141,567 16	97,031 12	4,823 4

der the Vaccination Act.	Payments on Account of the Registration Act.		Payments under the Parochial Assessments Act (for Surveys, Valuations, &c.), and Loans repaid under the same.	Payments for or towards the County Rate.	Payments for or towards the County and Local Police Forces.	Money Expended for all other Purposes.	Total Parochial Rates, &c., Expended.	Medical Relief.
Outlay for Register and Certificate Books.	Fees to Clergymen and Registrars.	Outlay for Register Offices, Books, Forms, and other Incidental Expenses.						
£. s.	£. s.	£. s.	£. s.	£. s.	£. s.	£. s.	£. s.	£. s.
..	0 13	..	..	22 6	..	..	122 4	4 4
..	1 6	..	..	54 19	..	151 1	462 6	7 0
..	..	..	..	5 11	..	..	10 18	..
..	..	1 11	..	39 16	..	4 18	247 13	5 0
..	0 4	..	..	23 7	..	3 1	46 6	0 17
.	6 15	..	..	114 12	..	10 14	595 19	10 10
..	1 11	..	..	38 15	..	37 12	275 10	1 11
..	2 8	..	..	46 11	..	4 12	257 4	0 15
..	2 15	..	..	46 5	..	13 6	308 14	..
..	..	0 2	..	..	..	..	24 4	..
..	..	0 3	..	19 3	..	..	58 15	..
..	..	0 7	..	17 18	..	..	82 4	..
..	..	..	..	8 1	..	..	41 16	..
..	..	..	..	24 5	..	..	24 5	..
..	0 16	..	..	26 9	..	0 15	146 10	..
..	..	..	..	9 5	..	9 13	63 17	..
..	..	2 9	..	57 9	..	..	301 9	..
..	..	..	..	16 19	..	..	44 19	..
..	0 9	..	..	22 0	..	1 1	70 12	..
..	..	..	..	6 3	19 15	4 13	44 7	..
..	27 5	..	..	251 18	..	108 13	1,822 3	35 1
..	4 10	..	..	..	..	..	206 16	0 4
..	0 10	..	..	29 0	..	2 11	51 8	..
..	0 10	..	..	7 15	..	25 15	105 4	..
..	..	0 11	..	67 1	..	88 8	257 11	..
..	0 2	..	..	..	..	..	85 16	..
..	..	..	..	9 18	..	1 9	19 13	..
..	0 10	0 1	..	35 8	..	..	75 7	..
..	15 6	..	..	452 19	..	49 16	1,602 7	25 0
..	6 7	0 10	..	170 10	..	4 18	852 3	66 4
1 4	0 1	25 16	..	621 6	..	349 4	3,526 7	..
..	7 13	..	..	..	319 4	46 7	977 6	13 5
..	2 5	..	..	..	178 4	..	749 12	..
..	14 8	0 17	..	718 13	..	34 8	1,522 12	16 16
0 4	46 16	..	..	866 6	..	335 13	4,732 9	42 0
..	54 11	..	..	1,048 15	..	16 7	4,084 5	196 2
23 8	323 2	23 2	..	8,812 15	..	238 16	35,733 13	411 12
..	4 11	..	..	276 5	..	12 8	540 4	13 12
..	20 17	0 6	..	473 7	..	89 17	2,892 14	10 7
36 7	1,015 19	191 11	329 14	26,568 2	891 16	5,051 19	136,180 13	1,877 6

Y

NAMES OF COUNTIES, PARISHES, &c.	Amount levied by Assessment.	Received from all other Sources, in Aid of Poor Rate.	Total Amount Received for the Relief, &c., of the Poor.
	£. *s.*	£. *s.*	£. *s.*
WALES.			
DENBIGH.			
Chirk Hundred.			
Chirk	515 12	..	515 12
Llansillin	550 1	..	550 1
Totals	1,065 13	..	
MONTGOMERY.			
Cawse Hundred, Lower Division.			
Forden	628 0	..	628 0
Leighton (part of) . . .	143 1	..	143 1
Middletown	53 5	..	53 5
Rhos Goch	33 8	..	33 8
Trelystan, or Woolstonmind .	69 19	1 0	70 19
Uppington	74 10	..	74 10
Cawse Hundred, Upper Division.			
Castle Caereinion, Upper and Lower	576 5	..	576 5
Cofronydd (part of) . . .	42 12	3 10	46 2
Montgomery Hundred, Lower Division.			
Aston	57 18	..	57 18
Castlewright	94 3	..	94 3
Churchstoke	900 0	..	900 0
Montgomery	597 7	2 8	599 15
Newton Hundred, Lower Division.			
Berriew	1,381 0	0 8	1,381 8
Newton Hundred, Upper Division.			
Llandysill	528 1	..	528 1
Llanmerewig	110 3	..	110 3
Pool Hundred.			
Guilsfield	1,261 11	7 9	1,269 0
Pool Borough.			
Cletterwood	183 0	10 2	193 2
Hope	118 8	..	118 8
Pool, Lower	380 16	..	380 16
Pool, Middle	891 10	..	891 10
Pool, Upper	488 15	..	488 15
Trewern	142 12	..	142 12
Totals	8,756 4	24 17	

for the Vaccination Act. Outlay for Register and Certificate Books.	Payments on Account of the Registration Act. Fees to Clergymen and Registrars.	Outlay for Register Offices, Books, Forms, and other Incidental Expenses.	Payments under the Parochial Assessments Act (for Surveys, Valuations, &c.), and Loans repaid under the same.	Payments for or towards the County Rate.	Payments for or towards the County and Local Police Forces.	Money Expended for all other Purposes.	Total Parochial Rates, &c., Expended.	Medical Relief.
£. s.	£. s.	£. s.	£. s.	£. s.	£. s.	£. s.	£. s.	£. s.
..	10 10	..	..	146 4	..	36 12	480 16	..
..		..	..	100 9	38 8	32 4	517 17	10 0
..	10 10	..	..	246 13	38 8	68 16	998 13	10 0
..	2 1	..	..	181 5	..	..	614 17	11 3
0 7	..	..	..	40 9	..	..	188 0	..
..	..	..	..	14 7	..	2 17	48 0	..
..	..	..	..	8 19	..	..	32 5	..
..	..	..	..	21 4	..	..	70 14	..
..	0 3	..	..	12 13	4 4	1 6	66 15	..
..	0 13	..	..	109 8	..	9 9	573 13	9 1
..	..	..	..	8 7	..	3 5	42 0	..
..	0 15	..	..	18 12	3 8	1 1	50 19	..
..	..	..	..	25 14	..	0 18	88 14	..
..	2 4	0 3	..	210 16	..	64 9	871 7	24 0
..	3 3	..	..	100 1	..	2 11	647 19	5 5
..	5 3	..	72 10	278 4	51 0	53 0	1,381 8	24 14
..	1 16	..	..	104 14	..	55 2	492 16	10 10
..	0 8	0 2	..	28 16	..	5 12	111 6	..
..	..	..	..	415 5	..	80 19	1,255 6	..
..	..	1 14	..	46 3	..	19 6	176 13	..
1 5	..	..	..	26 11	..	..	109 12	..
..	2 5	0 2	..	122 2	..	16 7	381 0	4 16
..	5 15	0 2	..	117 15	121 4	48 11	876 11	19 18
..	0 13	0 2	..	107 9	..	12 4	440 6	8 11
..	..	..	..	41 7	..	..	121 10	5 0
1 12	24 19	2 5	72 10	2,040 1	179 16	376 17	8,641 11	122 19

No. II.—STATEMENT, showing the Amount of Money Expended for the RELIEF and MAINTENANCE of the Poor, in each of the following Unions and Single Parishes, under the Provisions of the Poor Law Amendment Act, from the earliest year for which complete Abstracts have been received to the Year ended Lady-day, 1844; also the Amount expended for the like purpose in each of the Unions and Single Parishes, under Local Acts, from 1337 to 1844.

COUNTIES, UNIONS, &c.	Amount of Money Expended for the Relief and Maintenance of the Poor.							
	Years ended at Lady-day,							
	1837	1838	1839	1840	1841	1842	1843	1844
	£.	£.	£.	£.	£.	£.	£	£.
BEDFORD.								
Ampthill	5,591	5,969	6,299	6,312	6,126	6,038	6,225	6,068
Bedford	9,896	10,046	10,941	10,530	10,502	10,899	10,788	11,310
Biggleswade	7,337	8,555	8,113	7,788	8,272	8,645	9,455	9,450
Leighton-Buzzard	5,771	5,491	5,262	7,241	5,923	6,453	6,490	6,464
Luton	5,736	7,439	5,939	5,976	6,541	6,619	6,458	5,976
Woburn	4,693	4,825	5,093	4,941	5,209	5,165	5,769	5,201
BERKS.								
Abingdon	7,041†	8,334	8,098	8,291	7,946	7,802	7,806	7,853
Bradfield	..	7,896	6,994	8,017	8,760	8,733	9,305	8,526
Cookham	2,844	2,926	2,921	2,997	2,916	2,945	3,396	3,562
Easthampstead	1,973	2,100	2,278	2,452	2,637	3,295	2,772	1,754
Faringdon	6,346	6,134	7,860	6,951	6,814	7,266	7,463	6,855
Hungerford	8,359†	8,340	9,906	9,325	10,143	10,068	10,148	9,663
Newbury	9,280	9,651	10,573	11,766	13,015	13,674	13,336	12,703
Reading	5,600	4,622	4,896	4,963	5,336	5,430	5,048	4,899
Wallingford	6,982	7,267	7,629	8,016	8,507	8,571	9,455	8,417
Wantage	10,298	8,987	8,336	8,698	8,966	8,836	9,401	9,348
Windsor	5,353	5,234	5,579	5,944	7,410	6,948	6,927	6,661
Wokingham	5,195	5,508	5,880	6,588	7,145	7,860	7,952	7,721
BUCKINGHAM.								
Amersham	5,751	6,089†	7,173	8,196	8,618	8,733	9,011	7,792
Aylesbury	10,246	11,401	11,206	12,414	11,932	12,127	13,395	13,583
Buckingham	5,974	6,569	7,590	8,436	7,777	8,725	7,624	7,785
Eton	8,607	6,396	6,325	7,193	7,675	7,052	6,454	5,992
Newport-Pagnell	..	7,809	8,115	9,084	8,875	9,711	9,276	9,545
Winslow	4,722	4,490	4,987	4,776	5,267	5,036	5,455	5,568
Wycombe	..	14,975	15,847	16,179	16,356	17,931	19,004	17,695
CAMBRIDGE.								
Cambridge	4,846	5,359	7,017	9,599	7,868	8,014	8,949	9,252
Caxton and Arrington	3,831	5,012	5,724	5,277	5,191	5,328	5,400	5,400
Chesterton	5,923	9,145	8,940	9,617	9,834	10,813	10,266	9,866
Ely	6,656	6,126	6,966	7,253	7,569	7,774	7,274	7,266

NOTE.—The Expenditure for Unions, &c., under the Poor Law Amendment Act, is obtained from the Quarterly Abstracts, Form B 11, received from the Clerks to the Guardians, and includes In-maintenance, Out-relief, Establishment Charges, and Salaries, Workhouse Loans, repaid, and "other Expenses" immediately connected with Relief to the Poor; and the Expenditure for Places under Local Acts, from the Returns made annually by the Overseers of the Poor, and also for a few Unions from which Quarterly Abstracts have not been received.

Those Places marked thus (*) are under Local Acts.

Those Unions marked thus (†) have had additions of Parishes made to them in the years under which the marks are placed.

Those Unions marked thus (‡) have had Parishes separated from them in the years under which the marks are placed.

No. 2, (*continued*).—Statement, showing the Amount of Money Expended for the Relief and Maintenance of the Poor, in each of the following Unions and Single Parishes, under the Provisions of the Poor Law Amendment Act, from the earliest year for which complete Abstracts have been received to the Year ended Lady-day, 1844; also the Amount Expended for the like purpose in each, of the Unions and Single Parishes, under Local Acts, from 1837 to 1844.

COUNTIES, UNIONS, &c.	Amount of Money Expended for the Relief and Maintenance of the Poor.							
	Years ended at Lady-day.							
	1837	1838	1839	1840	1841	1842	1843	1844
CAMBRIDGE—*continued*	£.	£,	£.	£.	£.	£.	£.	£.
Linton	6,739	7,675	8,344	8,048	9,269	9,129	8,467	8,219
Newmarket . . .	11,152	12,789	15,120	15,251	14,451	14,456	13,735	13,474
North Witchford .	..	4,075	5,325	7,334	6,734	..	6,134	5,426
Whittlesey . . .	..	1,754	1,808	1,764	1,781	1,841	1,687	1,854
Wisbeach . . .	..	11,484†	11,858	15,013	14,388	14,896	14,681	14,602
CHESTER.								
Altrincham . . .	..	7,634‡	6,723	8,274	7,659	7,974	9,346	9,448
Boughton, Great .	..	..	7,530	7,905	8,448	9,066	9,604	9,452
Congleton . . .	..	7,745	6,839	6,896*	6,887	6,862	6,860	6,429
Macclesfield . . .	..	11,342	10,394	10,466	10,326	10,800	11,245	10,098
Nantwich . . .	..	8,749†	8,706	9,570	10,226	9,204	10,783	11,042
Northwich . . .	..	8,325‡	7,899	9,310	8,482	8,884	9,819	8,592
Runcorn	..	5,191	5,691	6,120	5,995	6,182	6,421	6,039
Stockport. . . .	..	..	..	10,647	11,951	17,075	23,595	16,643
Wirrall	..	3,127	3,448	2,798	2,998	2,931	2,873	2,670
*Chester, City of . .	3,585	3,829	4,369	4,734	5,101	7,708	6,232	5,967
CORNWALL.								
Austell, St. . . .	..	..	7,011	7,794	7,877	8,310	7,990	7,753
Bodmin	..	..	5,758	6,062	6,143	6,279	6,878	6,727
Camelford . . .	..	2,098	2,449	2,600	2,711	2,788	2,778	2,636
Columb, St. Major .	..	..	4,230	4,837	6,095	5,506	5,590	4,672
Falmouth . . .	..	..	5,344	5,552	5,588	5,638	5,377	5,011
Germans, St. . .	..	4,731	4,776	5,313	5,766	5,823	5,837	5,370
Helston	..	..	6,010	5,672	5,860	6,095	6,595	6,329
Launceston . . .	..	4,659	4,555	5,235	5,521	5,337	5,308	5,168
Liskeard	..	8,794	9,406	9,747	9,683	9,584	10,031	9,539
Penzance . . .	..	..	5,542	5,602	7,501	5,905	5,106	4,899
Redruth	..	..	7,307	6,877	8,421	6,196	7,163	6,032
Stratton	..	2,653	3,082	3,329	3,528	3,709	3,611	3,438
Truro	..	..	8,408	9,402	10,182	9,972	10,055	9,156
CUMBERLAND.								
Alston-with-Garrigill	..	..	1,413	1,304	1,500	1,229	1,270	1,323
Bootle	..	..	..	..	1,356	1,320	1,323	1,348
Brampton . . .	..	..	2,340	2,193	2,012	2,410	2,210	1,981
Carlisle	..	..	..	6,002	6,403	6,458	6,734	5,969
Cockermouth . .	..	..	..	6,577	7,183	7,279	7,539	7,405
Longtown . . .	..	..	2,527	2,751	2,689	3,061	3,148	2,963
Penrith	..	5,106	4,915	6,243	5,583	5,377	5,469	5,523
Whitehaven . . .	..	..	..	5,986	5,722	5,377	5,737	5,365
Wigton	..	..	4,220	4,682	4,779	4,441	4,303	3,880
DERBY.								
Bakewell . . .	..	..	..	6,011	6,080	8,345	7,984	6,963
Belper	..	..	6,161	6,440	8,021	8,207	7,332	6,867

No. 2, (*continued*).—Statement, showing the Amount of Money Expended for the Relief and Maintenance of the Poor, in each of the following Unions and Single Parishes, under the Provisions of the Poor Law Amendment Act, from the earliest year for which complete Abstracts have been received to the year ended Lady-day, 1844; also the Amount Expended for the like purpose in each of the Unions and Single Parishes, under Local Acts, from 1837 to 1844.

COUNTIES, UNIONS, &c.	Amount of Money Expended for the Relief and Maintenance of the Poor. Years ended at Lady-day.							
	1837	1838	1839	1840	1841	1842	1843	1844
	£.	£.	£.	£.	£.	£.	£.	£.
DERBY—*continued.*								
Chapel-en-le-Frith .	..	..	1,973	2,235	2,770	3,611	3,218	2,468
Chesterfield . . .	..	..	6,511	7,853	8,517	8,635	8,804	9,253
Derby	..	..	4,642	6,874	4,995	5,076	4,947	4,184
Glossop	..	..	1,127	1,447	1,599	1,520	1,914	1,312
Hayfield	..	..	1,469	1,858	1,990	2,423	2,442	2,195
Shardlow	..	..	6,318	6,708	6,514	7,082	8,249	8,078
DEVON.								
Axminster . . .	..	7,935	9,278	9,975	9,572	9,802	10,641	9,385
Barnstaple . . .	8,782	9,938	9,417	9,767	10,244	10,303	10,463	10,252
Bideford	5,201	5,224	5,932	6,218	6,657	6,288	6,495	5,735
Crediton . . .	..	9,953	11,133	11,930	11,223	11,428	11,290	10,021
East Stonehouse . .	..	..	..	2,306	2,450	2,413	2,485	2,193
Holsworthy . . .	..	2,904	3,350	3,431	3,744	3,785	3,635	3,426
Honiton	..	8,229	10,026	10,469	10,230	10,472	11,165	9,866
Kingsbridge . . .	..	9,117	10,172	9,816	9,947	9,612	10,326	9,214
Newton Abbot . .	..	12,953	13,938	15,999	15,067	15,125	14,418	13,303
Okehampton . . .	..	6,299	7,446	7,243	7,004	6,883	7,250	6,659
Plympton, St. Mary	..	7,066	7,563	8,140	8,155	9,026	8,135	7,320
South Molton . .	6,896	7,985	8,557	8,191	8,328	7,857	8,083	7,541
Tavistock . . .	..	6,394	7,460	8,046	8,167	7,467	7,768	7,450
Thomas, St.. . .	..	16,778	16,682	18,044	19,050	19,134	18,456	17,603
Tiverton	12,818	14,259	14,979	16,764	16,166	16,931	17,215	16,986
Torrington . . .	5,938	6,781	6,611	6,976	7,209	7,506	7,291	7,070
Totnes	..	11,897	12,536	13,179	13,546	13,803	13,878	11,211
*Exeter, City of . .	5,706	6,663	6,457	7,063	7,470	7,161	7,063	6,769
*Plymouth . . .	9,395	9,320	9,277	9,600	9,388	9,630	9,937	10,207
*Stoke Damerell . .	8,059	7,630	7,187	9,793	10,331	8,631	7,365	7,640
DORSET.								
Beaminster . . .	..	5,689	7,219	7,845	8,653	8,805	9,271	8,305
Blandford . . .	5,730	6,028	6,261	6,777	6,459	6,483	6,330	6,280
Bridport	3,878	4,753	6,571	6,398	6,979	7,587	7,948	6,910
Cerne	2,464	3,162	3,349	3,584	3,492	3,399	3,412	3,375
Dorchester . . .	4,251	6,118	6,313	6,316	6,379	6,700	6,478	6,728
Poole	4,191	3,684	4,001	5,037	4,826	4,824	4,848	4,584
Shaftesbury . . .	5,203	5,544	6,362	6,872	6,633	6,370	6,467	6,227
Sherborne . . .	3,194	4,003	5,383	5,805	5,942	6,009	5,992	5,895
Sturminster . . .	4,656	5,679	5,732	5,495	5,520	5,823	5,884	5,907
Wareham and Purbeck	4,879	6,511	8,516	8,549	8,694	8,273	8,268	8,075
Weymouth . . .	5,072	5,535	6,250	6,244	6,245	6,856	7,659	6,937
Wimborne and Cranborne	5,349	6,067	7,086	7,959	7,659	7,484	7,239	6,880
DURHAM.								
Auckland	..	3,212	3,225	3,137	2,982	3,102	3,605	3,759
Chester-le-Street .	..	5,095	4,964	4,969	4,902	4,585	4,749	4,830
Darlington . . .	..	5,252	5,533	5,208	5,108	5,527	5,696	5,755

No. 2, (*continued*).—Statement, showing the Amount of Money Expended for the Relief and Maintenance of the Poor, in each of the following Unions and Single Parishes, under the Provisions of the Poor Law Amendment Act, from the earliest year for which complete Abstracts have been received to the year ended Lady-day, 1844; also the Amount Expended for the like purpose in each of the Unions and Single Parishes, under Local Acts, from 1837 to 1844.

COUNTIES, UNIONS, &c.	Amount of Money Expended for the Relief and Maintenance of the Poor.							
	Years ended at Lady-day,							
	1837	1838	1839	1840	1841	1842	1843	1844
	£.	£.	£.	£.	£.	£.	£.	£.
DURHAM—*continued.*								
Durham	..	3,837	4,329	3,910	3,679	3,670	4,237	4,542
Easington . . .	..	1,029	1,144	1,185	1,231	1,307	1,500	1,749
Gateshead . . .	..	7,091	7,705	7,278	7,657	8,778	10,788	9,884
Houghton-le-Spring.	..	3,143	3,511	3,582	3,535	3,549	3,732	3,662
Lanchester . . .	..	2,014	2,100	2,250	2,188	2,425	2,266	2,400
Sedgefield . . .	..	1,680	1,633	1,790	1,612	1,603	1,734	1,868
South Shields . .	..	6,166	6,453	6,181	6,775	7,173	7,854	8,119
Stockton	..	5,390	5,455	5,270	5,104	5,552	5,829	5,784
Sunderland . . .	..	9,378	11,382	11,394	12,140	14,370	19,091	18,234
Teesdale . . .	..	5,138	5,599	6,273	5,814	5,655	6,181	5,509
Weardale . . .	..	3,665	3,848	3,833	3,672	3,514	3,250	3,778
ESSEX.								
Billericay . . .	4,936	4,908	4,878	5,049	8,097	6,051	5,429	5,879
Braintree . . .	8,085	9,610	10,306	11,619	11,180	10,411	10,381	9,446
Chelmsford . . .	12,570	13,468	16,050	16,496	14,665	15,107	15,235	15,596
Colchester . . .	7,170	7,767	7,399	6,902	7,517	7,588	7,783	7,679
Dunmow . . .	10,969	12,270	13,996	14,569	16,856	15,638	13,450	12,610
Epping	5,322	4,725	5,927	5,769	6,061	6,577	6,295	5,979
Halstead . . .	10,181	8,795	8,838	9,264	8,959	8,696	9,251	8,695
Lexden and Winstree	9,151†	9,506	9,509	8,797	8,679	8,612	8,689	8,219
Maldon	7,776	7,491	8,445	9,478	9,677	10,017	9,903	9,662
Ongar.	..	4,885	5,575	5,163	5,201	5,262	5,964	5,897
Orsett . . .	3,771	3,955	4,259	4,848	4,724	4,883	5,236	4,594
Rochford. . . .	4,973†	5,475	6,832	6,540	6,969	5,530	5,611	5,317
Romford . . .	..	8,211	8,033	9,151	11,693	10,117	9,794	9,775
Saffron Walden . .	9,292	10,255	10,569	11,209	10,874	11,375	12,058	11,281
Tendring . . .	9,035†	8,424†	11,594	12,985	11,756	10,835	10,481	9,592
West Ham . . .	..	10,108	9,767	10,504	10,861	13,160	12,208	11,322
Witham	5,069	5,531	6,163	5,780	4,974	4,996	4,945	5,483
GLOUCESTER.								
Cheltenham . . .	4,747†	5,501	5,885	6,628	6,580	8,455	8,694	8,198
Chipping Sodbury .	4,922	..	..	5,889	6,404	6,491	6,650	6,230
Cirencester . . .	5,921	6,659	6,407	6,993	7,312	7,009	6,975	6,667
Clifton	..	15,431	14,222	15,192	16,544	16,304	16,744	16,304
Dursley	..	7,259	7,551	8,623	9,507	9,156	9,398	8,622
Gloucester . . .	4,661	4,944	5,352	5,762	5,965	7,363	7,419	7,193
Newent	3,252	3,780	3,921	3,976	4,505	4,303	4,509	4,766
Northleach . . .	3,235	4,238	4,072	4,406	4,177	4,063	4,230	4,150
Stow-on-the-Wold .	2,998	3,776	3,631	3,591	3,634	3,546	3,747	3,775
Stroud	..	12,333	13,191	13,294	14,054	14,463	15,480	13,517
Tetbury	..	1,737	1,532	2,401	1,831	1,802	1,610	1,559
Tewkesbury . . .	4,492	4,181	6,935	5,015	4,997	5,023	5,452	4,920
Thornbury . . .	4,206	5,283	5,173	6,615	5,958	5,733	5,663	5,849
Westbury-on-Severn	2,364	3,020	2,938	3,109	3,170	3,233	3,200	3,132
Wheatenhurst .	3,687	4,107	2,553	2,799	2,938	3,212	2,998	2,578
Winchcombe . .	2,600	3,142	3,054	3,394	3,431	3,539	3,292	3,335
*Bristol, City of .	16,565	15,294	15,279	17,092	17,589	18,580	20,468	22,021

No. 2, (*continued*).—Statement, showing the Amount of Money Expended for the Relief and Maintenance of the Poor, in each of the following Unions and Single Parishes, under the Provisions of the Poor Law Amendment Act, from the earliest year for which complete Abstracts have been received to the year ended Lady-day, 1844; also the amount Expended for the like purpose in each of the Unions and Single Parishes, under Local Acts, from 1837 to 1844.

COUNTIES, UNIONS, &c.	Amount of Money Expended for the Relief and Maintenance of the Poor. Years ended at Lady-day.							
	1837	1838	1839	1840	1841	1842	1843	1844
	£.	£.	£.	£.	£.	£.	£.	£.
HEREFORD.								
Bromyard . . .	..	4,144	4,156	4,598	4,653	4,861	4,814	4,390
Dore	..	..	4,001	4,273	4,452	4,371	4,352	3,985
Hereford	..	7,440†	8,444	8,267	8,366	8,611	9,191	8,405
Kington	..	..	5,067	5,304	5,208	4,999	4,979	4,593
Ledbury	..	3,595	3,990	3,921	4,651	4,542	4,288	4,495
Leominster . . .	..	4,631	4,562	4,764	5,096	5,177	5,167	5,797
Ross	..	5,817	5,878	5,973	5,944	6,146	6,426	6,482
Weobly	..	3,067†	2,743	3,068	3,182	3,223	3,257	2,902
HERTFORD.								
Albans, St. . . .	3,910	4,040	4,035	4,111	4,884	3,803	3,991	3,865
Barnet	4,009†	5,367	5,193	5,525	5,625	5,730	5,992	5,980
Berkhampstead . .	..	3,353	3,554	3,974	4,385	4,558	4,503	4,020
Bishop Stortford .	8,447	9,844	10,840	10,675	11,247	11,320	11,592	10,739
Buntingford . .	2,468	3,049	3,167	3,354	2,895	3,123	3,064	3,409
Hatfield . . .	1,640	1,746	1,672	1,737	1,904	2,006	2,643	2,235
Hemelhempstead .	..	2,950	3,156	3,481	3,601	3,687	3,811	3,649
Hertford . . .	4,573	4,618	5,282	5,127	5,407	5,454	5,659	5,774
Hitchin . . .	7,818	8,712	8,044	8,377	9,430	9,867	9,762	8,882
Royston . . .	7,321	6,585	7,597	7,615	7,530	7,255	7,156	6,963
Ware . . .	5,925	6,323	5,918	6,087	7,948	10,066	8,387	7,596
Watford	4,294	4,829	4,969	6,759	5,497	5,529	6,181	5,825
Welwyn	726	841	876	888	894	820	790	784
HUNTINGDON.								
Huntingdon . . .	6,919	..	8,555	7,978	7,330	7,640	7,770	7,555
Ives, St. . . .	5,511	7,420	8,263	8,195	8,430	8,146	8,328	7,577
Neots, St. . . .	8,066	7,480	7,926	8,423	8,587	8,964	8,287	7,859
KENT.								
Ashford, East .	5,917	6,092	6,731	6,692	6,642	6,587	5,963	5,848
Ashford, West .	4,997	5,490	5,665	5,872	5,925	6,000	6,053	5,696
Blean	4,877	4,332	4,651	4,297	4,150	4,596	4,564	4,300
Bridge	5,241	4,764	4,045	4,257	4,637	4,797	4,830	4,318
Bromley	..	4,703	5,010	5,446	5,399	4,860	5,189	4,901
Cranbrook . . .	6,827	6,175	7,079	7,045	8,963	8,088	7,666	7,773
Dartford . . .	..	7,141	6,542	7,214	6,206	6,183	6,641	6,615
Dover	7,967†	7,267	7,888	7,858	7,813	8,033	7,657	7,689
Eastry	8,800	7,424	8,211	7,444	8,066	8,990	9,843	9,265
Elham	5,357†	5,210	5,256	5,502	5,412	5,535	5,565	5,275
Faversham . . .	7,109	6,323	6,829	7,428	7,652	7,321	7,360	6,959
Gravesend and Milton	2,756	2,455	2,668	2,707	2,933	2,912	3,137	3,332
Greenwich . . .	..	15,594	16,888	17,796	20,287	27,969	22,133	21,697
Hollingbourn . .	7,006	8,934	9,236	9,359	10,764	10,006	10,718	9,581
Hoo	1,828	1,903	1,397	1,454	1,385	1,371	1,329	1,278
Lewisham . . .	..	5,991	5,410	5,587	5,255	5,001	5,406	5,166
Maidstone . . .	..	12,456†	14,652	13,157	13,002	12,667	11,857	12,029
Malling	10,860	7,904	7,841	9,069	9,306	8,996	9,104	9,336
Medway	8,096†	8,314	9,562	10,016	9,633	9,841	9,907	8,472

No. 2, (*continued*).—Statement, showing the Amount of Money Expended for the Relief and Maintenance of the Poor, in each of the following Unions and Single Parishes, under the Provisions of the Poor Law Amendment Act, from the earliest year for which complete Abstracts have been received to the year ended Lady-day, 1844; also the Amount Expended for the like purpose in each of the Unions and Single Parishes, under Local Acts, from 1837 to 1844.

COUNTIES, UNIONS, &c.	Amount of Money Expended for the Relief and Maintenance of the Poor.							
	Years ended at Lady-day.							
	1837	1838	1839	1840	1841	1842	1843	1844
	£.	£.	£.	£.	[£.	£.	£.	£.
KENT—*continued.*								
Milton . . .	5,472	4,382	4,676	4,951	5,004	4,779	5,351	4,565
North Aylesford . .	5,400	6,788	6,152	5,576	5,763	5,698	5,911	5,644
Romney Marsh . .	2,766	3,608	3,026	2,947	3,014	2,987	3,194	3,106
Sevenoaks . . .	7,627	7,795	8,305	8,493	8,226	9,666	9,566	9,496
Sheppey	3,460	3,482	3,469	3,583	3,453	3,208	3,175	3,099
Tenterden . . .	6,569	7,402	7,190	5,783	6,066	6,262	6,687	5,794
Thanet, Isle of .	6,946	8,199	7,134	7,535	7,824	7,786	7,642	7,413
Tonbridge . . .	8,692	8,457	10,458	10,489	10,612	10,885	10,827	10,636
*Canterbury, City of	5,739	5,468	5,933	4,985	5,306	5,319	4,729	4,569
LANCASTER.								
Ashton-under-Lyne	..	5,339	6,047	8,016	9,179	9,298	11,776	10,065
Blackburn . . .	..	..	7,922	7,485	8,259	10,544	15,781	11,483
Bolton	..	..	..	..	18,699	18,723	24,698	16,926
Burnley	..	..	..	9,319	10,402	14,046	17,926	10,953
Bury	..	..	..	..	..	9,662	13,733	12,412
Chorley	..	..	..	6,031	6,689	6,597	10,014	8,699
Chorlton	..	..	5,613	5,098	6,299†	9,890	13,085	11,020
Clitheroe . . .	..	..	..}	8,699	6,911	8,100	10,351	7,439
Fylde, The . . .	..	..	..	3,375	3,688	4,168	4,995	4,245
Garstang . . .	..	..	..	3,852	3,744	4,115	5,243	5,088
Haslingden . . .	..	3,178	3,188	3,917	4,307	5,160	7,655	5,534
Lancaster . . .	..	..	..	..	6,266	6,596	7,505	6,551
Leigh	..	..	3,908	4,609	5,555	5,760	6,783	5,801
Liverpool . . .	32,020	36,564	36,719	40,361	32,069	35,581	42,536	50,678
Manchester . . .	..	..	..	..	..	53,415	51,119	49,589
Oldham	..	4,677	5,169	6,811	9,331	11,797	14,658	10,355
Ormskirk . . .	..	..	3,714	3,931	5,630	4,723	5,028	5,308
Prescot	..	..	..	5,593	7,504	7,681	8,216	7,154
Preston	..	..	..	12,379	13,410	17,962	23,509	16,975
Rochdale . . .	..	5,336	5,666	6,202	8,477	10,295	11,493	10,330
Salford	..	..	..	7,892	8,398	8,579	10,267	9,023
Todmorden . . .	..	3,025	3,753	4,440	5,029	5,836	9,039	7,231
Ulverstone . . .	..	6,227	7,537	7,710	7,697	7,682	8,371	7,486
Warrington . . .	..	..	5,437	6,397	7,459	8,063	9,384	8,537
West Derby . . .	..	..	4,945	5,177	5,818	8,267	8,808	7,998
Wigan	..	..	..	9,583	11,000	12,329	14,977	11,727
LEICESTER.								
Ashby-de-la-Zouch .	..	5,557	5,459	5,719	5,914	6,533	7,305	7,777
Barrow-upon-Soar .	..	..	5,978	6,116	6,780	7,067	7,570	7,367
Billesdon . . .	..	2,716†	2,842	2,869	3,139	3,181	3,336	2,997
Blaby	..	6,584	5,185	4,943	5,556	5,766	5,822	5,396
Hinckley . . .	3,632	5,304	5,020	4,725	7,270	6,993	10,059	6,747

NOTE.—The expenditure for Liverpool is taken from the annual Poor Rate Return.

No. 2. (*continued*).—Statement, showing the Amount of .... d for the Relief
Maintenance of the Poor, in each of the following U: .... parishes, under
Provisions of the Poor Law Amendment Act, from the earliest .... for which
Abstracts have been received to the year ended Lady-day, 1844; also the Amount
for the like purpose in each of the Unions and Single Parishes, under Local Acts, &c.
to 1844.

COUNTIES, UNIONS, &c.	Amount of Money Expended for the Relief and Maintenance of the Poor.							
	Years ended at Lady-day,							
	1837	1838	1839	1840	1841	1842	1843	1844
LEICESTER—*continued.*	£.	£.	£.	£.	£.	£.	£.	£.
Leicester . . .	..	14,612	12,291	12,764	13,311	16,301	20,254	19,56
Loughborough . .	..	..	6,604	7,086	7,241	7,623	8,200	7,03
Lutterworth . . .	4,410†	4,097	4,140	4,656	6,792	6,024	6,665	6,23
Market Bosworth .	3,984	5,498	5,240	4,808	4,913	5,517	6,160	5,83
Market Harborough .	8,260	7,849	7,614	7,507	7,678	7,765	8,180	8,29
Melton Mowbray .	..	5,793	5,024	4,896	4,806	5,271	5,167	5,13
LINCOLN.								
Boston	..	10,162	10,820	9,444	10,228	10,302	11,001	11,09
Bourn	4,310	4,076	4,543	5,021	5,223	5,254	5,660	5,96
Caistor	..	5,796	6,168	6,555	6,945	7,322	7,775	7,41
Gainsborough . .	..	5,481	6,629	7,134	7,546	7,405	7,140	7,63
Glandford Brigg .	..	7,113	8,346	7,356	7,811	7,980	8,707	8,98
Grantham . . .	5,822	6,083	5,474	6,018	6,499	6,056	6,103	6,14
Holbeach . . .	5,494	6,506	5,540	5,533	5,489	5,310	5,991	6,48
Horncastle . . .	..	7,555	8,867	7,999	8,111	8,144	8,680	9,17
Lincoln	..	6,280	7,681	7,115	7,984	7,191	7,893	7,63
Louth	..	..	10,959	10,421	10,440	10,265	10,876	11,23
Sleaford	..	6,111	5,705	5,504	6,043	6,137	6,669	6,83
Spalding . . .	4,959†	5,492	4,997	5,358	5,638	6,295	6,580	6,12
Spilsby	..	..	10,248	9,411	9,420	9,930	10,505	10,06
Stamford . . .	3,601	5,251	4,727	4,844	5,167	5,238	5,246	5,21
MIDDLESEX.								
Bethnal Green . .	..	12,516	10,676	10,157	11,590	14,093	14,918	11,99
Brentford . . .	..	8,684	9,998	13,527	11,738	13,809	14,744	13,65
Chelsea	..	..	..	..	..	..	11,378	9,66
Edmonton . . .	..	15,283	13,839	14,479	15,120	16,884	16,684	17,20
George, St., in-the-Ea-t . . . }	..	11,678	13,987	13,140	13,286	14,244	15,728	13,42
Hackney . . .	..	8,799	10,466	10,503	11,588	13,252	13,705	12,61
Hendon . . .	4,329	4,593	5,014	6,192	8,963	7,242	7,394	7,00
Holborn	..	11,485	8,667	9,923	9,775	8,936	9,028	8,63
Kensington . . .	..	..	20,940	21,618	25,641	22,931†	18,881	17,11
London, City . .	..	..	42,736	46,256	47,434	52,722	55,750	51,18
London, East . .	..	..	..	14,892	15,109	16,213	16,697	16,30
London, West . .	..	..	12,612	13,934	14,415	15,103	14,524	14,05
Martin's, St., in-the-Fields . . . }	..	..	..	..	..	12,320	11,606	10,87
Poplar	..	10,568	11,023	9,179	9,912	11,108	13,878	11,55
Staines	..	5,002	5,815	6,210	6,035	6,523	8,168	7,36
Stepney . . .	..	26,371	20,330	20,636	21,309	20,910	19,978	20,08
Strand	..	14,015†	12,981	13,703	14,404	15,172	15,168	13,50
Uxbridge . . .	..	5,570	5,916	5,718	5,873	6,121	6,412	5,99

* One quarter's expenditure of the Leicester Union is estimated on the average of the other
three quarters' in this year.

No. 2, (*continued*).—Statement, showing the Amount of Money Expended for the Relief and Maintenance of the Poor, in each of the following Unions and Single Parishes, under the Provisions of the Poor Law Amendment Act, from the earliest year for which complete Abstracts have been received to the Year ended Lady-day. 1844; also the Amount expended for the like purpose in each of the Unions and Single Parishes, under Local Acts, from 1837 to 1844.

COUNTIES, UNIONS, &c.	Amount of Money Expended for the Relief and Maintenance of the Poor. Years ended at Lady-day,							
	1837	1838	1839	1840	1841	1842	1843	1844
	£.	£.	£.	£.	£.	£.	£.	£.
MIDDLESEX—*cont.*								
Whitechapel	..	16,426	18,540	16,724	17,468	19,414	18,233	16,992
*Clerkenwell, James, St., and John, St.	10,104	10,674	11,122	10,901	11,279	13,225	13,513	12,066
*George, St., Hanover Square	15,005	13,790	13,655	13,701	14,455	16,100	16,007	16,664
*Giles, St., in-the-Fields, and George, St., Bloomsbury	13,081	13,424	13,446	13,109	14,176	14,583	16,019	14,596
*James, St., Westminster	9,636	9,135	9,273	9,891	10,460	10,567	11,083	11,114
*Leonard, St., Shoreditch	14,662	17,318	18,513	19,138	19,736	20,430	21,383	19,058
*Luke, St., Middlesex	9,244	9,635	10,627	12,571	13,996	15,205	15,058	13,558
*Margaret, St., and John, St., Westminster	8,276	9,349	8,065	8,876	9,625	9,107	9,302	10,735
*Mary, St., Islington	5,805	6,066	7,156	7,055	6,722	8,693	9,262	7,034
*Marylebone, St.	27,907	27,803	26,438	29,917	35,517	41,476	44,744	45,503
*Sepulchre, St.	1,638	1,799	1,603	1,557	1,416	1,553	1,684	1,695
*Pancras, St.	18,296	19,921	18,405	21,985	25,798	28,515	26,657	23,807
MONMOUTH.								
Abergavenny	..	3,457	3,906	4,815	6,052	6,326	8,149	7,408
Chepstow	..	4,063	5,323	5,200	5,358	5,273	5,537	5,375
Monmouth	..	5,340	5,396	5,907	5,894	5,597	5,831	5,699
Newport	..	5,604	6,155	6,976	7,921	7,490	8,076	8,323
Pontypool	..	3,206	3,421	3,218	3,316	3,757	4,497	4,615
NORFOLK.								
Aylsham	..	9,667	9,459	9,564	9,325	8,893	9,206	9,825
Blofield	5,511	6,041	5,106	5,135	4,990	5,264	5,199	5,525
Depwade	..	13,461	15,378	13,659	13,928	13,922	14,238	13,138
Docking	8,516	9,032	9,134	9,333	8,352	8,623	8,517	8,358
Downham	..	6,994	7,505	7,574	7,546	7,691	7,442	7,195
Erpingham	..	8,946	9,546	10,289	10,443	10,347	10,108	10,042
Faith, St.	6,504	5,838	6,211	6,853	7,327	6,985	7,731	7,580
Flegg, East and West	..	..	..	2,831	2,878	2,930	3,137	3,005
Forehoe	..	..	..	6,058	6,215	6,320	5,895	5,630
Freebridge Lynn	6,023	5,149	5,214	5,522	5,310	5,352	5,190	4,879
Guiltcross	7,406	7,469	7,725	7,552	6,568	6,690	6,820	6,870
Henstead	6,205	8,881	6,928	6,628	6,637	6,215	6,484	6,603
King's Lynn	6,412†	6,692	7,208	6,837	7,205	7,674	7,696	7,916
Loddon and Clavering	..	4,474	5,266	5,465	5,592	5,740	5,883	5,705
Mitford and Launditch	..	11,939	12,741	13,178	13,623	12,432	12,522	12,143
Swaffham	8,234†	8,681	8,265	7,938	7,683	7,826	7,829	7,623
Thetford	5,845	6,249	6,816	6,921	6,551	6,712	6,923	6,6?8
Tunstead & Happing	..	..	..	5,831	5,965	5,996	5,935	5,978

No. 2, (*continued*).—Statement, showing the Amount of Money Expended for the Relief Maintenance of the Poor, in each of the following Unions and Single Parishes, under Provisions of the Poor Law Amendment Act, from the earliest year for which comp Abstracts have been received to the Year ended Lady-day, 1844: also the Amount exper for the like purpose in each of the Unions and Single Parishes, under Local Acts, from 1 to 1844.

COUNTIES, UNIONS, &c.	1837	1838	1839	1840	1841	1842	1843	18
	£.	£.	£.	£.			£.	£.
Walsingham . .	..	9,762	11,317	11,340	12,245	11	11,796	11,24
Wayland . . .	6,140	5,715	6,209	6,017	5,658	5	5,884	5,91
Yarmouth, Great .	..	..	5,931	7,173	6,891	7	8,062	8,75
*Norwich, City of .	12,904	14,976	14,962	16,443	18,435	20,469	22,754	24,37
NORTHAMPTON.								
Brackley . . .	5,494	6,547	6,892	6,842	6,875	6,801	7,	7,00
Brixworth . .	6,849†	7,858	8,277	7,830	8,506	7,858	7,	7,83
Daventry . . .	8,760	9,369	9,467	9,143	8,810	9,680	9,	9,26
Hardingstone .		3,656	3,646	3,746	4,957	4,153	4,	4,39
Kettering . . .	8,664	8,940	9,759	9,999	12,282	9,214		9,02
Northampton .	5,679	7,348	7,097	6,336	6,031	7,871		8,18
Oundle . . .	5,619	5,837	5,814	5,824	5,934	6,417		6,77
Peterborough .	6,133	8,692	7,290	7,223	7,663	7,994†	10,501	11,56
Potterspury . .	3,597	4,025	3,811	3,409	3,739	4,081		4,02
Thrapston . .	5,235	5,477	5,988	7,164	7,511	6,425	825	6,24
Towcester . .	5,710	6,260	6,121	6,161	5,500	6,172	181	5,87
Wellingborough .	7,781	8,220	8,368	8,143	7,955	8,367	689	8,38
NORTHUMBERLAND.								
Alnwick . . .	..	6,001	5,324	5,162	5,114		5,923	5,60
Belford . . .	..	1,943	1,941	2,100	1,840	1,839	1,941	1,95
Bellingham . .	..	2,561	2,481	2,620	2,570	2,497	2,450	2,48
Berwick-on-Tweed .	..	6,837	6,492	7,015	6,166	6,162		6,73
Castle Ward . .	..	4,468	4,279	4,060	3,937	923		4,94
Glendale . . .	..	4,440	4,373	4,699	4,497	469	4,219	4,20
Haltwhistle . .	..	1,465	1,332	1,245	1,332	373	1,270	1,37
Hexham . . .	..	7,823	7,616	7,685	8,225†	8,350	8,390	8,13
Morpeth . . .	..	4,509	4,815	4,791	4,655	4,653	4,802	4,82
Newcastle-on-Tyne .	..	13,392	13,812	17,456	17,110	20,948	21,402	22,35
Rothbury . . .	..	3,275	3,267	3,311	3,191	3,062	3,113	3,05
Tynemouth . . .	..	10,534	10,555	10,407	10,613	10,275	10,494	10,76
NOTTINGHAM.								
Basford . . .	..	9,371	9,998	10,841	12,626	16,683	16,653	15,69
Bingham . . .	..	2,823	2,345	2,226	2,485	2,724	2,548	2,71
East Retford . .	..	4,370	5,843	5,484	5,592	5,811	6,006	5,83
Mansfield . . .	..	6,147†	6,359	7,213	7,632	7,703	8,596	7,26
Newark . . .	..	5,438	5,657	5,651	5,495		5,476	5,56
Nottingham . .	..	18,556	14,279	14,156	15,375	19,579	22,825	22,4
Radford . . .	..	1,850	2,416	3,176	3,219	3,298		3,49
Southwell . . .	..	5,155	5,282	5,418	5,182	5,318		5,64
Worksop . . .	..	4,195	5,180	4,739	5,067	4,751	5,029	5,53
OXFORD.								
Banbury . . .	12,746†	12,919	13,358	14,131	14,243	15,310	14,720	14,17
Bicester . . .	..	6,089	6,843	7,001	6,016	6,149	5,798	6,54

¶ No. 2, *(continued).*—Satement, showing the Amount of Money Expended for the Relief and Maintenance of the Poor in each of the following Unions and Single Parishes, under the Provisions of the Poor Law Amendment Act, from the earliest year for which complete Abstracts have been received to the Year ended Lady-day, 844 ; also the Amount expended for the like purpose in each of the Unions and Single Parishes, under Local Acts, from 1837 to 1844.

COUNTIES, UNIONS, &c.	Amount of Money Expended for the Relief and Maintenance of the Poor.							
	Years ended at Lady-day,							
	1837	1838	1839	1840	1841	1842	1843	1844
OXFORD—*continued.*	£.	£.	£.	£.	£.	£.	£.	£.
Chipping Norton .	5,602	8,248	7,866	7,333	7,169	7,585	7,090	7,171
Headington . . .	4,227†	4,707	4,779	4,979†	5,354	5,837	5,961	5,954
Henley	6,694	7,657	8,024	8,167	8,343	8,748	8,651	8,445
Thame	9,896	9,826	13,029	11,470	12,264	12,210	12,433	12,445
Witney	10,913	10,351	11,031	11,333	11,296	11,329	11,459	10,918
Woodstock . . .	5,347‡	7,188	6,704	6,770	6,959	7,237	6,869	6,870
*Oxford, City of .	3,111	3,195	4,080	4,889	4,889	4,562	5,664	5,698
RUTLAND.								
Oakham	..	4,165	3,764	3,896	4,000	4,074	4,062	4,316
Uppingham . . .	..	4,603	4,643	4,324	4,189	4,177	4,176	4,209
SALOP.								
Atcham	..	4,941	6,058	4,371	4,310	4,119	4,225	4,423
Bridgnorth . . .	..	3,372	3,705	3,563	3,690	3,825	4,030	4,022
Church Stretton .	..	1,825	1,739	2,137	2,070	1,746	2,192	2,532
Cleobury Mortimer .	..	2,316	2,283	2,584	2,720	2,383	2,443	2,628
Clun	..	2,924	3,062	3,117	3,111	3,034	3,295	3,471
Ellesmere . . .	..	5,312	4,214	4,130	4,085	4,029	4,468	4,703
Ludlow	..	5,466	6,658	7,241	8,008	6,868	6,354	6,538
Madeley	..	4,663	4,189	4,364	4,426	4,454	5,919	7,084
Market Drayton . .	..	3,188†	3,274	3,129	2,967	3,291	3,506	3,573
Newport	..	2,883	3,037	2,816	3,230	3,340	4,173	4,661
Shiffnal	..	3,101	3,234	3,180	3,307	3,266	4,073	4,564
Wellington . . .	..	3,288	3,285	3,464	4,369	4,783	6,509	7,778
Wem	..	3,077	3,193	3,162	3,178	3,218	3,635	3,653
*Shrewsbury, Town of	4,348	4,318	4,235	3,900	4,221	4,353	6,352	5,152
*Oswestry . . .	3,475	3,334	3,790	4,046	4,027	4,165	4,468	4,147
*Whitchurch . .	1,544	1,604	1,605	1,503	1,692	1,974	2,058	1,711
SOMERSET.								
Axbridge. . . .	8,195	9,451	10,559	10,980	11,483	11,499	11,382	10,647
Bath	..	12,254	13,512	13,989	14,111	13,804	13,536	13,222
Bedminster . . .	..	7,540	9,261	8,314	8,349	8,785	10,173	10,644
Bridgwater . . .	..	10,402	12,082	11,128	11,441	11,473	11,979	11,831
Chard	..	7,286	7,948	8,431	8,884	9,980	10,467	9,282
Clutton	7,534	8,191	8,959	9,268	10,508	10,367	10,666	9,753
Dulverton . . .	..	1,973	1,983	2,240	2,222	2,265	2,109	2,378
Frome	9,516	12,376	13,437	13,194	13,717	13,557	15,381	13,651
Keynsham . . .	..	6,030	7,065	7,453	8,013	7,933	8,323	8,218
Langport . . .	..	4,188	5,295	5,595	4,855	4,910	5,084	4,950
Shepton Mallet . .	8,709	10,024	9,861	10,852	10,843	11,778	12,554	13,106
Taunton	..	11,862	14,735	13,017	12,113	11,929	12,042	11,787
Wellington . . .	..	9,738	12,894	11,264	11,478	11,573	11,975	10,478
Wells	4,792	5,900	7,031	7,341	7,067	7,112	8,372	7,079
Williton	..	7,761	9,714	9,812	10,000	11,292	10,012	9,738
Wincanton . . .	10,577	10,935	12,352	12,557	11,775	11,626	11,838	11,853
Yeovil	..	8,050	9,470	9,677	9,785	9,783	9,795	9,207

No. 2, (*continued*).—Statement, showing the Amount of Money Expended for the Relief and Maintenance of the Poor, in each of the following Unions and Single Parishes, under the Provisions of the Poor Law Amendment Act, from the earliest year for which complete Abstracts have been received to the year ended Lady-day, 1844; also the Amount Expended for the like purpose in each of the Unions and Single Parishes, under Local Acts, from 1837 to 1844.

COUNTIES, UNIONS, &c	Amount of Money Expended for the Relief and Maintenance of the Poor. Years ended at Lady-day.							
	1837	1838	1839	1840	1841	1842	1843	1844
	£.	£.	£.	£.	£.	£.	£.	£.
SOUTHAMPTON— *continued.*								
Bury St. Edmunds	..	..	..	..	..	..	4,897	4,409
Cosford	7,694	7,122	7,259	6,404	6,102	5,818	6,008	5,356
Hartismere	10,454	9,250	8,273	8,553	9,291	10,021	10,197	9,565
Hoxne	9,252	7,595	8,270	7,299	7,169	7,246	7,330	7,853
Ipswich	8,561	8,808	9,938	10,293	10,261	10,025	11,281	11,150
Mildenhall	4,872	4,175	4,339	4,027	3,865	3,895	4,148	3,735
Mutford and Lothingland	..	..	..	4,169	4,043	3,823	4,196	4,289
Plomesgate	11,328	11,566	10,616	11,441	10,603	10,199	10,108	9,369
Risbridge	8,165	8,543	8,850	9,579	9,589	9,688	9,843	9,641
Samford	..	..	..	3,546	3,581	3,507	3,981	4,234
Stow	7,797	7,769	8,122	7,755	7,541	7,685	7,725	8,032
Sudbury	13,131	17,571	19,661	15,765	15,694	16,249	16,626	16,276
Thingoe	8,407	9,026	9,269	9,611	9,933	9,686	9,332	9,200
Wangford	5,315	5,270	5,445	5,240	5,405	5,761	5,992	5,962
Woodbridge	12,043	11,938	12,328	12,127	11,685	11,376	11,420	11,262
SURREY.								
Bermondsey	..	12,928	9,968	12,949	14,238	14,136	14,481	21,779
Camberwell	10,493	8,807	6,202	6,196	6,963	6,732	6,801	6,499
Chertsey	4,282	6,429	6,563	6,920	6,556	6,583	6,249	6,045
Croydon	..	9,856	10,192	9,935	10,532	10,242	11,698	10,174
Dorking	..	3,908	4,232	4,278	4,500	5,625	7,304	6,939
Epsom	..	6,489	8,872	7,637	7,642	7,593	7,774	8,427
George, St., the Martyr	..	..	..	13,295	14,052	13,901	13,735	13,103
Godstone	4,005	4,014	4,244	4,383	4,278	4,538	4,831	4,475
Guildford	..	11,520	10,706	11,845	13,026	12,600	12,792	12,643
Hambledon	..	5,089	5,751	6,391	6,515	6,200	6,706	6,421
Kingston	..	5,673	6,531	7,347	8,095	9,032	8,760	8,398
Lambeth	..	..	..	23,517	36,498	36,676	36,528	36,176
Olave's, St.	..	5,895	6,369	5,987	6,868	7,831	7,178	7,960
Reigate	..	..	7,190	6,572	6,527	6,902	7,652	7,270
Richmond	..	4,350	4,526	4,684	5,067	4,592	4,519	4,572
Rotherhithe	..	5,260	5,208	4,723	5,905	7,145	8,474	6,591
Saviour's, St.	..	..	..	13,375	12,164	12,453	13,224	11,905
Wandsworth and Clapham	..	13,876	12,149	12,890	13,644	13,469	13,833	13,924
*Newington, St. Mary	9,995	8,079	13,299	6,354	14,650	15,628	15,628	15,497
SUSSEX.								
Battle	5,751	6,435	7,542	7,913	9,166	8,576	8,359	7,835
Chailey	4,579	4,373	4,357	4,214	4,225	4,524	4,906	4,643
Cuckfield	6,667	7,105	7,866	7,516	7,803	8,018	7,971	7,786
Eastbourne	4,937	4,733	5,220	5,366	5,394	4,951	5,048	4,460
East Grinstead	6,992	6,871	6,945	6,603	6,174	6,402	6,727	6,638

§ In this year the salaries of Officers, &c., were included under the head of " Other Purposes."

No. 2, (*continued*).—Statement, showing the Amount of Money Expended for the Relief and Maintenance of the Poor, in each of the following Unions and Single Parishes, under the Provisions of the Poor Law Amendment Act, from the earliest year for which complete Abstracts have been received to the year ended Lady-day, 1844; also the Amount Expended for the like purpose in each of the Unions and Single Parishes, under Local Acts, from 1837 to 1844.

COUNTIES, UNIONS, &c.	Amount of Money Expended for the Relief and Maintenance of the Poor. Years ended at Lady-day.							
	1837	1838	1839	1840	1841	1842	1843	1844
	£.	£.	£.	£.	£.	£.	£.	£.
SUSSEX— *continued.*								
Hailsham	8,543	8,984	10,951	10,261	10,704	11,055	10,855	9,592
Hastings	4,696	5,493	7,799	5,921	5,416	5,873	6,145	5,466
Horsham	6,071	6,155	6,825	8,380	6,735	7,062	7,312	7,164
Lewes	3,682	3,936	4,285	4,201	4,089	4,087	4,307	4,275
Midhurst	6,327	6,042	6,768	6,865	7,408	7,948	7,472	6,640
Newhaven	2,475	1,927	2,267	2,610	2,391	2,482	2,653	2,539
Petworth	3,904	4,105	5,114	5,149	5,734	5,793	5,662	5,454
Rye	6,710	7,450	7,055	7,265	8,189	7,717	7,076	7,537
Steyning	4,572	5,046	4,990	4,828	4,904	4,717	5,223	4,885
Thakeham	2,884	3,372	3,518	3,881	3,851	3,659	4,037	3,687
Ticehurst	5,425	6,263	7,088	6,472	6,533	6,785	6,676	6,037
Uckfield	6,728	7,019	8,020	9,532	8,365	7,868	7,685	7,017
Westbourne	2,709	2,579	2,822	3,109	3,112	3,077	3,410	2,942
West Firle	1,940	1,889	1,988	2,211	2,434	2,394	2,379	2,219
Westhampnett	6,553	6,659	6,253	5,866	5,935	5,641	6,103	5,437
*Chichester, City of	1,345	1,813	2,048	2,981	2,030	2,576	2,783	2,407
*Brighton	12,385	14,817	17,499	16,723	16,661	18,929	18,273	18,650
WARWICK.								
Alcester	..	4,418	4,887	4,852	5,823	5,524	5,455	5,598
Aston	..	6,056	6,104	5,708	6,211	5,980	5,695	5,211
Atherstone	..	3,481	4,231	4,429	4,549	4,438	4,678	4,698
Foleshill	..	2,921	2,234	2,675	3,333	3,360	3,632	3,214
Meriden	..	3,037	3,213	3,695	3,936	4,320	4,468	4,347
Nuneaton	..	5,108	4,941	5,725	7,411	6,304	6,371	4,717
Rugby	..	5,158	5,231	5,467	5,667	5,825	5,960	6,018
Solihull	..	3,147	3,561	3,229	3,590	2,902	3,343	3,267
Southam	..	3,142	3,633	3,414	3,337	3,467	3,641	3,416
Stratford-on-Avon	..	7,291	7,723	7,805	7,126	6,842	7,202	7,209
Warwick	..	8,467	11,319	11,053	12,359	12,160	12,780	12,140
*Birmingham	32,837	43,889	38,986	39,836	27,013	24,881	27,013	28,79
*Coventry, City of	5,910	6,975	6,939	6,465	7,273	8,520	10,855	8,29
WESTMORELAND.								
East Ward	..	3,347	3,311	3,591	3,798	3,939	4,026	3,8
Kendal	..	9,492	9,191	10,566	11,470	12,068	12,793	12,7
West Ward	..	2,274	2,238	2,388	2,417	2,520	2,535	2,
WILTS.								
Alderbury	5,561	6,560	7,353	7,602	7,626	7,264	7,365	6,
Amesbury	3,295	3,640	3,935	4,103	4,257	4,221	4,117	3,
Bradford	5,775	6,196	7,452	7,424	7,550	9,678	11,182	8,
Calne	4,640	4,518	4,381	4,618	4,801	4,733	5,216	5,
Chippenham	7,054	6,984	7,411	7,778	7,759	8,129	8,612	8,
Cricklade and Wootton Bassett	5,586	6,829	7,085	6,813	6,417	6,276	6,329	6,

No. 2, (*continued*).—Statement, showing the Amount of Money Expended for the Relief and Maintenance of the Poor, in each of the following Unions and Single Parishes, under the Provisions of the Poor Law Amendment Act, from the earliest year for which complete Abstracts have been received to the year ended Lady-day, 1844; also the Amount Expended for the like purpose in each of the Unions and Single Parishes, under Local Acts from 1837 to 1844.

COUNTIES, UNIONS, &c.	Amount of Money Expended for the Relief and Maintenance of the Poor.							
	Years ended at Lady-day,							
	1837	1838	1839	1840	1841	1842	1843	1844
York, North Riding *—continued.*	£.	£.	£.	£.	£.	£.	£.	£.
Helmsley	..	..	2,732	2,829	2,804	3,084†	3,172	2,953
Leyburn	..	2,801	3,196	3,128	3,095	3,538	3,476	3,540
Malton	..	6,069	7,092	7,524	6,790	7,118	6,721	6,767
Northallerton	..	..	4,999‡	4,162	4,266	4,048	4,390	4,912
Pickering	..	2,746	2,811	2,773	3,070	3,182	2,940	2,928
Reeth	..	..	..	..	..	2,846	3,041	2,957
Richmond	..	4,567	5,070	5,036‡	3,694	4,204	4,038	4,212
Scarborough	..	4,531	4,320	4,708	4,787	5,175	5,552	5,080
Stokesley	..	..	3,716	3,677	3,444	3,435	3,526	3,485
Thirsk	..	3,373	3,683	3,396	3,352	3,610†	3,939	3,832
Whitby	..	4,554	4,796	4,880	5,173	4,992	4,803	4,608
York, West Riding.								
Bradford	..	..	..	17,388	20,106	25,490	28,514	25,477
Dewsbury	..	..	..	..	10,885	11,367	14,148	13,114
Doncaster	..	..	7,715	8,466	8,631	8,839	9,893	9,915
Ecclesall Bierlow	..	..	5,826	6,306	8,663	8,415	12,757	14,090
Goole	..	..	3,337	3,925	3,501	3,847	4,248	3,546
Halifax	..	..	10,986	13,774	16,987	17,584	19,920	18,459
Huddersfield	..	..	..	12,215	17,199	17,711	21,798	20,077
Keighley	..	..	..	5,675	6,634	7,441	8,191	7,285
Leeds Township	18,640	23,865	19,755	18,674	20,495	25,128	30,596	25,674
Pateley Bridge	..	..	2,648	2,678	2,798	2,992	3,226	3,003
Rotherham	..	..	5,519	6,609	7,520	7,248	9,536	10,841
Selby	..	..	4,342	4,445	4,853	6,221	5,402	5,575
Sedbergh	..	..	..	..	..	1,901	2,095	1,912
Settle	..	..	4,472	5,067	5,443	6,250	8,020	6,412
Sheffield	..	..	17,946	19,411	25,947	25,759	42,648	33,738
Skipton	..	..	7,894	7,347	8,543	9,803	10,706	8,585
Thorne	..	..	3,756	5,060	4,961	4,349	4,267	4,099
Wakefield	..	..	..	..	12,197	13,463	14,576	15,234
Wortley	..	..	..	3,755	4,699	5,057	5,679	7,459
Anglesey.								
Anglesey	..	..	11,867	12,678	13,081	13,401	13,257	13,269
Brecon.								
Brecknock	..	6,547	6,977	7,306	7,442	7,785	8,415	8,971
Builth	..	3,172	3,185	3,539	3,694	3,870	4,022	4,137
Crickhowell	..	1,682	1,902	2,133	2,185	2,539	3,189	3,327
Hay	..	3,811	3,721	3,866	4,017	4,126	3,800	3,785

No. 2, *(continued).*—Statement showing the Amount of Money Expended for the Relief and Maintenance of the Poor, in each of the following Unions and Single Parishes, under the Provisions of the Poor Law Amendment Act, from the earliest year for which complete Abstracts have been received to the year ended Lady-day, 1844; also the Amount Expended for the like purpose in each of the Unions and Single Parishes, under Local Acts, from 1837 to 1844.

COUNTIES, UNIONS, &c.	Amount of Money expended for the Relief and Maintenance of the Poor.							
	Years ended at Lady-day.							
	1837	1838	1839	1840	1841	1842	1843	1844
	£.	£.	£.	£.	£.	£.	£.	£.
CARDIGAN.								
Aberayron · · ·	··	··	3,292	4,025	3,976	3,795	3,922	3,730
Aberystwith · · ·	··	··	4,023	4,898	5,528	5,814	4,879	4,361
Cardigan · · ·	··	··	5,184	6,135	5,368	5,582	5,729	5,583
Lampeter · · ·	··	··	3,017	3,220	3,218	3,299	3,366	3,352
Tregaron · · ·	··	··	1,849	2,064	2,244	2,232	2,255	2,146
CARMARTHEN.								
Carmarthen · · ·	··	11,442	12,606	12,491	12,693	13,924	12,785	11,629
Llandilofawr. · ·	··	4,903†	5,271	5,204	5,132	5,423	5,761	5,499
Llandovery · · ·	··	3,860	4,416	4,622	4,371	4,386	4,432	4,303
Llanelly · · · ·	··	4,255‡	5,039	4,822	5,262	5,216	5,607	5,085
Newcastle-in-Emlyn	··	··	5,053	5,980	5,546	5,251	5,418	5,340
CARNARVON.								
Bangor and Beaumaris	··	··	5,421	5,872	6,112	6,174	6,471	6,378
Carnarvon · · ·	··	··	6,790	6,972	7,451	7,657	7,814	7,589
Conway · · · ·	··	··	··	··	4,572	4,914	4,865	4,836
Pwllheli · · · ·	··	··	5,483	6,566	5,725	6,680	5,932	6,419
DENBIGH.								
Llanrwst · · · ·	··	··	4,699	4,680	4,999	5,183	4,872	4,397
Ruthin · · · ·	··	··	8,402	8,779	8,593	7,840	8,007	7,818
Wrexham · · ·	··	··	9,796	8,898	8,450	10,204	10,640	10,581
FLINT.								
Asaph, St. · · ·	··	··	10,771	10,888	11,549	9,913	9,519	8,704
Holywell · · ·	··	··	8,858	9,589	11,881	10,981	11,009	11,289
GLAMORGAN.								
Bridgend and Cowbridge · · ·	··	5,233	5,623	5,316	5,605	6,052	6,212	7,033
Cardiff · · · ·	··	7,612	7,992	9,734	9,976	10,753	11,700	11,818
Merthyr-Tydvil · ·	··	6,109	5,966	6,144	6,417	7,814	9,820	9,163
Neath · · · ·	··	5,586	6,021	5,761	5,782	6,665	7,398	7,409
Swansea · · · ·	··	6,479	6,776	6,763	7,074	7,175	8,260	8,356
MERIONETH.								
Bala · · · · ·	··	2,380	2,455	2,758	2,692	2,543	2,598	2,566
Corwen · · · ·	··	3,812	4,016	4,484	4,398	4,829	4,158	4,527
Dolgelly · · · ·	··	··	5,224	5,202	5,562	5,786	5,749	5,654
Festiniog · · ·	··	··	4,195	4,474	4,602	4,823	4,928	5,013

No. 2, (*continued*).—Statement, showing the Amount of Money Expended for the Relief and Maintenance of the Poor, in each of the following Unions and Single Parishes, under the Provisions of the Poor Law Amendment Act, from the earliest year for which complete Abstracts have been received to the year ended Lady-day, 1844 ; also the Amount Expended for the like purpose in each of the Unions and Single Parishes, under Local Acts, from 1837 to 1844.

COUNTIES, UNIONS, &c.	Amount of Money Expended for the Relief and Maintenance of the Poor.							
	Years ended at Lady-day,							
	1837	1838	1839	1840	1841	1842	1843	1844
WILTS—*continued.*	£.	£.	£.	£.	£.	£.	£.	£.
Devizes	10,457	10,755	11,209	11,564	11,399	11,239	11,451	11,208
Highworth and Swindon . .	5,314	5,940	6,929	6,710	6,271	6,949	7,287	7,692
Malmesbury . . .	5,026	5,450	6,014	6,954	6,457	6,367	6,511	6,548
Marlborough . .	3,403	4,291	4,830	5,680	5,093	4,923	5,015	5,459
Melksham . . .	7,437	8,454	10,857	9,917	10,126	11,639	12,517	12,030
Mere	3,418	3,336	3,957	4,583	5,049	5,444	5,608	5,597
Pewsey	4,774	5,215	5,663	6,488	6,387	6,048	6,080	5,506
Tisbury	4,472	5,094	6,083	6,243	5,779	5,735	5,822	5,702
Warminster . . .	8,875	10,143	10,790	10,809	11,133	11,818	12,114	11,432
Westbury and Whorwellsdown . . .	4,639	6,486	6,088	8,065	7,617	7,581	8,201	7,719
Wilton	5,605	7,393	7,056	7,632	7,514	7,370	7,461	6,882
*New Sarum, City of.	3,989	3,920	4,423	4,670	4,531	4,358	4,610	4,628
WORCESTER.								
Bromsgrove . . .	..	4,881	6,668	6,877	6,581	6,932	7,449	6,771
Droitwich . . .	..	5,811	5,764	5,210	5,958	6,133	6,435	6,150
Dudley	..	9,762	9,732	9,866	10,679	11,177	14,963	16,603
Evesham . . .	..	3,899	5,124	4,562	4,571	4,784	4,919	4,707
Kidderminster . .	..	8,539	8,768	8,244	8,563	8,873	9,529	8,683
King's Norton . .	..	3,227	3,615	3,917	4,241	4,870	4,913	4,727
Martley	..	3,942	4,560	4,807	4,881	4,517	4,232	4,760
Pershore . . .	3,930†	3,838	4,943	4,383	4,086	4,095	4,134	4,011
Shipston-on-Stour .	..	8,815	9,098	8,949	8,803	8,877	8,622	7,791
Stourbridge . . .	..	6,795	7,261	6,591	6,578	6,839	8,807	9,398
Tenbury	..	2,116	2,253	2,625	2,549	2,463	2,508	2,465
Upton-on-Severn .	4,310	4,536	4,489	4,773	4,774	4,985	5,067	4,585
Worcester . . .	..	5,300	5,339	8,167	6,404	6,259	6,445	6,245
YORK, EAST RIDING.								
Beverley	..	5,015	5,666	4,998	5,055	5,563	5,811	5,834
Bridlington . . .	..	3,127	3,378	3,765	3,938	4,238	4,276	4,414
Driffield	..	4,764	5,242	4,876	5,118	5,421	5,842	5,765
Howden	..	4,769	4,691	4,747	5,193	4,812	4,721	4,768
Patrington . . .	..	2,968†	3,843	3,693	3,332	3,516	3,383	3,264
Pocklington . . .	..	4,999	5,029	5,279	5,397	5,411	5,669	5,650
Sculcoates. . . .	..	..	..	9,370	8,979	9,669	10,307	9,942
Skirlaugh . . .	..	..	3,779	4,168	4,345	4,176	3,746	3,742
York	..	..	9,897	9,813	10,260	10,659	11,624	11,597
*Kingston-upon-Hull	9,840	12,276	12,060	11,356	11,751	13,135	14,649	14,437
YORK, NORTH RIDING.								
Bedale	..	..	..	2,734	3,102	3,459	3,248	
Easingwold . . .	..	2,690†	3,006	3,470	3,122	2,935	2,957	2,921
Guisborough. . .	..	..	3,341	3,719	3,576	3,371	3,549	3,647

Z

No. 2, (*continued*).—Statement, showing the Amount of Money Expended for the Relief and Maintenance of the Poor, in each of the following Unions and Single Parishes, under the Provisions of the Poor Law Amendment Act, from the earliest year for which complete Abstracts have been received to the year ended Lady-day, 1844; also the Amount Expended for the like purpose in each of the Unions and Single Parishes, under Local Acts, from 1837 to 1844.

COUNTIES, UNIONS, &c.	Amount of Money Expended for the Relief and Maintenance of the Poor.							
	Years ended at Lady-day,							
	1837	1838	1839	1840	1841	1842	1843	1844
	£.	£.	£.	£.	£.	£.	£.	£.
SUSSEX—*continued.*								
Hailsham . . .	8,543	8,984	10,951	10,261	10,704	11,055	10,855	9,592
Hastings . . .	4,696	5,493	7,799	5,921	5,416	5,873	6,145	5,466
Horsham . . .	6,071	6,155	6,825	8,380	6,735	7,062	7,312	7,164
Lewes . . .	3,682	3,936	4,285	4,201	4,089	4,087	4,307	4,275
Midhurst . . .	6,327	6,042	6,768	6,865	7,400	7,948	7,472	6,640
Newhaven . . .	2,475	1,927	2,267	2,610	2,391	2,482	2,663	2,539
Petworth . . .	3,904	4,105	5,114	5,149	5,734	5,793	5,662	5,454
Rye	6,710	7,450	7,055	7,265	8,189	7,717	7,076	7,537
Steyning . . .	4,572	5,046	4,990	4,828	4,904	4,717	5,223	4,895
Thakeham . . .	2,884	3,372	3,518	3,881	3,851	3,659	4,037	3,687
Ticehurst . . .	5,425	6,263	7,088	6,472	6,533	6,785	6,676	6,037
Uckfield	6,728	7,019	8,020	9,532	8,365	7,858	7,583	7,017
Westbourne . .	2,709	2,579	2,822	3,109	3,112	3,077	3,410	2,942
West Firle . . .	1,940	1,889	1,988	2,211	2,434	2,394	2,379	2,219
Westhampnett . .	6,553	6,659	6,253	5,866	5,935	5,641	6,103	5,437
*Chichester, City of .	1,345	1,813	2,048	2,981	2,030	2,576	2,783	2,407
*Brighton	12,385	14,817	17,499	16,723	16,661	18,929	18,373	18,650
WARWICK.								
Alcester	..	4,418	4,887	4,852	5,823	5,524	5,458	5,598
Aston	..	6,056	6,104	5,708	6,211	5,980	5,696	5,211
Atherstone . . .	..	3,481	4,231	4,429	4,549	4,438	4,678	4,698
Foleshill	..	2,921	2,234	2,675	3,333	3,360	3,632	3,214
Meriden	..	3,037	3,213	3,695	3,936	4,320	4,468	4,347
Nuneaton . . .	..	5,108	4,941	5,725	7,411	6,304	6,371	4,717
Rugby	..	5,158	5,231	5,467	5,667	5,825	5,960	6,018
Solihull	..	3,147	3,561	3,229	3,590	2,902	3,343	3,267
Southam	..	3,142	3,633	3,414	3,337	3,467	3,641	3,416
Stratford-on-Avon .	..	7,291	7,723	7,805	7,126	6,842	7,302	7,208
Warwick . . .	..	8,467	11,319	11,053	12,359	12,160	12,780	12,146
*Birmingham . . .	32,837	43,889	38,986	39,836	27,013	24,881	27,013	28,733
*Coventry, City of. .	5,910	6,975	6,939	6,465	7,273	8,520	10,855	8,290
WESTMORELAND.								
East Ward . . .	..	3,347	3,311	3,591	3,798	3,939	4,026	3,840
Kendal	..	9,492	9,191	10,566	11,470	12,068	12,793	12,345
West Ward . . .	..	2,274	2,238	2,388	2,417	2,520	2,535	2,562
WILTS.								
Alderbury . . .	5,561	6,560	7,353	7,602	7,626	7,264	7,365	6,980
Amesbury . . .	3,295	3,640	3,935	4,103	4,257	4,221	4,117	3,910
Bradford	5,775	6,196	7,452	7,424	7,550	9,678	11,182	8,873
Calne	4,640	4,518	4,381	4,618	4,801	4,733	5,216	5,299
Chippenham . . .	7,054	6,984	7,411	7,778	7,759	8,129	8,612	8,547
Cricklade and Wootton Bassett . . .}	5,586	6,829	7,085	6,813	6,417	6,276	6,329	6,104

No. 2, (*continued*).—Statement; shewing the Amount of Money Expended for the Relief and Maintenance of the Poor, in each of the following Unions and Single Parishes, under the Provisions of the Poor Law Amendment Act, from the earliest year for which complete Abstracts have been received to the year ended Lady-day, 1844; also the Amount Expended for the like purpose in each of the Unions and Single Parishes, under Local Acts, from 1837 to 1844.

COUNTIES, UNIONS, &c	Amount of Money Expended for the Relief and Maintenance of the Poor.							
	Years ended at Lady-day.							
	1837	1838	1839	1840	1841	1842	1843	1844
	£.	£.	£.	£.	£.	£.	£.	£.
SOUTHAMPTON— *continued.*								
Bury St. Edmunds .	..	..	..	..	..	..	4,897	4,409
Cosford	7,694	7,122	7,259	6,404	6,102	5,818	6,008	5,356
Hartismere . .	10,434	9,250	8,273	8,553	9,291	10,021	10,197	9,565
Hoxne	9,252	7,595	8,270	7,299	7,169	7,246	7,330	7,853
Ipswich	8,561	8,808	9,938	10,293	10,261	10,025	11,281	11,150
Mildenhall . . .	4,872	4,175	4,339	4,027	3,865	3,895	4,148	3,735
Mutford and Lothing- land }	..	..	..	4,169	4,043	3,823	4,196	4,289
Plomesgate . . .	11,328	11,566	10,616	11,441	10,603	10,199	10,108	9,369
Risbridge . . .	8,165¾	8,543	8,850	9,579	9,589	9,688	9,843	9,641
Samford	..	..	..	3,546	3,581	3,507	3,981	4,234
Stow	7,797†	7,769	8,122	7,755	7,541	7,685	7,725	8,032
Sudbury . . .	13,131	17,571	19,661	15,765	15,694	16,249	16,626	16,276
Thingoe . . .	8,407†	9,026	9,269	9,611	9,933	9,686	9,332	9,200
Wangford . . .	5,315	5,270	5,445	5,240	5,405	5,761	5,992	5,962
Woodbridge . .	12,043	11,938	12,328	12,127	11,685	11,376	11,420	11,262
SURREY.								
Bermondsey . . .	..	12,928	9,968	12,949	14,238	14,136*	14,481	21,779
Camberwell . . .	10,493	8,807	6,202	6,196	6,963	6,732	6,801	6,499
Chertsey	4,282	6,429	6,563	6,920	6,556	6,583	6,249	6,045
Croydon	..	9,856	10,192	9,935	10,532	10,242	11,698	10,174
Dorking	..	3,908	4,232	4,278	4,500	5,625	7,304	6,939
Epsom	..	6,489	8,872	7,637	7,642	7,593	7,774	8,427
George, St., the } Martyr . . . }	..	..	..	13,295	14,052	13,901	13,735	13,103
Godstone . . .	4,005	4,014	4,244	4,383	4,278	4,538	4,831	4,475
Guildford . . .	..	11,520	10,706	11,845	13,026	12,600	12,792	12,643
Hambledon	..	5,089	5,751	6,391	6,515	6,200	6,706	6,421
Kingston. . . .	..	5,675	6,531	7,347	8,095	9,032	8,760	8,398
Lambeth	..	..	..	23,517	36,498	36,676	36,528	36,176
Olave's, St. . . .	..	5,895	6,369	5,987	6,868	7,831	7,178	7,960
Reigate	..	..	7,190	6,572	6,527	6,902	7,652	7,270
Richmond . . .	..	4,350	4,526	4,684	5,067	4,592	4,519	4,572
Rutherhithe . . .	..	5,260	5,208	4,723	5,905	7,145	8,474	6,591
Saviour's, St. . .	..	..	..	13,375	12,164	12,453	13,224	11,805
Wandsworth and } Clapham . . . }	..	13,876	12,149	12,890	13,644	13,469	13,833	13,924
*Newington, St. Mary	9,995	8,079	13,299	6,3546	14,650	15,628	15,628	15,497
SUSSEX.								
Battle	5,751	6,435	7,542	7,913	9,166	8,576	8,359	7,835
Chailey	4,579	4,373	4,357	4,214	4,225	4,524	4,906	4,643
Cuckfield. . . .	6,667	7,105	7,866	7,516	7,803	8,018	7,971	7,786
Eastbourne . . .	4,937	4,733	5,220	5,366	5,394	4,951	5,048	4,460
East Grinstead . .	6,992	6,871	6,945	6,603	6,174	6,402	6,727	6,638

§ In this year the salaries of Officers, &c., were included under the head of "Other Purposes."

No. 2, (*continued*).—Statement, showing the Amount of Money Expended for the Relief and Maintenance of the Poor, in each of the following Unions and Single Parishes, under the Provisions of the Poor Law Amendment Act, from the earliest year for which complete Abstracts have been received to the Year ended Lady-day, 1844 ; also the Amount Expended for the like purpose in each of the Unions and Single Parishes, under Local Acts, from 1837 to 1844.

COUNTIES, UNIONS, &c.	Amount of Money Expended for the Relief and Maintenance of the Poor.							
	Years ended at Lady-day.							
	1837	1838	1839	1840	1841	1842	1843	1844
SOUTHAMPTON.	£.	£.	£.	£.	£.	£.	£.	£.
Alresford . . .	4,369	4,423	4,560	5,032	4,662	4,437	4,280	4,142
Alton	4,586	4.694	5,089	5.475	5,385	5,344	5,281	4,830
Andover . . .	8,348	9,179	9,622	9,612	9,001	9,076	9,314	8,184
Basingstoke . .	9,425	8,839	10,015	9,200	9,749	9,775	10,291	9,784
Catherington . .	1,503	1,280	1,426	1,407	1,378	1,347	1,461	1,296
Christchurch . .	2,676	2,991	2,984	3,227	3,238	3,250	3,270	3,315
Droxford . . .	5,240	5,309	5,745	6,026	5,507	5,902	5,193	5,587
Fareham . . .	6,164	5,178	5,985	6,218	6,316	6,063	6,603	5,439
Fordingbridge . .	3,494	3,192	3,399	3,692	3,845	3,748	3,790	3,538
Hartley Wintney .	4.539	4,007	4,632	4,335	4,668	4,778	5,114	4,670
Havant	2,872	2,848	2,608	3,107	2,881	2,857	3,026	2,774
Hursley . . .	847‡	942	1,162	1,104	1,052	1,029	1,079	950
Kingsclere . .	3,767	4,565	3,872	3,915	4,161	4,393	4,431	4,410
Lymington . .	4,643	4,782	4,759	4,615	4,551	4,379	4,641	4,238
New Forest . .	3,508	4,943	5,598	6,206	6,259	6,413	6,751	6,440
Petersfield . .	3,212	3,686	3,580	3,772	4,064	4,183	4,624	4,499
Portsea Island . .	..	14,858	15,824	16,817	17,592	17,389	16,942	16,303
Ringwood . .	2,199	2,249	2,540	2,785	2,619	2,443	2.515	2,330
Romsey . . .	4,465	4,262	4,117	4,578	4,392	4,161	3,884	3,816
South Stoneham.	3,416	3,198	3,192	3,488	3,441	3,353	3,438	3,610
Stockbridge . .	3,383	3,534	3,521	3,382	3,394	3,352	3,345	3,047
Whitchurch . .	2,433	2,682	2,951	2,744	2,862	2,730	2,815	2,611
Winchester, New	6,862†	7,118	7,702	8,000	7,705	7,938	7,940	7,258
*Isle of Wight .	14,601	10,605	11,023	12,703	12,984	12,265	12,181	12,558
*Southampton .	6,276	7,116	7,574	6,746	7,539	7,136	7,902	7,628
STAFFORD.								
Burton-on-Trent .	..	..	7,269	7,857	7,106	7,409	7,379	7,663
Cheadle . . .	..	..	3.686	3,725	4,030	3,955	4,570	3,986
Leek	..	..	4,554	5,665	5,736	6,026	6,031	5,192
Lichfield . . .	..	5,950	5,691	5,886	6,188	6,555	7,124	7,135
Newcastle-under-Lyme	..	..	..	4,408	4,894	4,046	4,327	4,270
Penkridge . . .	..	2,900	3,059	2,928	4,160	3,325	4,008	4,193
Seisdon . . .	..	2,349	1,791	1,865	1,950	2,066	2,248	2,068
Stafford . . .	..	3,152†	4,216	7,586	4,327	4,585	4,564	4,448
Stoke-on-Trent . .	..	8,021	8,373	7,689	8,358	7,557	14,272	10,267
Stone	..	..	..	5,538	5,931	5,665	6,131	4,827
Tamworth . . .	..	3,997	4,247	4,509	4,598	5,043	5,327	5,470
Uttoxeter . . .	..	..	2,772†	3,782	3,259	3,258	3,453	3,416†
Walsall	..	5,527	5,911	5,831	6,278	6,204	9,049	7,855
West Bromwich .	..	5,247	5,755	6,888	7,910	8,277	10,333	13,244
Wolstanton and- Burslem . . }	..	..	..	6,837	7,450	7,749	12,974	9,142
Wolverhampton . .	..	6,534	6,786	9,567	7,504	7,252	11,122	9,929
SUFFOLK.								
Blything . . .	11,116	10,403	11,261	9,958	9,521	9,293	8,859	8,310
Bosmere and Claydon	7,510	7,098	7,774	7,483	7,151	7,610	8,394	8,015